Handbook of Research on Big Data Clustering and Machine Learning

Fausto Pedro Garcia Marquez
Universidad Castilla-La Mancha, Spain

A volume in the Advances in Data Mining and
Database Management (ADMDM) Book Series

Published in the United States of America by
    IGI Global
    Engineering Science Reference (an imprint of IGI Global)
    701 E. Chocolate Avenue
    Hershey PA, USA 17033
    Tel: 717-533-8845
    Fax: 717-533-8661
    E-mail: cust@igi-global.com
    Web site: http://www.igi-global.com

Library of Congress Cataloging-in-Publication Data

Names: Garcia Marquez, Fausto Pedro, editor.
Title: Handbook of research on big data clustering and machine learning /
  Fausto Pedro Garcia Marquez, editor.
Description: Hershey, PA : Engineering Science Reference (an imprint of IGI
  Global), [2020] | Includes bibliographical references.
Identifiers: LCCN 2019016785| ISBN 9781799801061 (hardcover) | ISBN
  9781799801078 (ebook)
Subjects: LCSH: Big data--Research--Handbooks, manuals, etc. | Cluster
  analysis--Research--Handbooks, manuals, etc. | Machine
  learning--Research--Handbooks, manuals, etc.
Classification: LCC QA76.9.B45 H366 2020 | DDC 005.7--dc23 LC record available at https://lccn.loc.gov/2019016785

This book is published in the IGI Global book series Advances in Data Mining and Database Management (ADMDM) (ISSN: 2327-1981; eISSN: 2327-199X).

British Cataloguing in Publication Data
A Cataloguing in Publication record for this book is available from the British Library.

All work contributed to this book is new, previously-unpublished material. The views expressed in this book are those of the authors, but not necessarily of the publisher.

For electronic access to this publication, please contact: eresources@igi-global.com.

Advances in Data Mining and Database Management (ADMDM) Book Series

David Taniar
Monash University, Australia

ISSN:2327-1981
EISSN:2327-199X

MISSION

With the large amounts of information available to organizations in today's digital world, there is a need for continual research surrounding emerging methods and tools for collecting, analyzing, and storing data.

The **Advances in Data Mining & Database Management (ADMDM)** series aims to bring together research in information retrieval, data analysis, data warehousing, and related areas in order to become an ideal resource for those working and studying in these fields. IT professionals, software engineers, academicians and upper-level students will find titles within the ADMDM book series particularly useful for staying up-to-date on emerging research, theories, and applications in the fields of data mining and database management.

COVERAGE

- Cluster Analysis
- Decision Support Systems
- Profiling Practices
- Text Mining
- Factor Analysis
- Educational Data Mining
- Data Warehousing
- Web-based information systems
- Data Mining
- Predictive Analysis

IGI Global is currently accepting manuscripts for publication within this series. To submit a proposal for a volume in this series, please contact our Acquisition Editors at Acquisitions@igi-global.com or visit: http://www.igi-global.com/publish/.

Titles in this Series

For a list of additional titles in this series, please visit:
https://www.igi-global.com/book-series/advances-data-mining-database-management/37146

Trends and Applications of Text Summarization Techniques
Alessandro Fiori (Candiolo Cancer Institute – FPO, IRCCS, Italy)
Engineering Science Reference • copyright 2020 • 335pp • H/C (ISBN: 9781522593737) • US $210.00 (our price)

Emerging Perspectives in Big Data Warehousing
David Taniar (Monash University, Australia) and Wenny Rahayu (La Trobe University, Australia)
Engineering Science Reference • copyright 2019 • 348pp • H/C (ISBN: 9781522555162) • US $245.00 (our price)

Emerging Technologies and Applications in Data Processing and Management
Zongmin Ma (Nanjing University of Aeronautics and Astronautics, China) and Li Yan (Nanjing University of Aeronautics and Astronautics, China)
Engineering Science Reference • copyright 2019 • 458pp • H/C (ISBN: 9781522584469) • US $265.00 (our price)

Online Survey Design and Data Analytics Emerging Research and Opportunities
Shalin Hai-Jew (Kansas State University, USA)
Engineering Science Reference • copyright 2019 • 226pp • H/C (ISBN: 9781522585633) • US $215.00 (our price)

Handbook of Research on Big Data and the IoT
Gurjit Kaur (Delhi Technological University, India) and Pradeep Tomar (Gautam Buddha University, India)
Engineering Science Reference • copyright 2019 • 568pp • H/C (ISBN: 9781522574323) • US $295.00 (our price)

Managerial Perspectives on Intelligent Big Data Analytics
Zhaohao Sun (Papua New Guinea University of Technology, Papua New Guinea)
Engineering Science Reference • copyright 2019 • 335pp • H/C (ISBN: 9781522572770) • US $225.00 (our price)

Optimizing Big Data Management and Industrial Systems With Intelligent Techniques
Sultan Ceren Öner (Istanbul Technical University, Turkey) and Oya H. Yüregir (Çukurova University, Turkey)
Engineering Science Reference • copyright 2019 • 238pp • H/C (ISBN: 9781522551379) • US $205.00 (our price)

Big Data Processing With Hadoop
T. Revathi (Mepco Schlenk Engineering College, India) K. Muneeswaran (Mepco Schlenk Engineering College, India) and M. Blessa Binolin Pepsi (Mepco Schlenk Engineering College, India)
Engineering Science Reference • copyright 2019 • 244pp • H/C (ISBN: 9781522537908) • US $195.00 (our price)

701 East Chocolate Avenue, Hershey, PA 17033, USA
Tel: 717-533-8845 x100 • Fax: 717-533-8661
E-Mail: cust@igi-global.com • www.igi-global.com

List of Contributors

Agrawal, Rashmi / *Manav Rachna International Institute of Research and Studies, India* 34

Al Janabi, Mazin A. M. / *EGADE Business School, Tecnologico de Monterrey, Mexico* 214

Alonso Moro, Jorge / *Universidad Europea de Madrid, Spain* 334

Assay, Benjamin Enahoro / *Delta State Polytechnic, Ogwashi-Uku, Nigeria* 345

Aydın, Mehmet Nafiz / *Kadir Has University, Turkey* 10

Bala, P. Shanthi / *Pondicherry University, India* 74

Berlanga, Antonio / *Grupo de Inteligencia Artificial Aplicada. Universidad Carlos III de
    Madrid, Spain* 311

Bogomolov, Timofei / *University of South Australia, Australia* 378

Bogomolova, Svetlana / *Business School, Ehrenberg-Bass Institute, University of South
    Australia, Australia* 378

Chander, Bhanu / *Pondicherry University, India* 50

Chavan, Pallavi Vijay / *Ramrao Adik Institute of Technolgy, India* 204

Chiou, Suh-Wen / *National Dong Hwa University, Taiwan* 231

Dhamodharavadhani S. / *Periyar University, India* 152

Fox, William / *College of William and Mary, USA* 100

Ganapathy, Jayanthi / *Anna University, India* 409

García Márquez, Fausto Pedro / *University of Castilla-La Mancha, Spain* 334

Gómez Muñoz, Carlos Quiterio / *Universidad Europea de Madrid, Spain* 334

K., Jayashree / *Rajalaskshmi Engineering College, India* 1

Korolkiewicz, Malgorzata W. / *University of South Australia, Australia* 378

Molina, José M. / *Grupo de Inteligencia Artificial Aplicada. Universidad Carlos III de Madrid,
    Spain* 311

N., Narmadha / *Periyar University, India* 366

Ninh, Anh / *College of William and Mary, USA* 100

Patricio, Miguel A. / *Universidad Carlos III de Madrid, Spain* 311

Perdahçı, Ziya Nazım / *Mimar Sinan Fine Arts University, Turkey* 10

R., Chithambaramani / *TJS Engineering College, India* 1

Ramezani, Niloofar / *George Mason University, USA* 135

Rather, Sajad Ahmad / *Pondicherry University, India* 74

Rathipriya R. / *Periyar University, India* 152

Rathipriya, R. / *Periyar University, India* 366

Rodríguez-Pardo, Carlos / *Grupo de Inteligencia Artificial Aplicada. Universidad Carlos III de
    Madrid, Spain* 311

Salunkhe, Aditya Suresh / *Ramrao Adik Institute of Technolgy, India* 204

Sönmez, Ferdi / *Istanbul Arel University, Turkey* 10

Taylan, Pakize / *Dicle University, Turkey* 177

V., Uma / *Pondicherry University, India* 409

Yamamoto, Masahide / *Nagoya Gakuin University, Japan* 279

Table of Contents

Preface xvii

Chapter 1
Big Data and Clustering Techniques 1
  Jayashree K., Rajalaskshmi Engineering College, India
  Chithambaramani R., TJS Engineering College, India

Chapter 2
Big Data Analytics and Models 10
  Ferdi Sönmez, Istanbul Arel University, Turkey
  Ziya Nazım Perdahçı, Mimar Sinan Fine Arts University, Turkey
  Mehmet Nafiz Aydın, Kadir Has University, Turkey

Chapter 3
Technologies for Handling Big Data 34
  Rashmi Agrawal, Manav Rachna International Institute of Research and Studies, India

Chapter 4
Clustering and Bayesian Networks 50
  Bhanu Chander, Pondicherry University, India

Chapter 5
Analysis of Gravitation-Based Optimization Algorithms for Clustering and Classification 74
  Sajad Ahmad Rather, Pondicherry University, India
  P. Shanthi Bala, Pondicherry University, India

Chapter 6
Analytics and Technology for Practical Forecasting 100
  William Fox, College of William and Mary, USA
  Anh Ninh, College of William and Mary, USA

Chapter 7
Modern Statistical Modeling in Machine Learning and Big Data Analytics: Statistical Models for
Continuous and Categorical Variables 135
  Niloofar Ramezani, George Mason University, USA

Chapter 8
Enhanced Logistic Regression (ELR) Model for Big Data 152
    Dhamodharavadhani S., Periyar University, India
    Rathipriya R., Periyar University, India

Chapter 9
On Foundations of Estimation for Nonparametric Regression With Continuous Optimization 177
    Pakize Taylan, Dicle University, Turkey

Chapter 10
An Overview of Methodologies and Challenges in Sentiment Analysis on Social Networks............ 204
    Aditya Suresh Salunkhe, Ramrao Adik Institute of Technolgy, India
    Pallavi Vijay Chavan, Ramrao Adik Institute of Technolgy, India

Chapter 11
Evaluation of Optimum and Coherent Economic-Capital Portfolios Under Complex Market
Prospects 214
    Mazin A. M. Al Janabi, EGADE Business School, Tecnologico de Monterrey, Mexico

Chapter 12
Data-Driven Stochastic Optimization for Transportation Road Network Design Under Uncertainty 231
    Suh-Wen Chiou, National Dong Hwa University, Taiwan

Chapter 13
Examining Visitors' Characteristics and Behaviors in Tourist Destinations Through Mobile Phone
Users' Location Data 279
    Masahide Yamamoto, Nagoya Gakuin University, Japan

Chapter 14
Machine Learning for Smart Tourism and Retail 311
    Carlos Rodríguez-Pardo, Grupo de Inteligencia Artificial Aplicada. Universidad Carlos III
        de Madrid, Spain
    Miguel A. Patricio, Universidad Carlos III de Madrid, Spain
    Antonio Berlanga, Grupo de Inteligencia Artificial Aplicada. Universidad Carlos III de
        Madrid, Spain
    José M. Molina, Grupo de Inteligencia Artificial Aplicada. Universidad Carlos III de
        Madrid, Spain

Chapter 15
Predictive Analysis of Robotic Manipulators Through Inertial Sensors and Pattern Recognition..... 334
    Jorge Alonso Moro, Universidad Europea de Madrid, Spain
    Carlos Quiterio Gómez Muñoz, Universidad Europea de Madrid, Spain
    Fausto Pedro García Márquez, University of Castilla-La Mancha, Spain

Chapter 16
Call Masking: A Worrisome Trend in Nigeria's Telecommunications Industry 345
Benjamin Enahoro Assay, Delta State Polytechnic, Ogwashi-Uku, Nigeria

Chapter 17
An Optimized Three-Dimensional Clustering for Microarray Data 366
Narmadha N., Periyar University, India
R. Rathipriya, Periyar University, India

Chapter 18
Identifying Patterns in Fresh Produce Purchases: The Application of Machine Learning
Techniques 378
Timofei Bogomolov, University of South Australia, Australia
Malgorzata W. Korolkiewicz, University of South Australia, Australia
Svetlana Bogomolova, Business School, Ehrenberg-Bass Institute, University of South
*   Australia, Australia*

Chapter 19
Urban Spatial Data Computing: Integration of GIS and GPS Towards Location-Based
Recommendations 409
Uma V., Pondicherry University, India
Jayanthi Ganapathy, Anna University, India

Compilation of References 432

About the Contributors 470

Index 476

Detailed Table of Contents

Preface xvii

Chapter 1

Big Data and Clustering Techniques 1
    Jayashree K., Rajalaskshmi Engineering College, India
    Chithambaramani R., TJS Engineering College, India

Big data has become a chief strength of innovation across academics, governments, and corporates. Big data comprises massive sensor data, raw and semi-structured log data of IT industries, and the exploded quantity of data from social media. Big data needs big storage, and this volume makes operations such as analytical operations, process operations, retrieval operations very difficult and time consuming. One way to overcome these difficult problems is to have big data clustered in a compact format. Thus, this chapter discusses the background of big data and clustering. It also discusses the various application of big data in detail. The various related work, research challenges of big data, and the future direction are addressed in this chapter.

Chapter 2

Big Data Analytics and Models 10
    Ferdi Sönmez, Istanbul Arel University, Turkey
    Ziya Nazım Perdahçı, Mimar Sinan Fine Arts University, Turkey
    Mehmet Nafiz Aydın, Kadir Has University, Turkey

When uncertainty is regarded as a surprise and an event in the minds, it can be said that individuals can change the future view. Market, financial, operational, social, environmental, institutional and humanitarian risks and uncertainties are the inherent realities of the modern world. Life is suffused with randomness and volatility; everything momentous that occurs in the illustrious sweep of history, or in our individual lives, is an outcome of uncertainty. An important implication of such uncertainty is the financial instability engendered to the victims of different sorts of perils. This chapter is intended to explore big data analytics as a comprehensive technique for processing large amounts of data to uncover insights. Several techniques before big data analytics like financial econometrics and optimization models have been used. Therefore, initially these techniques are mentioned. Then, how big data analytics has altered the methods of analysis is mentioned. Lastly, cases promoting big data analytics are mentioned.

Chapter 3

Technologies for Handling Big Data 34
    Rashmi Agrawal, Manav Rachna International Institute of Research and Studies, India

In today's world, every time we connect phone to internet, pass through a CCTV camera, order pizza online, or even pay with credit card to buy some clothes, we generate data and that "ocean of data" is popularly known as big data. The amount of data that's being created and stored on a universal level is almost inconceivable, and it just keeps growing. The amount of data we create is doubled every year. Big data is a critical concept that integrates all kinds of data and plays an important role for strategic intelligence for any modern company. The importance of big data doesn't revolve around how much data you have, but what you do with it. Big data is now the key for competition and growth for new startups, medium, and big enterprises. Scientific research is now on boom using big data. For the astronomers, Sloan Digital Sky Survey has become a central resource. Big data has the potential to revolutionize research and education as well. The aim of this chapter is to discuss the technologies that are pertinent and essential for big data.

Chapter 4

Clustering and Bayesian Networks 50
    Bhanu Chander, Pondicherry University, India

The goal of this chapter is to present an outline of clustering and Bayesian schemes used in data mining, machine learning communities. Standardized data into sensible groups is the preeminent mode of understanding as well as learning. A cluster constitutes a set regarding entities that are alike and entities from different clusters are not alike. Representing data by fewer clusters inevitably loses certain fine important information but achieves better simplification. There is no training stage in clustering; mostly, it's used when the classes are not well-known. Bayesian network is one of the best classification methods and is frequently used. Generally, Bayesian network is a form of graphical probabilistic representation model that consists of a set of interconnected nodes, where each node represents a variable, and inter-link connection represents a causal relationship of those variables. Belief networks are graph symbolized models that successfully model familiarity via transmitting probabilistic information to a variety of assumptions.

Chapter 5

Analysis of Gravitation-Based Optimization Algorithms for Clustering and Classification 74
    Sajad Ahmad Rather, Pondicherry University, India
    P. Shanthi Bala, Pondicherry University, India

In recent years, various heuristic algorithms based on natural phenomena and swarm behaviors were introduced to solve innumerable optimization problems. These optimization algorithms show better performance than conventional algorithms. Recently, the gravitational search algorithm (GSA) is proposed for optimization which is based on Newton's law of universal gravitation and laws of motion. Within a few years, GSA became popular among the research community and has been applied to various fields such as electrical science, power systems, computer science, civil and mechanical engineering, etc. This chapter shows the importance of GSA, its hybridization, and applications in solving clustering and classification problems. In clustering, GSA is hybridized with other optimization algorithms to overcome the drawbacks such as curse of dimensionality, trapping in local optima, and limited search space of conventional data clustering algorithms. GSA is also applied to classification problems for pattern recognition, feature extraction, and increasing classification accuracy.

Chapter 6

Analytics and Technology for Practical Forecasting 100

William Fox, College of William and Mary, USA
Anh Ninh, College of William and Mary, USA

With the importance of forecasting in businesses, a wide variety of methods and tools has been developed over the years to automate the process of forecasting. However, an unintended consequence of this tremendous advancement is that forecasting has become more and more like a black box function. Thus, a primary goal of this chapter is to provide a clear understanding of forecasting in any application contexts with a systematic procedure for practical forecasting through step-by-step examples. Several methods are presented, and the authors compare results to what were the typical forecasting methods including regression and time series in different software technologies. Three case studies are presented: simple supply forecasting, homicide forecasting, and demand forecasting for sales from Walmart.

Chapter 7

Modern Statistical Modeling in Machine Learning and Big Data Analytics: Statistical Models for Continuous and Categorical Variables... 135

Niloofar Ramezani, George Mason University, USA

Machine learning, big data, and high dimensional data are the topics we hear about frequently these days, and some even call them the wave of the future. Therefore, it is important to use appropriate statistical models, which have been established for many years, and their efficiency has already been evaluated to contribute into advancing machine learning, which is a relatively newer field of study. Different algorithms that can be used within machine learning, depending on the nature of the variables, are discussed, and appropriate statistical techniques for modeling them are presented in this chapter.

Chapter 8

Enhanced Logistic Regression (ELR) Model for Big Data 152

Dhamodharavadhani S., Periyar University, India
Rathipriya R., Periyar University, India

Regression model is an important tool for modeling and analyzing data. In this chapter, the proposed model comprises three phases. The first phase concentrates on sampling techniques to get best sample for building the regression model. The second phase is to predict the residual of logistic regression (LR) model using time series analysis method: autoregressive. The third phase is to develop enhanced logistic regression (ELR) model by combining both LR model and residual prediction (RP) model. The empirical study is carried out to study the performance of the ELR model using large diabetic dataset. The results show that ELR model has a higher level of accuracy than the traditional logistic regression model.

Chapter 9

On Foundations of Estimation for Nonparametric Regression With Continuous Optimization 177

Pakize Taylan, Dicle University, Turkey

The aim of parametric regression models like linear regression and nonlinear regression are to produce a reasonable relationship between response and independent variables based on the assumption of linearity and predetermined nonlinearity in the regression parameters by finite set of parameters. Nonparametric regression techniques are widely-used statistical techniques, and they not only relax the assumption of linearity in the regression parameters, but they also do not need a predetermined functional form as nonlinearity for the relationship between response and independent variables. It is capable of handling higher dimensional problem and sizes of sample than regression that considers parametric models because the data should provide both the model building and the model estimates. For this purpose, firstly, PRSS problems for MARS, ADMs, and CR will be constructed. Secondly, the solution of the generated problems will be obtained with CQP, one of the famous methods of convex optimization, and these solutions will be called CMARS, CADMs, and CKR, respectively.

Chapter 10

An Overview of Methodologies and Challenges in Sentiment Analysis on Social Networks............ 204
    Aditya Suresh Salunkhe, Ramrao Adik Institute of Technolgy, India
    Pallavi Vijay Chavan, Ramrao Adik Institute of Technolgy, India

The expeditious increase in the adoption of social media over the last decade, determining and analyzing the attitude and opinion of masses related to a particular entity, has gained quite an importance. With the landing of the Web 2.0, many internet products like blogs, community chatrooms, forums, microblog are serving as a platform for people to express themselves. Such opinion is found in the form of messages, user-comments, news articles, personal blogs, tweets, surveys, status updates, etc. With sentiment analysis, it is possible to eliminate the need to manually going through each and every user comment by focusing on the contextual polarity of the text. Analyzing the sentiments could serve a number of applications like advertisements, recommendations, quality analysis, monetization provided on the web services, real-time analysis of data, analyzing notions related to candidates during election campaign, etc.

Chapter 11

Evaluation of Optimum and Coherent Economic-Capital Portfolios Under Complex Market
Prospects 214
    Mazin A. M. Al Janabi, EGADE Business School, Tecnologico de Monterrey, Mexico

This chapter examines the performance of liquidity-adjusted risk modeling in obtaining optimum and coherent economic-capital structures, subject to meaningful operational and financial constraints as specified by the portfolio manager. Specifically, the chapter proposes a robust approach to optimum economic-capital allocation in a liquidity-adjusted value at risk (L-VaR) framework. This chapter expands previous approaches by explicitly modeling the liquidation of trading portfolios, over the holding period, with the aid of an appropriate scaling of the multiple-assets' L-VaR matrix along with GARCH-M technique to forecast conditional volatility and expected return. Moreover, in this chapter, the authors develop a dynamic nonlinear portfolio selection model and an optimization algorithm, which allocates both economic-capital and trading assets by minimizing L-VaR objective function. The empirical results strongly confirm the importance of enforcing financially and operationally meaningful nonlinear and dynamic constraints, when they are available, on the L-VaR optimization procedure.

Chapter 12

Data-Driven Stochastic Optimization for Transportation Road Network Design Under Uncertainty 231
    Suh-Wen Chiou, National Dong Hwa University, Taiwan

A data-driven stochastic program for bi-level network design with hazardous material (hazmat) transportation is proposed in this chapter. In order to regulate the risk associated with hazmat transportation and minimize total travel cost on interested area under stochasticity, a multi-objective stochastic optimization model is presented to determine generalized travel cost for hazmat carriers. Since the bi-level program is generally non-convex, a data-driven bundle method is presented to stabilize solutions of the proposed model and reduce relative gaps between iterations. Numerical comparisons are made with existing risk-averse models. The results indicate that the proposed data-driven stochastic model becomes more resilient than others in minimizing total travel cost and mitigating risk exposure. Moreover, the trade-offs among maximum risk exposure, generalized travel costs, and maximum equitable risk spreading over links are empirically investigated in this chapter.

Chapter 13

Examining Visitors' Characteristics and Behaviors in Tourist Destinations Through Mobile Phone Users' Location Data 279
Masahide Yamamoto, Nagoya Gakuin University, Japan

This chapter uses Mobile Kukan Toukei™ (mobile spatial statistics) to collect the location data of mobile phone users in order to count the number of visitors at specific tourist destinations and examine their characteristics. Mobile Kukan Toukei is statistical population data created by an operational data of mobile phone networks. It is possible to estimate the population structure of a region by gender, age, and residence using this service of the company. The locations and characteristics of the individuals obtained herein are derived through a non-identification process, aggregation processing, and concealment processing. Therefore, it is impossible to identify specific individuals. This chapter attempts to identify the number of visitors in different periods and their characteristics based on the location data of mobile phone users collected by the mobile phone company. In addition, it also attempts to demonstrate an alternative method to more accurately infer the number of visitors in specific areas.

Chapter 14

Machine Learning for Smart Tourism and Retail 311
Carlos Rodríguez-Pardo, Grupo de Inteligencia Artificial Aplicada. Universidad Carlos III de Madrid, Spain
Miguel A. Patricio, Universidad Carlos III de Madrid, Spain
Antonio Berlanga, Grupo de Inteligencia Artificial Aplicada. Universidad Carlos III de Madrid, Spain
José M. Molina, Grupo de Inteligencia Artificial Aplicada. Universidad Carlos III de Madrid, Spain

The unprecedented growth in the amount and variety of data we can store about the behaviour of customers has been parallel to the popularization and development of machine learning algorithms. This confluence of factors has created the opportunity of understanding customer behaviour and preferences in ways that were undreamt of in the past. In this chapter, the authors study the possibilities of different state-of-the-art machine learning algorithms for retail and smart tourism applications, which are domains that share common characteristics, such as contextual dependence and the kind of data that can be used to understand customers. They explore how supervised, unsupervised, and recommender systems can be used to profile, segment, and create value for customers.

Chapter 15
Predictive Analysis of Robotic Manipulators Through Inertial Sensors and Pattern Recognition 334
    Jorge Alonso Moro, Universidad Europea de Madrid, Spain
    Carlos Quiterio Gómez Muñoz, Universidad Europea de Madrid, Spain
    Fausto Pedro García Márquez, University of Castilla-La Mancha, Spain

Industrial robotics is constantly evolving, with installation forecast of about 2 million new robots in 2020. The predictive maintenance focused on industrial robots is beginning to be applied more, but its possibilities have not yet been fully exploited. The present study focuses on the applications offered by inertial sensors in the field of industrial robotics, specifically the possibility of measuring the "real" rotation angle of a robotic arm and comparing it with its own system of measure. The study will focus on the measurement of the backlash existing in the gearbox of the axis of a robot. Data received from the sensor will be analysed using the wavelet transform, and the mechanical state of the system could be determined. The introduction of this sensing system is safe, dynamic, and non-destructive, and it allows one to perform the measurement remotely, in the own installation of the robot and in working conditions. These features allow one to use the device in different predictive functions.

Chapter 16
Call Masking: A Worrisome Trend in Nigeria's Telecommunications Industry 345
    Benjamin Enahoro Assay, Delta State Polytechnic, Ogwashi-Uku, Nigeria

The phenomenon of call masking and other related infractions have assumed frightening dimension in Nigeria. Apart from depriving the government and telecoms companies of huge revenue, the sharp practices also constitute a security threat to the nation. In a bid to curb the menace, the Nigerian Communications Commission, the industry regulator, had to suspend six interconnect exchange licenses in February 2018 and bar 750,000 lines belonging to 13 operators from the national network suspected to have been involved in the criminal act. However, in spite of the measures taken by NCC, the sharp practices have continued unabated. It is against this backdrop that this chapter proffers solutions and recommends ways to nip the infractions in the bud and save the telecoms industry from imminent collapse.

Chapter 17
An Optimized Three-Dimensional Clustering for Microarray Data 366
    Narmadha N., Periyar University, India
    R. Rathipriya, Periyar University, India

This chapter focuses on discrete firefly optimization algorithm (FA)-based microarray data, which is a meta-heuristic, bio-inspired, optimization algorithm based on the flashing behaviour of fireflies, or lighting bugs. Its primary advantage is the global communication among the fireflies, and as a result, it seems more effective for triclustering problem. This chapter aims to render a clear description of a new firefly algorithm (FA) for optimization of tricluster applications. This research work proposes discrete firefly optimization-based triclustering model first time to find the highly correlated tricluster from microarray data. This model is reliable and robust triclustering model because of efficient global communication among the swarming particles called fireflies.

Chapter 18

Identifying Patterns in Fresh Produce Purchases: The Application of Machine Learning
Techniques 378

    Timofei Bogomolov, University of South Australia, Australia
    Malgorzata W. Korolkiewicz, University of South Australia, Australia
    Svetlana Bogomolova, Business School, Ehrenberg-Bass Institute, University of South
        Australia, Australia

In this chapter, machine learning techniques are applied to examine consumer food choices, specifically purchasing patterns in relation to fresh fruit and vegetables. This product category contributes some of the highest profit margins for supermarkets, making understanding consumer choices in that category important not just for health but also economic reasons. Several unsupervised and supervised machine learning techniques, including hierarchical clustering, latent class analysis, linear regression, artificial neural networks, and deep learning neural networks, are illustrated using Nielsen Consumer Panel Dataset, a large and high-quality source of information on consumer purchases in the United States. The main finding from the clustering analysis is that households who buy less fresh produce are those with children – an important insight with significant public health implications. The main outcome from predictive modelling of spending on fresh fruit and vegetables is that contrary to expectations, neural networks failed to outperform a linear regression model.

Chapter 19

Urban Spatial Data Computing: Integration of GIS and GPS Towards Location-Based
Recommendations 409

    Uma V., Pondicherry University, India
    Jayanthi Ganapathy, Anna University, India

Urban spatial data is the source of information in analysing risks due to natural disaster, evacuation planning, risk mapping and assessments, etc. Global positioning system (GPS) is a satellite-based technology that is used to navigate on earth. Geographical information system (GIS) is a software system that facilitates software services to mankind in various application domains such as agriculture, ecology, forestry, geomorphology analysis in earthquake and landslides, laying of underground water pipe connection and demographic studies like population migration, urban settlements, etc. Thus, spatial and temporal relations of real-time activities can be analysed to predict the future activities like predicting places of interest. Time analysis of such activities helps in personalisation of activities or development of recommendation systems, which could suggest places of interest. Thus, GPS mapping with data analytics using GIS would pave way for commercial and business development in large scale.

Compilation of References 432

About the Contributors 470

Index 476

Preface

Big Data and Management Science has been designed and done to synthesize the analytic principles with business practice and big data. Specifically, the book provides an interface between the main disciplines of engineering/technology and the organizational, administrative, and planning abilities of management. It is complementary to other sub-disciplines such as economics, finance, marketing, decision and risk analysis, etc.

The Advances in Analytics in Big Data synthesizes the analytic principles with Big Data and provides an interface between the main disciplines of engineering/economics and the organizational, administrative, and planning abilities of management. It is also complementary to other disciplines such as finance, marketing, decision and risk analysis. In this book each chapter discusses different topics in Advances in Business Analytics

This book will aim to provide relevant theoretical frameworks and the latest empirical research findings in the area. It will be written for professionals who want to improve their understanding of the strategic role of trust at different levels of the information and knowledge society, that is, trust at the level of the global economy, of networks and organizations, of teams and work groups, of information systems and, finally, trust at the level of individuals as actors in the networked environments.

This book is intended for engineers, economists and researchers who wish to develop new skills in management, or who employ the management discipline as part of their work. The authors of this volume describe their original work in the area or provide material for case studies successfully applying the management discipline in real life cases where is employed Bid Data.

Big data concept became a chief strength of innovation across academics, governments and corporates. Big data comprises massive sensor data, raw and semi-structured log data of IT industries and the exploded quantity of data from social media. Big data need big storage and this volume makes operations such as analytical operations, process operations, retrieval operations, very difficult and time consuming. One way to overcome these difficult problems is to have big data clustered in a compact format. Thus, Chapter 1 discusses the background of big data and clustering. It also discusses the various application of big data in detail. The various related work, research challenges of big data and the future direction would be addressed in this chapter.

Uncertainty is expressed as a situation in which many different outcomes of an option can take place in the decision-making process, but the probabilities of these different outcomes are unknown. When uncertainty is regarded as a surprise and an event in the minds, it can be said that individuals can change the future view. Market, financial, operational, social, environmental, institutional and humanitarian risks and uncertainties are the inherent realities of the modern world. Life is suffused with randomness and volatility; everything momentous that occurs in the illustrious sweep of history, or in our individual lives, is an outcome of uncertainty. An important implication of such uncertainty is the financial instability engendered to the victims of different sorts of perils. Chapter 2 is intended to explore big data analytics as a comprehensive technique for processing large amounts of data to uncover insights. Several techniques before big data analytics like financial econometrics and optimization models have been used. Therefore, initially these techniques are mentioned. Then, how big data analytics has altered the methods of analysis is mentioned. Lastly, cases promoting big data analytics are mentioned.

Big Data is a critical concept that integrates all kinds of data and plays an important role for strategic intelligence for any modern company. The importance of big data does not revolve around how much data you have, but what you do with it. Big data is now the key for competition and growth for new startups, medium and big enterprises. Scientific research is now on boom using big data. For the astronomers, Sloan Digital Sky Survey has become a central resource. Big data has the potential to revolutionize research and education as well. The aim of Chapter 3 is to discuss the technologies which are pertinent and essential for the big data.

Chapter 4 presents an outline of clustering and Bayesian schemes used in data mining, machine learning communities. Standardize data into sensible groups is preeminent modes of understanding as well as learning. A cluster constitutes set regarding entities which are alike and entities from different clusters are not alike. Representing data by fewer clusters inevitably loses certain fine important information but achieves better simplification. Basically, there is no training stage in clustering; mostly it is used when the classes are not well-known in prior. Bayesian network is one of the best classification method which is frequently used. Generally, Bayesian network is a form of graphical probabilistic representation model consist a set of interconnected nodes, where each node represents a variable and inter-link connection represents a causal relationship of those variables. Belief networks are graph symbolize models that successfully model familiarity estate via transmit probabilistic information to a variety of assumption.

Social media becomes very popular in everyday life. Hence, as a result, the database becomes huge. Therefore, many enterprises are shifting their analytical databases towards cloud instead of high-end proprietary machines and moving towards a cheaper solution. Hence, the concept of MapReduce comes into consideration that provides better scalability, fault tolerance, and flexibility in handling unstructured analytical data.

Chapter 5 shows the importance of GSA, its hybridization and applications in solving clustering and classification problems. In clustering, GSA is hybridized with other optimization algorithms to overcome the drawbacks such as curse of dimensionality, trapping in local optima and limited search space of conventional data clustering algorithms. GSA is also applied to classification problems for pattern recognition, feature extraction, and increasing classification accuracy.

With the importance of forecasting in businesses, a wide variety of methods and tools has been developed over the years to automate the process of forecasting. However, an unintended consequence of this tremendous advancement is that forecasting has become more and more like a black box function. Thus, a primary goal of Chapter 6 is to provide a clear understanding of forecasting in any application contexts with a systematic procedure for practical forecasting through step-by-step examples. Several methods are presented and the authors compare results to what were the typical forecasting methods including regression and time series in different software technologies. Three case studies are presented: simple supply forecasting, homicide forecasting, and demand forecasting for sales from Walmart.

Machine learning, big data, and high dimensional data are the topics we hear about frequently these days and some even call them the wave of the future. Therefore, it is important to use appropriate statistical models, which have been established for many years and their efficiency have already been evaluated, to contribute into advancing machine learning, which is a relatively newer field of study. Different algorithms that can be used within machine learning, depending on the nature of the variables, are discussed and appropriate statistical techniques for modeling them are presented in Chapter 7.

Regression model is an important tool for modeling and analyzing data. In Chapter 8, the proposed model comprises of three phases. First phase concentrates on sampling techniques to get best sample for building the regression model. Second phase is to predict the residual of Logistic Regression (LR) model using time series analysis method- Autoregressive. Third phase is to develop Enhanced Logistic Regression (ELR) model by combining the both LR model and Residual Prediction (RP) Model. The empirical study is carried out to the study the performance of the ELR model using large diabetic dataset. The results show that ELR model has higher level of accuracy than the traditional Logistic Regression model.

The aim of parametric regression models like linear regression and nonlinear regression are to produce a reasonable relationship between response and independent variables based on the assumption of linearity and predetermined nonlinearity in the regression parameters by finite set of parameters. Nonparametric regression techniques are widely-used statistical techniques and they are not only relax the assumption of linearity in the regression parameters, but they also do not need a predetermined functional form as nonlinearity for the relationship between response and independent variables. It capable of handling higher dimensional problem and sizes of sample than regression that considers parametric models because the data should provide both the model building and the model estimates. For this purpose, in Chapter 9, firstly, PRSS problems for MARS, ADMs and CR will be constructed. Secondly, the solution of the generated problems will be obtained with CQP, one of the famous methods of convex optimization, and these solutions will be called CMARS, CADMs and CKR respectively.

Chapter 10

The expeditious increase in the adoption of social media over the last decade, determining and analyzing the attitude and opinion of masses related to a particular entity has gained quite an importance. With the landing of the Web (2.0), many internet products like Blogs, Community Chatrooms, Forums, Microblog are serving as a platform for people to express themselves. Such opinion is found in the form of messages, user-comments, news articles, personal blogs, tweets, surveys, status updates etc. With sentiment analysis, it is possible to eliminate the need to manually going through each and every user comment by focusing on the contextual polarity of the text. Analyzing the sentiments could serve a number of applications like advertisements, recommendations, quality analysis, monetization provided on the Web services, real-time analysis of data, analyzing notions related to candidates during election campaign, etc. This is analysed in Chapter 10.

Chapter 11 examines the performance of liquidity-adjusted risk modeling in obtaining optimum and coherent economic-capital structures, subject to meaningful operational and financial constraints as specified by the portfolio manager. Specifically, the chapter proposes a robust approach to optimum economic-capital allocation, in a Liquidity-Adjusted Value at Risk (L-VaR) framework. This chapter expands previous approaches by explicitly modeling the liquidation of trading portfolios, over the holding period, with the aid of an appropriate scaling of the multiple-assets' L-VaR matrix along with GARCH-M technique to forecast conditional volatility and expected return. Moreover, in this chapter, the authors develop a dynamic nonlinear portfolio selection model and an optimization algorithm, which allocates both economic-capital and trading assets by minimizing L-VaR objective function. The empirical results strongly confirm the importance of enforcing financially and operationally meaningful nonlinear and dynamic constraints, when they are available, on the L-VaR optimization procedure.

A data-driven stochastic program for bi-level network design with hazardous material (hazmat) transportation is proposed in Chapter 12. In order to regulate the risk associated with hazmat transportation and minimize total travel cost on interested area under stochasticity, a multi-objective stochastic optimization model is presented to determine generalized travel cost for hazmat carriers. Since the bi-level program is generally non-convex, a data-driven bundle method is presented to stabilize solutions of the proposed model and reduce relative gaps between iterations. Numerical comparisons are made with existing risk-averse models. The results indicate that the proposed data-driven stochastic model becomes more resilient than others in minimizing total travel cost and mitigating risk exposure. More-over, the trade-offs among maximum risk exposure, generalized travel costs and maximum equitable risk spreading over links are empirically investigated in this chapter.

Chapter 13 uses "Mobile Kukan Toukei™" (mobile spatial statistics) to collect the location data of mobile phone users in order to count the number of visitors at specific tourist destinations and examine their characteristics. Mobile Kukan Toukei is statistical population data created by a mobile phone network. It is possible to estimate the population structure of a region by gender, age, and residence using this service of the company. The locations and characteristics of the individuals obtained herein are derived through a non-identification process, aggregation processing, and concealment processing. Therefore, it is impossible to identify specific individuals. This chapter attempts to identify the number of visitors in different periods and their characteristics based on the location data of mobile phone users collected by the mobile phone company. In addition, it also attempts to demonstrate an alternative method to more accurately infer the number of visitors in specific areas.

The unprecedented growth in the amount and variety of data it can be stored about the behaviour of customers has been parallel to the popularization and development of machine learning algorithms. This confluence of factors has created the opportunity of understanding customer's behaviours and preferences in ways that were undreamt of in the past. Chapter 14, the authors study the possibilities of different state-of-the-art machine learning algorithms for retail and smart tourism applications, which are domains that share common characteristics, such as contextual dependence and the kind of data that can be used to understand customers. They explore how supervised, unsupervised and recommender systems can be used to profile, segment and create value for customers.

Industrial robotics is constantly evolving, with installation forecast of about 2 million new robots in 2020. It is necessary to be more efficient in the processes, producing more in less time, which implies reducing the time of penalizing breakdowns of the plants. The predictive maintenance focused on in-dustrial robots is beginning to be applied more, but its possibilities have not yet been fully exploited. Chapter 15 focuses on the applications offered by inertial sensors in the field of industrial robotics, specifically the possibility of measuring the "real" rotation angle of a robotic arm and comparing it with its own system of measure. This could determinate the need to make actions plans to extend the life of industrial robots and avoid unwanted stops of production processes, which could only be solved through corrective actions. The study will focus on the measurement of the backlash existing in the gearbox of the axis of a robot. Data received from the sensor will be analysed using the Wavelet Transform, and the mechanical state of the system could be determined. The introduction of this sensing system is safe, dynamic and non-destructive, and it allows to perform the measurement remotely, in the own installa-tion of the robot and in working conditions. The data of the sensor can be stored to determine pattern of movements and compare them in the future with the current values. All these features allow to use the device in different predictive functions.

Chapter 16 discussed the phenomenon of call masking, and other related infractions have assumed frightening dimension in Nigeria. Apart from depriving the government and telecoms companies of huge revenue, the sharp practices also constitute security threat to the nation. In a bid to curb the menace, the Nigerian Communications Commission, the industry regulator, had to suspend six interconnect exchange licenses in February 2018 and bar 750,000 lines belonging to 13 operators from the national network suspected to have been involved in the criminal act. However, in spite of the measures taken by NCC, the sharp practices have continued unabated. It is against this backdrop that this chapter proffers solutions and recommends ways to nip the infractions in the bud and save the telecoms industry from imminent collapse.

Chapter 17 focuses on Discrete Firefly Optimization Algorithm (FA) based Microarray Data which is a meta-heuristic, bio-inspired, optimization algorithm based on the flashing behaviour of fireflies, or lighting bugs. Its primary advantage is the global communication among the fireflies, and as a result, it seems more effective for triclustering problem. This chapter aims to render a clear description of a new Firefly Algorithm (FA) for optimization of tricluster applications. this research work proposes Discrete Firefly Optimization based Triclustering model first time to find the highly correlated tricluster from microarray data. This model is reliable and robust triclustering model because of efficient global communication among the swarming particles called fireflies.

In Chapter 18, machine learning techniques are applied to examine consumer food choices, specifically purchasing patterns in relation to fresh fruit and vegetables. This product category contributes some of the highest profit margins for supermarkets, making understanding consumer choices in that category important not just for health, but also for economic reasons. Several unsupervised and supervised machine learning techniques, including hierarchical clustering, latent class analysis, linear regression, artificial neural networks, and deep learning neural networks are illustrated using the Nielsen Consumer Panel Dataset, a large and high-quality source of information on consumer purchases in the United States. The main finding from the clustering analysis is that households that buy less fresh produce are those with children – an important insight with significant public health implications. The main outcome from predictive modelling of spending on fresh fruit and vegetables is that contrary to expectations, neural networks failed to outperform linear regression models.

Finally, Chapter 19 studies the urban spatial data as the source of information in analysing risks due to natural disaster, evacuation planning, risk mapping and assessments etc. Global Positioning System (GPS) is a satellite based technology which is used to navigate on earth. It enables tracking of stationary and non-stationary objects in real world. Geographical Information System (GIS) is a software system that facilitates software services to mankind in various application domains such as agriculture, ecology, forestry, geomorphology analysis in earthquake and landslides, laying of underground water pipe connection and demographic studies like population migration, urban settlements etc. Spatial and temporal analysis of such human activities involves aggregation of spatial and temporal factors. Further, these factors act as prime elements in decision making on human activities when they are related. Thus, spatial and temporal relations of real time activities can be analysed to predict the future activities like predicting places of interest. Time analysis of such activities helps in personalisation of activities or development of recommendation systems which could suggest places of interest. Thus, GPS mapping with data analytics using GIS would pave way for commercial and business development in large scale.

Fausto Pedro García Márquez
University of Castilla-La Mancha, Spain

Chapter 1
Big Data and Clustering Techniques

Jayashree K.
Rajalaskshmi Engineering College, India

Chithambaramani R.
TJS Engineering College, India

ABSTRACT

Big data has become a chief strength of innovation across academics, governments, and corporates. Big data comprises massive sensor data, raw and semi-structured log data of IT industries, and the exploded quantity of data from social media. Big data needs big storage, and this volume makes operations such as analytical operations, process operations, retrieval operations very difficult and time consuming. One way to overcome these difficult problems is to have big data clustered in a compact format. Thus, this chapter discusses the background of big data and clustering. It also discusses the various application of big data in detail. The various related work, research challenges of big data, and the future direction are addressed in this chapter.

INTRODUCTION

Big data is the rapidly changing research areas which involved wide-ranging consideration from academia, industry, and government. The likely of changing the real world force the researchers to originate up with progressive learning methods to overawed the current issues. Big data is data having complexity, scalability, and diversity and it needs new methods, designs, analytics, and algorithms to succeed concealed knowledge and extract value from it. Big data analytics encompass the method of gathering, organizing and examining big data. It examines large datasets having a variety of data types to relate concealed patterns, customer favorites, market drifts, unknown associations and other useful commercial data. (Singh et al., 2018).

It becomes imperious to find a structure in a group of unlabeled data and this method is called Clustering. Clustering is the process of organizing the data into clusters whose members are similar in some

DOI: 10.4018/978-1-7998-0106-1.ch001

way while data in different clusters are dissimilar. (Jacob & Vijayakumar 2018). The problem of clustering is becoming more and more relevant in many areas. Currently, many different clustering algorithms have been developed. Their complexity depends on the dimensionality of the data, the volume of the clustering set, the scope of application, and so on. Clustering is an unsupervised learning technique and a useful technique that applied into many areas like marketing studies, DNA analysis, text mining and web documents classification (Goel, 2014)

The remainder of this chapter is organized as follows: Section 2 provides a general overview of big data and Clustering techniques; Section 3 discusses the related work. Section 4 discusses the challenges of big data and clustering. Section 5 presents the future research directions discussion and Section 6 concludes the chapter.

BACKGROUND

Big Data

Big data is a set of techniques and technologies that require new forms of integration to uncover large hidden values from large datasets that are diverse, complex, and of a massive scale (Hashem, 2015).

1. Volume refers to the amount of all types of data generated from different sources and continue to expand. The benefit of gathering large amounts of data includes the creation of hidden information and patterns through data analysis
2. Variety refers to the different types of data collected through sensors, smartphones, or social networks. Such data types include video, image, text, audio, and data logs, in either structured or unstructured format.
3. Velocity refers to the speed of data transfer. The contents of data constantly change because of the absorption of complementary data collections, introduction of previously archived data or legacy collections, and streamed data arriving from multiple sources (Berman, 2013).
4. Value refers to the process of discovering huge hidden values from large datasets with various types and rapid generation (Chen, 2014).

Importance of Big Data (Sasi Kiran 2015)

The government's emphasis is on how big data creates "value" – both within and across disciplines and domains. Value arises from the ability to analyze the data to develop actionable information. (Jinquan, 2011) suggests five generic ways that big data can support value creation for organizations.

1. Creating transparency by making big data openly available for business and functional analysis.
2. Supporting experimental analysis in individual locations that can test decisions or approaches, such as specific market programs.
3. Assisting, based on customer information, in defining market segmentation at more narrow levels.
4. Supporting real-time analysis and decisions based on sophisticated analytics applied to data sets from customers and embedded sensors.

5.   Facilitating computer-assisted innovation in products based on embedded product sensors indicating customer responses.

Clustering Techniques

Rodriguez et al, 2019 have discussed Machine learning encompasses different topics such as regression analysis, feature selection methods, and classification. Three main approaches can be considered for classification: supervised, semi-supervised and unsupervised classification. In supervised classification, the classes, or labels, of some objects are known earlier, defining the training set, and an algorithm is used to obtain the classification criteria. Semi-supervised classification deals with training the algorithm using both labeled and unlabeled data. They are commonly used when manually labeling a dataset becomes costly. Unsupervised classification, referred as clustering, deals with defining classes from the data without knowledge of the class labels. The purpose of clustering algorithms is to identify groups of objects, or clusters, that are more similar to each other than to other clusters. One of the most convenient and understandable approaches for Big data processing is clustering. Clustering is a process of partitioning a set of data into a set of meaningful sub-classes, called clusters. (Vijayalakshmi & Priya 2019).

Hierarchical Based Clustering Algorithms

The Various Hierarchical Clustering Algorithms (Sajana et al 2016)

- BIRCH - Balanced Iterative Reducing and Clustering using Hierarchies.: It is an agglomerative hierarchical algorithm which uses a Clustering Feature (CF-Tree) and incrementally adjusts the quality of sub clusters.
- CURE- Clustering Using REpresentatives: A hierarchy of Divisive approach is used and it selects well scattered points from the cluster and then shrinks towards the center of the cluster by a specified function. Adjacent clusters are merged successively until the no of clusters reduces to desired no of clusters.
- ROCK - Robust Clustering algorithm for Categorical attributes.: It is a hierarchical clustering algorithm in which to form clusters it uses a link strategy. From bottom to top links are merging together to form a cluster.
- Chameleon: It is an agglomerative hierarchical clustering algorithm of dynamic modeling which deals with two phase approach of clustering
- ECHIDNA: It is an agglomerative hierarchical approach for clustering the network traffic data
- SNN - Shared Nearest Neighbors: A hierarchy of top to bottom approach is used for grouping the objects.
- GRIDCLUST - GRID based hierarchical Clustering algorithm.: A clustering algorithm of hierarchical method based on grid structure.
- STING (Stastical Information Grid) Deshmukh & Ramteke 2017: It is a grid-based multi resolution clustering technique in which the embedded spatial area of input object is divided into rectangular cells. Statistical information regarding the attributes in each grid cell, such as the mean, maximum, and minimum values are stored as statistical parameters in the rectangular cells.

Density Based Clustering

The Various Density-Based Clustering Algorithms (Lakshmi et al 2018)

- DBSCAN (Density Based Spatial Clustering Application with Noise): DBSCAN is a clustering algorithm that is based on density. It uses two parameters such as ε and MinPts. ε stands for Eps – neighborhood of a point and MinPts denotes least amount of points in an Eps-neighborhood. Both of these parameters are specified by the user.
- Ordering Points to Identify Clustering Structure (OPTICS): OPTICS is an extension to DBSCAN. In this method points with the higher density are processed first and discover clusters of higher density first. It organizes each and every object in the database and stores the values of core and reachability distance. It maintains a record known as Order Seeds to construct the output ordering.
- Density – based Clustering (DENCLUE): DENCLUE is useful for datasets with great quantity of noise. It uses grid cells to form a cluster and manage these grid units in a structure called tree. Clusters can be defined accurately by classifying density attractors and two functions called influence function, density functions.

Partition Clustering Algorithms

- K-means (Kanungo et al, 2012): It starts with a random initial partition and keeps reassigning the patterns to clusters based on the similarity between the pattern and the cluster centers until a convergence criterion is met.

Multiple Machine Clustering (Suganya et al, 2018)

The various multiple machine clustering algorithms are parallel clustering and Map Reduce based clustering and it is brief as follows

- Parallel clustering: The parallel classification divides the data partitions that will be distributed on different machines
- MapReduce based clustering: MapReduce is a task partitioning mechanism for a distributed execution on a large number of servers. It works under the principle to decompose a task into smaller tasks and the tasks are then dispatched to different servers, and then the results are collected and consolidated.

RELATED WORK

Data originating from smartphones, desktops, sensors, digital documents etc. come under the purview of big data. Big data is characterized by its Volume, Variety, Velocity, Veracity, Validity and Volatility. The big data is gathered from different sources, so it is in several forms, including (Zanoon et al, 2017):

1. Structured data: It is the organized data in the form of tables or databases to be processed.

2. Unstructured data: It represents the biggest proportion of data; it is the data that people generate daily as texts, images, videos, messages, log records, click-streams, etc.
3. Semi-structured data: or multi-structured, It is regarded a kind of structured data but not designed in tables or databases, for example XML documents or JSON (Sremack 2015).

In (Alguliyev et al, 2018) five clustering methods such as k-means, multivariate Gaussian mixture, hierarchical clustering, spectral and nearest neighbor methods were studied. Four proximity measures such as Pearson and Spearman correlation coefficient, cosine similarity and the euclidean distance were used in the experiments. The algorithms were evaluated in the context of 35 gene expression data from either Affymetrix or cDNA chip platforms, using the adjusted rand index for performance evaluation. The multivariate Gaussian mixture method provided the best performance in recovering the actual number of clusters of the datasets. The k-means method displayed similar performance. In this same analysis, the hierarchical method led to limited performance, while the spectral method showed to be particularly sensitive to the proximity measure employed.

PACADBSCAN algorithm is a combination of partitioning-based DBSCAN and customized ant clustering algorithms that can splits the database into N groups based on the density of data, and then cluster each partition with DBSCAN (Ziang,2011). Chen 2017 proposed the use of MapReduce-based soft clustering for large datasets. A divide and conquer approach have been used to divide huge volumes of data into chunks, The MapReduce model causes each of map and reduce phase to work in autonomous of other running map and reduce phases which are run in parallel. Shafiq & Torunski, 2017 proposed a parallel K-Medoids clustering algorithm based on MR framework for doing clustering in huge database. Hidri et al 2017 proposed an enhanced FCM clustering algorithm using sampling mixed with split and merge strategy for clustering big data. Younghoon et al 2014 developed the DBCURE-MR. It is the DBCURE algorithm parallelized using MapReduce and it found several clusters in parallel. Ludwig & Simone A. (2015) have implemented a MapReduced-based fuzzy c-means clustering algorithm to explore the parallelization and scalability.

CHALLANGES OF BIG DATA AND CLUSTERING TECHNIQUES

Oussous 2018 have discussed Big Data challenges includes Big data management, Big data cleaning, Big data aggregation, Imbalanced systems capacities, Imbalanced big data, Big data analytics and Big data machine learning

Exploring high dimensional spaces in massive datasets is a great challenge to the researchers. The method of discovering relevant and meaningful information from high dimensional datasets has been complex and awkward. This is due to the four significant properties of the high dimensional data (Shanmugapriya, 2017).

- The size of a dataset producing the similar density of data points in an n-dimensional space rises exponentially with the dimensions
- A huge area is required to fit a fraction of the data points in a high dimensional space
- Almost every point is closer in a given group than to another sample point in a high dimensional space

- Every point is an outlier so that the distance between the prediction point and the center of the classified points increases

FUTURE RESEARCH DIRECTIONS

Nerurkara et al, 2018 have discussed that Clustering is a meta learning approach for getting into data and in various domains such as Market Research, E-Commerce, Social Network Analysis and Aggregation of Search Results amongst others. Multiple algorithms exist for organizing data into clusters however there is no universal solution to all problems. Each approach has its own favoritism and comes with certain advantages and disadvantages to a given analysis or application scenario.

(Chen, 2017) has discussed that due to the ability of handling impreciseness, uncertainty, and vagueness for real-world problems, soft clustering is more realistic than hard clustering. Soft clustering as a partitioning algorithm is well for big data due to the heterogeneous structure of very large data. Parallelism in soft clustering is potentially useful for big data. MapReduce has gained significant momentum from industry and academia in recent years.

(Pavithra et al, 2018) Improving the partition clustering algorithms such as K-means and FCM could be an interesting issue for future research.

Neves, 2015 has also pointed out

1. Big data API standardization to avert vendor lock-in platforms;
2. improving iterative and streaming algorithms;
3. improving fault-tolerance, neighborhood search, scalability and disaster recovery;
4. develop improved protocols for file transferring over the WAN; and
5. develop cloud abilities to adapt load peaks by providing elasticity to its consumers.

Das et al 2018 The followings are the future trends connected with medical big data analytics.

- Text analytics applications used for E-Hospital, E-Antibiotic, and identical case recovery functions: A huge amount of health-related information is unorganized as records, representations, medical or duplicate notes. Investigation articles, survey articles, medical references, and system guidance are wealthy sources for content analysis functions that intent to disclose ability by excavating these forms of content-based information.
- Genetic Applications: Genetic related information represents important amounts of genetic material arrangement information and utilizations are needed to examine and figure out the series in regards to better understanding of patient treatment.
- Excavate and study of Biosensors function: The current information about controlling home, tele-health, handheld and sensor-established Wi-Fi is well settled information origin for medical information.
- Applications Related to Social Media Investigation: The Social media will boost the connection between patients, specialist and society. Therefore, analysis is enforced to resolve this info to indicate emerging epidemic of disease, comfort of patient, and consent of patient to medical controls and analysis.

- Business and Organizational Designing Applications: Regulatory information like billing, organizing, and other harmful information exist an aggressively expanding origin of data. Analysis and optimization of this type of information can accumulate enormous amounts of money and increase the continuality of a healthcare capability.

CONCLUSION

With data increasing on a daily base, big data systems and in particular, analytic tools, have become a major force of innovation that provides a way to store, process and get information over petabyte datasets. Big data computing is an emerging data science paradigm of multidimensional information mining for scientific discovery and business analytics over large-scale infrastructure. The data collected/produced from several scientific explorations and business transactions often require tools to facilitate efficient data management, analysis, validation, visualization, and dissemination while preserving the intrinsic value of the data. This chapter describes the different clustering techniques. Thus, this has discussed about the future research direction involved in big data.

REFERENCES

Alguliyev, R., Imamverdiyev, Y., & Sukhostat, L. (2018). Weighted Clustering for Anomaly Detection in Big Data Optim. *Information and Computation*, *6*, 178–188.

Berman, J. J. (2013). Introduction. In Principles of Big Data. Morgan Kaufmann.

Chen, M. (2017). Soft clustering for very large data sets. *Comput Sci Netw Secur J.*, *17*(11), 102–108.

Chen, M., Mao, S., & Liu, Y. (2014). Bigdata:asurvey. *Mobile Networks and Applications*, *19*(2), 1–39.

Das, N., Das, L., & Rautaray,, S.S., & Pandey, M. (2018). Big Data Analytics for Medical Applications I.J. *Modern Education and Computer Science*, *2*, 35-42.

Deshmukh & Ramteke. (2015). Comparing the techniques of cluster analysis for big data. *International Journal of Advanced Research in Computer Engineering & Technology*, *4*(12).

Goel, A. (2014). Study of Different Partitioning Clustering Technique. International Journal for Scientific Research & Development, *2*(8).

Hashem, I. A. T., Yaqoob, I., Anuar, N. B., Mokhtar, S., Gani, A., & Ullah Khan, S. (2015). The rise of "big data" on cloud computing: Review and open research issues. *Information Systems*, *47*, 98–115. doi:10.1016/j.is.2014.07.006

Hidri, M. S., Zoghlami, M. A., & Ayed, R. B. (2017). Speeding up the large-scale consensus fuzzy clustering for handling Big Data. *Fuzzy Sets and Systems*.

Jacob, S.S., & Vijayakumar, R. (2018). Modern Techniques used for Big Data Clustering: A Review. *International Journal of Engineering Science Invention*, *7*(6), 1-5.

Jiang, H., Li, J., Yi, S., Wang, X., & Hu, X. (2011). Expert Systems with Applications A new hybrid method based on partitioning-based DBSCAN and ant clustering. *Expert Systems with Applications, 38*(8), 9373–9381. doi:10.1016/j.eswa.2011.01.135

Jinquan. (2011). Hitune: dataflow-based performance analysis for big data cloud. Proc. of the 2011 USENIX ATC, 87-100.

Kanungo, T., Mount, D. M., Netanyahu, N. S., Piatko, C. D., Silverman, R., & Wu, A. Y. (2012). A local search approximation algorithm for k-means clustering. *18th Annual ACM Symposium on Computational Geometry*, 10-18.

Lakshmi, T. M., Sahana, R. J., & Venkatesan, V. R. (2018). Review on Density Based Clustering Algorithms for Big Data Integrated Intelligent Research (IIR). *International Journal of Data Mining Techniques and Applications, 7*(1), 13–20. doi:10.20894/IJDMTA.102.007.001.003

Ludwig & Simone, A. (2015). MapReduce-based fuzzy c-means clustering algorithm: Implementation and scalability. *International Journal of Machine Learning and Cybernetics, 6*, 923–934.

Nerurkar, P., Shirke, A., Chandane, M., & Bhirud, S. (2017). Empirical Analysis of Data Clustering Algorithms. *6th International Conference on Smart Computing and Communications.*

Neves, P.C., & Bernardino, J. (2015). Big Data in Cloud Computing: features and issues. *Open Journal of Big Data, 1*(2).

Oussous, A., Benjelloun, F., Ait Lahcen, A., & Belfkih S. (2018). Big Data technologies: A survey. *Journal of King Saud University – Computer and Information Sciences, 30*, 431–448.

Pavithra, P., Nandhini, R., & Suganya. (2018). A Research on Different Clustering Algorithms and Techniques. *International Journal of Trend in Scientific Research and Development, 2*(5).

Rodriguez M.Z., Comin, C.H., Casanova, D., Bruno, O.M., Amancio D.R., & Costa, L.F. (2019). Clustering algorithms: A comparative Approach. *PLoS One.*

Sajana, T., Sheela Rani, C. M., & Narayana, K. V. (2016). A Survey on Clustering Techniques for Big Data Mining. *Indian Journal of Science and Technology, 9*(3).

Sasi Kiran, J., Sravanthi, M., Preethi, K., & Anusha, M. (2015). Recent Issues and Challenges on Big Data in Cloud Computing. IJCST, 6(2).

Shafiq, M. O., & Torunski, E. (2016). A Parallel K-Medoids Algorithm for Clustering based on MapReduce. *Proceedings of 2016 15th IEEE International Conference on Machine Learning and Applications*, 502-507.

Shanmugapriya, B. (2017). Clustering Algorithms for High Dimensional Data – A Review. *International Journal of Computer Science and Information Security, 15*(5).

Singh, S. P., & Jaiswal, U. C. (2018). Machine Learning for Big Data: A New Perspective. *International Journal of Applied Engineering Research, 13*(5), 2753-2762.

Suganya, R., Pavithra, M., & Nandhini, P. (2018). *Algorithms and Challenges in Big Data Clustering. International Journal of Engineering and Techniques, 4*(4), 40–47.

Vijayalakshmi, K., & Priya, M. (2019). A K- Nearest Neighbors' based on Clustering for High Performances and High Volumes of the Data. *International Journal of Scientific Research & Engineering Trends, 5*(3).

Younghoon, K., Kyuseok, S., Min-Soeng, K., & Sup, L. J. (2014). DBCURE-MR: An efficient density-based clustering algorithm for large data using MapReduce. *Information Systems, 42*, 15–35. doi:10.1016/j.is.2013.11.002

Zanoon, N., Al-Haj, A., & Khwaldeh, S. M. (2017). Cloud Computing and Big Data is there a Relation between the Two: A Study. *International Journal of Applied Engineering Research, 12*, 6970-6982.

Chapter 2
Big Data Analytics and Models

Ferdi Sönmez

ⓘ https://orcid.org/0000-0002-5761-3866
Istanbul Arel University, Turkey

Ziya Nazım Perdahçı
Mimar Sinan Fine Arts University, Turkey

Mehmet Nafiz Aydın
Kadir Has University, Turkey

ABSTRACT

When uncertainty is regarded as a surprise and an event in the minds, it can be said that individuals can change the future view. Market, financial, operational, social, environmental, institutional and humanitarian risks and uncertainties are the inherent realities of the modern world. Life is suffused with randomness and volatility; everything momentous that occurs in the illustrious sweep of history, or in our individual lives, is an outcome of uncertainty. An important implication of such uncertainty is the financial instability engendered to the victims of different sorts of perils. This chapter is intended to explore big data analytics as a comprehensive technique for processing large amounts of data to uncover insights. Several techniques before big data analytics like financial econometrics and optimization models have been used. Therefore, initially these techniques are mentioned. Then, how big data analytics has altered the methods of analysis is mentioned. Lastly, cases promoting big data analytics are mentioned.

INTRODUCTION

Uncertainty is expressed as a situation in which many different outcomes of an option can take place in the decision-making process, but the probabilities of these different outcomes are unknown. When uncertainty is regarded as a surprise and an event in the minds, it can be said that individuals can change the future view. Market, financial, operational, social, environmental, institutional and humanitarian risks and uncertainties are the inherent realities of the modern world. Life is suffused with randomness and volatility; everything momentous that occurs in the illustrious sweep of history, or in our individual lives, is an outcome of uncertainty. An important implication of such uncertainty is the financial insta-

DOI: 10.4018/978-1-7998-0106-1.ch002

bility engendered to the victims of different sorts of perils. This chapter is intended to explore big data analytics as a comprehensive technique for processing large amounts of data to uncover insights. Several techniques before big data analytics like financial econometrics and optimization models have been used. Therefore, initially these techniques are mentioned. Then, how big data analytics has altered the methods of analysis is mentioned. Lastly, cases promoting big data analytics are mentioned.

Financial Econometric Models

This sub-section involves a comprehensive series of techniques using financial econometrics and practical applications of these techniques. This sub-section opens up the experimental subjects and techniques meet the finance, forecasting and sampling requirements including continuous-time-period sampling and an introduction to inference. The main topics of financial econometric models are Market Efficiency, Return Predictability, ARCH, GARCH, value at risk, volatility clustering, asset returns, Single and Variable linear Models, Cointegration, Conditional Heteroskedasticity, Market Microstructure, Event Analysis, Case Study Analysis Predictability, Capital Asset Pricing Models, Multi-Factor Pricing Models, Present-Price Relations, Intertemporal Equilibrium Models, and Maturity Structure Models.

Studies that examine conditional return predictability dependent on the magnitude of the information signal can be divided into two groups (Ulusavas, 2010). The first group is the ones that examine price patterns following large one-day price changes and the second group are the ones that deals with the investment strategies designed to exploit large one-day price changes. The first group, which examined price patterns following large one-day price changes, found mixed evidence. Although most of the studies found evidence of overreaction following large positive and negative one-day price change events, only a few of them found evidence of under reaction to negative price change events. However, it was noted that in the face of transaction costs, these predictable patterns do not have economic significance. The studies in the second group dealt with whether contrarian strategies or momentum strategies make abnormal profits. A contrarian investment strategy sells past winners and buys past losers relying on price reversals but a momentum strategy sells past losers and buys winners that rely on price continuations for profitability. Most of these studies documented price continuations and price reversals for different return intervals. However, these transaction intensive strategies might not be profitable if transaction costs are taken into account. Also, the contrarian investment strategies, which rely on short-term price movements, may be a manifestation of the bid-ask bounce effect.

The concept of Market Efficiency (ME) was first introduced by Fama (1965) and has been continuously studied ever since then. ME is one of the basic concepts of financial economics. It argues that in active markets, securities are invested in the best possible way by market participants. According to the Efficient Market Hypothesis, it is stated that in the active markets it is very difficult to obtain a return on market returns only with the help of past price information, (Fama, 1970). In this context; financial econometric models and machine learning techniques have also emerged as experiments where ME is experimentally tested. It refers to the instantaneous and full incorporation of all available information and expectations by market participants into financial asset prices at any given time. Therefore, in an efficient market, investors should not be able to develop investment strategies that will consistently generate abnormal profits. Bachelier (2011) described this by saying "past, present and even discounted future events are reflected in market price, but often show no apparent relation to price changes". The concept of ME is built on the "random walk theory", which claims that financial asset price changes are independent of each other and are driven by new information that arrives at the market on a random basis. Since the term "efficiency" is ambiguous, it is worth shedding some light on what it means from a capital markets stand point. There are three types of efficiency in capital markets: operational efficiency, allocational efficiency and informational efficiency. Operational efficiency (transactional efficiency) emphasizes the way resources are employed to facilitate the operation of the market. If a market facilitates the achievement of a Pareto optimal allocation of resources, it is called allocationally efficient. Under Pareto optimality, funds should be effectively allocated to the most productive investments and stock markets should provide a mechanism to channel scarce resources among computing real investments (Saraoglu, 2017).

Financial time series analysis is based on understanding how the mechanism that controls time series data works (Lkhagva, et al.., 2006). The financial time series, which are the time series of financial systems that generate data flows by the hour, minute or even by shorter periods, have a special economic value in real time as well as being frequent frequencies (Ican, 2013). This economic value has led to storing of financial time series and transferring to related parties. The returns on investment (ROI) series obtained weekly or with a higher frequency are not really independent (Teräsvirta, 2009). In this series although the observations are irrelevant or almost unrelated, the yield series contain a high degree of dependence. One of the most popular ways to explain this dependence with parameters is the autoregressive conditional heteroskedasticity (ARCH) or generalized autoregressive conditional heteroskedasticity (GARCH) model. Time series may show great volatility under some conditions or periods. Under these conditions, the assumption of constant variance is not appropriate. There are many examples of how we might want to predict the conditional variance of a series. The holders of the assets may want to consider the rate of return or the variance over the period in which the asset is held. If an asset is planned to be bought at time t and sold at time t + 1, unconditional variance will be insignificant in this case. For this reason, the distinction between conditional and unconditional variance is shown first. The ARCH models are applied to model interest rates, exchange rates, stock prices and stock index returns (Teräsvirta, 2009). The prediction of the volatility of these series is different from the prediction of the conditional average of a process because volatility, i.e. the target to be predicted, cannot be observed. The main issue that needs to be addressed here is how to measure volatility. In the modeling of financial time series, the GARCH model, which was independently proposed by Bollerslev (1986) and Taylor (1986), is used instead of the ARCH model. In this model, the conditional variance is also a linear function of its delays and is expressed by Teräsvirta (2009) as:

$$h_t = \alpha_0 + \sum_{j=1}^{q} \alpha_j \varepsilon_{t-j}^2 + \sum_{j=1}^{p} \beta_j h_{t-j}$$

The GARCH process has a constant average. If there is variance, the process is a weak stationary process. The GARCH process can be a precise stationary process without the weak stationarity feature that requires constant, mean, variance and auto covariance to be constant and unchanged over time. Precise stationary requires that the distribution function of any set of ε_t be constant under time transitions. Finite moments are not required for precise stationarity (Yang, 2001).

The storage and transmission of large quantities of financial data was only possible through the advancement of database technology and information infrastructure. However, it has come a long way thank to big data analytics. In parallel with this development, practitioners have started to use machine learning techniques as a solution approach to more demanding problems. The reason for this is that models can be applied to explain the observed characteristics of real-life data, and they can provide a distributed estimate of future observational values in the time series. The features based on observations in the financial time series reflect the characteristics of the data set and are addressed under three heading given below.

- Kurtosis: This criterion is a parameter that describes the graphical representation of the probability distribution of real-valued random variables. Kurtosis is calculated as:

$$kurt(X) = \frac{E[(X - \mu)^4]}{\sigma^4}$$

Here, kurt is the kurtosis, X represents the random variable, μ represents the mean of the random variable X, and σ represents the standard deviation of X. The distribution of financial assets is generally more uniform than the normal distribution. In other words, the average is more than the normal distribution. This increases the standard deviation by having a thicker tail than the normal distribution. The increase in the size of the fluctuations experienced with the integration process in the financial markets causes the time series to move away from stationary. Normal distribution is one of the methods of financial time series distribution. It is necessary to have an auxiliary function in determining the distribution of the overall risk level. The most important indicators of this distribution are kurtosis and skewness values.

- Volatility Cluster: Mandelbrot (1963) mentioned that large changes in the prices of financial assets traded in financial markets are followed by large changes, while small changes are followed by small changes, namely, volatility clusters. This indicates that price changes are affected by each other, that is to say, they are not independent. Two different time series are shown in the following two graphs. In the first graph, there is no volatility clustering, while in the second there is volatility clustering.
- Leverage Impact: The amount of volatility of the financial asset is related to the change in the price of the financial asset, that is to say, the volatility created by the decrease in the price of the financial asset is higher than the volatile created by the increase in the price of the financial asset.

Black Sholes Model

In 1997, the Black-Scholes model, which awarded Fisher Black and Myron Scholes the Nobel Prize for economy, was introduced to calculate the prices of European-based options based on non-dividend stocks (Paul and Baschnagel, 2013). The model has been developed to calculate whether the amount paid or collected when purchasing or selling an option is reasonable.

The original Black-Scholes model was designed for stock options. However, the model can be adapted to other assets by making minor changes. Black-Scholes model is used for foreign exchange options, as in foreign exchange options by central banks. In order to be able to adapt the model to foreign exchange options, the risk-free interest rate of both currencies that are subject to the option is required. For this reason, the Garman-Kohlhagen model emerged that had been adjusted according to these requirements.

Knightian Uncertainty

F. H. Knight distinguished between risk and uncertainty in his work "Risk Uncertainty and Profit" written in 1921. Following Knight's work, the economy separated risk and uncertainty. Potential risk effects can be expressed as the known outcomes of past experiences so that future values and objective probabilities can be related to these outcomes (Langlois and Cosgel, 1993). Therefore, the values of the alternative results and occurrence probabilities are becoming known. According to Knight, although risks can be reduced by empirical and statistical estimation methods, uncertainties cannot be completely removed. Knight states that the probability factor cannot be defined empirically and that the issue of uncertainty cannot be grasped in this way. Moreover, probability calculation can be done with two different approaches: logical-mathematical approach and statistical approach. The cost of risk acceptance can be determined in advance for both approaches. Knight, pioneered a third possibility of accountability, and called estimators, in which it was not possible to predetermine size and effect. Knight claimed that past events will shed light on what will happen in the future and that predictions will come to the fore when ignorance is dominated by the decisions of the individual, suggesting a mode of behavior involving convictions based on incomplete and partial knowledge, and decisions based on intuitive reasoning. Because, according to Knight, uncertainty stems from partial knowledge.

What Knight particularly emphasized is that the theory of probability cannot help in predicting the economic consequences of decisions made in an uncertain environment. Furthermore, it is not possible to completely eliminate uncertainty, which is defined as the information disruptions of the business, while it is possible to reduce the risks by empirical and statistical estimation methods. Uncertainty can be thought of as one of the important contributions to the theory of economics, as 'a factor that cannot be replaced with information' as opposed to 'incomplete information'.

Optimization Models

Optimization is the process of selecting the best solution for a problem, subject to various constraints, from a set of available alternatives. Decision variables are the set of values that represent the decisions to be made and implemented (e.g., type of technology to invest in, number of stocks to be invested). Optimization under uncertainty has been extensively studied in stochastic programs, the optimal control theory, Markov decision processes, statistical decision theory and stochastic dynamic programming.

Deterministic mathematical programming is an important research field in modeling and analyzing the systems that involve complex decision making that cannot be handled through non-mathematical and non-computational approaches (e.g., intuition, experience based). This research field can be restrictive in its practicality, because of the assumption that the model parameters are always known with certainty. For example, in supply chain networks, the supply process is not always precise because of fluctuations or disruptions that might happen during the period of supply. These fluctuations can occur due to seasonality, quality problems, transportation problems or disruptions in supply resources. In production planning, the production capacity is not precise because of the unexpected events that can happen during production, or unexpected changes in production requirements such as specific tools, machines, etc. Deterministic mathematical programming cannot account for these uncertainties and their effect on the solution except in a few instances and only to a certain degree such as in the case of linear programming where sensitivity analysis can be employed. Furthermore, deterministic mathematical models do not consider possible future scenarios that are subject to changes in parameter values when optimizing problems (Chiralaksanakul and Mahadevan, 2007). Therefore, SP models are introduced as an extension of deterministic mathematical programs in order to deal with uncertain parameters in the system.

Although the aforementioned techniques are related to the proposed work in coping with uncertainty, the authors do not discuss these methods because the theory of these techniques are developed and improved independently from Stochastic Programming (SP) literature (Chiralaksanakul and Mahadevan, 2007; Aydin, 2012). In today's business environment, companies around the world are struggling with decision making under uncertainty related to their supply chain and production planning and often resort to myopic planning or consider very few "most likely" scenarios for their long-term planning. SP problems with recourse were first introduced by Dantzig in 1955 for mathematical programs with uncertainties (Dantzig, 2010). Since then, SP has become one of the most important methods to optimize systems that include uncertain parameters or variables in some or all aspects of the model. The most important assumption in SP is that the probability distributions of the random variables are known. A commonly used objective of the SP is to identify a feasible solution that is optimal for the expected value function over all possible realizations (Solak, 2007). Other objectives include identification of robust solutions and solutions that are optimal with respect to a pre-specified trade-off between the expected value function and its variability.

In order to determine the size of an SP problem, the dimensions of the mathematical model and the number of realizations of random vectors need to be considered. If the model's random vectors have continuous distribution or have infinitely many dimensions, then the optimization of such SP models are typically impossible. One alternative is to approximate the uncertainty through scenario aggregation or discretizing the continuous probability distributions. In the multi-stage model, the complexity continues to escalate because in this model the problem size also grows exponentially with the number of decision stages subject to uncertainty.

When the SP models are very large or the underlying mixed-integer problem is difficult, solving the SP as a single mathematical programming problem is impractical due to computational restrictions. Often, decomposition-based methods are adjusted to break the problem down to sub problems. These sub problems are then solved iteratively while enforcing those aspects of the problem relaxed for decomposition. One such decomposition method is the Progressive Hedging Algorithm (PHA) (Rockafellar & Wets, 1991). SP models are decomposed by scenarios rather than by time stages. PHA converges to the optimal solution when SP models convex programs. In cases where the decisions are integer, PHA is used as a heuristic method (Lokketangen & Woodruff, 1996; Fan & Liu 2010; Watson & Woodruff 2011).

Machine Learning

The machine learning model can be defined as a search for computational methods to test new knowledge skills and new ways to organize existing knowledge (Witten et al.., 2005). Different learning strategies are used in learning systems. The system that will do the learning and the learning algorithm used will vary depending on these strategies. In general, there are two basic strategies to learn from training data.

In the first strategy, Supervised Learning, the entire training data was labeled (Witten et al., 2005). This labeling process is usually done by an external mechanism (usually a human) and is therefore called consultative learning. The creation of a set of input-output pairs (training sample) of the training set is an example of advisory learning. Artificial neural networks, decision trees, bass learning, support vector machines are the most frequently used counseling methods. Artificial neural networks are a mixed model based on the model of human neurons. A neural network predicts one or more output with a given input set (Bramer, 2007). In decision trees that provide an advantage for decision makers in terms of easy interpretation and intelligibility, the learned model is shown as classification rules or decision tree. Independent features are separated into classes by the divide-and-conquer algorithm (Witten et al., 2005). The aim is to keep the depth of the tree at a minimum while grouping together data as similar as possible while the tree is being constructed. Thus, when the complexity (entropy) is reduced to a minimum, the gain at the maximum level (obtained information) is obtained. The Bayesian methods calculate the possible aggregation distribution. In some applications, data do not have class labels. In this case, the structure in the data has to be discovered. The second strategy, Unsupervised Learning, shows only input values in the system. And the system is expected to learn the relationships between the parameters in the examples themselves. However, no information is provided about what the correct outputs are. This type of learning tries to find rules in untagged training data, to retrieve cluster tags and sometimes to remove poultry numbers.

Support Vector Machines

Support Vector Machines (SVM), which is a machine learning method, is based on statistical learning theory and structural risk minimization principle (Bramer, 2007). Compared with other classification methods, SVM is a preferred method with high reliability, robustness to learning by heart, and levels of success in nonlinear classification, even though the training period is quite long (Celik, 2017). SVM is a consultative learning algorithm that aims to maximize the margin between support vectors that are determined dependent on the decision line. SVMs do not require assumptions of statistical estimation methods. SVMs can be used to classify entities as bankruptcy risk estimation and credit risk estimation.

Neural Networks

Artificial neurons, which have a structure similar to that of biological neurons, form artificial neural networks (NNs) by forming bonds between them, just as they are in biological neurons. The fact that many of the systems used in daily life have nonlinear structures render conventional methods ineffective in solving these problems, which increases the use of NNs in almost every field (Sönmez & Bülbül, 2015). Interest in NNs is increasing day by day in all areas of life, with features such as learning to possess, generalization, adaptability, speed, fault tolerance and non-linearity in solving complex problems. NN learns with examples. NNs will be able to generalize the problem using real events. Successful results cannot be achieved if the event cannot be shown to the network in all its aspects. It's not that the network is troubled; it's not showing well to the network. In order for NN to work safely, training and performance needs to be tested first. NNs can produce information by generalizing about unseen samples (Bramer, 2007). After being trained, NNs may produce results, even if there are missing data in the incoming new samples. NNs have a Distributed Memory that the information is spread over the network, and the values of the connections of the cells with each other show the knowledge of the network. NNs can model non-linear relationships that are difficult or impossible to model mathematically.

Genetic Algorithms

The basis of Genetic Algorithms (GA) is based on the survival and adaptation of the best. GA is a search method (Kartal, 2015) obtained by computer application that is created by simulating the conservation of nature and natural selection principle. Probability has a fundamental role for the genetic algorithm, which is a stochastic algorithm. The most important feature of GA, which is closely related to the concepts of natural selection and natural genetic mechanism, is to select new solutions to be produced in a probabilistic manner according to the fitness value of the existing solutions (the value of the objective function). The generation of the initial population uses probabilistic methods for selection of individuals for genetic operations in populations and the selection of points on the selected individual to apply genetic operators such as crossing or mutation. Parameter selection is another important step in GA because parameters have a significant effect on the performance of the genetic algorithm. Many studies have been carried out on these parameters, also called control parameters (Witten et al., 2005). The success or failure of the GA depends on the choice of these parameter values. GAs are among the methods used in bankruptcy prediction models, because the search space is large and complex, it is difficult to solve with existing information, the problem cannot be expressed by a certain mathematical model, and it is effective and useful when the desired result is not obtained from traditional optimization methods (Bramer, 2007).

Bayesian Models

Bayesian belief networks, which are a result of progress in artificial intelligence studies, provide decision makers with cognitive maps in the decision making process. Although the relationships expressed in Bayesian belief networks do not necessarily have to be causal, they are quite effective when causal. Bayesian belief networks use the advantages of not requiring strict statistical assumptions, graphically presenting a set of conditional independence constraints between a given number of variables and their corresponding conditional probability distributions in a chain-like fashion. Bayesian belief networks are casual maps that present a specialist's knowledge with some kind of graph based on probability theory. Bayesian belief networks are used to determine the importance and priority of causal factors along with the use of missing information and details. They provide practicality in analyzing variable and complex systems as the main advantage when historical data is acquired. Compared to other information maps, Bayesian belief networks use Bayes' theorem to find certainty factors for the interaction between decision variables.

By the 1980s, probability-based approaches have begun to be used and the commonly used logit and probit models have been developed. Neural networks models and genetic algorithms began to be used in 1990 when artificial intelligence became widespread in the 1990s. In the 2000s, the Hazard and Bayesian Approaches, which can be interpreted more easily with increasing environmental uncertainty and include uncertainty modeling, have begun to be used in modeling firms' failures.

Big Data

Big data is a business intelligence technique that differs from others of its kind. The term big data was first used by computer scientists in the mid 90's. The progress of technology and the rapid development of the Internet have made the power of knowledge come to the forefront (Dincerden, 2017). Many different types of data, including social media posts, continuously recorded log files, meteorological data, sensor data, GPS data, and space data are increasing constantly. Big data is a large collection of data clusters that consist of complex structures. It is not entirely possible to use conventional methods in processing big data. New techniques are being developed to store, process, analyze and visualize this type of data. The acquisition of meaningful data from big data communities and the useful information gained during the data analysis process help companies and organizations gain richer and deeper insights and a competitive edge. For this reason, big data applications should be analyzed and implemented as accurately as possible. The data are growing at a great speed, making it difficult to process large amounts of exabytes. The main difficulty in transporting such large quantities of data is the rapid increase in volumes compared to computing resources. The term big data, used today, is an inadequate term as it only indicates the size of the data and not its other existing features. Big data structures can be defined by associating with the following properties known as the 4Vs (Gandomi & Haider, 2015; Dincerden, 2017).

- Volume: Volume refers to the magnitude of data. The magnitude of data produced in recent years has increased tremendously. Due to its volume, big data cannot be analyzed by using conventional data processing methods, as these methods usually have high time complexities. While many traditional business intelligence algorithms are used to process gigabytes and terabytes, petabytes can be processed using big data analytics. However, volume definitions are relative and vary according to factors such as time and data type. What is considered to be big data today may not be so in the future, as storage capacities will increase and allow bigger data sets to be captured.
- Velocity: The increase in the collection speed of the data collected daily makes it necessary to develop technologies and methods that enable storage operations to be performed in a shorter time. Big data cannot be analyzed using traditional methods, which have high time complexities, due to its velocity. While previous data warehouses are updated weekly and evolved with daily updates, new technologies including big data are used to cope with the decision making speed and incoming data rate of new data.
- Variety: The growing variety of data sources leads to the accumulation of various information, such as structural and non-structural textures. Today, there is a wide variety of content to be analyzed, including social media comments, blogs, medical record notes, photographs, videos, textual data, as well as new types of digitizing data. The variety of data is due to continually emerging technologies. Data structure is generally evaluated as structured, semi-structured or non-structured.
- Value: The critical issue today is the development of new technologies that offer new ways of creating value by transforming raw data into information. Users can use and run stored queries and therefore extract important results from the filtered data obtained and also sort the data by size. These reports help companies discover business trends that can change their strategies. The data stored by different institutions and organizations is used for the data analyses of these institutions and organizations. The results obtained from the analyses serve as a guide for companies to achieve a higher profit rate. Above all, the analysis of the instantaneous data for the financial sector and its sub-sectors is of the utmost value, as it offers great advantages over other competitors.

Big Data Sources

Archives, sensor data, machine log data, social media, public web, business applications, data storage, various media, and various documents can be considered as big data sources. Data sets are growing rapidly due to the equipment that generates digital data getting cheaper and the data sources becoming more widespread. Traditional structured data was easier to store and analyze with the existing Relational Database Management Systems (RDBMS) even in large volumes. This structured data is now joined by semi-structured data such as XML and RSS feeds and unstructured data, which comes from diverse data sources including various different sensors and also web sources such as logs, click streams and mostly social media and comes in various data types such as texts, photos, videos and audio. Streaming data analytics is a sub-concept of big data analytics that specializes in processing streaming data. Most of the time streaming data comes from continuous data sources that analytics has to be done on flowing data which can either be structured or unstructured. This is different than the traditional store and process systems. In the traditional systems input data is first stored in a database, file system or memory which can be based on the nature of the system.

Big Data Analytics

Big data analytics (Gandomi & Haider, 2015) is a general term used for advanced data analysis techniques such as statistical analysis, data mining, machine learning, natural language processing, text analysis, and data visualization. Big data analysis is the implementation of advanced data analysis techniques to analyze large volumes of data. The concept of big data analytics involves the latest technology in data analysis and processing, in order to rapidly create valuable information from various data types (Gandomi & Haider, 2015; Dincerden, 2017). Based on the literature, the evolution of big data analytics is illustrated in Figure 1.

The following features form the basis of life cycle management of the big data analytics.

- Including structured data, semi-structured and unstructured data.
- Complex and dynamically changing data relationships.
- Achieving semantic via data and relationships.
- Increased development of the data model in the whole data cycle for a better expandability.

Figure 1. Evolution of big data analytics
(Arunachalam et al., 2018)

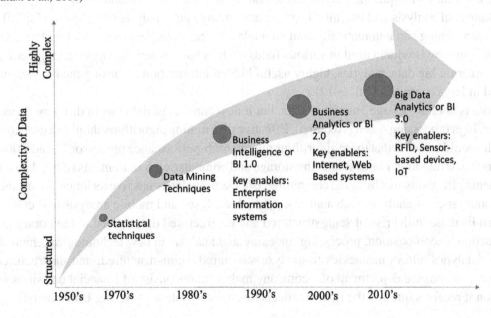

- Timely and error-free data development effect.
- Data distribution in different regions as multi-source and heterogeneous.

In big data analysis, a large amount of data that can affect an operation must first be analyzed. However, the complexity of the data to be analyzed and the need for specific algorithms to support such processes for various applications are difficult to analyze. Big data analytics has two main purposes: to understand the relationships between different properties and to develop effective methods of data mining that can accurately predict future observations.

Today, there are various devices that produce large amounts of data. A big data analytics platform is needed analyze such data. There are several vendors providing big data analytics platforms and software:

1. Actian Analytics Platform
2. Amazon Web Service
3. Cloudera Enterprise Bigdata
4. Google BigQuery
5. Hortonworks Data Platform
6. IBM Bigdata Analytics,
7. HP Bigdata
8. MapR
9. Microsoft Bigdata
10. Oracle Bigdata Analytics
11. Pivotal Bigdata
12. SAP Bigdata Analytics
13. Tableau Software bigdata
14. Teradata Bigdata Analytics

The speed of access to structured and unstructured data has also increased over time. However, there is a great need for techniques that can analyze and deliver such large amounts of data quickly. Data mining, statistical analysis and machine learning are among such analysis techniques (Cil, 2012). For example, data mining can automatically find valuable and interesting patterns in a big data set. In this respect, data mining is widely used in various fields such as basic sciences, engineering, medicine and trade. By utilizing big data analytics, highly useful hidden information regarding the business world is uncovered in large quantities (Cil, 2012).

Big Data is not only a large amount of data, but it also consists of data bits in different formats. For this reason, high processing speed is required. Effective data mining algorithms should be used to analyze big data. It should be noted that these algorithms require high-performance processors. In addition, some facilitators are developing. For example, the storage and computation requirements of big data analytics are now being effectively met by cloud computing. Big Data Analytics has five technical fields, including Big Data analysis, test analysis, web analysis, network analysis, and mobile analysis (Cil et al., 2013). There is an increase in the rise of semi-structured and unstructured data related to temporary and one-time extraction, decomposition, processing, indexing and analysis in new technological environments. Big Data Analytics allows businesses to analyze structured, semi-structured, and unstructured data. For instance, the finance department of a company makes more consistent financial decisions with the information it receives through the financial decision support system using Big Data Analytics.

Big data analysis can be applied to specific data types. However, computer science and many traditional statistical techniques are still widely used in Big Data analysis (Cil et al., 2013). There are a number of techniques that can actually be used when a project is launched. Several traditional data analysis methods used to analyze Big Data are briefly reviewed below.

- Data Mining: There are a range of different financial information systems tools. Data mining is one of these tools and is considered very important. Data mining is the process of extracting hidden information in a multitude of states and variants of data using a combination of statistical analysis techniques and artificial intelligence algorithms. Furthermore, data mining is a tool for discovering information and data mining techniques are used in financial decision-making processes (Uzar, 2013). The aim of data mining is to create decision-making models for predicting future behavior based on the analysis of past activities. Data mining is a multidisciplinary field that bridges many technical fields such as data base technology, statistics, artificial intelligence, machine learning, pattern recognition and data visualization.

- Association rule: The analysis of association rules is one of the widely used methods of data mining. It is the process of extraction of rules based on associations, relations and correlations between the data. Interesting relationships between data objects and synchronous situations are investigated. As an example of an association rule, customers who buy X and Y products can buy C product with 80% probability can be given as an example for an association rule. These kinds of association rules are meaningful if the situation related to the objects in question is frequently repeated (Birand et al.., 2012). These techniques, however, are also important in the context of the acquisition of valuable information from various events which seem not to have remarkable relations (Uzar, 2013). The discovery of some relationships that are not immediately noticeable among the various qualities in a database, where a large number of databases are stored, can help in strategic decision making. However, deriving these relationships from a large number of data, which is called cooperative mining, is not a simple process.

- Clustering Analysis: The clustering analysis provides summary information to the investigator by grouping the ungrouped data by their similarities. Grouping according to specific criteria allows creating upper groups that provide summary information by decreasing the data. In clustering analysis, there is no distinction between dependent and independent variables, unlike other highly variable techniques (Erduran, 2017). Clustering analysis is similar to Discriminant Analysis because it is often used to group data. However, the groups are pre-determined in the separation analysis and do not change during the analysis. The facts that the dependent / independent variable is not differentiated and the objects are brought together because of their characteristics are similar to factor analysis.

- Text Mining: One of the successful analysis tools developed to make meaningful aggregate of information gathered from textual data sources is text mining, a version of data mining. Text mining is defined as the automatic extraction of information from different written sources, the extraction of key items and the creation of links or hypotheses to form new facts with the information extracted. Text mining, which is different from web search, can be described as a variation of data mining. The most important feature that distinguishes text mining from data mining is the extraction of information from natural language texts rather than structured databases (Hearst, 1999). Text mining is the process of converting irregular text formatted data into digital form and extracting the qualified information in it. In the literature, it is also known as text data mining and knowledge discovery from textual databases (Oguz, 2009). Other widely used and well known methods are regression analysis and statistical analysis.

Social Media Analytics and Sentiment Analytics

According to the research of We Are Social, a global social agency, there are 4 billion internet users active around the world today; with 3 billion of these users active on Social Media (We Are Social, 2018). Social Networks are graph structures that consist of social actors/agents and relationships between these actors. Social networks are often self-organizing, complex and emergent. (Newman, 2010) Most social networks are not randomly distributed networks, where relationships between actors are distributed randomly but Scale-free networks, where relations are distributed according to a power law (Yilmaz, 2017). Social network analysis assumes that relationships among groups are important. Social network analysis evaluates, analyzes, and visually presents which nodes are communicating with each other, what facilitates the flow of information between these nodes based on the forms of relations between nodes. The social networking approach uses mathematical graph theory and statistical analysis techniques. However, it differs from the classical statistical methodology by examining its actors as a community rather than individuals. The actors that form the community and the relations, information, experiences between the actors are of fundamental interest to network theory. Each inter-node relation is represented with its own graph. In the original graphical model, the dots on the graphic represent the actors, and the lines connecting the points that represent the relationship between the actors are called the relationship.

Sentiment analysis is the measurement of people's attitude according to their writings with respect to a topic or context. The writings may include emotions, ratings, and perceptions. Sentiment analysis relies on natural language processing and machine learning to make sense of documents and classify them accordingly.

Sentiment analysis is onerous due to the high complexity of natural languages, as expressions are often hard to quantify and similar ideas can be written in many different ways which makes it hard for a computer to analyze pattern in the text. In addition to these difficulties, sentiment can be expressed with no apparent positive or negative words. With the rise of social media and the online abundance of ratings and reviews, online opinions have become an important issue for business and politics. Sentiment analysis can measure public opinions and provide intelligence using a large amount of data available online.

Use Cases

Banking and finance sector have very suitable use cases for big data projects. Fraud use cases, audit use cases, credit risk reporting, customer analytics, customer based pricing are samples of use cases. Agencies like The Securities Exchange Commission (SEC), which is maintaining fair and orderly functioning of securities markets and facilitating capital formation, is monitoring financial market activity by using network analytics and non-linear programming in big data platforms. A fraud use case and a credit risk analysis use case are mentioned below.

Fraud Use Case

Despite all the precautions taken to prevent fraud, it still continues to take place in various forms. In terms of supervisors and business management, it is important to reveal the fraud in time (Silahtaroglu,

2016; Akdemir, 2016). With the development of technology, the examination process has progressed over time, and by searching through data, proactively searching for abnormalities that may be a sign of cheating has come to the forefront. Thus, possible tricks can be detected at early stages and the operator can overcome this process with minimal harm. The banking and finance sector has suitable use cases for big data studies. Fraud crimes, credit ratings, audit use cases, credit risk analyses, customer analytics, are samples of use cases. Two of the greatest advantages brought to this sector by big data are real-time monitoring of transactions and fraud detection.

Studies carried out on national and international level to detect and prevent fraud crimes, which are almost as old as human history, are promising. However, it is known that the losses caused by fraudulent events in social and economic terms continue throughout the world (Levi & Burrows, 2008). Efforts to reduce fraud in every country and industry continue to increase. To this end, an effective system needs to be built and managed, in particular by making information sharing transparent between interested parties. At this point, governance and information systems have a vital importance.

The banking and securities sector has very suitable use cases for big data projects. Fraud use cases, audit use cases, credit risk reporting, customer analytics, customer based pricing are samples of use cases. The Securities Exchange Commission (SEC) monitors financial market activity by using network analytics and non-Linear Programming (NLP) in big data platforms. This enables to detect illegal trading activities in the financial markets.

Undoubtedly, one of the sectors that stand out both in economic terms and potential fraud issues is insurance. It is estimated that the loss due to fraud in this sector is billions of dollars (Thornton et al., 2014) and it is considered that especially accident-related fraud cases are a serious problem for the economy and institutions of a country. In connection with the detection of fraud, the effective use of information and communication technologies (ICT) offers new opportunities, but it is a daunting task to identify staged accident fraud cases.

In recent years, the role of ICT on the agenda of corporations and companies has been to contribute to business intelligence. In the insurance sector, large-scale digital transformation projects have been initiated to change the traditional way of doing business and to eliminate the clutter of legacy systems. While technology-focused solutions seem to create new opportunities to detect fraud, new fraud tactics emerge due to the weaknesses of information systems in many sectors where digital data are used. In other words, existing information systems are based on business processes, making it difficult to detect fraudulent traffic accidents and events.

International software vendors have been adding relational analysis-based software modules for fraud detection to their product ranges and are executing joint projects with the leading companies in the insurance industry. There seem to be a limited number of software products in the world that claim to be able to detect potential staged accident fraud cases. It is believed that fraudsters often exploit their interactions with humans and objects for criminal deceptions that lead to personal or financial gain.

In order to identify the complex relationships that are easily lost within information systems one needs to employ network science (that is, the science of networked relations), which enables scientists to discover new mathematical models for describing, predicting, and prescribing things and their inter-actions embedded in complex systems.

Stochastic based approaches to fraud detection have been adopted by using machine learning techniques. Srivastava et al. (2008) adopt stochastic approach to credit card fraud detection by using Hidden Markov Model. They present results that the model is successful for detecting fraudulent credit card purchases where the digital trace data is based on sequence of operations in credit card transactions. The model essentially reflects the normal behavior of a cardholder and in case the next transaction does not comply with the expected behavior it is considered to be fraudulent. Maes et al. (2002) applied artificial neural networks and Bayesian belief networks to credit card fraud detection and showed promising results on real-world financial data. The data used is provided by Europay International that licenses the MasterCard credit card brand in Europe. The dataset consists of credit card transactions with useful features that are anonymized. The proposed method, so-called Receiver Operating Curve (ROC), is claimed to successfully classify fraudulent transactions.

Abdallah et al. (2016) emphasized that the prevention and detection features of information systems are both needed to support protection mechanisms against fraud. Each fraud context, such as health, traffic accidents and finance, has distinguishing characteristics and is subjected to investigation in terms of various approaches and techniques. For instance, Van Vlasselaer et al.. (2016) proposed a network-based approach for detecting security fraud. Our approach as we elaborate with a use case below is similar to such approach, but we give special importance on validity issues for using digital trace data from a network science perspective (Aydin et al., 2018).

Akoglu et al. (2015) argue that earlier works on time series analysis for detecting anomalies can be associated with such statistical techniques as an auto-regressive or integrated moving average process (ARMA or ARIMA). They also provide a review on time series and data streams related fraud detection in the context of graph model. Graph-based fraud detection that uses time series data is also labeled as dynamic or temporal network analysis. Essentially dynamic time series of graph data can be considered as the aggregation of static graphs in which each snapshot may correspond to a slice of data. Regarding for fraud detection by static graphs one can use a bipartite graph for network representation. As shall be elaborated further our case is a demonstration of how to use bipartite graph model for stage accident fraud in the insurance domain.

As a case study, we consider the accident report service of Insurance Information and Monitoring Center (IIMC) of Turkey. According to the Center's official web site (www.sbm.org.tr), the Turkish government founded IIMC to collect all insurance data in a shared data base for the purpose of protecting the rights of insurance companies and the rights of the public sector. One of the missions of the Center is the prevention of fraud. The Center carries out projects to identify organized insurance fraud. The fraud initiative was first limited to "crash-for-cash" fraud detection in motor vehicle accidents (Button & Brooks, 2016), and later use cases were extended to other branches such as health, fire, life and individual accident insurance as well.

The Center provides a special online service that allows insurance companies and individuals to report accidents. We obtained information regarding what gets logged into the IIMC database as insurance companies interact with each other through the service. We learned that there are eight distinct stages in the claim evaluation process before the decision is made to pay a claim. Each accident reported to the system is assigned a unique accident identification number, which is the only piece of information that IIMC use to differentiate between accidents.

Reported vehicle collisions between drivers are rare incidents as drivers take every evasive action possible to avoid accidents, especially ones that result in loss of life and property. If we think about who we have been involved in an accident with, we might have been involved in collisions with a few drivers or around a dozen drivers at most and there are thousands of drivers in the district we live. This means that almost every driver that we could potentially be involved in an accident with, we do not collide with. Or, almost every possible collision between drivers in the World is non-collision, that is, avoidance, it is not registered in the data base; so data collected by centers like IIMC in this respect is sparse; as opposed to dense data in a world where every driver is colliding with each other Moreover, the relation between collision and evasive action was studied by Fuji and Tanaka (1971) who inferred that only one evasive action in 100,000 may fail.

Many systems can be regarded as networks, sets of things and their interactions. In a graphic representation of a network, nodes (or vertices) are the things of interest, and interacting nodes are joined in pairs by arcs (or links). A network is a mathematical object specifically designed to represent sparse data, and network science is concerned with analyzing and modeling such systems (Newman, 2010).

Let us regard the sparse data of recorded the vehicle accidents on the IIMC data base as a network. To emphasize this, from now on, we will refer to the network produced by the drivers who have been involved in accidents as the "faulty evasive action network" (FEAN). To put it simply, accident occurrence means concurrent failure of evasive action by one or several drivers. In FEAN the objects of interest are the drivers, and the drivers are joined in pairs by arcs if they fail to take evasive action, i.e., were involved in an accident.

The network science approach to sparse data turns the staged accident fraud detection problem into pattern recognition on FEAN, in which the task is to identify the structural patterns within the network associated with normative accident events, and consequently pinpoint the unusual patterns that go against the grain. What shape does the FEAN take? Mathematically, if we assume that a collision between two drivers occurs one in 100,000 encounters, the probability of multiple accidents happening between the same driver as to be next to none (i.e., around one in ten billion). Thus, we can hypothesize that the vanishingly small probability of multiple accidents between the same drivers result in a network that takes a tree like structure, in which root nodes correspond to the drivers who tend to be involved in at least three (possibly more) accidents and the leaf nodes correspond to the drivers who were involved in (at most) two accidents. The next question is what unusual patterns does the network reveal? Following the same line of reasoning we can hypothesize that the exceedingly rare loop structures that signify multiple accidents between the same drivers are strong candidates for crash-for-cash staged fraud.

The dataset that we collected from one of the insurance companies constitutes a select part of the event-based digital trace data retrieved from the IIMC. In the data set, the recorded stages relate to the trace left by the process of evaluating accident insurance claims in the automobile category of the insurance industry. By its very nature, trace data is longitudinal data, as the recorded stages occur in time. So, the network structure that we produced is an aggregation of events over a period of time, namely eight years and two months. The network we produced is an aggregation of approved insurance claims only, that is, either private insurance companies or the IIMC Commission for Automobile Accidents or both agreed to pay claim compensation for material and physical damage via the insured vehicle depending on the claims filed.

Technically speaking, we model FEAN as a special kind of tree network that is a forest. Forests are acyclic tree networks. That is, there is no pathway that starts and ends in the same driver node. By definition, all forests are two-mode (bipartite) networks having no loops or multiple edges. The model permits us to combine both the drivers who are involved in an accident and the accident identification number assigned to the reported accident event. The model is indicative of both the general forest structure of FEAN and IIMC. Unusual patterns within FEAN may indicate possible fraud cases.

A typical scenario for fraudulent reporting of automobile accidents, commonly referred to as staged accident fraud, is given as follows: Suppose that two fraudsters, who will be referred to as A and B, report two staged accidents. In order not to be caught by the authorities, A and B allegedly drive different cars and different districts are selected for the staged accidents. The districts may or may not be within the same city. IIMC logs the chassis numbers (abbreviated to C, see the Figure 2) of the cars, and the district of the accident (abbreviated to L, see the Figure 2) which is incorporated into the FEAN model.

Unusual patterns such as this loop (Figure 2) within FEAN may indicate possible fraud cases. Drivers A and B report that they were involved in two road accidents, in two distinct locations, L_1 and L_2 while driving different cars C_1, C_2, C_3, and C_4. In an FEAN of 3,974,190 nodes and 3,024,772 edges reconstructed from IIMC data of paid claims we have observed 955,625 disconnected network components. Each network component contains at least one accident event. Of these 955,625 components 5,555 of them contain loop structures such as shown in Figure 2. We have devised an algorithm that searches for fraudster networks based on location and vehicle chassis numbers. The algorithm detected 28 network components that contain accident events for which both the districts of the events and all chassis numbers differ. In other words, according to what is filed to IMMS two drivers were involved in two accident events while driving four different cars in two different districts.

More sophisticated algorithms can be devised that can incorporate the time of the accident events as well to search for fraudster networks.

However, a graphical model alone, no matter how sophisticated it is, cannot be expected to accurately determine staged insurance fraud. Each and every fraudster network detected by the FEAN model begs verification, which is the important role of loss adjusters, who should always have the last word in fraudulent claims.

Credit Risk Analytics Use Case

Based on the needs of the organizations in the sector and the continually innovative solutions in the industry, revealing new infrastructure and applications, and shaping works with successful Research and Development activities are inevitable. Consequently, volume of credit, important and inevitable source of support for activities or financial needs of organizations and individuals, has experienced tremendous growth in recent years. The increase of the volume of the loan portfolio has brought significant gains for financial institutions, especially banks.

Improvement of the ability to manage sectoral, economic and geopolitical risks and further changes will contribute to economic recovery and development across organizations, sectors and even countries.

Figure 2. Fraudster network

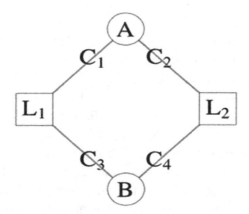

Credit risk is one of the major risks faced by finance sector, especially commercial banks, and has an important effect on the profitability ratios. Credit rating refers to a relative opinion on the credit worthiness of an independent and aforementioned entity created by credit rating agencies or groups on the credit risk of the borrower, where the party is a state, financial institution, company or a financial asset issued (Zan et al, 2004). In other words, the rating is the activity of rating and classification of the risk status and pay ability of enterprises or capital market institutions, with capital market instruments representing the indebtedness, principal money, interest and similar liabilities in the light of certain criteria by credit rating agencies. Above-mentioned rating activity is conducted by examining, evaluating and classifying the ability of businesses or countries to meet the financial obligations of their liquidity, profitability and financial structure by taking into account the sectoral, economic, financial, political and social conditions (Zan et al, 2004; Wang et al, 2018). Credit rating is an important source of information on the risk to the parties involved (Zan et al, 2004; Kılıçaslan and Giter, 2016). This reduces the representation costs resulting from not having equal information between the parties and contributes to the more effective and effective work of the markets (Kılıçaslan and Giter, 2016). Opportunities for investors, exporters and other entrepreneurs have emerged with the increase in the credit supply and demand in the financial markets together with globalization and this has led to the opening of new national and international markets to the banks, especially banks and credit markets. The fact that credit marketing institutions do not fully recognize the region, the sector and the customer has brought various challenges which leads to high emphasis on credit rating (Shi et al, 2016).

Consequently, the credit rating or scoring systems are extremely important in the decision making process for banks and other financial institutions that lend to customers. In today's intense competition environment, in order to perform financial analysis for clients, financial institutions are forced to rely on very high costs and tend to use software packages and solutions, or to trust the methodologies of their staff, which may not be analytical or academic or even not based on present methodologies. An increase in the number of potential applicants has helped to develop the automated credit approval procedures. Financial institutions constitute various internal credit assessment models that reveal the relationships between variables affecting credit scoring. In the literature, statistics and machine learning techniques for credit ratings have been widely studied. According to the findings obtained from previously mentioned studies, while statistical methods like discriminant analysis, linear regression, and ANOVA are very effective in the selection of variables, the machine learning techniques are effective in ensuring provision. Such methods have become increasingly more important in recent years with the growth in commercial loans. Although there are a wide range of applied statistical methods in the literature, they are limited due to commercial confidentiality. Since data collection is difficult, the development of the customer credit rating model has been implemented later on compared to commercial credit rating. Banks must diminish the risk in their operations, since the financial crisis reveals the current banking risk. In recent years, many financial institutions and researchers have examined many different credit rating models, due to the publicly available data in some countries (Wang et al, 2018). In bank loans, scope of credit rating models used are not broad scope and banks mainly adopt the mortgage method. Damage becomes inevitable when the mortgaged property is depreciated. Banks should make better use of their capital and capital should include the data in the database. Banks should use customer data in better ways. The Bank relies on model and algorithm in lending business and direct marketing, not on machine learning (Wang et al, 2018). Multivariate discriminant analysis and logistic regression (LR) have been used as statistical methods to determine the credit worthiness. Many studies (Sheen, 2005; Landajo et al., 2007) showed that the decision trees or NNs, exhibit more consistent results regarding the determination of bankruptcy and the estimation of credit worthiness than discriminant analysis or logistic regression. However, some studies (Hsieh, 2004; Lee & Chen, 2005) focused on the strengths of different models, including hybrid methodologies. Studies related with credit scoring and credit rating problems have shown that machine learning techniques are superior to statistical techniques (Luo et al, 2017; Wang et al, 2018). Decision certainty on the applicant's credit score/rating or worthiness minimizes potential losses and helps to increase the lending capacity of financial institutions. Additionally, this increase has also helped the development of advanced techniques that control the financial health of the borrower and intervening great accuracy on credit scoring and rating.

As a case study we consider loan data for issuing the decision on the assessment of customers' demand for credit and acceptance of loan requests. The purpose of the credit score model is to classify the credit applicants in seven groups: starting from those who will be able to pay back liabilities (good credit rating or good performance class) and ending with those who will fail to fulfill the financial obligations and need to be deprived of credit as a consequence the high risk (bad credit rating or low performance class). Hence, the credit score represents a person's likelihood of being able to pay back the loan. Poor credit worthiness shows that there is a high risk on a loan, and thus may lead to the rejection of application or high interest rates for borrowing.

The dataset that we collected from (Kaggle Inc., 2019) involves 74 attributes and 887,000 instances. It has been seen that it is possible to use up to 34 variables, which are re-examined in the original data set, as the input variable and 1 variable as the class variable which shows the customer's discrete class. 7 discrete classes for estimation have been created for the class variable. We have removed irrelevant attributes that may affect the accuracy of classification. Variables that cannot be converted to numeric values or non-categorical variables are excluded from the data set. We have run ANOVA on the data set. The variable has been considered relevant and informative with regard to the credit rating decision on the basis of the difference (significant / low p-value). We have eliminated attributes with relatively high p-values. Also, rows and columns with many missing values have been neglected. As a consequence, we selected 34 attributes with 100,000 instances. We have used scalar normalization to scale numeric attributes between 0 and 1. MLP and SVM classifiers have been used. Levenberg-Marquardt Back Propagation Algorithm is preferred because it has an effective learning algorithm with little computational time for each iteration (Anyaeche and Ighravwe, 2013; Lavanya and Parveentaj, 2013), since we have been dealing with a big dataset in this case study.

To provide reliable estimation and to minimize the impact of data dependence on credit rating model development, k-fold cross-validation (10-fold) is used. Here, the entire credit data set is randomly separated into 10 subunits and layers of approximately equal size. After one of the 10 groups is separated as a test group, the remaining 9 (k-1) groups are trained on each fold. After training is completed, accuracy performance is calculated on the test group. This process is repeated 10 times so that the remaining groups taken as test data set at least once. Finally, the average of 10 different accuracy values is taken. Consequently, each model has been trained and tested by 10 times. It is contemplated that a prediction obtained from 10-fold cross validation will be more reliable than a prediction that is commonly applied using a single validation set.

The SVM classifier has obtained prediction accuracy comparable to that of MLP as around 85%. However, the MLP classifier was slightly slower and less accurate (81%) than the SVM classifier. Machine learning classification and feature selection methods have been applied in Python environment.

CONCLUSION

Big data analytics is used in the finance field for purposes such as estimation of stock prices, pricing of company treasuries, portfolio management, direct marketing, and credit dealing, understanding and managing financial risk, forecasting exchange rates, and credit rating. Big data analytics is also used to predict financial distress and crises. Risks and uncertainties are driving factors of financial distress and crises. Market, financial, operational, social, environmental, institutional and humanitarian risks and uncertainties are the inherent realities of the modern world. Several techniques like financial econometrics and optimization models have been used to uncover insights on risks and uncertainties. Basically, this chapter is intended to explore big data analytics as a comprehensive technique for processing large amounts of data to uncover insights. Elaborate use cases have been given for the readers to derive full understanding of the importance of the subject. Moreover, the focus is on how big data has altered the methods of conventional analysis techniques in these cases. The chapter has tried to illustrate with detailed examples of how big data models help managers to manage risk.

REFERENCES

Abdallah, A., Maarof, M. A., & Zainal, A. (2016). Fraud detection system: A survey. *Journal of Network and Computer Applications*, *68*, 90–113. doi:10.1016/j.jnca.2016.04.007

Abdou, H. A. (2009). Genetic programming for credit scoring: The case of Egyptian public sector banks. *Expert Systems with Applications*, *36*(9), 11402–11417. doi:10.1016/j.eswa.2009.01.076

Akdemir, C. (2016). *Detecting Fraud by Using Data Mining Techniques and an Application in Retail Sector* (Doctoral Dissertation). Marmara University Social Sciences Institute, Istanbul, Turkey.

Akoglu, L., Tong, H., & Koutra, D. (2015). Graph based anomaly detection and description: A survey. *Data Mining and Knowledge Discovery*, *29*(3), 626–688. doi:10.100710618-014-0365-y

Arunachalam, D., Kumar, N., & Kawalek, J. P. (2018). Understanding big data analytics capabilities in supply chain management: Unravelling the issues, challenges and implications for practice. *Transportation Research Part E, Logistics and Transportation Review*, *114*, 416–436. doi:10.1016/j.tre.2017.04.001

Aydin, M. N., Kariniauskaite, D., & Perdahci, N. Z. (2018). Validity Issues of Digital Trace Data for Platform as a Service: A Network Science Perspective. Proceedings of Trends and Advances in Information Systems and Technologies. WorldCIST'18 2018. doi:10.1007/978-3-319-77703-0_65

Bachelier, L. (2011). *Louis Bachelier's theory of speculation: the origins of modern finance*. Princeton, NJ: Princeton University Press; doi:10.1515/9781400829309

Birant, D., Kut, A., Ventura, M., Altınok, H., Altınok, B., Altınok, E., & Ihlamur, M. (2012). *A New Approach for Quality Function Deployment: An Application*. Paper presented at Akademik Bilisim 2010, Mugla, Turkey.

Bramer, M. (2007). *Principles of data mining*. London: Springer.

Button, M., & Brooks, G. (2016). From 'shallow'to 'deep'policing:'crash-for-cash'insurance fraud investigation in England and Wales and the need for greater regulation. *Policing and Society, 26*(2), 210–229. doi:10.1080/10439463.2014.942847

Celik, S. (2017). Applying Web Usage Mining for the Analysis of Web Log Files. *Istanbul Business Research, 46*(1), 62–75.

Chiralaksanakul, A., & Mahadevan, S. (2007). Decoupled approach to multidisciplinary design optimization under uncertainty. *Optimization and Engineering, 8*(1), 21–42. doi:10.100711081-007-9014-2

Cil, I. (2012). Consumption universes based supermarket layout through association rule mining and multidimensional scaling. *Expert Systems with Applications, 39*(10), 8611–8625. doi:10.1016/j.eswa.2012.01.192

Cil, I., & Turkan, Y. S. (2013). An ANP-based assessment model for lean enterprise transformation. *International Journal of Advanced Manufacturing Technology, 64*(5-8), 1113–1130. doi:10.100700170-012-4047-x

Dantzig, G. B. (2010). Linear programming under uncertainty. In *Stochastic programming* (pp. 1–11). New York, NY: Springer. doi:10.1007/978-1-4419-1642-6_1

Dincerden, E. (2017). *Is Zekasi ve Stratejik Yonetim.* Istanbul: Beta Basım Dagitim Co.

Fama, E. F. (1965). The behavior of stock-market prices. *The Journal of Business, 38*(1), 34–105. doi:10.1086/294743

Fama, E. F. (1970). Efficient capital markets: A review of theory and empirical work. *The Journal of Finance, 25*(2), 383–417. doi:10.2307/2325486

Fan, Y., & Liu, C. (2010). Solving stochastic transportation network protection problems using the progressive hedging-based method. *Networks and Spatial Economics, 10*(2), 193–208. doi:10.100711067-008-9062-y

Fujii, Y., & Tanaka, K. (1971). Traffic capacity. *Journal of Navigation, 24*(4), 543–552. doi:10.1017/S0373463300022384

Gandomi, A., & Haider, M. (2015). Beyond the hype: Big data concepts, methods, and analytics. *International Journal of Information Management, 35*(2), 137–144. doi:10.1016/j.ijinfomgt.2014.10.007

Hearst, M. A. (1999). Untangling Text Data Mining. In *Proceedings of the 37th Annual Meeting of the Association for Computational Linguistics on Computational Linguistics.* Association for Computational Linguistics. 10.3115/1034678.1034679

Hsieh, N.-C. (2005). Hybrid mining approach in the design of credit scoring models. *Expert Systems with Applications, 28*(4), 655–665. doi:10.1016/j.eswa.2004.12.022

Ican, O. (2013). *Determining the Functional Structure of Financial Time Series by Means of Genetic Learning.* Anadolu University, Graduate School of Social Sciences.

Kaggle Inc. (2019). *Loan data set.* [Data file]. Retrieved from https://www.kaggle.com/prateikmahendra/loan-data

Kartal, B. (2015). *Financial Portfolio Optimization with Artifical Bee Colony Algorithm.* Istanbul University, Social Sciences Institute.

Kılıçaslan, H., & Giter, M. S. (2016). Kredi Derecelendirme ve Ortaya Çıkan Sorunlar [Credit Rating and Emerging Issues]. *Maliye Araştırmaları Dergisi, 2*(1), 61–81.

Landajo, M., Andres, J. D., & Lorca, P. (2007). Robust neural modeling for the cross-sectional analysis of accounting information. *European Journal of Operational Research, 177*(2), 1232–1252. doi:10.1016/j.ejor.2005.10.064

Langlois, R. N., & Cosgel, M. M. (1993). Frank Knight on risk, uncertainty, and the firm: A new interpretation. *Economic Inquiry, 31*(3), 456–465. doi:10.1111/j.1465-7295.1993.tb01305.x

Lee, T.-S., & Chen, I.-F. (2005). A two-stage hybrid credit scoring model using artificial neural networks and multivariate adaptive regression splines. *Expert Systems with Applications, 28*(4), 743–752. doi:10.1016/j.eswa.2004.12.031

Levi, M., & Burrows, J. (2008). Measuring the impact of fraud in the UK: A conceptual and empirical journey. *British Journal of Criminology, 48*(3), 293–318. doi:10.1093/bjc/azn001

Lkhagva, B., Suzuki, Y., & Kawagoe, K. (2006, April). New time series data representation ESAX for financial applications. In *22nd International Conference on Data Engineering Workshops (ICDEW'06)* (pp. x115-x115). IEEE. 10.1109/ICDEW.2006.99

Løkketangen, A., & Woodruff, D. L. (1996). Progressive hedging and tabu search applied to mixed integer (0, 1) multistage stochastic programming. *Journal of Heuristics, 2*(2), 111–128. doi:10.1007/BF00247208

Luo, C., Wu, D., & Wu, D. (2017). A deep learning approach for credit scoring using credit default swaps. *Engineering Applications of Artificial Intelligence, 65*, 465–470. doi:10.1016/j.engappai.2016.12.002

Maes, S., Tuyls, K., Vanschoenwinkel, B., & Manderick, B. (2002). *Credit card fraud detection using Bayesian and neural networks.* Paper presented at 1st International Naiso Congress on Neuro Fuzzy Technologies, Havana, Cuba.

Mandelbrot, B. B. (1963). The variation of certain speculative prices. *The Journal of Business, 24*, 392–417.

Newman, M. (2010). *Networks: an introduction.* Oxford, UK: Oxford University Press. doi:10.1093/acprof:oso/9780199206650.001.0001

Paul, W., & Baschnagel, J. (2013). *Stochastic processes.* Heidelberg, Germany: Springer. doi:10.1007/978-3-319-00327-6

Rockafellar, R. T., & Wets, R. J. B. (1991). Scenarios and policy aggregation in optimization under uncertainty. *Mathematics of Operations Research, 16*(1), 119–147. doi:10.1287/moor.16.1.119

Saraoglu, A. C. (2017). *Stock Price Reactions to Dividend Changes: a Comparative Test of Signalling Theory and Market Efficiency in The Emerging Emea Stock Markets* (Doctoral Dissertation). Kadir Has University, Istanbul, Turkey.

Sheen, J. N. (2005). Fuzzy financial profitability analyses of demand side management alternatives from participant perspective. *Information Sciences, 169*(3-4), 329–364. doi:10.1016/j.ins.2004.05.007

Shi, B., Chen, N., & Wang, J. (2016). A credit rating model of microfinance based on fuzzy cluster analysis and fuzzy pattern recognition: Empirical evidence from Chinese 2,157 small private businesses. *Journal of Intelligent & Fuzzy Systems, 31*(6), 3095–3102. doi:10.3233/JIFS-169195

Silahtaroglu, G. (2016). *Veri madenciliği*. Istanbul: Papatya Press.

Solak, S. (2007). *Efficient solution procedures for multistage stochastic formulations of two problem classes*. Georgia Institute of Technology.

Sönmez, F., & Bülbül, S. (2015). An intelligent software model design for estimating deposit banks profitability with soft computing techniques. *Neural Network World, 25*(3), 319–345. doi:10.14311/NNW.2015.25.017

Srivastava, A., Kundu, A., Sural, S., & Majumdar, A. (2008). Credit card fraud detection using hidden Markov model. *IEEE Transactions on Dependable and Secure Computing, 5*(1), 37–48. doi:10.1109/TDSC.2007.70228

Teräsvirta, T. (2009). An Introduction to Univariate GARCH Models. In T. Mikosch, J. P. Kreiß, R. Davis, & T. Andersen (Eds.), *Handbook of Financial Time Series*. Heidelberg, Germany: Springer. doi:10.1007/978-3-540-71297-8_1

Thornton, D., van Capelleveen, G., Poel, M., van Hillegersberg, J., & Mueller, R. (2014, April). *Outlier-based health insurance fraud detection for us medicaid data*. Paper presented at 16th International Conference on Enterprise Information Systems, ICEIS 2014, Lisbon, Portugal.

Ulusavas, O. (2010). *Short Term Predictable Patterns Following Price Shocks Conditional On Characteristics of Information Signals, Foreign Investment and Investor Confidence: Evidence from Istanbul Stock Exchange* (Doctoral Dissertation). Yeditepe University, Istanbul, Turkey.

Uzar, C. (2013). *The Usage of Data Mining Technology in Financial Information System: an Application on Borsa Istanbul* (Doctoral Dissertation). Dokuz Eylül University Social Sciences Institute, Izmir, Turkey.

Van Vlasselaer, V., Eliassi-Rad, T., Akoglu, L., Snoeck, M., & Baesens, B. (2016). Gotcha! Network-based fraud detection for social security fraud. *Management Science, 63*(9), 3090–3110. doi:10.1287/mnsc.2016.2489

Wang, D., Zhang, Z., Bai, R., & Mao, Y. (2018). A hybrid system with filter approach and multiple population genetic algorithm for feature selection in credit scoring. *Journal of Computational and Applied Mathematics, 329*, 307–321. doi:10.1016/j.cam.2017.04.036

Watson, J. P., & Woodruff, D. L. (2011). Progressive hedging innovations for a class of stochastic mixed-integer resource allocation problems. *Computational Management Science, 8*(4), 355–370. doi:10.100710287-010-0125-4

Witten, I. H., Paynter, G. W., Frank, E., Gutwin, C., & Nevill-Manning, C. G. (2005). KEA: Practical Automated Keyphrase Extraction. In Design and Usability of Digital Libraries: Case Studies in the Asia Pacific (pp. 129-152). IGI Global.

Yildiz, E. G. (2017). *Analysis of Online Customer Complaints by Data Mining* (Doctoral Dissertation). Trakya University Social Sciences Institute, Edirne, Turkey.

Yilmaz, S. E. (2017). *Evaluation of the Ability of the Social Network Analysis Method about Establishment of the Relations and Contradictions in Prescribing Characteristics, with the Real World Data* (Doctoral Dissertation). Istanbul University, Institute of Health Science, Istanbul, Turkey.

Zan, H., Hsinchun, C., Chia-Jung, H., Wun-Hwa, C., & Soushan, W. (2004). Credit rating analysis with support vector machines and neural networks: A market comparative study. *Decision Support Systems*, *37*(4), 543–558. doi:10.1016/S0167-9236(03)00086-1

Chapter 3
Technologies for Handling Big Data

Rashmi Agrawal

ⓘ https://orcid.org/0000-0003-2095-5069

Manav Rachna International Institute of Research and Studies, India

ABSTRACT

In today's world, every time we connect phone to internet, pass through a CCTV camera, order pizza online, or even pay with credit card to buy some clothes, we generate data and that "ocean of data" is popularly known as big data. The amount of data that's being created and stored on a universal level is almost inconceivable, and it just keeps growing. The amount of data we create is doubled every year. Big data is a critical concept that integrates all kinds of data and plays an important role for strategic intelligence for any modern company. The importance of big data doesn't revolve around how much data you have, but what you do with it. Big data is now the key for competition and growth for new startups, medium, and big enterprises. Scientific research is now on boom using big data. For the astronomers, Sloan Digital Sky Survey has become a central resource. Big data has the potential to revolutionize research and education as well. The aim of this chapter is to discuss the technologies that are pertinent and essential for big data.

INTRODUCTION

In today's world, every time we connect phone to internet, pass through a CCTV camera, order pizza online or even pay with credit card to buy some clothes, we generate data and that "Ocean of Data" is popularly known as Big Data. The amount of data that's being created and stored on a universal level is almost inconceivable, and it just keeps growing. The amount of data we create is doubled every year. Big Data is a critical concept that integrates all kinds of data and plays an important role for strategic intelligence for any modern company. The importance of big data doesn't revolve around how much data you have, but what you do with it. Big data is now the key for competition and growth for new startups, medium and big enterprises. Scientific research is now on boom using big data. For the astronomers, Sloan Digital Sky Survey has become a central resource. Big data has the potential to revolutionize re-

DOI: 10.4018/978-1-7998-0106-1.ch003

search and education as well. A commonly quoted axiom is that "big data is for machines; small data is for people." Big data is in its initial phase now and much more is to be discovered yet. The voluminous, varied and scattered data cannot be handled by traditional approaches and techniques and it prompted the development of various technologies which are required for handling big data. These technologies help the businesses (Pathak and Agrawal, 2019) and organizations (Agrawal and Gupta, 2017) for their specific and varied purposes. The future of big data can be imagined like the central nervous system of the planet. NoSQL is a non-relational database management system and designed for distributed data stores like Google or Facebook which collects terabits of data every day for their users. In these cases, storing data in fixed schema may not provide join and horizontal scalability.

In today's moment data access and capturing through other parties is much easier such as Facebook, Google+ and others. Data has been increasing exponentially in some scenarios like Personal user information, social graphs, geo location data, user-generated content and machine logging (Agrawal and Gupta, 2018). To run these services in order, processing of huge data is required which SQL database can't handle hence evolution of NoSQL databases happened. As organizations have become more familiar with the capabilities of big data analytics solutions, they have begun demanding faster and faster access to insights. For these enterprises, streaming analytics with the ability to analyze data as it is being created, is something of a holy grail. They are looking for solutions that can accept input from multiple disparate sources, process it and return insights immediately — or as close to it as possible. This is particular desirable when it comes to new IoT deployments, which are helping to drive the interest in streaming big data analytics.

The aim of this chapter is to discuss the technologies which are pertinent and essential for the big data. The important technologies for big data are-

1. Distributed and Parallel Computing
2. Schema less Databases
3. Map Reduce
4. Hadoop
5. Cloud Computing
6. Artificial Intelligence
7. Edge Computing
8. Blockchain

DIMENSIONS OF BIG DATA

The general accord of the day is that there are explicit attributes available to define big data in an explicit manner. Generally, in most of big data circles, these are called the four V's: volume, variety, velocity, and veracity.

Big Data has a lot of prospective for organizations and hence almost all big and middle level organizations are continuously looking to find the ways to apply its techniques in their organizations. For accelerating Big Data initiatives, Capgemini and Cloudera have announced an extended partnership recently. To smear this initiative, they have formed an infographic which outline five dimensions to define and characterize Big Data. Some of the important dimensions of big data are described here-

1. **Volume-** The main characteristic feature or dimension of big data is its sheer volume. The term Volume refers to the amount of data an organization or an individual collects and/or generates. Currently, to qualify as big data, a minimum of 1 terabyte is the threshold of big data which stores as much data as would fit on 1,500 CDs or 220 DVDs, which is quite enough to store approximately 16 million Facebook images (Gandomi & Haider, 2015). The vast amounts of data are generated every second. E-commerce, social media, and various sensors produce high volumes of unstructured data in the form of various audio, images, and video files. Today big data is also generated by machines, networks and human interaction on systems and the volume of data to be analyzed is massive.

2. **Variety-** It is one the most attractive dimension in technology as almost every information is digitized now a days. Traditional data types or structured data include information in a structured way like date, amount, and time which can be easily fit neatly in a relational database. Structured data is augmented by unstructured data. The modern day data like Twitter feeds, you tube videos, audio files, MRI images, web pages, web logs and anything else that can be captured and stored and does not require any meta model for its structure to access it later on.

Unstructured data is an essential concept in big data. To understand the difference between structured and unstructured data, we can compare these two types of data and we can see that a picture, a voice recording, a tweet — these all are different in their function and usage but express ideas and thoughts based on human understanding. One of the major goals of big data is to make sense from this unstructured data.

3. **Velocity-** It refers to the frequency of incoming data that is required to be processed. The flow of data is massive and continuous. The velocity of data increases over time. In 2016, approximately 5.5 million new devices were connected every day for collecting and sharing data. The improved data streaming potential of linked devices will persist to gather speed in future. Streaming application like Amazon Web Services Kinesis is an example of an application that handles the velocity of data.

4. **Veracity-** It refers to the reliability of the data. Given the increasing volume of data being generated at an unparalleled rate, it is common that data contains noise. Veracity means trustworthiness of the data that is to be analyzed. Uncertainty and unreliability arise due to incompleteness, inaccuracy, latency, inconsistency, subjectivity, and deception in data.

In addition to these four dimensions, there are two additional dimensions which are keys for operationalising the data.

5. **Volatility-** This big data dimension refers that for how long this data is valid and for how long it should be stored.

6. **Validity-** The dimension validity in big data means that data in use should be correct and accurate. If one wants to use the results for decision making, validity of big data sources and subsequent analysis must be accurate.

Table 1. Distributed and parallel computing

	Distributed Computing	Parallel Computing
Memory	Tightly coupled shared memory	Distributed memory
Control	Global clock control SIMD, MIMD	No global clock control Synchronization algorithms needed
Focus Point	Performance Scientific computing	Performance(cost and scalability) Reliability/availability Information/resource sharing
Fault tolerance	Built in	Needs additional code
Level of abstraction	High	Both Low level and high level
I/O Usage	Comparatively higher	Comparatively lower

TECHNOLOGIES FOR HANDLING BIG DATA

The voluminous, varied and scattered data cannot be handled by traditional approaches and techniques and it prompted the development of various technologies which are required for handling big data. These technologies help the businesses and organizations for their specific and varied purposes. This section focuses on basics of these technologies and their role and relevance in handling big data.

1. Distributed and Parallel Computing

In distributed computing,(Assunção, Calheiros, Bianchi, Netto, & Buyya, 2015) computing tasks are distributed across the multiple computing resources. The sharing of these tasks in distributed computing increases the speed and efficiency of the system. Therefore distributed computing is considered faster and efficient over traditional computing. The major issues in distributed computing are transparency, scalability and reliability/fault tolerance (Gupta and Agrawal, 2017). The applications which suits distributed framework are map only applications that have very less or negligible message passing between procedures or processes.

In parallel computing, to improve the processing capability of a computer system, additional computational resources are added. It helps in dividing complex computations into subtasks which is easy to handle individually by processing units which are running in parallel. The major issues in parallel computing are data sharing, process coordination, Distributed versus centralized memory, single shared bus versus network with many different topologies and Fault tolerance/reliability. Most applications and algorithms which encompass halo exchange are well-matched to be applied with parallel structures.

2. Schema less Databases

Traditional databases like sql are not capable of handling such a large volume of data while handling the applications related to big data. In modern day technology these schema less databases are capable enough to play with the real time applications and can provide answers to complex queries while handling big data. These databases are known as schema less databases as they don't follow a fixed schema for a database. These are popularly known as NoSQL databases. Some of the common NoSqL databases are MongoDB, Cassandra, Neo4j etc.

Table 2. Difference between RDBMS and NoSQL

RDBMS	NoSQL
• Data is stored in a relational model, with rows and columns. • A row contains information about an item while columns contain specific information, • Follows fixed schema. Meaning, the columns are defined and locked before data entry. In addition, each row contains data for each column. • Supports vertical scaling. Scaling an RDBMS across multiple servers is a challenging and time-consuming process. • Atomicity, Consistency, Isolation & Durability(ACID) Compliant	• Data is stored in a host of different databases, with different data storage models. • Follows dynamic schemas. Meaning, you can add columns anytime. • Supports horizontal scaling. You can scale across multiple servers. Multiple servers are cheap commodity hardware or cloud instances, which make scaling cost-effective compared to vertical scaling. • Not ACID Compliant.

NoSQL is a non-relational database management systems (Bhogal & Choksi, 2015, Gupta, 2018)and designed for distributed data stores like Google or Facebook which collects terabits of data every day for their users. In these cases, storing data in fixed schema may not provide join and horizontal scalability.

In today's moment data access and capturing through other parties is much easier such as Facebook, Google+ and others. Data has been increasing exponentially in some scenarios like Personal user information, social graphs, geo location data, user-generated content and machine logging. To run these services in order, processing of huge data is required which SQL database can't handle hence evolution of NoSQL databases happened.

- **Social-***Network Graph*
  ◦ Each user record: UID1, UID2
  ◦ Separate records: UID, first name, last name, about, hobbies, age ...
  ◦ Task: Find all friends of friends of friends of ... friends of a given user.
- Wikipedia pages:
  ◦ Large collection of documents
  ◦ Combination of structured and unstructured data
  ◦ Task: Retrieve all pages regarding cricket of IPL before 2011.

Big Data Capability

NoSQL databases are not constrained to only working with big data. However, an enterprise-class NoSQL solution can scale to manage large volumes of data from terabytes to petabytes. In addition to storing large volumes of data, it delivers high performance for data velocity, variety, and complexity.

To provide enterprise-class solution, a NoSQL database must offer continuous availability without any single point of failure. The NoSQL solution delivers intrinsic uninterrupted availability.

Following key features must be included in any NoSQL database-

- All nodes in a cluster must be able to serve read request even if some machines are down.
- A NoSQL database must be capable of easily replicating and segregating data between different physical shelves in a data center to avoid hardware outages.
- A NoSQL database must support data distribution designs that are multi-data centers, on-premises or in the cloud.

Figure 1. CAP theorem

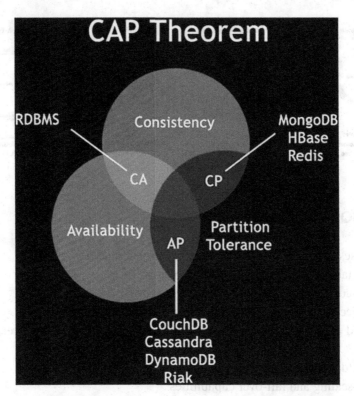

To understand the NoSQL databases, we must understand the CAP theorem which states the requirements of creating a distributed system. CAP theorem(C- Consistency, A- Availability, P-Partition Tolerance) states that every NoSQL database must fulfill at least 2 of these 3 requirements. Therefore current NoSQL databases follow the different combinations of the C, A, P from the CAP theorem. Different combinations of CA, CP and AP are-:

- **CA -** Single site cluster. When any partition occurs, system fails.
- **CP –**This model provides the consistency but some of the data may not be accessible at a particular point of time.
- **AP -** Under partitioning some of the data returned may be inaccurate but rest of the data is available.

The term eventual consistency guarantees that if no new updates are made to a given data item eventually all accesses to that item will return the last updated value. Eventually consistent services provide weak consistency using BASE

- Basically Available, Soft state, Eventual consistency
- Basically available indicates that the system guaranteed availability (CAP theorem)
- Soft state indicates that the state of the system may change over time, even without input
- Eventual consistency indicates that the system will become consistent over time

Figure 2. Types of NoSQL databases

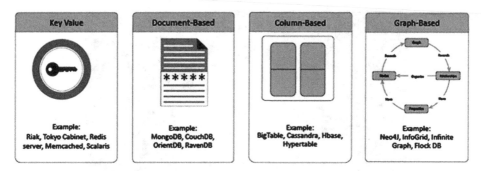

Features of NoSQL Databases

- NoSQL databases generally do not follow the relational model
- Do not provide tables with flat fixed-column records
- Work with self-contained (hierarchical) aggregates or BLOBs
- No need for object-relational mapping and data normalization
- No complex and costly features like query languages, query planners,referential integrity, joins, ACID
- Several NoSQL databases can be executed in a distributed fashion
- Providing auto-scaling and fail-over capabilities
- Often ACID is sacrificed for scalability and throughput
- Often no synchronous replication between distributed nodes is possible, e.g.
- asynchronous Multi-Master Replication, peer-to-peer, HDFS Replication
- Only providing eventual consistency

There are four most common categories of NoSQL databases. Each of these has its own specific features and limitations(Oussous, Benjelloun, Lahcen, & Belfkih, 2015). There is not a single solution which is best from others rather these databases are designed to solve specific problems. The four types of databases are-

- Key-value stores- Redis, Dynamo, Riak. etc
- Column-oriented- Google's BigTable, HBase and Cassandra
- Graph- OrientDB, Neo4J, Titan.etc
- Document oriented- MongoDB, CouchDB etc

The other NoSQL systems are Object DB, XML DB, Special Grid DB and Triple store.
Figures 2-5 represent the four types of NoSQL databases.

3. Map Reduce

Before MapReduce large scale data processing was difficult in order to manage data parallelization, distribution, I/O scheduling and fault tolerance. MapReduce is a processing technique and a program

Figure 3. Key value store

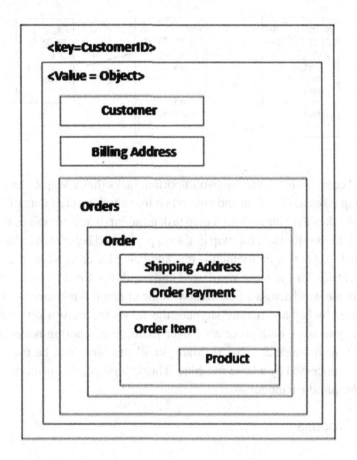

Figure 4. Graph database

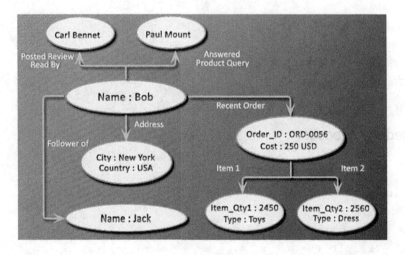

Figure 5. Document oriented database

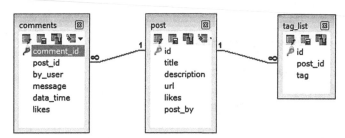

model for distributed computing. There are two important tasks that a MapReduce algorithm contains-Map and Reduce. Map takes a set of data and converts it into another set of data of tuples with key/value pairs. The reduce task takes the output from a map task as an input and combines the output of map into a smaller set of tuples. In MapReduce, the map is always performed before the reduce task. Reduce phase starts with intermediate key/value pair which is one key/value for each word in all files being grouped (including multiple entries for the same word) and ends with finalized key value pairs which has one key/value for each unique word across all the files with the number of instances summed into this entry.. Starting pairs are sorted by key and iterator supplies the values for a given key to reduce the function.

MapReduce is easy to scale data processing over multiple computing nodes(Subramaniyaswamy, Vijayakumar, Logesh, & Indragandhi, 2015). Many small machines can be used to process jobs that normally could not be processed by a large machine. The data processing primitives are called mappers and reducers in the MapReduce model

Example of *Map Process*

```
def map(key,value):
        list=[ ]
        for a in value:
                if test:
                        list.append((key,x))
        return list
```

Example of Reduce *Process*

```
def map(key,list of values):
        result=0
        for a in list of values:
                result + = a
        return (key, result)
```

MapReduce is typically used by yahoo for webmap application which uses Hadoop. Facebook uses Hive data center to provide business statistics. Rackspace analyzes server log files.

This approach is better as it creates an abstraction for dealing with complex overhead. The computations are simple, the overhead is messy. The programs are much smaller and easier to use as the overheads are removed. Requirement of testing reduces to a great extent as MapReduce libraries can be assumed to work properly therefore only user code needs to be tested.

Table 3 represents the key benefits of MapReduce.

4. Hadoop

Hadoop is Apache's top level project which is an open source implementation of framework for data storage and provides assurance for reliability and scalability(O'Driscoll, Daugelaite, & Sleator, 2013). Hadoop provides highly available and flexible architecture for big data computation. It supports data-intensive distributed applications, licensed under the Apache v2 license.

Important Features of Hadoop

- Flexibility
- Scalability
- Availability
- Fault Tolerance
- Use commodity hardware
- Move computation rather than data
- Distributed, with centralization
- Written in Java
- Also supports Ruby and Python

Hadoop architecture is known as HDFS (Hadoop distributed file system) where the nodes are divided into three categories: Name node, Data node and Secondary name node. Name nodes run TaskTracker to accept and reply to MapReduce tasks. By default Hadoop replicated each data block three times and stores in data node. Secondary name node works like a reservoir and comes into picture in while handling critical situations. It maintains each log activity. Hadoop distributed file system has been tailored to meet

Table 3. Benefits of MapReduce

Benefit	Description
Speed	Due to the parallel processing Map Reduce can complete the task in minutes which my take days to complete.
Recovery	The JobTracker module keeps track of the jobs which are running in parallel and if one copy of the data is not available it provides another copy of the data to the assigned node.
Simplicity	Developers can write applications in their language of choice (C, C++, Java or python)
Scalability	As Map Reduce can handle petabytes of data which runs on Hadoop cluster, it offers a great scalability.
Minimal data motion	MapReduce moves compute processes to the data on HDFS and not the other way around.

Figure 6. Hadoop name node and data node

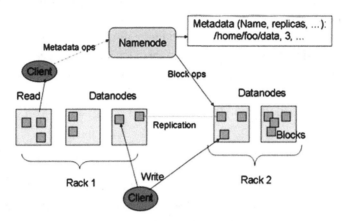

the needs of MapReduce. It is targeted towards many reads as writes are more costly. It provides a high degree of data replication as by default writes three times therefore no need to implement the RAID on the data nodes. The name node stores metadata for the files, like the directory structure of a typical file system. The server holding the NameNode instance is reasonably critical.

Presently Hadoop is in use in most of the organizations where big data is handled. Some of the well-known organizations are:-

- Yahoo!
- Facebook
- Amazon
- Netflix

Examples of scalability-

- Yahoo!'s Search Webmap runs on 10,000 core Linux cluster and powers Yahoo! Web search
- FB's Hadoop cluster hosts 100+ PB of data (July, 2012) & growing at ½ PB/day (Nov, 2012)

5. Cloud Computing

Big data and cloud computing, both technologies are valuable to their own but many business organizations are in compete to combine both of these technologies to reap more business benefits. As discussed in the previous sections, big data handles the data which is in structured, unstructured or semi structured form and the important aspects of big data are described through its V's like volume, velocity, variety, veracity and value.

Cloud computing offer services to the users on *pay as you go* model(Yang, Huang, Li, Liu, & Hu, 2017). Three primary services offered by the cloud computing are- IaaS (Infrastructure as a service), PaaS (platform as a service) and SaaS (Software as a service). Figure 7 depicts the relationship between big data and cloud computing.

Based on the service types, big data and cloud computing relationship can be categorized into three:-

Figure 7. Relationship between big data and cloud computing
(source: www.whizlabs.com)

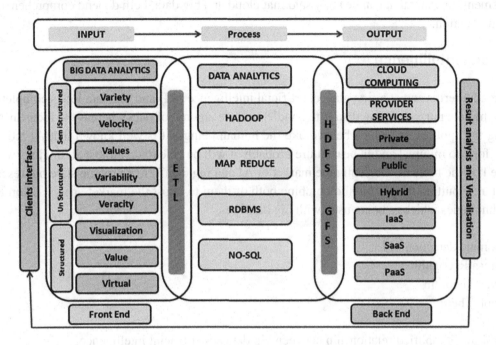

1. **IaaS in Public Cloud** - As IaaS is a very cost effective solution for the enterprises where the cloud provider bears complete cost for providing IT infrastructure at a minimal cost. Utilizing this cloud service for handling big data for an organization enables them for unlimited storage and computing power.

2. **PaaS in Private Cloud** - The PaaS cloud service providers eliminates the need for dealing with complex hardware and software which is very difficult while handling terabytes of data.

3. **SaaS in Hybrid Cloud**- For the organizations involved in business analysis, analyzing data related to social media is an essential parameter. The SaaS cloud vendors provide an excellent cloud environment for conducting such kind of analysis in a cost effective manner.

Big data relationship with cloud computing can be better understood with the following benefits-

1. **Simplified Infrastructure**- Cloud computing provides infrastructure without the need of handling technical complexities which can also be scaled as per the need of the business.

2. **Security and Privacy**- By offering different type of cloud storage by cloud service providers the big data is kept secure and private. Further the big data solutions like Hadoop offers third party services and infrastructure making the system secure.

3. **Enhanced Analysis**- Cloud aids to integrate data from various sources and analyst prefer to analyze data available over cloud sources.

4. **Lower Cost**- Both technologies conveys value to organizations by reducing the proprietorship and thus lower down the enterprise purpose cost.

5.   **Virtualization**- Virtualized applications provides multiple benefits and abridges big data management. In general, it can be aptly said that cloud and big data, both depend comprehensively on virtualization.

6. Artificial Intelligence

In the broader terms and at a first glance, artificial intelligence (AI) and big data looks completely different as the sole purpose of big data is to handle massive amount of data whereas the focus in AI is on designing the applications which behave like the human beings. It is well known that AI reduces the human efforts to minimal and in near future probably it will be able to do almost all the jobs which are performed by the humans. Currently the market of AI and big data is in its rookie state but researchers are constantly putting their efforts to combine both of them to boost the market analysis. Some of the mjor technologies which re being used with big data are-

- Anomaly detection
- Pattern Recognition
- Bayes Theorem
- Graph Theory

Fig 8 shows simplified relationship between big data and artificial intelligence.
Impacts of Big Data on AI:
Following are the key aspect of AI through which we can easily understand the impact of Big data on AI-

Figure 8. Relationship between big data and artificial intelligence

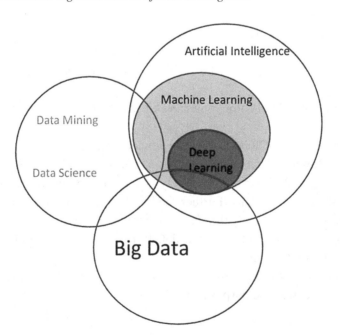

- Availability of low-cost and highly reliable large-scale memory devices
- Voice and image processing algorithms
- Exponential increase in computational power
- Machine learning from actual data sets, not just sample data
- Open-source programming languages and platforms

7. Edge Computing

Edge computing can be defined as a network of small data centers which stores desperate data locally i.e.in the vicinity. Typically it is performed by IoT devices. Edge computing embraces potential for enterprises, predominantly in supporting their IoT implementations. However, edge also raises some security concerns. Artificial intelligence applications and the incipient 5G communication network comprehensively be governed by edge computing. Edge is the future of big data. Some of the major applications are- Sorting the signal from the noise, and applying real-time learning requires Edge Computing, delivered by robust, customizable systems. Figure 9 represents the model of edge computing.

8. Block Chain Technology

Block chain technology is a decentralized system of records of transactions which can be modified anytime without changing the records. Block chain comprises of two words block and chain which means it is sequence of blocks that share some certificates (data). This technology is used for secure communication between two parties in that particular block. This technology was invented by Satoshi Nakamoto in 2008(Nakamoto, 2008). The framework of block chain technology encompasses following components:

1. **Blocks:** These are the building blocks of block chain technology to store the transactions in a cryptographic hash function. Cryptographic hash function is takes input message of any length and produces the hash function. The two blocks are linked via a hash function forming a chain. Whenever a new transaction is added in the database it is updated in the new block. The previous blocks are removed.
2. **Timestamps:** Every block in a block chain has timestamp associated with it. A shorter block time means faster transactions.

Figure 9. Edge computing

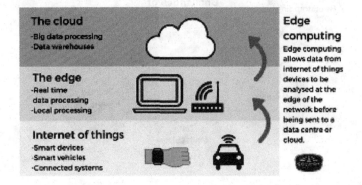

3. **Decentralization:** A block chain system is decentralized in nature which means all the nodes are generated in form of a tree. There is no central point of failure in the system.

4. **Private block chain:** These block chains need protection from external attacks as they cannot rely on the any anonymous factors.

Figure 10 shows the challenges faced by block chain technology.

CONCLUSION

By uploading the data over the server, blockchain eliminates the hazardous processors which accompany that data being hide on the halfway. If device needs unified purposes of vulnerability that can be abused by computer specialists. The present internet has privacy problems which can be known to everyone. The overall device depends on "username " architecture to secure our user tasks and sources on the internet. Blockchain privacy procedures use encryption mechanism. The main thing for use of the encryption standards is that it is open access and private "keys". A "public key" is a users' location over blockchain. Bitcoins transfers data to system and get stored with a location having physical address. The "private key" shows a secret key which gives permissions to their Bitcoin. Saving our data over the blockchain which is honest and valid, and making secure of our advanced sources will need in defending of our private key by processing out, and making it available in wallet. By blockchain discovery, the internet brings out other level of usefulness. Till date clients can communicate with each other or can communicate with service providers — Bitcoin transfers in 2017 arrived at the midpoint with around $2 billion US daily.

Figure 10. Challenges of block chain technology

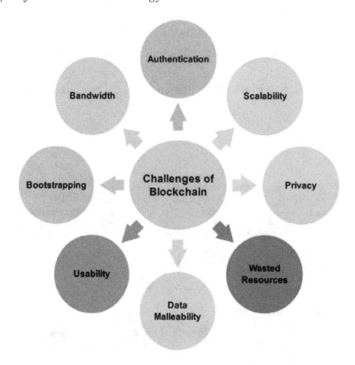

These technologies are pertinent and essential for the big data. Without understanding these, it will be a strenuous task to get the solutions which involve big data. Lot of work has been carried out by researchers over a period of time but still there are many promising fields which can be further improved by fully utilizing the potential of these technologies.

REFERENCES

Agrawal, R., & Gupta, N. (2017). Educational Data Mining Review: Teaching Enhancement. In Privacy and Security Policies in Big Data (pp. 149-165). IGI Global.

Agrawal, R., & Gupta, N. (Eds.). (2018). *Extracting Knowledge from Opinion Mining*. IGI Global.

Assunção, M. D., Calheiros, R. N., Bianchi, S., Netto, M. A. S., & Buyya, R. (2015). Big Data computing and clouds: Trends and future directions. *Journal of Parallel and Distributed Computing*. doi:10.1016/j.jpdc.2014.08.003

Bhogal, J., & Choksi, I. (2015). Handling Big Data Using NoSQL. *Proceedings - IEEE 29th International Conference on Advanced Information Networking and Applications Workshops, WAINA 2015.* 10.1109/WAINA.2015.19

Gupta, N., & Agrawal, R. (2017). Challenges and Security Issues of Distributed Databases. In *NoSQL* (pp. 265–284). Chapman and Hall/CRC.

Gupta, N., & Agrawal, R. (2018). NoSQL security. *Advances in Computers*, *109*, 101–132. doi:10.1016/bs.adcom.2018.01.003

Nakamoto, S. (2008). *Bitcoin: A Peer-to-Peer Electronic Cash System*. Satoshi Nakamoto Institute.

O'Driscoll, A., Daugelaite, J., & Sleator, R. D. (2013). "Big data", Hadoop and cloud computing in genomics. *Journal of Biomedical Informatics*, *46*(5), 774–781. doi:10.1016/j.jbi.2013.07.001 PMID:23872175

Oussous, A., Benjelloun, F., Lahcen, A. A., & Belfkih, S. (2015). *Comparison and Classification of NoSQL Databases for Big Data*. Big Data Analytics.

Pathak, S., & Agrawal, R. (2019). Design of Knowledge Based Analytical Model for Organizational Excellence. *International Journal of Knowledge-Based Organizations*, *9*(1), 12–25. doi:10.4018/IJKBO.2019010102

Subramaniyaswamy, V., Vijayakumar, V., Logesh, R., & Indragandhi, V. (2015). Unstructured data analysis on big data using map reduce. *Procedia Computer Science*, *50*, 456–465. doi:10.1016/j.procs.2015.04.015

Yang, C., Huang, Q., Li, Z., Liu, K., & Hu, F. (2017). Big Data and cloud computing: Innovation opportunities and challenges. *International Journal of Digital Earth*, *10*(1), 13–53. doi:10.1080/17538947.2016.1239771

Chapter 4
Clustering and Bayesian Networks

Bhanu Chander

ⓘ https://orcid.org/0000-0003-0057-7662

Pondicherry University, India

ABSTRACT

The goal of this chapter is to present an outline of clustering and Bayesian schemes used in data mining, machine learning communities. Standardized data into sensible groups is the preeminent mode of understanding as well as learning. A cluster constitutes a set regarding entities that are alike and entities from different clusters are not alike. Representing data by fewer clusters inevitably loses certain fine important information but achieves better simplification. There is no training stage in clustering; mostly, it's used when the classes are not well-known. Bayesian network is one of the best classification methods and is frequently used. Generally, Bayesian network is a form of graphical probabilistic representation model that consists of a set of interconnected nodes, where each node represents a variable, and inter-link connection represents a causal relationship of those variables. Belief networks are graph symbolized models that successfully model familiarity via transmitting probabilistic information to a variety of assumptions.

INTRODUCTION

Clustering is one of the classification task introduced on a finite set of objects. Clustering is unsupervised learning model; therefore like other unsupervised machine learning models, it will generate a definite model structure in collected works of unlabelled data/information. Clearly, clustering could be the progression of systematizing objects in the direction of groups whose members are look-alike in the same way. Systematizing data points into reasonable groups is the major fundamental task of understanding and learning. In 1970 Tyron stated regarding clustering as "understanding our real-world requires conceptualizing the similarities and difference among entities that compose it". Following that In 1974 Everett stated definition for cluster as "A Cluster is aggregation of points in the test space such that the distance among any two points in the cluster is less than the distance among any points in the cluster

DOI: 10.4018/978-1-7998-0106-1.ch004

and any point not in it" or "Cluster may be described as connected regions of a multi-dimensional space containing a relatively high density of points, separated from other such regions by a region containing a relatively low density of points". From the above-mentioned definitions, the objects to be organized as a cluster are characterized as points in the measurement field. If we see a cluster in the paper it is easily recognizable but we cannot clear how it is made, because of clusters made due to different objects harmonized into clusters with consideration of special intentions or measurement metrics in intellect. It is trouble-free to give a determined explanation for cluster however it is complicated to give a practical explanation for the cluster. Shapes and sizes of clusters different based on data reveal methods moreover timely cluster membership also changes. Numbers of clusters depend on the resolution by means of which we analysis data (Rokash 2005; Pavel et al 2002; Satya et al., 2013; Kaur et al., 2014; suman et al., 2014; Mehrotra et al., 2017; Anil k et al., 1990).

Clustering groups data instance into dissimilar subgroups in a corresponding way with the aim of related instance handled collectively while peculiar instance fit special groups. After that, instances structured toward as professional representations to facilitate characterize the inhabitants being sampled. Given a set of data instances/points and group them into suitably represented cluster where points contained by each cluster are related to each other moreover points from special clusters are unrelated. A data point which takes the main role in clustering is in high dimensional space furthermore relationship of that above-mentioned data point defined using a distance quantifies like Jaccard, Euclidean, edit distance, cosine, etc. basically clustering shape well-designed formation like a set of subgroups $C=C1, C2....CK$ of D means where: $D = Uki=1$ Ci and Ci $\cap$ Cj $= \phi$ for i Not-equal to j. Therefore whichever data point in D feels right to accurately one and only single subgroup. Clustering operation considered necessary in assorted data mining tasks. Clustering data points known from earliest human stages where human could do a performance in well-known distinctiveness of mean as well as objects categorize them with nature? Clusters customer behavior based on their purchase history. Clusters products based on the sets of customers who purchased them. Clusters documents based on comparable words or shingles. Clusters DNA sequence based on edit distance. Hence, it embraces an assortment of systematic regulations from math, statistics to life sciences along with genetics every one applied special terms to illustrate the topologies produced using this analysis. Starting biological taxonomy to medicinal syndromes moreover genetics genotypes to mechanized class machinery- but the dilemma is indistinguishable construction categories of entities and assigning individuals to suitable groups contained by it (Deepti et al., 2012; Mehrotra et al., 2017; Anil k et al., 1990; Sohrab et al.,2012; Omer et al., 2018; Sanjay et al., 2011).

Clustering methods provide more advantages than traditional grouping procedures. In clustering, a specific idea continuously forms groups. Humans regard as first-rate cluster seekers in two or three-dimensional data but here problem came where a dissimilar individual cannot able to identify same structure in cluster data, for this a similarity measurement is applied among objects in specified data. More importantly, clustering methods separate data points in a fraction of time. The speed, time, reliability along with the consistency of individual, specific clustering algorithms to systematize data together characterizes an irresistible motivation to utilize it. Clustering methods effectively utilize in divide and conquer policy for the reduction of the computational complexity of various decision-making procedures in pattern recognition.

The goal of this chapter is to present an outline of clustering and Bayesian schemes used in data mining, machine learning communities. Standardize data into sensible groups is preeminent modes of understanding as well as learning. A cluster constitutes set regarding entities which are alike and entities from different clusters are not alike. Clustering an unsupervised learning exercise where one instance investigates toward recognizing a fixed set of departments termed as clusters, headed for express information. Representing data by fewer clusters inevitably loses certain fine important information but achieves better simplification. Basically, there is no training stage in clustering; mostly it's used when the classes are not well-known in prior. Clustering procedure and many other procedures mostly have a close relation moreover clustering frequently used in statistics as well as in applied sciences. Typical applications include speech and character recognition, data compression in image processing, information retrieval, text mining, web applications, spatial database applications, DNA analysis in computational biology and many more.

Bayesian network is one of the best classification methods in data mining and Machine learning communities which is frequently used in text mining, intrusion and anomaly detection, fraud detection, information retrieval and many more. Generally, a Bayesian network is forms of graphical probabilistic representation model consist of a set of interconnected nodes, where each node represents a variable and inter-link connection represents a causal relationship of those variables. At the movement of making vital decisions, it is reasonable to look for instruction from remains that have proficiency in relevant field/ domain of knowledge. The particular experts/consultants grant-based on their concentrated knowledge, familiarity and any other on-hand source of information. Probabilistic models also have acknowledged considerable attention, although predominantly they not able to outfit for tentative expert knowledge of their representation along with reasoning. Moreover, knowledge of models is characterized by causal relationships stuck between variables along with their allied probability measures. These probability measures may be situated on conventional probabilities, Bayesian probabilities or an amalgamation of twain.

Belief networks are graph symbolize models that successfully model familiarity estate; they endow with a constructive tool for interfering assumption from on-hand information via transmit probabilistic information to a variety of assumption.

IDENTIFY CLUSTER

Classification as well as clustering both deep-seated missions of data mining and machine learning. Where both implemented as supervised or unsupervised learning depends on the application domain. Veyssieres in 1998 stated classification goal is predictive and coming to clustering it is descriptive. In view of the fact that classification groups reproduce some point of a reference set of classes, an important part about assessment in extrinsic. Whereas clustering discovers new strategies, which are interested and their assessment are intrinsic. Clustering might be base on similarity or distance quantity, however, the final result is the same, for the reason that similarity measurements are strongly unenthusiastically associated with distance measurements. Distance positioned algorithms depend upon a design that data points within the same cluster estranged by somewhat small distances, while cluster data points of a dissimilar cluster are at a superior distance from each other. Coming to similarity-based algorithms, propose data points which are comparable to each other must fit inside the similar cluster, here got a clear idea about smaller distance data points are presumed to be more similar than bigger distance data point similarity (Mehrotra et al., 2017; Aggarwal 2013; Pavel 2002; Wang et al., 2017; He et al., 2017; Fahad 2014; Everitt 1977).

Clustering is one of the most important procedure in machine learning as well as data mining. There are many algorithms extensively applied in text, image, computer visualization, outlier detection, and forecast observation. In view of the fact that clustering is collecting similar data points together, so desirable type of measure required, which can accurately decide whether two data points are similar or not. Most of the above-mentioned domains use distance or similarity measurement for accurate clustering. Some of them are described below:

Distance Measurement

Many of classification, as well as clustering procedures, exercise on the distance to decide likeness or unlikeness among any pair of objects or data points. Present two outstanding varieties of procedures utilized in the direction of describe the relationship those are distance measurement and similarity measurement. A valid dimension must be real symmetric moreover achieve its least important in case of the exact vector (Rokach 2005).

Minkowski Distance Measurement

Given two m-dimensional data objects ai = (ai1, ai2. . . aim) and bj = (bj1,bj2, . . ., bjm), with the help of Minkowski distance measurement distance among above mentioned data objects can be calculated as

d(ai, bj) = (| ai1 −bj1| e + | ai2 − bj2| e + . . . + | aim − bjm| e)1/e.

Here e- indicates Euclidean distance among two data objects or points. However, distance measurement effect the overall clustering analysis. Means choice of dependencies on measurement units may affect cluster results; to avoid this data should be in standardizing formation. Standardize data contain all data objects or points have equal weights moreover each-every data objects consigned with a weight according to its impact (Rokach 2005; Han et al., 2001).

For suppose if our data in mixed, categorical, ordinal, binary formation then corresponding distance measurements will be quite different from remaining distance measurement principles. For example, our data contains binary attributes then distance measurement can take place with the help of a contingency table. If the binary attribute is symmetric where data has equal variables then simpler co-efficient similarity distance measurement can be applicable for dissimilarity among two objects or data points. Rather than this if our binary attribute is asymmetric then Jaccard distance measurement is applicable.

$$d(a_i, b_j) = \frac{r+s}{q+r+s+t}$$

When two data attributes, points are nominal or insignificant. Then simply matching approach applicable mean total number of attributes or points minus the number of matches divided by the total quantity of data attributes or points. Other than this create a binary attribute for every state of each insignificant and compute their respective similarity the same as mentioned above.

$$d(a_i, b_j) = \frac{p-m}{p}$$

For suppose our data is ordinal attributes, where attributes are in sequential values in a meaningful way. For these attributes or points are turned into numeric rates and mapping into [0, 1] range.

Similarity Function

Similarity function is the alternating procedure for distance measurement where it compares two attributes or data points. Moreover, similarity function must be symmetrical and produce huge value when xi, as well as xj parallel to each other in addition, provides principal value for exact vectors.

Cosine Measure

If a viewpoint among two vectors is momentous appraise of their likeness, the normalized interior invention may perhaps an appropriate likeness appraise:

$$s(a_i, b_j) = \frac{a_i^T \cdot b_j}{a_i \cdot b_j}$$

Pearson Correlation Measure

The standardize Pearson correlation is described as

$$s(a_i, b_j) = \frac{\left(a_i - \bar{a}_i\right)^T \cdot \left(b_j - \bar{b}_j\right)}{a_i - \bar{a}_i \cdot b_j - \bar{b}_j}$$

Extended Jaccard Measure

The extensive Jaccard measure was offered by

$$s(a_i, b_j) = \frac{a_i^T \cdot b_j}{a_i^2 + b_j^2 - a_i^T \cdot b_j}$$

Dice Coefficient Measure

The dice coefficient measure is related to the extensive Jaccard measure and it is described as

$$s(a_i, b_j) = \frac{2a_i^T \cdot b_j}{x_i^2 + b_j^2}$$

CLASSIFICATION OF CLUSTERING METHODS

Clustering is a type of classification imposed on set of finite objects/instances. Cluster investigation is the main process of taxonomy objects/instances which have meaning in perspective of a specific problem. After that data objects/instances represented into a specified organization, based on that characterize the population sample. As stated above clustering is the special nature of classification where the relationship among objects/instances is symbolized in a proximity matrix where columns as well as rows shown as data objects/instances. Data instances/objects could be exemplified as patterns, points in m-dimensional space. However the proximity as distance among data objects as well as data points with the help of Euclidean, Mahalanobis distances. Clustering classification procedure separated into various formations such as *Exclusive and Non-exclusive* – In an exclusive, classification is partition set of data points/instances. Where each-every data point/object belongs truly to solitary cluster or sub-set. Coming to Non-exclusive, classification which is also pronounced as overlapping cluster classification where data objects/instances are assigned to numerous sub-sets or clusters. *Intrinsic and extrinsic* – Intrinsic classification is also known as unsupervised learning cluster algorithm where it does not have any category label partition for data objects/instances. It mainly makes use of the proximity matrix on behalf of classification. One simple procedure to estimate intrinsic cluster classification is continuously observed how the cluster labels connected to data instances/objects while clustering process, match them and assigned a priori. Extrinsic cluster partitions simply reverse of intrinsic classification; it employs category labels and proximity matrix. *Hierarchical and partitioned* – the above mentioned intrinsic as well as extrinsic are sub-divided into hierarchical and partitioned cluster classifications as a result of kind structure institute on the data. Hierarchical is a fixed sequence of separations while partitioned classification is single partition (Anil 1990; Dewdneg 1986; Pavel 2002; ; Carlsson 2010; Velmurugan et al., 2011; Keogh 2001; Jain 2010).

There are various kind algorithms developed for the purpose of explanation about intrinsic and extrinsic cluster classifications. A little few of primary algorithmic options are listed as: *Serial and Simultaneous* – As the name indicates Serial processes holds data patterns one after another, while Simultaneous classification performs with the entire pattern set at the same time. *Graph-theory and Matrix algebra* – Some methods/procedures could explain with help of graph theory such as terms completeness, connectedness for characterizing classification. Some more special algorithms explained in terms of algebraic notations such as mean-squared-error, sum-of-squared-error, etc. *Monothetic and Ploythetic* – Monothetic classification algorithms use feature one-by-one, where polythetic classification process takes all feature at once. These two methods show very interesting variation in the clustering process. *Agglomerative and Divisive* – In Agglomerative method, hierarchical takes place where each object/instances in its own cluster and also takes place progressively merge cluster into one single larger cluster. Divisive is completely reverse of agglomerative classification cluster, it starts with all available data instances/objects as one cluster then starts sub-dividing small clusters (Anil 1990; Dewdneg 1986; Pavel 2002; ; Carlsson 2010; Velmurugan et al., 2011; Keogh 2001; Jain 2010).

Compare to other data mining as well as machine learning techniques, clustering has a very close connection with them moreover with other disciplines. In statistics and science background clustering has been used outstandingly. Classical usage clustering comes into action into pattern recognition framework in 1973. After those clustering techniques incorporated in typical appliances like speech and character recognitions, most importantly machine learning-based clustering algorithms applied in computer vision and image segmentation procedures in 1986. Clustering has also used as an image compression process in 1992 which was also well-known as vector quantization.

Grouping data points into clusters are depending at the principle of minimization of inter-class likeness as well as maximizing intraclass similarity. A high-quality clustering method fabricates high-quality clusters with great intra-class similarity like one another inside similar cluster low inter-class similarity. Dissimilar to the objects in extra clusters the worth of a cluster end result depends on both similarity measure which was employed moreover its execution and performance process. Additionally, the excellence of clustering also considered via its capability to realize some or entire hidden pattern (Mehrotra et al., 2017; Pavel 2002; Satya et al., 2013; Kaur et al., 2014; suman et al., 2014).

Nearest Neighbor Clustering

A K-NN algorithm has been developed for different kind of problems, based on the main inspiration that individual similarity of its majority of k owns adjacent or nearest neighbor. This scheme provides huge weight-age to neighboring data points, but computationally more expensive than other techniques although summarizes properties of large data sets into small accurate with limited numerical characteristics. This procedure most widely used in classification tasks where points are labeled with a similar label as a greater number of their K-NN which is same as a supervised learning process. The algorithm always starts with solitary fresh data point at a time and label it with a new-fangled data point, this process iteratively labels all the instant neighbors of labeled points whose measurement is less important than a threshold which builds upon on distances among labeled data points in that cluster. At the end of iteration step recreation labeling points placed on the majority of their k instant neighbors; such as boundaries of identified clusters or results of merging some clusters.

Partition Clustering

Partition algorithms determine clusters either iteratively relocate points among subsets or identifying areas deeply colonized with data. In briefly partition algorithm attempts to decompose N objects keen on k clusters suchlike partition develop a definite principle meaning. Each-cluster characterizes with the center of gravity of that cluster like k-means clusters. Otherwise closest point/instance to the gravity center like k-medoids. As mentioned above explanations k stating points are randomly selected and repositioning proposal iteratively applied on points among clusters to optimize clustering standard. One main drawback of partition clustering is there are numerous possible solutions. The sum-squared-error, minimization squared error, scatter criteria and Euclidean distances of points from bordering cluster centroid (Deepti et al., 2012; Pavel 2002).

K-Means Algorithm

K- Means clustering algorithm is a well-known clustering algorithm that perfectly categorizes each cluster through its cluster centroid. Simply center of each cluster is considered as a mean of the entire instances/ points fit into that cluster. K-means algorithm introduced by Hartigan and Wong in the year 1975 and 1979 respectively. The algorithm represents each of k clusters centroid by the mean of its points and results shown as symmetric clusters like spheres as three-dimensional data. The main objective function in k means is the sum of inconsistencies among point and its corresponding centroid expressed in the course of appropriate distance. Since k means algorithm is partitioned based clustering, algorithm initiate by means of fundamental cluster centers, which are chosen randomly or in consonance to any method. According to each-iteration, every instance is allocating to the closest cluster center according to predefined Euclidean distance among two data points/instances. Subsequently, cluster midpoint is re-calculated, if the partitioned error is not condensed by means of rearrangement centers on that movement there is a chance for stop search operation (Mehrotra et al., 2017; Berkin et al., 2002).

K means clustering process is most widely applied in statistical as well as science domains, there are numerous problems for which k means algorithm not satisfactory. The algorithm shows best results with a geometric, statistical sense for binary attributes and with categorical data, it shows worst results compare to other mechanisms. K means algorithms also work same as gradient-descent process which starts by a primary set of k cluster-centers and iteratively updates it so as to decrease the error function. The algorithm is trouble-free, uncomplicated and straightforward base on the hard foundation of investigation of variances. Although it is the best algorithm for clustering but suffers with some natural deduces like as noted above only numerical attributes are covered, it is not clear what a good k to chose, most of the results depend on the initial guess of centroid, procedure is sensitive with outliers such that data significantly manipulate the centroid calculation, resulting cluster could be unequal, procedure has lack of scalability, incapability to pledge with cluster random shape size plus density, sensitivity initialization, poor cluster descriptors, dependence on user to indicate number of clusters (Mehrotra et al., 2017; Berkin et al., 2002; Anil et al., 1990).

The marvelous fame of k means clustering brings rebirth to lots of additional expectations as well as modifications. Addition of Mahalanobis distance provides great results in hyper-ellipsoidal clusters. Instead of sum error, maximum correlations of intracluster variance produce great values. K - Means algorithm starting steps as follows first chose fractions of clusters (K) second arbitrarily create k clusters as well as cluster centers then allot each instance/point to closest cluster center later than again compute fresh cluster centers and finally repeat above mentioned steps till some coherence decisive factor met.

K – Medoid Algorithm

Unlike k means, k - medoid algorithm - cluster illustrated via one of its points. Simply cluster illustrated by its medoid which is most centrally positioned point/objects in that cluster. There are two most popular medoid algorithms that are Partition around medoid (PAM) and Clustering Large Appliances (CLARA). PAM algorithm - randomly selects an object as medoid in each cluster thereafter remaining non-selected points/objects are harmonized to closest medoid which is most related. PAM continually substitutes every medoid with non-objective made medoid. Compare to k means algorithm PAM is expensive regarding finding medoid and compare with remaining complete data set at every-iteration of algorithm step. CLARA employs various samples which are each subjected to PAM. Entire data points are allocated to resulting medoid and then the objective function is computed to retain the best system of medoid. Ng and Han in 1994 further progressed CLARA as Clustering Large Appliances based upon RANdomized Search (CLARANS) authors consider a graph where node symbolizes K medoid and an edge symbolizes the connection of pair nodes if they disagree by accurately single medoid, here every node as potential to set K medoids. Selecting an arbitrary node as base CLARANS chose random search to produce neighbors and randomly checks for max-neighbor. If any neighbor produces enhanced partition results, process prolong with that newly established node or else local minima can initiate and algorithm start again until num-local minima found (Anil et al., 1990; Han et al., 1994; Ester et al., 1995; Mehrotra et al., 2017; Pavel 2002; Satya et al., 2013; Kaur et al., 2014; suman et al., 2014).

Probabilistic Clustering

In probabilistic clustering search proposed in 1998, data points are taken as independently from a mixture model from various probabilistic distributions. In this algorithm data points are engendered by two processes first accidentally pick a probability model; secondly, draw a point shape subsequent distribution. The region throughout the mean of each distribution function constructs a cluster. Each data point contains its own attributes along with hidden/unknown cluster-ID.

Each point assumed to be a relationship with only one cluster. From the above discussion, a key possession of probabilistic clustering is a mixture model that be capable of logically comprehensive to clustering heterogeneous information. For the reason that mixture model has comprehensible probabilistic basis and purpose of a high-quality proper number of clusters (k) becomes to the well-mannered mission. From data mining viewpoint excessive parameter set cause over-fitting, while from a probabilistic point of view; the number of parameters can be addressed inside Bayesian structure. Although there some important feature for Probabilistic algorithm those are: algorithm can able to knob records of complex formation. It can be closed as well as a resume with successive groups of data since clusters illustration totally special from sets of points moreover at any phase of iterative progression the intermediate mixture representation can be utilized to allot cases; it results without difficulty interpretable cluster system.

Fuzzy Clustering

Classical clustering procedures create data partitions, where each partition contains each instance belongs to only one cluster. Hence clustering provides hard clustering with disjoint operations. Fuzzy clustering is an extension to disjoint operation moreover suggests a soft-clustering plan. In this fuzzy clustering plan, each-every data point connection in the business of all clusters with some type of membership function. Each cluster is a fuzzy set of the entire patterns. Simply, in fuzzy clustering data points/instances has a fixed degree of belonging to clusters which are completely special from belonging entirely to one solitary cluster. Those points which are located at the edge of a cluster have might be in the luster with less degree than points in the cluster in the center of the cluster (Mehrotra et al., 2017; Deepthi 2012; Anil et al., 1990; Bezdesk 1981).

Fuzzy c-means (FCM) is the most popular fuzzy clustering algorithm; FCM produces better results than hard disjoint k-means algorithm moreover avoid local-minima but still converge toward local-minima of square error criterion. Moreover, the utmost crucial trouble of fuzzy clustering is designing of relationship functions, dissimilar choices take based on similarity decompositions and centroids of clusters. A fuzzy c-shell algorithm, as well as an adaptive variant, is for detecting circular and elliptical boundaries respectively.

From the above-mentioned details of all clustering algorithms we can conclude that partition-based clustering has some advantages as well as some disadvantages those are: *Advantages* – Partition based clustering classification methods are moderately scalable and effortless. Moreover appropriate for data sets with solid sphere-shaped clusters which are well-set. *Dis-advantages* – frequent interrupts in local minima, in-ability toward deal through non-convex clusters with unstable volume and density. The theory of distance among points in high dimensional spaces is unclear, high sensitivity to initialization phase and noise as well as outliers.

Density-Based Partition Clustering

Density clustering, based on local density conditions groups adjacent data points/instances into cluster rather than proximity connecting objects. Points those belong to each cluster taken from a definite probability distribution. Dense base cluster procedures have low noise tolerance moreover dense regions being separated through low-level density noise regions besides discovering non-convex clusters. Mainly density-based clusters classify respective clusters along with respective distribution parameters furthermore discover clusters of the random figure which are not essentially convex. In partition clustering, Euclidean distance is used in open-set decomposed to set of related components. For finite set, partition entails impressions like connectivity, density and boundary those strongly associated with points bordering neighbors. If cluster defined or designed as connected component increases in any path that density leads, so it's capable of discovering clusters of arbitrary shapes. A single dense cluster consists of two adjacent areas with extensively dissimilar densities moreover its shows lack of interpretability (Ester 1996; Ertoz 2003; pearl 1988; Pavel 2002; Deepti et al., 2012).

Notably, two density-based clustering algorithms are there: First method pin-on density to a training data point and Re-viewed like density-based connectivity examples like DBSCAN, GDBSCAN, and OPTICS. Second method pin-on density to a point in the attribute space and give an explanation in subsection density functions example DENCLUE.

Density-Based Connectivity

In density-based connectivity, the two mentioned terms density as well as connectivity measure in-premises of local distribution from adjacent neighbors. Here Density-Based Spatial Clustering of Applications with Noise (DBSCAN) shows the core objective of density-based connectivity by targeting low dimensional spatial data. DBSCAN seeks for reachable core objects data points and factorized to maximal associated peripherals as clusters. Those data points which are associated with none of the core objects acknowledged as outliers or noise and separated from remaining clusters. The non-core points within a cluster represent its own boundary. DBSCAN can discover arbitrary shaped clusters, there is no need for any limitations on dimension or attributes type because core objects are interior points and processing is autonomous of data sort. Note DBSCAN relies on locality frequency calculation to describe the perception of a core object. Whereas several other contain comprehensive objects like polygons as a substitute of points moreover strength of point can be utilized instead of a simple count as well. These things escort to GDBSCAN that uses similar parameters as DBSCAN. There is no clear-cut way to fit two parameters ε and MinPts to data. The method Ordering Points To Identify the Clustering Structure (OPTICS) adjusts this dispute by constructing increased order of data which is reliable with DBSCAN. Moreover OPTICS consider as DBSCAN addition in course of dissimilar local densities, more mathematically approach think about an accidental variable equivalent to the distance from a point to its adjacent neighbor and find out its possibility distribution (Ester 1996; Anil et al., 1990; Ertoz 2003; pearl 1988; Pavel 2002; Deepti et al., 2012).

Density Function

Density Function proposed by Hinneburg & Keim in 1998, changed the prominence from computing densities binds to data points, to compute density functions define over the underlying attribute space. Authors prepared an algorithm DENCLUE (DENsity-based CLUstEring). DENCLUE make use of an influence function to express the impact of a point in relation to its neighborhood whereas the

the overall density of data space is a summation of influence functions from the entire data. By the side with DBCLASD, DENCLUE has a solid statistical foundation. DENCLUE uses a density function, focus on local maxima of density functions entitled density-attractors furthermore employ a taste of gradient hill-climbing procedure used for finding them. In addition to center-defined clusters, arbitrary-shape clusters are defined as continuity along with sequences of points whose local densities are not smallest than the prearranged threshold (Anil et al., 1990; Pavel 2002).

Compare to remaining clustering methods Density-based clustering has some advantages and disadvantages: *Advantages* – Finding irresponsible-shaped clusters by means of changeable size, moreover resistance against noise, outliers. *Dis-advantages* – High sensitivity for the setting of input parameters, poor cluster descriptors, not fits for high-dimensional data sets since the curse of dimensionality circumstance.

Hierarchical Clustering

Partition based and Density-based clustering methods produce single partition, other than this Hierarchical clustering methods produce a sequence of clusters, a solitary all-encompassing cluster on the top position while singleton clusters with individual points at the bottom. As per name Hierarchical can formed in both directions top-down known as Divisive or bottom-up known as agglomerative. Generally, each-iteration programmed with divide a pair of clusters based on convinced criteria then measure proximity flanked-by clusters. After the specified number of clusters has been formed merging or splitting function stops. Both the merging and splitting performed according to preferred similarity measures, based on these similarity measurements hierarchical clustering further divided: *Single-link-clustering* - single link clustering is too call as nearest neighbor, connectedness or minimum distance method. The distance among any pair-off clusters is minimum or the same to shortest distance from some member of one cluster to some member of remaining clusters. In addition, suppose data consist of similarities and that similarity difference of particular pair of the cluster is considered being a furthermost relationship from any member of solitary cluster to any member of the additional cluster. Single link clustering described in terms of connected sub-graphs. *Complete-link-clustering* – Complete link clustering uses complete sub-graphs also named as diameter, furthest nearest neighbor and maximum method. The method consists of distance among any two clusters is the highest distance from any member of one cluster to any member of remaining clusters which is completely reverse to single-link clustering. *Average-link-clustering* - Average link clustering is named as regular distance variance method, believe the distance between any two clusters equivalent to average variance from members of one cluster or members of any remaining clusters (Rokach 2005; Mehrotra et al., 2017; Sohrab et al.,2012; Omer et al., 2018; Sanjay et al., 2011; Wang et al., 2017).

An image of hierarchical clustering is much familiar to a human being to understand than a list of abstract symbols. The dendrogram is one variety tree-like construction to provide a well-situated image of clustering. Dendrogram tree includes layers of nodes where each node symbolizes cluster. Lines which are attached nodes representing clusters those are nested into one another. Hierarchical clustering final outcome is dendrogram, which represents a nested grouping of objects along with similarity levels of those groups' changes. At much-loved similarity level cut on the dendrogram provides clustering of that data objects.

Agglomerative Clustering

Agglomerative clustering starts with small clusters each consist of a single element and successively merge all clusters to form one huge cluster. Each object primarily symbolizes its individual cluster, after that clusters successively merged until specified cluster structure is achieved. Two similar clusters will take part if there distance measurement is nearest to each-other. The procedure continuous till specified clusters are formed satisfactorily otherwise terminated when the next merger cluster is small compared with previous merger result. Like k means algorithm agglomerative method does not involve any external single-minded parameter for the number of clusters (k), it provides the same result for each iteration. But the main draw-back is it needs huge computational complexity as well as we have to determine how deep we go from root to down path for declaring a node is a genuine cluster (Guha 1998; Rokach 2005; Mehrotra et al., 2017).

Balanced Iterative Reducing and Clustering Using Hierarchies (BIRCH)

In BIRCH method hierarchical data structures called cluster feature (CF) tree which store in leaves, no leaf nodes stock sum of CF of owned children. It compresses data toward small sub-clusters and then executes clustering with these reviews rather than unprocessed data. Just the once CF tree is Fabricated, any hierarchical or portioning algorithm could utilize it to execute clustering. Compare with other hierarchical clustering classification BIRCH is sensibly quick but drawbacks in data order sensitivity and incapability to deal with a no-spherical cluster with changeable sizes (Deepti et al 2012; Zhang 1996; Guha 1998).

Clustering With Representatives (CURE)

CURE discusses two processes, first – instead of the single centroid, clusters represent by a predetermined number of clusters with well-scattered points. Second – data points minimize towards their respective cluster centers with a constant factor. While performing each iteration, pair of clusters those have close representative points are merged. CURE deal with arbitrary shape clusters with dissimilar shape, size moreover minimization process spray effects of outliers and noise (Deepti et al 2012; Zhang 1996; Guha 1998).

Divisive Clustering

In Divisive clustering all objects/instances fit-in single cluster. Thereafter each cluster separated into sub-clusters those again sequentially separated to their sub-clusters. This process stops only when it has the desired set of clusters formed. Avoiding wide-ranging distance computations at lowest levels involve to facilitate Divisive algorithm would be more computational well-organized than agglomerative clustering.

Hierarchical clustering classification has some noted Advantages as well as Disadvantages those listed here: *Advantages* – it is well-suited for problems involving like linkages and taxonomy, non-isotropic clusters, including well-separated, chain-like and concentric cluster. Shows flexibility regarding granularity levels, allow the ability to choose different partition according to similarity levels. *Dis-advantages* – inability to look back and undo previously done work, inability to scale-well with a large amount of data, Lack of interpretability regarding the cluster descriptors (Deepti et al., 2012, Anil et al., 1990; Rokach 2005).

Grid-Based Method

The above-mentioned algorithms depend on concepts like density, boundary, and connectivity those need certain definitions. We have another option to deriving the topology from the principal feature/attribute space. In order toward restraining search combination, multi-rectangular fragments are measured. The methods which are portioning space commonly call as Grid-based-method. All incremental as well as relocation algorithms flexible regard to data requires. Whereas density-based methods produce a good outcome in the company of numerical attributes and grid-based methods have a good outcome in the company of characteristics of unrelated type (Schikuta 1997; Aggarwal 2013; Pavel 2002).

BANG-clustering by Schikuta & Erhart in 1997 improves the hierarchical algorithm. Grid-based fragment employs headed for summarizing data. These fragments stored in an exclusive BANG-structure that is a grid-directory integrate divergent scales. From grid-directory, a dendrogram is straightforwardly designed. The STING algorithm (Statistical Information Grid-based method) by Wang et al. in 1997 workings through numerical attributes (spatial data). In doing so, STING creates data reviews in a way related to BIRCH. Nonetheless, collect statistics in hierarchical tree nodes that are grid-cells.

EVOLUTION CRITERIAS IN CLUSTERING

Various methods applied to build accurate certain clustering methods in various domains. To determine a certain clustering is excellent or not is a most problematical moreover contentious problem. In the year of 1964 Fact, Bonner stated that at hand No unique description/definition for first-rate clustering. The evaluation criteria commonly depend on spectator (Dudal 2001; Deepti et al., 2012; Pavel 2002). However, there are some popular evaluation criteria proposed listed below:

External Quality Criteria

External quality will help to examine the structure of the cluster match with the predetermined arrangement of attributes/instances.

- *Mutual information-based measure:* Mutual statistics mostly utilized as an external measure for clustering methods. The n-instances/attributes clustered via C and referred to objective attribute t whose field is dom(t)

$$C = \frac{2}{m} \sum_{l=1}^{g} \sum_{h=1}^{k} m_{l,h} \log_{g,k} \left(\frac{m_{l,h} \cdot m}{m_{.,l} \cdot m_l} \right)$$

Here, $m_{l,h}$ specify the number of instances that are in a cluster C_l, C_h. moreover $m_{.,l}$, m_l specify entire quantity instances in C_h, C_l.

- *Precision-Recall measure:* Precision recall measure is one of the popular external quality criteria measurements for evaluating cluster where information retrieval approach takes place. The results of the cluster are the outcome of a requested query for a specific class. From the name precision-recall measure, precision provides a fraction of correctly retrieved instances/attributes, at the same time recall provides a small part of properly retrieve instances/attributes absent of all available instances/attributes.

- *Rand Index:* Rand index proposed by Rand in 1971, it is trouble-free cluster evaluation criteria modeled to differentiate provoked cluster structure-1 (CS-1) with a given cluster structure-2 (CS-2). For more clarity w be the number of instances/attributes allocated to identical cluster inside CS-1 as well as identical cluster inside CS-2. X indicates a number of instances of a cluster inside CS-1, but not in a similar cluster inside CS-2. And y is no of pair of instances/attributes which are similar cluster inside CS-2, but not in a similar cluster inside CS-1. Moreover, z is No of pair instances/attributes that assign to dissimilar clusters in both CS-1 as well as CS-2. From above-mentioned w,x is taken as agreements whereas y, z are dis-agreements. Rand index varied among 0 or 1 if any case two partitions concurs completely Rand index will be shown as 1.

$$\text{Rand Index} = \frac{w + x}{w + x + y + z}$$

Internal Evaluation Criteria

An internal evaluation criterion does not go away any outside information apart from data itself. It mostly measures intra-cluster correlation or inter-cluster separation or amalgamation of both procedures.

- *Sum of Squared Error (SSE):* SSE is straightforward as well as most extensively use a criterion for clustering, premeditated as

$$SSE = \sum_{k=1}^{k} \sum_{\forall xi \in C} x_i - \mu_k^2$$

Here, Ck is a set of instances in cluster k; μk is vector mean of cluster k.

- *Scatter criteria:* Scatter criteria defined from scattering matrices, between scatter clustering and summation

$$S_k = \sum_{x \in Ck} \left(x - \mu_k \right) \left(x - \mu_k \right)^T$$

- ◦ *The trace criterion:* Representing the within-cluster scatter
- ◦ *Determinant criterion:* Roughly Measures the square of the Scattering volume
- ◦ *Invariant criterion*: Basic linear invariants of the scatter matrices
- *Condorcet's criterion:* Condorcet's standard comes into the action in 1785 as Condorcet's solution applied to the ranking crisis.
- *The C-C criterion:* it is an inclusion to Condorcet's criterion represent as follows.
- *Category Utility metric:* It is defined by Gluck and corter in 1985 which shows enlargement of the anticipated amount of feature values that are properly predicted in given clustering. Category utility measured is handy in those problems which enclose a comparatively little number of nominal features each encompass diminutive cardinality.
- *Edge cut metric:* If there are any restrictions on certain cluster size, edge cut minimization problem provides the best results for avoiding the problem in clustering. In this case, excellence is measured as the ratio of remainder edge weights to the whole precut edge weights, thus min-cut measure is revised to penalize imbalanced structures.

CLUSTERING LARGE DATASETS

Clustering large set of data set is a very hard task. There is a huge number of applications in data mining which contains hundreds to thousands of objects. Clustering such high dimensional instances are a tremendously difficult task moreover it is prognostic learning. Majority of the algorithms presented above cannot hold large data sets. To avoid the problem of clustering large data sets a probable explanation is simply slightly sacrificing adaptability of clusters to execute more well-organized modifications of the clustering algorithm. Particularly in clustering, large range of dimensionality holds two problems. First, no matter what definition of similarity, some attendance regarding irrelevant attributes reduce hope on the clustering learning process. Attendance and quantity of unrelated attributes grow with increasing size. Second, dimensionality curse – adjoining neighbor uncertainty turn into insecure where the distance amid the nearest neighbor turn into impossible to differentiate from distance to the majority of points. Thus, the creation of clusters originated on the perception of proximity is uncertain in such circumstances (Aggarwal 2000; Pavel 2002).

Dimensionality Reduction: when the conversation in relation to high dimensionality, many stated spatial clustering algorithms confide on the sign of spatial data-sets in view of a quick search of the nearest neighbor. There are two most general-purpose procedures used to cut-down dimensionalities those are: *attribute transformations* – trouble-free functions of existent attributes, *Domain Decomposition* – segregates data into subgroups with help of low-cost association measure, as a result, high dimensional calculation happens over minor datasets. This approach essentially applicable in high dimensional, outsized data sets.

Subspace Clustering

Subspace clustering well-against to fine-tune through high dimensional data set. Clustering with Quest (CLIQUE) is elemental in subspace clustering for numerical attributes moreover It ties thoughts of density, grid-based clustering algorithms. Another algorithm Entropy-based clustering algorithm (EN-CLUS) follows the same procedure but employs different criteria for sub-space selection. That particular criterion is relevant from entropy associated considerations: the subspace extended by attributes with entropy slighter than a threshold considered first-rate for clustering. Merging Adaptive Finite Intervals (MAFIA) extensively change CLIQUE. It initiates through one data pass to create adaptive grids in every dimension. Projected Clustering (PROCUS) connections by a separation C a low-dimensional subspace such that projection of C into subspace is a fixed cluster. Oriented projected cluster generation (ORCLUS) make use related process of predictable clustering, although utilizes non-axes comparable subspaces of great dimensional space (Aggarwal 2000; Berry 1995; Pavel 2002; Goil 1999; Aggarwal 1999; Keogh 2001; Hinneburg 1999).

Co-Clustering

A motivating inspiration of fabricating attribute grouping coincidence through clustering of points themselves directly headed for the perception of co-clustering. It is instantaneous clustering of mutual-points as well as their attributes. This path overturns great effort: to advance clustering of points pedestal on their attributes, it endeavors to cluster attributes pedestal on points. Co-clustering data points and attributes are also named like bi-dimensional clustering, conjugate clustering, simultaneous clustering, and distributional clustering.

CLUSTERING APPLIANCES

Clustering algorithms most widely used in industrial as well as scientific domains. From the past clustering has been utilized in natural human activities such as grouping students in college or school, customers based on purchase history, books in the library and many more. Clustering is also found applications in various disciplines such as biology, life sciences, physical sciences, geology, marketing, chemistry and information retrieval. Especially in computer science clustering plays a significant role in image processing and pattern recognition. Clustering also useful in spatial data analysis, document taxonomy, cluster web data to find out groups of related access patterns, segmentation of range images, selecting features for clustering in images, image segmentation, image registration, grammatical inference more-over speech and speaker recognition.

BAYESIAN NETWORK

As a result of important innovations in scientific, industrial and computer science and engineering domains human being living in a satisfactory way. However, there are large choices of improbability take place in numerous real-life applications that will handle with expert systems. At the moment Bayesian Network (BN) one of the most leading expert system that allows expert systems via exploiting probability as determine of improbability/unpredictability (Pearl 1988; Diez 2014; Kriey 2001; Kaewprag et al., 2017; Wang et al., 2003). Whenever taking an important decision, most of us consult experts who have a broad range of domain knowledge in that field for better advice. These experts base on their experience, knowledge or any available information gave a suggestion, advice. After that, we analyze to clarify whether our decision is correct or not, to make it better what we have to do. There comes huge interest to make automate above mentioned human reasoning process. Then the birth of expert system models takes place which makes the model knowledge of interest and their corresponding association with offered data (Kaewprag et al., 2017; Levng et al., 2000; Wooldridge et al., 2003).

Bayesian network is modeled from a concept from expert knowledge and there has been emergent curiosity in learning the structure of Bayesian network for data-mining appliances. The fundamental scheme is Bayesian model is to display probabilistic dependencies as well as independencies resulting from the available data in a summarizing way (Fenz et al., 2012; Pearl 1988; Diez 2014; Hackerman et al., 1996). Moreover Bayesian network likely to produce more important information about the domain than visualization which was made on correlations and distance measurements. Compare to models like undirected edges, Bayesian models display models which can easily understand by human beings more spontaneously (Cai et al., 2016; Kaewprag et al., 2017). Most present methods of expert systems consist of decision trees, the rule-based, artificial neural network represents for Knowledge modeling and clustering, density estimation, taxonomy practices employed to analyses above mentioned models.

Bayesian network is Directed Acyclic Graph (DAG) where nodes exemplify subjective variables toward trouble and links exemplify correlation among them. This whole operation is done along with a probability distribution upon mentioned variables to accomplish the disjointing feature which specifies the joint possibility allocation of Bayesian network as multiplication likelihood of each node conditioned on its predecessors [1, 2, 4]. In DAG, each node represent a random variable, each edge from X to Y represents that exactly and straightly manipulates Y, officially each variable X is autonomous of its non-Descendents specified its parents. Moreover, each node has a conditional probability distribution. For example, the DAG: P to Q to R, both P and R will stay independent if Q is not known but suppose as soon as Q is known both P and Q turns to dependent. If all the conditional independencies in the probability distribution must be represented in the DAG and vice-versa, then only the Bayesian network is said to be a perfect map of the probability distribution (Kaewprag et al., 2017; Cai et al., 2016; Krieg et al., 2001; Diez 2014).

With apply of the chain rule, a joint probability distribution can be articulated as

$$P\left(X_1,....X_n\right) = P\left(X_1\right)\prod_{i=2}^{n}P\left(X_i \, / \, X_1,....X_n\right)$$

Bayesian network affords compacted demonstration of a joint probability distribution as follows

$$P\left(X_1,....X_n\right) = \prod_{i=1}^{n}P\left(X_i \, / \, parents\left(X_i\right)\right)$$

There are two most popular stages to build Bayesian network (BN) those are structural learning and parameter approximation. The design must be familiar that will show the manner of qualitatively representing probabilistic correlations between mentioned variables. And the next thing the parameter rough calculation builds the conditional probability for each node. When building Bayesian Network there are two fundamental manners are available those are Automatic and manual. The automatic process involves through utilizing a data-set after that applying any of frequent algorithms which capitulate mutually outline as well as the conditional probability that would be quick and well-situated. Coming to Manual procedure that includes above-mentioned steps, constructing a network in-assistance of human professional also that adds subsequent conditional probabilities. For the reason that the nonexistence of definite data often forces an applicant to attain probabilities from human professional estimations. The manual procedure is time-consuming as well as probabilities acquirement is sometimes complex and biased(Kaewprag et al., 2017).

Advantages of Bayesian Network

Advantages with Bayesian network models are capture both independence and conditional independence wherever they exist, extract full information of full joint between variables whenever dependencies exist. The inference operation in BN: forgiven some variables and set of query variables, do the appropriate posterior distribution on above-mentioned query variables. Bayesian network is a perfect method through enumeration means it computes the exact answer for a given query. There are some approximate inferences methods which provide an answer which is close to the exact answer. Here approximate inference is NP-hard problem but these work well for most real-time appliances.

PROBABILISTIC MODEL

Probabilistic models have equal attraction or notices since most part of models proficient to provide data for undecided expert knowledge in own illustration with reasoning. Simply probabilistic form is an encoding of probabilistic information in several domains of attention, such that each attractive sentence/statement/proposition will calculate in harmony with essentials of probability language. These sentences are characterized by interconnected random/stochastic variables contained by the model. Most of these models knowledge may represent through major association among variables and their associated probability measures as Bayesian, classical or combination of both probabilities. Bayesian probability approaches make use of grade of a person's confidence that an event takes place, not like as other genuine probability that the event will occur. Bayesian probability approaches depend on properties of the person not on an event. Classical probability depends on replicated trials to determine physical probabilities for particular events (Kaewprag et al., 2017; Krieg 2001; Pearl 1988).

Probability language is well-matched to reasoning under uncertainty, which endows with an appropriate framework for processing improbability association among the variables of a probabilistic model. It has four primitive relationships as likelihood, relevance, causation, and conditioning. Likelihood is quantified how feasibly/probable that an event will take place. Two events turn into appropriate when the regular result is observed, that is, A and B are appropriate if both are reasons of C. Causation expresses outline dependence among events. An incident is a conditional base on the second event if its probability is distorted as a result of knowledge of the second events state. A dependence model is a probabilistic model in which affiliation among every variable captured. Means it captures dependency among a mixture of events along with data that models represent.

BELIEF NETWORKS

Belief networks represent pictorial representation of methods which confine association-ships among the model variables those straightforwardly interact. Does belief updating of each variable through limiting each the local neighborhood those are directly connected with it. Clearly, the method states that the variable does not straightforwardly see that do not subject to it. Belief networks can be represented in both undirected as well as directed graphs, but the directed acyclic graph has better depiction, flexible and wide range of probabilistic independencies. Casual belief networks are one of Directed acyclic graph characterizes independence knowledge for the network. Here the causality or directionality shows hierarchical structural tree toward the network. Simply casual belief network is built with numerous types of nodes; the root node has no-parents as well as leaf node has no children. Where the nodes or variables that are foundations for particular node known as the parent of that node. Child node is straightforwardly affected or inclined by particular connected parent node (Kaewprag et al., 2017; Krieg 2001; Pearl 1988).

Bayesian Belief Network

Bayesian belief network (BBN) is out of the ordinary kind of casual belief network, is one of the promising form which aims to provide a decision-support framework for problems involving ambiguity, complication, and probabilistic reason. BBN can also be known as probabilistic cause-effect models, belief network, Graphical probability network, and casual probability network. Mostly BBN applied in situations that involve statistical presumption. With help of statements with probabilities of events, the abuser can obtain some evidence, means events which are essentially observed and wants to update its own belief in the collaboration or outcome probability of other events, which has not yet observed. For this BBN utilizes both probability calculus as well as famous Bayes theorem to proficiently propagate the verification throughout the network, in this way update strength of belief in the occurrence of the unobserved events.

To know how BBN is working and how to recognize things how they model - take variables and model a situation, dependency among variables will know to make function although our understanding of what is going to happen is imperfect. So there is only one choice to express things is Probabilistic way. The probabilistic-way aims to be a sign of the truth that some states in our designed model sphere will be liable to occur more recurrently in the reason of when other states are also in attendance. As discussed above Bayesian Belief Network (BBN) utilized in modeling likelihood/probabilistic presumption regarding model domains that are characterized through inbuilt complication and improbability. Because an imperfect understanding of the field/domain, knowledge and randomness behavior of the domain this improbability will occur. A well-designed and parameterized BBN has a rational framework to inference for a modeled domain ((Kaewprag et al., 2017; Krieg 2001; Lecave 2003; Cai 2016; Pearl 1988).

Advantages and Limitations

BBN has advantages than some other methods those dealing with improbability and limited data. Those are –

- *Modular Design* – Pre-arranged designed network structure, BBN's productively extract or assume the concept of modularity, the composite system is built through uniting simpler parts.
- *Future scenario testing* – Mostly BBN's endow with the supreme structure to test most likely/ probable consequences of potential events or state of affairs.
- Combining *different types of data* – Well-designed Bayesian probability or Bayes theorem conclude a rational technique that combines together subjective and quantitative data.

- *Predictions are amenable to risk analysis* – BBN's state predictable product as the probability that forms the root in favor of risk analysis.
- *Formal structuring our understanding* - BBNs are supportive in favor of challenging expert to coherent what they recognize in relation to the model domain, and to tie individuals influences into dependence networks. Besides remarkable advantages BBN has some limitations also those are listed below –
- *Large BBNs can become Unmanageable* – BBN's become hard to deal with huge problems for the reason that number of conditional probabilities should be specific and speedily turn into tremendously huge as the conceptual possibility of problem increases. In those situations designed model turns to become tricky to manage and many of probabilities well not characterize so, we will take expert judgment in those situations.
- *Potential to over-emphasize* – In some applications objective data is absent; BBN is no superior to a simple statement of an educated guess, if have subjective judgment is available, it is an advantage to rely on multiple experts and average their predictable probabilities to reproduce the comparative improbability in collective beliefs (Krieg 2001).

Building Bayesian Belief Network

The designer of Bayesian Belief Network (BBN) has to identify network structure and probabilities for own application. In 1996 author Heckerman stated most important following steps in designing Bayesian Belief Network those are: Select data that are carrying great weight and meaningful in the context of the model, identify goals of the model, identify all possible sources which might be relevant to achieving goals. Organize preferred data into variables that have equally special and cooperatively exhaustive states (Hackerman 1996; Fenz 2012; Diez 2014).

- *Selecting Structure* - Bayesian belief networks fascinated to obtain estimations of confidence for events which are not detectable or detectable at an improper expenditure. In the selected variable network, there is essential to determine the causal structure among the variables. While shaping causality it is essential that proper conditional probabilities moreover dependencies should be well-known among information variables as well as assumption variables.
- *Probabilities* – Bayesian structure uses two probabilities namely prior and conditional probabilities might be Bayesian or else physical, where Bayesian likelihoods derive from prior knowledge plus physical likelihoods studied from existing data. Here the probability measurement is progression of determining the degree otherwise likelihood of each variable. Although one main distress regards Bayesian, as well as physical probability measurement, are precision.
- *Undirected relations* – In rare cases not able to decide the track/direction of arcs, means two or more than two events are conditional however neither cause via other. Moreover, it might not handy to discover an ordinary reason. This could direct to networks containing a mix of directed and undirected arcs or relation like as chain graphs.
- *The Noisy* – If a variable with multiple parents it is not easy to conclude the conditional probability. It is like disjunctive relations among binary variables which mean variables with only two variables.
- *Divorcing* – Divorcing is nothing but reducing the number of combination states of a variable with numerous parents after that amount of likelihoods will be calculated.

REFERENCES

Aggarwal, C. C., & And Yu, P. S. (2000). Finding generalized projected clusters in high dimensional spaces. *SIGMOD Record, 29*(2), 70–92.

Aggarwal, C.C., Hinneburg, A., & Keim, D.A. (2000). On the surprising behavior of distance metrics in high dimensional space. *IBM Research report*, RC 21739.

Aggarwal, C. C., Procopiuc, C., Wolf, J. L., Yu, P. S., & And Park, J. S. (1999a). Fast algorithms for projected clustering. *Proceedings of the ACM SIGMOD Conference*, 61-72.

Aggarwal, C. C., Wolf, J. L., & And Yu, P. S. (1999b). A new method for similarity indexing of market basket data. *Proceedings of the ACM SIGMOD Conference*, 407-418.

Aggarwal & Reddy. (2013). *Data Clustering: Algorithms and Applications*. CRC Press.

Berkhin, P. (2002). Survey of Clustering Data Mining Techniques. Accrue Software.

Berry, M., Dumais, S., Landauer, T., & O'Brien, G. (1995). Using linear algebra for intelligent information retrieval. *SIAM Review, 37*(4), 573–595.

Bezdek, J. C. (1981). *Pattern Recognition with Fuzzy Objective Function Algorithms*. Norwell: Kluwer Academic Publishers. doi:10.1007/978-1-4757-0450-1

Bothtner, U., Milne, S. E., & Kenny, G. N. (2002). Bayesian probabilistic network modeling of remifentanil and propofol interaction on wakeup time after closed-loop controlled anesthesia. *Journal of Clinical Monitoring and Computing, 17*, 31–36. PMID:12102247

Cai, X., Perez-Concha, O., & Coiera, E. (2016). Real-time prediction of mortality, readmission, and length of stay using electronic health record data. *Journal of the American Medical Informatics Association, 23*, 553–561. PMID:26374704

Carlsson, G., & Mémoli, F. (2010). Characterization, stability and convergence of hierarchical clustering methods. *Journal of Machine Learning Research, 11*, 1425–1470.

Chakraborty & Nagwani. (2011). Analysis and Study of Incremental DBSCAN Clustering Algorithm. *International Journal of Enterprise Computing and Business Systems, 1*(2).

Cheng, C., Fu, A., & And Zhang, Y. (1999). Entropy-based subspace clustering for mining numerical data. Proceedings of the 5th ACMSIGKDD, 84-93.

Díez, F. J. (2014). *Introducción a los Modelos Gráficos Probabilistas*. UNED.

Duda, P. E. H., & Stork, D. G. (2001). *Pattern Classification*. New York: Wiley.

Ertöz, Steinbach, & Kumar. (2003). Finding clusters of different sizes, shapes, and densities in noisy, high dimensional data. *SDM SIAM*.

Ester, M., Kriegel, H. P., Sander, J., & Xu, X. (1996). A density-based algorithm for discovering clusters in large spatial databases with noise. In *Proceedings of the 2nd International Conference on Knowledge Discovery and Data Mining*. AAAI Press.

Ester, M., Kriegel, H.-P., Sander, J., & Xu, X. (1996). A Density-Based Algorithm for Discovering Clusters in Large Spatial Databases with Noise. *Proceeding of 2nd international Conference on Knowledge Discovery and date Mining (KDD 96)*.

Everitt, B., Landau, S., Leese, M., & Stahl, D. (2011). *Cluster Analysis*. Wiley Series in Probability and Statistics. doi:10.1002/9780470977811

Fahad. (2014). A Survey of Clustering Algorithms for Big Data: Taxonomy and Empirical Analysis. *IEEE Trans. Emerging Topics in Computing, 2*(3), 267-79.

Fenz, S. (2012). An ontology-based approach for constructing Bayesian networks. *Data & Knowledge Engineering, 73*, 73–88. doi:10.1016/j.datak.2011.12.001

Goil, S., Nagesh, H., & And Choudhary, A. (1999). *MAFIA: Efficient and scalable subspace clustering for very large data sets*. Technical Report CPDC-TR-9906-010, Northwestern University.

Guha, S., Rastogi, R., & Shim, K. (1998). CURE: an efficient clustering algorithm for large databases. *Proceedings of the 1998 ACM SIGMOD international conference on Management of data*, 73-84. 10.1145/276304.276312

Guha, S., Rastogi, R., & Shim, K. (1998). Cure: An efficient clustering algorithm for large databases. *Proceedings of the 1998 ACM SIGMOD International Conference on Management of Data*, 73–84.

Han, J., & Kamber, M. (2001). *Data Mining: Concepts and Techniques*. Morgan Kaufmann Publishers.

He, R. (2017). A Kernel-Power-Density Based Algorithm for Channel Multipath Components Clustering. *IEEE Transactions on Wireless Communications, 16*(11), 7138–7151.

Heckerman, D. (1996). *A Tutorial on Learning With Bayesian Networks*. Technical Report MSR-TR-95-06, Microsoft Corporation.

Hinneburg, A., & Keim, D. (1999). Optimal grid-clustering: Towards breaking the curse of dimensionality in high-dimensional clustering. *Proceedings of the 25th Conference on VLDB*, 506-517.

Jain, A. (2010). Data clustering: 50 years beyond K-means. *Pattern Recognition Letters, 31*(8), 651–666. doi:10.1016/j.patrec.2009.09.011

Jain, A. K., & Dubes, R. C. (1988). *Algorithms for Clustering Data*. Upper Saddle River, NJ: Prentice-Hall.

Jain & Dubes. (1990). *Algorithms for Clustering Data*. Prentice hall advanced references series, Michigan state University.

Kaewprag, P., Newton, C., & Vermillion, B. (2017). Predictive models for pressure ulcers from intensive care unit electronic health records using Bayesian networks. *BMC Medical Informatics and Decision Making, 17*(Suppl 2), 65. PMID:28699545

Kalisch, M., Fellinghauer, B. A., & Grill, E. (2010). Understanding human functioning using graphical models. *BMC Medical Research Methodology, 10*, 14. PMID:20149230

Keogh, E., Chakrabarti, K., & Mehrotra, S. (2001). Locally adaptive dimensionality reduction for indexing large time series databases. *Proceedings of the ACMSIGMOD Conference*.

Krieg. (2001). A Tutorial on Bayesian Belief Networks. Surveillance Systems Division Electronics and Surveillance Research Laboratory.

Lacave, C., & Diez, F. J. (2003). *Knowledge Acquisition in PROSTANET-A Bayesian Network for Diagnosing Prostate Cancer*. Berlin: Springer-Verlag. doi:10.1007/978-3-540-45226-3_182

Leung, H., & Wu, J. (2000). Bayesian and Dempster-Shafer target identification for radar surveillance. *IEEE Transactions on Aerospace and Electronic Systems, 36*(2), 432–447. doi:10.1109/7.845221

Malhotra, K. G., Mohan, C. K., & Huang, H. (2017). *Anomaly detection principles and algorithms. Terrorism, Security, and Computation*. Springer.

Maninderjit, K., & Garg, S. K. (2014). Survey on Clustering Techniques in Data Mining for Software Engineering. *International Journal of Advanced and Innovative Research, 3*, 238–243.

Narmanlioglu, O., & Zeydan, E. (2018). Mobility-Aware Cell Clustering Mechanism for Self-Organizing Networks. *Access IEEE, 6*, 65405–65417. doi:10.1109/ACCESS.2018.2876601

Nistal-Nuño. (2018). *Tutorial of the probabilistic methods Bayesian networks and influence diagrams applied to medicine*. Wiley.

Pearl, J. (1988). *Probabilistic Reasoning in Intelligent Systems: Networks of Plausible Inference*. San Francisco, CA: Morgan Kaufmann.

Rokach, L., & Maimon, O. (2005). Clustering Methods. In O. Maimon & L. Rokach (Eds.), *Data Mining and Knowledge Discovery Handbook*. Boston, MA: Springer.

Sathya, R., & Abraham, A. (2013). Comparison of supervised and unsupervised learning algorithms for pattern classification. *Int J Adv Res Artificial Intell, 2*(2), 34–38. doi:10.14569/IJARAI.2013.020206

Sisodia, D., Singh, L., & Sisodia, S. (2012). Clustering Techniques: A Brief Survey of Different Clustering Algorithms. *International Journal of Latest Trends in Engineering and Technology, 1*(3).

Sohrab Mahmud, Md., Mostafizer Rahman, Md., & Nasim Akhtar, Md. (2012). Improvement of K-means Clustering algorithm with better initial centroids based on weighted average. *7th International Conference on Electrical and Computer Engineering*, 647-650.

Strehl, A., Ghosh, J., & Mooney, R. (2000). Impact of similarity measures on web-page clustering. *Proc. AAAI Workshop on AI for Web Search*, 58–64.

Suman & Mittal. (2014). Comparison and Analysis of Various Clustering Methods in Data mining On Education data set using the weak tool. *International Journal of Emerging Trends & Technology in Computer Science, 3*(2).

Velmurugan, T., & Santhanam, T. (2011). A survey of partition based clustering algorithms in data mining: An experimental approach. *Inf Technol J, 10*(3), 478–484. doi:10.3923/itj.2011.478.484

Wang, Q., Ai, B., He, R., Guan, K., Li, Y., Zhong, Z., & Shi, G. (2017). A Framework of Automatic Clustering and Tracking for Time-Variant Multipath Components. *IEEE Communications Letters, 21*(4), 953–956. doi:10.1109/LCOMM.2016.2637364

Wang, Y., & Vassileva, J. (2003). Bayesian Network-Based Trust Model. *Proceedings of the IEEE/WIC International Conference on Web Intelligence (WI'03)*. 10.1109/WI.2003.1241218

Zhang, T., Ramakrishnan, R., & Livny, M. (1996). BIRCH: an efficient data clustering method for very large databases. *Proceedings of the 1996 ACM SIGMOD international conference on Management of data*, 103-114. 10.1145/233269.233324

Chapter 5
Analysis of Gravitation–Based Optimization Algorithms for Clustering and Classification

Sajad Ahmad Rather
Pondicherry University, India

P. Shanthi Bala
ⓘ https://orcid.org/0000-0003-0576-4424
Pondicherry University, India

ABSTRACT

In recent years, various heuristic algorithms based on natural phenomena and swarm behaviors were introduced to solve innumerable optimization problems. These optimization algorithms show better performance than conventional algorithms. Recently, the gravitational search algorithm (GSA) is proposed for optimization which is based on Newton's law of universal gravitation and laws of motion. Within a few years, GSA became popular among the research community and has been applied to various fields such as electrical science, power systems, computer science, civil and mechanical engineering, etc. This chapter shows the importance of GSA, its hybridization, and applications in solving clustering and classification problems. In clustering, GSA is hybridized with other optimization algorithms to overcome the drawbacks such as curse of dimensionality, trapping in local optima, and limited search space of conventional data clustering algorithms. GSA is also applied to classification problems for pattern recognition, feature extraction, and increasing classification accuracy.

INTRODUCTION

With the advancement of computing technology, the researchers can easily solve complex real-world problems in the domain of optimization. Further, the researchers are inspired by nature to solve complicated computational problems. They are classified into evolutionary algorithms (EA) and Swarm Intelligence (SI) based algorithms as shown in figure 1. The EAs are based on Darwinian Theory of natural selection.

DOI: 10.4018/978-1-7998-0106-1.ch005

Figure 1. Classification of nature inspired computational algorithms

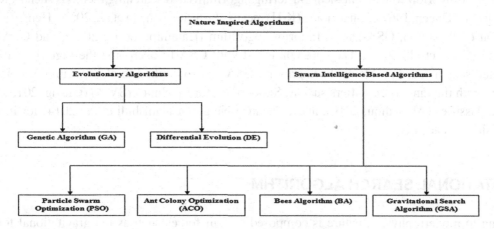

The examples include Genetic Algorithms (GA) (Holland, 1975), Differential Evolution (Storm et al., 1995), etc. Furthermore, SI based algorithms mimic the physical and natural processes for mathematical modeling of the optimization algorithm. They have the properties of information interchange and non-centralized control structure. Some examples of SI based algorithms are Particle Swarm Optimization (PSO) (Kennedy et al., 1995), Ant Colony Optimization (ACO) (Dorigo et al., 1991), Bees Algorithm (Jung, 2003; Karaboga, 2005) and Gravitational Search Algorithm (GSA) (Rashedi et al., 2009).

Gravitational search algorithm (GSA) is a physics-based optimization algorithm inspired by Newton's laws of motion and gravity. It is a powerful heuristic optimization method which shows good results for non-linear optimization problems. The conceptual and theoretical foundation of GSA is based on the concept of mass interactions which states that "A particle in the universe attracts every other particle with a force that is directly proportional to the product of their masses and inversely proportional to the square of the distance between them". The masses are considered as objects that interact and cooperate with each other through the gravitational force. The position of the heavy mass gives the global optimum solution as it has the highest fitness value.

GSA is good at finding the global optima but has the drawbacks of slow convergence speed and getting stuck in local minima in the last few iterations. In order to overcome these problems, GSA is hybridized with other swarm based optimization algorithms such as PSO, ACO, DE, etc. The GSA has been used to solve various optimization problems in different domains of study such as clustering, classification, feature selection, routing, image processing, etc.

Clustering is the technique of grouping similar data samples based on similarity index and distance measure. It is also a popular data analysis technique. On the other hand, Classification is the process of categorizing the data into groups based on mathematical information and is useful for obtaining potential features from the complex dataset. Today, the most part of the world is interconnected by social media such as Facebook, Twitter, etc. It results in the generation of the voluminous and huge amount of data. This raw data is multidimensional in nature and has large complexity. The branch of artificial intelligence that deals with the analysis and processing of complex data is called as data science and the data items that are present in variety of formats can be efficiently handled using Big data. It is a hot topic in computer science community today (Chira et al., 2014). The clustering and classification are the fundamental techniques for finding potential patterns in the big data.

The GSA is hybridized with classical clustering algorithms and searching methods such as K-means clustering (MacQueen, 1967), K-harmonic (K-H) means clustering (Zhang et al., 2000), Heuristic Search (Hatamlou et al., 2011), GSA-Data Clustering algorithm (Hatamlou et al., 2012), and GSA-Kernel Clustering (C. Li et al., 2014). They are combined with GSA to overcome the high dimensionality and limited search space problems. Furthermore, GSA is also applied to classification problems and combined with the famous classifiers such as Support Vector Machines (SVM) (Ghang, 2015), Neural Network classifier (Ahmadlou, 2010), and K-Nearest Neighbor (Jamshidi et al., 2014) for increasing the precision and accuracy.

GRAVITATIONAL SEARCH ALGORITHM

According to modern physics, nature is composed of four forces such as the gravitational force, the strong nuclear force, the electromagnetic force and the weak nuclear force. As per classical Newtonian mechanics, the law of universal gravitation is stated as "the gravitational force between two masses is directly proportional to the product of their masses and inversely proportional to the square of the distance between them" (Halliday, D., Resnick, R., & Walker, J., 2000).

If M_1 and M_2 are two point masses, R is the distance between them, then the gravitational force, F is calculated using Eq.1.

$$F = G\left(\frac{M_1 M_2}{R^2}\right) \tag{1}$$

The "gravitational constant" G, is used for adjusting the accuracy of the search and is given by Eq. 2.

$$G(t) = G(t_0)\frac{t_0^{\beta}}{t}, \beta < 1 \tag{2}$$

Where G(t) is the gravitational constant with respect to time interval t, β is a coefficient and G(t_0) is the initial value of the gravitational constant.

As per Newton's second law of motion, "The acceleration (a) of the agent is directly proportional to the force (F) applied by the agent and inversely proportional to the mass (M) of the agent" and it is calculated using Eq.3.

$$a = \frac{F}{M} \tag{3}$$

Now, the standard Gravitational Search Algorithm (GSA) can be stated as:

Let $X = \{x_1, x_2, x_3 \dots, x_n\}$ be a system with 'n' agents, such that $x_i \in \mathcal{R}^n$. The force between mass i and j can be written as:

$$F_{ij} = G(t) \frac{m_{pi}(t) m_{aj}(t)}{R_{ij}(t) + \in} \left(x_j^d(t) + x_i^d(t) \right) \tag{4}$$

Here, $m_{pi}(t)$ is the passive gravitational mass and $m_{aj}(t)$ is the active gravitational mass. $R_{ij}(t)$ is the Euclidian Distance and $\in$ is a constant with a small value in 'd' dimensional space.

The total force exerted on agent i due to other masses is found using Eq.5.

$$F_i^d(t) = \sum_{j=1, j \neq i}^{m} \gamma_j F_{ij} \tag{5}$$

whereas γ_j belongs to [0, 1].

In GSA, the location of the heavy mass gives the global optimum (solution to the optimization problem). The normalized mass m_i is mathematically represented in Eq.6.

$$m_i(t) = \frac{f_i(t) - w(t)}{b(t) - w(t)} \tag{6}$$

whereas $f_i(t)$ is the fitness function, w(t) and b(t) are the worst and best fitness values respectively.

In GSA it is assumed that total mass M_i is equivalent to the active gravitational mass, passive gravitational mass, and inertial mass. The total mass can be calculated using Eq.7.

$$M_i(t) = \frac{m_i(t)}{\sum_{j=1}^{m} m_j(t)} \tag{7}$$

The gravitational force is directly proportional to the product of masses according to Eq.1.So, it is the heavy mass that is having the high gravitational field and it attracts maximum agents towards itself. Due to high fitness value of heavy mass, it helps in getting the global optimum and avoid the problems of getting stuck in local optima and the premature convergence. Also, it gives the elitism criterion to the GSA algorithm i.e. only one best solution will execute force in all directions at the end of the last iteration. Hence, Eq.4 can be modified using Eq.8.

$$F_i^d(t) = \sum_{j \in \kappa, j \neq i}^{m} \gamma_j F_{ij}(t) \tag{8}$$

The GSA consists of the agents which are continuously changing their positions from time t to t+1. So, in GSA, the agents are attracting each other with a gravitational force and all the agents are getting attracted towards the heavy mass. In order to find the global optimum, the position (x_i^d) and velocity (

v_i^d) of the agents is updated in every iteration. These can be represented mathematically as in Eq.9 and Eq.10.

$$v_i^d \left(t+1\right) = \gamma_j v_i^d \left(t\right) + a_i^d \left(t\right) \tag{9}$$

$$x_i^d \left(t+1\right) = x_i^d \left(t\right) + v_i^d \left(t+1\right) \tag{10}$$

The pseudo-code of GSA is as follows:

1. Initialize the search space randomly in an 'n' agent system as:

$$X = \left\{x_1, x_2, x_3 \ldots, x_n\right\}$$

while all agents attract the single heavy mass **do**

2.   Calculate the fitness function, $m_i \left(t\right)$.
3.   Update the gravitational constant, G.
4.   Find the Gravitational force, F_{ij} by using equation (4).
5.   Calculate the acceleration, $a_i^d \left(t\right)$ with the help of equation (3).
6.   Update the velocity: v_i^d.
7.   Update agent positions: $x_i^d \left(t+1\right)$.

   end

The GSA pseudo-code can be represented diagrammatically as shown in figure 2. The searching process starts with the random initialization of agents in the dynamic. The agents attract each other with a gravitational force in all directions having some velocity and acceleration. All agents in the system have some fitness value and the agent with high fitness value i.e. global optimum. The searching process stops with finding the heavy mass that attracts all other forces i.e. the best solution.

GSA VARIANTS

The GSA is an optimization algorithm in which masses are in the form of agents. These agents can be represented using different ways. The agents in GSA variants are continuous, discrete, and binary. The various forms of GSA are also used to solve the multi-modal, multi-objective, and constraint-based optimization problems. The modified versions of GSA include quantum-based and anti-gravity based GSA.

Figure 2. Stepwise gravitational search algorithm

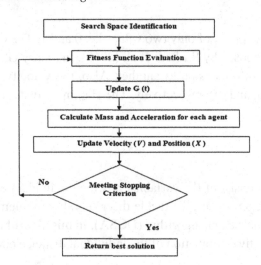

Continuous GSA

The standard GSA is proposed by Esmat Rashedi et al. in 2009 for solving continuous optimization problems. Also, GSA is a memoryless algorithm because it takes into consideration only the current position of the agents. The GSA is combined with PSO (Memory based algorithm) in order to give the memory characteristics to the GSA. This is done by combining the velocity of PSO with the GSA velocity (Mirjalili et al., 2012).

Another version of continuous GSA is based on the antigravity force. The GSA operates with both gravity and antigravity forces in order to have more agents around the feasible solutions (Khajooei et al., 2016). The GSA also utilizes the concepts of attractive and repulsive forces to attract agents present in the neighborhood and repel the bad solutions (Zandevakili et al., 2017).

Table 1. GSA variants

Variants	Year	References
Continuous GSA	2009, 2012	Rashedi et al., 2009; Mirjalili et al., 2012
Binary GSA	2010	Rashedi et al. 2010
Discrete GSA	2012, 2014	Shamsudin et al., 2012; Dowlatshahi et al., 2014
Quantum based GSA	2012, 2014	Ibrahim et al., 2012; B. Ji et al., 2014
Constraint based GSA	2013, 2014	Yadav et al., 2013; Poole et al., 2014
Multimodal GSA	2011,2014, 2017	Yadav et al., 2011; Yazdani et al., 2014; Haghbayan et al., 2017
Multi-objective GSA	2010, 2012	Hassanzadeh et al., 2010; Nobahri et al., 2012

Binary GSA

Binary optimization problems consist of only two values i.e. 0 and 1. The GSA handles these problems by using its binary version proposed by Rashedi et al. (2010). In binary GSA, the agents have only two values, when moving from one dimension to another. Also, the velocity, acceleration, and force are calculated by the Eqs. (3), (4), and (9), respectively. The Hamming distance is used for calculating the distance between the agents.

Discrete GSA

The discrete value problems consist of the variables in which individual elements can be represented mathematically by vector integer values. To tackle discrete value problems, Shamsudin et al. (2012) proposed a discrete gravitational search algorithm (DGSA). In this algorithm, acceleration and velocity are calculated by random selective summation of the individual distance components and it depends on the direction of the velocity.

The Iranian researchers Dowlatshahi et al. (2014) have given another version of DGSA in which agent movement is traced by using undirected graph. The fitness of the agents is calculated using arc-tan and sigmoid functions.

Quantum Based GSA

The quantum theory is a wave mechanical model which describes the nature at subatomic levels. Quantum computing (QC) is the new growing field of computer science which uses the concepts of superposition and entanglement. In QC, the system is represented by qubits or quantum bits which are superposition of different wave states. The gravitational search algorithm is also combined with quantum computing for increasing the quality of feasible solutions (Soleimanpour et al., 2012a; 2014b). In the proposed algorithm, the agents mimic the behavior of quantum waves in which movement function is directly dependent on the kbest set.

Meanwhile, Ibrahim et al., (2012) presented a binary version of quantum-based GSA for increasing the diversification capabilities of the gravitational search algorithm.

Quantum based GSA has been utilized for solving various problems in scheduling and integer programming (B. Ji et al. 2014) and power systems (A.A. Ibrahim et al., 2014).

Constraint Based GSA

A constraint optimization problem consists of equality and inequality functions which are used for optimizing the objective function. The main feature of constraint-based problems is a penalty function which operates in parallel with the objective function. It is used for evaluating the feasible solutions that are within the boundaries of the system. Whenever an agent violates the system characteristics, it gets penalized.

The constraint-based GSA is proposed by Yadav et al. (2013) in which penalty function is in the form of computing violations. Also, GSA has been applied to dynamic constraint optimization problems (K. Pal et al., 2013). In the proposed algorithm, the feasible solutions are given in a reference set. Whenever the agent produces a bad solution it is penalized with distance measures i.e. it is thrown away from the neighborhood of the feasible solution in order to maintain the integrity and elitism of the whole system.

The GSA is combined with swarm based approaches for solving constraint optimization problems (Poole et al., 2014).

Multi-Modal GSA

Multimodality of an optimization algorithm is defined as the optimizing ability of an algorithm to find the multiple global optima after a specified number of iterations. The optimization algorithms deal with multimodal problems by dividing the searching space into different groups. Each group is having unique global optima of its own. The niche GSA is proposed by Yazdani et al. in 2014 for multimodal optimization. The unique feature of this algorithm is that every agent exerts force to its nearest neighbor only because its global optima will be present in a local group. The active gravitational mass is calculated through vector masses consisting of KNN agents.

Differential Evolution (DE) algorithm is combined with GSA to form a co-swarm to deal with multimodal problems (Yadav et al., 2011). Additionally, Haghbayan et al. in 2017 combined GSA having the nearest neighbor property with hill valley algorithm (Ursem, 1999) to detect niches in the searching space by dividing it into different groups.

Multi-Objective GSA

The optimization algorithms have to face the test of multiple objectives, high dimensionality and computational complexities for solving the real-world problems. The multi-objective optimization problems consist of multiple features that need to be optimized after the specified number of iterations. The special feature of multi-objective problems is a pool of constant solutions having optimal fitness values called as dominant or Pareto optimal solutions.

The multi-objective GSA is proposed by Hassanzadeh et al. in 2010 by using the concepts of mutation and elitism. In the proposed algorithm, the dominant solutions are stored in an archive having a grid structure. Additionally, Nobahri et al. in 2012 proposed non- dominated sorting GSA. It consists of an external archive for constant solutions to prevent them from external moving agents. Abbasian et al. in 2015 proposed cluster-based multi-objective GSA. The main feature of this algorithm is a cluster-based archive for storing Pareto solutions.

Multi-objective GSA has been utilized and found useful in solving different problems in the field of engineering optimization such as power systems (Ajami et al., 2013; Bhattacharya et al., 2012), gas production(Ganesan et al., 2013), electrical engineering (Baniassadi et al., 2011; Abbasian et al., 2012) and networks (Rubio-largo et al., 2013).

ADVANTAGES AND DISADVANTAGES OF GSA

The GSA is a recent optimization algorithm which is gaining a lot of popularity in the research community due to its efficiency and optimization capability.

Advantages

The various advantages of Gravitational Search Algorithm are

- Simple implementation.
- Suitable swarm-based algorithm for solving non-linear optimization problems.
- It takes less computational time.
- Generation of feasible solutions.
- Adaptive learning capability.
- Gives high precision results.

Disadvantages

The various disadvantages of Gravitational Search Algorithm are

- The GSA operators are complex in nature.
- The searching capability of GSA gets slower in the last iterations of the algorithm.
- It is not flexible due to the inactivity after convergence.
- Randomized nature of Gravitational operator (G) in the algorithm.

In order to overcome drawbacks, GSA is hybridized with other swarm based optimization algorithms. The strong features of other algorithms will overwhelm the limitations in the GSA. Due to hybridization, the performance and accuracy of the GSA gets increased by folds.

GSA HYBRIDIZATION

Hybridization is the technique of modifying the mathematical structure of the parent algorithm by using another optimization algorithm(s) so that the limitations of the parent algorithm can be removed. The main advantage of hybridization is to increase the search space and the problem-solving domain of the algorithm. It also improves the exploration and exploitation capabilities of the algorithm.

Table 2 shows the scope of GSA and its hybridization with other meta-heuristic algorithms and methods in order to tackle different application domain problems.

Neural Networks

The Genetic algorithm is the evolutionary algorithm based on Darwin's theory of natural selection and it uses different operators such as crossover, selection, mutation, etc. for the optimization process. The GSA is combined with a genetic algorithm for training the neural network (NN). It is utilized for performing the global search in order to find the global optimum and then genetic algorithm is used for performing the local search around the solution. The hybrid algorithm shows better performance than the Backpropagation algorithm (Sun & Zhang, 2013).

The gravitational search algorithm is combined with a neural network for solving the famous Wessinger's equation. It is achieved by training the perceptron neural network. The sigmoid function is used

Table 2. Scope of GSA hybridization

Application Domain	Techniques
Neural Networks	GA-PSO, NN-GSA, PSO-GSA
Power Systems	PSO-GSA, QBGSA, GSA-FAPSO
Routing	GSA-PSO
Optimization	KNN-GSA, AIS-GSA, DE-GSA, CHAOS-GSA, PSO-GSA

as a fitness function. The hybridized method shows the generalized solution to the problem (Ghalambaz et al., 2011). Moreover, GSA is hybridized with PSO for training the multilayer feed forward neural network (FNN). The hybridization results in good convergence speed and avoidance from the "trapping in local optima" problem for GSA (Mirjalili, Hashim, Sardroudi & H.M., 2012).

Power Systems

GSA and Particle Swarm Optimization (PSO) are used to solve load dispatch problem in power systems by considering some constraints such as Generator rate, transmission loss, etc. The proposed algorithm shows better performance than other power system optimization algorithms (Jiang, Ji, & Shen, 2014).

The gravitational search algorithm is also combined with Quantum based theories to increase the diversity in the agent population and overcome the premature convergence problem. The hybrid Quantum based gravitational search algorithm (QBGSA) is compared with other heuristic algorithms for performance evaluation (Soleimanpour-moghadam et al., 2011).

The gravitational search algorithm also finds its application in utility systems where it is hybridized with PSO to increase the profit margins in utility systems. In the proposed algorithm, the local searching and good convergence properties of GSA are combined with the global searching capability of PSO. To handle the nonlinearity of the system, the concepts of fuzzy logic are included in the PSO i.e. Fuzzy adaptive particle swarm optimization (FAPSO). The hybrid algorithm is evaluated on standard benchmark functions and tested on the real-world problem (Rajagopal et al., 2018).

Routing

The GSA is a memoryless algorithm i.e. it's searching operator considers only the current position of the agents. This problem can be solved by using PSO which is a memory based algorithm because it uses the pbest and gbest operators which are powerful searching operators having good exploitation capability. The pbest is used for local exploitation of the particles and gbest is utilized for getting the global optimum from the feasible solutions. To increase the quality of the optimal solutions, the social operators i.e. pbest and gbest of the PSO are combined with GSA operators. The improved GSA-PSO hybrid algorithm is used for solving path planning global optimization problem (Pei et al., 2012).

Optimization

Optimization is the technique of selecting the most feasible solution for the given problem. The GSA is also hybridized with other algorithms for solving the optimization problems in different fields.

The Binary version of GSA is hybridized with KNN (K-Nearest Neighbor) for increasing the classification accuracy. The hybrid method is evaluated on several UCI machine learning datasets (Xiang et al., 2015).

The artificial immune system algorithm is inspired by the defense mechanism of the human body against outside intervention by harmful agents i.e. viruses and bacteria. It uses the concepts of antibody diversity and vaccination. As GSA is a swarm based technique, it shows efficient results on large sets of problems. But GSA has the drawback of getting stuck in local optima in last iterations. To overcome this problem GSA is hybridized with AIS (Artificial Immune System) (Yu et al., 2011).

GSA has also been hybridized with differential evolution optimization algorithm for solving unconstrained problems. The hybrid algorithm uses Differential Evolution (DE) operators such as crossover, mutation, selection, etc which work with the gravity and velocity operators of the GSA for getting the global optimum and increase the speed of convergence. The GSA-DE hybrid algorithm is evaluated on different datasets and benchmark functions (Xiangtao et al., 2011).

Every optimization algorithm uses two concepts for its searching process i.e. exploration and exploitation. Exploration means randomized initialization of inputs for the algorithm and exploitation means using the searching inputs for getting the global optimum. The chaotic maps are used to increase the exploration and exploitation properties of the gravitational search algorithm. The hybrid algorithm is tested on various benchmark functions and shows appreciable performance (Mirjalili et al., 2017).

Both PSO and GSA are Swarm Intelligence (SI) algorithms. The first one is based on the social behavior of birds and fishes and the second one is based on the universal law of gravitation and laws of motion. The agent positions are updated by using the equations of velocity and acceleration from PSO and GSA, respectively. Gravitational operators are used for increasing the fitness value of the particles in the PSO algorithm. The hybrid PSO-GSA hybrid algorithm results in the decrease in computational cost and increase in the feasibility and efficiency of the PSO (Shanhe et al., 2018).

GSA IN CLUSTERING

Clustering is the technique of grouping similar data samples based on distance and similarity criterion of the data points. Clustering is a statistical data analysis task which has been employed in many areas such as information retrieval, data mining, bioinformatics, data compression, etc. Clustering is a general task that can be achieved using different algorithms. These algorithms use various measures to find the similarity index among data clusters such as the distance between the clusters, statistical distribution, the density of the data objects, etc.

Many optimization algorithms have been utilized for clustering such as ABC (Karaboga et al., 2011), ACO (Shelokar et al., 2004), BB-BC (Erol et al., 2006), etc. Clustering is a multi-objective optimization problem and there does not exist a single method or algorithm that solves all clustering problems as it involves trial and failure principle for getting disjoint clusters in a single dataset. In this section, the gravitation search algorithm has been applied to the clustering problems to overcome the drawbacks of classical clustering algorithms, optimize the clustering accuracy and solve real-world clustering problems in various fields of study.

The clustering algorithms have been classified into various models such as hierarchical based, centroid-based, distribution based, etc. In the research literature, there are at least 100 published clustering algorithms. They cannot be used on all data sets because each clustering algorithm has some domain and boundaries. The k-means, K-harmonic means, Density-based spatial clustering of applications with noise (DBSCAN); clustering algorithms are being used widely with a gravitational search algorithm (GSA).

K- Means Algorithm

It is a centroid-based clustering method which divides the dataset into different cells called as Voronoi cells. The k-means algorithm uses k- vector concept such that dataset has k- cluster centers and all clusters have data objects. The main function of this algorithm is that the cluster centers should have a minimum distance from each other. It uses Lloyd's algorithm for getting the approximate solutions and to find the local optima. It is an NP hard problem.

The main drawback of the algorithm is that it requires a number of clusters to be known before initialization of the algorithm. Also, the size of the cluster objects should be the same. The main advantages of the k-means algorithm include its theoretical simplicity and resemblance with classification algorithms such as a nearest neighbor classifier.

Density-Based Spatial Clustering of Applications with Noise (DBSCAN)

It is a density-based clustering method. If there are data objects in a particular dimensional space, the DBSCAN algorithm clusters the data objects based on how much the cluster is densely populated. It uses Euclidean distance to separate the data clusters among each other. Also, the data objects that are present at the boundaries are considered as outliers.

The main advantages of DBSCAN algorithm are that the initialization of the algorithm is independent of the number of clusters. It can find the cluster of any shape i.e. polygon independence. Further, it uses the concept of outliers that is efficient in dealing with redundant and noise inducing data objects. It uses a number of parameters that can be changed easily. The parameters are employed for analyzing the boundary data through database querying.

There are also some drawbacks to the DBSCAN algorithm: it has non-deterministic nature i.e. there are some data objects which do not fall in any cluster. So, it increases the noise level of the algorithm. It faces the problem of "curse of dimensionality". Further, it becomes inefficient when the data density separation increases. Also, the distance measure is only selected after applying it on the dataset.

GSA Hybrid Algorithms for Clustering

The gravitational search algorithm is an optimization algorithm that has adaptive learning capability. It is due to the inertial mass which is against the mass movement. It makes the masses to move into the local neighborhood region. In other words, the heavy mass moves slowly and its inertial nature attract large point masses towards itself. The adaptive learning capability gives the clustering property to the GSA.

The GSA is combined with other optimization algorithms and methods to overcome clustering problems and solve real-world problems. The k-Harmonic clustering is the most commonly used clustering algorithm because it has simple implementation and takes fewer iterations. But there is a major drawback in K-harmonic algorithm i.e. its dependency on initial states of the data centers. The reason for this problem is that cluster centers are unable to move out from the density of data due to the strong attraction between data objects and the nearest center. Here, GSA helps the clustering algorithm (i.e. KH means) to get away from local optima problem and also increases its convergence speed (Minghao et al., 2011).

Table 3. GSA hybridization algorithms for clustering

GSA Hybrid Clustering Techniques	Reference
k-Harmonic Means-GSA	Minghao et al., 2011
GSA-Data Clustering	Han et al., 2014
k-Means-GSA	Hatamlou et al., 2012
GSA-Heuristic Search (HS)	Li et al., 2014
GSA-Kernel Clustering	Hatamlou et al., 2011
Grouping GSA	Dowlatshahi et al., 2014
GSA- Automatic Clustering	Kumar et al., 2014
Bird Flock GSA-Data Clustering	Han et al., 2017

The majority of the optimization algorithms have issues when dealing with multidimensional data. Both PSO and GSA have clustering properties. The hybrid algorithm uses the exploitation capability of PSO and exploration property of GSA for updating the velocity. The position is updated through a mobility factor which in turn is used to improve the final accuracy and the convergence speed of the PSOGSA. It is also used in microarray data for cluster analysis (Han et al., 2014).

K-means is another famous data clustering algorithm. But it has the problem of getting stuck in local optima. To overcome this glitch, K-means is hybridized with GSA, which has the capability of finding global optimum in less iteration. The result of hybridization is faster convergence speed in GSA and overcoming of "trapping in local optima" problem in the k-means algorithm. The hybrid algorithm is compared with other swarm-based algorithms (Hatamlou et al., 2012).

The inertial mass operator in GSA has the clustering properties because it is the heavy mass that is having high fitness value and attracts other agents towards itself. So, the gravitational search algorithm is combined with other clustering methods to solve clustering problems. The GSA-HS is the hybrid clustering technique in which GSA is used for finding the optimal solutions for the clustering problem and heuristic search (HS) for exploitation of the search space (Li et al., 2014).

The clustering can be divided into data clustering and kernel clustering. There are various algorithms for data clustering but very few in kernel clustering. A support vector machine (SVM) is a supervised machine learning technique commonly utilized for fault diagnosis when fault samples are known. The GSA has been hybridized with semi-supervised SVM for diagnosis of both known and unknown faults (Hatamlou et al., 2011).

The gravitational search algorithm has also been applied to multi-variate clustering problems in order to increase the intra-cluster similarity and decrease the inter-cluster similarity. The GSA uses grouping encoding scheme to cluster the similar data items. The Grouping GSA (GGSA) is applied to various UCI benchmark test functions and compared with other optimization algorithms (Dowlatshahi et al., 2014).

In practical real-life problems, the information is not available about the number of clusters present in the dataset. The gravitational search algorithm is combined with automatic clustering to determine the prior information about the clusters in the dataset. The hybrid algorithm uses the concepts of threshold setting and weighted cluster centroid computation. It has been applied to image segmentation problem (Kumar et al., 2014).

The data clustering algorithm introduced by Han et al., 2017 is a combination of gravitational search algorithm and diversity mechanism inspired by the collective behavior of birds. This hybrid algorithm is called as Bird Flock Gravitational Search Algorithm (BFGSA) which uses three new concepts of initialization, identification of nearest neighbors, and orientation change for getting the optimal clusters in the dataset. The initialization step is used for exploration of the search space and orientation change step updates the position of the agents based on the nearest agent candidate solutions. The novel hybrid data clustering algorithm has been applied to the 13 UCI machine learning benchmark data sets and compared with ACO, PSO, Firefly, and K-means algorithms.

GSA IN CLASSIFICATION

Classification is the process of categorizing the data into groups based on mathematical information. It is basically a technique of finding the patterns in data and is a pattern recognition method.

Classification consists of features or independent variables and outcomes or dependent variables. It is a supervised machine learning technique i.e. where the training set of observations are available in advance. The algorithmic and mathematical implementation of classification is done through a classifier. The classifier is a correspondence or mapping function that connects data objects and class labels.

The main issue in all classification algorithms is accuracy and precision. The optimization algorithms are best suited for this task. The various optimization algorithms have been already employed for classification such as decision tree, artificial neural network, ABC, etc. The gravitational search algorithm has also been applied to classification problems and hybridized with other optimization algorithms and classifiers to increase the classification accuracy, classification precision, optimal classifier design, and prototype generation.

The main task of classification is to find the patterns in a dataset and group them into categories by using a mathematical tool i.e. a classifier. There are various well-known classifiers that have the features of evaluating and characterizing the unknown values present in the data set. The examples include support vector machines, k-nearest neighbors classifier, Naive Bayes classifier, etc. The gravitational search algorithm is hybridized with the above algorithms for solving the computational problems and overcoming its limitations.

Support Vector Machines

The support vector machine (SVM) is the supervised learning model that is utilized for regression analysis and detection of unlabelled data. The basic principle in SVM is that it divides the points in a finite dimensional space into two classes separated by a hyper plane. The data items which are distant from the hyper plane line are having low generalization error. The SVM uses the kernel function to evaluate the dot product of the feature vectors in order to lower computation load.

The applications of support vector machines include text grouping, image classification and segmentation, handwriting recognition and protein classification in the field of biological sciences.

However, SVM requires full dataset categorization. Besides, the probabilities of the class membership function is not standardized and it is applicable for only two class problems. Further, if applied for other types of problems then whole classifier algorithm needs extensive changes, and also reverse evaluation of the parameters is complex.

Naive Bayes Classifier

It is a mathematical model which is based on Bayes probability theorem which analytically confirms the independence of the data object instances. The main principle of naive bayes classifier is feature independence i.e. the particular value of a feature vector is independent of the value of other feature vectors if the class label is known. It is mainly a supervised learning technique of classification that uses the maximum likelihood for parameter estimation.

The various advantages of naive bayes classifier are it needs less training data for categorization; it works well in the multi-dimensional space and gives accurate results. It has been employed to solve the problems of gender classification and document classification. The main drawback of naive bayes classifier is class probability estimation (Niculescu-Mizil et al., 2005).

K- Nearest Neighbors Classifier

It is a non- probabilistic technique in classification. It is employed for regression analysis too. The main idea behind KNN classifier states that if there are finite feature vectors in the k dimensional space with instances having known class labels then the feature instance will fall into the class that is near to it based on Euclidean distance. It is a supervised learning technique and the simplest form of classification technique in artificial intelligence. The main feature of KNN classifier is its local searching capability. The computation is preceded by the classification task. This type of learning is called lazy learning. The matching matrix is used for estimating the classification accuracy in KNN classifier.

The main advantages of KNN classifier are multi-objective classification and low error rates. Further, the curse of dimensionality is overcome through data reduction technique. KNN classifier gives consistent results as compared to Bayes classifier (Cover et al.,1967). The obvious drawbacks of KNN classifier include: initialization of the algorithm totally depends on the value of k, high computation cost as compared to other classifiers such as K-D tree and distance measures are not standardized.

GSA Hybrid Algorithms for Classification

The gravitational search algorithm is a global optimization algorithm having high convergence speed. The heavy mass operator in GSA is having the property of local searching i.e. it searches the agents that are near and attracts them towards itself because of having high fitness function value. So, it is the heavy mass that moves slowly and is having the high gravitational field than other masses. This feature of GSA is highly utilized in tackling classification problems. The GSA is also hybridized with other optimization algorithms and classifiers in order to increase the classification accuracy and precision.

The GSA is used for classification of data with Support vector machine (SVM). Both versions of GSA i.e. continuous and binary logic based are combined with SVM in order to increase the classification accuracy. The hybrid algorithm is tested on famous UCI benchmark test functions and shows more performance than already available classifiers (Sarafrazi et al., 2013).

The GSA is combined with K-nearest neighbor (KNN) for the classification of data. The GSA provides the randomized initialization of the search space and increases the optimization of the features. The hybrid technique is tested on 12 benchmark datasets (Jamshidi et al., 2014). Prototype generation is the process of reducing the dimension of the class samples used for decision making. The GSA is hybridized with K- nearest neighbor for classification of prototypes (Rezaei et al., 2014; 2015).

Table 4. GSA hybridization algorithms for classification

GSA Hybrid Classifier	References
GSA-Support Vector Machine (SVM)	Sarafrazi et al., 2013
GSA-Intervals Number (IN) KNN	Jamshidi et al., 2014
GSA-Neural Network Classifier	Rezaei et al., 2014
Improved Binary GSA-SVM	Rezaei et al., 2015
GSA-Optimum Path Forest (OPF)	Papa et al., 2011
Evolutionary GSA	Ramos et al., 2012
Improved GSA-KNN	Xiang et al., 2015
MGSA-FSS (Feature Subset Selection)	Han et al., 2014
Binary Quantum GSA	Barani et al., 2017

Feature selection is one of the fundamental steps in the classification process in data mining. It extracts the important features from the data set that can reduce the dimensionality and search space of the problem. It is carried out using GSA, a swarm based technique and Optimum-Path Forest (OPF), a powerful pattern recognition method. The GSA acts as the optimization tool that helps in finding the pattern in the search domain and maximizes the output given by OPF (Papa et al., 2011).

The GSA is used for selecting the appropriate features for identifying the frauds in power distribution systems. The GSA is combined with Harmony search and PSO for feature selection. The hybrid algorithm increases the recognition rates and finds the illegal consumer profiles (Ramos et al., 2012).

In solving the feature selection problems, the performance of the algorithms gets deteriorated due to the curse of dimensionality problem. The GSA is used for reducing the size of the datasets by selecting the appropriate features. It also uses the chaotic maps for increasing the exploitation process and sequential programming for boosting the exploration process, respectively (Xiang et al., 2015).

Also, MGSA (Modified Gravitational Search Algorithm) is used for feature subset selection (FSS) by using the concepts of chaotic maps (QM) and sequential quadratic programming (SQP). The QM is utilized for getting the diversity of the agents and SQP is used for optimal exploitation of the agents. The FSS-GSA is stochastic in nature and is applicable when domain knowledge is not available. The MGSA algorithm is tested on 10 CEC 2005 benchmark test functions and compared with other classification techniques such as GA, PSO, and GSA for Classification accuracy check (Han et al., 2014).

It is also hybridized with K-nearest neighbor algorithm for selecting the potential features that can reduce the dimension and increase the accuracy of the dataset (Barani et al., 2017).

PERFORMANCE EVALUATION AND ASSESSMENT

The qualitative analysis of the gravitational search algorithm is done by comparing its quantitative results with existing clustering methods. The various performance metrics for clustering are Davies–Bouldin index, Dunn index, and Silhouette coefficient.

Davies–Bouldin Index

In clustering, the data items are scattered in the given dimensional space. The data items form the various clusters having their own centroids. The clusters having less intra-cluster distance and more inter-cluster distance are considered efficient. The performance metric utilized for calculating intra and inter cluster similarity is known as Davies–Bouldin index. So, the clustering algorithm having a low value of Davies–Bouldin index is considered efficient. It is mathematically represented by using the Eq. (11):

$$DB = \frac{1}{n}\sum_{i=1}^{n} \max_{j \neq i} \left(\frac{\sigma_i + \sigma_j}{d\left(c_i, c_j\right)} \right) \tag{11}$$

Whereas n is the number of clusters in a problem space, $\left\langle \sigma_i, \sigma_j \right\rangle$ is the distance between the data items and the centroid; $d\left(c_i, c_j\right)$ is the distance between the centroids.

Dunn Index

In the clustering process, when the data items are in close proximity to the centroid then, the cluster is said to be dense. It also means that the intra cluster distance is less and intra cluster similarity is more. The Dunn Index shows how much a cluster is densely populated by the data elements i.e. large intra-cluster distance and identifies the clusters having minimum inter-cluster distance. It is a ratio of minimum inter-cluster distance between two centroids and the maximum intra-cluster distance between the centroid and data elements. It is mathematically calculated by using the Eq. 12:

$$D = \frac{\min_{1 \leq i \leq j \leq n} d\left(i, j\right)}{\max_{1 \leq k \leq n} d'\left(i, j\right)} \tag{12}$$

In the equation, n is the number of clusters, <i,j> are the clusters and d(i, j) is the distance between the clusters. Also, $d'\left(i, j\right)$ is the intra-cluster distance between the data items and centroid of the cluster, k. The clustering algorithm having high value of the Dunn Index is considered more reliable and efficient.

Silhouette Coefficient

The Silhouette is the graphical representation of the data items in the cluster. Moreover, the Silhouette coefficient is the measure of calculating intra-cluster distance. The data items that are close to the centroid will have the high Silhouette coefficient and vice versa. It is calculated by using Eq. 13:

$$s\left(i\right) = \frac{b\left(i\right) - a\left(i\right)}{\max\left\{a\left(i\right), b\left(i\right)\right\}} \tag{13}$$

Here s(i) is the Silhouette coefficient. Here, i is a data item present in the cluster, a(i) is the distance between the data item (i) and the cluster i.e. intra-cluster distance. Also, b(i) is the smallest distance between the data item(i) and the data items of the other cluster. The value of a(i) should have to be small i.e. low intra-cluster distance and b(i) must have more value because it gives positive value to the s(i) which means data item is properly clustered. If s(i) have the negative value, it indicates the outlier or noise present in the cluster.

The gravitational search algorithm and its variants are also applied to classification problems in order to overcome the limitations of existing classifiers. The classification is the pattern recognition technique which is used for categorizing the data elements based on mathematical information. So, classification power is directly proportional to the categorization and grouping of data objects by the classifier.

There are various classical classification algorithms used by researchers for classification of data such as SVM, Decision Tree, Artificial Neural Network Classifier and optimization algorithms based classifiers such PSO, ABC, DE etc. The GSA is also utilized for classification task to overcome the classification problems and it is also combined and hybridized with other swarm based optimization algorithm to increase the classification precision. The metrics for performance estimation are Confusion matrix, Precision and recall, and Receiver operating characteristic (ROC).

Confusion Matrix

It is a two-dimensional matrix that shows the performance of the classifier. The rows in the table represent the data objects or instances of the predicted class and the columns indicate the data objects of the actual class. In case of supervised learning, it is called as Error matrix and in unsupervised learning it is called as a matching matrix.

The confusion matrix is used for checking the classification accuracy of the classifier. In other words, it indicates the percentage of the data objects successfully classified and categorized by the classifier. The example of the measure that uses the error matrix for evaluating the classification accuracy of the classifier is the Kappa Coefficient.

Precision and Recall

The precision and recall are both measures of relevance of the classifier. The precision indicates the data items truly classified by the classifier from the selected instances. It is also known as positive predictive value (PPV). On the other hand, the recall represents the data items successfully categorized by the classifier from all instances. It is also known as sensitivity or true positive rate (TPR).

In simple terms, the precision shows the exactness and quality of the classification algorithm whereas recall shows the completeness and quantity of the classifier. The precision and recall can be represented statistically using Eq. 14 and 15.

$$\text{Precision=PPV}= \frac{TP}{TP + FP} \tag{14}$$

$$\text{Recall=TPR=} \frac{TP}{TP + FN} \tag{15}$$

Where TP indicate true positives i.e. the data items classified successfully; FP is the false positives i.e. the data items classified incorrectly and FN is the false negatives i.e. the data items that are incorrectly rejected by the classifier for classification.

The precision and recall is the measure for checking the classification precision of the classifier. The measures that use the concepts of the precision and recall are F-measure, Matthews correlation coefficient, Markedness, etc.

Receiver Operating Characteristic (ROC)

It is the graphical representation of the classification ability of the classifier. The ROC curve is plotted by using the concepts of recall and selectivity on X axis and Y axis respectively. The recall is also called as true positive rate (TPR) and selectivity is also known as false positive rate (FPR) in machine learning. The TPR can be represented mathematically by Eq. 15. The TFR can be calculated as:

$$\text{TNR=} \frac{TN}{TP + FP} \tag{16}$$

Where TN is the True Negatives i.e. the data items that are correctly rejected by the classifier for classification.

In simple terms, the ROC curve is utilized for selecting the optimal classifier and rejects the suboptimal classifier. The measure that uses the concept of ROC is Z- score.

The performance measures mentioned above such as Davies-Buildin Index, Confusion Matrix, etc are assessment measures for clustering and classification. There are other metrics such as classification rank, Hopkins statistic, etc mentioned in research literature but they are not widely used by the researchers.

CONCLUSION

Gravitational search algorithm (GSA) is a population-based heuristic optimization algorithm. It can be concluded that GSA are suitable for solving clustering and classification problems. It provides better performance than conventional clustering and classification algorithms. Also, it overcomes the drawbacks such as high dimensionality and trapping in local optima of clustering and classification problems.

In this chapter, the focus is mainly on the comprehensive survey of GSA in solving clustering and classification. But GSA has the potential to solve these problems in new emerging fields of study such as IoT, Cloud Computing, Network security, etc. with high accuracy and precision. GSA can be combined with new optimization algorithms such as Butterfly Algorithm and Grey Wolf Algorithm to produce new clustering and classification algorithms that can improve clustering efficiency and additionally classification accuracy and precision.

REFERENCES

Abbasian, M. A., & Nezamabadi-pour, H. (2012). Multi objective gravitational search algorithm using non-dominated Fronts. *J. Electr. Eng.*, *41*(1), 67–80.

Abbasian, M. A., Nezamabadi-pour, H., & Amoozegar, M. (2015). A clustering based archive multi objective gravitational search algorithm. *J. Fund. Inf.*, *138*, 387–409.

Ahmadlou, M., & Adeli, H. (2010). Enhanced probabilistic neural network with local decision circles: A robust classifier. *Integrated Computer-Aided Engineering*, *17*(3), 197–210. doi:10.3233/ICA-2010-0345

Ajami, A., & Armaghan, M. (2013). A multi-objective gravitational search algorithm based approach of power system stability enhancement with UPFC. *Journal of Central South University*, *20*(6), 1536–1544. doi:10.100711771-013-1645-1

Baniassadi, Z., Nezamabadi-pour, H., & Farsangi, M. M. (2011). A multi-objective solution of gravitational search algorithm for benchmark functions and placement of SVC. *Intell. Syst. Electr. Eng.*, *1*(1), 59–78.

Barani, F., Mirhosseini, M., & Nezamabadi-pour, H. (2017). Application of binary quantum-inspired gravitational search algorithm in feature subset selection. *Applied Intelligence*, *47*(2), 304–318. doi:10.100710489-017-0894-3

Bhattacharya, A., & Roy, P. K. (2012). Solution of multi-objective optimal power flow using gravitational search algorithm. *IET Generation, Transmission & Distribution*, *6*(8), 751–763. doi:10.1049/iet-gtd.2011.0593

Chira, C., Sedano, J., Camara, M., Prieto, C., Villar, J. R., & Cor-chado, E. (2014). A cluster merging method for time series microarray with product values. International Journal of Neural Systems, 24(6).

Cover, T. M., & Hart, P. E. (1967). Nearest neighbor pattern classification. *IEEE Transactions on Information Theory*, *13*(1), 21–27. doi:10.1109/TIT.1967.1053964

Dorigo, M., Maniezzo, V., & Colorni, A. (1991). *Positive Feedback as a Search Strategy*. Technical Report no. 91016. Politecnico di Milano.

Dowlatshahi, M. B., & Nezamabadi-pour, H. (2014). GGSA: A grouping gravitational search algorithm for data clustering. *Engineering Applications of Artificial Intelligence*, *36*, 114–121. doi:10.1016/j.engappai.2014.07.016

Dowlatshahi, M. B., Nezamabadi-pour, H., & Mashinchi, M. (2014). A discrete gravitational search algorithm for solving combinatorial optimization problems. *Information Sciences*, *258*, 94–107. doi:10.1016/j.ins.2013.09.034

Erol, O. K., & Eksin, I. (2006). A new optimization method: Big Bang–Big Crunch. *Advances in Engineering Software*, *37*(2), 106–111. doi:10.1016/j.advengsoft.2005.04.005

Ganesan, T. (2013). Swarm intelligence and gravitational search algorithm for multi-objective optimization of synthesis gas production. *Appl. Energy*, *103*, 368–374.

Ghalambaz. (2011). A hybrid neural network and gravitational search algorithm method to solve well known wessinger's equation. *International journal of MAIMM Engineering*, 5.

Haghbayan, P., Nezamabadi-pour, H., & Kamyab, S. (2017). A niche GSA method with nearest neighbor scheme for multimodal optimization. *Swarm and Evolutionary Computation*, 35, 78–92. doi:10.1016/j.swevo.2017.03.002

Halliday, D., Resnick, R., & Walker, J. (2000). *Fundamentals of Physics* (6th ed.). Delhi: Wiley.

Han. (2014). Feature subset selection by gravitational search algorithm optimization. *Inf. Sci.*, *81*, 28-146.

Han, X., Chang, X. M., Quan, L., Xiong, X. Y., Li, J. X., Zhang, Z. X., & Liu, Y. (2014). Feature subset selection by gravitational search algorithm optimization. *Inf. Sci.*, *281*, 128–146. doi:10.1016/j.ins.2014.05.030

Han, X., Quan, L., Xiong, X. Y., Almeter, M., Xiang, J., & Lan, Y. (2017). A novel data clustering algorithm based on modified gravitational search algorithm. *Engineering Applications of Artificial Intelligence*, *61*, 1–7. doi:10.1016/j.engappai.2016.11.003

Hassanzadeh, H. R., & Rouhani, M. (2010). A multi-objective gravitational search algorithm. *Computational Intelligence, Communication Systems and Networks (CICSyN), Second International Conference.*

Hatamlou, Abdullah, & Othman. (2011). Gravitational Search Algorithm with Heuristic Search for Clustering Problems. *Proceeding of 3rd IEEE on Data Mining and Optimization (DMO)*, 190 – 193.

Hatamlou, A., Abdullah, S., & Nezamabadi-pour, H. (2012). A combined approach for clustering based on K-means and gravitational search algorithms. *Swarm and Evolutionary Computation*, *6*, 47–55. doi:10.1016/j.swevo.2012.02.003

Ho, Y., & Pepyne, D. (2002). Simple explanation of the no-free-lunch theorem and its implications. *Journal of Optimization Theory and Applications*, *155*(3), 549–570. doi:10.1023/A:1021251113462

Holland, J. H. (1975). *Adaptation in Natural and Artificial Systems*. Ann Arbor, MI: University of Michigan Press.

Ibrahim, A. A., Mohamed, A., & Shareef, H. (2012). A novel quantum-inspired binary gravitational search algorithm in obtaining optimal power quality monitor placement. *Journal of Applied Sciences (Faisalabad)*, *12*(9), 822–830. doi:10.3923/jas.2012.822.830

Ibrahim, A. A., Mohamed, A., & Shareef, H. (2014). Optimal power quality monitor placement in power systems using an adaptive quantum-inspired binary gravitational search algorithm. *International Journal of Electrical Power & Energy Systems*, *57*, 404–413. doi:10.1016/j.ijepes.2013.12.019

Jamshidi, Y., & Kaburlasos, V. G. (2014). gsaINknn: A GSA optimized, lattice computing knn classifier. *Engineering Applications of Artificial Intelligence*, *35*, 277–285. doi:10.1016/j.engappai.2014.06.018

Ji, B., Yuan, X., Li, X., Huang, Y., & Li, W. (2014). Application of quantum-inspired binary gravitational search algorithm for thermal unit commitment with wind power integration. *Energy Conversion and Management*, *87*, 589–598. doi:10.1016/j.enconman.2014.07.060

Jiang, J., Ji, Z., & Shen, Y. (2014). A novel hybrid particle swarm optimization and gravitational search algorithm for solving economic emission load dispatch problems with various practical constraints. *International Journal of Electrical Power & Energy Systems*, *55*, 628–644. doi:10.1016/j.ijepes.2013.10.006

Karaboga, D. (2005). *An Idea based on Honey Bee Swarm for Numerical Optimization*. Technical Report TR06. Computer Engineering Department, Engineering Faculty, Erciyes University.

Karaboga, D., & Ozturk, C. (2011). A novel clustering approach: Artificial bee colony (ABC) algorithm. *Applied Soft Computing*, *11*(1), 652–657. doi:10.1016/j.asoc.2009.12.025

Kennedy, J., & Eberhart, R. C. (1995). In Particle swarm optimization. *Proceedings of IEEE International Conference on Neural Networks*. 10.1109/ICNN.1995.488968

Khajooei, F., & Rashedi, E. (2016). *A New Version of Gravitational Search Algorithm with Negative Mass*. Academic Press.

Knagenhjelm, P., & Brauer, P. (1990). Classification of vowels in continuous speech using MLP and a hybrid network. *Speech Communication*, *9*(1), 31–34. doi:10.1016/0167-6393(90)90042-8

Kumar, V., Chhabra, J. K., & Kumar, D. (2014). Automatic cluster evolution using gravitational search algorithm and its application on image segmentation. *Engineering Applications of Artificial Intelligence*, *29*, 93–103. doi:10.1016/j.engappai.2013.11.008

(2014). Kumar, Yugal, & Sahoo, G. (2014). A Review on Gravitational Search Algorithm and its Applications to Data Clustering. *I.J. Intelligent Systems and Applications*, *6*, 79–93. doi:10.5815/ijisa.2014.06.09

Kurzynski, M. W. (1983). The optimal strategy of a tree classifier. *Pattern Recognition*, *16*(1), 81–87. doi:10.1016/0031-3203(83)90011-0

Li, C., & Zhou, J. (2014). Semi-supervised weighted kernel clustering based on gravitational search for fault diagnosis. *ISA Transactions*, *53*(5), 1534–1543. doi:10.1016/j.isatra.2014.05.019 PMID:24981891

MacQueen, J. (1967). Some methods for classification and analysis of multivariate observations. In *Proceedings of Fifth Berkeley Symposium on Mathematics Statistics and Probability*. University of California Press.

Minghao, H. (2011). A novel hybrid K-harmonic means and gravitational search algorithm approach for clustering. *Expert Systems with Applications*, *38*(8), 9319–9324. doi:10.1016/j.eswa.2011.01.018

Mirjalili, S., & Gandomi, A. (2017). Chaotic gravitational constants for the gravitational search algorithm. *Applied Soft Computing*, *53*, 407–419. doi:10.1016/j.asoc.2017.01.008

Mirjalili, S., & Hashim, M. (2012). Training feed forward neural networks using hybrid particle swarm optimization and gravitational search algorithm. *Applied Mathematics and Computation*, *218*(22), 1125–11137. doi:10.1016/j.amc.2012.04.069

Niculescu-Mizil, A., & Caruana, R. (2005). *Predicting good probabilities with supervised learning*. ICML. doi:10.1145/1102351.1102430

Nobahari, H., Nikusokhan, M., & Siarry, P. (2012). A multi-objective gravitational search algorithm based on non-dominated sorting. *International Journal of Swarm Intelligence Research*, *3*(3), 32–49.

Papa, J. (2011). Feature selection through gravitational search algorithm. *Acoustics Speech and Signal Processing (ICASSP), IEEE International Conference.*

Pei, L., & HaiBin, D. (2012). Path planning of unmanned aerial vehicle based on improved gravitational search algorithm. *Science China, 55*, 2712–2719.

Rajagopal, Anamika, Vinod, & Niranjan. (2018). *gsa–fapso-based generators active power rescheduling for transmission congestion management.* Academic Press.

Ramos, C. C. O., de Souza, A. N., Falcao, A. X., & Papa, J. P. (2012). New insights on nontechnical losses characterization through evolutionary-based feature selection. *IEEE Transactions on Power Delivery, 27*(1), 40–146. doi:10.1109/TPWRD.2011.2170182

Rashedi, E., Nezamabadi-pour, H., & Saryazdi, S. (2009). GSA: A Gravitational Search Algorithm. *Information Sciences, 179*(13), 2232–2248. doi:10.1016/j.ins.2009.03.004

Rashedi, E., Nezamabadi-Pour, H., & Saryazdi, S. (2010). BGSA: Binary gravitational search *algorithm. Natural Computing, 9*(3), 727–745. doi:10.100711047-009-9175-3

Rezaei, M., & Nezamabadi-pour, H. (2014). *A prototype optimization method for nearest neighbor classification by gravitational search algorithm. Intelligent Systems.* ICIS.

Rezaei, M., & Nezamabadi-pour, H. (2015). Using gravitational search algorithm in prototype generation for nearest neighbor classification. *Neurocomputing, 157*, 256–263. doi:10.1016/j.neucom.2015.01.008

Rubio-Largo, A., & Vega-Rodriguez, M. A. (2013). *A multi-objective approach based on the law of gravity and mass interactions for optimizing networks.* Lect. Notes Comput. Sci., 7832, 13–24).

Sarafrazi, S., & Nezamabadi-pour, H. (2013). Facing the classification of binary problems with a GSA-SVM hybrid system. *Mathematical and Computer Modelling, 57*(1-2), 270–278. doi:10.1016/j.mcm.2011.06.048

Seifi, F., Kangavari, M. R., Ahmadi, H., Lotfi, E., Imaniyan, S., & Lagzian, S. (2008). Optimizing twins decision tree classification using genetic algorithms. *7th IEEE International Conference on Cybernetic Intelligent Systems*, 1–6. 10.1109/UKRICIS.2008.4798957

Shamsudin, H. C. (2012). A fast discrete gravitational search algorithm. *Computational Intelligence, Modeling and Simulation (CIMSiM), Fourth International Conference.*

Shanhe, Wenjin, & Yanmei. (2018). An improved hybrid particle swarm optimization with dependent random coefficients for global optimization. *33rd Youth Academic Annual Conference of Chinese Association of Automation (YAC)*, 666-672.

Shelokar, P. S., Jayaraman, V. K., & Kulkarni, B. D. (2004). An ant colony approach for clustering. *Analytica Chimica Acta, 509*(2), 187–195. doi:10.1016/j.aca.2003.12.032

Soleimanpour-moghadam, M., & Nezamabadi-pour, H. (2012). An improved quantum behaved gravitational search algorithm. *Electrical Engineering (ICEE), 20th Iranian Conference.* 10.1109/IranianCEE.2012.6292446

Soleimanpour-moghadam, M., Nezamabadi-pour, H., & Farsangi, M. M. (2011). A quantum behaved gravitational search algorithm. *Proceeding of Int. Conf. Computational Intelligence and Software Engineering*.

Soleimanpour-moghadam, M., Nezamabadi-pour, H., & Farsangi, M. M. (2014). A quantum inspired gravitational search algorithm for numerical function optimization. *Inf. Sciences, 267*, 83–100. doi:10.1016/j.ins.2013.09.006

Storn, R., & Price, K. (1995). *Differential Evolution – A simple and Efficient Heuristic for Global Optimization over Continuous Spaces*. International Computer Science Institute.

Sun & Zhang. (2013). A hybrid genetic algorithm and gravitational using multilevel thresholding. *Pattern Recognition and Image Analysis*, 707–714.

Ursem, R. K. (1999). Multinational evolutionary algorithms. *Proceedings of Congress of Evolutionary Computation*, 1633–1640.

Wu, J. Y. (2011). MIMO CMAC neural network classifier for solving classification problems. *Applied Soft Computing, 11*(2), 2326–2333. doi:10.1016/j.asoc.2010.08.013

Xiang, J., Han, X. H., Duan, F., Qiang, Y., Xiong, X. Y., Lan, Y., & Chai, H. (2015). A novel hybrid system for feature selection based on an improved gravitational search algorithm and k-NN method. *Applied Soft Computing, 31*, 293–307. doi:10.1016/j.asoc.2015.01.043

Xiangtao, Yin, & Ma. (2011). Hybrid differential evolution and gravitation search algorithm for unconstrained optimization. *International Journal of Physical Sciences, 6*, 5961–5981.

Yadav, A., & Kim, J. H. (2014). A niching co-swarm gravitational search algorithm for multi-modal optimization. *Proceedings of Fourth International Conference on Soft Computing for Problem Solving*. 10.1007/978-81-322-1771-8_55

Yazdani, S., & Nezamabadi-pour, H. (2011). A new gravitational solution for multimodal optimization. *18th Iranian Conference on Electrical Engineering*.

Yazdani, S., Nezamabadi-pour, H., & Kamyab, S. (2014). A gravitational search algorithm for multimodal optimization. *Swarm and Evolutionary Computation, 14*, 1–14. doi:10.1016/j.swevo.2013.08.001

Yu, Ying, & Wang. (2011). Immune gravitation inspired optimization algorithm. *International Conference on Intelligent Computing, Springer*.

Zandevakili, H., Rashedi, E., & Mahani, A. (2017). Gravitational search algorithm with both attractive and repulsive forces. *Soft Computing*. doi:10.100700500-017-2785-2

Zhang, B., Hsu, M., & Dayal, U. (2000). K-harmonic means. *International Workshop on Temporal, Spatial, and Spatio-temporal Data Mining*.

Zhang, Y., & Zhou, W. (2015). Multifractal analysis and relevance vector machine-based automatic seizure detection in in-tracranial. *International Journal of Neural Systems, 25*(6). doi:. doi:10.1142/S0129065715500203

ADDITIONAL READING

Dorigo, M., Maniezzo, V., & Colorni, A. (1996). The ant system: Optimization by a colony of cooperating agents. *IEEE Transactions on Systems, Man, and Cybernetics. Part B, Cybernetics*, *26*(1), 29–41. doi:10.1109/3477.484436 PMID:18263004

Kalinlia, A., & Karabogab, N. (2005). Artificial immune algorithm for IIR filter design Engineering. *Applied Artificial Intelligence*, *18*(8), 919–929. doi:10.1016/j.engappai.2005.03.009

Kennedy, J., & Eberhart, R. (1995). Particle swarm optimization. In IEEE *International Conference on Neural Networks*, 1942–1948. 10.1109/ICNN.1995.488968

Kirkpatrick, S., Gelatto, C. D., & Vecchi, M. P. (1983). Optimization by simulated annealing. *Science*, *220*(4598), 671–680. doi:10.1126cience.220.4598.671 PMID:17813860

Lavika, S., Sharthak, & Satyajit. (2016). Hybridization of gravitational search algorithm and biogeography based optimization and its application on grid scheduling problem. *Ninth International Conference on Contemporary Computing (IC3)*, 1-6.

Li, C., & Zhou, J. (2011). Parameters identification of hydraulic turbine governing system using improved gravitational search algorithm. *Energy Conversion and Management*, *52*(1), 374–381. doi:10.1016/j.enconman.2010.07.012

Simon, D. (2008). Biogeography-Based Optimization. *IEEE Transactions on Evolutionary Computation*, *12*(6), 702–713. doi:10.1109/TEVC.2008.919004

Tang, K. S., Man, K. F., Kwong, S., & He, Q. (1996). Genetic algorithms and their applications. *IEEE Signal Processing Magazine*, *13*(6), 22–37. doi:10.1109/79.543973

KEY TERMS AND DEFINITIONS

Classification: Classification is the process of categorizing the data into groups based on mathematical information. It is a pattern recognition technique (i.e., finding the meaningful informational patterns from the outlier and noisy data).

Clustering: Clustering is the technique of grouping similar data samples based on distance and similarity criterion. Clustering is a statistical data analysis task which has been employed in many areas such as information retrieval, data mining, bioinformatics, data compression, etc.

Exploitation: It is the process of finding the feasible solution around the candidate solutions in the search space. This step is used by all the optimization algorithms in order to find the local optima. The high exploitation power of an algorithm indicates its effectiveness and high convergence rate.

Exploration: It is the ability of the optimization algorithm to randomly initialize the search space. Basically, it is the first step in every optimization algorithm because it shows the range i.e. the lower and upper limits of the algorithm. The high exploration power of an algorithm indicates its fewer chances of getting trapped in the local optima.

Gravitational Search Algorithm (GSA): It is a meta-heuristic algorithm for global optimization based on the law of interaction of masses.

Heuristic Algorithms: The techniques that are used for finding the optimal solution around the feasible solutions are called Heuristics. The algorithms which mimic the natural systems are called as Heuristic Algorithms. These algorithms have the properties of working in a parallel manner and information interchange among the agents. They are probabilistic in nature and do not have central control.

Hybridization: It is the technique of modifying the mathematical structure of the parent algorithm by using another optimization algorithm(s) so that the limitations of the parent algorithm can be removed.

Optimization: It is the technique of selecting the most feasible solution for the given problem. The nature-inspired algorithms such as GSA, PSO, GA, etc. are the best examples of optimization.

Particle Swarm Optimization (PSO): It is a nature-inspired algorithm which mimics the behavior of a flock of birds or fishes. It uses the concepts of local best and global best in getting the optimal solution. The iteration procedure is used to improve the quality of candidate solutions.

Swarm Intelligence (SI): It is the field of artificial intelligence in which the population is in the form of agents which search in a parallel fashion with multiple initialization points. The swarm intelligence-based algorithms mimic the physical and natural processes for mathematical modeling of the optimization algorithm. They have the properties of information interchange and non-centralized control structure.

Chapter 6
Analytics and Technology for Practical Forecasting

William Fox
College of William and Mary, USA

Anh Ninh
College of William and Mary, USA

ABSTRACT

With the importance of forecasting in businesses, a wide variety of methods and tools has been developed over the years to automate the process of forecasting. However, an unintended consequence of this tremendous advancement is that forecasting has become more and more like a black box function. Thus, a primary goal of this chapter is to provide a clear understanding of forecasting in any application contexts with a systematic procedure for practical forecasting through step-by-step examples. Several methods are presented, and the authors compare results to what were the typical forecasting methods including regression and time series in different software technologies. Three case studies are presented: simple supply forecasting, homicide forecasting, and demand forecasting for sales from Walmart.

INTRODUCTION TO FORECASTING

What is forecasting? We assume that forecasting is concerned with making predictions about future observations based upon past data. Mathematically, there are many algorithms that one might use to make these predictions: *regression (linear and nonlinear)*, *exponential smoothing* (time series) model, *autoregressive integrated moving average* (ARIMA) model to name a few that we will illustrate in this chapter.

Applications of forecasting might include the following:

- Operations management in business such as forecast of product sales or demand for services
- Marketing: forecast of sales response to advertisement procedures, new item promotions etc.
- Finance & Risk management: forecast returns from investments or retirement accounts

DOI: 10.4018/978-1-7998-0106-1.ch006

- Economics: forecast of major economic variables, e.g. GDP, population growth, unemployment rates, inflation; monetary & fiscal policy; budgeting plans & decisions
- Industrial Process Control: forecasts of the quality characteristics of a production process
- Demography: forecast of population; of demographic events (deaths, births, migration); forecasting languages demand, forecasting crime or homicides

To facilitate the process of deciding which forecasting process to use, we employ the following mathematical modeling approach within the decision process.

Steps in the Modeling and Decision Process

We adopt the framework for the mathematical modeling process (adapted from Giordano et al, 2014) which works very well in the decision-making contexts with a few minor adjustments as shown in the following steps:

Step 1. Define the main objective for the forecasting tasks

Step 2. Make assumptions and choose relevant variables

Step 3. Collection of data if necessary

Step 4. Choose the right forecasting model.

Step 5. Run the model

Step 6. Perform model testing and sensitivity analysis

Step 7. Perform a common sense test on the results

Step 8. Consider both strengths and weaknesses to your modeling process.

Step 9. Present the results to the decision maker.

We discuss each of these nine steps in a little more depth.

Step 1. Understand the problem or the question asked. To make a good decision you need to understand the problem. Identifying the problem to study is usually difficult. In real life no one walks up to you and hands you an equation to be solved, usually, it is a comment like, "we need to make more money", or "we need to improve our efficiency". We need to be precise in our understanding of the problem to be precise in the formulation of the mathematics to describe the situation.

Step 2a. Make simplifying assumptions. Start by brain storming the situation, making a list of as many factors, or variables, as you can. However, keep in mind that we usually cannot capture all these factors influencing a problem. The task is simplified by reducing the number of factors under consideration. We do this by making simplifying assumptions about the factors, such as holding certain factors as constants. We might then examine to see if relationships exist between the remaining factors (or variables). Assuming simple relationships might reduce the complexity of the problem.

Once you have a shorter list of variables, classify them as independent variables, dependent variables, or neither.

Step 2b. Define all variables and provide their respective units. It is critical to clearly define all your variables and provide the mathematical notation and units for each one.

Step 3. Acquire the data. We note that acquiring the data is not an easy process.

Step 4. Construct the model. Using the tools in this text and your own creativity to build a mathematical model that describes the situation and whose solution helps to answer important questions.

Step 5. Solve and interpret the model. We take the model constructed in Steps 1 - 4 and solve it. Often this model might be too complex so we cannot solve it or interpret it. If this happens, we return to Steps 2 - 4 and simplify the model further.

Step 6. Perform sensitivity analysis and model testing. Before we use the model, we should test it out. We must ask several questions. Does the model directly answer the question or does the model allow for the answer to the question(s) to be answered? During this step, we should review each of our assumptions to understand the impact on the mathematical model's solution if the assumption is incorrect.

Step 7. Passing the common sense test. Is the model useable in a practical sense (can we obtain data to use the model)? Does the model pass the common sense test? We will say that we "collaborate the reasonableness" of our model.

Step 8. Strengths and Weaknesses. No model is complete with self-reflection of the modeling process. We need to consider not only what we did right but we did that might be suspect as well as what we could do better. This reflection also helps in refining models.

Step 9. Present results and sensitivity analysis to the Decision Maker. A model is pointless if we do not use it. The more user-friendly the model the more it will be used. Sometimes the ease of obtaining data for the model can dictate its success or failure. The model must also remain current. Often this entails updating parameters used in the model.

Our plan stems from the modeling approach which is an iterative approach as we move to refine models. Therefore, starting with least squares regression and "moving" models from time series we transition to the more formal machine learning methods.

Machine Learning

We have found and teach that ***machine learning*** has many definitions. Machine learning can range from almost any use of a computers (machine) performing calculations and analysis measures to the applications of artificial intelligence (AI) or neural networks in the computer's calculations and analysis methods. In this chapter, we adapt the definition from Huddleston and Brown (2018),

"The defining characteristic of machine learning is the focus on using algorithmic methods to improve descriptive, predictive, and prescriptive performance in real-world contexts. An older, but perhaps more accurate, synonym for this approach from the statistical literature is algorithmic modeling (Breiman 2001). This algorithmic approach to problem solving often entails sacrificing the interpretability of the resulting models. Therefore, machine learning is best applied when this trade-off makes business sense, but is not appropriate for situations such as public policy decision-making, where the requirement to explain how one is making decisions about public resources is often essential."

Huddleston and Brown (2018) provide a nice schematic that we present as Figure 1.

We concentrate in this chapter with the supervised learning aspect only and in particular, those regression and time series models that we can readily apply to the forecasting tasks.

Figure 1. Overview of machine learning paradigms: supervised, unsupervised, and reinforcement learning. This illustration provides a summary of the data needed to train the model, the format of the resulting model output, and a list of algorithms often used for this class of problem. Algorithms listed are addressed in this chapter, except Q Learning, which is omitted due to space limitations. (Huddleston et al, 2018)

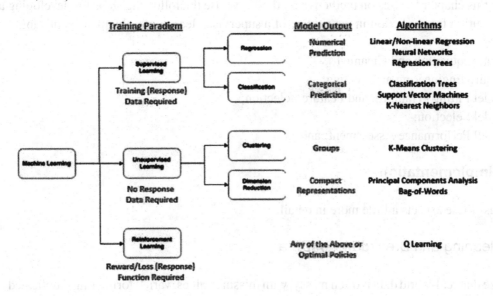

According to Huddleston et al (2018).

"Machine learning is an emerging field, with new algorithms regularly developed and fielded. Specific machine learning techniques are usually designed to address one of the three types of machine learning problems introduced here, but in practice, several methods are often combined for real-world application. As a general rule, unsupervised learning methods are designed to be descriptive, supervised learning methods are designed to be predictive, and reinforcement-learning methods are designed to be prescriptive" (Breinman, 2001).

This difference in modeling focus yields the following list of guiding principles for algorithmic modeling, some of which are based on Breiman's (2001) influential article:

- *"There are likely to be many models with demonstrated predictive power.*
- *Analysts should investigate and compete as many models as possible.*
- *Analysts should measure the performance of models on out-of-sample test datasets using a procedure that mimics the real-world situation in which the model will be applied.*
- *Predictive accuracy on out-of-sample test data, not goodness of fit on training data, is the primary criterion for how good a model is, however...*
- *Predictive power is not the only criteria upon which model selection is made; we routinely also consider model interpretability, speed, deployability, and parsimony."*

Technology is a key aspect in all these algorithms. Where appropriate and applicable we will present examples using MAPLE, R, MINITAB, and EXCEL to compute our output. Each has some strengths and weaknesses in forecasting. We point out here that in comparing the technologies for time series that the values differ slightly across the technologies.

Since this chapter focuses on predictive methods, we use the following steps for developing an algorithmic solution for prediction in the context of a supervised learning problem, as applicable:

- Data Acquisition and Cleaning;
- Feature Engineering and Scaling;
- Model Fitting (Training) and Feature Selection;
- Model Selection;
- Model Performance Assessment; and

Model Implementation

We discuss these aspects a little more in detail.

Data Cleaning and Breakdown of Data

We realize that real-world data is often messy, with missing values, varied formatting, duplicated records, etc. We have all experienced it even with collecting simple data from a class of students. Did they use lbs. or did they use kg in their weights? Data obtained from unknown sources or over the internet might require considerable time reformatting for computer use. For most supervised learning problems, data acquisition and cleaning will end with the data stored in a two-dimensional table where the rows of the table represent observations and the columns represent the features of those observations. For supervised learning problems, at least one column must represent the response variable or class (the item that will be predicted). This response variable is often referred to as the dependent variable in statistical regression and as the target variable in machine learning. The forecasting model can be stated using the mathematical relationship:

y (the response variable) =f(x, the predictors).

In general, data needs to be divided into training, validation and test sets. The training set is for model construction, the validation set is to tune the parameters, if any, and the test set is to check the model effectiveness.

Feature Engineering

Feature engineering is a heuristic process of creating new input features for the machine-learning problem. It is considered as an effective approach to improving predictive models since it helps isolate key information; introduce valuable patterns via domain knowledge. However, this topic is quite open ended; and thus, it will not be explored in details in this chapter. Note that for many problems, feature engineering might be worth exploring.

Model Fitting

Regression (adapted from Fox, et al, 2019)

In general, we suggest using the following steps in regression analysis.

Step 1. Enter the data *(x, y), obtain a scatterplot of the data,* and note the trends.
Step 2. If necessary, transform the data into "y" and "x" components.
Step 3. Build or compute the regression Equation. Obtain all the output. Interpret the ANOVA output for *R^2, F-test, and P-values for coefficients.*
Step 4. Plot the regression function and the data to obtain a visual fit.
Step 5. Compute the predictions, the residuals, percent relative error as described later.
Step 6. Insure the predictive results passes the common sense test.
Step 7. Plot the residual versus prediction to determine model adequacy.

We discuss several methods to check for model adequacy. First, we suggest your predictions pass the "common sense" test. If not, return to your regression model as we shown with our exponential decay model. The residual plot is also very revealing. Figure three shows possible residual plot results where only random patterns indicate model adequacy from the residual plot perspective shown in figure 2. Linear, curve, or fanning trend indicate a problem in the regression model. Affix and Azen (1979) have a good and useful discussion on corrective action based upon trends found. Percent relative error also provides information about how well the model approximates the original values and it provides insights into where the model fits well and where it might not fit well. We define the percent relative error with Equation (1),

$$\%RE = \frac{100\left|y_a - y_p\right|}{y_a} \tag{1}$$

where y_a is the observed value and y_p is the predicted value.

Simple Least Squares Regression

The method of least-squares curve fitting, also known as **ordinary least squares** and **linear regression**, is simply the solution to a model that minimizes the sum of the squares of the deviations between the observations and predictions. Least squares will find the parameters of the function, *f(x)* that will minimize the sum of squared differences between the real data and the proposed model, shown in Equation (2).

$$\text{Minimize } SSE = \sum_{i=1}^{n}(y_i - f(x_i))^2 \tag{2}$$

The use of technology: Excel, R, MINITAB, JUMP, MAPLE, MATLAB are a few software packages that will perform regression.

Figure 2. Patterns for residuals (a) no pattern (b) curved pattern (c) outliers (d) fanning pattern (e) linear trend

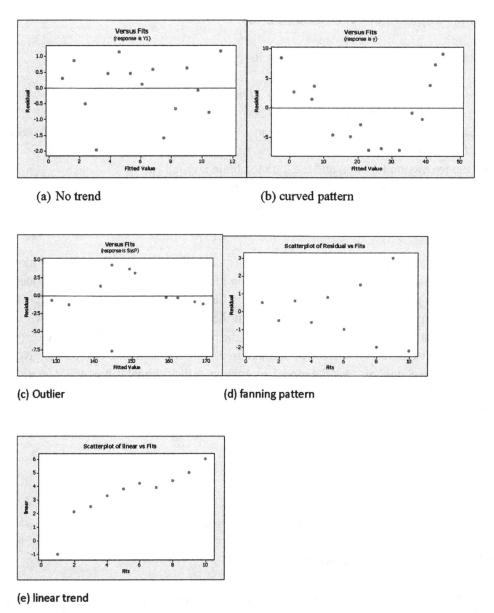

(a) No trend

(b) curved pattern

(c) Outlier

(d) fanning pattern

(e) linear trend

Example 1. Regression of recoil data (adapted from Fox et al, 2019)

We can then perform simple linear regression on this recoil data and produce tables presenting coefficient estimates and a range of diagnostic statistics to evaluate how well the model fits the data provided.

We visualize this estimated relationship by overlaying the fitted line to the spring data plot. This plot shows that the trend line estimated by the linear model fits the data quite well as shown in Figure 3. The relationship between R^2 and the linear correlation coefficient ρ is that $R^2 = (\rho)^2$.

Table 1.

	Estimate	Std. Error	t Value	Pr(>|t|)
x	0.001537	1.957e-05	78.57	4.437e-14
(Intercept)	0.03245	0.006635	4.891	0.0008579

Table 2. Fitting linear model: y ~ x

Observations	Residual Std. Error	R^2	Adjusted R^2
11	0.01026	0.9985	0.9984

Table 3. Analysis of variance table

	Df	Sum Sq	Mean Sq	F Value	Pr(>F)
x	1	0.6499	0.6499	6173	4.437e-14
Residuals	9	0.0009475	0.0001053	NA	NA

Exponential Decay Modeling

Introducing hospital recovery data from a typical hospital (data from Neter et al. 1996, Fox et al. 2019). The data that we use is provided in Table 4.

Plotting the table of recovery data shows that once again, the structure of the data is amenable to statistical analysis. We have two columns, T (number of days in the hospital) and Y (estimated recovery

Figure 3. Regression plot of spring data

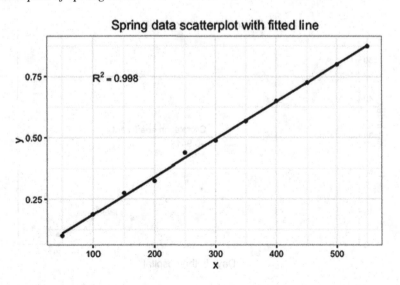

Table 4. Patient recovery time

T	2	5	7	10	14	19	26	31	34	338	45	52	53	60	65
y	54	50	45	37	35	25	20	16	18	13	8	11	8	4	6

index) and we want to generate a model that predicts how well a patient will recover as a function of the time they spend in the hospital. Using Excel we can compute the correlation coefficient of $\rho = -0.941$.

Once again, creating a scatter plot, Figure 4, of the data helps to visualize how closely the estimated correlation value matches the overall trend in the data.

In this example, we will demonstrate linear regression, polynomial regression, and then exponential regression in order to obtain a useful model.

Linear Regression of Hospital Recovery Data

It definitely appears that there is a strong negative relationship: the longer a patient spends in the hospital, the lower their recovery index. Next, we fit an OLS model to the data to estimate the magnitude of the linear relationship.

OLS modeling shows that there is a negative and statistically significant relationship between time spent in the hospital and patient recovery index. However, ordinary least-squares regression may not be the best choice in this case for two reasons. First, we are dealing with real-world data: a model that can produce (for example) negative estimates of recovery index is not applicable to the underlying concepts our model is dealing with. Second, the assumption of OLS, like all linear models, is that the magnitude of the relationship between input and output variables stays constant over the entire range of values in the data. However, visualizing the data suggests that this assumption may not hold --- in fact, it appears

Figure 4. Scatterplot of days in the hospital and recovery index

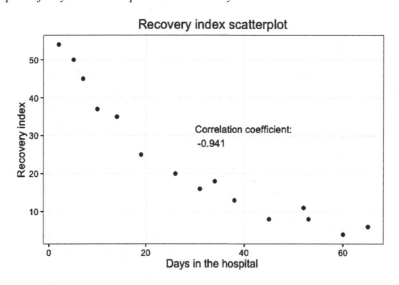

Table 5.

	Estimate	Std. Error	t Value	Pr(>|t|)
T	-0.7525	0.07502	-10.03	1.736e-07
(Intercept)	46.46	2.762	16.82	3.335e-10

Table 6. Fitting linear model: Y ~ T

Observations	Residual Std. Error	R^2	Adjusted R^2
15	5.891	0.8856	0.8768

that the magnitude of the relationship is very high for low values of *T* and decays somewhat for patients who spend more days in the hospital.

To test for this phenomenon, we examine the residuals of the linear model. Residuals analysis can provide quick visual feedback about model fit and whether the relationships estimated hold over the full range of the data. We calculate residuals as the difference between observed values *Y* and estimated values Y^*, or $Y_i - Y_i^*$. We then normalize residuals as percent relative error between the observed and estimated values, which helps us compare how well the model predicts each individual observation in the data set:

These data can also be plotted to visualize how well the model fits over the range of our input variable. The residuals can be plotted and willshow a curvilinear pattern, decreasing and then increasing in magnitude over the range of the input variable. This means that we can likely improve the fit of the model by allowing for non-linear effects. Furthermore, the current model can make predictions that are substantively nonsensical, even if they were statistically valid. For example, our model predicts that after 100 days in the hospital, a patient's estimated recovery index value would be -29.79. This has no common sense, as the recovery index variable is always positive in the real world. By allowing for non-linear terms, perhaps we can also guard against these types of illogical predictions.

Quadratic Regression of Hospital Recovery Data

Note that including a quadratic term can be regarded as feature engineering, i.e., it modifies the model formula:

Table 7. Analysis of variance table

	Df	Sum Sq	Mean Sq	F Value	Pr(>F)
T	1	3492	3492	100.6	1.736e-07
Residuals	13	451.2	34.71	NA	NA

Table 8. Residual analysis

T	Y	Index	Predicted	Residuals	Pct_Relative_Error
2	54	1	44.96	9.04	16.74
5	50	2	42.7	7.3	14.60
7	45	3	41.19	3.81	8.47
10	37	4	38.94	-1.94	-5.24
14	35	5	35.93	-0.93	-2.66
19	25	6	32.16	-7.16	-28.64
26	20	7	26.9	-6.9	-34.50
31	16	8	23.13	-7.13	-44.56
34	18	9	20.88	-2.88	-16.00
38	13	10	17.87	-4.87	-37.46
45	8	11	12.6	-4.6	-57.50
52	11	12	7.33	3.67	33.36
53	8	13	6.58	1.42	17.75
60	4	14	1.31	2.69	67.25
65	6	15	-2.45	8.45	140.83

$$Y = \beta_0 + \beta_1 x + \beta_2 x^2$$

Fitting this model to the data produces separate estimates of the effect of T itself as well as the effect of T^2, the quadratic term.

Including the quadratic term improves model fit as measured by R^2 from 0.88 to 0.98 --- a sizable increase. To assess whether this new input variable deals with the curvilinear trend, as saw in the residuals from the first model, we now calculate and visualize the residuals from the quadratic model.

Table 9.

	Estimate	Std. Error	t Value	Pr(>|t|)
T	-1.71	0.1248	-13.7	1.087e-08
I(T^2)	0.01481	0.001868	7.927	4.127e-06
(Intercept)	55.82	1.649	33.85	2.811e-13

Table 10. Fitting linear model: Y ~ T + I(T^2)

Observations	Residual Std. Error	R^2	Adjusted R^2
15	2.455	0.9817	0.9786

Table 11. Analysis of variance table

	Df	Sum Sq	Mean Sq	F Value	Pr(>F)
T	1	3492	3492	579.3	1.59e-11
I(T^2)	1	378.9	378.9	62.84	4.127e-06
Residuals	12	72.34	6.029	NA	NA

Again, a residual plot can be obtained and it will show that the trend has disappeared. This means that we can assume the same relationship holds whether $T = 1$ or $T = 100$. However, we are still unsure if the model produces numerical estimates that pass the common-sense test. The simplest way to assess this is to generate predicted values of the recovery index variable using the quadratic model, and plot them to see if they make sense.

To generate predicted values in R, we can pass the quadratic model object to the **predict()** function along with a set of hypothetical input values. In other words, we can ask the model what the recovery index would look like for a set of hypothetical patients who spend anywhere from zero to 120 days in the hospital.

We can then plot these estimates to conveniently access whether they pass the common-sense test for real-world predictive values as shown in Figure 5.

The predicted values curve up toward infinity (see Figure 5); clearly, this is a problem. The quadratic term we included in the model leads to unrealistic estimates of recovery index at larger values of T. Not only is this unacceptable for the context of our model, but it is unrealistic on its face. After all, we understand that people generally spend long periods in the hospital for serious or life-threatening condi-

Table 12. Residual analysis of quadratic model

T	Y	Index	Predicted	Residuals	Pct_Relative_Error
2	54	1	52.46	1.54	2.85
5	50	2	47.64	2.36	4.72
7	45	3	44.58	0.42	0.93
10	37	4	40.2	-3.2	-8.65
14	35	5	34.78	0.22	0.63
19	25	6	28.67	-3.67	-14.68
26	20	7	21.36	-1.36	-6.80
31	16	8	17.03	-1.03	-6.44
34	18	9	14.79	3.21	17.83
38	13	10	12.21	0.79	6.08
45	8	11	8.44	-0.44	-5.50
52	11	12	6.93	4.07	37.00
53	8	13	6.77	1.23	15.38
60	4	14	6.51	-2.51	-62.75
65	6	15	7.21	-1.21	-20.17

Figure 5. Polynomial regression plot (quadratic polynomial)

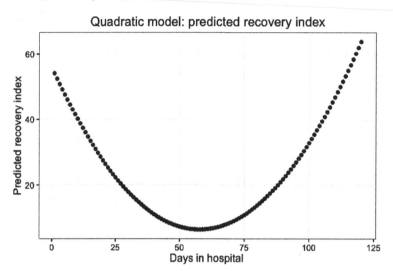

tions such as severe disease or major bodily injury. As such, we can assess that someone who spends six months in the hospital probably should not have a higher recovery index than someone who was only hospitalized for a day or two.

Exponential Decay Modeling of Hospital Recovery Data

We build a model that both accurately fits the data and produces estimates that pass the common-sense test by using an exponential decay model. This modeling approach lets us model relationships that vary over time in a non-linear fashion --- in this case, we want to accurately capture the strong correlation for lower ranges of T, but allow the magnitude of this relationship to decay as T increases, as the data seems to indicate.

Generating non-linear models in **R** is done using the non-linear least squares or NLS function, appropriately labeled **nls()**. This function automatically fits a wide range of non-linear models based on a functional form designated by the user. It is important to note that when fitting an NLS model in **R**, minimizing the sum of squares

$$\sum_{i=1}^{n}\left(y_i - a\left(\exp\left(bx_i\right)\right)\right)^2$$

is done computationally rather than analytically. That means that the choice of starting values for the optimization function is important --- the estimates produced by the model may vary considerably based on the chosen starting values (Fox, 2012). As such, it is wise to experiment when fitting these non-linear values to test how robust the resulting estimates are to the choice of starting values. We suggest using a ln-ln transformation of this data to begin with and then transforming back into the original xy space to obtain "good" estimates. The model, $ln(y)=ln(a)+bx$, yields $ln(y) = 4.037159-0.03797\,x$. This translates into the estimated model: $y=56.66512e^{(-.03797x)}$. Our starting values for (a,b) should be $(56.66512,-0.03797)$.

Table 13. Parameter estimates

a	b
58.61	-.03959

residual sum-of-squares: 1.951

This starting value can be found by performing linear regression on a ln-ln transformation of the model and converting back to the original space (see, Fox, 1993, 2012).

Fitting nonlinear regression model: $Y \approx a \cdot e^{bT}$

The final model is $y=58.61e^{-0.03959x}$. Overlaying the trend produced by the model on the plot of observed values (see Figure 6), we observe that the NLS modeling approach fits the data very well.

Once again, we can visually assess model fit by calculating and plotting the residuals. Figures 7a-7b, show the same residuals plotted along both days in the hospital T and recovery index Y.

In both cases we see that there is no easily distinguishable pattern in residuals. Finally, we apply the common-sense check by generating and plotting estimated recovery index values for a set of values of T from 1 to 120.

The predicted values generated by the exponential decay model make intuitive sense. As the number of days a patient spends in the hospital increases, the model predicts that their recovery index will decrease at a decreasing rate. This means that while the recovery index variable will continuously decrease, it will not take on negative values (as predicted by the linear model) or explosively large values (as predicted by the quadratic model). It appears that the exponential decay model not only fit the data best from a purely statistical point of view, but also generates values that pass the common-sense test to an observer or analyst shown in Figure 6.

Figure 6. Exponential regression model and data

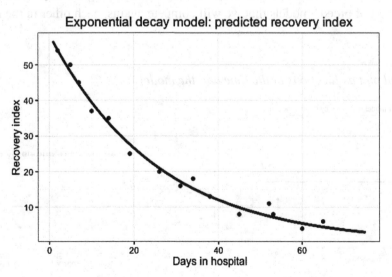

Table 14. Residual analysis of exponential model

T	Y	Index	Predicted	Residuals	Pct_Relative_Error
2	54	1	52.46	-0.14	-0.26
5	50	2	47.64	1.92	3.84
7	45	3	44.58	0.58	1.29
10	37	4	40.2	-2.44	-6.59
14	35	5	34.78	1.34	3.83
19	25	6	28.67	-2.62	-10.48
26	20	7	21.36	-0.93	-4.65
31	16	8	17.03	-1.17	-7.31
34	18	9	14.79	2.75	15.28
38	13	10	12.21	-0.01	-0.08
45	8	11	8.44	-1.86	-23.25
52	11	12	6.93	3.52	32.00
53	8	13	6.77	0.81	10.13
60	4	14	6.51	-1.45	-36.25
65	6	15	7.21	1.53	25.50

Sinusoidal Regression with Demand Data

Therefore, using regression techniques is much more than just running the model. Analysis of the results needs to be accomplished by analysts involved in the problem.

This involves a multi-step "contest" for choosing a model from the many (perhaps thousands when considering all the different combinations of features) available:

- Model Fitting: We fit and perform *feature selection* and parameter optimization for each of the modeling methods (algorithms) under consideration on a *training dataset*. The output of this step is a list of "best of breed" models that we will compete against each other in the next step.

Figure 7. Residual plot as functions of the time and the model

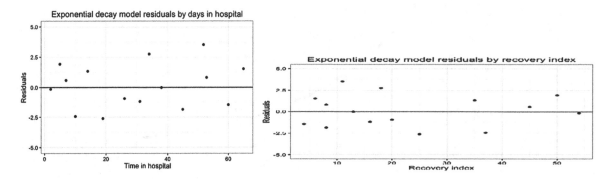

- Model (Algorithm) Selection: We compete the "best of breed" models against each other on an out-of-sample *validation dataset*. The best performing algorithm (on a range of criteria) is chosen for implementation.
- Model Performance Assessment: We assess the performance of our selected approach on an out-of-sample *test dataset*. This gives us an unbiased estimate for how well the algorithm will perform in practice.
- Model (Algorithm) Implementation: The selected algorithm is applied to the full dataset (i.e. training, validation, and test datasets, now combined) so that the model we deploy uses all available information

Training, testing and validation are key aspects as well as error analysis.

According to Huddleston et al (2018) "In the context of time series forecasting, we make a clear distinction between a prediction and a forecast. A prediction is defined as an assertion (often probabilistic) that a specific event will take place whereas a forecast is an assertion of how much of something will occur over a specified geographic area and period of time. In this context, the nightly weather "forecast" might include a prediction about the high temperature for the following day and a forecast for the amount of rain. We provide a brief discussion of some frequently used approaches here and recommend forecasting techniques.

Time Series Models

Time series model fitting is similar in many ways to predictive regression modeling but is unique in that previous observations of the response variable are often the most important predictive feature for the forecast. The statistical term for this use of previous observations of the response variable is *autoregression.*(*Box et al, 0* Fitting time series models often involves modeling the four components of a time series: the *trend*, *seasonality effects* (rises and falls in the data on a fixed pattern, often due to the effects of weather), *cycles* (rises and falls in the data that fall outside of a fixed pattern), and *noise*.[35] Fitting and evaluating time series models also requires the use of rolling horizon design due to the time dependency inherent in these problems.

The three most common methods used for time series forecasting are *time series regression*, *exponential smoothing*, and *Auto-Regressive Integrated Moving Average (ARIMA) models*. Time series regression extends basic regression to include auto- regression against previous observations of the response variables. Time series regression also facilitates the use of other variables (i.e. another time series) as predictive features. For example, various studies have related temperature and weather effects to crime occurrence and so predicted temperature over the next week could be incorporated into a forecasting model using time series regression. ARIMA models extend basic auto-regressive modeling to account for trends and other effects.

Measure of effectiveness, especially for exponential smoothing in time series, according to MINITAB©19 are defined by the following, any of which can be minimized in an optimization procedure:

MAPE

Mean absolute percentage error (MAPE) measures the accuracy of fitted time series values. MAPE expresses accuracy as a percentage.

Formula

$$\frac{\sum \dfrac{y_i - \hat{y}_t}{y_t} \times 100\% \left(y \neq 0\right)}{n}$$

Notation

See Table 15.

MAD

Mean absolute deviation (MAD) measures the accuracy of fitted time series values. MAD expresses accuracy in the same units as the data, which helps conceptualize the amount of error.

Formula

$$\frac{\sum_{t=1}^{n} \left|y_t - \hat{y}_t\right|}{n}$$

Notation

See Table 16.

MSD

Mean squared deviation (MSD) is always computed using the same denominator, n, regardless of the model. MSD is a more sensitive measure of an unusually large forecast error than MAD.

Table 15.

Term	Description
y_t	actual value at time t
$\hat{y}_t$	fitted value
n	number of observations

Table 16.

Term	Description
y_t	actual value at time t
$\hat{y}_t$	fitted value
n	number of observations

Formula

$$\frac{\sum_{t=1}^{n} \left| y_t - \hat{y}_t \right|^2}{n}$$

Notation

See Table 17.

Exponential Smoothing

Exponential smoothing is a non-parametric technique that develops a forecast for the next period by using the immediately previous forecast and the immediately previous observation as the predictor variables according the following formula:

New Forecast = α(Previous Forecast) + (1 − α)(Observed Value).

The parameter α is a tuning parameter that places more weight either on the previous forecast or the previous observation, taking on values between 0 and 1. This model form results in a recursive relationship with previous forecasts, with the effects of previous forecasts decaying exponentially backwards in time. Hence the name for the algorithm. Fitting an exponential smoothing model is relatively simple and straightforward as it requires only the optimization of the weighting parameter a. Basic exponential smoothing has been extended to account for trend and seasonal effects in an algorithm but our examples will only be basic single term exponential smoothing. Good discussion is also in Box-Jenkins (1976).

We choose the best value for α so the value which results in the smallest MAPE, MAD, or MSE.

Table 17.

Term	Description
y_t	actual value at time t
$\hat{y}_t$	fitted value
n	number of observations

Table 18.

Time	yt	S(α=0.1)	Error	Error Squared
1	71			
2	70	71	-1.00	1.00
3	69	70.9	-1.90	3.61
4	68	70.71	-2.71	7.34
5	64	70.44	-6.44	41.47
6	65	69.80	-4.80	23.04
7	72	69.32	2.68	7.18
8	78	69.58	8.42	70.90
9	75	70.43	4.57	20.88
10	75	70.88	4.12	16.97
11	75	71.29	3.71	13.76
12	70	71.67	-1.67	2.79

Example 1. Let us illustrate this principle with an example. Consider the following data set consisting of 12 observations taken over time:

The sum of the squared errors (SSE) = 208.94. The mean of the squared errors (MSE) is the SSE /11 = 19.0.

The MSE was again calculated for α=0.5 and turned out to be 16.29, so in this case we would prefer an α of 0.5 or an α of 0.1. Can we do better? We could apply the proven trial-and-error method. This is an iterative procedure beginning with a range of α between 0.1 and 0.9. We determine the best initial choice for αand then search between α−Δ and α+Δ. We could repeat this perhaps one more time to find the best α to 3 decimal places. However, we can employ optimization on α.

In this case, α=0.9 is best with a MSE value of 12.9506, MSD is the Minitab plot in Figure 8.

But there are better search methods, such as the Leven-Marquardt or a gradient search procedure. These are nonlinear optimizing schemes that minimize the sum of squares of residuals (Fox, 2012). In general, most well designed statistical software programs should be able to find the value of α that minimizes the MSE. The plots in Figure 8 show the visual comparison.

Example 2. We optimize α for another example.

Using a program to optimize α involves machine learning techniques in this simple example.

We find the best α is 0.65621 with a MAD of 10.0824, seen from Figure 9. We graphically depict this using MINITAB and note that the MAD value is slightly different. We see a good fit with the Figure 10 from MINITAB.

Figure 8. Exponential smoothing plots with α=0.9

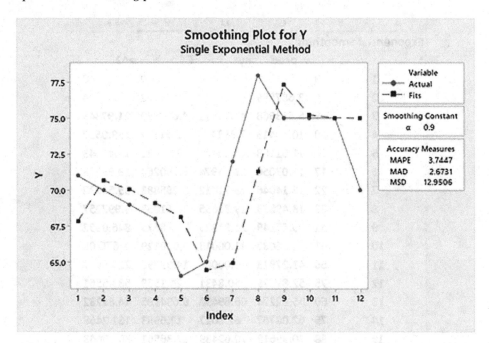

Autoregressive Integrated Moving Average (ARIMA)

ARIMA stands for auto-regressive integrated moving average and is specified by these three order parameters: *(p, d, q)*. The process of fitting an ARIMA model is sometimes referred to as the Box-Jenkins method. For more discussion, see Box-Jenkins (1976).

An auto regressive (AR(p)) component is referring to the use of past values in the regression equation for the series *Y*. The auto-regressive parameter *p* specifies the number of lags used in the model. For example, AR(2) or, equivalently, ARIMA(2,0,0), is represented as

Such a model has hyperparameters p, q and, d.

- p is the order of the AR model
- q is the order of the MA model
- d is the differencing order (how often we difference the data)

The ARMA and ARIMA combination is defined as

$$X_t = c + \varepsilon_t + \sum_{t=1}^{p}\varphi_i X_{t-i} + \sum_{i=1}^{q}\theta_i \epsilon_{t-i}$$

where φ_1, φ_2 are parameters for the model.

Figure 9. Screenshot from Excel

Exponential Smoothing

t	y	y_pred	ny	ϵ	e^2
1	3	3	3	0	0
2	5	3.687589	3	2	4
3	9	5.513968	4.312411	4.687589	21.97349
4	20	10.49419	7.388432	12.61157	159.0517
5	12	11.01188	15.66421	3.66421	13.42643
6	17	13.07056	13.25974	3.740264	13.98958
7	22	16.14046	15.71412	6.285883	39.51232
8	23	18.49873	19.83895	3.161053	9.992257
9	51	29.67249	21.91325	29.08675	846.0392
10	41	33.56683	41.00013	0.000129	1.67E-08
11	56	41.27923	41.00004	14.99996	224.9987
12	75	52.87225	50.8431	24.1569	583.5561
13	60	55.32274	66.69498	6.694985	44.82282
14	75	62.08767	62.3017	12.6983	161.2468
15	88	70.99619	70.63439	17.36561	301.5643
				141.1532	2424.174
				10.08237	173.1553
alpha	0.656205				

The *d* represents the degree of differencing in the **integrated** (*I(d)*) component. Differencing a series involves simply subtracting its current and previous values *d* times. Often, differencing is used to stabilize the series when the stationarity assumption is not met, which we will discuss below.

ARIMA methodology does have its limitations. These models directly rely on past values, and therefore work best on long and stable series. Also note that ARIMA simply approximates historical patterns and therefore does not aim to explain the structure of the underlying data mechanism.

We will not describe any further the ARIMA models and suggest the reader seeing the additional readings for more information.

Case Studies of Time Series Data

We use several data sets from the literature: one small data set, stock prices (MINITAB, 2019), and one larger data set, Walmart sales from Kaggle.com (Walmart Recruiting, n.d.).

Case Study 1: Typical Supply/Demand Shipping Data (Fox, et al, 2019)

Consider a situation where we have shipping data that we need to model to estimate future results.

First, we obtain the correlation, $\rho = 0.6725644$.

Figure 10. MINITAB graphical output

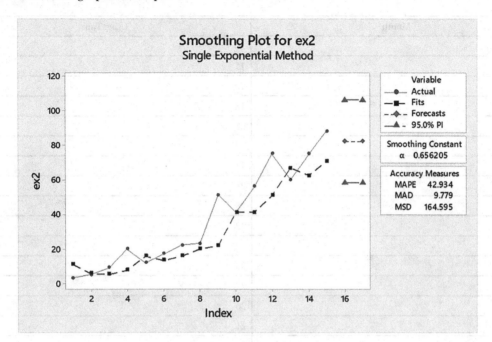

Once again, we can visualize the data in a scatter plot to assess whether this positive correlation is borne out by the overall trend.

Visualizing the data, Figure 11, we see that there is a clear positive trend over time in shipping usage. However, examining the data in more detail suggests that a simple linear model may not be best-suited to capturing the variation in these data. One way to plot more complex patterns in data is through the use of a trend line using polynomial or non-parametric smoothing functions.

Plotting a trend line generated via a spline function shows that there seems to be an oscillating pattern, Figure 12, with a steady increase over time in the shipping data.

Sinusoidal Regression of Shipping Data

R, as well as other software, treats sinusoidal regression models as part of the larger family of nonlinear least-squares (NLS) regression models. This means that we can fit a sinusoidal model using the same **nls**() function and syntax as we applied earlier for the exponential decay model. The functional form for the sinusoidal model we use here can be written as:

$$Usage = a * \sin\left(b * time + c\right) + d * time + e$$

This function can be expanded out trigonometrically as:

$$Usage = a * time + b * \sin\left(c * time\right) + d * \cos\left(c\left(time\right)\right) + e$$

Table 19.

Month	UsageTons
1	20
2	15
3	10
4	18
5	28
6	18
7	13
8	21
9	28
10	22
11	19
12	25
13	32
14	26
15	21
16	29
17	35
18	28
19	22
20	32

Figure 11. Scatterplot of shipping data

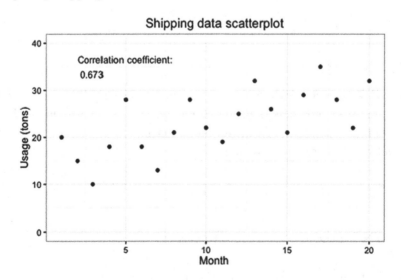

Figure 12. Shipping data with data points connected show an oscillating trend

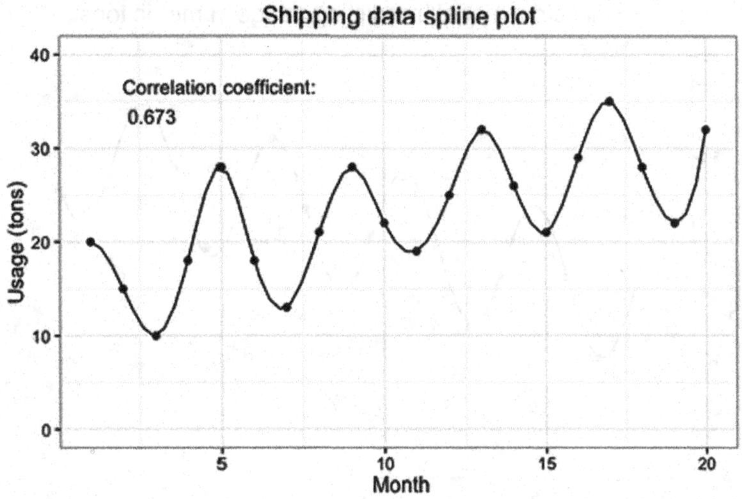

Shipping data spline plot

The preceding equation can be passed to **nls()** and **R** will computationally assess best-fit values for the $a, b, c, d,$ and e terms. It is worth stressing again the importance of selecting good starting values for this process, especially for a model like this one with many parameters to be simultaneously estimated. Here, we set starting values based on pre-analysis of the data. It is also important to note that because the underlying algorithms used to optimize these functions differ between Excel and R, the two methods produce models with different parameters but nearly identical predictive qualities. The model can be specified in **R** as follows.

Fitting nonlinear regression model:

$$UsageTons \sim a \cdot Month + b \cdot \sin(c \cdot Month + d \cdot \cos(c \cdot Month) + e$$

The model found is shown in Figure 13.

Plotting the trend line produced by the sinusoidal model shows that this modeling approach fits the data much better, Figure 13, accounting for both the short-term seasonal variation and the long-term increase in shipping usage.

Analysis of model residuals bears this out, and also highlights the difference in solving method between Excel and **R**. The model fitted in **R** has different parameter estimates and slightly worse model fit (average percent relative error of 3.26% as opposed to the 3.03% from the Excel-fitted model) but the overall trend identified in the data is virtually identical.

Table 20. Parameter estimates

a	b	c	d	e
0.848	6.666	1.574	0.5521	14.19

We have a residual sum-of-squares: 1.206

Figure 13. Overlay of regression model and data

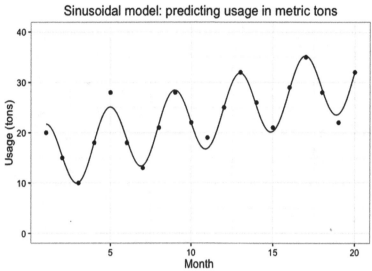

Table 21. Residual analysis

Month	Usage Tons	Predicted	Residuals	Pct_Relative_Error
1	20	21.7	-1.7	-8.50
2	15	15.29	-0.29	-1.93
3	10	10.07	-0.07	-0.70
4	18	18.2	-0.2	-1.11
5	28	25.08	2.92	10.43
6	18	18.61	-0.61	-3.39
7	13	13.47	-0.47	-3.62
8	21	21.67	-0.67	-3.19
9	28	28.47	-0.47	-1.68
10	22	21.93	0.07	0.32
11	19	16.87	2.13	11.21
12	25	25.13	-0.13	-0.52
13	32	31.85	0.15	0.47
14	26	25.25	0.75	2.88
15	21	20.67	0.33	1.57
16	29	28.59	0.41	1.41
17	35	35.24	-0.24	-0.69
18	28	28.57	-0.57	-2.04
19	22	23.67	-1.67	-7.59
20	32	32.06	-0.06	-0.19

Figure 14. Exponential smoothing of supply/demand data

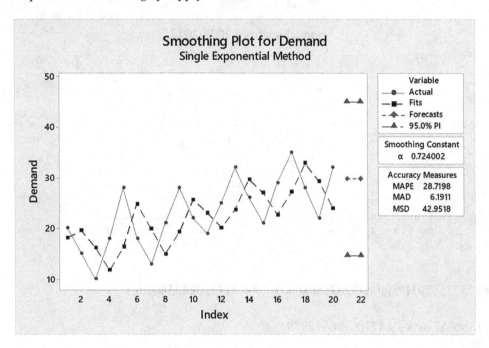

Time Series With Exponential Smoothing

We apply the exponential smoothing model for a single exponential smoothing. We optimize for α. We use the Solver and find the optimal α value is 0.724002. We find the best α is 0.724002 and the optimal MAD is 5.10935, optimizing is done in Excel. Figure 14 from MINITAB shows the relative accuracy. Again, we note the slight differences between Excel's measures and MINITAB's.

We estimate the next time permit and obtain a value of 27.90505. After the next time period arrives, we can compare to our estimates to determine which model does better and (perhaps) use that model for the next time period estimate.

Case Study 2: Homicides in Hampton VA Future Predictions
(Source: Daily Press, Hampton, Virginia, March 4, 2018)

Data was provided in a story in the Daily Press concerning homicides in Hampton VA and Newport News VA. The purpose was to provide comparative information and not to predict anything. However, let's analyze the homicide data in Hampton and try to forecast the number of homicides at least in 2018.

First, we plot the time series and then we plotted the data from 2003-2017 as displayed in figure 15.

We first use moving average ARIMA model to forecast the future. We train with the data from 2003-2016 and test with the data point from 2017 since the 2018 data is not yet available. Our ARIMA model predicts 20 homicides and we had only 17 in Hampton. The percent relative error is 17.6%.

Next, we use sine regression in MAPLE to model and predict. Even varying our initial inputs estimates we obtain the same sine regression model (see Figure 16) as:

Figure 15. Time series plot of homicide data

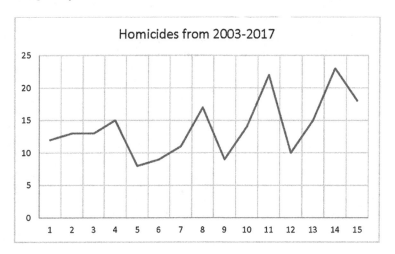

y= -3.97687527582931*sin(4.33262380863333*x+.514250245580131)

+.524461138685776*x+9.47706296518979

Using sine regression our percent relative absolute error is 8.55%. In this case the regression model was slightly better in predicting over the ARIMA model.

Figure 16. Screenshot from MAPLE's output

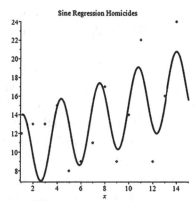

Figure 17. Plot of Walmart data

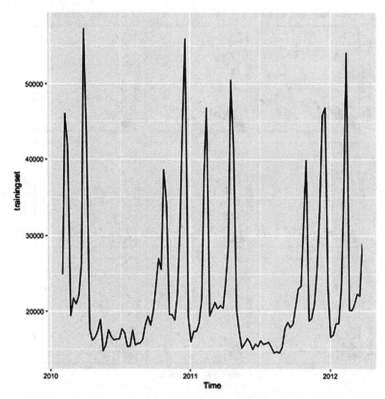

Case Study 3: Walmart Demand with One Store

We work with historical sales data for 45 Walmart stores located in different regions available on Kaggle. com. For demonstration, we only show performance for weekly demand forecasting of a single store from this dataset using the automatic forecast package in R. In total, there are 143 weeks of data, starting from 2010-02-05 to 2012-10-26. We use 113 weeks as the training set and 30 weeks as the test set.

To visualize the weekly demand time-series, we use the following time plot., Figure 7.17 and the autocorreltation plots in figure 7.18.

Next, we plot the autocorrelation, Figure 18. Each graph shows D_t plotted against D_{t-k} for different values of k. Recall that the autocorrelations are the correlations associated with these scatterplots. Together, the autocorrelations at lags 1, 2, . . ., constitute the autocorrelation function plot or ACF. The training data plot is shown in Figure 7.19

First, we are applying three simple forecasting methods to the dataset and report four different measures of forecasting accuracy.

1. **Mean method:** Forecast of all future demands is equal to mean of historical data (Box 1).
2. **Naive method:** Forecasts equal to last observed demand (Box 2).
3. **Drift method:** Forecasts equal to last demand plus average change. This method is equivalent to extrapolating the line between the first and last observations (Box 3).

Figure 18. Autocorrelation plots

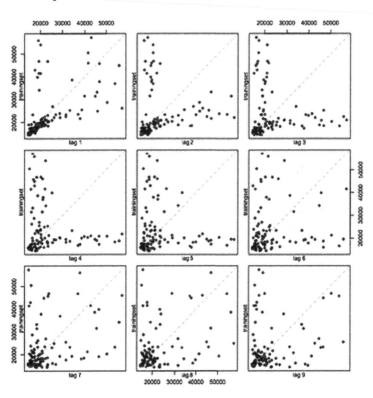

Figure 19. Series training set data plot

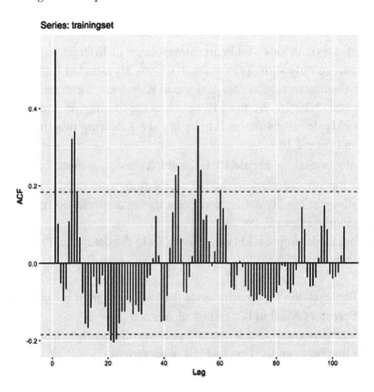

Box 1.

	RMSE	MAE	MAPE	MASE
Training set	10147.859	7453.852	30.89842	1.404549
Test set	8589.083	6512.135	31.99593	1.227098

Box 2.

	RMSE	MAE	MAPE	MASE
Training set	9620.207	5306.938	20.85188	1.000000
Test set	11965.421	11179.685	60.01608	2.106617

Box 3.

	RMSE	MAE	MAPE	MASE
Training set	9620.14	5299.117	20.82762	0.9985264
Test set	12427.93	11729.988	62.98930	2.2103119

Next, we use the ***ets*** package from R., which implements the innovations state space models for exponential smoothing developed by Rob Hyndman (Hyndman and Athanasopoulos, 2018). In summary, this package selects the best exponential smoothing models out of roughly 30 different models. We obtain a plot, Figure 20.

Next, we use the ARIMA model from R. The auto.arima function fit the best ARIMA model to any univariate time series data and the plot is shown in Figure 21.

Compared to the all the methods so far, ARIMA has the best performance in all performance metric. We also perform a post-analysis of residuals, see figure 22.

Finally, we fit a neural network to the time-series data. It also has quite competitive performance. We see the plot in Figure 23.

CONCLUSION

As has been shown in the many examples in this chapter, training machines (i.e. computers) to "learn" via the application of algorithmic modeling has a wide variety of very diverse applications. This chapter has also demonstrated that even though the algorithmic procedures employed to "fit" these models can be automated to a certain extent, the machines still require significant input from analysts for their "training". While individual machine learning algorithms provide a framework for approaching a particular class of problem, choosing the right machine learning algorithm for any particular problem is a highly complex and iterative process that requires significant expertise, judgement, and often the active participation of domain experts and users of your results. Often, for best results, multiple machine learning algorithms, as well as best practices for data storage, data engineering, and computing will be needed. Practitioners are well advised to algorithmically model in teams that incorporate statisticians, operations research analysts, computer scientists, data engineers, data scientists, and domain experts to form a comprehensive unit dedicated to training the machines to "learn" to solve the right problems in best way.

In modeling the analyst must know the purpose of the model. Is it to predict the short term, predict in the long term, interpolate, or just estimate? In other words, how accurate must our model be. All these answers affect the modeling choice we make for analyzing the data in any forecasting situations.

Figure 20. R's plot and forecasts

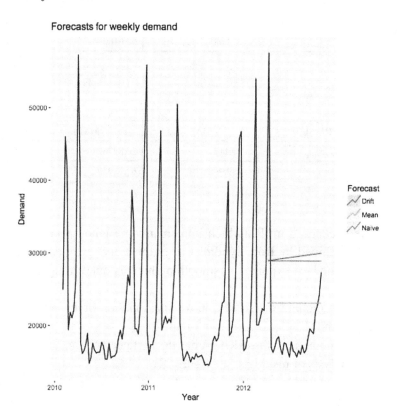

Box 4.

	RMSE	MAE	MAPE	MASE
Training set	9578.881	5275.023	20.72777	0.9939861
Test set	11964.911	11179.090	60.01260	2.1065048

Box 5.

	RMSE	MAE	MAPE	MASE
Training set	4502.625	2191.082	9.008531	0.4128712
Test set	8797.632	4017.068	19.315153	0.7569465

Figure 21. Arima plot

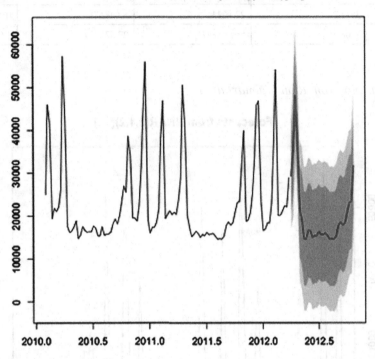

Figure 22. Best Arima plot

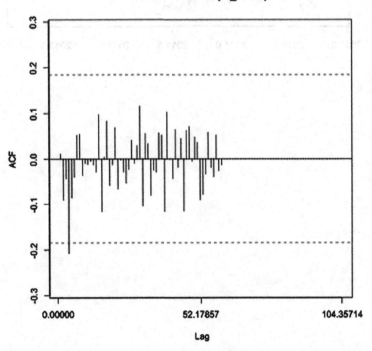

Box 6.

	RMSE	MAE	MAPE	MASE
Training set	3815.251	2208.116	8.647171	0.4160809
Test set	7108.422	5454.581	27.527417	1.0278208

Figure 23. Forecasts plot from R on Walmart data

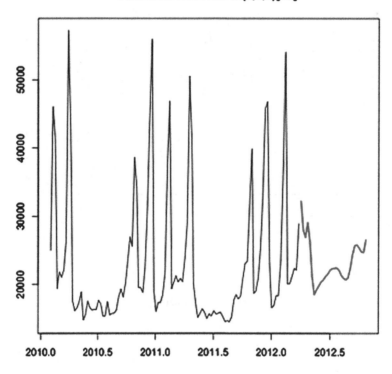

REFERENCES

Affi, A., & Azen, S. (1979). *Statistical Analysis* (2nd ed.). London, UK: Academic press.

Box, G., & Jenkins, G. (1976). *Time series analysis: forecast and control*. Hoboken, NJ: John Wiley & Sons.

Breiman, L. (2001). Statistical Modeling: The Two Cultures. *Statistical Science, 16*(3), 199–231. doi:10.1214s/1009213726

Devore, J. (2012). *Probability and Statistics for Engineering and the Sciences* (8th ed.). Belmont, CA: Cengage Publisher.

Fox, W. P. (1993). The Use of Transformed Least Squares in Mathematical Modeling. *Computers in Education Journal, III*(1), 25–31.

Fox, W. P. (2011). Using Excel for nonlinear regression. *COED Journal, 2*(4), 77–86.

Fox, W.P. (2011). Using the EXCEL Solver for Nonlinear Regression. *Computers in Education Journal, 2*(4), 77-86.

Fox, W. P. (2012). *Mathematical Modeling with Maple*. Boston, MA: Cengage Publishers.

Fox, W. P. (2012). Issues and Importance of "Good" Starting Points for Nonlinear regression for Mathematical Modeling with Maple: Basic Model Fitting to Make Predictions with Oscillating Data. *Journal of Computers in Mathematics and Science Teaching, 31*(1), 1–16.

Fox, W. P. (2012). Importance of "good" starting points in nonlinear regression in mathematical modeling in Maple. *JCMST, 31*(1), 1–16.

Fox, W. P. (2018). *Mathematical Modeling for Business Analytics*. Boca Raton, Fl.: CRC Press.

Fox, W. P., & Christopher, F. (1996). Understanding Covariance and Correlation. *PRIMUS (Terre Haute, Ind.), VI*(3), 235–244. doi:10.1080/10511979608965826

Fox, W. P., & Hammond, J. (2019). Advanced Regression Models: Least Squares, Nonlinear, Poisson and Binary Logistics Regression Using R. Data Science and Digital Business, 221-262.

Giordano, F., Fox, W., & Horton, S. (2013). *A First Course in Mathematical Modeling* (5th ed.). Boston, MA: Cengage Publishers.

Huddleston, S., & Brown, G. . (2018). INFORMS Analytics Body of Knowledge. John Wiley & Sons and Naval Postgraduate School updated notes.

Hyndman, R., & Athanasopoulos, A. (2018). *Forecasting: principles and practices* (2nd ed.). OTexts. Retrieved from https://otexts.com/fpp2/ets.html

Johnson, I. (2012). *An Introductory Handbook on Probability, Statistics, and Excel*. Retrieved from http://records.viu.ca/~johnstoi/maybe/maybe4.htm

MINITAB ©. (2019). Retrieved from https://support.minitab.com/en-us/minitab/18/help-and-how-to/graphs/how-to/time-series-plot/before-you-start/example/

Neter, J., Kutner, M., Nachtsheim, C., & Wasserman, W. (1996). Applied Linear Statistical Models (4th ed.). Irwin Press.

Walmart Recruiting - Store Sales Forecasting. (n.d.). Retrieved from https://www.kaggle.com/c/walmart-recruiting-store-sales-forecasting/data

Chapter 7
Modern Statistical Modeling in Machine Learning and Big Data Analytics:
Statistical Models for Continuous and Categorical Variables

Niloofar Ramezani

George Mason University, USA

ABSTRACT

Machine learning, big data, and high dimensional data are the topics we hear about frequently these days, and some even call them the wave of the future. Therefore, it is important to use appropriate statistical models, which have been established for many years, and their efficiency has already been evaluated to contribute into advancing machine learning, which is a relatively newer field of study. Different algorithms that can be used within machine learning, depending on the nature of the variables, are discussed, and appropriate statistical techniques for modeling them are presented in this chapter.

INTRODUCTION

Machine learning is an important topic these days as it involves a set of many different methods and algorithms that are suited to answer diverse questions about a business or problem. Therefore, choosing an algorithm is a critical step in the machine learning process to ensure it truly fits the solution proposed in answering a problem at hand (Segal, 2004). To better understand machine learning algorithms and when each algorithm needs to be used, it is helpful to understand them within the framework of statistics and separate them into two main groups based on the data and the format of their outcomes. These two types of machine learning methods are classification and regression for categorical and continuous response variables, respectively. Within this book chapter, we will differentiate these two types and mention related algorithms and statistical techniques that can be used to answer real world problems.

DOI: 10.4018/978-1-7998-0106-1.ch007

Then the concept of high-dimensional data and some of the methods that are appropriate for handling such data will be discussed.

An outline of the sections and subsections within this chapter are discussed below. First, the continuous approaches are discussed and regression algorithm and regression algorithm, as the most commonly used approach for such scenarios, is explained. Such methods help modeling the continuous response variables. On the other hand, generalized linear models and classification techniques assist researchers to model discrete, binary, and categorical responses. While discussing the statistical models, which are appropriate in predicting the categorical response variables, binary logistic regression as well as multinomial and ordinal logistic regression models are introduced and discussed here. These models can assist researchers and applied practitioners in modeling binary and categorical response variables. Within the section that discusses ordinal logistic models, different logit models are briefly discussed. These logit functions are cumulative logit, adjacent-categories logit, and continuation-ratio logit.

The next section of this chapter is dedicated to introducing and discussing dimension reduction methods. Dimension reduction techniques applied within the two classification and regression algorithms, paired with the analytically powerful computers, will assist researchers in handling data sets with higher dimensions of variables and observations efficiently within a reasonable timeline. Different models to address each set of techniques are introduced in this chapter to provide different statistical and research tools that can be used by researchers and practitioners in machine learning and data analysis. Selected dimension reduction methods are discussed in this chapter. These subsections are principal components analysis, decision trees and their use in building random forest, regression decision trees and random forest for continuous responses, classification decision trees and random forest for categorical responses, LASSO and ridge regression, and finally cluster analysis.

This chapter adopts an introductory and educational approach, rather than rushing into the programming or data analysis details, to familiarize the readers with different data scenarios and the proper statistical and machine learning algorithms to appropriately model the data. The author believes the first step in ensuring the quality, correctness, and reliability of any quantitative analysis is to learn about the characteristics of the data, by exploring them, and then choosing the proper statistical and machine learning approach to model the data. Years of teaching statistics, data analytics, and quantitative methodology, as well as providing statistical consultation, have taught the author the importance of strengthening the foundations of statistical knowledge of students, clients, or data analysts before diving into running codes and printing output to ensure the accuracy of the results. This chapter is meant to educate the readers about the correct modeling options to minimize the chances of choosing the wrong methods of data analysis while exploring and modeling real-world data.

CONTINUOUS DATA

When dealing with continuous data and predicting such outcome measures, regression approaches and algorithms can be used. Linear regression is by far the simplest and most popular example of a regression algorithm used in many fields. Though it is often underrated due to its simplicity, it is a flexible prediction tool. Regression trees and support vector regressions are more advanced algorithms within the framework of regression that can be used for high dimensions of data.

Regression

Every machine learning problem is an optimization problem. This means we want to find either a maximum or a minimum of a specific function of predictors and responses. This function is usually called the loss function, which is defined for each machine learning algorithm we use. A regression function can be optimized using the same procedure. Linear regression is widely used in different supervised machine learning problems and focuses on regression problem. Linear regression uses the optimization technique in linear programming. This means linear regression is generally considered as an optimization problem. Concepts such as regression help with investigating and establishing a relationship between the vast amounts of data required for learning through the relationships that exist among different variables in a model. If we have an explanatory or predictor variable and a response variable, we would like to make predictions of the expected values of the response variable based on the observed values of the explanatory variable. If we fit a line to the data, which is called regression line if it is the best and most optimal fit, then we can use this line's equation in predicting the response variable by estimating the coefficients of the regression model. This is achievable by executing an iterative process that updates the coefficients, which are now considered the parameters of the model, at every step by reducing the loss function as much as possible. Once we reach the minimum point of the loss function, we can say that we have completed the iterative process and estimated the parameters.

For the simple linear regression model, we use only one predictor variable to predict the response. In this case, we will end up with two coefficients; the intercept and the slope. Within multiple linear regression, we can have multiple predictors that together they can explain a higher amount of the variation of the response. The multiple regression model can be written as below,

$$Y = \beta_0 + \beta_1 X_1 + \beta_2 X_2 + \beta_3 X_3 + ... + \beta_k X_k + \epsilon,$$

Where Y is the response, $X_1, X_2, ..., X_k$ are k predictors, β_0 is the intercept of the regression line, $\beta_1, \beta_2, ..., \beta_k$ are the slopes, and ϵ is the random error term.

In order to solve the linear regression problem, we will use the same iterative algorithm and minimize the loss function. The main difference will be that we will end up with multiple β coefficients instead of only two, which was the case for a simple linear regression. Least square estimation is the most common algorithm, and one of the most efficient techniques, used to minimize the loss function and estimate the best coefficients for the regression model (Montgomery, Peck & Vining, 2012). Many assumptions need to be checked before fitting the regression model to the data which is not the main focus of this chapter. For more details on the regression assumptions and how to fit a regression model, see Montgomery et al. (2012). We also recommend reading chapters 2 and 3 of "The elements of statistical learning" book by Friedman, Hastie, and Tibshirani (2001) to learn more about structured regression models within supervised learning and linear methods for regression, respectively. Chapter 3 of "An introduction to statistical learning with application in R" by James, Witten, Hastie, and Tibshirani (2013) provides examples and applications of regression. Applications of this method can be found in almost any field.

CATEGORICAL DATA

When dealing with categorical outcomes, the assumption of normality is not met and therefore, the linear regression approaches cannot be fitted to such data anymore. Additionally, the relationship between the response variable and predictors is no longer linear, hence more advanced models than linear approaches need to be adopted to appropriately model this nonlinear relationship. Binary, multinomial, and ordinal logistic regression approaches are some examples of the robust predictive methods to use for modeling the relationship between non-normal discrete response and the predictors. Readers can consult Ramezani and Ramezani (2016) that discusses multiple methods and algorithms to fit predictive models to non-continuous non-normal responses. Agresti (2007) is another resource that is recommended if readers are interested in learning more details regarding such techniques. These methods are briefly discussed below.

Binary classification in machine learning will model binary responses while multi-label classification captures everything else, and is useful for customer segmentation, audio and image categorization, and text analysis for mining customer sentiment (James, Witten, Hastie & Tibshirani, 2013). Algorithms like naive Bayes, decision trees, logistic regression, kernel approximation, and K-nearest neighbors are among the methods that can be used within this framework. Within this chapter, these models will be expanded and tools for fitting such models will be provided. We briefly discuss two of the most important models within logistic regression in this chapter.

Binary Logistic Regression

Logistic regression allows one to form a multiple regression relation between a dependent variable and several independent variables. Logistic regression is useful for predicting the presence or absence of a characteristic or outcome based on values of a set of predictor variables. The advantage of logistic regression is that, through the addition of an appropriate link function to the usual linear regression model, the variables may be either continuous or discrete, or any combination of both types and they do not necessarily have normal distributions. Where the dependent variable is binary, the logit link function is applicable (Atkinson & Massari, 1998). Logistic regression coefficients can be used to estimate ratios for each of the independent variables in the model (Lee, 2005).

Quantitatively, the relationship between the occurrence and its dependency on several variables can be expressed as:

$$p = 1 \Big/ {1 + e^{-z}},$$

where p is the probability of an event occurring. The probability varies from 0 to 1 on an S-shaped curve and z is the linear combination. It follows that logistic regression involves fitting an equation of the following form to the data:

$$z = \beta_0 + \beta_1 X_1 + \ldots + \beta_k X_k,$$

where β_0 is the intercept of the model, the

$$\beta_i \left(i = 0, 1, 2, \ldots, k \right)$$

are the slope coefficients of the logistic regression model, and the

$$X_i \left(i = 0, 1, 2, \ldots, k \right)$$

are the independent variables.

In logistic regression, probability of the outcome is measured by the odds of occurrence of an event. Change in probability is not constant (linear) with constant changes in X. This means that the probability of a success (Y = 1) given the predictor variable (X) is a non-linear function, specifically a logistic function.

The most common form of logistic regression uses the logit link function so it is easily understandable to show the logistic regression equation as

$$logit \left(p \right) = \beta_0 + \beta_1 X_1 + \ldots + \beta_k X_k.$$

Different methods are then applied to do the analysis of the logistic regression model, which are explained in detail in different books like Hosmer and Lemeshow (2013) and Agresti (2007). Application of this method can be found in different fields such as education and biology (Peffer & Ramezani, 2019), psychology and education (Cokluk, 2010), and geographical information system (Lee, 2005).

Ordinal Logistic Regression

Ordinal logistic regression models have been applied in recent years in analyzing data with ranked multiple response outcomes. Ordered information has been increasingly used in health indicators but their use in the public health is still rare (Abreu et al., 2009). This may be attributed to these models' complexity, assumptions validation, and limitations of modeling options offered by statistical packages (Lall, 2002).

The multinomial logistic regression model is an extension of the binomial logistic regression model. This type of model is used when the dependent variable has more than two nominal (unordered) categories. When the response categories are ordered, a multinomial regression model still can be used. According to Agresti (2007), the disadvantage is that some information about the ordering is thrown away. An ordinal logistic regression model preserves that information, but it is slightly more involved (Ramezani, 2015).

There are different logit functions such as Cumulative Logit, Adjacent–Categories Logit, and Continuation Ratio Logit which are used within regression models to provide useful extensions of the multinomial logistic model to ordinal response data. Each of these models are briefly explained below, based on the description of Ramezani (2015), and notations used in Agresti (2007).

Cumulative Logit Models

The cumulative logit function used in ordinal multinomial logistic models is as below which basically models categories $\leq j$ versus categories $> j$, where j is the cut-off point category decided by the data analyst or researcher based on the research question. This division dichotomizes the multiple categories that exists within each categorical response by aggregating the before and after categories at a certain point.

$$logit\left(P\left(Y \leq j\right)\right) = \log\left(\frac{P\left(Y \leq j\right)}{P\left(Y > j\right)}\right) = \log\left(\frac{P\left(Y \leq j\right)}{1 - P\left(Y \leq j\right)}\right)$$

$$= \log\left(\frac{\pi_1 + \cdots + \pi_j}{\pi_{j+1} + \cdots + \pi_J}\right), for\ j = 1, \cdots, J-1$$

Using this logit function, the cumulative logit based ordinal logistic regression model can be written as below

$$\log it\left(P\left(Y \leq j\right)\right) = \alpha_j + \sum_{k=1}^{K}\beta_k X_k.$$

Adjacent–Categories Logit Models

The adjacent-categories logit function used in ordinal multinomial logistic models is as below modeling two adjacent categories

$$\log\left(\frac{P\left(Y = j\right)}{P\left(Y = j+1\right)}\right) = \log\left(\frac{\pi_j}{\pi_{j+1}}\right).$$

Using this logit function, the adjacent-categories logit model is as below

$$\log\left(\frac{\pi_j}{\pi_{j+1}}\right) = \alpha_j + \sum_{k=1}^{K}\beta_k X_k.$$

Within this model, only adjacent categories will be used in odds resulting in using local odds ratios for interpretations, whereas within the cumulative logit models, the entire response scale is used for the model and cumulative odds ratio is used for their interpretation.

Continuation–Ratio Logit

The continuation-ratio logit function used in ordinal multinomial logistic models is as below

$$logit\left(\omega_j\left(X\right)\right) = \log\left(\frac{P\left(Y=j\right)}{P\left(Y \geq j+1\right)}\right)$$

$$= \log\left(\frac{\pi_j}{\pi_{j+1} + \cdots + \pi_J}\right), for\ j = 1,\cdots,J-1$$

where

$$\omega_j\left(X\right) = \frac{\pi_j\left(X\right)}{\pi_j\left(X\right) + \cdots + \pi_J\left(X\right)}.$$

Using this logit function, the continuation-ratio logit model is as below

$$logit\left(\omega_j\left(X\right)\right) = \alpha_j + \sum_{k=1}^{K}\beta_k X_k.$$

As described in Agresti (2007), this model is useful when a sequential mechanism determines the response outcome. Mechanisms like survival through various age periods would be suitable for such models. For more details and examples about the application of these models to real data see Ramezani (2016).

DIMENSION REDUCTION

When dealing with high dimensional data, methods such as principal component analysis, cluster analysis, discriminant analysis, and random forest are highly recommended (Wickham & Grolemund, 2016). Radom forest can be used for both categorical and continuous variables in two forms of classification random forest and regression random forest, respectively. Breiman (2001) proposed random forests, which uses decision trees. In addition to constructing each tree using a different bootstrap sample of the data, random forests change how the classification or regression trees are constructed to build the most optimal group of trees. This strategy turns out to perform very well compared to many other classifiers, including discriminant analysis, support vector machines and neural networks, and is robust against overfitting of the data (Liaw & Wiener, 2002).

Principal Component Analysis

Pearson (1901) and Hotelling (1933) introduced principal component analysis (PCA) to describe the variation in a set of multivariate data in terms of a set of uncorrelated variables. PCA is a variable dimension-reduction tool that can be used to reduce a large set of variables to a small set of new variables that still contains most of the information in the large set while reducing the dimension of the data. PCA is a mathematical procedure that transforms a number of correlated variables into a smaller number of uncorrelated variables called principal components. This will assist researchers with the multicollinearity issue that can negatively affect regular multiple linear regression models through creating a new set of uncorrelated variables. Multicollinearity happens when predictors are correlated with each other (Montgomery et al., 2012).

Among the newly created components of PCA, the first principal component accounts for as much of the variability in the data as possible, and each succeeding component accounts for as much of the remaining variability as possible.

Figure 1 shows a sample of a Scree plot, which is a widely used plot within PCA. Scree plots can list eigenvalues or percentage of variances as criteria of component selection. As seen on the following scree plot, the percentage of variance of the data explained by each component is listed on the Y-axis. The first principal component explains 42 percent of the variance, which is a significant amount of explained variation. This guarantees that this is the most important component, hence the first principal component, which should be kept in the model. The second principal component explains 18 percent of the variance, which in addition to the first one, these two principal components explain 60 percent of the model variation. Therefore, if someone wishes to ensure that 80 percent of variation is being captured, four components should be chosen and possibly used in future models. Of course, if the researchers are wishing to capture higher variation of the data, they would need to choose to keep higher number of components in their model.

The shape of scree plot and number of principal components, and how much variance each explains, vary in each data set but following the same steps can help researchers choose the appropriate number of principal components to use.

Within PCA, we typically have a data matrix of n observations on p correlated variables $x_1, x_2, \ldots x_p$. PCA looks for a transformation of the x_i into p new variables that are uncorrelated (Jolliffe, 2011). Principal component analysis is useful for finding new, more informative, uncorrelated features while reducing dimensionality by rejecting low variance features. One important point that should be considered by researchers is to make sure PCA is applied on data that have approximately the same scale in each variable.

For more details on this topic see Jolliffe (2011) and Wold, Esbensen, and Geladi (1987). "A user's guide to principal components" is another informative book by Jackson (2005) regarding PCA and its application, which we recommend reading. Chapter 8 of "Applied Multivariate Statistical Analysis" by Johnson and Wichern (2002) is another reference that provides more technical information about principal component analysis. Dunteman's book "Principal components analysis" shows interesting applications of PCA in social sciences (1989). Articles such as Raychaudhuri, Stuart, and Altman (1999) and Wiegleb (1980) provide examples of applications of PCA in microarray experiments within sporulation time series and ecological research, respectively.

Decision Trees and Random Forest

Random forest is an ensemble classifier that consists of many decision trees and outputs the class that is the mode of the class's output by individual trees. The term came from random decision forests, that was first proposed by Tin Kam Ho in 1995. The method combines Breiman's "bagging" idea and the random selection of features.

Figure 1. Scree plot using percentage of variances as component selection criterion

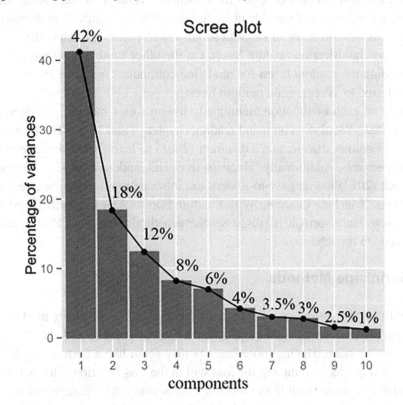

Decision trees, used in building random forests, are individual learners that are combined. They are one of the most popular learning methods commonly used for data exploration. We discuss some of the advantages of random forest here. It is one of the most accurate learning algorithms available. For many data sets, it produces a highly accurate classifier while running efficiently on large databases and handling thousands of input variables without variable deletion. It gives estimates of what variables are important in the classification. Additionally, it generates an internal unbiased estimate of the generalization error as the forest building progresses. Also, random forest has an effective method for estimating missing data and maintains accuracy when a large proportion of the data are missing. It has methods for balancing error in class population unbalanced data sets.

Generated forests can be saved for future use on other data. Moreover, prototypes are computed that give information about the relation between the variables and the classification. It computes proximities between pairs of cases that can be used in clustering, locating outliers, or give interesting views of the data by scaling. The capabilities of the above can be extended to unlabeled data, leading to unsupervised clustering, data views and outlier detection. Finally, it offers an experimental method for detecting variable interactions.

Some of the disadvantages of random forests are that they have been observed to overfit for some data sets with noisy classification or regression tasks. For data including categorical variables with different number of levels, random forests are biased in favor of those attributes with more levels. Therefore, the variable importance scores from random forest are not reliable for this type of data (Segal, 2004).

A tree is called a classification tree when the dependent variable is categorical and it is called a regression tree when the dependent variable is continuous. When classification decision trees are used while building the random forest for modeling categorical response variables, the respective random forest is referred to as classification random forest. On the other hand, when regression decision trees are used while building the random forest for modeling continuous response variables, the respective random forest is referred to as regression random forest.

For more details on each of the aforementioned random forest models, see Breiman (2001) and Liaw and Wiener (2002). We also recommend reading chapters 9 and 15 of "The elements of statistical learning" book by Friedman, Hastie, and Tibshirani (2001) to learn more about regression trees and random forests, respectively. Additionally "Decision trees and random forests: a visual introduction for beginners" by Smith (2017) has an easy-to-understand introduction to decision trees, random forests, and their applications. "Machine Learning With Random Forests And Decision Trees: A Visual Guide For Beginners" book by Hartshorn (2016) discusses these methods from a machine learning perspective, which we recommend to the readers.

Regression Shrinkage Methods

Two extensions of linear regression are ridge regression and LASSO, which are used for regularization. When applying multiple linear regression models, more features could be added to the model compared to the simple linear regression. Having more features may seem like a perfect way for improving the accuracy of the trained model by reducing the loss within the loss function. This is because the model that will be trained will be more flexible and will take into account more parameters that can potentially explain more variation of the response variable. On the other hand, we need to be extremely careful while adding more features to the model as this may increase the likelihood of overfitting the data. As we know, every research study, and the related data set, can have noisy samples as the samples are taken at random. Such noisy samples may lead to inaccuracies within each fitted model and hence it can lead to a low-quality model if not trained carefully. The model might end up memorizing the noise that exists within the noisy data set instead of learning the trend of the data. Overfitting can happen in linear models as well when dealing with multiple features. If not filtered and explored up front, some features can be more destructive to the accuracy of the model than helpful, repeat information that are already expressed by other features, and add high noise to the data set.

Therefore, statisticians have always tried assisting the applied researchers in avoiding overfitting. One of the most common mechanisms for avoiding overfitting is called regularization. A regularized machine learning model is a model that its loss function contains another element that should be minimized as well. The loss function includes two elements. The first one is what is used within regular linear regression models; it is the sum of the distances between each prediction and its ground truth or the observed value. The second element added to the loss function which is used in Ridge regression and LASSO models is the regularization term. It sums over squared β values and multiplies it by another parameter λ. The reason for doing that is to "punish" the loss function for high values of the coefficients β and prevent the overfitting of the regression models while using many variables in building it.

In general, simple models are better than complex models and usually do not face overfitting issues. Therefore, we should try to simplify the model as much as possible. The goal of the iterative process is to minimize the loss function. By punishing the β values, we add a constraint to minimize them as much as possible. Chapters 3 and 10 of "The elements of statistical learning" book by Friedman, Hastie, and

Tibshirani (2001), as well as chapter 6 of "An introduction to statistical learning with application in R" by James, Witten, Hastie, and Tibshirani (2013), discuss shrinkage, related methods and examples using R, which is a statistical programing language.

Ridge Regression

There is a gentle trade-off between fitting the model and at the same time making sure that we are not overfitting it. This approach is called Ridge regression.

Ridge regression is an extension for linear regression. It is basically a regularized linear regression model, which was explained above. The λ parameter, also called tuning parameter, is a scalar that should be learned as well, using a method called cross validation, which is beyond the topic of this chapter.

An important fact we need to notice about ridge regression is that it enforces the β coefficients to be lower, but it does not enforce them to be zero. So, it shrinks them to zero but does not set them equal to zero. That is, it will not get rid of irrelevant features and variables but rather minimize their impact on the trained model to reduce the likelihood of the overfitting.

Another way to look at it, beyond the overfitting issue, is that having many variables at play in a multiple linear regression sometimes poses a problem of choosing the inappropriate variables for the linear model, which gives undesirable and unreliable output as a result. Ridge regression can help overcoming this issue. This method is a regularization technique in which an extra variable (tuning parameter) is added and optimized to offset the effect of multiple variables in linear regression, which can reduce the noise.

As described above, ridge regression essentially is an instance of linear regression with regularization. Mathematically, the model with ridge regression is given by

$$Y = X\beta + \epsilon$$

where Y is the dependent variable, X is the independent variable or a matrix of all predictors if there are multiple independent variables (features), β represents all the regression coefficients and ϵ represents the residuals or errors. Based on this, the variables are now standardized by subtracting the respective means and dividing by their standard deviations.

The tuning parameter (λ) is now included in the ridge regression model as part of regularization. The higher the value of λ is, the residual sum of squares tend to be closer to zero. The lower the λ is, the solutions conform to least square method. In simpler words, this parameter helps the model in deciding the effect of coefficients. λ is estimated using a technique called cross-validation.

For more details regarding ridge regression, LASSO, and their application in machine learning see Hastie, Tibshirani, and Wainwright (2015). Earlier applications of this method can be found in Marquardt and Snee (1975), Mahajan, Jain, and Bergier (1977), and Price (1977).

Lasso Method

Least absolute shrinkage and selection operator, abbreviated as LASSO, is a linear regression technique which also performs regularization on variables in consideration. LASSO is another extension built on regularized linear regression, but with a small difference. The only difference from ridge regression is that the regularization term is in absolute value. Setting the coefficient equal to zero, when the tuning parameter allows the model to do so, has a huge impact on the results. LASSO method overcomes the disadvantage of ridge regression by not only punishing high values of the coefficients β, but actually setting them to zero if they are not relevant. Therefore, one might end up with fewer features included in the model than originally entered into the model, which is a huge advantage. This also qualifies the LASSO to be considered a variable selection technique.

In fact, it almost shares a similar statistical analysis evident in ridge regression, except it differs in the regularization values. This means, it considers the absolute values of the sum of the regression coefficients (hence the 'shrinkage' feature). It even sets the coefficients to zero which reduces the errors and noise completely. In the ridge equation mentioned earlier, the error component has absolute values instead of squared values.

This method was proposed by Professor Robert Tibshirani. Tibshirani said, *Lasso minimizes the residual sum of squares to the sum of the absolute value of the coefficients being less than a constant. Because of the nature of this constraint, it tends to produce some coefficients that are exactly 0 and hence gives interpretable models.*

In his journal article titled *Regression Shrinkage and Selection via the Lasso,* Tibshirani gives an account of this technique with respect to various other statistical models such as all subset selection and ridge regression. He goes on to say that LASSO can even be extended to generalized linear regression models and tree-based models. In fact, this technique provides possibilities of even conducting statistical estimations. This method is widely applied in different fields. For more details about LASSO, its applications and extensions, we recommend "Statistical learning with sparsity: the lasso and generalizations" by Tibshirani and Wainwright (2015). Grouped LASSO, an extension of the LASSO technique, is frequently used in biomedical studies such as Lin, Wang, Liu, and Holtkamp (2013) and Rao, Nowak, and Rogers (2013).

Cluster Analysis

Clustering is a case reduction technique and can be viewed as a way of grouping together data samples that are similar in some way according to some criteria that researchers pick. Both similarities and dissimilarities can be used while defining different clusters and grouping cases together. It also is a form of unsupervised learning meaning that we generally do not have examples demonstrating how the data should be grouped together and instead the data guide us through this grouping based on the characteristics of them.

Therefore, one can say that clustering is a method of data exploration and a way of looking for patterns or structure in the data that are of interest. The goal is to group together "similar" data and the important question is how to find the similarities and dissimilarities and use them to group the data.

There exists no single answer in how to define the similarities. It depends on what we want to find or emphasize in the data; this is one reason why clustering can be a flexible tool based on what researchers need. The similarity measure is often more important than the clustering algorithm used in the data exploration as if the similarity is not measured properly, the clustering algorithm cannot do anything to fix that issue. Measures such as Pearson correlation coefficient and Euclidean distance are some examples of measures that quantifies the similarities among the data points.

Instead of talking about similarity measures and using them to define the clusters within the cluster analysis, we often equivalently refer to dissimilarity measures. Jagota (2013) defines a dissimilarity measure as a function $f(x, y)$ such that $f(x, y) > f(w, z)$ if and only if x is less similar to y than w is to z. This is always a pair-wise measure:

$$d_{euc}(x, y) = \sqrt{\sum_{i=1}^{n}(x_i - y_i)^2}$$

where n is the number of dimensions in the data vector.

Sometimes researchers care more about the overall shape of variables rather than the actual magnitudes of dissimilarities. In that case, we might want to consider cases similar when they are "up" and "down" together based on the measured variable of interest. In that case, Pearson linear relationship can be used as a measure of the overall shape.

$$\rho(x, y) = \frac{\sum_{i=1}^{n}(x_i - \overline{x})(y_i - \overline{y})}{\sqrt{\sum_{i=1}^{n}(x_i - \overline{x})^2}\sqrt{\sum_{i=1}^{n}(y_i - \overline{y})^2}}$$

$$\overline{x} = \frac{1}{n}\sum_{i}^{n}x_i$$

$$\overline{y} = \frac{1}{n}\sum_{i}^{n}y_i$$

Within this calculation, the variables are shifted down by subtracting the means and then scaling them by dividing them by the standard deviations. This will standardize our data and make them have the mean of zero and standard deviation of one regardless of the unit of measurement. Pearson linear correlation is a measure that is invariant to vertically scaling and shifting of the expression values. The values are always between –1 and +1, where -1 shows a perfect negative linear correlation between two variables and +1 shows a perfect positive linear correlation between two variables. This is a similarity measure, but we can easily make it into a dissimilarity measure as below by defining d,

$$d = \frac{1 - \rho(x, y)}{2}$$

Pearson linear correlation only measures the degree of a linear relationship between two variables. If one wants to measure other relationships, there are many other possible measures.

Different clustering algorithms include, but are not limited to, hierarchical agglomerative clustering, K-means clustering and quality measures, and self-organizing maps.

To read more about this model and its applications in different fields, we recommend the following books and articles to the readers of this chapter. Books such as "Cluster Analysis for Researchers" by Charles Romesburg (2004) provides detailed information about this method and includes multiple examples. "Cluster analysis for applications: probability and mathematical statistics: a series of monographs and textbooks" by Michael R. Anderberg (2014) is another book discussing the applications of this method in detail. Chapter 12 of "Applied Multivariate Statistical Analysis" by Johnson and Wichern (2002) is another reference that provides more technical information about clustering methods. Additionally, we recommend reading chapters 13 and 14 of "The elements of statistical learning" book by Friedman, Hastie, and Tibshirani (2001) to learn more about unsupervised learning and clustering algorithms.

Articles such as Punj and Stewart (1983), Ketchen and Shook (1996), and Sturn, Quackenbush, and Trajanoski (2002) provide interesting examples of application of culuster analysis in marketing research, strategic management research, and microarray data and bioinformatics, respectively.

CONCLUSION

To summarize, in this chapter, we tried to assist reader in the understanding of different statistical methods and using their algorithms within machine learning and data analytics. We organized and explained various statistical strategies and algorithms based on the type of response variables used in each model. We first explained models used for modeling of continuous and categorical response variables and then moved on to explaining different approaches used for dimension reduction while working with various types of response and predictors when dealing with high dimensional data. These techniques can assist researchers in modeling of the big data, describing them and making inferences about them, and predicting the behavior of the data. Different approaches, based on the type of the variables involved in a study, were presented to help working with data sets in different dimensions and formats, reduce the dimensions of a big data set, and get efficient results. Once these methods are understood and the differences become clear, the data analysis stage is much easier to perform and many resources are available for programming and modeling in different software packages.

FUTURE RESEARCH DIRECTIONS

Different statistical algorithms and machine learning approaches were introduced, and discussed, in this chapter. Categorical statistical methods, especially ordinal logistic models, and classification approaches, such as classification random forest, are among the models not used by researchers as often as they should duo to their complexities and longer run time using different software packages. The computational burden and time-consuming nature of the existing algorithms for such approaches, based on the current computational capabilities, make such methods less popular among applied researchers and practitioners and therefore results in the use of less appropriate models by researchers when dealing with categorical and discrete response variables. This happens in both low and high dimensional data analysis.

Author suggests, and are currently working on, developing more powerful algorithms, which are computationally more advanced in terms of programming, that can handle applying such methods more efficiently, computationally. Developing such algorithms can encourage researchers to use these more appropriate models, which can guarantee reliable results, rather than using faster algorithms that ignore the categorical nature of variables to optimize the speed of the computation procedure.

We propose the development of such computationally efficient algorithms, in addition to using them within random forest, in neural network, deep learning, and artificial intelligence areas of research. Such methods and their application in neural network and deep learning can greatly benefit researchers in handling high dimensional data with varying types of variables.

ACKNOWLEDGMENT

This research received no specific grant from any funding agency in the public, commercial, or not-for-profit sectors. The author would like to thank Dr. Ali Ramezani and Dr. Iman Raeesi Vanani for their assistance with research and the compilation of this chapter.

REFERENCES

Agresti, A. (2007An Introduction To Categorical Data Analysis (2nd ed.). Wiley.

Anderberg, M. R. (2014). *Cluster analysis for applications: probability and mathematical statistics: a series of monographs and textbooks* (Vol. 19). Academic Press.

Breiman,L.(2001).Breiman.Randomforests.*MachineLearning*,*45*(1),5–32.doi:10.1023/A:1010933404324

Cokluk, O. (2010). Logistic Regression: Concept and Application. *Educational Sciences: Theory and Practice*, *10*(3), 1397–1407.

Dunteman, G. H. (1989). *Principal components analysis (No. 69)*. Sage. doi:10.4135/9781412985475

Friedman, J., Hastie, T., & Tibshirani, R. (2001). *The elements of statistical learning* (Vol. 1). New York: Springer Series in Statistics.

Hartshorn, S. (2016). *Machine Learning With Random Forests And Decision Trees: A Visual Guide For Beginners*. Kindle Edition.

Hastie, T., Tibshirani, R., & Wainwright, M. (2015). *Statistical learning with sparsity: the lasso and generalizations*. CRC Press. doi:10.1201/b18401

Hosmer, D., & Lemeshow, S. (2013). *Applied Logistic Regression* (3rd ed.). Willey Series in Probability and Statistics. doi:10.1002/9781118548387

Hosmer, D., Lemeshow, S., & May, S. (2008). Regression Modeling of Time-to-Event Data. Willey Series in Probability and Statistics, second edition. doi:10.1002/9780470258019

Jackson, J. E. (2005). *A user's guide to principal components* (Vol. 587). John Wiley & Sons.

Jagota, A. (2013). *Machine Learning Basics Kindle Edition* [Kindle Fire version]. Retrieved from Amazon.com.

James, G., Witten, D., Hastie, T., & Tibshirani, R. (2013). *An introduction to statistical learning* (Vol. 112). New York: Springer.

Johnson, R. A., & Wichern, D. W. (2002). Applied multivariate statistical analysis: Vol. 5. *No. 8*. Upper Saddle River, NJ: Prentice Hall.

Jolliffe, I. (2011). Principal component analysis. In *International encyclopedia of statistical science* (pp. 1094–1096). Berlin: Springer. doi:10.1007/978-3-642-04898-2_455

Ketchen, D. J. Jr, & Shook, C. L. (1996). The application of cluster analysis in strategic management research: An analysis and critique. *Strategic Management Journal, 17*(6), 441–458. doi:10.1002/(SICI)1097-0266(199606)17:6<441::AID-SMJ819>3.0.CO;2-G

Lee, S. (2005). Application of logistic regression model and its validation for landslide susceptibility mapping using GIS and remote sensing data. *International Journal of Remote Sensing, 26*(7), 1477–1491. doi:10.1080/01431160412331331012

Liaw, A., & Wiener, M. (2002). Classification and regression by randomForest. *R News, 2*(3), 18–22.

Lin, H., Wang, C., Liu, P., & Holtkamp, D. J. (2013). Construction of disease risk scoring systems using logistic group lasso: Application to porcine reproductive and respiratory syndrome survey data. *Journal of Applied Statistics, 40*(4), 736–746. doi:10.1080/02664763.2012.752449

Mahajan, V., Jain, A. K., & Bergier, M. (1977). Parameter estimation in marketing models in the presence of multicollinearity: An application of ridge regression. *JMR, Journal of Marketing Research, 14*(4), 586–591. doi:10.1177/002224377701400419

Marquardt, D. W., & Snee, R. D. (1975). Ridge regression in practice. *The American Statistician, 29*(1), 3–20.

Montgomery, D. C., Peck, E. A., & Vining, G. G. (2012). *Introduction to linear regression analysis* (Vol. 821). John Wiley & Sons.

Peffer, M. E., & Ramezani, N. (2019). Assessing epistemological beliefs of experts and novices via practices in authentic science inquiry. *International Journal of STEM Education, 6*(1), 3. doi:10.118640594-018-0157-9

Price, B. (1977). Ridge regression: Application to nonexperimental data. *Psychological Bulletin, 84*(4), 759–766. doi:10.1037/0033-2909.84.4.759

Punj, G., & Stewart, D. W. (1983). Cluster analysis in marketing research: Review and suggestions for application. *JMR, Journal of Marketing Research, 20*(2), 134–148. doi:10.1177/002224378302000204

Ramezani, N. (2015). Approaches for missing data in ordinal multinomial models. In *JSM Proceedings, Biometrics section, New Methods for Studies with Missing Data Session*. Alexandria, VA: American Statistical Association Journal.

Ramezani, N. (2016). Analyzing non-normal binomial and categorical response variables under varying data conditions. In *Proceedings of the SAS Global Forum Conference*. Cary, NC: SAS Institute Inc.

Ramezani, N., & Ramezani, A. (2016). *Analyzing non-normal data with categorical response variables. In proceedings of the Southeast SAS Users Group Conference*. Cary, NC: SAS Institute Inc.

Rao, N., Cox, C., Nowak, R., & Rogers, T. T. (2013). Sparse overlapping sets lasso for multitask learning and its application to fmri analysis. In Advances in neural information processing systems (pp. 2202-2210). Academic Press.

Raychaudhuri, S., Stuart, J. M., & Altman, R. B. (1999). Principal components analysis to summarize microarray experiments: application to sporulation time series. In Biocomputing 2000 (pp. 455-466). Academic Press. doi:10.1142/9789814447331_0043

Romesburg, C. (2004). *Cluster analysis for researchers*. Lulu.com.

Segal, M. R. (2004). *Machine learning benchmarks and random forest regression*. Academic Press.

Smith, C. (2017). *Decision trees and random forests: a visual introduction for beginners*. Blue Windmill Media.

Sturn, A., Quackenbush, J., & Trajanoski, Z. (2002). Genesis: Cluster analysis of microarray data. *Bioinformatics (Oxford, England)*, *18*(1), 207–208. doi:10.1093/bioinformatics/18.1.207 PMID:11836235

Wickham, H., & Grolemund, G. (2016). *R for data science: import, tidy, transform, visualize, and model data*. O'Reilly Media, Inc.

Wiegleb, G. (1980). Some applications of principal components analysis in vegetation: ecological research of aquatic communities. In *Classification and Ordination* (pp. 67–73). Dordrecht: Springer. doi:10.1007/978-94-009-9197-2_9

Wold, S., Esbensen, K., & Geladi, P. (1987). Principal component Analysis. *Chemometrics and Intelligent Laboratory Systems*, *2*(1-3), 37–52. doi:10.1016/0169-7439(87)80084-9

Chapter 8
Enhanced Logistic Regression (ELR) Model for Big Data

Dhamodharavadhani S.
Periyar University, India

Rathipriya R.
Periyar University, India

ABSTRACT

Regression model is an important tool for modeling and analyzing data. In this chapter, the proposed model comprises three phases. The first phase concentrates on sampling techniques to get best sample for building the regression model. The second phase is to predict the residual of logistic regression (LR) model using time series analysis method: autoregressive. The third phase is to develop enhanced logistic regression (ELR) model by combining both LR model and residual prediction (RP) model. The empirical study is carried out to study the performance of the ELR model using large diabetic dataset. The results show that ELR model has a higher level of accuracy than the traditional logistic regression model.

INTRODUCTION

In the emerging data analytics for big data, regression analysis is one of them used in this research work. It mainly focuses the two class classification problems in the big data. The regression techniques are applicable only for minimal dataset having around some hundreds of records which is evident from the literature. So, the application of regression for big data is also a challenging task. The regression analysis is chosen because they entirely based on the variable dependency.

The data classification will be meaningful when that approach considers the relationships among the attributes. In that sense, the regression analysis is chosen in this research. This entire study deals with the logistic regression for big data having two class problem. Acquiring the knowledge by applying the regression to the entire large dataset is complex, so the sampling is one of the solutions to acquire the knowledge from the large dataset. The first phase data is sampled and then the regression analysis is performed on those samples. It concentrates on sampling techniques to get best sample for building the

DOI: 10.4018/978-1-7998-0106-1.ch008

regression model. Second phase is to predict the residual of Logistic Regression (LR) model using time series analysis method- Autoregressive. Third phase is to develop Enhanced Logistic Regression (ELR) model by combining the both LR model and Residual Prediction (RP) Model. The empirical study is carried out to the study the performance of the ELR model using large diabetic dataset. The results show that ELR model has higher level of accuracy than the traditional Logistic Regression model

Chapter Organization

The rest of the chapter is organized as follows: First section describes the literature study done for this research work. Second section deals with the methods and material used for the logistic regression analysis on big data. The experimental results of the proposed work are discussed in third section. Finally, summarizes this research work and suggests some ideas for future extension.

REVIEW OF LITERATURE

In the literature survey, the previous research contributions are studied. A lot of machine learning techniques are used for data analysis. They are discussed further in this chapter

(Strack, et al., 2014), An multivariate logistic regression is used to fit the relationship between the measurement of HbAlc early readmission while controlling for covariates such as demographics, severity and type of the dieses and type of admission. Results show that the measurement of HbAlc was performed frequently (18.4%) in the inpatient setting.

(Combes.C, Kadari.F, & Chaabane.S, 2014), A linear regression to identify the factors (variable) characterizing the length of stay (LOS) in Emergency department(ED) in- order to propose model to predict the length of stay.

(NM, T, P, & S, 2015), Using the predictive analysis algorithm in Hadoop and Map Reduce goal of their research deals with the study of diabetic treatment in HealthCare industry using big data analytics. The predictive analysis system of diabetic treatment is produce greats in healthcare. They mainly focused the patients in the rural area to generate proper treatment at low cast.

(Luo, 2016), The machine learning predictive model is using the electronic medical record dataset from practice fusion diabetes classification competition containing patient records from all 50 states in the united states. They explained the prediction result for 87.4% of patients who were correctly predicted by the model to have type 2 diagnoses with the next year.

(Carter & Potts, 2014), The poission regression and the negative binomial model for predicting length of stay were age, gender, consltant, discharge destination applying a negative binomial model to the variable was successful. The models can be successfully created to help improve resource planning and from which a simple decision support system can be produced to help patient explanation on length of stay.

(Ho, et al., 2016), An T Test, Chi square test and multivariate Logistic Regression analysis the variables in aciute stroke can predict in hospitality and help decision makes in clinical practice musing Nanogram. The nanogrames may help physicians in risk prediction in hospital mortality.

(Duggal & Kharti, 2016), The problem of predicting the risk of readmission was framed as a binary classification problem and several available prediction models were developed. This work explained a complex, high dimensional, clinical dataset provided by an Indian hospitals identify the readmission of patient with diabetes within 30 days of discharge.

(Sushmita, Khulbe, Hasan, & Newman, 2015), The Machine Learning Algorithm goal of this study was a dual predictive modeling effort that utilities healthcare data to predict the risk and cost of any hospital readmission ("all cause"). Machine learning algorithm to do predict for risk and cost of 30 day readmission.

(Zhang, Shoa, & Xi, 2014), An classification model, if the result is "Bad", which means the patient is likely to be readmitted within 30 days doctors and nurses can try to adjust the features of the patient (Time in hospital, No of lab procedures, no of medications). After personalizing the treatment, the model can be run once again to see the result is changed to "Good".

(Glugnn, Owens, Bennett, Healy, & Silke, 2014), A multivariate logistic regression is using for patients without diabetes, abnormal serum glucose is independently predictive of an increased mortality among the broad cohort of acute emergency medical patient similar disturbances of glucose homeostasis for patient with diabetes do not confer equivalent adverse prognostic implications.

In this chapter, analysis of logistic regression, a machine learning technique in the field data analysis is summarized briefly.

METHODS AND MATERIALS

Big Data

The term "Big Data" often refers simply to the use of predictive analytics user behavior analytics, or certain other advanced data analytics methods that extract value from data, and seldom to a particular size of data set. More and more data are increasing continuously in diverse fields such as social networks or smart communications. This is an opportunity at the same time, this bring us the confusion of information because it is difficult to analyze the big data. But, many researches for big data analysis have been studied in diverse domains such as text and data mining. The McKinsey defined big data is a collection of data which cannot be control by tradition database system because of its enormous size.

Big data includes text, audio, and video as well as tradition data types. That is, the format of big data is not regular but irregular. In the infrastructure and management for big data, we need the data storing and controlling technologies for large data saving and retrieving, this is beyond traditional technologies of data structure and database.

In big data analysis there is many problems. One of them is how to apply statistical analysis to the huge data at once. It takes time and effort to analyze all big data at a time. In general, the statistical methods have computing limitation to manipulate extremely large data set in big data.

Big data technologies are important in provides more accurate analysis, which may lead to more concrete decision making results in greater operational efficiencies, cost reduction, and reduced risks for the business. The big data is requiring an infrastructure that can manage and process huge volumes of structured and unstructured data in real time and can perfect data privacy and security. It is not a single technique or a tool it involves many areas of business and technology (Jun, Lee, & Ryu, 2015).

Characteristics of Big Data

Big data is important because it enables organizations to gather, store, manage, and manipulate vast amount data at the right speed, at the right time, to gain the right insight as in the figure 1.

Figure 1. Characteristics of big data

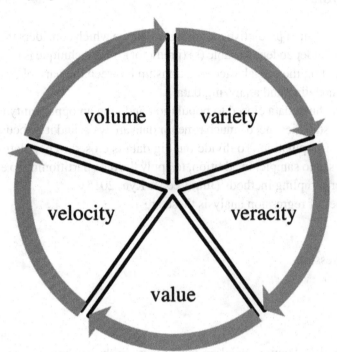

- **Volume:** Refers to the size of data that has been created from all the sources.
- **Velocity:** Refers to the speed at which data is generated, stored, analyzed and processed. An emphasis is being put recently on supporting real time big data.
- **Variety:** Refers to the different types of data being generated. It is common now that most data is unstructured data cannot be easily categories or tabulated as in the table1.
- **Variability:** Refers to how the structure and meaning of data constantly change especially when dealing with data generated from natural language analysis for example.
- **Value:** Refers to the possible advantage big data can offer a business based on good big data collection of management and analysis (Nuarmi, Neyadi, Mohamed, & A1-jaroodi, 2015).

The above mentioned basic 5 Vs of Big Data. They also have 54 Vs characteristics of big data like Venue, Vocabulary, Vendible, Validity, Volatility, Verbosity, Vagueness, Vanity, Voracity and so on (S.Dhamodharavadhani, 2018).

Table 1. Types of big data

Types of Data	Description	Example
Structured data	It is in defined format	Database, Sql
Semi-structured data	It is like structured but not in rigid structured	XML, NoSql database
Unstructured data	It has no structured data	Mail messages, Photos, Videos and Audio files

Regression Analysis

Regression analysis is a form of predictive modeling technique which considers the relationship between a dependent (target) and independent variable (s) (predictor). This technique is used for forecasting, time series modeling and finding the causal effect relationship between the variables. Regression analysis is an important tool for modeling and analyzing data.

In big data to get the huge data closed to population and gain an opportunity to analyze the population. But the traditional statistical needs much time for data analysis, and it is focused on the sample data analysis for inference of population. To divide the big data is closed to population into some sub data sets with small size closed to sample. In addition, to apply the data partitioning to estimate the parameter in regression model for sampling methods (Jun, Lee, & Ryu, 2015).

There are three types of regression analysis these are,

1. Linear regression
2. Multi-Linear regression
3. Logistic regression

Linear Regression

It is one of the most widely known modeling techniques. In this technique, the dependent variable is continuous, independent variable(s) can be continues and discrete, and nature of regression line is linear. Linear Regression establishes a relationship between dependent variable (Y) and one or more independent variables (X) using a best t straight line (also known as regression line) (Park & Hyeoun Ae, 2013).

Multi-Linear Regression

A regression with two or more explanatory variables is called a multiple regression. Multiple regression models thus describe how a single response variable Y depends linearly on a number of predictor variables.

Logistic Regression

In logistic regression, a mathematical model of a set of explanatory variable is used to predict a logit of the dependent variable. The logistic regression analysis studies the association between a categorical dependent variable and set of independent variables. The name logistic regression is used when the dependent variable has only two values, such as '0' and '1' or 'Yes' or 'No' (Park & Hyeoun Ae, 2013).

Logistic regression is one of the statistical methods, for analyzing a dataset. The main process of learning from data is to analyze data by logistic methods such as time series modeling. In Big data is analyzed the efficient methods for logistic regression is a good analytical process. Logistic regression is a classification algorithm as in the figure 2.

First, extract the sample from big data, to analyze the sample using logistic regression. In Logistic regression, a population is defined as a collection of total elements in the subject of study, and cannot analyze the population because of its analyze cost or changeable. But in Big data it is easily analyze a data set closed to the population.

Figure 2. Logistic regression for big data

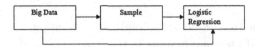

It is caused by the development of computing large data and decreasing in price of data storage. But, the computing burdens of big data analysis such as logistic regression methods have a limitation for analyzing big data. To overcome this limitation, a model is proposed using logistic regression for big data analysis (Jun, Lee, & Ryu, 2015).

In this research, the logistic regression is used for analyzing big data. The logistic regression is a classification algorithm, for these processes are used to predict a binary outcome "0" and "1".

Sampling

Sampling is related with the selection of a subset of individuals from within a population to estimate the characteristics of whole population (Charles Teddie & Fen yu, 2007).

The sampling techniques are,

1. Sequence sampling
2. Random sampling
3. Cluster sampling
4. Systematic sampling
5. Stratified sampling

Sequence Sampling

The sequential sampling methods can be implemented efficiently on computers and are particularly adaptable to selecting samples as a file is read or as a process takes place (R.Chromy).

Random Sampling

In the random sampling method, each unit included in the sample has equal chance of inclusion in the sample. This technique provides the unbiased and better estimate of the parameters if the population is homogeneous (Singh, Ajay S, Masuku, & Micah B, 2014).

Cluster Sampling

The Cluster sampling is a sampling method where the entire population is divided into groups, or clusters and a random sample of these clusters are selected. All observations in the selected clusters are included in the sample.

Systematic Sampling

In this method of sampling, the first unit of the sample selected at random and the subsequent units are selected in a systematic way. If there are N units in the population and n units are to be selected, then R = N/n (the R is known as the sampling interval). The first number is selected at random out of the remainder of this R (Sampling Interval) to the previous selected number.

Stratified Sampling

Stratified sampling is useful method for data collection if the population is heterogeneous. In this method, the entire heterogeneous population is divided in to a number of homogeneous groups, usually known as Strata, each of these groups is homogeneous within itself, and then units are sampled at random from each of these stratums. The sample size in each stratum varies according to the relative importance of the stratum in the population (Singh, Ajay S, Masuku, & Micah B, 2014).

There are different types of sampling methods also there now, in this research using only three sampling techniques such as sequential sampling, random sampling without replacement and sampling using clustering.

LOGISTIC REGRESSION (LR) USING SAMPLING TECHNIQUES

Logistic Regression (LR)

Logistic regression is a simple tool to analyze the effect of covariates on a binary outcome. This model sometimes called the logistic model or logit model, analyzes the relationship between multiple independent variables and a categorical dependent variable, and estimates the probability of occurrence of an event by fitting data to a logistic curve (Park & Hyeoun Ae, 2013).

Logistic regression is a part of a larger class of algorithms known as the generalized linear model (glm). The logistic regression is one of the statistical methods.

Logit (p) is the log (to base e) of the odds ratio or likelihood ratio for the dependent variable is 1. In symbol, it is defined in the equation (1)

$$logit\left(p\right) = \log\left(\frac{p}{1-p}\right) = lm\left(\frac{p}{1-p}\right) \tag{1}$$

Where as p can only range from 0 to 1, logit (p) scale range from negative infinity to positive infinity and is symmetrical around the logit. The formula below the relationship between the usual regression equation (a+bx....), which is a straight line formula, and the logistic regression equation (2).

The form of the logistic regression equation is

$$logit\left(p\left(x\right)\right) = \log\left(\frac{\left(p\left(x\right)\right)}{1 - p\left(x\right)}\right) = a + b1x + b2x2 + \ldots \tag{2}$$

This looks just a linear regression and although logistic regression finds a "best fitting" equation. The least squared deviations criterion for the best fit, it uses a maximum likelihood method, which maximizes the pbability of getting the observed results given the fitted regression coefficient. P can be calculated with the following equation (3),

$$P = \frac{e^{a+b_1x_1+b_2x_2\ldots}}{1 + e^{a+b_1x_1+b_2x_2}\ldots}. \tag{3}$$

Where

P= the probability that a case is in a particular category,
E= the base of natural algorithm,
a = the constant of the equation and,
b= the coefficient of the predictor variable.

There are two types of Logistic regression

1. The binary logistic regression is typically used when the dependent variable is dichotomous and the independent variables are either continuous or categorical.
2. The multinomial logistic regression is used when the dependent variable is not dichotomous and is comprised of more than two categories.

In addition, we apply this data partitioning to estimate the parameters in regression model (Park & Hyeoun Ae, 2013).

Sampling Methods

A sample can be defined as a group of relatively smaller number of people selected from a population is called as sampling. The process through which a sample is extracted from a population is called as sampling. In investigation it is impossible to assess every single element of a population so a group of people (smaller in number than the population) is selected for the assessment. The more the sample is representative of the population, the higher is the accuracy of the inference and better is the results are generalizable (Alvi, 2016).

In our research three different sampling methods are used, they are Sequential Sampling, Random Sampling, and k-means clustering based Sampling.

Sequential Sampling

In sequential sampling plan is sequence of samples taken from the given dataset and number of samples is determined by the resulting sampling (R.Chromy). In big data era, one can get huge data closed to population, and gain an opportunity to analyze the population. But traditional logistic regression needs much time for data analysis, and it is focused on the sample data analysis for inference of population.

To divide the big data population into number of sub data sets as samples. These divided data sets are proper to statistical analysis. In this thesis the logistic regression, a machine learning method is chosen for big data analysis. It is a popular model for data analysis (Jun, Lee, & Ryu, 2015) as in the Figure 3.

Random Sampling

The word random itself describes the procedure used to select elements (participates, test items) for a sample. The main goal of all sampling methods is to get a representative sample from the population, and this sampling technique should be based on the random sample selection method. In the random sampling, all elements of a population have equal chances to be selected to sample (Uitter, 1984).

The samples can be drawn in two possible ways,

1. Random Sampling with Replacement: The sampling units are chosen without replacement in the sense that the units once chosen are not placed back in the population.
2. Random Sampling without Replacement: The sampling units are chosen with replacement in the sense that the units are placed basic in the population as in the figure 4.

The simple random sampling without replacement is used as one of the sampling method for dividing big data in this work.

Sampling Using Clustering

Clustering is grouping a set of objects in such a way that objects in the same group (called cluster) are more similar (objective dependant) to each other than in other groups (clusters) (L.v.Bijuraj, 2013).

Clustering aims at identifying and extracting significant groups in underlying data. Clustering is a division of data into groups of similar objects. The four main classes of clustering algorithms are Partitioning methods, Hierarchical methods; Density based Clustering and Grid-based Clustering. Clustering analysis has become an important technique in exploratory data Analysis, Pattern Recognition, Machine

Figure 3. Sequential sampling

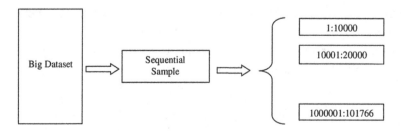

Figure 4. Random sampling without replacement

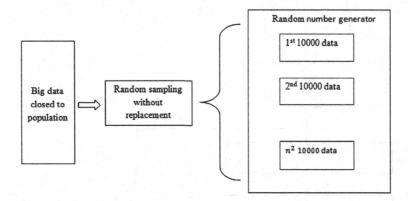

Learning, Neural Computing, and other fields. For Clustering there are number of algorithms available but in this proposed work the K-Means algorithm is used.

THE BASIC K-MEANS ALGORITHM

The K-Means clustering technique is simple, and begins with a description of the basic algorithm. First choose k initial centroids, where k is a user specified parameter. It represents the number of clusters desired. Each point is then assigned to the closest centroid, and each collection of points assigned to a centroid is a cluster. The centroid of each cluster is then updated based on the points assigned to the cluster (Sanjoy Chawla & Aristides Glonis). To repeat the assignment and updates steps until clusters remains idle, or equivalently, until the centroids remain the same. K-Means is formally described by Algorithm 1 as in the figure 5.

Algorithm: Basic K-Means Algorithm

1. Select K points as initial centroids.
2. Repeat
    a. From K clusters by assigning each point to its closest centroid.
    b. Recomputed the centroid of each cluster.

Until centroids remains idle.

In this thesis, K-Means clustering method is used for sampling (i.e. grouping the given population into samples.)

Performance Measures

The measure is a systematic and replicable process by which objects or events are quantified and/or classified with respect to a particular dimension.

Figure 5. Clustering model

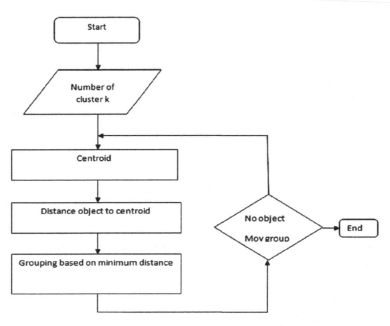

Deviance

Deviance is a measure of goodness of fit of a generalized linear model. The null deviance shows how well the response is predicted by the model with nothing but an intercept. The residual deviance is measure for the lack of fit of model taken as a whole data. It shows how well the response is predicted by the model when the predictors are included.

From your example, it can be seen that the deviance goes up by 3443.3 when 22 predictor variables are added (note: degrees of freedom = no. of observations – no. of predictors). This increase in deviance is evidence of a significant lack of fit.

AIC

The Akaike Information Criterion (AIC) is another measure of goodness of fit that takes into account the ability of the model to fit the data. It provides a method for assessing the quality of your model through comparison of related models. It's based on the Deviance, but penalizes you for making the model more complicated. Much like adjusted R squared, it's intent is to prevent from including irrelevant predictors. If you have more than one similar candidate models (where all of the variables of the simpler model occur in the more complex models), then you should select the model that has the smallest AIC. The estimation of the β_i based on least squares and the maximum likelihood estimates are identified (Hu, 2007). Then the RSS is a residual sum of squares as in equation (4).

$$AIC = n + n\log2\pi + n\log\left(\frac{RSS}{n}\right) + 2(p+1) \qquad (4)$$

PROPOSED WORK: ELR MODEL FOR REGRESSION

The proposed work is developing enhanced logistic regression (ELR) model by combining the both LR model and RP model. First to apply the different sampling techniques for LR model to get the best fit LR model. The regression results from different sampling methods are compared and quantified based on the error measure. Second is to predict the residual using time series model. Residual is the difference between the actual and predicted values of the predictors. It is used to understand the model and improve the model fitting. The figure 6 shows the work flow of ELR model.

Sequential Sampling Algorithm

The sample size 'n' is selected from a sampling frame of 'N' sampling by selecting 'n'. Sequential methods require each sampling unit in the sampling frame to be considered in the order and a probabilistic decision reached for the sample (R.Chromy).

Algorithm

Step 1: Develop an ordered sampling frame of 'N' sampling units
Step 2: Select a unit with probability proportional to its size to receive the label 1.
Step 3: Continue labeling serially to the end of the sampling frame.
Step 4: Assign the next serial label to the first unit at the beginning of the list and continue until all sampling units are labeled.
Step 5: Apply the sequential sample selection algorithm. Starting with the sampling unit labeled 1 (R.Chromy).

Random Sampling Algorithm

To selecting a simple random sample of size 'n' from 'N' involves sequentially comparing conditional probabilities of selection for each unit labeled i=1,2,3,...N with minimum random number (Uitter, 1984)

$$\frac{N-u}{N+1-1} \geq v_i. \tag{5}$$

where, u is the number selected from the first (i-1) units. Sampling unit 'i' is included when the inequality is satisfied. It is calculated using the equation (5).

Algorithm

Step 1: [Generate U] Generate a random variants 'U' that is uniformly dtributed between '0' and '1'
Step 2: [Test] if NU>n, go to step 4
Step 3: [Select] To select the next record in the file N: =N-1. If n >0, then return to step 1; otherwise the sample is complete and the algorithm terminates.

Figure 6. ELR model

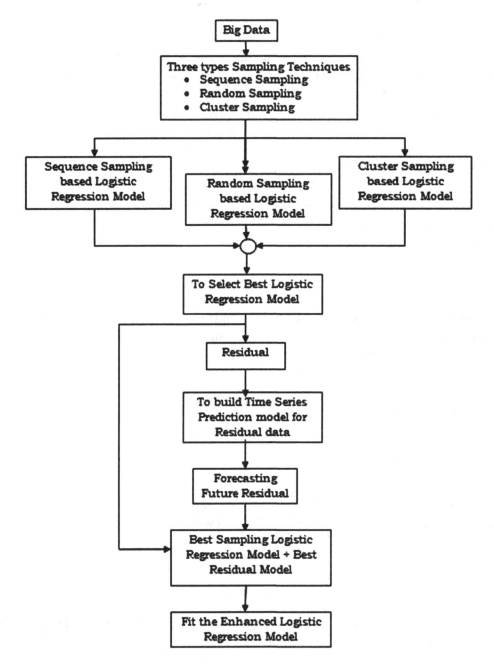

Step 4: [Don't select] Skip over the next record (do not include it in the sample), set N: =N-1, and return to step 1.

Before the algorithm is run, each record in the file has the same chance of being selected for the sample. Furthermore, the algorithm never runs off the end of the file before 'n' records have been chosen. If at some point in the algorithm n=N, then each of the remaining n records in the file will be selected for the sample with probability one. The average number of uniform random variables generated by algorithm S is (N+1) n/ (n+1) and the average running time is O(n) (Uitter, 1984).

Cluster Sampling Algorithm

The cluster analysis procedure is analyzed to determine the properties of the data set and the target variable. It is typically used to determine how to measure similarity distance (Sanjoy Chawla & Aristides Glonis).

Algorithm

Input: Set of points X= { $X_1, X_{2...}, X_n$ }

A distance function d: X×X→R
  Number k and l

Output: A set of k cluster center c

  A set of l outliers L⊆X

1. $C_{0 \leftarrow \{K \text{ } Random \text{ } points \text{ } of \text{ } X\}}$
2. $i \leftarrow 1$
3. While (no convergence achieved) do
4. Compute $d(X / C_{i-1})$, for all $x \in X$
5. Re-order the points in X such that $d(x_{1|C_{i-1}}) \geq ... \geq d(X_{n/C_i-1})$
6. $L_{i \leftarrow \{x_{1...x_n}\}}$
7. $X_{i \leftarrow X|L_{i=\{x_{i+1...x_n}\}}}$
8. For (j∈{1...k})do
9. $P_{j \leftarrow} \{X \in X_{i/c} \text{ } (x/C_{i-1}) = (i-1,j)\}$
10. $(i,j \leftarrow means(P_j))$
11. $C_{j \leftarrow} \{C_{i,1...C_{i,K}}\}$
12. $j \leftarrow i+1$

K-Means Clustering Based Logistic Regression Analysis

The steps in the proposed approach k-means based Logistic Regression analysis is discussed in this section (Jun, Lee, & Ryu, 2015)

Step 1: Dividing big data (Sampling)

Dividing the big data (population) into 'm' subsets (samples) using three sampling techniques such as sequential sampling, random sampling without replacement and sampling using clustering.

Step 2: Performing logistic regression analysis
    i.   Computing logistic regression parameters for 'm' samples
    ii.   Aggregating 'm' regression parameters to estimate the regression parameters of the entire dataset.
Step 3: Evaluating model
    i.   To compare the regression results of three sampling approaches.
    ii.   Computing the confidence interval of regression parameter for three approaches
    iii.   Checking whether all averaged parameters is included in the confidence interval (Jun, Lee, & Ryu, 2015)

The comparison of the results is studied based on the AIC measure, null deviance of data, Residual Deviance of the data.

Residual Prediction (RP) Using Time Series Model

Residual is the difference between the actual and predicted values of the predictors. It is used to understand the model and improve the model fitting. Minimal residual value is the best regression model. The residual error is calculated as

Residual = actual value – predicted value

To build a model of the residual error time series and predict the expected error for future model. The predicted error can be subtracted from the model prediction and in turn provide an additional lift in performance. A simple and effective model of residual error is autoregression time series model. This model has some number of lagged error values are used to predict the error at the next time step. These lag errors are combined in a autoregression model of the direct time series observations.

Autoregression of the residual error time series is called a Moving Average (MA) model but more different from moving average smoothing. It process, except on lagged residual error rather than lagged raw observations.

ENHANCED LOGISTIC REGRESSION MODEL (ELR)

This model is developing enhanced logistic regression (ELR) model by combining the both LR model and RP model. First to apply the different sampling techniques for LR model to get the best fit LR model. The minimal residual is called as best fit regression model. Second is to predict the residual using time series model. Then to combine the LR and RP model

Experimental Study

In the experiment, the Y_i represents the value of dependent variable and X_j represents value of independent variable in the ith sample and j[th] parameter in the equation is (6)

The simple logistic regression model used is denoted below,

$$Y_i = \beta_0 + \beta_1 x_1 + \beta_2 x_2 + \ldots \beta_n x_n \tag{6}$$

The error terms i=1, 2, 3,…N are assumed to be independent variables having a normal distribution with mean E(i)=0 and constant variance var(i)= σ^2. The variance is one, $\sigma^2 = 1$, that is, the error terms i=1,2,….N from a normal distribution with mean 0 and variance 1 denoted by N(0,1). The population size N was 1, 01,766 data are divide the population into 11 sub population, So the size of each sub population was 10,000.

Dataset Description

The data set represents 10 years (1999-2008) of clinical care data at 130 US hospitals. It includes over 9 features representing patient and hospital outcomes. This information was extracted from the database that satisfied the following data (Yifan & Sharma).

1. It is an inpatient encounter (a hospital admission)
2. It is a diabetes encounter, that is, one during which any kind of diabetes was enclosed to the system as a diagnosis.
3. The length of stay was at least 1 day and at most 14 days.
4. Laboratory tests were performed during the encounter.
5. Medications were administrated during the encounter.

The data contains the attributes such as 'number_outpatient', 'number_emergencg', 'number inpatient', 'num_procedures', 'num_medications', 'lab procedures', 'time_in_hospital', 'age', 'readmitted'.

Data Preprocessing

The age attribute of the dataset is a converted into categorical data using the scale as in the table 2.

Results and Discussion

The experimental results of the three different proposed approaches Sequence Sampling based Logistic Regression, Random Sampling based Logistic Regression and Cluster Sampling based Logistic Regression are discussed in this section. The derived models of these three proposed approaches are given in the tables 3, 4 and 5.

The logistic regression is applied for each sample in all the approaches and the specific models are derived for each sample. Finally the models of the samples are aggregated to derive the overall model for the dataset. For each approach the dataset is divided into 10 samples.

Table 2. Age conversion scale

Range	0-10	11-20	21-30	31-40	41-50	51-60	61-70	71-80	81-90	91-100
Value	1	2	3	4	5	6	7	8	9	10

The performance of the derived models is analyzed using the null deviance, residual deviance and AIC measures. The higher Deviance value of the model represents the poor performance whereas the deviance value should be lowered to get better results.

The Null deviance and Residual deviance obtained for the first proposed approach is 4301.282 on 9250 degrees of freedom and 4015.475 on 9242 degrees of freedom.

The null deviance shows how well the response variable is predicted by a model that includes only the intercept (grand mean) where as residual with inclusion of independent variables. The table 6 shows that addition of 2 (9250-9242=8) independent variables decreased the deviance to 9242 from 4015.475, a significant reduction in deviance. The residual deviance reduced by 285.807 with a loss of degrees of freedom.

The Null deviance and Residual deviance obtained for the second proposed approach is 6988.5 on 10175 degrees of freedom and 6851.34 on 10167 degrees of freedom. The deviance is measure the "goodness of fit" of a model. The higher numbers indicates the bad fit.

The null deviance shows how well the response variable is predicted by a model that includes only the intercept (grand mean) where as residual with inclusion of independent variables. The table 6 shows that addition of 2 (10175-10167=8) independent variables decreased the deviance to 10167 from 6851.34, a significant reduction in deviance. The residual deviance reduced by 137.167 with a loss of degrees of freedom.

Similarly, the Null deviance and Residual deviance obtained for the third proposed approach is 917.1136 on 9250 degrees of freedom and 888.8191 on 9242 degrees of freedom. The deviance is measure the "goodness of fit" of a model. The higher numbers indicates the bad fit.

The null deviance shows how well the response variable is predicted by a model that includes only the intercept (grand mean) where as residual with inclusion of independent variables. The figure 7 shows that addition of 2 (9250-9242=8) independent variables decreased the deviance to 9242 from 888.8191, a significant reduction in deviance. The residual deviance reduced by 28.2945 with a loss of degrees of freedom.

From the three approaches the values of Null deviance, Residual deviance and AIC is minimal to the Cluster Sampling based Logistic regression. Deviance is a measure of "goodness of fit" of a model. The Null deviance shows how well the response variable is predicted by a model that includes only the intercept whereas residual deviance with inclusion of independent variables. If Null Deviance and

Residual Deviance are small, it gives good fitness of the Model. Deviance is higher numbers always indicates bad fit. The measure of clustering sampling Null deviance (917.1136), Residual deviance (6851.34) is smaller deviance to provides a good fit of the data while compare to random and sequence sampling as in the figure 7.

From the three approaches the values of Null deviance, Residual deviance and AIC is minimal to the Cluster Sampling based Logistic regression. From this it evident that the Cluster sampling based logistic regression approach outperforms the other two approaches.

Table 3. Derived models using sequence sampling based logistic regression

Sample Number	Derived Models
1	$Y_1 = -0.04540X_1 - 0.12963X_2 - 0.05631X_3 + 0.032334X_4 - 0.05308X_5 - 0.01716X_6 - 0.00976 X_7 - 0.01309X_8$
2	$Y_2 = -0.05564X_1 - 0.13548 X_2 - 0.05209 X_3 + 0.015455 X_4 - 0.02577 X_5 - 0.03306 X_6 - 0.00659 X_7 - 0.01335 X_8$
3	$Y_3 = -0.05527 X_1 - 0.11390 X_2 - 0.07234 X_3 + 0.021147 X_4 - 0.03153 X_5 - 0.03414 X_6 - 0.01012 X_7 - 0.00947 X_8$
4	$Y_4 = -0.02496 X_1 - 0.11080 X_2 - 0.05938 X_3 + 0.005493 X_4 - 0.03984 X_5 - 0.03562 X_6 - 0.00344 X_7 - 0.01080 X_8$
5	$Y_5 = -0.02609 X_1 - 0.11396 X_2 - 0.03415 X_3 + 0.017030 X_4 - 0.01557 X_5 + 0.030977 X_6 - 0.00789 X_7 - 0.01832 X_8$
6	$Y_6 = -0.02652 X_1 - 0.11283 X_2 - 0.05871 X_3 + 0.013976 X_4 - 0.02144 X_5 - 0.01261 X_6 - 0.00145 X_7 - 0.01869 X_8$
7	$Y_7 = -0.02132 X_1 - 0.10845 X_2 - 0.03665 X_3 + 0.010657 X_4 - 0.01357 X_5 - 0.00964 X_6 - 0.00539 X_7 - 0.02094 X_8$
8	$Y_8 = -0.00206 X_1 - 0.01169 X_2 - 0.00339 X_3 + 0.001938 X_4 - 0.00437 X_5 + 0.0003150 X_6 - 0.000004 X_7 - 0.00205 X_8$
9	$Y_9 = -0.01767 X_1 - 0.12342 X_2 - 0.02284 X_3 + 0.008795 X_4 - 0.04209 X_5 - 0.00126 X_6 - 0.00289 X_7 - 0.02074 X_8$
10	$Y_{10} = -0.02513 X_1 - 0.12920 X_2 - 0.03429 X_3 + 0.014172 X_4 - 0.04792 X_5 - 0.00859 X_6 - 0.00187 X_7 - 0.02139 X_8$
11	$Y_{11} = -0.01484 X_1 - 0.10857 X_2 - 0.04604 X_3 + 0.0110597 X_4 - 0.07059 X_5 - 0.03540 X_6 + 0.000686 X_7 - 0.02205 X_8$
Aggregated Model	$Y = -0.03032 X_1 - 0.11847 X_2 - 0.04607 X_3 - 0.015440 X_4 - 0.03684 X_5 - 0.01394 X_6 - 0.00444 X_7 - 0.01724 X_8$

Residual Prediction Using AutoRegressive Model

An autoregressive (AR) model predicts future value based on past value. It's used for forecasting when there is some correlation between values in a time series and the values that precede and succeed them. The process is basically a linear regression of the data in the current series against one or more past values in the same series. In this phase cluster sampling based logistic regression model residual is taken for prediction. The figure 8 shows the time series model of residual.

The table 9 shows residual prediction using AR model. It represented as actual residual is compared by the predicted residual values for each model. This model has minimal predicted error. Based on this prediction to forecasting the future residual value using AR forecast model.

The table 10.shows forecast the future residual value using AR forecast model.

Enhanced Logistic Regression Model

In this phase to combining the both LR model and Residual Prediction (RP) Model. The table 11 shows enhanced logistic regression model is better than traditional logistic regression model

Table 4. Derived models using random sampling based logistic regressions

Sample Number	Derived Models
1	$Y_1 = -0.00400X_1 -0.23851X_2 -0.04238X_3 +0.00200X_4 - 0.033148 - X_5 0.001410X_6 -0.018340X_7 -0.01624X_8$
2	$Y_2 = -0.02160X_1 -0.23178X_2 -0.07282X_3 +0.09812X_4 -0.27200X_5 -0.04063X_6 + 0.02233X_7 -0.06972X_8$
3	$Y_3 = -0.03765X_1 -0.27878X_2 -0.05872X_3 +0.01202X_4 -0.00489X_5 +0.04065X_6 +0.02475X_7 -0.08141X_8$
4	$Y_4 = -0.03268X_1 -0.52005X_2 -0.05863X_3 -0.00785X_4 -0.07234X_5 +0.001499X_6 -0.02655X_7 -0.07496X_8$
5	$Y_5 = -0.06999X1 -0.32120X_2 -0.16564X_3 +0.01956X_4 -0.17227X_5 +0.09429X_6 -0.13117X_7 +0.01878X_8$
6	$Y_6 = 0.01858X_1 -0.30299X_2 -0.36360X_3 -0.02807X_4 - 0.05484X_5 -0.04100X_6 -0.07391X_7 -0.07536X_8$
7	$Y_7 = 0.04542X_1 -0.51738X_2 -0.22220X_3 +0.06125X_4 -0.01264X_5 +0.01720X_6 -0.24078X_7 -0.08365X_8$
8	$Y_8 = -0.04975X_1 -0.59491X_2 -0.15446X_3 +0.05467X_4 -0.10180X_5 -0.02266X_6 -0.10581X_7 +0.02014X_8$
9	$Y_9 = -0.02962X_1 -0.13273X_2 +0.000103X_3 -0.21800X_4 +0.065556X_5 +0.083311X_6 -0.02325X_7 +0.07239X_8$
10	$Y_{10} = -0.00268X_1 -0.22407X_2 -0.01008X_3 +0.003256X_4 -0.13186X_5 -0.02139X_6 +0.033562X_7 -0.01002X_8$
Aggregated Model	$\mathbf{Y= -0.01408X_1 -0.33624X_2 -0.11483X_3 -0.02034X_4 -0.07239X_5 +0.011268X_6 -0.05025X_7 -0.03001X_8}$

CONCLUSION

In this work, an Enhanced Logistic regression model for analyzing the big data. The performance of the proposed work is studied with different sampling method. From the study, it has been observed that ELR model gives better result compared to traditional LR model. For big data, ELR model is the ideal approach for analyzing the Big data.

ACKNOWLEDGMENT

The first author acknowledges the UGC- Special Assistance Programme (SAP) for the financial support to her research under the UGC-SAP at the level of DRS-II (Ref.No.F.5-6/2018/DRS-II (SAP-II)), 26 July 2018 in the Department of Computer Science.

REFERENCES

Alvi, M. (2016). *A Manual For Selecting Sampling Techniques In Research*. MPRA Munich Personal RepPEC Archive.

Table 5. Derived models using cluster sampling based logistic regression

Random Number	Derived Models
1	$Y_1 = -0.00400X_1 -0.23851X_2 -0.04238X_3 +0.00200X_4 - 0.033148 - X_5 0.001410X_6 -0.018340X_7 -0.01624X_8$
2	$Y_2 = -0.02160X_1 -0.23178X_2 -0.07282X_3 +0.09812X_4 -0.27200X_5 -0.04063X_6 + 0.02233X_7 -0.06972X_8$
3	$Y_3 = -0.03765X_1 -0.27878X_2 -0.05872X_3 +0.01202X_4 -0.00489X_5 +0.04065X_6 +0.02475X_7 -0.08141X_8$
4	$Y_4 = -0.03268X_1 -0.52005X_2 -0.05863X_3 -0.00785X_4 -0.07234X_5 +0.001499X_6 -0.02655X_7 -0.07496X_8$
5	$Y_5 = -0.06999X1 -0.32120X_2 -0.16564X_3 +0.01956X_4 -0.17227X_5 +0.09429X_6 -0.13117X_7 +0.01878X_8$
6	$Y_6 = 0.01858X_1 -0.30299X_2 -0.36360X_3 -0.02807X_4 - 0.05484X_5 -0.04100X_6 -0.07391X_7 -0.07536X_8$
7	$Y_7 = 0.04542X_1 -0.51738X_2 -0.22220X_3 +0.06125X_4 -0.01264X_5 +0.01720X_6 -0.24078X_7 -0.08365X_8$
8	$Y_8 = -0.04975X_1 -0.59491X_2 -0.15446X_3 +0.05467X_4 -0.10180X_5 -0.02266X_6 -0.10581X_7 +0.02014X_8$
9	$Y_9 = -0.02962X_1 -0.13273X_2 +0.000103X_3 -0.21800X_4 +0.065556X_5 +0.083311X_6 -0.02325X_7 +0.07239X_8$
10	$Y_{10} = -0.00268X_1 -0.22407X_2 -0.01008X_3 +0.003256X_4 -0.13186X_5 -0.02139X_6 +0.033562X_7 -0.01002X_8$
Aggregated Model	**$Y = -0.01408X_1 -0.33624X_2 -0.11483X_3 -0.02034X_4 -0.07239X_5 +0.011268X_6 -0.05025X_7 -0.03001X_8$**

Table 6. Sequence sampling deviance values

Sample No	Null Deviance	Residual Deviance	AIC
1	4589.9	4328.4	20025
2	4840.4	4489.8	20391
3	4851.1	4496.2	20405
4	4634.1	4371.3	20124
5	4645.8	4415.0	20223
6	4585.0	4304.3	19969
7	4553.3	4289.6	19935
8	4582.6	4236.8	19811
9	4607.8	4244.2	19828
10	4591.6	4232.1	19800
11	832.50	762.53	3548.5
Mean	**4301.282**	**4015.475**	**18550.86**

Table 7. Random sampling deviance values

Sample No	Null Deviance	Residual Deviance	AIC
1	9179.7	9094.9	9112.9
2	1533.3	1499.0	1517
3	10548	10449	10647
4	8952.0	8719.3	8737.3
5	10817	10637	10655
6	4174.2	4099.4	4117.4
7	7980.9	7748.3	7766.3
8	7476.7	7172.8	7190.8
9	3270.5	3184.4	3202.4
10	5952.7	5859.3	5877.3
Mean	**6988.5**	**6851.34**	**6864.34**

Table 8. Cluster sampling deviance values

Cluster Sampling	Null Deviance	Residual Deviance	AIC
1	980.56	956.87	4932
2	972.75	935.53	4706.5
3	959.44	933.45	4684.2
4	967.28	942.79	4783.8
5	1023.14	987.75	5249.7
6	1012.36	970.67	5075.3
7	1010.04	981.93	5190.6
8	1010.8	985.2	5223.8
9	989.54	5267.7	3270.5
10	946.06	922.57	4567
11	188.07	179.71	996.11
Mean	**917.1136**	**888.8191**	**4606.974**

Bchenne, S., Jacob, D., & Henze, G. P. (2011). Sampling Based On SOBOL, Sequences For Month Carlo Techniques Applied To Builing Simulations. *12th Conference Of international Building Performance Simulation Association.*

Bijuraj, L. v. (2013). Clustering And Its Application. *Proceedings Of National Conference On New Horizones in.it-NCNHIT.*

Carter, E. M., & Potts, H. w. (2014). *Predicting Length Of Stay From An Electronic Patient Record System: A Primary Total Knee Replacement Example.* Crter And Potts BMC Medical Informatics And Decision Making.

Figure 7. Performance of LR with different sampling method

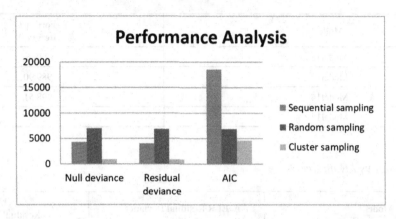

Figure 8. Residual time series plot

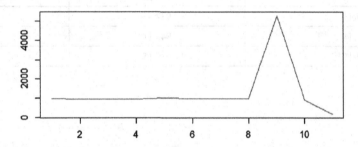

Table 9. Residual prediction using AR model

Model	Actual Residual Deviance	Predicted Residual Deviance
Model1	956.87	950.12
Model2	935.53	936.30
Model3	933.45	932.95
Model4	942.79	943.11
Model5	987.75	986.15
Model6	970.67	970.12
Model7	981.93	980.00
Model8	985.2	984.81
Model9	5267.7	5198.9
Model10	922.57	923.91
Model11	179.71	176,99

Table 10. Residual forecast using AR model

Model	Forecast Residual
Model12	1278.58
Model13	989.90
Model14	998.51
Model15	1098.91

Table 11. ELR model vs LR model

Model	ELR Residual Deviance	LR Residual Deviance
Model1	950.12	1499.0
Model2	936.30	10449
Model3	932.95	8719.3
Model4	943.11	10637
Model5	986.15	1499.0

Combes, C., Kadari, F., & Chaabane, S. (2014). Predicting Hospital Length of Stay Using Regression Models: Application To Emergency Department. *10eme Conference Francophone de Modelisation, optimization et Simulation-MOSIM'14.*

Dhamodharavadhani, S., Gowri, R., & Rathipriya, R. (2018). Unlock Different V's of Big Data for Analytics. *International Journal on Computer Science and Engineering, 06*(04), 183–190.

Duggal, R., & Kharti, S. K. (2016). Impact Of Selected Pre-Processing Techniques On Prediction Of Risk Of Early Readmission For Diabetic Patient In India. *International Journal Of Diabetes In Developing Countries.*

Glugnn, N., Owens, L., Bennett, K., Healy, M. L., & Silke, B. (2014). Glucose As A Risk Predictior In Acute Medical Emergency Admissions. Elsevier. *Diabetes Research and Clinical Practice.*

Ho, W.-M., Lin, J.-R., Wang, H.-H., Liou, C.-W., Chang, K. C., Lee, J.-D., ... Lee, T.-H. (2016). Prediction OF In-Hospital Stroke Mortality In Critical Care Unit. *SpringerPlus, 5*(1), 1051. doi:10.118640064-016-2687-2 PMID:27462499

Hu, S. (2007). *Akaike Information Criterrion.* Academic Press.

Jun, S., Lee, S. J., & Ryu, J.-B. (2015). A Divide Regression Analysis For Big Data. *International Journal Of Software Enginnering And Its Applications.*

Jung, Kang, & Heo. (2014). Clustering Performance Comparission Using K-means And Expectation MaximiZation Algorithm. *Bio Technology And Biotechnological Equipment, 28.*

Luo, G. (2016). *Automatically Expalining Machine Learning Prediction Results: A Demonstration On Type 2 Diabetes Risk Prediction.* Luo Health Inf Sci Syst.

Mukhajee, S., & Shaw, R. (2016). *Big Data, Concept, Applications, Challenges And Future Scope* (Vol. 5). International Journal Of Advanced Research In Computer And Communication Engineering.

NM, D. S., T, E., P, S., & S, L. (2015). Predictive Methodology For Diabetic Data Analysis In Big Data. *Procedia Computer Science.*

Nuarmi, E. A., Neyadi, H. A., Mohamed, N., & A1-jaroodi, J. (2015). Application Of Bigdata To Smart-cities. *Springer Open Journal.*

Owais, S. S., & Hussein, N. S. (2016). *Extract Five Categories CPIVW From The 9v's Characteristics of Big data.* Academic Press.

Park & Hyeoun. (2013). An Introduction To Logistic Regression From Basic Concepts To Interpretation with Particular Attension To Nursing Domin. *J Korean Acad Nurs, 43.*

Singh, A. S., Masuku, & Micah, B. (2014). Sampling Techniques And Determination Of Sample Size in applied Statistical Research: An Overview. *International Journal Of Economics, Commerce And Management.*

Strack, B., DeShazo, J. P., Gennings, C., Olmo, J. L., Ventura, S. J., & Cios, K. (2014). *Impact OF HbAlc Measurement on Hospital Readmission Rates: Analysis of 70,000 Clinical Database Patient Records.* Hindawi Publishing Corporation BioMed research International.

Sushmita, S., Khulbe, G., Hasan, A., & Newman, S. (2015). *Predicting 30-Day Risk And Cost Of "All Cause" Hospital Readmissions.* The Workshop Of The Thirtieth AAA 1 Conference On Artificial Intelligence Expanding The Boundaries Of Health Informatics Using A1: Technical Report ws-16-08.

Teddie & Yu. (2007). Mixed Methods Sampling A Typology with examples. *Journal Of Mixed Methods Research, 1.*

Uitter, J. S. (1984). Faster Methods for Random Sampling (Vol. 27). Academic Press.

Zhang, H., Shoa, L., & Xi, C. (2014). Predicting The Treatement Effect in Diabetes Patient Using Classification Models. *International Journal Of Digital Content Technology And Its Applications, 8.*

Chapter 9
On Foundations of Estimation for Nonparametric Regression With Continuous Optimization

Pakize Taylan

Dicle University, Turkey

ABSTRACT

The aim of parametric regression models like linear regression and nonlinear regression are to produce a reasonable relationship between response and independent variables based on the assumption of linearity and predetermined nonlinearity in the regression parameters by finite set of parameters. Nonparametric regression techniques are widely-used statistical techniques, and they not only relax the assumption of linearity in the regression parameters, but they also do not need a predetermined functional form as nonlinearity for the relationship between response and independent variables. It is capable of handling higher dimensional problem and sizes of sample than regression that considers parametric models because the data should provide both the model building and the model estimates. For this purpose, firstly, PRSS problems for MARS, ADMs, and CR will be constructed. Secondly, the solution of the generated problems will be obtained with CQP, one of the famous methods of convex optimization, and these solutions will be called CMARS, CADMs, and CKR, respectively.

DOI: 10.4018/978-1-7998-0106-1.ch009

INTRODUCTION

The traditional nonlinear regression model (NRM) fits the model (Bates & Watts, 1988; Seber & Wild, 1989).

$$y_i = f\left(\beta, x_i^T\right) + \varepsilon_i, \tag{1}$$

where $\beta = \left(\beta_1, \beta_2, ..., \beta_p\right)^T$ is a p-vector for unknown parameters that must be estimated by nonlinear least square estimation method, $x_i = \left(x_{i1}, x_{i2}, ...x_{ip}\right)^T$ is a p-vector of explanatory variables of the ith observations, say y_i, and $f\left(\cdot\right)$ is an suitable function that depends on the explanatory variables and parameters. The function $f\left(\cdot\right)$ that establishes relationship between the average of the response variable y and the explanatory variables, is predetermined. Here, ε_i are random errors that describes deviation from the function f and observations y and it is supposed that they are independent and distributed with $N\left(0, \sigma^2\right)$ where σ^2 is constant variance. Nonlinear model is a parametric model and it is supposed that set of unknown parameters β is finite. If we have parameters β, future estimations of x, will be independent of data obtained from observation. For this reason β holds everything you need to know about the data and the complexity of the model will be finite even the amount of data used is infinite. This situation makes NLR model not very flexible. Nonparametric regression (NPR) is established based on the information ensured from the data and it needs larger sizes sample than regression using parametric models like linear and nonlinear regression models because the data should provide both the model building and the model estimates. Nonparametric models suppose that the distribution of data cannot be described by considering such a finite dimensional parameters. But they can usually be desribed by supposing an infinite dimensional β. The amount of information that β can hold about the data can increase as the amount of data increases. This makes NPR more flexible.

The general NPR model (Fox, 2001) is written as

$$y_i = f\left(x_i\right), i = 1, 2, ..., n \tag{2}$$

where $x_i = \left(x_{i1}, x_{i2}, ...x_{ip}\right)^T$ is p- vector of explanatory variables for ith realization, but the function f is unspecified unlike NRM. Moreover, the aim of NPR is to produce a model directly for the relationship between response variable and explanatory variables through function f, rather than for estimating parameters. Generally, it is supposed implicitly that f is a smooth, continuous function when NPR is used for data analysis. The standart assumption for NPR is that $\varepsilon_i \sim N\left(0, \sigma^2\right)$, as in NRM.

In low dimensional $(p \leq 2)$ situations global parametric modeling (GPM) techniques based on the piecewise and local parametric fitting, and roughness penalty may be successfully implemented. The piecewise parametric fitting approximates regression function f by using different type of parametric functions, each described on a different subregion of the domain U. Commonly used parametric functions are low order polynomials whose popular ones are splines. In this metod, approximation function has a constraints such as being everywhere continuous, and having continuous low order derivatives. The number of subregions and the lowest order derivative allowed being discontinuous at subregion boundaries provide a tradeoff between flexibility and smoothness of the approximation of f, say $\hat{f}$. The process is accomplished by establishing a set of basis functions, and to fit the coefficients of the basis function expansion to the data by employing ordinary least-squares. Piecewise parametric modeling can be extented to higher dimensions $(p > 2)$ and can be seen as simple in principle, but it is very hard to apply in practice.

Local parametric approximations ("smoothers") take the form (Friedman, 1991)

$$\hat{f}(x) = h\left[x\left|\{\hat{c}_j(x)\}_{j=1}^l\right.\right], l \le p, \tag{3}$$

where h is a simple parametric function and $\hat{c}_j$ are estimation of parameters c_j. In this approach, the parameters take different values according to the each assessment point x and they are obtained by locally weighted least-squares fitting

$$\{\hat{c}_j(x)\}_{j=1}^l = \underset{\{\hat{c}_j\}_{j=1}^l}{\arg\min} \sum_{i=1}^n w(x, x_i)\left[y_i - h\left(x_i\left|\{c_j\}_{i=1}^l\right.\right)\right]^2. \tag{4}$$

The weight function $w(x, x')$ is selected to set the dominant mass on points x' 'near' to x. The features of the approximation are mostly specified by the selection of w and to a smaller degree by the particular parametric function h employed. the choice of an suitable weight function w for the problem at hand makes it difficult to apply local parametric methods at higher dimensions. This based on f and thus is generally unknown. Roughness penalty approximations are defined by

$$\hat{f}(x) = \underset{h}{\arg\min}\left\{\sum_{i=1}^n [y_i - h(x_i)]^2 + \rho R(h)\right\}, \tag{5}$$

here, $R(h)$ is a penalty function on the "roughness" of the function $h(x)$ and it increases with the increase of the function. The minimization process is carried out over all h for which $R(h)$ is defined. The parameter ρ is the smoothing or penalty parameter, which governs the tradeoff between the roughness of h and its accuracy to the data. There are similarities between the features of roughness penalty methods and those of kernel methods, employing an suitable kernel function K with ρ governing the bandwidth $s(x)$. Thus, this approximations will have the same basic limitations in high dimensional settings.

As described in the above-introduced methods, it is very difficult to fit the general NPR when the number of predictors is larger than two 2. These difficulties are related to the variance of nonparametric estimators since generally, nonparametric methods are negatively affected from variance that scales exponentially with the number of predictors p. This is called the curse of dimensionality that is invented by Bellman (1961). Therefore, more restrictive models should be used. In this context, we will consider *Additive Models* (ADMs) (Buja, Hastie, & Tibshirani, 1989) fitted by backfitting algorithm that uses scatterplot smoother as a building block in Section 2. and *Multivariate Adaptive Regression Splines* (MARS) developed by Friedman (1991) for estimating unspecified NPR f in Section 3. For the ADMs, firstly we will consider B-splines (Boor, 1978) basis function as a smooth functions, and construct Penalized Residual Sum of Squares (*PRSS*) for it. Secondly we will solve *PRSS* by *Conic Quadratic Programming* (CQP) (Ben-Tal & Nemirovski, 1987) which is a *Convex Optimization* method (Boyd & Vandenberghe, 2004). MARS is a data based approach for estimating multivariate NPR function Eq.(2) to overcome some of the limitations associated methods mentioned above. This approach employs two algorithms so called backward step and forward step. Taylan et al. (2010) developed an alternative for forward step algorithm by *PRSS* and CQP considered in this chapter. Finally, we propose *Kernel Regressions* (KR) (Schölkopf, Smola, & Müller, 1999) for obtain regression function f. But KR has troubles related with computational and statistical efficiency in high dimensionally problem. To overcome this distress, regression function considered in additive way by employing ADMs. Then, *PRSS* problem is formed to be solved by elegant framework of CQP.

BACKGROUND

Estimation, prediction, and classification problems using NPR frequently arise in the scientific areas, such as finance, computational biology, medicine, and medicine. GPM techniques can give successful and effective results if the works in these areas contain low dimensional predictor or explanatory variables. Otherwise, these methods do not yield beneficial results. For high dimensional situations some flexible regression methods should be considered. In this chapter, some nonparametric regression techniques that take into account the advantages of CQP from continuous optimization techniques will be discussed.

MAIN FOCUS OF THE CHAPTER

Related Works

Today, hundreds of research studies have examined NPR approaches in modeling and classification of different data sets. K-nearest-neighbors (kNN) approach (Mucherino, Papajorgji, & Pardalos, 2009) is the most basic and popular ones and it is very efficient and effective classifier for classification data. It classify samples in the data set based on the class of their nearest neighbor. It is not surprising to find numerous studies in science, technology and economics using kNN. (Jabbar, Deekshatulua, & Chandra, 2013) combined kNN with genetic algorithm for effective classification of heart diseases that cause death in India. Their algorithm improved the accuracy in diagnosis of heart disease according to the experimental results. Imandoust and Bolandraftar (2013) used kNN classification method, which is more than other methods, for forcasting financial distress after the global financial crisis in Iran. Smoothing splines are also popular method, such as kNN, ensure a flexible way of estimating the underlying regression function f. Smoothing splines are implemented based on the smoothing parameter which its selection has great importance. Because they are adjusted via this parameter chosen by trial and error, selecting a value that adjusts smoothness against accuracy for the data used. Many methods of choising smoothing parameter are based on the minimization of the Mean-Squared Error (MSE) of the fit by using a formula that gives a value close to the mean-square error or by some form of *Cross-Validation* (CV) (Refaeilzadeh, Tang, & Liu, 2009) such as *Generalized Cross-Validation* (GCV) (Golub, Heath, & Wahba, 1979) that is the most common method for determining the smoothing parameter. GCV was developed by Golub et al. (1979) for selecting of Ridge Parameter. Lee (2003) dealt with different smoothing parameter choice techniques, including two so-called risk estimation procedures have never been declared in the literature, in his simulation study. One of the his remarkable experimental observation was that the popular method, GCV, was outperformed by an advanced *Akaike Information criterion* (AIC) (Burnham & Anderson, 2002), that shares the same assumptions and computational complexity. Parametric regression obtains the set of parameter estimates that fit the data best for a predetermined family of functions for estimation of regression function f. This method provide easily explainable models performing an useful work of interpreting the variation in the data set. However, the selected family of functions can impose excessive restriction can impose excessive restriction for some types of data set. Fan and Gijbels (1996) presented some examples in that even a 4th-order polynomial was fail to obtain satisfactory fits. Higher order fits may be considered, but this can be caused to numerical inconsistency and instability problem. A more dynamic method modeling such as local polynomial regression method can overcome this challenge. In this method a low-order weighted least squares (WLS) regression is considered at each point of interest predictor, say x_0 employing data in the neighborhood of x_0. Stone (1977) presented a class of weight functions employed to estimate the conditional probability of a response variable Y given a corresponding value for X. Especially, Stone proposes a weight function that specifies positive values to only the k observations with X-values closest to the point of interest, x_0, where "closest" is assigned using some pseudo-metric which is subject to regularity conditions. One of the powerful NPR method is ADMs, employing backfitting algorithm. Buja et al. (1989) showed that backfitting is the Gauss-Seidel iterative method to solve a set of normal equations associated with the ADMs. They demonstrated conditions for consistency and nondegeneracy. Also, they verified that convergence for the backfitting and related algorithms for a class of smoothers that includes cubic spline smoothers. In order to make the theoretical properties of this method more understandable, especially the use of backfitting algorithm for estimators, Opsomer et al. (1997) explored properties of ADMs fitted by local polynomial regression. In their study, they not only presented sufficient conditions for the asymptotic existence of unique estimators for the bivariate ADMs but also computed asymptotic approximations to the bias and the variance of a homoskedastic bivariate additive model with local polynomial terms. Extention of ADMs are provided by Generalized additive models (GAMs)(Hastie & Tibshirani,1986) that ensures a flexible technique to detect nonlinear covariate effects in exponential family models and other likelihood-based regression models. GAMs extends generalized linear model GLM (Nelder & Wedderburn, 1972) by replacing the linear predictor $\eta = \sum_{j=1}^{p} \beta_j X_j$ with the additive predictor $\eta = \sum_{j=1}^{p} S_j \left(X_j \right)$ where $S_j \left(X_j \right)$ is an unspecified smooth function that can be estimated by any so called scatterplot smoother, in an iterative procedure called the local scoring algorithm. A running mean, kernel estimate and splines are examples of scatterplot smoother (Reinsch, (1967), Wahba and Wold (1975), Cleveland (1979), and Silverman (1985) for discussions of smoothing techniques). Another famous and widely used nonparametric technique is Multivariate Adaptive Regression Splines (MARS) which introduced by Friedman (1991) and it is a flexible regression modeling for high dimensional data. MARS is a data based method since it takes the form of an expansion in product spline basis functions, where the number of basis functions as well as the parameters associated with each one prompt (product degree and knot locations) are automatically determined by the data. This method is inspired by the recursive partitioning (RP) approach for regression and holding the same features with it. Unlike RP, however, this procedure generates continuous models that have continuous derivatives through the above-mentioned algorithms. It has more power and flexibility to model relationships that are nearly additive or involve interactions in at most a few variables.

ADDITIVE MODEL (ADM)

A significant particular situation of the general model Eq. (2) is nonparametric simple regression, where there is only one predictor. Nonparametric simple regression is often called 'scatterplot smoothing' because an significant application is to tracing a smooth curve through a scatterplot of y_i against x_i. Since there are difficulties in the fit of the general NPR model and to display the fitted model when there are many predictors, more restrictive models have been developed. One such model is the additive regression model (Buja et al., 1989; Hastie & Tibshirani, 1990)

$$y_i = S_0 + \sum_{j=1}^{p} S_j\left(x_{ij}\right), i = 1,..,n, \tag{6}$$

where the partial-regression functions S_j are supposed to be smooth, and are to be estimated from the data. Here, the functions S_j are mostly considered to be splines, i.e., piecewise polynomial, since, e.g., polynomials themselves have a too strong or early asymptotic to $\pm\infty$ and by this they are not satisfying for data fitting. The standard convention consists in assuming at X_j that $E\left(S_j\left(X_j\right)\right) = 0$ when considering ADMs for data fitting, since otherwise there will be a free constant in each of the functions S_j

ADMs have a strong motivation as a useful data analytic tool. Each function is estimated by an algorithm proposed by *Friedman and Stuetzle* (1981) and called *backfitting* (or *Gauss-Seidel*) *algorithm*. As the estimator for S_0, the arithmetic mean (average) of the output data is used:

$$\hat{S}_0 = ave(y_i \mid i = 1,...,n) := (1 / n)\sum_{i=1}^{n} y_i .$$

This procedure depends on the partial residual against x_{ij}:

$$r_{ij} = y_i - \hat{S}_0 - \sum_{k \neq j} \hat{S}_k\left(x_{ik}\right), \tag{7}$$

and consists of estimating each smooth function by holding all the other ones fixed (Hastie & Tibshirani, 1987). To prove its ***convergence***, Buja et al. (1989) used the normal equation for an arbitrary solution $\tilde{S}$ to reduce the problem to the solution of a corresponding homogeneous system.

Since each variable is represented in Eq. (6), the model retains an important interpretive feature of the linear model: the variation of the fitted response surface holding all but one predictor fixed does not depend on the values of the other predictor. In practice this means that once the additive model is fitted to data, we can plot the p coordinate functions separately to examine the roles of the predictors in modeling the response. Such simplicity does not come free; the additive model is almost always an approximation to the regression surface, but hopefully a useful one. When fitting a linear regression model, we generally do not believe that the model is correct. Rather we believe that it will be a good first order approximation to the true surface, and that we can uncover the important predictors and their roles using to approximations. ADMs are more general approximations. Figure 1 shows to what extent the additive model for age and base deficit is an approximation to the bivariate response surface. In this case it appears that a possibly important bumb in the regression surface is lost in the additive approximation. On the other hand, the average trend in each variable is well represented.

In our approach to estimate each smooth function $\hat{S}_0$ we use penalized residuals sum of squares (*PRSS*) that consider B-spline basis function (De Boor, 1978) that provide stable solution for high dimensional data and CQP (Ben-Tal & Nemirovski, 1987) which is a very important modern class convex programming.

The Penalized Residual Sum of Squares Problem (*PRSS*) for ADMs

For the ADMs, *PRSS* has the following form:

$$PRSS(S_0, S_1, ..., S_p) := \sum_{i=1}^{n} \left\{ y_i - S_0 - \sum_{j=1}^{p} S_j(x_{ij}) \right\}^2 + \sum_{j=1}^{m} \varphi_j \int_{c}^{d} \left[S_j''(t_j) \right]^2 dt_j, \tag{8}$$

where the first sum measures "goodness of data fitting", the second sum means "penalties" and is defined by the functions' curvatures. In the case of separation of variables, the interval bounds may also depend on j, i.e., they are intervals $[c_j, d_j]$. We recall that one basic idea of the additive models just consists in a model with variables separated. In Eq. (8), $\varphi_j \geq 0$ are tuning or *smoothing* parameters and represent a tradeoff between the first and the second term. Large values of φ_j yield smoother curves, smaller values result in more fluctuation. The goal of smoothness is sometimes also called stability, robustness

Figure 1. Perspectives plots of the additive and bivariate surfaces
(Hastie & Tibshirani, 1990)

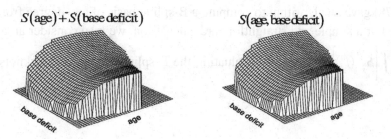

or regularity; in fact, in the theory of inverse problems one wants to guarantee that the estimation is sufficiently stable with respect to noise and other forms of perturbation.

It can be shown that the minimize of *PRSS* is an additive spline model (Hastie & Tibshirani, 1987). Several type spline function may be imposed into *PRSS* for estimation of function S_j. Simple choices of basis functions are the truncated power series basis. The truncated power bases are conceptually simple. However, they are not attractive numerically, because they often yield big rounding problems. Therefore, in this study we will use the B-spline bases which lead to efficient elegant computations even when the number of knots is large (De Boor, 1978). B-splines consist of polynomial pieces, which are connected in a special way. In a B-spline, each control point is associated with a basis function. Then, the curve is defined by

$$S_j(z) := \sum_{u=1}^{r} \lambda_u^j B_{u,k}(z), z \in [c_j, d_j]. \tag{9}$$

Here, $\lambda_1^j; \lambda_2^j, ..., \lambda_r^j$ are r control parameters and

$$B_{1,k}(z), B_{2,k}(z), ..., B_{r,k}(z)$$

are r basis functions of degree k (order $k+1$). Let a knot vector $z = (z_1, z_2, ..., z_q)$ be a sequence with

$$z_u \in [c_j, d_j], c_j \le z_u < z_{u+1} \le d_j,$$

and $k = q - r - 1$. This determines the values of z at which the pieces of curve connect to each other.

Zero and k degree *B*-splines basis function to estimate each smooth function f_j are defined by

$$B_{u,0}(z) = \begin{cases} 1, & z_u \le t < z_{u+1} \\ 0, & otherwise, \end{cases} and \; B_{u,k}(z) = \frac{z - z_u}{z_{u+k} - z_u} B_{u,k-1}(z) + \frac{z_{u+k+1} - z}{z_{u+k+1} - z_{j+1}} B_{u+1,k-1}(z) (k \ge 1); \tag{10}$$

for $k \ge 2$. Its derivative, wherever defined, is given by (De Boor, 1978; Eilers & Marx, 1996).

$$\frac{d}{dt} B_{u,k}(z) = \frac{k}{t_{u+k} - z_u} B_{u,k-1}(z) - \frac{k}{t_{u+k+1} - t_{u+1}} B_{u+1,k-1}(z). \tag{11}$$

De Boor (1978) gave an algorithm to compute a B-spline basis of any degree from a B-spline basis of lower degree. For a simple and straightforward calculation, we may consider an approximative discreted form of $\int \left[S_j''(t_j) \right]^2 dt_j$, e.g., by evaluating the B-splines $S_j''(\cdot)$ at the knots x_{ij}. To be more precise:

Either, we integrate between the end points $a < b$, uniformly for all j; in this case, we would add some further nodes $x_{ij} \in [c, d]$ in addition to our cluster points x_{ij} which are located in the interior of $I_j := [c_j, d_j]$. Now, we get the following approximative evaluation:

$$\int \left[S_j''(t_j) \right]^2 dt_j \cong \sum_{i=1}^{n-1} \left[S_j''(x_{ij}) \right]^2 (x_{i+1j} - x_{ij}) = \sum_{i=1}^{n-1} \left[S_j''(x_{ij}) w_i \right]^2,$$

where

$$w_i := \sqrt{x_{i+1j} - x_{ij}} \, (i = 1, 2, ..., n-1).$$

Then, *PRSS* becomes

$$PRSS(S_0, S_1, ..., S_p) := \sum_{i=1}^{n} \left\{ y_i - S_0 - \sum_{j=1}^{p} S_j(x_{ij}) \right\}^2 + \sum_{j=1}^{p} \varphi_j \sum_{i=1}^{n-1} \left[S_j''(x_{ij}) w_i \right]^2. \tag{12}$$

We want to minimize Eq. (12) using *B*-spline for each function S_j, through the *PRSS* which is used to estimate S_j. Therefore, we explicitly insert the parametrical form Eq. (9) of the functions S_j into Eq. (8) and we take $B_{u,k} := B_u$ for abbreviate, then Eq. (12) looks as follows:

$$PRSS(S_0, S_1, ..., S_p) := \sum_{i=1}^{n} \left\{ y_i - S_0 - \boldsymbol{B}_i \lambda \right\}^2 + \sum_{j=1}^{p} \varphi_j \sum_{i=1}^{n-1} \left[\boldsymbol{B}_i^{j''} w_i \lambda^j \right]^2 \tag{13}$$

where

$$\lambda^j := \left(\lambda_1^j, ..., \lambda_r^j \right)^T, \lambda = \left(\lambda^{1T}, ..., \lambda^{pT} \right)^T, B_i^j := \left(B_1(x_{ij}), ..., B_r(x_{ij}) \right),$$

$$B_i := \left(B_i^1, ..., B_i^p \right),$$

$$B_i^{j''} = \left(B_1''(x_{ij}), ..., B_r''(x_{ij}) \right) (i = 1, 2, ..., n-1; j = 1, 2, ..., p).$$

Let assume that S_0 is fixed via the estimation by the arithmetic mean of the values y_i and then our problem takes the following brief form:

$$PRSS(\lambda^1,...,\lambda^p) := \sum_{i=1}^{n} \left\{ y_i - \hat{S}_0 - B_i\lambda \right\}^2 + \sum_{j=1}^{p} \varphi_j \left\| \bar{B}^j \lambda^j \right\|^2$$

$$= \sum_{i=1}^{n} \left\{ b_i - B_i\lambda \right\}^2 + \sum_{j=1}^{p} \varphi_j \left\| \bar{B}^j \lambda^j \right\|^2 \qquad (14)$$

$$= \left\| B\lambda - b \right\|^2 + \sum_{j=1}^{p} \varphi_j \left\| \bar{B}^j \lambda^j \right\|^2$$

where

$$b_i = y_i - \hat{S}_0 (i = 1, 2, ..., n), b = \left(b_1, ..., b_n \right)^T$$

and

$$B = (B_1^T, ..., B_n^T)^T$$

with

$$\bar{B}^j = \left(B_1^{j\,''T} w_1, ..., B_{n-1}^{j\,''T} w_{n-1} \right)^T.$$

PRSS noticeably, may be considering as *Lagrange function* associated with the lagrange multipliers φ_j and constraints

$$\sum_{i=1}^{n-1} \left[B_i^{j\,''} w_i \lambda^j \right]^2 - M_j \leq 0$$

where $M_j > 0$ being some prescribed upper bounds for the corresponding sum curvature terms. Intending to keep the curvature integrals as small as possible, this bound can be interpreted as an "(error) tolerance" and it can be selected by the practitioner with the help of model-free or model-based methods (Hastie, Tibshirani, & Friedman, 2001). For the *Lagrangian dual problem* we may refer to (Taylan & Weber, 2007). Any solution or iteratively approximate solution of *PRSS* problem serves for determining the smoothing or regularization parameters φ_j, in particular, parameter the λ^j and, as a result functions S_j will be found.

An Alternative to the Choice for Smoothing Parameters with CQP (CADMs)

As mentioned in subsection 2.1, *PRSS* problem contains smoothing parameters φ_j with which we may easily influence the smoothness of a fitted curve. Therefore, they have to be estimated. For this, there are three possible methods which are called Generalized Cross Validation (GCV), Akaike information criteria (AIC) (Burnham & Anderson, 2002) and minimization of an UnBiased Risk Estimator (UBRE) (Craven & Wahba, 1979). In this subsection, we will give an alternative tecnique that takes advantage of convex optimization. Convex programming deals with problems consisting of minimizing a convex function over a convex set. Such problems arise frequently in many different application fields and have many important properties, like strong duality theory and the fact that any local minimum is a global minimum. These programs are not only computationally tractable but they also have theoretically efficient solution methods. Convex programming consists of several important specially structured classes of problems such as semidefinite programming (SDP), CQP, and geometric (GP) programming (Ben-Tal & Nemirovski, 1987). As mentioned earlier, we will consider (CQP) for determining smoothing parameters φ_j and, therefore functions S_j.

A CQP, also known as second-order cone programming (SOCP) is a conic problem

$$\underset{\alpha}{minimize}\ c^T\alpha, where\ A\alpha - b \in K, \tag{15}$$

for which the cone K is a direct product of several *"Lorentz cones"*:

$$L^{n_i+1} = \left\{\alpha = (\alpha_1, \alpha_2, ..., \alpha_{n_i+1})^T \in \mathbb{R}^{n_i+1} \mid \alpha_{n_i+1} \geq \sqrt{\alpha_1^2 + \alpha_2^2 + ... + \alpha_{n_i}^2}\right\}(n_i \geq 1, n_i \in \mathbb{N}). \tag{16}$$

More generally, partitioning the data matrix $\left[A_i; b_i\right]$ by

$$\left[A_i; b_i\right] = \begin{bmatrix} D_i & d_i \\ p_i^T & q_i \end{bmatrix},$$

then, its standart form may be written as

$$\underset{\alpha}{minimize}\ c^T\alpha, such\ that \left\|D_i\alpha - d_i\right\|_2 \leq p_i^T\alpha - q_i \quad (i = 0, 1, 2, ..., k). \tag{17}$$

After small introduction of CQP, then the standard form of *PRSS* problem Eq. (13) subject to the constrained curvature condition may be reinterpreted as the following constrained optimization problem:

$$\underset{\lambda}{minimize}\ \left\|B\lambda - b\right\|_2^2, such\ that \left\|\bar{B}^j\lambda^j\right\|_2^2 \leq M_j \quad (j = 1, 2, ..., p), \tag{18}$$

where $\left\|\bullet\right\|_2^2$ denote Euclidean norm squared. Here, B is an $n \times nr$ matrix of B-splines basis functions, λ is an nr - vector of control parameters, b is an n - vector of new responses

$$b_i = y_i - \hat{S}_0 \ (i = 1, 2, ..., n),$$

$\bar{B}^j$ is an $n - 1 \times r$ -matrix of multiplications of w_i and derivative of B- splines basis functions for jth, variables and λ^j is an r-vector of control parameters for jth variables. Then, optimization problem Eq. (13) may be written equivalent to:

$$\underset{s,\lambda}{minimize}\, s, such\, that \left\| B\lambda - b \right\|_2^2 \leq s^2, t \geq 0, \left\| \bar{B}^j \lambda^j \right\|_2^2 \leq M_j (j = 1, 2, ..., p) \tag{19}$$

or

$$\underset{t,\lambda}{minimize}\, s, such\, that \left\| B\lambda - b \right\|_2 \leq s, \left\| \bar{B}^j \lambda^j \right\|_2 \leq \sqrt{M_j} (j = 1, 2, ..., p). \tag{20}$$

In fact, it may be noted that optimization problem Eq. (20) is such a CQP program with the following properties if it is compared with the standard form of CQP problem Eq. (17):

$$c = \left(1, 0^T \right)^T, x = \left(s, \lambda^T \right)^T, D_0 = \left(0, B \right), d_0 = b, p_0 = \left(1, 0, ..., 0 \right)^T, q_0 = 0,$$

$$D_j = (0, \bar{B}^j), d_j = 0, p_j = 0 \text{ and } q_j = -\sqrt{M_j} (j = 1, 2, ..., p).$$

In order to obtain the optimality condition for the problem Eq. (20), it should be reformulated as follows:

$$\underset{s,\lambda}{minimize}\, s, such\, that$$

$$\chi := \begin{pmatrix} 0 & B \\ 1 & 0^T \end{pmatrix} \begin{pmatrix} s \\ \lambda \end{pmatrix} + \begin{pmatrix} -b \\ 0 \end{pmatrix},$$

$$\eta_j := \begin{pmatrix} 0 & \bar{B}^j \\ 0 & 0^T \end{pmatrix} \begin{pmatrix} s \\ \lambda \end{pmatrix} + \begin{pmatrix} 0 \\ \sqrt{M_j} \end{pmatrix}, \tag{21}$$

$$\chi \in L^{n+1}, \eta_j \in L^n \, (j = 1, 2, ..., p),$$

where L^{n+1}, L^n are the $(n + 1)$- and n-dimensional ice-cream (or second-order, or Lorentz) cones. The *dual problem* for the primal problem Eq.(20) may be formulated as

$$\underset{\omega_0, \omega_1, \omega_2, ..., \omega_p}{maximize}(b^T, 0)\, \omega_0 + \sum_{j=1}^{p} \left(0^T, -\sqrt{M_j} \right) \omega_j such\, that$$

$$\begin{pmatrix} 0^T & 1 \\ B^T & 0 \end{pmatrix} \omega_0 + \sum_{j=1}^{p} \begin{pmatrix} 0^T & 0 \\ \bar{B}^{jT} & 0 \end{pmatrix} \omega_j = \begin{pmatrix} 1 \\ 0 \end{pmatrix}, \tag{22}$$

$$\omega_0 \in L^{n+1}, \omega_j \in L^n (j = 1, 2, ..., p).$$

Moreover,

$$(s, \lambda, \chi, \eta_1, \ldots, \eta_p, \omega_0, \omega_1 \ldots, \omega_p)$$

is a *primal dual optimal solution* (Ben-Tal & Nemirovski, 1987) if and only if

$$
\chi := \begin{pmatrix} 0 & B \\ 1 & 0^T \end{pmatrix} \begin{pmatrix} s \\ \lambda \end{pmatrix} + \begin{pmatrix} -b \\ 0 \end{pmatrix},
$$

$$
\eta_j := \begin{pmatrix} 0 & \overline{B}^j \\ 0 & 0^T \end{pmatrix} \begin{pmatrix} s \\ \lambda \end{pmatrix} + \begin{pmatrix} 0 \\ \sqrt{M_j} \end{pmatrix},
$$

$$
\begin{pmatrix} 0^T & 1 \\ B^T & 0 \end{pmatrix} \omega_0 + \sum_{j=1}^{p} \begin{pmatrix} 0^T & 0 \\ \overline{B}^{jT} & 0 \end{pmatrix} \omega_j = \begin{pmatrix} 1 \\ 0 \end{pmatrix}, \tag{23}
$$

$$
\omega_0^T \chi = 0, \omega_j^T \eta_j = 0 (j = 1, 2, \ldots, p),
$$

$$
\chi \in L^{n+1}, \eta_j \in L^n (j = 1, 2, \ldots, p),
$$

$$
\omega_0 \in L^{n+1}, \omega_j \in L^n (j = 1, 2, \ldots, p).
$$

MULTIVARIATE ADAPTIVE REGRESSION SPLINE (MARS)

Multivariate Adaptive Regression Spline (MARS) is a method to estimate general functions of high dimensional arguments given sparse data (Friedman, 1991); MARS is an adaptive procedure because the selection of basis functions is data-based and specific to the problem at hand. This algorithm is a NPR procedure that makes no specific assumption about the underlying functional relationship between the dependent and independent variables. A special advantage of MARS lies in its ability to estimate the contributions of the basis functions so that both the additive and the interactive effects of the predictors are allowed to determine the response variable. For this model an algorithm was proposed by Friedman (1991) as a flexible approach to high dimensional nonparametric regression, based on a modified recursive partitioning methodology. MARS uses expansions in piecewise linear basis functions of the form

$$
c^+(x, \phi) = [+(x - \phi)]_+, c^-(x, \phi) = [-(x - \phi)]_+, \tag{24}
$$

where $[q]_+ := \max \{0, q\}$ and ϕ is an univariate knot. Each function is piecewise linear, with a knot at the value ϕ, and it is called a *reflected pair*. For visualization see Figure 2.

MARS uses collection of functions comprised of reflected pairs from the set basis function $\wp$:

$$
\wp := \left\{ (X_j - \phi)_+, (\phi - X_j)_+ \mid \phi \in \left\{ x_{1,j}, x_{2,j}, \ldots, x_{n,j} \right\}, j \in \left\{ 1, 2, \ldots, p \right\} \right\} \tag{25}
$$

If all of the input values are distinct, then set $\wp$ contains $2np$ basis functions where n is number of observation. MARS model for $f(x)$ has the form

Figure 2. A basic element in the regression with MARS
(Taylan, Weber, & Ozkurt, 2010):

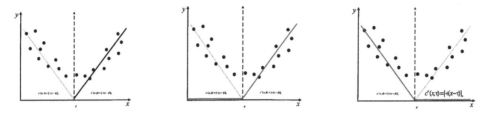

$$y = \beta_0 + \sum_{m=1}^{M} \beta_m \psi_m(x) + \varepsilon. \tag{26}$$

Here, $\psi_m \ (m = 1, 2, ..., M)$ are basis functions from $\wp$ or products of two or more such functions, ψ_m is taken from a set of M linearly independent basis elements, and β_m are the unknown coefficients for the mth basis function $(m = 1, 2, ..., M)$ or for the constant 1 ($m = 0$). Provided the observations represented by the data

$$(x_i, y_i)(i = 1, 2, ..., n),$$

the form of the mth basis function is as follows:

$$\psi_m(x) := \prod_{j=1}^{K_m} \left[s_{\kappa_j^m} \cdot \left(x_{\kappa_j^m} - \phi_{\kappa_j^m} \right) \right]_+, \tag{27}$$

where K_m is the number of truncated linear functions multiplied in the mth basis function, $x_{\kappa_j^m}$ is the input variable corresponding to the jth truncated linear function in the mth basis function, $\phi_{\kappa_j^m}$ is the knot value corresponding to the variable $x_{\kappa_j^m}$, and $s_{\kappa_j^m}$ is the selected sign $+1$ or -1.

The MARS algorithm for estimating the model function $f(x)$ consists of the forward stepwise algorithm and *backward* stepwise algorithm (Friedman, 1991): the aim of the forward stepwise algorithm is to search the basis function and it takes place with the constant basis function, the only one present initially. At each step, the split that minimized some *"lack of fit" criterion* from all the possible splits on each basis function is chosen. The process stops when a user-specified maximum number of basis function, M_{max} is reached. At the end of this process we have a large expression in (3.3). This model typically overfits the data and so a *backward* deletion procedure is applied. The purpose of this algorithm is to prevent from over-fitting by decreasing the complexity of the model without degrading the fit to the data. Therefore, the backward stepwise algorithm involves removing from the model basis functions that contribute to the smallest increase in the residual squared error at each stage, producing an optimally estimated model $\hat{f}_\tau$ with respect to each number of terms, called τ. Here, τ expresses some *complexity* of estimation. To estimate the optimal value of τ, generalized cross-validation can be used which shows the lack of fit when using MARS. This criterion is defined by

$$GCV := \frac{\sum_{i=1}^{n}(y_i - \hat{f}_\tau(x_i))^2}{(1 - M(\tau)/n)^2},\tag{28}$$

where $M(\tau) := u + d\,K$ (Craven & Wahba, 1979). Here, n is the number of sample observations, u is the number of linearly independent basis functions, K is the number of knots selected in the forward process, and d is a cost for basis-function optimization as well as a smoothing parameter for the procedure.

Taylan et al. (2010) suggested an alternative method instead of the backward stepwise algorithm to estimate the function $f(x)$. In their method that stated the following subsection, they propose to write *PRSS* problem by collecting maximum number of basis function based on the forward *stepwise algorithm* for estimating each smooth function. Then they treat it as a conic optimization problem which can be solve by famous method interior points (Karmarkar, 1984).

The *PRSS* Problem for MARS

Let us assume that $M_{\max}$ basis functions having been accumulated in the *forward* stepwise algorithm. We will employ *PRSS* that contains regularization terms in addition to the least-squares estimation in order to control the lack of fit from the viewpoint of the *complexity* of the estimation problem. For the MARS model, *PRSS* has the following form:

$$PRSS := \sum_{i=1}^{n}\left(y_i - f(\bar{x}_i)\right)^2 + \sum_{m=1}^{M_{\max}} \rho_m \sum_{\substack{|\varphi|=1 \\ \varphi=(\varphi_1,\varphi_2)}}^{2} \sum_{\substack{r<v \\ r,v\in V(m)}} \int \theta_m^2 \left[D_{r,v}^{\varphi}\psi_m(t^m)\right]^2 dt^m,\tag{29}$$

where

$$(\bar{x}_i, \bar{y}_i)(i = 1, 2, ..., n)$$

are the data points,

$$V(m) := \left\{\kappa_j^m \mid j = 1, 2, ..., K_m\right\}$$

is the variable set associated with the mth basis function ψ_m (cf.(28)),

$$t^m = \left(t_{m_1}, t_{m_2}, ..., t_{m_{K_m}}\right)^T$$

represents the vector of variables which contribute to the *m*th basis function ψ_m. Furthermore, we refer to

$$D^\varphi_{r,s}\psi_m(t^m) := \frac{\partial^\varphi \psi_m}{\partial^{\varphi_1} t^m_r \partial^{\varphi_2} t^m_v}(t^m)$$

for

$$\varphi = (\varphi_1, \varphi_2), \quad |\varphi| := \varphi_1 + \varphi_2, \quad \text{where} \quad \varphi_1, \varphi_2 \in \{0,1\}.$$

Furthermore, for convenience, it is used the integral symbol " $\int$ " as a dummy in the sense of $\int_{Q^m}$ where Q^m is some appropriately large K_m-dimensional parallelpipe where the integration takes place. Finally, since all the regarded derivatives of any function ψ_m exist except on a set of measure 0, the integrals and entire optimization problems are well defined.

The optimization problem Eq.(29) bases on the **tradeoff** between both *accuracy*, i.e., a small sum of error squares, and *not too high a complexity*. This tradeoff is established through the regularization parameters ρ_m. The second goal on a small complexity encompasses two parts. If we consider the representations Eq. (26) and Eq. (27) in Eq. (29), then the objective function Eq. (29) will be of the following form:

$$PRSS = \sum_{i=1}^n \left(\bar{y}_i - \theta_0 - \sum_{m=1}^M \theta_m \psi_m(\bar{x}^m_i) - \sum_{m=M+1}^{M_{max}} \theta_m \psi_m(\bar{x}^m_i) \right)^2$$
$$+ \sum_{m=1}^{M_{max}} \rho_m \sum_{\substack{|\varphi|=1 \\ \varphi=(\varphi_1,\varphi_2)}}^2 \sum_{\substack{r<v \\ r,v \in V(m)}} \int \theta_m^2 \left[D^\varphi_{r,v}\psi_m(t^m) \right]^2 dt^m, \tag{30}$$

where

$$\bar{x}_i = (\bar{x}_{i,1}, \bar{x}_{i,2}, ..., \bar{x}_{i,p})^T$$

denotes any of the input vectors and

$$\bar{x}^m_i = (\bar{x}_{i,\kappa_1}, \bar{x}_{i,\kappa_2}, ..., \bar{x}_{i,\kappa_{K_m}})^T$$

stands for the corresponding projection vectors of $\bar{x}_i$ onto those coordinates which contribute to the *m*th basis function ψ_m, they are related with the *i*th output $\bar{y}_i$. We recall that those coordinates are collected in the set $V(m)$. Let us note that the second-order derivatives of the piecewise linear functions

ψ_m $(m = 1, 2, ..., M)$ and, hence, the regularization terms related, are vanishing. Now, we can rearrange the representation of *PRSS* as follows:

$$PRSS = \sum_{i=1}^{n} \left(y_i - \theta^{\mathrm{T}} \psi(\bar{d}_i) \right)^2 + \sum_{m=1}^{M_{max}} \varphi_m \sum_{\substack{|\varphi|=1 \\ \varphi=(\varphi_1, \varphi_2)}}^{2} \sum_{\substack{r<s \\ r,v \in V(m)}} \int_{Q^m} \theta_m^2 \left[D_{r,v}^{\varphi} \psi_m(t^m) \right]^2 dt^m, \tag{31}$$

where

$$\psi(\bar{d}_i) := \left(1, \psi_1(\bar{x}_i^1), ..., \psi_M(\bar{x}_i^M), \psi_{M+1}(\bar{x}_i^{M+1}), ..., \psi_{M_{max}}(\bar{x}_i^{M_{max}}) \right)^T,$$

$$\theta := \left(\theta_0, \theta_1, ..., \theta_{M_{max}} \right)^{\mathrm{T}}$$

with the point

$$\bar{d}_i := (\bar{x}_i^1, \bar{x}_i^2, ..., \bar{x}_i^M, \bar{x}_i^{M+1}, \bar{x}_i^{M+2}, ..., \bar{x}_i^{M_{max}})^T$$

in the argument.

To approximate the multi-dimensional integrals

$$\int_{Q^m} \theta_m^2 \left[D_{r,v}^{\varphi} \psi_m(t^m) \right]^2 dt^m,$$

discretized forms of them is considered. For this, our data point

$$(\bar{x}_i, \bar{y}_i)(i = 1, 2, ..., n)$$

with $\bar{x}_i \in \mathbb{R}^d$ are given. In natural way, these input data

$$\bar{x}_i = (\bar{x}_{i,1}, \bar{x}_{i,2}, ..., \bar{x}_{i,p})^T$$

generate a subdivision of any sufficiently large parallelpipe Q of $\mathbb{R}^d$ which contains each of them as elements. Let Q be a parallelpipe which encompasses all our input data; we represent it by

$$Q = \left[a_1, b_1 \right] \times \left[a_2, b_2 \right] \times ... \times \left[a_p, b_p \right] = \prod_{j=1}^{p} Q_j,$$

where

$$Q_j =: \left[a_j, b_j\right], a_j \leq \overline{x}_{i,j} \leq b_j \, (j = 1, 2, ..., p; \; i = 1, 2, ..., n).$$

Without loss of generality, we may assume $a_j < \overline{x}_{i,j} < b_j$. For all j we reorder the coordinates of the input data points:

$$\overline{x}_{i_1^j, j} \leq \overline{x}_{i_2^j, j} \leq \cdots \leq \overline{x}_{i_n^j, j},$$

where

$$i_\delta^j = 1, 2, ..., n (\delta = 1, 2, ..., n; \; j = 1, 2, ..., p),$$

and $\overline{x}_{i_\delta^j, j}$ is jth component of $\overline{x}_{i_\delta^j}$, the i_δ^j th input vector after reordering. Without loss of generality we may assume $\overline{x}_{i_\delta^j, j} \neq \overline{x}_{i_\varsigma^j, j}$ for all $\delta, \varphi = 1, 2, ..., N$ with $\delta \neq \varsigma$; i.e.,

$$\overline{x}_{i_1^j, j} < \overline{x}_{i_2^j, j} < \cdots < \overline{x}_{i_n^j, j} \, (j = 1, 2, ..., p).$$

Then, *PRSS* can be rearranged in the following form:

$$
\begin{aligned}
PRSS &\approx \sum_{i=1}^{n} \left(y_i - \theta^{\mathrm{T}} \psi(\overline{d}_i) \right)^2 \\
&+ \sum_{m=1}^{M_{max}} \rho_m \sum_{\substack{|\varphi|=1 \\ \alpha=(\varphi_1,\varphi_2)}}^{2} \sum_{\substack{r<v \\ r,v \in V(m)}} \sum_{(\delta^{\kappa_j})} \theta_m^2 \left[D_{r,v}^{\varphi} \psi_m \left(\overline{x}_{i_{\delta^{\kappa_1^m}}, \kappa_1^m}, \overline{x}_{i, \kappa_2^m}, ..., \overline{x}_{i_{\delta^{\kappa_{K_m}^m}}, \kappa_{K_m}^m} \right) \right]^2 \prod_{j=1}^{K_m} \left(\overline{x}_{i_{\delta^{\kappa_j}+1}^{\kappa_j^m}, \kappa_j^m} - \overline{x}_{i_{\delta^{\kappa_j}}^{\kappa_j^m}, \kappa_j^m} \right),
\end{aligned}
\tag{32}
$$

where

$$(\delta^{\kappa_j})_{j \in \{1,2,...,K_m\}} \in \{0, 1, 2, ..., n+1\}^{K_m}.$$

Details of discrietizaton made for integral can be found in Taylan et al. (2010).

Let us introduce some more notation related with the sequence (δ^{κ_j}):

$$\hat{x}_i^m = \left(\overline{x}_{l_{\sigma^{\kappa_1}}^{\kappa_1^m}, \kappa_1^m}, \overline{x}_{l_{\sigma^{\kappa_2}}^{\kappa_2^m}, \kappa_2^m}, ..., \overline{x}_{l_{\sigma^{\kappa_{K_m}}}^{\kappa_{K_m}^m}, \kappa_{K_m}^m} \right), \quad \Delta \hat{x}_i^m := \prod_{j=1}^{K_m} \left(\overline{x}_{l_{\sigma^{\kappa_j}+1}^{\kappa_j^m}, \kappa_j^m} - \overline{x}_{l_{\sigma^{\kappa_j}}^{\kappa_j^m}, \kappa_j^m} \right). \tag{33}$$

By Eq. (33), *PRSS* can be approximated *PRSS* as

$$PRSS \approx \sum_{i=1}^{n} \left(y_i - \theta^{\mathrm{T}} \psi(\bar{d}_i) \right)^2 + \sum_{m=1}^{M_{\max}} \rho_m \theta_m^2 \sum_{i=1}^{(n+1)^{K_m}} \left(\sum_{\substack{|\varphi|=1 \\ \alpha=(\varphi_1,\varphi_2)}}^{2} \sum_{\substack{r<v \\ r,v \in V(m)}} \left[D_{r,v}^{\varphi} \psi_m(\hat{x}_i^m) \right]^2 \right) \Delta \hat{x}_i^m. \tag{34}$$

For a short representation, we can rewrite the approximate relation Eq. (32) as

$$PRSS \approx \left\| y - \psi(\bar{d})\theta \right\|_2^2 + \sum_{m=1}^{M_{\max}} \rho_m \sum_{i=1}^{(n+1)^{K_m}} L_{im}^2 \theta_m^2, \tag{35}$$

where

$$\psi(\bar{d}) = \left(\psi(\bar{d}_1), ..., \psi(\bar{d}_N) \right)^T$$

is an $(n \times (\mathit{œ}_{\max} + 1)) - $ matrix and the numbers L_{im} are defined by

$$L_{im} := \left[\left(\sum_{\substack{|\varphi|=1 \\ \varphi=(\varphi_1,\varphi_2)}}^{2} \sum_{\substack{r<v \\ r,v \in V(m)}} \left[D_{r,s}^{\varphi} \psi_m(\hat{x}_i^m) \right]^2 \right) \Delta \hat{x}_i^m \right]^{1/2}.$$

Now, the problem *PRSS* can be considered as a *Tikhonov regularization problem* (TGP)(Aster, Borchers, & Thurber, 2013). For this aim we take into account formula Eq.(35) again, arranging it as follows:

$$
\begin{aligned}
PRSS &\approx \left\| y - \psi(\bar{d})\theta \right\|^2 + \sum_{m=1}^{M_{\max}} \rho_m \sum_{i=1}^{(n+1)^{K_m}} L_{im}^2 \theta_m^2 \\
&= \left\| y - \psi(\bar{d})\theta \right\|^2 + \rho_1 \left\| L_1 \theta_1 \right\|_2^2 + \rho_2 \left\| L_2 \theta_2 \right\|_2^2 + ... + \rho_{M_{\max}} \left\| L_{M_{\max}} \theta_{M_{\max}} \right\|_2^2,
\end{aligned}
\tag{36}
$$

where

$$L_m := \left(L_{1m}, L_{2m}, ..., L_{(n+1)^{K_m},m} \right)^T \ (m = 1, 2, ..., M_{\max}).$$

But, rather than a singleton, there is a finite sequence of the *tradeoff* or regularization parameters $\rho = \left(\rho_1, \rho_2, ..., \rho_{M_{\max}} \right)^T$ such that this equation is not yet a TGP with a single such parameter. For this reason, let us make a uniform penalization by taking the same ρ for each derivative term. Then, our approximation of *PRSS* can be rearranged as

$$PRSS \approx \left\| y - \psi(\overline{d})\,\theta \right\|_2^2 + \rho \left\| L\theta \right\|_2^2, \tag{37}$$

where L is an $(M_{max}+1) \times (M_{max}+1)$-diagonal matrix with first column $L_0 = 0_{(n+1)^{K_m}}$ and the other columns being the vectors L_m introduced above. Furthermore, θ is an $((M_{max}+1) \times 1)$-parameter vector to be estimated through the data points. Thus *PRSS* problem was be converted a classical TGP with regularization parameter ρ.

Solution of *PRSS* Problem for MARS With CQP (CMARS)

The PRSS or TGP Eq.(37) can be tackled as CQP problem mentioned in Subsection 2.1.and we call its solution as CMARS. Actually, based on an convenient selection of a bound *T*, we express problem Eq. (37) similarly to the problem Eq. (18) as follows:

$$\underset{\theta}{minimize} \left\| \psi(\overline{d})\,\theta - y \right\|_2^2 \ such\ that \left\| L\theta \right\|_2^2 \leq T. \tag{38}$$

Also, the optimization problem Eq. (38) equivalently can be written as follows:

$$\underset{s_1,\theta}{minimize}\ s_1, such\ that \left\| \psi(\overline{d})\,\theta - y \right\|_2^2 \leq s_1^2, s_1 \geq 0, \left\| L\theta \right\|_2^2 \leq T, \tag{39}$$

or, equivalently again,

$$\underset{s_1,\theta}{minimize}\ s_1, such\ that \left\| \psi(\overline{d})\,\theta - y \right\|_2 \leq s_1 . \left\| L\theta \right\|_2 \leq \sqrt{T}. \tag{40}$$

As you can easily see, we have a CQP problem with the following properties again:

$$c = (1, 0_{M_{max}+1}^T)^T,\ x = (s_1, \theta^T)^T,\ D_1 = (0_N, \psi(\overline{d})),\ d_1 = y,\ q_1 = 0,$$

$$p_1 = (1, 0, ..., 0)^T,\ D_2 = (0_{M_{Max}+1}, L),\ d_2 = 0_{M_{max}+1},\ p_2 = 0_{M_{max}+2},\ q_2 = -\sqrt{T}.$$

The dual problem and for optimization problem Eq. (40) can be formulated similar to Eq. (22) as follows:

$$maximize(y^T, 0)\,\omega_1 + \left(0_{M_{max}+1}^T, -\sqrt{T}\right)\omega_2$$

$$such\ that \begin{pmatrix} 0_N^T & 1 \\ \psi(\bar{d})^T & 0_{M_{max}+1} \end{pmatrix}\omega_1 + \begin{pmatrix} 0_{M_{max}+1}^T & 0 \\ L^T & 0_{M_{max}+1} \end{pmatrix}\omega_2 = \begin{pmatrix} 1 \\ 0_{M_{max}+1} \end{pmatrix}. \tag{41}$$

$$\omega_1 \in L^{N+1}, \omega_2 \in L^{M_{max}+2}.$$

Additionally similar to Eq. (23), $(s_1, \theta, \chi, \eta, \omega_1, \omega_2)$ is a *primal dual optimal solution* if and only if

$$\chi := \begin{pmatrix} 0_N & \psi(\bar{d}) \\ 1 & 0_{M_{max}+1}^T \end{pmatrix}\begin{pmatrix} s_1 \\ \theta \end{pmatrix} + \begin{pmatrix} -y \\ 0 \end{pmatrix},$$

$$\eta := \begin{pmatrix} 0_{M_{max}+1} & L \\ 0 & 0_{M_{max}+1}^T \end{pmatrix}\begin{pmatrix} s_1 \\ \theta \end{pmatrix} + \begin{pmatrix} 0_{M_{max}+1} \\ \sqrt{M} \end{pmatrix},$$

$$\begin{pmatrix} 0_N^T & 1 \\ \psi(\bar{d})^T & 0_{M_{max}+1} \end{pmatrix}\omega_1 + \begin{pmatrix} 0_{M_{max}+1}^T & 0 \\ L^T & 0_{M_{max}+1} \end{pmatrix}\omega_2 = \begin{pmatrix} 1 \\ 0_{M_{max}+1} \end{pmatrix}, \tag{42}$$

$$\omega_1^T\chi = 0, \omega_2^T\eta = 0,$$

$$\omega_1 \in L^{N+1}, \omega_2 \in L^{M_{max}+2},$$

$$\chi \in L^{N+1}, \eta \in L^{M_{max}+2}.$$

KERNEL REGRESSION (KR)

Kernel regressions are weighted average estimators that use kernel functions as weights. These techniques can be considered of as explicitly supplying estimates of the regression function or conditional expectation by stating the nature of the local neighborhood, and of the class of regular functions fitted locally. The local neighborhood is stated by a *kernel function* $K_\lambda\left(x_0, x\right)$ which dedicates weights to points x in a region around x_0 where the parameter λ checks the width of the neighborhood. The simplest form of kernel estimate is the Nadaraya-Watson weighted average (Schölkopf et al., 1999).

$$\hat{f}(x_0) = \frac{\sum_{i=1}^n K_\zeta\left(x_0, x_i\right)y_i}{\sum_{i=1}^n K_\zeta\left(x_0, x_i\right)}, \tag{43}$$

where

$$K_\zeta\left(x_0, x_i\right) := K\left(\|x_i - x_0\|_2/\zeta\right)$$

a kernel function defined as $K : \mathbb{R} \to \mathbb{R}$, providing

$$\int K\left(x\right)dx = 1, \; K\left(-\boldsymbol{x}_0\right) = K\left(\boldsymbol{x}_0\right). \tag{44}$$

For obtaining kernel estimator for regression function f, many $K\left(\cdot\right)$ are possible. Most used kernel functions for $x_i \in \mathbb{R}^p$ are Uniform, Epanechnikov, Gaussian, Quartic (biweight), and Tricube (triweight) given as follows:

1. $K\left(x\right) = \dfrac{1}{2}1_{\left(\|x\|\leq 1\right)}$,

2. $K\left(x\right) = \dfrac{3}{4}\left(1 - \|x\|^2\right)1_{\left(\|x\|\leq 1\right)}$,

3. $K\left(x\right) = \dfrac{1}{\sqrt{2\pi}}\exp\left(-\dfrac{\|x\|^2}{2}\right)$

4. $K\left(x\right) = \dfrac{15}{16}\left(1 - \|x\|^2\right)^2 1_{\left(\|x\|\leq 1\right)}$,

5. $K\left(x\right) = \dfrac{35}{32}\left(1 - \|x\|^2\right)^3 1_{\left(\|x\|\leq 1\right)}$.

In general, the local regression estimate of $f(x_0)$ can be estimated as $f_{\hat{\beta}}(x_0)$, where $\hat{\beta}$ minimizes residual sum of squares (RSS),

$$RSS\left(f_\beta, x_0\right) = \sum_{i=1}^{n} K_\zeta\left(x_0, x_i\right)\left(y_i - f_\beta\left(x_i\right)\right)^2 \tag{45}$$

where f_β can be considered some parameterized function, such as a low-order polynomial or splines.

Extention of Kernel smoothing to high dimensionally problem causes computational and statistical efficiency concerns when p is large, (say, larger than 10). Boundary impacts are greatly exaggerated as p increases, since the fraction of data points near the boundary grows rapidly. Therefore, less flexible models should be used in high dimensions. The additive models mentioned above is one of example of such models. For this reason for estimating regression function f_β, n our approach, we propose to consider f_β in additive way where each smooth function $f_\beta(x_{ij})$ considered as B-spline basis function in our approach.

The *PRSS* Problem for KR

For estimation of regression function f_β we will use the *PRSS* again to control the complexity of the problem. The *PRSS* problem for KR can be written as follows:

$$PRSS\left(f_{\beta}, x_0\right) = \sum_{i=1}^{n} K_{\zeta}\left(x_0, x_i\right)\left\{y_i - \beta_0 - \sum_{j=1}^{p} f_j(x_{ij})\right\}^2 + \sum_{j=1}^{p} \varphi_j \int_c^d \left[f_j''(t_j)\right]^2 dt_j. \tag{46}$$

If the B- splines bases functions for $f_j(x_{ij})$ and discretized forms of integrals are considered in *PRSS*, then *PRSS* look as follows:

$$PRSS\left(\beta^1, ..., \beta^p, x_0\right) = \sum_{i=1}^{n} K_{\zeta}\left(x_0, x_i\right)\left\{y_i - \beta_0 - B_i\beta\right\}^2 + \sum_{j=1}^{p} \varphi_j \sum_{i=1}^{n-1}\left[B_i^{j''} w_i \beta^j\right]^2, \tag{47}$$

where dimensions of all matrices and all vectors has the same as the corresponding vectors and matrices in Eq. (13). If the mathematical operations performed in Eq. (13) are performed in Eq.(4.5), thus *PRSS* look as

$$PRSS\left(\beta^1, ..., \beta^p, x_0\right) := \sum_{i=1}^{n} K_{\zeta}\left(x_0, x_i\right)\left\{y_i - \widehat{\beta}_0 - B_i\beta\right\}^2 + \sum_{j=1}^{p} \varphi_j \left\|\bar{B}^j \beta^j\right\|^2$$

$$= \sum_{i=1}^{n} K_{\zeta}\left(x_0, x_i\right)\left\{b_i - B_i\beta\right\}^2 + \sum_{j=1}^{p} \varphi_j \left\|\bar{B}^j \beta^j\right\|^2$$

$$= \left(B\beta - b\right)^T K_{\zeta}\left(B\beta - b\right) + \sum_{j=1}^{p} \varphi_j \left\|\bar{B}^j \beta^j\right\|^2 \tag{48}$$

$$= \left\|A\beta - a\right\|_2^2 + \sum_{j=1}^{p} \varphi_j \left\|\bar{B}^j \beta^j\right\|^2,$$

where $A = K^{1/2}B$, $a = K^{1/2}b$ and $K^{1/2}$ is $n \times n$-diagonal matrix with ith diagonal element $\left[K_{\zeta}\left(x_0, x_i\right)\right]^{1/2}$.

Indeed, based on an convenient choice of a bound T_1, the problem can be expressed as

$$\underset{s_{12}, \beta}{minimize}\ s_2, such\ that \left\|A\beta - a\right\|_2 \leq s_2, \left\|\bar{B}^j \beta^j\right\|_2 \leq \sqrt{T_j}\ (j = 1, 2, ..., p), \tag{49}$$

which is a CQP problem with

$$c = \left(1, 0^T\right)^T, x = \left(s_2, \beta^T\right)^T, D_0 = \left(0, A\right), d_0 = a, p_0 = \left(1, 0, ..., 0\right)^T, q_0 = 0,$$

$$D_j = (0, \bar{B}^j), d_j = 0, p_j = 0$$

and

$$q_j = -\sqrt{T_j}\ (j = 1, 2, ..., p).$$

Dual problem and optimality conditions for problem Eq. (40) can be formed similar to Eqs. (22) (23),(40), (42).

Solution Methods for CQP

To obtain solutions for convex optimization problems (Boyd & Vandenberghe, 2004), in particular, CQP problems, classical polynomial time algorithms may be employed. However, these algorithms have some drawbacks since they don't consider information on the objective function and the constraints in a global sense. That's, they consider only local information for them..

CQP problems are "well-designed" convex problems, therefore, interior point methods (Nemirovski & Todd, 2008) can be used to solve them. This method is firstly introduced by Karmarkar (1984) and it was firstly employed for linear programming in 1984. Then, over the years, since these algorithms and software for linear programming have turn into quite advanced, its extensions have beginned to be employed for more general classes of problems, such as convex quadratic programming, nonconvex and nonlinear problems over sets that can be characterized by self-concordant barrier functions. These algorithms are depend on the given (primal) and the dual problem as well. They consider the structure of the problem in a global sense by providing a more better complexity bounds and display a much better practical result and performance.

The complexity of the method to obtain solution for an optimization problem (P)

$$\underset{\alpha \in \mathbb{R}^n}{minimize} \left\{ c^T \alpha : \left\| D_i \alpha - d_i \right\|_2 \leq p_i^T \alpha - q_i, d_i \in \mathbb{R}^{n_i}, (i = 0,1,2,...,k); \left\| \alpha \right\|_2 \leq M \right\}, \text{(P)}$$

is of great importance, and it is a measure of the efficiency of a method to obtain a accurate solution on the basis of the running time $Compl(P, \varepsilon *)$ - the number of elementary operations performed by the method when solving optimization problem (P) within accuracy $\varepsilon *$. This characteristic depends on data

$$Data(P) := \left[n; k;; n_1,...,n_k; c; D_1, d_1, p_1, q_1;...; D_k, d_k, p_k, q_k; M \right]$$

and size

$$Size(P) := \dim Data(P) = \left(k + \sum_{i=1}^{k} n_i \right)(n+1) + k + n + 3$$

for optimization problem (P). Then. the arithmetic complexity of $\varepsilon *$-solution for problem (P) is given by

$$Compl(P, \varepsilon *) := O(1)(k+1)^{1/2} n \left(n^2 + k + \sum_{i=1}^{k} n_i^2 \right) Digits(P, \varepsilon *).$$

CONCLUSION

This chapter gives a support and new contribution to the NPR approximation of data in the multivariate situations. *ADMs, MARS and KR* has been proposed by considering *PRSS* problem for them. Then, alternative solutions produced by modern and practical techniques of continuous optimization, particularly, CQP, turned into reachable and employable. Thus not only a connection has been established between NPR which is a method of statistical learning and data mining and inverse problems, but the robust instruments submitted for well- designed convex optimization problems. We hope that we provide a good light and service to the theoretical and practical studies that will be carried out in every field of science and technology that conducts data analysis by considering alternative solutions tecniques mentioned in this chapter.

REFERENCES

Aster, R. C., Borchers, B., & Thurber, C. H. (2013). *Parameter estimation and inverse Problems*. New York, NY: Academic Press.

Bates, D. M., & Watts, D. G. (1988). *Nonlinear regression analysis and its applications*. Hoboken, NJ: Wiley Sons. doi:10.1002/9780470316757

Bellman, R. E. (1961). *Adaptive control processes*. Princeton, NJ: Princeton University Press. doi:10.1515/9781400874668

Ben-Tal, A., & Nemirovski, A. (1987). *Lectures on modern convex optimization: Analysis, algorithms and engineering applications. MOS-SIAM Series Optimization*. Philadelphia, PA: Philadelphia Society for Industrial and Applied Mathematics.

Boyd, S., & Vandenberghe, L. (2004). *Convex optimization*. Cambridge, UK: Cambridge University. doi:10.1017/CBO9780511804441

Buja, A., Hastie, T., & Tibshirani, R. (1989). Linear smoothers and additive models (with discussion). *Annals of Statistics*, *17*(2), 453–555. doi:10.1214/aos/1176347115

Burnham, K. P., & Anderson, D. R. (2002). *Model selection and multimodel inference: A practical Information-theoretic approach*. New York, NY: Springer Verlag.

Cleveland, W. S. (1979). Robust locally weighted regression and smoothing Scatter plots. *Journal of the American Statistical Association*, *74*(368), 829–836. doi:10.1080/01621459.1979.10481038

Craven, P., & Wahba, G. (1979). Smoothing noisy data with spline functions: Estimating the correct degree of smoothing by the method of generalized cross-validation. *Numerische Mathematik*, *31*(4), 377–403. doi:10.1007/BF01404567

De Boor, C. (1978). *Practical guide to splines*. New York, NY: Springer Verlag. doi:10.1007/978-1-4612-6333-3

Eilers, P. H. C., & Marx, B. D. (1996). Flexible smoothing with B-splines penalties. *Statistical Science*, *11*(2), 89–121. doi:10.1214s/1038425655

Fan, J., & Gijbels, I. (1996). *Local polynomial modelling and its applications.* London, UK: Chapman & Hall.

Fox, J. (2001). *Multiple and generalized nonparametric regression, series: Quantitative applications in the social sciences.* London, UK: SAGE Publications.

Friedman, J. H. (1991). Multivariate adaptive regression splines. *Annals of Statistics, 19*(1), 1–141. doi:10.1214/aos/1176347963

Friedman, J. H., & Stuetzle, W. (1981). Projection pursuit regression. *Journal of the American Statistical Association, 76*(376), 817–823. doi:10.1080/01621459.1981.10477729

Golub, G. H., Heath, M., & Wahba, G. (1979). Generalized Cross-Validation as a method for choosing a good Ridge Parameter. *Technometrics, 21*(2), 215–223. doi:10.1080/00401706.1979.10489751

Hastie, T., & Tibshirani, R. (1986). Generalized Additive Models. *Statistical Science, 1*(3), 297–318. doi:10.1214s/1177013604

Hastie, T., & Tibshirani, R. (1987). Generalized additive models: Some applications. *Journal of the American Statistical Association, 82*(398), 371–386. doi:10.1080/01621459.1987.10478440

Hastie, T., Tibshirani, R., & Friedman, J. H. (2001). *The element of statistical learning.* New York, NY: Springer Verlag. doi:10.1007/978-0-387-21606-5

Hastie, T. J., & Tibshirani, R. J. (1990). *Generalized additive models.* New York, NY: Chapman and Hall.

Imandoust, S. B., & Bolandraftar, M. (2013). Application of k-nearest neighbor (kNN) approach for predicting economic events: Theoretical background. *International Journal of Engineering Research and Applications, 3*(5), 605–610.

Jabbar, M. A., Deekshatulua, B. L., & Chandra, P. (2013). Classification of Heart Disease Using K-Nearest Neighbor and Genetic Algorithm. In *Proceedings of International Conference on Computational Intelligence: Modeling Techniques and Applications* (CIMTA) 2013 (*vol. 10*, pp. 85 – 94). Kalyani, India: Elsevier Ltd. 10.1016/j.protcy.2013.12.340

Karmarkar, N. (1984). A new polynomial-time algorithm for linear programming. *Combinatorica, 4*(4), 373–395. doi:10.1007/BF02579150

Lee, T. C. M. (2003). Smoothing parameter selection for smoothing splines: A simulation study. *Computational Statistics & Data Analysis, 42*(1-2), 139–148. doi:10.1016/S0167-9473(02)00159-7

Mucherino, A., Papajorgji, P. J., & Pardalos, P. M. (2009). K-nearest neighbor classification. In *Data mining in agriculture. Springer Optimization and Its Applications, 34.* New York, NY: Springer. doi:10.1007/978-0-387-88615-2_4

Nelder, J. A., & Wedderburn, R. W. M. (1972). Generalized linear models. *Journal of Royal Statistical Society. A, 135*(3), 370–384. doi:10.2307/2344614

Nemirovski, A., & Todd, M. J. (2008). Interior-point methods for optimization. *Acta Numerica, 17*, 191–234. doi:10.1017/S0962492906370018

Opsomer, J., & Ruppert, D. (1997). Fitting a bivariate additive model by local polynomial regression. *Annals of Statistics*, 25(1), 186–211. doi:10.1214/aos/1034276626

Refaeilzadeh, P., Tang, L., & Liu, H. (2009). Cross-Validation. In L. Liu & M. T. Özsu (Eds.), *Encyclopedia of Database Systems*. Boston, MA: Springer.

Reinsch, C. H. (1967). Smoothing by spline functions. *Numerische Mathematik*, 10(3), 177–183. doi:10.1007/BF02162161

Schölkopf, B., Smola, A., & Müller, K. R. (1999). *Kernel principal component analysis: Advances in kernel methods-support vector learning*. Cambridge, MA: MIT Press.

Seber, G. A. F., & Wild, C. J. (1989). *Nonlinear regression*. New York, NY: Wiley and Sons. doi:10.1002/0471725315

Silverman, B. W. (1985). Some aspects of the spline smoothing approach to non-parametric regression curve fitting. *Journal of the Royal Statistical Society. Series B. Methodological*, 47(1), 1–21. doi:10.1111/j.2517-6161.1985.tb01327.x

Stone, C. (1977). Consistent nonparametric regression. *Annals of Statistics*, 5(4), 595–645. doi:10.1214/aos/1176343886

Taylan, P., Weber, G.-W., & Beck, A. (2007). New approaches to regression by generalized additive models and continuous optimization for modern applications in finance, science and technology. *Optimization*, 56(5-6), 675–698. doi:10.1080/02331930701618740

Taylan, P., Weber, G. W., & Ozkurt, F. Y. (2010). A new approach to multivariate adaptive regression splines by using Tikhonov regularization and continuous optimization. *Top (Madrid)*, 18(2), 377–395. doi:10.100711750-010-0155-7

Wahba, G., & Wold, S. (1975). A completely automatic French curve: Fitting spline functions by cross-validation. *Communications in Statistics*, 4(1), 1–17. doi:10.1080/03610927508827223

Chapter 10
An Overview of Methodologies and Challenges in Sentiment Analysis on Social Networks

Aditya Suresh Salunkhe

Ramrao Adik Institute of Technolgy, India

Pallavi Vijay Chavan

Ramrao Adik Institute of Technolgy, India

ABSTRACT

The expeditious increase in the adoption of social media over the last decade, determining and analyzing the attitude and opinion of masses related to a particular entity, has gained quite an importance. With the landing of the Web 2.0, many internet products like blogs, community chatrooms, forums, microblog are serving as a platform for people to express themselves. Such opinion is found in the form of messages, user-comments, news articles, personal blogs, tweets, surveys, status updates, etc. With sentiment analysis, it is possible to eliminate the need to manually going through each and every user comment by focusing on the contextual polarity of the text. Analyzing the sentiments could serve a number of applications like advertisements, recommendations, quality analysis, monetization provided on the web services, real-time analysis of data, analyzing notions related to candidates during election campaign, etc.

DOI: 10.4018/978-1-7998-0106-1.ch010

Figure 1. General classification of sentiments

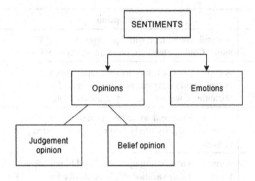

INTRODUCTION

The Cambridge dictionary defines sentiments as, "an opinion, thought, or an idea based on a feeling about a particular situation, or an approach of thinking about something" (Cambridge University Press, 2008).

Types of Sentiments

There are primarily two ways one can classify the sentiments being expressed in text.

1. **Opinions:** This is something that the subject believes/decides. For instance, liked/disliked/expensive/low quality/affordable etc.
2. **Emotions:** This is something that the subject perceives or feels. For instance, happy/sad/satisfied/relaxed etc.

In this chapter we shall focus only on the opinions rather than emotions. Merriam-Webster dictionary has defined an opinion as ''a judgment, a view or appraisal formed in the mind about a particular entity'', or ''a belief that is stronger than an impression but less strong than positive knowledge''

Thus there are 2 types of opinions:

- Judgement opinion: desirable/undesirable/disgusting/good/bad.
- Belief opinion: Possibly/likely/mostly/probably/true/false

Their internal structure can be defined with the help of a quadruple at minimum (Hovy, 2015).

- Topic = topic which is being considered.
- Holder = individual, group, institution holding or making the opinion.
- Claim = statement which is in regard with the topic.
- Valence (judgment opinions): – Positive/Negative/Neutral.
- Valence (belief opinions): – Believed/Disbelieved/Unsure/Neutral.

Table 1. Categorical classification of emoticons

Emoji	Description	Category
☺	A simple round face with open eyes and broad smile. Conveys humour, pleasure and good vibes.	Smileys and People
☕	A cup of a hot beverage usually represents tea or coffee. Used to express sentiments related to food, restaurants, warmness, hunger, appetite. etc.	Food and Beverages
⚽	A round, black and white ball used in the game of football usually used to express sports related sentiments.	Sports & Activities.
✈	Airplane transcending upwards. Used to represent travel, overseas vacation or phone/device on airplane mode.	Travel & Places.
🏳	Contains a range of internationally recognised flags of countries & organisations. Usually used while conveying national/international news/ events, political opinions etc.	Flags and Countries

- **Definition:** Opinion is a decision made by the holder i.e. person, group or an organization as a whole about a topic. One can add additional factors such as strength, facets, and conditions to the quadruple to extend the structure.
- Strength of opinion: It is difficult to establish strength across different holders.
- Facet of topic: It is used for narrowing down the topic and differentiate between its sub-facets. For example, not the "overall delivery time" but the time required for "product dispatch" for a particular goods delivery company.
- Argument/Reasoning: This opens up the argument structure. "I find the service quality poor because, (reason)"

Sentiment Analysis through Emoticons:

Apart from above two, emoticons are also been used nowadays while expressing opinions And highly reflect the attitude of the subject, for example has stated emoji having effect on results of elections, stocks etc. (Ljubesic and Fiser, 2016). Pairing writer's sentiment to the use of the emoticons can provide a better understanding of user sentiments. Another major advantage is the limited sets of emoji compared to infinite possibility of words. We can take advantage of this and introduce a template database with annotations for every possible emoji. Further rules to correlate the sentiment based on a set/combination of emoji could be used.

BACKGROUND

Defining the opinion is one of the major challenge in sentiment analysis. Many linguists of different times have tried to define subjectivity. One of the prominent definition among existing definitions is been given by Randolph Quirk. Quirk has defined private state as "something that is not accessible to verification or objective" (Quirk, Greenbaum, and Syartyik, 1985). Emotions, personal opinions, attitude, speculations and many more form these private states. A pioneer in Natural Language Processing (NLP), Weibe has used this definition of Quirk where private state is narrative. According to her, private state is a tuple defined as: (p, attitude, object, and experiencer) (Pang and Lee, 2008). For practical purposes, a simpler version of this definition where only the polarity and goal state are in focus is used. In general terms, sentiments are positive or negative individual opinions with several unique properties that set them apart from the general text.

SENTIMENT ANALYSIS METHODS

Sentimental Analysis can be carried out majorly in 3 different ways: Supervised, Semi supervised, unsupervised techniques. Naïve Bayesian, SVM and decision trees are the most predominantly used supervised approaches.

Use of Semi-Supervised Polarity Dictionary

- **Polarity (Definition):** Cambridge dictionary has defined polarity as: "the quality of having two poles/extreme opposite values" (Cambridge University Press, 2008).

To determine the sentimental polarity of any news or online blog response, we first create a polarity dictionary, consisting of terms and their respective polarities. This polarity dictionary uses a semi-supervised dictionary approach in which first a dictionary of considerably small size is constructed using a few seed words. The polarity to the seed words are assigned manually. After which, we add new words to the polarity dictionary using co-occurrence frequency with words in a polarity dictionary.

Polarity Dictionary Construction

Bootstrap method is used for construction of polarity dictionary of semi-supervised nature. A bootstrap method focuses on both small unlabelled data and large unlabelled data, the small labelled data is basically the initial dictionary with few seed words entered manually. Here we assume that all sentences in an article are of the same polarity. This assumption is strict because some sentences may include adversative conjunction & negation. Since the expressions change a context in an article, our assumption is not correct. Under the assumption candidates which are added in the polarity dictionary are selected according to co-occurrence frequency with words in the polarity dictionary. We begin by making a small initial polarity dictionary which has some words present in that polarities determined manually. Hence, human efforts are required to make the initial dictionary. The dictionary consists of both positive and negative words. We call a dictionary for positive words a 'positive polarity dictionary' and a dictionary for negative words a 'negative polarity dictionary'. After that, we measure how many times a new word which is not added in the dictionary occurs with words in positive or negative polarity dictionary in the same sentence. If a word occurs with positive words and negative words in the same sentence, we count co-occurrence frequency for both polarities. Many words occur with words in a positive polarity dictionary and in a negative polarity dictionary though we exclude sentences including negation and adversative conjunction. Thereby to measure a bias of co-occurrence we use a rate of co-occurrence with a positive or a negative polarity dictionary. And based upon the rate of co-occurrence we estimate a polarities of a word not added in the polarity dictionary. Finally we determine the polarity of word that became candidates after previous operation and add them to the polarity dictionary. In this approach we determine two thresholds, T1 and T2. Where T1 and T2 represent positive and negative thresholds. When R1 of a word is over T1, the word is added in the positive polarity dictionary, When R2 of a word is greater than T2, and we add the word to the negative polarity dictionary. The thresholds lie in between 0.5-1.0 (Ljubesic and Fiser, 2016). We don't use words whose occurrence frequency is less than 10 since co-occurrence frequency for such words is not reliable. This process is repeated several times to increase the size of the polarity dictionary. The process terminates when it reaches the saturation point i.e. no new words are being added to the dictionary. In case the process isn't stopping, we can introduce a maximum loop condition.

Sentimental Analysis Using Polarity Dictionary

We begin by counting the frequency of the positive words and negative words. Then we compare them quantitatively. If a text has more positive words as compared to negative words, the polarity of the entire article is positive. When there are more negative words compared to positive ones, the polarity of the article is negative. When the frequency of the positive and negative words is same or when there are no positive or negative words at all the article is considered as neutral. Hence, all article are classified as either positive, negative, or neutral. We explain a process to determine a polarity of an article using an example:

"The product is very good, after sales service is supreme but price is unaffordable"

Here the words "good" and "supreme' account for positive polarity whereas "unaffordable" accounts for negative polarity. Since the number of positive polarities are greater than negative polarities, the overall polarity of the sentence is considered as positive. In this step we neglect impact, negation and adversative conjunction and use all sentence to decide polarity of articles. This methodology was experimented for data acquired from Centillion Co. and an accurate polarity of 45% of total news was obtained (Ljubesic and Fiser, 2016).

Sentiment Classification Based on Support Vector Machine (SVM)

In this approach, the sentence is first splitted into 3 parts: the starting part of the comment, the middle part of the comment and the terminating/concluding part of the comment. Then mark the sentences with labels according to their position in the comment. The first sentence is marked as 'f', the middle sentence which forms the centre of the comment is marked as 'm' and the last sentence is marked as 'l'. Then through Jeiba Chinese Software, the words were segmented. To improve the accuracy, noun, verb, adjective, adverb etc. were introduced (Mizumoto, Yanagimoto, and Yoshioka, 2012). Every forum review set ri where $\mathbf{R}= \{r1, r,..., rm\}$ of several completed sentences$<si1,si2,...sin>$ (Wang, Zheng, Liu, 2012). In the next step, the review is divided into 3 parts: the first sentence, middle sentence, last sentence. The weight is then calculated based on the part of the sentence at the paragraph following to which polarity is calculated of the review 'i'

$(ri)=\Sigma(sij)wijnj=1$. Suppose two sentiment labels are used *Rpos* and the other is *Rnega*. When $sij \in Rpos, (sij)=1$; else if $sij \in Rnega, P(sij)=-1$. If $(ri)>0, ri$ is the +1. Else, ri is the -1. We can acquire weights as wij through the formula as follows: $wi= ((r \in Rpos \wedge si \in Rpos) \vee (r \in Rneg \wedge si \in Rneg))$. Following to this, we use SVM as classifier to train the model. This method when tested for shares trading on SSE and SZSE. At first, the information crawling software to get comments of every stocks on Easymoney stock forum was used. When compared to the traditional semantic method which gave an accuracy of 53.1%, this method gave an accuracy of 80.7% (Wang, Zheng, Liu, 2012).

Sentence Level Sentiment Analysis

A rule base analysis is essential for performing sentence level sentiment analysis. This method focuses on analysing the various intricacies and levels of granularity (Zhang and Bu, 2017). Negation rules are used here for the purpose of sentiment extraction. Thus the presence of words like no, never, not, negative etc. account for negative polarity of the sentence. Further various combinations of verbs or adjectives such as unstable, inefficient, stop etc. can be put to use to improve accuracy.

Feature Level Sentiment Analysis

This method is used when an overall or aggregate notion about the product/service to improve knowledge about predicting its stock outcomes is to be found. In this intelligent analysis, each feature is assigned some score/weightage. For instance, a positive review is assigned a positive weightage score. A more positive comment/review is assigned a more weighted score. In similar fashion, a negative feature is assigned a negative score. The overall/ aggregate review is judged on the factor of aggregate of the individual scores. Thus if the aggregate score is positive, the entire review is considered positive. If the aggregate score is negative, the entire review is considered negative. Feature analysis is an approach based on the mathematical formula or statistics which acts as a base for the entire prediction of the sentiment feature.

Word Level Sentiment Analysis

One of the most widely used and high performance sentimental analysis technique. Encoding is done effectively between the classes and the words. For instance, (Satisfactory, good, excellent, brilliant) => positive sentiments. A number of databases are used that represent a relationship between adjectives and its respective classes. Extraction of adjectives comes under lexical analysis of the sentiment (Zhang and Bu, 2017). Two classes are formed for the purpose of identifying the positive and negative reviews. The overall efficiency of Word-level Sentiment Analysis approach depends on the wholesomeness of the wordlist/adjective database put to use.

The steps further involved are as follows:

Relevant documents are considered.

- Irrelevant words such as are, we, am, for etc. are eliminated and keywords are extracted.
- From these extracted keywords, adjectives and keywords that reflect opinions are identified.
- Opinion class is determined and weightage is designated to each keyword. The opinion class comprising of higher number of keywords is assigned a higher weightage and vice versa.
- Overall/ aggregate weight depends on each opinion class based on which overall resulting decision is taken.

It is an effective, simple technique and thereby quite extensively used algorithm for document classification.

Challenges in Sentiment Analysis

1. Fast paced change in data sets: Creating a robust classifier that works for the ever changing mentality and opinions reflected through the reviews and comments online is difficult. Thus features used for classification so far may soon become irrelevant in near future. The amount and the type of user data collected every day is changes at an unprecedented rate. Another drawback could be people expressing their views towards the utility or service implicitly with no or less words of sentiments

rather than doing it explicitly. This worsens the situation and furthermore makes it challenging. Another problem that may make the problem more difficult is it is difficult to differentiate transient important features from recurring ones. It is important to keep a track of these features as they may disappear and reappear in the future. Another problematic situation arises when there is inconsistency in the datasets. Machine learning often assumes clean, well-distributed data sets for the purpose of experimentation. However the real life datasets aren't that well-distributed (Raghuvanshi and Patil, 2016).

2. Each product is referred using different names sometimes in same document and many a times across various documents. This is a serious issue of entity resolution and is not yet solved. Anaphora handling is another major challenge in sentiment analysis. For instance, the terms "mileage" and "fuel efficiency" have same meanings and refer to same aspects of a car.

3. Texts with spelling mistakes, grammatical errors, improper use of tense, punctuation mistakes, use of slangs etc. account as noisy data. Classification of such a data is still a major challenge in sentiment analysis.

4. Many a times, statements which put forth the factual aspects of the products are made. Currently, the approaches which are employed focuses only on the subjective nature of the statements. There's a need of algorithms that could attach context scores & focus on the objective (factual) part of the statement for efficient classification and better understanding.

5. Challenges related to interpretation: There has been lack of harmony in the online behaviour of the masses and their actual behaviour in practice. For instance, a person/group writing negative comments about the online food delivery service may still continue to use it despite of their opinion on internet perhaps because it's the only service available in their neighbourhood. This thus doesn't affect monetarily and neither hampers the sales.

6. Presence of links: If we take an example of twitter, many a times the tweets redirect the readers to certain websites, profiles, articles etc. through browser links. While the parent tweet may fail to reflect sentiments of the users, it may be contained in the redirected site. These links cannot be identified by the current methods. Those links are crucial and represent the tweet in its complete sense. Without referring two those links, it becomes impossible to detect the sentiments even for a human annotator (Ebrahimi, Yazdayar, and Sheth, 2017).

7. Content related challenges: Recently there has been an advent in the use of hashtags. These hashtags are quite volatile in nature and hence need distant control which is training a dataset on periodically labelled training set (Ebrahimi, Yazdayar, and Sheth, 2017).

People tend to use a quite access of these hashtags on various online platforms such as twitter to express their opinion about a product or entity. Hashtags are also used for emotion detection through machine learning approach (Go, Bhayani, and Huang, 2009). Due to its dynamic nature, the quantity, quality and freshness of the labelled data plays an important role in constructing a robust classifier with reliability.

8. Many a times the presence of bots on social media platform hamper the authenticity of the data obtained for sentiment analysis. A bot is a computer generated algorithm that tries to imitate the human behaviour by generating biased content on social & news distribution related platforms (Wang et. al, 2012). Though measures are been taken to track down and ban bots, this still poses a serious threat to the idea of sentiment analysis.

9. Use of sarcasm can be an issue while mining responses for the analysis. For instance, the classifier may consider both the comments "I love the way the after sales service of car 'X' ignores me" and "I love the in-built music stereo system of car X" as similar when in practical world, they clearly don't comply similar notions (Lee, Eoff, Cayerlee, 2011).

10. Unclear target of emotion could also lead to ambiguity. For instance, for a company 'X' trying to find about the opinions of masses about a newly released feature in their car, comments like "I hate the traffic outside showroom X" or "The music taste of employees working in day-shift of showroom X is poor" might lead to problems while classification.

MISINFORMATION IN SENTIMENTS OVER SOCIAL MEDIA

These days most of the review sites, public discussions, forums etc. are affected more & more due to widespread of misinformation. Misinformation usually aims at hampering the business or goodwill of an individual, group or an organization by misleading them & thereby causes anomalies in the sentiment analysis. To tackle this, several data-driven solutions have been suggested since reviews can strongly affect the decisions of uninformed people visiting the website for advice. Today with the introduction to the Web 2.0, it is possible for every individual to diffuse his/her opinions over internet without requiring any form of trusted security verifications. One of the proposed methodology is analysis of the features connected to the reviewers and reviews & to learn about their distinct characteristics. Literature shows that it has led to it has led to successful identification of malicious or falsely generated content. One method is to compare the features of a singleton review ad check for the occurrence of multiple reviews with similar features which then is used to determine the creditability factor. For instance, if there's single negative review among a set of hundreds of positive reviews, the creditability of that single review is low. However if there are multiple reviews of same nature, the creditability factor increases (Fontanaraya, Pasi, Viviani, 2017).

From a historical point of view creditability is often associated with truth worthiness, reliability, accuracy etc. The features or the characteristics which are considered for the purpose of evaluation are linguistic parameters associated with the text. One of the approach is to analyze the reviews based on the meta-data. For instance analyzing the reviews based upon its rating (1-5 stars) or the period during which the review/comment was made (Fontanaraya, Pasi, Viviani, 2017). The latter is done to ensure that the comments/reviews made far in the past on a particular service/ product aren't considered especially since several updates have been already done to it. The classifiers used for the same are supervised and unsupervised. Unsupervised classifiers are in general less effective but useful in cases where a pre-determined dataset is not required. Supervised classifiers are in general more effective and employ review & reviewer centric features. To evaluate this a supervised model based on Random Forests has been developed. This model can be used efficiently on large public datasets.

FUTURE RESEARCH DIRECTIONS

For future research, we would evaluate the effectiveness of each of the above proposed methodologies against various test scenarios for the purpose of sentence and phrase-level analysis of sentiments. We also aim to employ these methods individually on different types of content such as stock markets, news articles, twitter feed, product reviews and test their effectiveness on an individual level. Further this research could also be directed for analyzing the abstract features of a document such as topic, genre, type of content etc.

Works which have been previously done have mostly focused on the semantic and syntactic features there has been a minimal use of the stylistic features such as vocabulary rich measures, character/word length, frequencies of special characters, lexical features at word level etc. Thus more light could be thrown on these parameters (Abbasi, Chen, and Salem, 2008).

Web-based crawling for sentiment analysis has a potential of research extension since most of the web-pages with undiscovered content contain diverse sentiments. Discovery of such mixed sentiments is important in various domains especially sales, politics, marketing etc. New metrics can be designed to gather, identify & evaluate such diverse emotions (Gural et. al, 2014).

CONCLUSION

This chapter gives a brief insight to the understanding of the term 'sentiment'. Further, the need to analyse the user generated data reflecting their opinions about a utility/service to get insights of their reviews were discussed. Various methodologies that can be employed for the classification of the data mined from the internet along with their efficiencies were discussed. SVM of all the discussed methods turned out to give most accurate results. Lastly we came up with the various challenges related to the classification of the data. Sentiment analysis is a promising field and overcoming these challenges and moving towards a more robust classifier would result in better mining of human sentiments from an industrial standpoint.

REFERENCES

Abbasi, A., Chen, H., & Salem, A. (2008). Sentiment Analysis in Multiple Languages: Feature Selection for Opinion Classification in Web Forums. ACM Transactions on Information Systems, 26(3), 12. *doi:10.1145/1361684.1361685*

Cambridge University Press. (2008). Cambridge online dictionary. Author.

Ebrahim*i, M., Yazdavar, A., & Shet*h, A. (2017). Challenges of Sentiment Analysis for dynamic events. IEEE Intelligent Systems, 32(5), 70–75. doi:*10.1109/MIS.2017.3711649*

Fontanarava, J., Pasi, G., & Viviani, M. (2017). Feature Analysis for Fake Review Detection through Supervised Classification. International Conference on Data Scien*ce and Advanced Analytics. 10.1109/ DSAA.2017.51*

Go, A., Bhayani, R., & Huang, L. (2009). Twitter sentiment classification using distant supervision. CS224N Project Report, 1(12).

Hovy, E. H. (2015). What are Sentiment, Affect, and Emo*tion? Applying the Methodology of Michael Zock to Sentiment Analysis. Springer International Publishing* Switzerland. doi:10.1007/978-3-319-08043-7_2

Joshi, A., Bhattacharya, P., & Mark, J. (2017). Automatic Sarcasm Detection: A Survey. ACM Computing Surveys, 50(5).

Lee, K., Eoff, B. D., & Caverlee, J. (2011). Seven Months with the Devils: *A Long-Term Study of Content Polluters on Twitter. ICWSM.*

*Ljubesic, N., & F*iser, D. (2016). A global analysis of emoji *usage. ACL.*

*Mizumoto, K., Ya*nagimoto, H., & Yoshioka, M. (2012). IEEE/ACIS 11th International Conferenc*e on Computer and Information Science. IEEE.*

Pang, B., & Lee, L. (2008). Opinion mining and sentiment analysis. Foundation and Trend*s in Information Retrieval, 2(1-2), 1–135.*

Qu*i*rk, R., Greenbaum, S. G. L., & Svartvik, J. (1985). A comprehensive grammar of the English language. Longman.

Raghuvanshi, N., & Patil, J. M. (2016). A Brief Review on Sentiment Analysis. International *Conference on Electrical, Electronics, and Optimization Techniques (ICEEOT). IEEE Conferences.*

Vural, A. G., Cambazoglu, B. B., & Karagoz, P. (2014). Sentiment-Focused Web Crawling. ACM Trans*actions on the Web, 8(4), 22.* doi:10.1145/2644821

Wang, H. W., Zheng, L. J., & Liu, Z. Y. (2012). Sentiment feature selection from Chinese online reviews. China Jo*urnal of Information Systems, 11.*

Wang, W. (2012). Harnessing twitter big data for automatic emotion identification. Privac*y, Security, Risk and Trust (PASSAT), International Conference on Social Computing (SocialCom) IEEE.*

Zhang, Y., & Bu, H. (2017). Can extracted features from stock forum amount for the stock return? In*ternational Conference on Service Systems and Service Management.*

Chapter 11
Evaluation of Optimum and Coherent Economic–Capital Portfolios Under Complex Market Prospects

Mazin A. M. Al Janabi

 https://orcid.org/0000-0002-2249-932X

EGADE Business School, Tecnologico de Monterrey, Mexico

ABSTRACT

This chapter examines the performance of liquidity-adjusted risk modeling in obtaining optimum and coherent economic-capital structures, subject to meaningful operational and financial constraints as specified by the portfolio manager. Specifically, the chapter proposes a robust approach to optimum economic-capital allocation in a liquidity-adjusted value at risk (L-VaR) framework. This chapter expands previous approaches by explicitly modeling the liquidation of trading portfolios, over the holding period, with the aid of an appropriate scaling of the multiple-assets' L-VaR matrix along with GARCH-M technique to forecast conditional volatility and expected return. Moreover, in this chapter, the authors develop a dynamic nonlinear portfolio selection model and an optimization algorithm, which allocates both economic-capital and trading assets by minimizing L-VaR objective function. The empirical results strongly confirm the importance of enforcing financially and operationally meaningful nonlinear and dynamic constraints, when they are available, on the L-VaR optimization procedure.

INTRODUCTION AND OUTLINE

The significance of assessing the market risk of portfolios of financial securities has long been acknowledged by academics and practitioners. In recent years, the growth of trading activities and instances of financial market upheavals has prompted new research underlining the necessity for market participants to develop reliable dynamic portfolio management and risk assessment methods and algorithms. In measuring market risk of trading portfolios, one technique advanced in the literature involves the use

DOI: 10.4018/978-1-7998-0106-1.ch011

of Value at Risk (VaR) models that ascertain how much the value of a trading portfolio would plunge, in monetary terms, over a given period of time with a given probability as a result of changes in market prices. From a portfolio market risk point of view, VaR faces some major difficulties. Three of the most researched and discussed issues are the non-normal behavior of market returns, volatility clustering and the impact of illiquid securities (Al Janabi, 2013, and 2014). The effect of the latter on portfolio risk management and dynamic economic-capital allocation under market liquidity constraints is the key focus of this chapter[1].

Indeed, methods for measuring market (or trading) risk have been well developed and standardized in the academic as well as the banking world. Asset liquidity trading risk, on the other hand, has received less attention from researchers, perhaps because it is less significant in developed countries where most of the market risk methodologies were originated. Nonetheless, the combination of the recent rapid expansion of emerging markets' trading activities and the recurring turbulence in those markets, in light of the aftermaths of the sub-prime financial crisis, has propelled asset liquidity trading risk to the forefront of market risk management research and development (Al Janabi, 2008, 2010, and 2013).

To address the above deficiency, in this chapter we characterize trading risk for emerging equity markets by using a multivariate Liquidity-Adjusted Value at Risk (L-VaR) approach that focuses on the modeling of optimum L-VaR under the notion of illiquid and adverse market conditions and by exercising different correlation factors and liquidity horizon periods[2]. The overall objective of this chapter is to construct different equity portfolios, which include several stock markets indices of the Gulf Cooperation Council (GCC) zone, and to evaluate the risk characteristics of such a portfolio besides examining an optimization algorithm process for assessing economic-capital's optimum (efficient) and coherent market portfolios[3]. To this end, we propose a general trading risk model that accounts for the characteristics of the series of equity price returns—for example, fat tails (leptokurtosis), skewness, correlation factors, and liquidity horizons—and adequately forecasts market risk within a short time horizon. To that end, the modeling techniques and optimization algorithms are based on Al Janabi model for market liquidity risk management (Al Janabi, 2008; Madoroba and Kruger, 2014).

LITERATURE REVIEW AND OBJECTIVES OF PRESENT RESEARCH STUDY

Based on studies to date, there is little agreement as to the best method for developing VaR risk measures. However, literature related to VaR is continually growing as researchers attempt to reconcile several pending issues. The prior literature on VaR and portfolio risk management has been focused on two distinct lines of research. The first category focuses mainly on the use of different VaR models for market and credit risk management and for selecting optimum portfolios within VaR framework, whereas the second category emphasizes the development of asset liquidity risk as an integral part of market risk and, therefore, leads to several approaches for the estimation of L-VaR. Below we discuss some of the relevant literature classified according to the above two categories.

Literature Review on Optimum Portfolio Selection Within a Value at Risk (VaR) Structure

The literature on measuring financial risks and volatility using VaR models is extensive, yet Jorion (2007) and Dowd et al. (2004) should be pointed out for their integrated approach to the topic. The general recognition and use of large scale VaR models has initiated a considerable literature including statistical descriptions of VaR and assessments of different modeling techniques. For a comprehensive survey, and the different VaR analysis and techniques, one can refer to Jorion (2007).

On another front, other authors have investigated the use of VaR for the selection of optimum portfolios and for active portfolio management. For instance, Campbell et al. (2001) develop a an optimum portfolio selection model which maximizes expected return subject to a downside risk constraint rather than standard deviation alone. The suggested model allocates financial assets by maximizing expected return conditional on the constraint that the expected maximum loss should be within the VaR limits set by the risk manager. Additionally, the authors develop a performance index similar to the Sharpe ratio, which for the special case when expected returns are assumed to be normally distributed provides almost identical results to the mean-variance approach. In another study, Yiu (2004) examines the optimum portfolio problem by imposing VaR as a dynamic constraint. This approach provides a path to control risks in the optimum portfolio and to satisfy the requirement of regulators on the assessment of market risks. Furthermore, the VaR constraint is derived for some risky assets plus a risk-free asset and is imposed continuously over time and the problem is formulated as a constrained utility maximization problem over a period of time. Under this formulation and the obtained numerical results, the author argues that investments in risky assets are optimally reduced by the imposed VaR constraint. This is due to the fact that the VaR constraint is applied over time so that there is a direct relationship between the VaRs and portfolio holdings at each instant. Finally, in a relatively recent study, Alexander and Baptista (2008) look at the impact of adding a VaR constraint to the problem of an active manager who seeks to outperform a benchmark by a given percentage. In doing so, the authors minimize the tracking error variance (TEV) by using the model of Roll (1992). As such, the authors obtain three main results. First, portfolios on the constrained mean-TEV boundary still display three-fund separation; however the weights of the three funds when the constraint binds differ from those in Roll's model. Second, the VaR constraint mitigates the problem that when a manager seeks to outperform a benchmark using the mean-TEV model, he or she selects a portfolio that is mean-variance inefficient. Finally, when short-sales are not permitted, the extent to which the constraint decreases the optimum portfolio's efficiency loss can still be noteworthy but is less significant than when short-sales are permitted.

Literature Related to Liquidity-Adjusted Value at Risk (L-VaR) Modeling

The combination of the latest swift expansion of emerging markets' trading activities and the persistent turbulence in those markets has impelled liquidity trading risk to the vanguard of market risk management research and development. To this end, within the VaR framework, Jarrow and Subramanian (1997) provide a market impact model of liquidity by considering the optimal liquidation of an investment portfolio over a fixed horizon. They derive the optimal execution strategy by determining the sales schedule that will maximize the expected total sales values, assuming that the period until liquidation is given as an exogenous factor.

Bangia et al. (1999) approach liquidity risk from another angle and provide a model of VaR adjusted for what they call exogenous liquidity—defined as common to all market players and unaffected by the actions of any one participant. It comprises such execution costs as order processing costs and adverse selection costs resulting in a given bid-ask spread faced by investors in the market. On the contrary, endogenous liquidity is specific to one's position in the market, depends on one's actions, and varies across market participants.

Finally, in his research papers, Al Janabi (2013 and 2014) establishes a robust modeling framework and algorithms for the measurement, management and control of trading risk. This literature provides real-world risk management techniques and strategies (drawn from a practitioner viewpoint) that can be applied to equity trading portfolios in emerging markets. The intent is to propose a robust modeling technique for including of liquidation trading risk in standard VaR analysis and to capture the liquidity risk arising due to illiquid trading positions by obtaining an L-VaR estimation. The key methodological contribution is a different and less conservative liquidity scaling factor than the conventional root-*t* multiplier[4].

Objectives of Present Research Chapter

In spite of the increasing importance of the GCC financial markets, there is very little published research in this respect and particularly within liquidity trading risk management context. Moreover, to the best of our knowledge, no work has been published yet in any international literature on liquidity risk management and coherent economic-capital allocation that takes into account the GCC countries as a case study in advanced risk management applications. As such, this chapter aims to capture liquidity risk arising due to illiquid trading positions and to obtain L-VaR and coherent economic-capital assessments.

This chapter shows that the performance of efficient and coherent economic-capital portfolios depends on the expected return, individual L-VaR positions, liquidity horizons of each trading asset, and the set of portfolio weights. Moreover, in this work, the relative performance of the L-VaR and economic-capital selection model is compared in a dynamic asset allocation framework. The objective of the dynamic asset allocation is to find the optimum equity asset allocation mix by minimizing L-VaR and economic-capital subject to the imposition of operational and financial constraints based on fundamental asset management considerations.

The implemented methodology and risk assessment algorithms can aid in advancing risk management practices in emerging markets, particularly in the wake of the sub-prime credit crunch and the subsequent 2007-2009 financial turmoil. In addition, the proposed quantitative risk management techniques and optimization algorithms can have important uses and applications in expert systems, machine learning, smart financial functions, and financial technology (FinTech) in big data environments. Likewise, it can aid in the development of regulatory technology (RegTech) for the global financial services industry, and can be of interest to professionals, regulators, and researchers working in the field of finance and FinTech; and for those who want to improve their understanding of the impact of innovative quantitative risk management techniques and optimization algorithms on regulatory challenges for financial services industry and its effects on global financial stability.

THEORETICAL FOUNDATIONS OF L-VAR AND ECONOMIC-CAPITAL USING AL JANABI MODEL

A Parametric L-VaR Approach for the Assessment of Trading Risk Exposure

To calculate VaR using the parametric method, the volatility of each risk factor is extracted from a predefined historical observation period and can be estimated using GARCH-M model. The potential effect of each component of the portfolio on the overall portfolio value is then worked out. These effects are then aggregated across the whole portfolio using the correlations between the risk factors (which are, again, extracted from the historical observation period) to give the overall VaR value of the portfolio with a given confidence level. As such, for a single trading position the absolute value of VaR can be defined in monetary terms as follows (Al Janabi, 2010, 2013 and 2017)[5]:

$$VaR_i = | (\mu_i - \alpha * \sigma_i) \text{ (Mark-to-Market Value of Asset}_i * Fx_i) | \tag{1}$$

where μ_i is the expected return of the asset, α is the confidence level (or in other words, the standard normal variant at confidence level α) and σ_i is the conditional volatility of the return of the security that constitutes the single position and can be estimated using a GARCH-M model. While the *Mark-to-Market Value of Asset*$_i$ indicates the amount of investment in asset i, Fx_i denotes the unit foreign exchange rate of asset i. If the expected return of the asset, μ_p is very small, then equation (1) can be reduced to:

$$VaR_i = | \alpha * \sigma_i * \text{Mark-to-Market Value of Asset}_i * Fx_i | \tag{2}$$

Indeed, equation (2) includes some simplifying assumptions, yet it is routinely used by researchers and practitioners in the financial markets for the estimation of VaR for a single trading position.

Trading risk in the presence of multiple risk factors is determined by the combined effect of individual risks. The extent of the total risk is determined not only by the magnitudes of the individual risks but also by their correlations. Portfolio effects are crucial in risk management not only for large diversified portfolios but also for individual instruments that depends on several risk factors. For multiple assets or portfolio of assets, VaR is a function of each individual security's risk and the correlation factor [$\rho_{i,j}$] between the returns on the individual securities as follows:

$$VaR_P = \sqrt{\sum_{i=1}^{n} \sum_{j=1}^{n} VaR_i VaR_j \rho_{i,j}} = \sqrt{[VaR]^T [\rho][VaR]} \tag{3}$$

This formula is a general one for the calculation of VaR for any portfolio regardless of the number of securities. It should be noted that the second term of the above formula is rewritten in terms of matrix-algebra—a useful form to avoid mathematical complexity, as more and more securities are added.

Incorporating Asset Liquidity Risk Into L-VaR Models

In effect, if returns are independent and they can have any elliptical multivariate distribution, then it is possible to convert the VaR horizon parameter from daily to any t–day horizon, such as:

$$VaR(t - day) = VaR(1 - day)\sqrt{t} \tag{4}$$

The above formula was proposed and used by *J.P. Morgan* in their earlier *RiskMetrics*[TM] method (1994). This methodology implicitly assumes that liquidation occurs in one block sale at the end of the holding period and that there is one holding period for all assets, regardless of their inherent trading liquidity structure. In order to take into account the full illiquidity of equity assets (that is, the required unwinding period to liquidate an asset) we define the following:

t = number of liquidation days (t–days to liquidate the entire equity asset fully)
σ_{adj}^{2} = variance of the illiquid equity trading position; and
σ_{adj} = liquidity risk factor or standard deviation of the illiquid equity trading position.

The proposed approach assumes that the trading position is closed out linearly over t-days and hence it uses the logical assumption that the losses due to illiquid trading positions over t-days are the sum of losses over the individual trading days. Moreover, we can assume with reasonable accuracy that asset returns and losses due to illiquid trading positions are independent and identically distributed (*iid*) and serially uncorrelated day–to-day along the liquidation horizon and that the variance of losses due to liquidity risk over t-days is the sum of the variance (σ_i^2, for all $i = 1,2...,t$) of losses on the individual days, thus:

$$\sigma_{adj}^{2} = \left(\sigma_1^2 + \sigma_2^2 + \sigma_3^2 + ... + \sigma_{t-2}^2 + \sigma_{t-1}^2 + \sigma_t^2\right) \tag{5}$$

In fact, the square root-t approach (equation [4]) is a simplified special case of equation (5) under the assumption that the daily variances of losses throughout the holding period are all the same as first day variance, σ_1^2, thus

$$\sigma_{adj}^{2} = \left(\sigma_1^{2} + \sigma_1^{2} + \sigma_1^{2} + \cdots + \sigma_1^{2}\right) = t\sigma_1^{2}.$$

As such, for this special linear liquidation case and under the assumption that the variance of losses of the first trading day decreases linearly each day (as a function of t) we can derive from equation (5) the following:

$$\sigma_{adj}^{2} = \left(\left(\frac{t}{t}\right)^{2}\sigma_1^2 + \left(\frac{t-1}{t}\right)^{2}\sigma_1^2 + \left(\frac{t-2}{t}\right)^{2}\sigma_1^2 + ... + \left(\frac{3}{t}\right)^{2}\sigma_1^2 + \left(\frac{2}{t}\right)^{2}\sigma_1^2 + \left(\frac{1}{t}\right)^{2}\sigma_1^2\right) \tag{6}$$

In the general case of t-days, the variance of the liquidity risk factor is given by the following mathematical functional expression of t:

$$\sigma_{adj}^{2} = \sigma_1^2\left(\left(\frac{t}{t}\right)^{2} + \left(\frac{t-1}{t}\right)^{2} + \left(\frac{t-2}{t}\right)^{2} + ... + \left(\frac{3}{t}\right)^{2} + \left(\frac{2}{t}\right)^{2} + \left(\frac{1}{t}\right)^{2}\right) \tag{7}$$

To calculate the sum of the squares, it is convenient to use a short-cut approach. From mathematical finite series, the following relationship can be obtained:

$$\left(t\right)^2 + \left(t-1\right)^2 + \left(t-2\right)^2 + ... + \left(3\right)^2 + \left(2\right)^2 + \left(1\right)^2 = \frac{t\left(t-1\right)\left(2t+1\right)}{6} \tag{8}$$

Hence, after substituting equation (8) into equation (7), the following can be achieved:

$$\sigma^2_{adj} = \sigma^2_1 \left[\frac{1}{t^2}\left\{\left(t\right)^2 + \left(t-1\right)^2 + \left(t-2\right)^2 + ... + \left(3\right)^2 + \left(2\right)^2 + \left(1\right)^2\right\}\right] \text{ or } \sigma^2_{adj} = \sigma^2_1 \left(\frac{\left(2t+1\right)\left(t+1\right)}{6t}\right) \tag{9}$$

Accordingly, from equation (9) the liquidity risk factor can be expressed in terms of volatility (or standard deviation) as:

$$\sigma^2_{adj} = \sigma_1 \left\{\sqrt{\frac{1}{t^2}\left[\left(t\right)^2 + \left(t-1\right)^2 + \left(t-2\right)^2 + ... + \left(3\right)^2 + \left(2\right)^2 + \left(1\right)^2\right]}\right\} \text{ or } \sigma_{adj} = \sigma_1 \left\{\sqrt{\frac{\left(2t+1\right)\left(t+1\right)}{6t}}\right\} \tag{10}$$

Likewise, in order to perform the calculation of L-VaR under illiquid market conditions, it is possible to use the liquidity factor of equation (10) and define the following:

$$L - VaR_{adj} = VaR\sqrt{\frac{\left(2t+1\right)\left(t+1\right)}{6t}} \tag{11}$$

where VaR = Value at Risk under liquid market conditions and; $L\text{-}VaR_{adj}$ = Value at Risk under illiquid market conditions. As a matter of fact, the number of liquidation days (t) necessary to liquidate the entire equity assets fully is related to the choice of the liquidity threshold and in actual practices it is generally estimated as:

$$t = |Total\ Trading\ Position\ Size\ of\ Asset_i\ /\ Daily\ Trading\ Volume\ of\ Asset_i|,\ s.t.\ t \geq 1.0 \tag{12}$$

In order to calculate the L-VaR for the full trading portfolio under illiquid market conditions $\left(L - VaR_{P_{adj}}\right)$, the above mathematical formulation can be extended, with the aid of equation (3), into a matrix-algebra form to yield the following:

$$L - VaR_{P_{adj}} = \sqrt{\left[L - VaR_{adj}\right]^T \left[\rho\right]\left[L - VaR_{adj}\right]} \tag{13}$$

On another front, the annual economic-capital necessary to support trading activities under illiquid normal and severe market settings can be defined as:

$$Economic\ capital(EC) = \left(\frac{\alpha_{EC}}{\alpha}\right)\sqrt{H}\sqrt{\rho_{BU}}\sqrt{\sum_{i=1}^{n}\sum_{j=1}^{n}L - VaR_i L - VaR_j \rho_{i,j}}$$

$$= \left(\frac{\alpha_{EC}}{\alpha}\right)\sqrt{H}\sqrt{\rho_{BU}}\sqrt{\left[L - VaR_{adj}\right]^T \left[\rho\right]\left[L - VaR_{adj}\right]}$$

(14)

where α_{EC} is the economic-capital quantile of 3.43, α is the daily VaR quantile as illustrated in equation (1), H is the number of active trading days in the year, ρ_{BU} is the correlation factor required to account for the diversification benefit provided by having the equity trading risk unit as one of a number of diversified financial businesses.

ASSESSMENT OF RISK EXPOSURE AND ECONOMIC-CAPITAL

In this chapter, database of daily return of six GCC stock markets' main indicators (indices) are gathered, filtered and adequately adapted for the creation of relevant inputs for the calculation of all risk factors. Historical database (of more than six years) of daily closing index levels, for the period 17/10/2004-22/05/2009, are assembled for the purpose of carrying out this research study and further for the construction of market and liquidity risk management parameters. The selected datasets fall within the most critical period of the 2007-2009 global financial crisis. The total numbers of indices that are considered in this work are seven indices, detailed as follows:

DFM General Index (United Arab Emirates; Dubai Financial Market General Index); ADSM Index (United Arab Emirates, Abu Dhabi Stock Market Index); BA All Share Index (Bahrain, All Share Stock Market Index); KSE General Index (Kuwait, Stock Exchange General Index); MSM30 Index (Oman, Muscat Stock Market Index); DSM20 Index (Qatar, Doha Stock Market General Index); SE All Share Index (Saudi Arabia, All Share Stock Market Index).

Moreover, in this work index returns are defined as $R_{i,t} = ln(P_{i,t}) - ln(P_{i,t-1})$ where $R_{i,t}$ is the daily return of index i, ln is the natural logarithm; $P_{i,t}$ is the current level of index i, and $P_{i,t-1}$ is the previous day index level. Furthermore, for this particular research study we have chosen a confidence interval of 95% (or 97.5% with "one-tailed" loss side) and several liquidation time horizons to compute L-VaR. Furthermore, an iterative optimization-algorithm software package is programmed for the purpose of creating trading portfolios of the above indices and consequently for carrying out L-VaR and economic-capital scenario-analysis under extreme illiquid market conditions and by implementing different correlation factors. The analysis of data and discussions of relevant findings and results of this research study are organized and explained as follows:

Optimization of Economic-Capital's Optimum (Efficient) and Coherent Portfolios

Optimized portfolios do normally not perform as well in practice as one would expect from theory. For example, they are often outperformed by simple allocation strategies such as the equally weighted portfolio (Jobson and Korkie, 1981) or the global minimum variance portfolio (Jorion, 1991). It is well documented (Michaud, 1989) that mean-variance optimizers, if left to their own devices, can sometimes lead to unintuitive portfolios with extreme positions in asset classes. Consequently, these "optimized" portfolios are not necessarily well diversified and exposed to unnecessary ex-post risk (Michaud, 1989). Therefore, large estimation errors in expected returns and/or variances/covariances will introduce errors in the optimized portfolio weights (Fabozzi et al., 2006).

In this work, we develop a model for optimizing portfolio risk-return with economic-capital constraints using realistic operational and financial scenarios and conduct a case study on optimizing equity portfolios of the six GCC stock markets. The case study shows that the optimization algorithm, which is based on quadratic programming techniques, is very stable and efficient in handling different liquidity horizons and correlation factors. Moreover, the approach can tackle large number of equity securities and rational fund management scenarios. Indeed, the economic-capital risk management constraints can be used in various applications to bound percentiles of loss distributions.

Essentially, our approach is a robust enhancement to the classic Markowitz mean-variance approach, where the original risk measure, variance, is replaced by L-VaR and economic-capital algorithms. The task is attained here by minimizing economic-capital, while requiring a minimum expected return subject to several financially meaningful operational constraints.

Constrained Optimization of Economic-Capital's Efficient and Coherent Portfolios

The optimization process is based on the definition of economic-capital as the minimum possible loss over a specified time horizon within a given confidence level. The iterative-optimization modeling algorithm solves the problem by finding the market positions that minimize the loss, subject to the fact that all constraints are satisfied within their boundary values. For the sake of simplifying the optimization algorithm and thereafter its analysis, a volume trading position limit of 10 million AED (UAE Dirhams) is assumed as a constraint—that is the equity trading entity must keep a maximum overall market value of different equities of no more than 10 million AED (between long and short-sales positions). As such, Figures (1) and (2) provide evidence of the empirical economic-capital's efficient frontiers (under *1*-day and *10*-days liquidation horizons respectively) defined using a 97.5% confidence level. As mentioned above, the optimum portfolio selection is performed by relaxing the short sale constraint, for the different equity assets.

On the other hand, efficient portfolios cannot always be attained (e.g. short-sales without realistic lower boundaries on x_i) in the day-to-day real-world portfolio management operations and, hence, the fund manager should establish proactive coherent portfolios under realistic and restricted dynamic budget constraints, detailed as follows:

- Total trading volume (between long and short equity trading positions) is 10 million AED.
- Asset allocation for long equity trading position varies from 10% to 100%.
- Asset allocation for short equity trading position varies from -10% to -60%.
- Liquidity horizons for all equities are kept constant according to the following indicated values for each market: DFM General Index (3 days); ADSM Index (3 days); BA All Share Index (4 days); KSE General Index (3 days); MSM30 Index (5 days); DSM20 Index (6 days); SE All Share Index (3 days).

Figure 1. Demonstrates the empirical optimum (efficient) frontier of economic-capital portfolios under 1-day liquidation horizon by relaxing short-sales constraints (i.e., allowing both long and short-sales trading positions).
Source: *Figure (1) is designed by the author using an in-house developed software.*

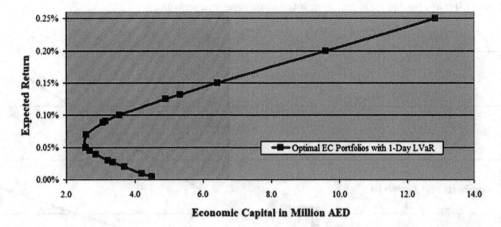

Now the asset allocation weights are allowed to take negative or positive values, however, since arbitrarily high or low percentages have no financial sense, we determined to introduce lower and upper boundaries for the weights and in accordance with reasonable trading practices. Furthermore, for comparison purposes and since the endeavor in this work is to minimize economic-capital subject to specific expected returns, we decide to plot economic-capital versus expected returns and not the reverse, as is commonly done in the various portfolio management literature. Accordingly, it is worthy of note that the four benchmark portfolios (coherent portfolios [1], [2], [3] and [4]) are noticeably located way off from the efficient frontiers as indicated in Figures (3). This is because financially and operation-

Figure 2. Demonstrates the empirical optimum (efficient) frontier of economic-capital portfolios under 10-day liquidation horizon by relaxing short-sales constraints (i.e., allowing both long and short-sales trading positions)
Source: *Figure (2) is designed by the author using an in-house developed software.*

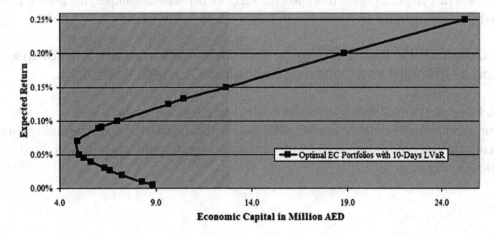

Figure 3. Depicts the empirical optimum (efficient) frontier of Economic-Capital Portfolios and Coherent Portfolios by relaxing short-sales constraint (i.e., allowing both long and short-sales trading positions). The four-benchmark coherent portfolios [1], [2], [3] and [4] are located off the efficient frontier, albeit to a different degree.
Source: *Figure (3) is designed by the author using an in-house developed software.*

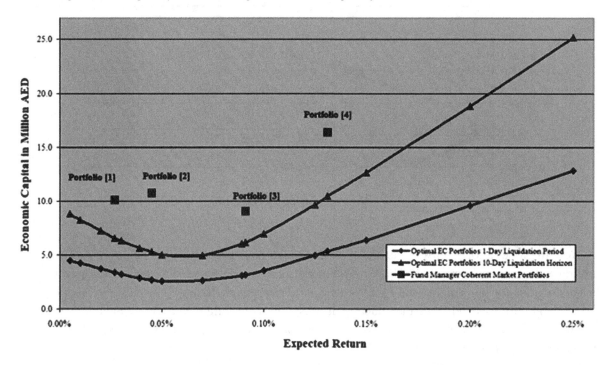

ally real-world investment considerations make it unlikely that a trading portfolio will behave exactly as theory predicts. Imperfections such as restriction on long and short trading positions, total trading volume and liquidation horizons make it unlikely to create an efficient equity-trading portfolio. Thus, the fund manager should apply active strategies in order to earn excess returns. These considerations are especially relevant for individual fund managers who may spread their trading positions across a few securities. Nevertheless, the elegance and compelling logic of the theory prompt attempts to apply the theory even though practitioners recognize the variance between the simplifying assumptions of the theory and the realities of the world.

Modus Operandi for the Risk-Engine and Optimization Algorithm for the Selection of Efficient and Coherent Economic-Capital's Portfolios

In this backdrop and to maximize its utility as a modeling algorithm for the selection and management of efficient and coherent economic capital portfolios, we have constructed the portfolio management tool such that the proposed risk-engine and robust scenario optimization-algorithms proceed according to the following steps[6]:

Step (1) of the Optimization Algorithm for the Selection of Efficient & Coherent Economic-Capital's Portfolios

In this first step of the modus operandi, we define a non-linear dynamic risk-function (i.e. objective function) of multivariable. For this purpose, the non-linear dynamic risk-function can be defined as a vector of the followings:

1. The amount of monetary investment in each asset-class;
2. Closeout periods (or unwinding periods) of each asset-class and the overall closeout periods of efficient and coherent portfolios;
3. Overall trading volume of efficient and coherent portfolios;
4. Constrained asset allocation proportions according to contemporary financial markets regulations and subject to the imposition of rational and meaningful operational and financial boundaries;
5. Downside risk constraints so that additional risk resulting from any non-normality and illiquid assets may be used to estimate the characteristics of efficient and coherent portfolios. This enables a much more generalized framework to be developed, with the distributional assumption most appropriate to the type of financial assets to be employed, and which can be of crucial value for more accurate market risk assessment during market stress periods and particularly when liquidity dries-up;
6. Correlation coefficients among all asset classes;
7. Expected returns of efficient and coherent portfolios;
8. Confidence level of estimated parameters under different scenarios and market settings;
9. Portfolio managers' choices of a combination of long/short-sales trading asset positions.

Step (2) of the Optimization Algorithm for the Selection of Efficient & Coherent Economic-Capital's Portfolios

In the second step of the modus operandi, we define the corresponding robust scenario optimization algorithm, which is based on quadratic programming techniques, subject to applying meaningful financial and operational meaningful constraints. Furthermore, in the development of portfolio investment policy there are many types of constraints that can be considered as an integral part of the optimization process. These constraints are drawn from rational financial investment considerations and can be used in various applications to bound percentiles of loss distributions; and it can include constraints on the asset classes that are allowable and concentration limits on investments. Moreover, in making the asset allocation decision, consideration must be given to any risk-based capital requirements. For this objective, the scenario optimization algorithms can be defined as a minimization algorithmic process of the dynamic objective risk-function and as follows:

1. The minimization process is attained here by minimizing the objective risk-function while requiring minimum expected returns subject to imposing several rational and meaningful financial and operational constraints;
2. As a minimum, the bounding limits may include the following:
   a. The expected return of the target efficient and coherent portfolios;
   b. The total volume of efficient and coherent portfolios;
   c. The amount of monetary asset-allocation of each asset-class;

    d.   Portfolio managers' choices of long-only positions or a combination of long/short-sales trading positions;

    e.   Closeout or unwinding liquidity horizons of each asset-class and/or the overall closeout periods of efficient and coherent portfolios.

Step (3) of the Optimization Algorithm for the Selection of Efficient and Coherent Economic-Capital's Portfolios

In this final phase of the modus operandi, we validate and compare the output results of efficient and coherent portfolios obtained in Step (2) with the requirements of efficient and coherent portfolios defined in Step (1). To this end, we rerun the optimization-engine until a new convergence to meaningful coherent portfolios is reached. At this stage, new coherent portfolios with meaningful asset allocations structures, that satisfy the boundary conditions defined in Step (2), are fulfilled accordingly.

CONCLUSION

This chapter extends previous approaches to optimization problems with L-VaR constraints. In particular, the suggested approach can be used for minimizing L-VaR under several budget constraints and ultimately for determining the amount of economic-capital necessary to sustain financial operation without subjecting the trading unit to violation of capital adequacy. Furthermore, multiple L-VaR constraints with various unwinding liquidation periods and correlation factors can be used to shape the profit/loss distribution. In some cases, the mean-variance optimizations are highly unstable, that is, small changes in the input assumptions can lead to large changes in the solutions.

As such, in this work, the optimization algorithm is formulated by finding a set of portfolios that minimize economic-capital subject to a given expected returns, trading volume and liquidity horizons. To this end, the economic-capital's risk function is constrained by a downside risk measure in addition to several operational constraints such as total volume, long and short trading positions, equity asset allocation weight factors, and liquidity unwinding periods.

Our modeling technique is a roust enhancement of the classic Markowitz mean-variance approach, where the original risk measure, variance, is replaced by L-VaR and economic-capital algorithms and by guaranteeing minimum expected return under different liquidation horizons. This modeling approach and optimization algorithms, which are based on Al Janabi model, can aid in solving some of the real-world trading dilemmas under adverse market conditions: when liquidity dries up; correlations factors switching signs; and the incorporation of non-normal distribution of assets' returns in risk measurement. This model has important uses and applications to portfolio management and can be useful to different markets participants, financial markets regulators and policymakers.

In addition, the implemented methodology and risk assessment algorithms can aid in advancing risk management practices in emerging markets, particularly in the wake of the sub-prime credit crunch and the subsequent 2007-2009 financial turmoil. In addition, the proposed quantitative risk management techniques and optimization algorithms can have important uses and applications in expert systems, machine learning, smart financial functions, and financial technology (FinTech) in big data environments. Likewise, it can aid in the development of regulatory technology (RegTech) for the global financial services industry, and can be of interest to professionals, regulators, and researchers working in the field of finance and FinTech; and for those who want to improve their understanding of the impact of innovative quantitative risk management techniques and optimization algorithms on regulatory challenges for financial services industry and its effects on global financial stability.

CONFLICT OF INTEREST

The author declares no conflict of interest in this chapter.

REFERENCES

Al Janabi, M. A.M. (2008, Summer). Integrating Liquidity Risk Factor into a Parametric Value at Risk Method. *Journal of Trading*, 76-87.

Al Janabi, M. A. M. (2010). Incorporating Asset Liquidity Effects in Risk-Capital Modeling. *Review of Middle East Economics and Finance*, 6(1), 3. doi:10.2202/1475-3693.1258

Al Janabi, M. A. M. (2013). Optimal and Coherent Economic-Capital Structures: Evidence from Long and Short-Sales Trading Positions under Illiquid Market Perspectives. *Annals of Operations Research*, 205(1), 109–139. doi:10.100710479-012-1096-3

Al Janabi, M. A. M. (2014). Optimal and investable portfolios: An empirical analysis with scenario optimization algorithms under crisis market prospects. *Economic Modelling*, 40, 369–381. doi:10.1016/j.econmod.2013.11.021

Al Janabi, M. A. M. (2019). Theoretical and Practical Foundations of Liquidity-Adjusted Value-at-Risk (LVaR): Optimization Algorithms for Portfolios Selection and Management. In N. Metawa, M. Elhoseny, A. E. Hassanien, & M. K. Hassan (Eds.), *Expert Systems: Smart Financial Applications in Big Data Environments*. London, UK: Taylor & Francis Group. doi:10.4324/9780429024061-1

Al Janabi, M. A. M., Arreola-Hernández, J. A., Berger, T., & Nguyen, D. K. (2017). Multivariate dependence and portfolio optimization algorithms under illiquid market scenarios. *European Journal of Operational Research*, 259(3), 1121–1131. doi:10.1016/j.ejor.2016.11.019

Alexander, G., & Baptista, A. M. (2008). Active portfolio management with benchmarking: Adding a value-at-risk constraint. *Journal of Economic Dynamics & Control*, 32(3), 779–820. doi:10.1016/j.jedc.2007.03.005

Amihud, Y., Mendelson, H., & Pedersen, L. H. (2005). Liquidity and Asset Prices. *Foundations and Trends in Finance*, 1(4), 269–364. doi:10.1561/0500000003

Angelidis, T., & Benos, A. (2006). Liquidity adjusted value-at-risk based on the components of the bid-ask spread. *Applied Financial Economics*, 16(11), 835–851. doi:10.1080/09603100500426440

Arreola-Hernández, J., Al Janabi, M. A. M., Hammoudeh, S., & Nguyen, D. K. (2015). Time lag dependence, cross-correlation and risk analysis of U.S. energy and non-energy stock portfolios. *Journal of Asset Management*, 16(7), 467–483. doi:10.1057/jam.2015.33

Arreola-Hernandez, J., Hammoudeh, S., Khuong, N. D., Al Janabi, M. A. M., & Reboredo, J. C. (2016). Global financial crisis and dependence risk analysis of sector portfolios: A vine copula approach. *Applied Economics*, *49*(25), 2409–2427. doi:10.1080/00036846.2016.1240346

Bangia, A., Diebold, F., Schuermann, T., & Stroughair, J. (1999). *Modeling Liquidity Risk with Implications for Traditional Market Risk Measurement and Management*. Working Paper, The Wharton School, University of Pennsylvania.

Campbell, R., Huisman, R., & Koedijk, K. (2001). Optimal portfolio selection in a Value-at-Risk framework. *Journal of Banking & Finance*, *25*(9), 1789–1804. doi:10.1016/S0378-4266(00)00160-6

Cochrane, J. H. (2005). *Asset Pricing*. Princeton, NJ: Princeton University Press.

Dowd, K., Blake, D., & Cairns, A. (2004, Winter). Long-Term Value at Risk. *The Journal of Risk Finance*, 52-57.

Fabozzi, F. J., Focardi, S., & Kolm, P. (2006, Spring). Incorporating Trading Strategies in the Black-Litterman Framework. *Journal of Trading*, 28-37.

Hisata, Y., & Yamai, Y. (2000). *Research toward the practical application of liquidity risk evaluation methods*. Discussion Paper, Institute for Monetary and Economic Studies, Bank of Japan.

Jarrow, R., & Subramanian, A. (1997). Mopping up Liquidity. *Risk (Concord, NH)*, *10*(12), 170–173.

Jobson, J. D., & Korkie, B. M. (1981). Putting Markowitz Theory to Work. *Journal of Portfolio Management*, *7*, 70–74.

Jorion, P. (1991). Bayesian and CAPM Estimators of the Means: Implications for Portfolio Selection. *Journal of Banking & Finance*, *15*(3), 717–727. doi:10.1016/0378-4266(91)90094-3

Jorion, P. (2007). *Value At Risk: The New benchmark for Managing financial Risk* (3rd ed.). McGraw-Hill.

Le Saout, E. (2002). *Incorporating liquidity risk in VaR models*. Working Paper, Paris 1 University.

Madhavan, A., Richardson, M., & Roomans, M. (1997). Why do security prices change? A transaction-level analysis of NYSE stocks. *Review of Financial Studies*, *10*(4), 1035–1064. doi:10.1093/rfs/10.4.1035

Madoroba, S. B. W., & Kruger, J. W. (2014). Liquidity effects on value-at-risk limits: Construction of a new VaR model. *Journal of Risk Model Validation*, *8*(4), 19–46. doi:10.21314/JRMV.2014.127

Markowitz, H. (1959). *Portfolio Selection: Efficient Diversification of Investments*. New York: John Wiley.

Meucci, A. (2009). Managing Diversification. *Risk (Concord, NH)*, *22*(5), 74–79.

Michaud, R. O. (1989). The Markowitz Optimization Enigma: Is 'Optimized' Optimal? *Financial Analysts Journal*, *45*(1), 31–42. doi:10.2469/faj.v45.n1.31

Morgan Guaranty Trust Company. (1994). *RiskMetrics-Technical Document*. New York: Morgan Guaranty Trust Company, Global Research.

Roch, A., & Soner, H. M. (2013). Resilient price impact of trading and the cost of illiquidity. *International Journal of Theoretical and Applied Finance*, *16*(6), 1–27. doi:10.1142/S0219024913500374

Roll, R. (1992). A mean/variance analysis of tracking error. *Journal of Portfolio Management, 18*(4), 13–22. doi:10.3905/jpm.1992.701922

Ruozi, R., & Ferrari, P. (2013). *Liquidity Risk Management in Banks: Economic and Regulatory Issues.* Springer Briefs in Finance. doi:10.1007/978-3-642-29581-2

Takahashi, D., & Alexander, S. (2002). Illiquid Alternative Asset Fund Modeling. *Journal of Portfolio Management, 28*(2), 90–100. doi:10.3905/jpm.2002.319836

Yiu, K. F. C. (2004). Optimal portfolios under a value-at-risk constraint. *Journal of Economic Dynamics & Control, 28*(7), 1317–1334. doi:10.1016/S0165-1889(03)00116-7

ENDNOTES

[1]   Economic-capital (or risk-capital) can be defined as the minimum amount of equity capital a financial entity needs to set aside to absorb worst losses over a certain time horizon with a certain confidence level. This is with the objectives of sustaining its trading operations activities and without subjecting itself to insolvency matters. Economic-capital can be assessed with an internal method and modeling techniques such as L-VaR. Economic-capital differs somehow from regulatory capital, which is necessary to comply with the requirements of Basel II & III committees on capital adequacy. However, building an internal market risk modeling techniques to assess economic-capital can significantly aid the financial entity in complying with Basel II and Basel III capital adequacy requirements (Al Janabi, 2013, and 2014).

[2]   In accordance with the latest Basel capital accords, financial institutions are permitted to develop their own internal risk models for the purposes of providing for adequate risk measures. Furthermore, internal risk models can be used in the determination of economic capital that banks must hold to endorse their trading of securities. The advantage of such an approach is that it takes into account the relationship between various asset types and can accurately assess the overall risk, including liquidity risk and firm-specific factors, for a whole combination of trading assets. As such, the notion of an internal risk model is the fact that the regulators allow financial institutions to develop their own risk models and use their own parameters instead of using models and parameters mandated by the regulatory bodies. The key benefits of internal risk models are convenience for the financial institutions, the ability of the financial entities to account for firm-specific factors, and lower regulatory costs.

[3]   In this chapter, the concept of coherent market portfolios refers to rational portfolios that are contingent on meaningful financial and operational constraints. In this sense, coherent market portfolios do not lie on the efficient frontiers as defined by Markowitz (1959), and instead have logical and well-structured long/short asset allocation proportions.

[4]   For other relevant literature on liquidity, asset pricing and portfolio choice and diversification one can refer as well to Ruozi and Ferrari (2013); Roch and Soner (2013); Angelidis and Benos (2006); Berkowitz (2000); Madhavan et al. (1997); Hisata and Yamai (2000); Le Saout (2002); Amihud et al. (2005); Takahashi and Alexander (2002); Arreola-Hernández, et al. (2017); Arreola-Hernández, et al. (2015); Cochrane (2005); and Meucci (2009), among others.

[5]   The L-VaR model applied here is based on that proposed by Al Janabi (2013) and Al Janabi et al. (2017). For further discussion on L-VaR literature and models, see Madoroba and Kruger (2014). In their paper, Madoroba and Kruger (2014) review and compare ten liquidity risk VaR models, including Al Janabi model. For further details on the mathematical derivation and rational usefulness of Al Janabi model, refer to Al Janabi (2008, 2013, and 2014) and Al Janabi et al. (2017) research papers.

[6]   For further details on this modus operandi, with full mathematical and optimization algorithms, we refer the readers to Al Janabi (2019) research paper.

Chapter 12
Data–Driven Stochastic Optimization for Transportation Road Network Design Under Uncertainty

Suh-Wen Chiou

https://orcid.org/0000-0003-4743-7544

National Dong Hwa University, Taiwan

ABSTRACT

A data-driven stochastic program for bi-level network design with hazardous material (hazmat) transportation is proposed in this chapter. In order to regulate the risk associated with hazmat transportation and minimize total travel cost on interested area under stochasticity, a multi-objective stochastic optimization model is presented to determine generalized travel cost for hazmat carriers. Since the bi-level program is generally non-convex, a data-driven bundle method is presented to stabilize solutions of the proposed model and reduce relative gaps between iterations. Numerical comparisons are made with existing risk-averse models. The results indicate that the proposed data-driven stochastic model becomes more resilient than others in minimizing total travel cost and mitigating risk exposure. Moreover, the trade-offs among maximum risk exposure, generalized travel costs, and maximum equitable risk spreading over links are empirically investigated in this chapter.

INTRODUCTION

For most urban road networks, transportation of hazardous material (hazmat) is of primary concern to decision makers due to serious safety, human health, and environmental risks associated with the release of hazmat. Because of the danger associated with the accidental release of hazmat, the people living and working around the roads heavily used for hazmat thus incur most of the risk during transportation. The reliability of a transportation road network with signal settings for hazmat traffic thus heavily depends on its vulnerability to a dangerous mix of probabilistic threats such as lane closure and road capacity loss. A

DOI: 10.4018/978-1-7998-0106-1.ch012

multi-objective program has long been regarded as one of the most popular approaches to tackle a hazmat network design problem where the interest of stakeholders is in conflict. For example, Zhao and Verter (2015) presented a bi-objective model for the location and routing problem to simultaneously minimize the total environment risk and the total cost. A weighted goal programming was employed to solve the location-routing problem with a case study in the Chongqing of southwest China. Zhang and Huang (2013) considered a multi-objective program for greenhouse gas emissions control from municipal solid waste management facilities. Two conflicting objectives are integrally considered, including minimization of total system cost and minimization of total greenhouse gas emissions from waste management facilities. The multi-objective program often assumes that the multiple objectives which are established by the same decision makers and located at the same level. As the objectives have to be optimized simultaneously, a tradeoff needs to be determined for compromising the multiple objectives. On the other hand, the bi-level decision-making follows a leader and follower relationship and attempts to sequentially optimize the objectives according to the levels of decision makers. Since multi-objective programs can hardly solve the problems with multiple decision makers at different levels, a bi-level decision making program has recently been noticed. He et al. (2011) gave a mixed-integer bi-level programming model for municipal solid waste management and greenhouse gases control with decision-makers at different levels. Empirical comparisons were made among various bi-level single objective decision-making models and multi-objective models. More recently, Gang et al. (2015) proposed a multi-objective bi-level location planning problem for stone industrial parks with a hierarchical structure under a random environment. The proposed model captured cost uncertainties and multiple decision makers with conflicting interests and solved by adaptive chaotic particle swarm optimization.

For a signal-controlled road network, one direct approach usually adopted by government to regulate the risks associated with hazmat shipment is the prohibition on the use of certain roads by hazmat traffic. A more amiable and flexible policy for regulators on effective road control can be achieved through appropriate signal design. Ukkusuri et al. (2010) introduced a dynamic system optimal model for isolated signal-controlled junctions. Despite a mean-variance based model is formulated to quantify network performance over the range of possible scenarios, the network effect of route choice from travelers is not taken into account. Cheng et al. (2006) presented a parallel algorithm for coordinated traffic control with certain traffic flow and compared performance of proposed approach with that of conventional hill-climbing method. Numerical results have shown significant travel delay savings can be achieved through better signal design. Zhang et al. (2013) recently presented a bi-objective model for coordinated traffic signals to minimize traffic delay and the risk associated with human exposure to traffic emissions. Numerical computations were performed for coordinated traffic signal design along an example arterial. However, no account of effect of route choice from travelers to signal settings was taken into account. In effect, the signal-controlled road network available for the carriers' operations is determined by the regulator. Most regulators do not have the authority to impose routes on hazmat carriers. Therefore, transportation risk of hazmat is an outcome of the carriers' route choice over the available signal-controlled network. While the authority is primarily concerned about mitigation of public risk, the carriers are more interested in minimizing transport costs. The routes in a signal-controlled road network with minimum travel delay would often be considered by carriers for hazmat transport. While hazmat transport risks can be reduced by limiting access on urban city roads to hazmat traffic, carriers will incur increased costs due to limited routing available. Planning to both cope with mitigation of public risk induced by hazmat shipments on population exposure and minimization of travel cost incurred by carriers becomes one of the most challenging issues facing decision makers. Considering the rationale response of carriers, Kara and Verter (2004) were the first ones to propose a deterministic bi-level network design model for hazmat transportation with single objective of risk minimization. A bi-level problem of minimizing population exposure risk is addressed by banning hazmat traffic from traveling on certain segments of road network. At the upper level, the local authority minimizes total transportation risk imposed on the population centers due to heavy hazmat traffic through the prohibition on the use of certain road segments. At the lower level, the carriers minimize their total travel distance through route choice over the available road network. In Kara and Verter (2004) an application of the proposed model is also presented. Numerical results have shown significant reduction in population exposure can be achieved through effective government interventions on the use of road segments by hazmat traffic while the carriers incurred more increased travel costs compared to the use of minimum cost routes. Erkut and Gzara (2008) improved the hazmat network design problem as a bi-objective bi-level problem. They generalized the risk-minimization problem to a bi-objective model by including the travel cost in the regulator's objective function at the upper level. They proposed a heuristic algorithm that exploits the network flow structure at both levels to effectively solve the deterministic bi-objective hazmat network design problem. As a result, a substantial improvement in computational performance has been achieved for suboptimal solutions for hazmat network design problem. Moreover, Verter and Kara (2008) presented a deterministic path-based formulation for a hazmat network design problem which aims to minimize hazmat transport risk without threatening the economic viability of transportation. A set of alternative routes for each hazmat shipment is constructed where only those routes that are acceptable to the carriers are included. A compromise solution between the regulator and the carriers is sought in terms of transport risks and travel cost during the policy decision-making process.

Despite traditional risk model taking the form of expected consequence of incidents is regarded as the most-widely used one in literature of modeling transport risk of hazmat (Verter and Kara, 2008; Alp, 1995; Jin and Batta, 1997), the development of risk-averse models for low probability but high risk hazmat routing has attracted the attention of researchers only fairly recently (Erkut and Ingolfsson, 2005; Bell, 2000; Gopalan et al., 1990). Erkut and Ingolfsson (2000) introduced three catastrophe-avoidance models for hazmat routing. The first model is the maximum risk model aiming to avoid catastrophes by minimizing the maximum risk along a route. The second model incorporates the variance of consequence along a route into route choice, and the third one minimizes the expected consequence using a convex utility function. It is shown that all three models can be solved as typical shortest path problems, and the first is recommended as an appropriate one in terms of computational tractability. By assuming that route usage probabilities and link accident probabilities are two person non-cooperative and zero-sum players in the mixed strategy Nash game, Bell (2000) proposed an alternative to reduce the maximum risk along a route. A mixed route strategy by sharing shipments among routes is considered to effectively reduce the maximum population exposure under uncertain probability of incidents. As a result, it generates the potential link usage probabilities and most vulnerable links with potentially high accident probabilities. For a global planning for hazmat shipments, one of the main problems is finding minimum risk routes whilst assuring an equitable distribution of the risk on the interested area (Current and Ratick, 1995; Marianov and ReVelle, 1998) following a well-defined work of Keeney (1980). For example, Zografos and Davis (1989) are the first authors to propose a multi-objective model to minimize total risk, and travel time where equity distribution of the risk is achieved by constraining the capacity of the road links. More recently, Kang et al. (2014) proposed a generalized hazmat route planning with VaR (value at risk) and equality considerations. Given entire probability distribution of incidents a priori, Kang et al. presented a least probability model under specified confidence level to mitigate the expected consequence for a multi-trip multi-hazmat transport. Numerical computations have shown more optimal routes between origin and destination of a pair can be conveniently obtained with varying level of confidence level although entire distribution of incident probability is known a priori. Moreover, Bianco et al. (2009) gave a bi-level flow model for hazmat transportation network design to consider both total risk minimization and risk equity for various levels of different government authorities. A linear bi-level programming model was proposed to minimize total risk at region level (the lower level) while local authorities (the upper level) want the risk to be the lowest and thus force the regional authorities to assure also risk equity. A single-level mixed integer linear program was presented to effectively solve the bi-level linear problem and numerical results were obtained using commercial optimization software.

In this chapter, a data-driven stochastic bi-level program (DDSBL) is proposed for hazmat transportation network design in order to effectively regulate the risk associated with hazmat transportation and minimize total transportation cost whilst assuring equitable risk distribution on interested area. At the lower level problem, the cost minimum routes in a risk neutral model for hazmat carriers are developed. The risk minimum routes in the risk-averse models are also investigated. A stochastic risk model is presented for hazardous materials with low probability but high consequence. The maximum risk exposure of population adjacent to selected routes of hazmat and that over entire road network can be minimized. At the upper level, travel delays in a transportation road network are explicitly considered and mathematically expressed. The generalized travel cost for carriers of hazmat traffic can be minimized over entire road network through better policies. In order to effectively reduce hazmat risk on every link, an equity constrained stochastic model is proposed to simultaneously tackle transport risk and generalized travel cost while equitable risk distribution over entire road network is achieved by constraining the maximum capacity of links. For a general bi-level problem, as mentioned in the literature (Luo et al., 1996; Dempe, 2003) only local solutions can be found due to the non-linearity of the constraints at the lower level problem. At the best of author's knowledge, there is very limited work in the literature to simultaneously tackle transport risk and generalized travel cost for hazmat traffic in urban road network using a data-driven approach. In this chapter, we intend to fill this gap. A bi-objective performance measure for hazmat transport can be evaluated using a well-known traffic model. The stochastic risk model is presented to determine the risk exposure for decision makers at the upper level. A risk equity constrained stochastic model is proposed to simultaneously tackle multi-criteria performance measure and maximum risk exposure of population over entire road network. The multi-objective performance index for the proposed DDSBL can be solved by a data-driven optimization model as detailed in this chapter. Due to the non-convexity of DDSBL, a data-driven bundle method is proposed to reduce relative gap of bound between iterations. A gradient-based method is also proposed to stabilize solutions and effectively solve DDSBL with reasonable computational efforts. Numerical computations are performed using a modest example road network at initial data sets.

The contributions made from this chapter can be briefly stated as follows. First, a data-driven stochastic program is presented. A multi-objective bi-level hazmat network design is proposed to simultaneously mitigate average risk exposure and reduce travel delay while guaranteeing equitable risk spreading. Equity distribution of the risk is achieved by constraining the capacity of the road links. A stochastic risk model is proposed to determine the maximum risk exposure for hazmat carriers at the lower level problem. Next, a risk equity constrained stochastic model is proposed to simultaneously tackle multi-criteria performance measure and maximum risk exposure of population over entire road network. Due to kinky structure of the DDSBL, a gradient-based method is proposed to stabilize solutions and effectively solve the problem with reasonable computational efforts. Finally, numerical computations are performed using an example road network to demonstrate the superiority of proposed bundle strategy. Empirical comparisons are also made with other risk-averse models to evaluate the effectiveness of the proposed stochastic model. The rest of the chapter is organized as follows. Section 2 introduces a multi-objective hazmat network design problem with signal settings. In Section 3, a risk equity constrained stochastic optimization is introduced. Alternative risk-averse models for hazmat network design are also presented in Section 4. Directional derivatives are given in Section 5. In Section 6, a data-driven bundle method aiming to effectively reduce relative gaps between iterations is presented and detailed in steps. In Section 7, numerical experiments are performed using a moderate example road network. In order to understand the effectiveness and robustness of the proposed model, comparisons are also empirically made with other risk models. Conclusions for this paper and extensions of the proposed model to topics of interest are briefly summarized in Section 8.

A MULTI-OBJECTIVE HAZMAT NETWORK DESIGN PROBLEM

A multi-objective hazmat network design problem with signal control is considered in this section. The risk analyses of hazmat transport to decision makers at lower level are conducted first. A stochastic risk model (SRM) is presented to determine the maximum risk exposure of population for hazmat carriers. A multi-objective maximum risk model integrating with explicit signal delay is proposed to determine total generalized travel cost for hazmat carriers. A least multi-objective SRM is given for which total generalized travel cost can be minimized over entire road network with signal control. A variational inequality is formulated for general hazmat traffic flow in which the marginal travel cost for hazmat carriers is employed. Notation used throughout this paper is stated first.

Notation

Let $G(N, L)$ denote a directed road network, where N represents a set of fixed time signal controlled junctions and L represents a set of links denoted by (i, j), $\forall (i, j) \in L$. Each traffic stream approaching any junction is represented by its own link.

W - a set of origin-destination (OD) pairs.

R_w - a set of routes between OD pair w, $\forall w \in W$.

$T = [T_w]$ - the matrix of travel demands for origin-destination pair w, $\forall w \in W$.

ζ - the reciprocal of the common cycle time

$\zeta_{\min}$, $\zeta_{\max}$ - the minimum and maximum reciprocal of the common cycle time.

$\theta = [\theta_{am}]$ - the vector of starts of green for various links as proportions of cycle time where θ_{am} is start of next green for signal group a at junction m.

$\varphi = [\varphi_{am}]$ - the vector of durations of green for various links as proportions of cycle time where φ_{am} is the duration of green for signal group a at junction m.

τ_{abm} - the clearance time between the end of green for signal group a and the start of green for incompatible signal group b at junction m.

$\Psi = \left(\zeta, \theta, \varphi\right)$ - the set of signal setting variables, respectively for the reciprocal of common cycle time, start and duration of greens.

$\lambda_{(i,j)}$ - duration of effective green for link (i,j).

$\lambda_{\min}$ - the minimum green.

$\Omega_m(a,b)$ - collection of numbers 0 and 1 for each pair of incompatible signal groups at junction m; where $\Omega_m(a,b) = 0$ if the start of green for signal group a precedes that of b and $\Omega_m(a,b) = 1$, otherwise.

$D_{(i,j)}$ - the rate of delay on link (i,j).

$S_{(i,j)}$ - the number of stops per unit time on link (i,j).

W_D - weighting factor for rate of delay.

W_S - weighting factor for number of stops.

M_D - monetary factor associated with $D_{(i,j)}$.

M_S - monetary factor associated with $S_{(i,j)}$.

$\rho_{(i,j)}$ - maximum degree of saturation for link (i,j).

$s_{(i,j)}$ - saturation flow on link (i,j).

γ - the maximum risk equity on links.

$q_{(i,j)}$ - incidental probability of accidental release of hazmat on link (i,j).

$e_{(i,j)}$ - incidental consequence of accidental release of hazmat on link (i,j).

$f_{(i,j)}$ - hazmat traffic flow on link (i,j).

h_k - hazmat traffic flow on route k between OD trips, $\forall k \in R_w, w \in W$.

Λ - a link-route incidence matrix with entry $\Lambda^k_{(i,j)} = 1$ if route k uses link (i,j), and $\Lambda^k_{(i,j)} = 0$ otherwise, $\forall (i,j) \in L$, $\forall k \in R_w, w \in W$.

Γ - an OD-route incidence matrix with entry $\Gamma^w_k = 1$ if path k connects OD trip w, $\forall w \in W$, and $\Gamma^w_k = 0$ otherwise, $\forall k \in R_w, w \in W$.

$c_{(i,j)}$ - travel time on link (i,j).

$c^0_{(i,j)}$ - un-delayed travel time on link (i,j).

$d_{(i,j)}$ - average delay on link (i,j).

C_k - travel time on route k, i.e. $C_k = \sum\limits_{(i,j) \in L} \Lambda^k_{(i,j)} c_{(i,j)}$, $\forall k \in R_w, w \in W$.

σ - converting factor from risk to monetary factor.

σ_c - converting factor from expected risk to travel cost.

The Cost Minimum Route Optimization (CM)

For a signal-controlled road network, the travel time on link (i, j) can be calculated as a sum of un-delayed travel time $c^0_{(i,j)}$ on the link and the average delay $d_{(i,j)}$ incurred by hazmat traffic at the down-stream junction, i.e.

$$c_{(i,j)}(f, \Psi) = c^0_{(i,j)} + d_{(i,j)}(f, \Psi) \tag{1}$$

The cost minimum routes (CM) for hazmat carriers among pairs of OD $w, \forall w \in W$ can be found through a system optimum as follows.

$$\underset{f}{Min} \sum_{(i,j) \in L} f_{(i,j)} c_{(i,j)}(f, \Psi) \tag{2}$$

subject to

$$\sum_{k \in R_w} h_k = T_w, \forall w \in W$$

$$f_{(i,j)} = \sum_{w \in W} \sum_{k \in R_w} \Lambda^k_{(i,j)} h_k, \forall (i,j) \in L$$

$$h_k \geq 0, \forall k \in R_w, w \in W$$

Let

$$\Omega = \{f : f = \Lambda h, \Gamma h = T, h \geq 0\}$$

For any hazmat traffic flow f^* solving cost minimization (2), let $\Sigma_{CM}(\Psi)$ denote a solution set for hazmat traffic flow f^*, i.e. $f^* \in \Sigma_{CM}(\Psi)$.

A Bi-Objective Risk Model

According to Erkut and Verter (1998), the expected consequence due to hazmat transport on link (i, j), can be generalized as a following form: let $r_{(i,j)}$ denotes a public risk with probability $q_{(i,j)}$ of accidental release for hazmat to population exposure on link (i, j) we have

$$r_{(i,j)} = e_{(i,j)} q_{(i,j)} \tag{3}$$

The bi-objective cost $c_{(i,j)}^G$ on a link (i,j) can be expressed as the following weighted sum model.

$$c_{(i,j)}^G(f,\Psi) = c_{(i,j)}(f,\Psi) + \sigma_c r_{(i,j)} \tag{4}$$

The corresponding route cost in relation to (3) and (4) can be expressed as follows. Let r_k denote the route cost for hazmat carriers on route k, $\forall k \in R_w, \forall w \in W$, we have

$$r_k = \sum_{(i,j)\in L} r_{(i,j)} \Lambda_{(i,j)}^k \tag{5}$$

Similarly, Let $C_k^G(f,\Psi)$ denote the bi-objective route cost for hazmat carriers on route $k, \forall k \in R_w, \forall w \in W$, we have

$$C_k^G(f,\Psi) = \sum_{(i,j)\in L} c_{(i,j)}^G(f,\Psi) \Lambda_{(i,j)}^k \tag{6}$$

The bi-objective total travel cost for hazmat carriers in a signal-controlled road network can be expressed a following weighted sum model,

$$TC^G(f,\Psi,q) = \sum_{(i,j)\in L} f_{(i,j)} c_{(i,j)}^G(f,\Psi)$$

$$= \sum_{(i,j)\in L} f_{(i,j)} c_{(i,j)}(f,\Psi) + \sigma_c \sum_{(i,j)\in L} f_{(i,j)} e_{(i,j)} q_{(i,j)} \tag{7}$$

or in a vector form

$$TC^G(f,\Psi,q) = fc(f,\Psi) + \sigma_c feq \tag{8}$$

A Maximum Risk Model (MM)

Since the distribution of occurrence of probability q in (8) is not always available, the expected consequence of incident on a signal-controlled network can be approximated by a maximum risk model. According to Erkut and Ingolfsson (2000), a maximum risk link along a chosen route k can be identified as a following form: for every route k, $\forall k \in R_w, \forall w \in W$

$$r_k^M = \underset{(i,j)\in k}{Max}\left\{r_{(i,j)}\right\} \tag{9}$$

Thus a least maximum risk model (MM) along a path k' can be expressed as follows.

$$\underset{k \in R_w, w \in W}{Min} \; r_k^M = \underset{k \in R_w, w \in W}{Min} \; \underset{(i,j) \in k}{Max} \left\{ r_{(i,j)} \right\} \tag{10}$$

Find a route k' with a least risk such that for every route k, $\forall k \in R_w, \forall w \in W$, we have

$$k' = \arg \underset{k}{Min} \, r_k^M \tag{11}$$

A Maximum Risk Model with Mixed Routes (MM2)

Erkut and Ingolfsson (2000) considered mixed routes and proposed an alternative to reduce the maximum risk along a route. A mixed route strategy by sharing shipments among routes is introduced to effectively reduce the maximum population exposure under uncertain probability of incidents. By assuming that route usage probabilities and link accident probabilities are two person non-cooperative and zero-sum players in the mixed strategy Nash game, Bell (2000) on the other hand presented a simple linear min-max model to measure a maximum risk for a single OD trip among various routes. As a result, it generates the potential link usage probabilities and most vulnerable links with potentially high accident probabilities. Considering a mixed route strategy between a specified OD trip w, $\forall w \in W$, Bell (2000) generalized a min-max model (10) as a following form using game theoretic approach. Let p_k denote path use probability for a trip w such that

$$1 = \sum_{k \in R_w} p_k \tag{12}$$

Let $p_{(i,j)}$ denote a link use probability such that for every link by definition, we have

$$p_{(i,j)} = \sum_{k \in R_w} \Lambda_{(i,j)}^k p_k \tag{13}$$

The expected consequence in (3) with link use probability $p_{(i,j)}$ can be re-expressed in a following form:

$$r_{(i,j)} = p_{(i,j)} e_{(i,j)} q_{(i,j)} \tag{14}$$

subject to (12) and (13).

A maximum risk model $r^M(p)$ with a mixed-route selection probability p_k, $\forall k \in R_w$ between a specified OD trip w can be described as a following form: for any link use probability $p_{(i,j)}$, $\forall(i,j) \in L$ satisfying (12) and (13), we have

$$r^M(p) = \underset{q_{(i,j)}}{Max} \sum_{(i,j) \in L} r_{(i,j)} = \underset{q_{(i,j)}}{Max} \sum_{(i,j) \in L} p_{(i,j)} e_{(i,j)} q_{(i,j)} \qquad (15)$$

subject to

$$1 = \sum_{(i,j) \in L} q_{(i,j)}$$

Therefore, a least probabilistic maximum risk model (MM2) over entire road network can be re-expressed as follows.

$$\underset{p_{(i,j)}}{Min} r^M(p) = \underset{p_{(i,j)}}{Min} \underset{q_{(i,j)}}{Max} \sum_{(i,j) \in L} p_{(i,j)} e_{(i,j)} q_{(i,j)} \qquad (16)$$

subject to

$$\sum_{(i,j) \in L} q_{(i,j)} = 1$$

and

$$\sum_{k \in R_w} p_k = 1$$

together with

$$p_{(i,j)} = \sum_{k \in R_w} \Lambda^k_{(i,j)} p_k$$

A Stochastic Risk Model (SRM)

For a signal-controlled road network, a multi-objective maxi-sum risk model is presented by combining signal delay at downstream junction and a following stochastic maxi-sum risk model. Assuming that the occurrence of accidental release for hazmat is barely to be known a priori, a stochastic risk model is introduced according to (15).

$$\underset{q}{Max} \sum_{(i,j) \in L} f_{(i,j)} e_{(i,j)} q_{(i,j)} \tag{17}$$

subject to

$$1 = \sum_{(i,j) \in L} q_{(i,j)}$$

According to (7), a multi-objective maximum risk model $TC^M(f, \Psi)$ taking account of signal delay $c(f, \Psi)$ can be described as a following weighted sum model.

$$TC^M(f, \Psi) = \underset{q}{Max} TC^G(f, \Psi, q)$$

$$= \sum_{(i,j) \in L} f_{(i,j)} c_{(i,j)}(f, \Psi) + \sigma_c \underset{q_{(i,j)}}{Max} \sum_{(i,j) \in L} f_{(i,j)} e_{(i,j)} q_{(i,j)} \tag{18}$$

subject to

$$\sum_{(i,j) \in L} q_{(i,j)} = 1.$$

Or in a vector form:

$$TC^M(f, \Psi) = \underset{q}{Max} TC^G(f, \Psi, q) = fc(f, \Psi) + \sigma_c \underset{q}{Max} feq$$

The occurrence of probability $q_{(i,j)}$ in (18) maximizing total risk for hazmat traffic over entire road network under signal setting can be determined in the following manner

$$q^M = \arg\underset{q}{Max} \sum_{(i,j) \in L} f_{(i,j)} c_{(i,j)}(f, \Psi) + \sigma_c \sum_{(i,j) \in L} f_{(i,j)} e_{(i,j)} q_{(i,j)} \tag{19}$$

subject to

$$\sum_{(i,j) \in L} q_{(i,j)} = 1$$

Now we have a multi-objective Stochastic Risk Model (SRM):

$$TC^M(f, \Psi) = \sum_{(i,j) \in L} f_{(i,j)} c_{(i,j)}(f, \Psi) + \sigma_c \sum_{(i,j) \in L} f_{(i,j)} e_{(i,j)} q^M_{(i,j)} \tag{20}$$

Or in a vector form,

$$TC^M(f, \Psi) = fc(f, \Psi) + \sigma_c f \ eq^M \tag{21}$$

Therefore, a least multi-objective SRM can be determined as follows.

$$\underset{f}{Min} \underset{q}{Max} \sum_{(i,j) \in L} f_{(i,j)} c_{(i,j)}(f, \Psi) + \sigma_c \sum_{(i,j) \in L} f_{(i,j)} e_{(i,j)} q_{(i,j)} \tag{22}$$

subject to

$$\sum_{k \in R_w} h_k = T_w, \forall w \in W$$

$$f_{(i,j)} = \sum_{w \in W} \sum_{k \in R_w} \Lambda^k_{(i,j)} h_k, \forall (i,j) \in L$$

$$h_k \geq 0, \forall k \in R_w, w \in W$$

$$\sum_{(i,j) \in L} q_{(i,j)} = 1$$

According to (19) and (20), it implies

$$\underset{f}{Min} \sum_{(i,j) \in L} f_{(i,j)} c_{(i,j)}(f, \Psi) + \sigma_c \sum_{(i,j) \in L} f_{(i,j)} e_{(i,j)} q^M_{(i,j)} \tag{23}$$

subject to

$$\sum_{k \in R_w} h_k = T_w, \forall w \in W$$

$$f_{(i,j)} = \sum_{w \in W} \sum_{k \in R_w} \Lambda^k_{(i,j)} h_k, \forall (i,j) \in L$$

$$h_k \geq 0, \forall k \in R_w, w \in W$$

The resulting hazmat traffic flow f thus can be determined by a worst-case incident probability q^M such that total risk is minimized. That is

$$f(\Psi) = \arg\underset{f' \in \Omega}{Min}\, TC^M(f', \Psi) \tag{24}$$

and let $\Sigma_{SRM}(\Psi)$ denote a solution set for hazmat flow satisfying (23).

A Variational Inequality

For a minimization problem (23), it can be generalized as a variational inequality if and only if the gradient of objective function with respect to hazmat traffic is available. It turns out that a marginal cost for risk model in (21) can be expressed as follows.

$$\tilde{c}(f, \Psi) = \nabla_f TC^M(f, \Psi) = c(f, \Psi) + f\nabla c(f, \Psi) + \sigma_c e q^M \tag{25}$$

The optimization problem (25) can be equivalently expressed as a following variational inequality: for every hazmat traffic flow $f' \in \Omega$, it is to find a hazmat traffic flow f, $f \in \Omega$ with a most obnoxious incident probability q^M such that

$$\tilde{c}(f, \Psi)(f' - f) \geq 0 \tag{26}$$

According to (25), for every hazmat traffic flow $f' \in \Sigma_{SRM}(\Psi)$, it implies

$$\tilde{c}(f', \Psi) = c(f', \Psi) + f'\nabla c(f', \Psi) + \sigma_c e q^M \tag{27}$$

A MULTI-OBJECTIVE STOCHASTIC OPTIMIZATION PROBLEM

A multi-objective performance measure of a transportation road network with signal settings can be evaluated using a well-known traffic model TRANSYT (Vincent et al., 1980). The performance measure in TRANSYT is represented as a sum for signal-controlled traffic streams of a weighted linear combination of estimated rate of delay and number of stops per unit time. For traffic streams with certain traffic conditions, calculations of indicator of traffic condition can be referred to recent results (Chiou, 2003). In order to find solutions for a data-driven stochastic bi-level program (DDSBL), a SRM in (17) can be employed at the upper level of DDSBL. The bi-objective performance measure for DDSBL can be therefore expressed as a weighted sum of maximum risk and a linear combination of the rate of delay and the number of stops for each link.

A Delay-Minimizing Signal Setting Problem

Let P be a performance index for a transportation road network with signal settings $\Psi = \left(\zeta, \theta, \varphi \right)$ and traffic flow f. It can be generally expressed via function P_0 in terms of signal timings and network flow in the following way.

$$\underset{\Psi, f}{Min} P = P_0(\Psi, f) \tag{28}$$

subject to $\Psi \in \Pi$

The set Π defines the constraints of signal settings as follows. For a signal-controlled network, the cycle time constraint is expressed as

$$\zeta_{\min} \leq \zeta \leq \zeta_{\max} \tag{29}$$

For each signal controlled junction m, the phase a green time for all signal groups at junction can be expressed as

$$\lambda_{\min} \zeta \leq \varphi_{am} \leq 1 \tag{30}$$

For a risk equity constrained road network, the maximum risk of links can be achieved by constraining the maximum capacity of all links leading to junction, i.e. for any link $(i, j) \in L$, find a maximum γ such that

$$f_{(i,j)} \leq \gamma \rho_{(i,j)} s_{(i,j)} \lambda_{(i,j)} \tag{31}$$

Let $\mu = \dfrac{1}{\gamma}, \gamma \neq 0$ denote a flow factor associated with hazmat traffic on link (i, j). Thus (31) can be re-expressed as

$$\mu f_{(i,j)} \leq \rho_{(i,j)} s_{(i,j)} \lambda_{(i,j)} \tag{32}$$

Taking account of behavior response, (32) becomes

$$f_{(i,j)}(\mu) \leq \rho_{(i,j)} s_{(i,j)} \lambda_{(i,j)} \tag{33}$$

In (33), it implies to find a minimum factor μ associated with hazmat traffic flow such that maximum equitable risk distribution γ in capacity constraint (31) can be achieved at current signal control. The clearance time τ_{abm} for incompatible signal groups a and b at junction m can be expressed as

$$\theta_{am} + \varphi_{am} + \tau_{abm}\zeta \le \theta_{am} + \Omega_m(a,b) \tag{34}$$

The performance index is taken to be a sum of a linear combination of the rate of delay and the number of stops per unit time for each link. It is also evaluated from TRANSYT and can be expressed as follows.

$$P = \sum_{(i,j)\in L} D_{(i,j)}(\Psi,f)W_D M_D + S_{(i,j)}(\Psi,f)W_S M_S \tag{35}$$

A min-max delay-minimizing signal setting optimization problem can be expressed as follows.

$$\underset{\mu}{Max}\underset{\Psi,f}{Min}\, P = \sum_{(i,j)\in L} D_{(i,j)}(\Psi,f)W_D M_D + S_{(i,j)}(\Psi,f)W_S M_S \tag{36}$$

subject to

$$\zeta_{min} \le \zeta \le \zeta_{max}$$

$$\lambda_{min}\zeta \le \varphi_{am} \le 1,\ \forall m \in N$$

$$f_{(i,j)}(\mu) \le \rho_{(i,j)}s_{(i,j)}\lambda_{(i,j)},\ \forall (i,j) \in L$$

$$\theta_{am} + \varphi_{am} + \tau_{abm}\zeta \le \theta_{am} + \Omega_m(a,b),\ \forall m \in N$$

A Risk Equity Constrained Stochastic Model

For hazmat traffic in a signal-controlled road network, a risk equity constrained stochastic model can be expressed as a following form. Let $|L|$ denote a cardinality of links. It implies

$$\underset{\mu}{Max}P = \frac{1}{|L|}\sum_{(i,j)\in L} f_{(i,j)}e_{(i,j)} \tag{37}$$

subject to

$$\zeta_{min} \le \zeta \le \zeta_{max}$$

$$\lambda_{min}\zeta \le \varphi_{am} \le 1,\ \forall m \in N$$

$$f_{(i,j)}(\mu) \leq \rho_{(i,j)} s_{(i,j)} \lambda_{(i,j)}, \ \forall (i,j) \in L$$

$$\theta_{am} + \varphi_{am} + \tau_{abm} \zeta \leq \theta_{am} + \Omega_m(a,b), \ \forall m \in N$$

A Data-Driven Stochastic Bi-Level Program

Considering two single objective problems (36) and (37) with constraints in (29)- (34), a data-driven multi-objective signal control with risk equity constraint can be expressed in the following weighted sum stochastic model.

$$P_0(\Psi, f(\Psi,\mu)) = \sum_{(i,j) \in L} D_{(i,j)}(\Psi, f) W_D M_D + S_{(i,j)}(\Psi, f) W_S M_S + \sigma \frac{1}{|L|} \sum_{(i,j) \in L} f_{(i,j)} e_{(i,j)} \tag{38}$$

For hazmat traffic flow in (24), i.e. $f \in \Sigma_{SRM}(\Psi)$, the performance index in (28) can be represented as P_{SRM}. A weighted sum in (40) of maximum risk, P_{SRM}^e and a linear combination of the rate of delay and the number of stops per unit time, P_{SRM}^c for each link can be expressed as follows.

$$P_{SRM} = P_{SRM}^c + \sigma P_{SRM}^e \tag{39}$$

A data-driven stochastic bi-level program (DDSBL) aiming to minimize total travel delays and mitigate stochastic risk whilst assuring equitable risk spreading over entire road network can be expressed as a follows.

$$\underset{\Psi,f}{Min} \underset{\mu}{Max} P_0(\Psi, f(\Psi,\mu)) = \sum_{(i,j) \in L} D_{(i,j)}(\Psi, f) W_D M_D + S_{(i,j)}(\Psi, f) W_S M_S + \sigma \frac{1}{|L|} \sum_{(i,j) \in L} f_{(i,j)} e_{(i,j)} \tag{40}$$

subject to

$$\zeta_{\min} \leq \zeta \leq \zeta_{\max}$$

$$\lambda_{\min} \zeta \leq \varphi_{am} \leq 1, \ \forall m \in N$$

$$f_{(i,j)}(\mu) \leq \rho_{(i,j)} s_{(i,j)} \lambda_{(i,j)}, \ \forall (i,j) \in L$$

$$\theta_{am} + \varphi_{am} + \tau_{abm} \zeta \leq \theta_{am} + \Omega_m(a,b), \ \forall m \in N$$

and

$$f \in \Sigma_{SRM}(\Psi)$$

Or in form of (39)

$$\underset{\Psi, f}{Min} \underset{\mu}{Max} P_{SRM} = P_{SRM}^c + \sigma P_{SRM}^e \tag{41}$$

subject to

$$\zeta_{\min} \leq \zeta \leq \zeta_{\max}$$

$$\lambda_{\min} \zeta \leq \varphi_{am} \leq 1, \ \forall m \in N$$

$$f_{(i,j)}(\mu) \leq \rho_{(i,j)} s_{(i,j)} \lambda_{(i,j)}, \ \forall (i,j) \in L$$

$$\theta_{am} + \varphi_{am} + \tau_{abm} \zeta \leq \theta_{am} + \Omega_m(a,b), \ \forall m \in N$$

and

$$f \in \Sigma_{SRM}(\Psi)$$

A Data-Driven Bi-Level Constrained Minimization

For a maximum factor μ^*, the bi-level min-max model (41) can be re-expressed as a following bi-level constrained optimization problem:

$$\underset{\Psi, f}{Min} P_{SRM} = P_{SRM}^c + \sigma P_{SRM}^e \tag{42}$$

subject to

$$\zeta_{\min} \leq \zeta \leq \zeta_{\max}$$

$$\lambda_{\min} \zeta \leq \varphi_{am} \leq 1, \ \forall m \in N$$

$$f_{(i,j)}(\mu^*) \leq \rho_{(i,j)} s_{(i,j)} \lambda_{(i,j)}, \ \forall (i,j) \in L$$

$$\theta_{am} + \varphi_{am} + \tau_{abm}\zeta \leq \theta_{am} + \Omega_m(a,b), \ \forall m \in N$$

and

$$f \in \Sigma_{SRM}(\Psi)$$

ALTERNATIVE RISK-AVERSE MODELS

Considering the lower level problem in Section 2, in this section, various alternative risk stochastic models are considered: the cost minimum route model (CM) in (2), the least risk maximum model (MM) in (10) and mixed-route least risk maximum model in (16). First, a CM-based risk equity constrained optimization model can be expressed below where a risk-neutral flow is determined by a cost minimum model (CM) (2).

$$\underset{\Psi,f}{Min} P_{CM} = \sum_{(i,j) \in L} D_{(i,j)}(\Psi,f)W_D M_D + S_{(i,j)}(\Psi,f)W_S M_S + \sigma \frac{1}{|L|} \sum_{(i,j) \in L} f_{(i,j)} e_{(i,j)} \tag{43}$$

Or like in the form of (42), it can be expressed below.

$$\underset{\Psi,f}{Min} P_{CM} = P_{CM}^c + \sigma P_{CM}^e \tag{44}$$

subject to

$$\zeta_{\min} \leq \zeta \leq \zeta_{\max}$$

$$\lambda_{\min}\zeta \leq \varphi_{am} \leq 1, \ \forall m \in N$$

$$f_{(i,j)}(\mu^*) \leq \rho_{(i,j)} s_{(i,j)} \lambda_{(i,j)}, \ \forall (i,j) \in L$$

$$\theta_{am} + \varphi_{am} + \tau_{abm}\zeta \leq \theta_{am} + \Omega_m(a,b), \ \forall m \in N$$

and

$$f \in \Sigma_{CM}(\Psi)$$

Second, a MM-based risk equity constrained model can be expressed below where a risk-averse flow is defined by a risk maximum model (MM) in (9). According to (9) and (10), a least maximum risk route k' can be determined such that for every route $k, k \in R_w$ between OD pair $w, w \in W$, we have

$$k' = \arg \underset{k}{Min} \underset{(i,j) \in L}{Max} \left\{ r_{(i,j)} \right\} \tag{45}$$

Let $h_{k'} = T_w$, thus for every link $(i, j), (i, j) \in L$, we have

$$f_{(i,j)} = \Lambda^{k'}_{(i,j)} h_{k'} \tag{46}$$

Let $\Sigma_{MM}(\Psi)$ denote a solution set for hazmat flow satisfying (45) and (46). Then a MM-based risk equity constrained optimization model can be expressed below.

$$\underset{\Psi, f}{Min} \, P_{MM} = \sum_{(i,j) \in L} D_{(i,j)}(\Psi, f) W_D M_D + S_{(i,j)}(\Psi, f) W_S M_S + \sigma \frac{1}{|L|} \sum_{(i,j) \in L} f_{(i,j)} e_{(i,j)} \tag{47}$$

Or like in the form of (44), it can be expressed below.

$$\underset{\Psi, f}{Min} P_{MM} = P^c_{MM} + \sigma P^e_{MM} \tag{48}$$

subject to

$$\zeta_{\min} \leq \zeta \leq \zeta_{\max}$$

$$\lambda_{\min} \zeta \leq \varphi_{am} \leq 1, \, \forall m \in N$$

$$f_{(i,j)}(\mu^*) \leq \rho_{(i,j)} s_{(i,j)} \lambda_{(i,j)}, \, \forall (i,j) \in L$$

$$\theta_{am} + \varphi_{am} + \tau_{abm} \zeta \leq \theta_{am} + \Omega_m(a,b), \, \forall m \in N$$

and

$$f \in \Sigma_{MM}(\Psi)$$

Furthermore, for a least maximum risk model with mixed routes (MM2) given in Bell (2000) and specified in (16), the least maximum risk hazmat flow can be determined as follows.

$$\underset{f_{(i,j)}}{Min} \underset{q_{(i,j)}}{Max} \sum_{(i,j)\in L} f_{(i,j)} e_{(i,j)} q_{(i,j)} \tag{49}$$

subject to

$$1 = \sum_{(i,j)\in L} q_{(i,j)}$$

$$\sum_{k\in R_w} h_k = T_w, \ \forall w \in W$$

and

$$f_{(i,j)} = \sum_{w\in W} \sum_{k\in R_w} \Lambda^k_{(i,j)} h_k$$

Let $\Sigma_{MM2}(\Psi)$ denote a solution set for hazmat flow satisfying (49). Then a MM2-based risk equity constrained model can be expressed below where a risk-averse flow is determined by a least mixed-route risk maximum model (MM2) in (49).

$$\underset{\Psi,f}{Min} \ P_{MM2} = \sum_{(i,j)\in L} D_{(i,j)}(\Psi,f)W_D M_D + S_{(i,j)}(\Psi,f)W_S M_S + \sigma \frac{1}{|L|} \sum_{(i,j)\in L} f_{(i,j)} e_{(i,j)} \tag{50}$$

Or like in the form of (48), it can be expressed below.

$$\underset{\Psi,f}{Min} P_{MM2} = P^c_{MM2} + \sigma P^e_{MM2} \tag{51}$$

subject to

$$\zeta_{\min} \leq \zeta \leq \zeta_{\max}$$

$$\lambda_{\min} \zeta \leq \varphi_{am} \leq 1, \ \forall m \in N$$

$$f_{(i,j)}(\mu^*) \leq \rho_{(i,j)} s_{(i,j)} \lambda_{(i,j)}, \ \forall (i,j) \in L$$

$$\theta_{am} + \varphi_{am} + \tau_{abm}\zeta \leq \theta_{am} + \Omega_m(a,b), \ \forall m \in N$$

and

$$f \in \Sigma_{MM2}(\Psi)$$

DIRECTIONAL DERIVATIVES FOR HAZMAT TRAFFIC FLOW

As notably mentioned in the literature (Luo et al., 1996; Dempe, 2003) that the responding flow in (26) may not always be differentiable, it would be preventive from direct use of sensitivity analysis results. However, the direction of change in signal settings $\Delta\Psi$ that occurs in responding flow f^* in (26) can be evaluated by first-order directional derivatives when applied to traffic equilibria. Regarding semi-differentiability of solution set $\Sigma_{SRM}(\Psi)$ for responding flow f^*, it can be adapted from (Dontchev and Rockafellar, 2002) and stated below without proof for brevity.

Theorem 1. (Semi-differentiability of solution set for responding flow) Suppose the solution set $\Sigma_{SRM}(\Psi)$ for (26) is convex. Then the following properties are equivalent:

1. $\Sigma_{SRM}(\Psi)$ is single-valued and Lipschitz continuous.
2. Directional derivatives $D\Sigma_{SRM}(\Psi)$ is single-valued on $\Delta\Psi = 0$. Then the solution set $\Sigma_{SRM}(\Psi)$ for responding flow in (26) is semi-differentiable and $D\Sigma_{SRM}(\Psi)$ is piecewise linear. The perturbation Δf of responding flow with respect to change in signal setting variables $\Delta\Psi$ can be therefore determined by a following linearized variational inequality. Introduce

$$\Omega(\Delta\Psi) = \{\Delta f : \Delta f = \Lambda(\Delta h), \Gamma(\Delta h) = 0, \exists \Delta h \in K_0\} \tag{52}$$

and

$$K_0 = \left\{ \Delta h : \begin{array}{ll} (i)\Delta h_k \ free, & if \ h_k^* > 0, \\ (ii)\Delta h_k \geq 0, & if \ h_k^* = 0, \tilde{C}_k = \pi_w, \forall k \in R_w, \forall w \in W \\ (iii)\Delta h_k = 0, & if \ h_k^* = 0, \tilde{C}_k > \pi_w \end{array} \right\} \tag{53}$$

In (53), $\tilde{C}_k$ denotes a marginal cost on route k and π_w denotes a minimum cost for OD trip w. For every flow perturbation in set (52), i.e. $f' \in \Omega(\Delta\Psi)$, a directional derivative Δf along a direction $\Delta\Psi$ can be determined such that

$$(\nabla_\Psi \tilde{c}(f, \Psi^*)\Delta\Psi + \nabla_f \tilde{c}(f, \Psi^*)\Delta f)(f' - \Delta f) \geq 0 \tag{54}$$

The gradients $\nabla_\Psi \tilde{c}(f, \Psi^*)$ and $\nabla_f \tilde{c}(f, \Psi^*)$ in (54) are evaluated at Ψ^* when perturbations in $\Delta\Psi$ are specified. According to Rademacher's theorem in Clarke et al. (1998), the Lipschitz solution set $\Sigma_{SRM}(\Psi)$ is differentiable almost everywhere, i.e. the responding flow avoiding points of both zero measure and at which the solution set is not differentiable. The generalized gradients for responding flow with respect to perturbation $\Delta\Psi$ can be characterized below.

Theorem 2 (Generalized gradient for responding flow) Let Σ be any set of zero measure, and let Σ_f be the set of points at which responding flow f fails to be differentiable. For every $\Psi^{(i)} \notin \Sigma$ and $\Psi^{(i)} \notin \Sigma_f$, let co denote a convex hull, it implies

$$\partial_\Psi \Sigma_{SRM}(\Psi^*) = co\left\{\lim_{i\to\infty}\nabla_\Psi f(\Psi^{(i)}) : \Psi^{(i)} \to \Psi^*\right\} \tag{55}$$

A Single-Level Constrained Optimization

According to results in (55), the generalized gradients for performance measure in (38) can be calculated

$$\nabla_\Psi P_0 = (\nabla_\Psi D(\Psi,f) + \nabla_f D(\Psi,f)\nabla_\Psi f(\Psi))W_D M_D +$$

$$(\nabla_\Psi S(\Psi,f) + \nabla_f S(\Psi,f)\nabla_\Psi f(\Psi))W_S M_S + \sigma \frac{1}{|L|}\nabla_\Psi f(\Psi)e \tag{56}$$

Now, a data-driven bi-level constrained model (42) can be reduced into a data-driven single-level constrained optimization model with a maximum factor μ^*

$$\underset{\Psi}{Min}\,\bar{P}_1(\Psi) = \sum_{(i,j)\in L} D_{(i,j)}(\Psi)W_D M_D + S_{(i,j)}(\Psi)W_S M_S + \sigma\frac{1}{|L|}\sum_{(i,j)\in L} f_{(i,j)}(\Psi,\mu^*)e_{(i,j)} \tag{57}$$

subject to

$$\zeta_{\min} \le \zeta \le \zeta_{\max}$$

$$\lambda_{\min}\zeta \le \varphi_{am} \le 1,\, \forall m \in N$$

$$f_{(i,j)}(\Psi,\mu^*) \le \rho_{(i,j)}s_{(i,j)}\lambda_{(i,j)},\, \forall (i,j) \in L$$

$$\theta_{am} + \varphi_{am} + \tau_{abm}\zeta \le \theta_{am} + \Omega_m(a,b),\, \forall m \in N$$

The generalized gradients in terms of (57) for $\bar{P}_1$ with respect to signal settings can be obtained.

$$\nabla_\Psi \bar{P}_1 = \nabla_\Psi P \tag{58}$$

For a given direction $\Delta\Psi = \hat{\Psi} - \Psi$, according two following mathematical properties, the generalized gradient in (58) can be determined when a sub-gradient $g \in \partial\bar{P}_1(\Psi)$ exists.

Definition 1 (Semi-smoothness) We say the objective function $\bar{P}_1(\Psi)$ in (57) is semi-smooth if $\bar{P}_1(\Psi)$ is locally Lipschitz and the limit

$$\lim_{g \in \partial\bar{P}_1(\Psi+t\Delta), \Delta \to \Delta\Psi, t \downarrow 0} \left\{ g\Delta \right\} \tag{59}$$

exists for every direction Δ in the neighborhood of signal settings Ψ.

Lemma 1 (Directional derivatives for semi-smooth functions) Suppose $\bar{P}_1(\Psi)$ in (57) is a locally Lipschitzian function and directional derivative $D\bar{P}_1(\Psi^*; \Delta\Psi)$ exists for every direction $\Delta\Psi$ in the change of Ψ^*. Then

1. $D\bar{P}_1(\cdot; \Delta\Psi)$ is Lipschitzian.
2. 2. For any direction $\Delta\Psi$ in the neighborhood of Ψ^*, there exists a sub-gradient $g \in \partial\bar{P}_1(\Psi^*)$ such that

$$D\bar{P}_1(\Psi^*; \Delta\Psi) = g\Delta\Psi \tag{60}$$

According to **Theorem 2**, let Σ be any set of zero measure, and let $\Sigma_{\bar{P}_1}$ be the set of points at which the objective function $\bar{P}_1$ fails to be differentiable. For every $\Psi^{(i)} \notin \Sigma$ and $\Psi^{(i)} \notin \Sigma_{\bar{P}_1}$, the generalized gradient of performance $\bar{P}_1(\Psi)$ can be expressed whenever a sub-gradient $g \in \partial\bar{P}_1(\Psi^*)$ exists.

$$\partial_\Psi \bar{P}_1(\Psi^*) = co\left\{ \lim_{i \to \infty} \nabla_\Psi \bar{P}_1(\Psi^{(i)}) : \Psi^{(i)} \to \Psi^* \right\} \tag{61}$$

In (61) the generalized gradient of $\bar{P}_1(\Psi)$ can be characterized as a convex hull of all points of the form $\lim_{i \to \infty} \nabla\bar{P}_1(\Psi^{(i)})$ where the subsequence $\{\Psi^{(i)}\}$ converges to a limit value $\bar{P}_1(\Psi^*)$. For some signal settings $\Psi^{(i)}$, the generalized gradient of $\bar{P}_1(\Psi^{(i)})$ can be obtained as follows.

$$\nabla_\Psi \bar{P}_1^{(i)} = (\nabla_\Psi D^{(i)} + \nabla_f D^{(i)} \nabla_\Psi f^{(i)}) W_D M_D + (\nabla_\Psi S^{(i)} + \nabla_f S^{(i)} \nabla_\Psi f^{(i)}) W_S M_S + \frac{1}{|L|} \sigma \nabla_\Psi f^{(i)} e \tag{62}$$

Therefore for a direction $\Delta\Psi^{(i)}$ in the neighborhood of signal setting, for any sub-gradient $g \in \partial\bar{P}_1(\Psi^{(i)})$ the directional derivative $D\bar{P}_1(\Psi^{(i)}; \Delta\Psi^{(i)})$ can be calculated as follows.

$$D\bar{P}_1(\Psi^{(i)}; \Delta\Psi^{(i)}) = g\Delta\Psi^{(i)} \tag{63}$$

A TRACTABLE COMPUTATIONAL SOLUTION SCHEME

For DDSBL (41) with optimal signal control $\Psi^{(i)}$, a maximum factor $\mu^{(i)}$ can be determined by solving a following linear programming problem.

$$\underset{\mu}{Max}\,\underline{P_1}(\mu) = \sum_{(i,j)\in L} D_{(i,j)}^{(i)} W_D M_D + S_{(i,j)}^{(i)} W_S M_S + \sigma\frac{1}{|L|}\sum_{(i,j)\in L} f_{(i,j)}(\Psi^{(i)},\mu)e_{(i,j)} \tag{64}$$

subject to

$$f_{(i,j)}(\Psi^{(i)},\mu) \leq \rho_{(i,j)}s_{(i,j)}\lambda_{(i,j)}^{(i)},\ \forall (i,j)\in L$$

Therefore a single-level constrained optimization model with a maximum factor $\mu^{(i)}$ in (57) can be solved when the generalized gradients in (62) are available at $(\Psi^{(i)},\mu^{(i)})$.

A Data-Driven Bundle Method

Bundle methods are the most promising methods for non-smooth optimization (Kiwiel, 1990; Shor, 1998). The information around current iterate together with the past are collected and accumulated in bundles in order to establish a polyhedral approximation of the objective function at the actual iterate. Because of implicit form of equilibrium constraints, a general bi-level problem is usually not a convex program as mentioned in the literature (Luo et al., 1996). Due to the kinky structure of the performance function in the single-level constrained optimization, the model (57) for single iterate could be possibly not precise for approximating the performance function in (57). Thus more information collected around current signal settings will be mobilized to acquire a more reliable model for (57). While non-smooth optimization problem can be effectively solved by the bundle methods as noticed in the literature, applications of bundle methods to bi-level signal control and road network design problems have not received much attention in the field of transportation. In order to effectively solve a proposed DDSBL problem, a data-driven bundle method is firstly investigated.

A cutting plane model for upper bound $\overline{P_1}(\cdot)$ in (57) at signal settings $\Psi^{(k)}$ along a perturbed direction $\Delta\Psi^{(k)}$ can be constructed using a bundle of past computed gradients in the following form:

$$\left\{\overline{P_1}(\Psi^{(i)}), g^{(i)}, \Psi^{(i)}; g^{(i)} \in \partial\overline{P_1}(\Psi^{(i)}), 1 \leq i \leq k\right\}$$

The generalized gradient of an upper bound estimate $\overline{P_1}(\cdot)$ can be determined by (62). Let $\overline{P_1}^{(k)}$ denote a linear approximation of $\overline{P_1}(\Psi)$ close to $\Psi^{(k)}$ at iteration $i, 1 \leq i \leq k$ we have

$$\overline{P_1}^{(k)} \approx \underset{1\leq i\leq k}{Max}\left\{g^{(i)}(\Psi - \Psi^{(i)}) + \overline{P_1}(\Psi^{(i)})\right\} \tag{65}$$

Let

$$\varepsilon_{i,k} = \overline{P}_1(\Psi^{(k)}) - (\overline{P}_1(\Psi^{(i)}) + g^{(i)}(\Psi^{(k)} - \Psi^{(i)}))$$

denote an error bound for a linear approximation of $\overline{P}_1(\Psi^{(k)})$. A linear approximation of $\overline{P}_1^{(k)}$ for (57) can be expressed in terms of bundle gradients

$$\overline{P}_1^{(k)} \approx \underset{1 \leq i \leq k}{Max} \left\{ g^{(i)}(\Psi - \Psi^{(k)}) - \varepsilon_{i,k} \right\} + \overline{P}_1(\Psi^{(k)}) \tag{66}$$

Therefore the single-level constrained optimization model (57) can be approximated as a following cutting plane model $\hat{P}_1^{(k)}$

$$\underset{\Psi \in \Pi}{Min} \hat{P}_1^{(k)} = \underset{1 \leq i \leq k}{Max} \left\{ g^{(i)}(\Psi - \Psi^{(k)}) - \varepsilon_{i,k} \right\} + \overline{P}_1(\Psi^{(k)}) \tag{67}$$

A sequence of iterates $\left\{ \Psi^{(k)} \right\}$ for a minimization problem (57) can be determined in accordance with a projection operator $\Pr(\cdot)$ and a step length $l, 0 < l < 2$ as follows.

$$\Psi^{(k+1)} = \Pr_{\Pi}(\Psi^{(k)} + l\Delta\Psi^{(k)}), k = 1, 2, \ldots \tag{68}$$

In (67), $\Delta\Psi^{(k)}$ can be determined as a following quadratic model.

$$\underset{\Delta\Psi^{(k)}}{Min} \nu + \frac{1}{2} \left\| \Delta\Psi^{(k)} \right\|^2 \tag{69}$$

subject to

$$g^{(i)}\Delta\Psi^{(k)} - \varepsilon_{i,k} + \overline{P}_1(\Psi^{(k)}) \leq \nu, 1 \leq i \leq k$$

A Tractable Computation Scheme

A proposed DDSBL in (41) can be solved by a tractable computation scheme proposed in this section. For a maximum flow factor μ^* satisfying capacity constraint (33) can be determined by (64). The corresponding signal control can be determined by a data-driven single-level optimization in (57). Followed by results given in previous section, a cutting plane model in (67) is proposed to determine optimal solutions for DDSBL locally. The performance measure in (38) can be continuously improved from iteration to iteration until the directional derivatives for $\overline{P}_1(\Psi^{(k)})$ in (63) vanishes. A tractable computation scheme solving DDSBL in (57) can be detailed as follows.

Step 0. Start with initial signal settings $\Psi^{(k)}$ with flow factor $\mu^{(k)}$. Set index $k = 0$, and stopping threshold ε. Set an upper bound $\bar{P}_1^{(0)} = \infty$ and a lower bound $\underline{P}_1^{(0)} = -\infty$.

Step 1. Solve a maximization problem (64) with $\Psi^{(k)}$ to obtain a maximum flow factor $\mu^{(k+1)}$. Update the lower bound estimate $\underline{P}_1^{(k)}$.

Step 2. Construct a cutting plane model (67) for $\bar{P}_1(\Psi^{(k)})$ using generalized gradients in (62).

Step 3. Solve a quadratic model in (69) to elaborate next movement $\Psi^{(k+1)}$ by (68) along tentative direction.

Step 4. Update the upper bound estimate $\bar{P}_1^{(k)}$ using new solution $\Psi^{(k+1)}$. Calculate the corresponding directional derivatives $D\bar{P}_1^{(k)}$ via (63).

Step 5. Optimality condition check: If $D\bar{P}_1^{(k)} > -\varepsilon$, go to Step 6. Otherwise, move step $k \to k+1$ and continue Step 1

Step 6. Bound check: let $\delta^{(k)} = \bar{P}_1^{(k)} - \underline{P}_1^{(k)}$. If $\delta^{(k)} \leq \varepsilon$, then optimal solution is $\Psi^{(k)}$ with a maximum flow multiplier $\mu^{(k)}$ and stop. Otherwise go back to Step 1 and move step $k \to k+1$.

NUMERICAL EXPERIMENTS

Numerical computations are primarily performed at an example urban road network for the following three objectives: to demonstrate the stability of solutions, to evaluate trade-offs among economic viable cost, maximum risk exposure and risk equity factor for DDSBL in (40), and to demonstrate the superiority of DDSBL over other alternatives.

Input Data

A moderate example road network is chosen for illustration as given in Fig. 1 (Allsop and Charlesworth, 1977). In this example road network, it includes 22 pairs of OD trip-ends, 23 links and 6 signal-controlled junctions. Initial travel demand data for various pairs of OD are given in Table 1. The cruise travel times along link are also given in Table 2. The average travel speed for hazmat traffic on link is supposed to be 15m/s. Thus the average length on a link can be calculated as the product of average speed and cruise travel time along the link. Assuming incidental consequence of accidental release of hazmat is measured by average population exposure along a link, the population exposure is set 20 units per 500m. Therefore, the incidental consequence of accidental release of hazmat along a link can be computed accordingly. Using typical values found in practice, the minimum green time for each signal-controlled group is 7s, and the clearance times are 5s between incompatible signal groups. The maximum cycle time is set at 180s. Implementations for carrying out the following computations were made on DELL T7610, Intel Xeon 2.5GHz processor with 32GB RAM under Windows 7 OS using C++ compiler. The stopping criterion is set when the relative difference in the objective function value is less than 0.15%. Two sets of initial signal setting are given in Table 3 together with initial performance index measured with converting factor $\sigma = 1$. Numerical results are summarized in Tables 4-7 and also plotted in Figs 2-17.

Solutions for DDSBL

Numerical computation results for solving DDSBL at two distinct initial signal settings are given in Tables 4-7. Details about how to achieve a good solution using a tractable solution scheme are plotted in Figs. 2-3 and 10-11 for two initial settings. As seen in Table 6, taking the first initial data set for example, the computation takes 16 iterations to determine a local optimal solution for DDSBL. As also seen in Fig. 2, the upper and lower bound estimates for the performance measure in (40) were respectively improved as the computation proceeds. In particular, the directional derivatives, as seen in Table 6, were progressively improved with significance as new signal settings are found from iteration to iteration. The corresponding gaps between upper and lower bounds for the performance measure were increasingly reduced as observed in Table 6 and in Fig. 3. The optimal solutions can be found following Steps 5-6 when relative difference between two bounds vanishes. As was seen in Fig. 3, on the one hand, the percent relative ratios of two bounds difference were in decrease from iteration to iteration. On the other hand, the directional derivatives in (63) were particularly increased until the stopping condition is satisfied for Step 5. The whole computation stops when relative difference ratio of two bounds in Step 6 is within a predetermined value. The risk equity factor defined in (31) was improved significantly from initial value of 0.971 to that of 0.682 using SRM as indicated in Tables 3-4 and 6. The corresponding flow factors associated with hazmat traffic in (33) were also improved from initial value of 1.03 to that of 1.467 as also observed in Table 6. As was seen in Table 4, SRM-based signal control successfully improved the value of performance measure of $3318 from initial value of $5250 with the very lowest CPU time of 201s as compared to other alternatives.

For the 2nd data set, as it shown in Table 7 the proposed data-driven bundle strategy takes 17 iterations to determine good signal control with a very low risk equity factor of 0.677. The directional derivatives in (63) were reduced from iteration to iteration with significance. The upper and lower bound estimates in Table 7 and also in Fig. 10 were respectively improved as computation proceeds. As observed in Fig. 11, the trade-off between relative difference ratio of two bound estimates and directional derivatives were progressively improved as iteration proceeds. Details about directional derivatives in Fig. 11 were also given in Table 7 from iteration to iteration. The risk equity factor defined in (31) was improved significantly from initial value of 0.966 to that of 0.677 using SRM as indicated in Tables 3, 5 and 7. The corresponding flow factors associated with hazmat traffic in (33) were also improved from initial value of 1.035 to that of 1.477 as also observed in Table 7. As was seen in Table 5, SRM-based signal control successfully improved the value of performance measure of $3319 from initial value of $7870 with the very lowest CPU time of 197s as compared to other alternatives.

Evaluation of Trade-Offs Among Risk, Cost, and Equity

As it has been widely noticed, the trade-offs among public risk, travel cost and risk equity spreading over entire road network are of great interest to policy makers. The trade-offs among risk, cost and equity factor for DDSBL using SRM are also obviously observed in Figs. 4-6 at first data set iteratively. As observed in Figs. 4-5, the risk for (40) can be considerably reduced under effective signal control despite generalized travel cost was in increase from iteration to iteration. As also seen in Fig. 6, the performance measure was greatly reduced whilst the flow factor μ was in steady increase. Details about how trade-offs between performance measure and risk equity evolved from iteration to iteration were also given in Tables 6 and 7 respectively for 1st and 2nd data sets. Similar results for 2nd data set are also given in Figs. 12-14.

Comparisons of Risk-Averse Based Models

For various risk models investigated in previous section, numerical comparisons are made in this section. The risk-neutral cost minimum (CM) is one economic viable objective generally selected by carriers to determine routes for hazmat transport. According to the performance measure with a fixed value of σ, the performance measure using x model to evaluate behavioral response of carriers at the lower level problem can be stated as follows.

$$P_x = P_x^c + \sigma P_x^e \tag{70}$$

where $x \in \{CM, MM, MM2, MS\}$. For example, when $x = CM$, the performance measure can be expressed as in (44) for which DDSBL can be solved by a risk-neutral cost minimum model. Comparisons of performance measure and risk equity for various risk models were made and the corresponding results were plotted in Figs. 7-8 and 15-16 respectively for 1st and 2nd data sets. As seen in Figs. 7-8, the proposed SRM achieved more comparable results as those did the risk-averse MM and MM2 based models whilst guaranteeing much lower risk equity as compared to that did the risk-neural CM based model. Trade-offs between risk and flow factor μ were also obviously observed in Fig. 9 among various risk models. As seen in Fig. 9, taking the first initial data for example, MM achieved the least risk and CM achieved a most one whilst MM obtained a largest flow factor and CM obtained a least one. The proposed SRM seems to achieve more compromised solutions between two extreme bounds. Comparisons were also made for relative effectiveness of risk-averse models given in (42), (48) and (51) and that of cost minimum model in (44). Three computation indices for generalized travel, the maximum risk exposure and risk equity spreading were introduced in percentages as follows. Let γ_x^c describe a percent relative ratio of cost reduction for x model over CM. It implies

$$\gamma_x^c = 100 * \left(\frac{P_x^c - P_{CM}^c}{P_{CM}^c} \right) \% \tag{71}$$

Similarly, let γ_x^e describe a percent relative ratio of maximum risk exposure reduction for x model over CM, i.e.

$$\gamma_x^e = 100 * \left(\frac{P_x^e - P_{CM}^e}{P_{CM}^e} \right) \% \tag{72}$$

Also, let γ_x^s describe a percent relative ratio of risk equity reduction for x model over CM, i.e.

$$\gamma_x^s = 100 * \left(\frac{\gamma_x - \gamma_{CM}}{\gamma_{CM}} \right) \%$$

(73)

In (73), γ_x represents the risk equity for x model. Details of comparisons are given in the last three lows of Tables 4-5 respectively for 1st and 2nd data sets. Taking the first initial data set for example, as shown in Table 4, MM taking no account of economic viable cost for carriers at lower level problem, was incurred a highest cost loss ratio of 54.76% among alternatives whilst achieved a largest risk reduction ratio of 28.5%. While MM2 performed slightly better than did MM by providing multiple routes for carriers at the lower level problem, it was incurred a relatively high cost loss ratio of 36.9% whilst achieving a relative risk reduction advantage of 28.2%. The proposed SRM achieved a relatively low cost loss ratio of 5.95% whilst guaranteeing a relative low risk equity loss ratio of 18.13% because SRM took full account of generalized travel cost for carriers and public risk exposure along travelled routes. The similar results can be observed in Table 5 for the second initial data set. As a result, the proposed SRM produced a similar result of 28% risk reduction whilst incurred with the least cost loss ratio of nearly 2% among all alternatives.

CONCLUSION AND DISCUSSION

In this chapter, a data-driven stochastic bi-level program (DDSBL) for hazmat network design problem is proposed to regulate three following conflicting objectives: minimization of risk associated with hazmat transportation, and minimization of transportation costs while guaranteeing risk equity spreading over entire road networks. Since multi-objective programs can hardly solve the problems with multiple decision makers at different levels, a bi-level decision making program was considered. Assuming the occurrence of incident probability of accidental release of hazmat is unknown, a stochastic risk model (SRM) was considered. The bi-objective travel cost for carriers took account of signal delay at downstream junctions and maximum risk along travelled route. An equity constrained stochastic model was also proposed to simultaneously tackle multi-criteria performance measure and average risk exposure of population over entire road network whilst guaranteeing equitable risk distribution. Due to the non-convexity of DDSBL, a data-driven bundle strategy was proposed to reduce relative gaps between iterations. According to more recent work in Chiou (2016), formulations of various risk-averse models with the objective to reduce the maximum risk for hazmat carriers were considered. Numerical computations were performed using a modest example road network at two initial signal settings. Computational results strongly demonstrated the superiority of proposed data-driven bundle method to solve DDSBL with reasonable computational efforts. As compared to other alternatives, the proposed SRM consistently exhibited a highly considerable cost advantage over those did the alternatives. The proposed SRM becomes more risk amiable in all cases whilst incurred the least cost loss of all models.

ACKNOWLEDGMENT

The author would like to give her great gratitude to Editor in Chief: Professor Fausto Pedro García Márquez for his arrangement about this book chapter. The work reported in this paper has been supported via grant number: MOST 107-2221-E-259-006 from Taiwan National Science Council.

REFERENCES

Allsop, R. E., & Charlesworth, J. A. (1977). Traffic in a signal-controlled road network: An example of different signal timings inducing different routeings. *Traffic Engineering & Control*, *18*, 262–264.

Alp, E. (1995). Risk-based transportation planning practice: Overall methodology and a case example. *INFOR*, *33*(1), 4–19. doi:10.1080/03155986.1995.11732263

Bell, M. G. H. (2000). A game theory approach to measuring the performance reliability of transport networks. *Transportation Research Part B: Methodological*, *34*(6), 533–546. doi:10.1016/S0191-2615(99)00042-9

Bianco, L., Caramia, M., & Giordani, S. (2009). A bilevel flow model for hazmat transportation network design. *Transportation Research Part C, Emerging Technologies*, *17*(2), 175–196. doi:10.1016/j.trc.2008.10.001

Cheng, S. F., Epelman, M. A., & Smith, R. L. (2006). CoSIGN: A parallel algorithm for coordinated traffic signal control. *IEEE Transactions on Intelligent Transportation Systems*, *7*(4), 551–564. doi:10.1109/TITS.2006.884617

Chiou, S.-W. (2003). TRANSYT derivatives for area traffic control optimisation with network equilibrium flows. *Transportation Research Part B: Methodological*, *37*(3), 263–290. doi:10.1016/S0191-2615(02)00013-9

Chiou, S.-W. (2016). A bi-objective bi-level signal control policy for transport of hazardous materials in urban road networks. *Transportation Research Part D, Transport and Environment*, *42*, 16–44. doi:10.1016/j.trd.2015.09.003

Clarke, F., Ledyaev, Y., Stern, R., & Wolenski, P. (1980). *Nonsmooth Analysis and Control Theory*. New York: Springer-Verlag.

Current, J., & Ratick, S. (1995). A model to assess risk, equity and efficiency in facility location and transportation of hazardous materials. *Location Science*, *3*(3), 187–201. doi:10.1016/0966-8349(95)00013-5

Dempe, S. (2003). Annotated bibliography on bilevel programming and mathematical programs with equilibrium constraints. *Optimization*, *52*(3), 333–359. doi:10.1080/0233193031000149894

Dontchev, A. L., & Rockafellar, R. T. (2002). Ample parameterization of variational inclusions. *SIAM Journal on Optimization*, *12*(1), 170–187. doi:10.1137/S1052623400371016

Erkut, E., & Gzara, F. (2008). Solving the hazmat transport network design problem. *Computers & Operations Research*, *35*(7), 2234–2247. doi:10.1016/j.cor.2006.10.022

Erkut, E., & Ingolfsson, A. (2000). Catastrophe avoidance models for hazardous materials route planning. *Transportation Science, 34*(2), 165–179. doi:10.1287/trsc.34.2.165.12303

Erkut, E., & Ingolfsson, A. (2005). Transport risk models for hazardous materials: Revisited. *Operations Research Letters, 33*(1), 81–89. doi:10.1016/j.orl.2004.02.006

Erkut, E., & Verter, V. (1998). Modeling of transport risk for hazardous materials. *Operations Research, 46*(5), 625–664. doi:10.1287/opre.46.5.625

Gang, J., Tu, Y., Lev, B., Xu, J., Shen, W., & Yao, L. (2015). A multi-objective bi-level location planning problem for stone industrial parks. *Computers & Operations Research, 56*, 8–21. doi:10.1016/j. cor.2014.10.005

Gopalan, R., Batta, R., & Karwan, M. (1990). The equity constrained shortest path problem. *Computers & Operations Research, 17*(3), 297–307. doi:10.1016/0305-0548(90)90006-S

He, L., Huang, G. H., & Lu, H. W. (2011). Greenhouse gas emissions control in integrated municipal solid waste management through mixed integer bilevel decision making. *Journal of Hazardous Materials, 193*, 112–119. doi:10.1016/j.jhazmat.2011.07.036 PMID:21816539

Jin, H., & Batta, R. (1997). Objectives derived from viewing hazmat shipments as a sequence of independent Bernoulli trials. *Transportation Science, 31*(3), 252–261. doi:10.1287/trsc.31.3.252

Kang, Y., Batta, R., & Kwon, C. (2014). Generalized route planning model for hazardous material transportation with VaR and equity considerations. *Computers & Operations Research, 43*, 237–247. doi:10.1016/j.cor.2013.09.015

Kara, B. Y., & Verter, V. (2004). Designing a road network for hazardous materials transportation. *Transportation Science, 38*(2), 188–196. doi:10.1287/trsc.1030.0065

Keeney, R. (1980). Equity and public risk. *Operations Research, 28*(3-part-i), 527–534. doi:10.1287/ opre.28.3.527

Kiwiel, K. C. (1990). Proximity control in bundle methods for convex nondifferentiable minimization. *Mathematical Programming, 46*(1-3), 105–122. doi:10.1007/BF01585731

Luo, Z. Q., Pang, J. S., & Ralph, D. (1996). *Mathematical Programs with Equilibrium Constraints.* Cambridge, UK: Cambridge University Press. doi:10.1017/CBO9780511983658

Marianov, V., & ReVelle, C. (1998). Linear non-approximated models for optimal routing in hazardous environments. *The Journal of the Operational Research Society, 49*(2), 157–164. doi:10.1057/palgrave. jors.2600506

Shor, N. (1998). *Nondifferentiable Optimization and Polynomial Problems.* Boston: Kluwer Academic Publishers. doi:10.1007/978-1-4757-6015-6

Ukkusuri, S. V., Ramadurai, G., & Patil, G. (2010). A robust transportation signal control problem accounting for traffic dynamics. *Computers & Operations Research, 37*(5), 869–879. doi:10.1016/j. cor.2009.03.017

Veter, V., & Kara, B. Y. (2008). A path-based approach for hazardous transport network design. *Management Science, 54*(1), 29–40. doi:10.1287/mnsc.1070.0763

Vincent, R. A., Mitchell, A. I., & Robertson, D. I. (1980). *User Guide to TRANSYT, TRRL report, LR888*. Crowthorne: Transport and Road Research Laboratory.

Zhang, L., Yin, Y., & Chen, S. (2013). Robust signal timing optimization with environmental concerns. *Transportation Research Part C, Emerging Technologies, 29*, 55–71. doi:10.1016/j.trc.2013.01.003

Zhang, X., & Huang, G. (2013). Optimization of environmental management startegies through a dynamic stochastic possibilistic multiobjective program. *Journal of Hazardous Materials, 246-247*, 257–266. doi:10.1016/j.jhazmat.2012.12.036 PMID:23313898

Zhao, J., & Verter, V. (2015). A bi-objective model for the used oil location-routing problem. *Computers & Operations Research, 62*, 157–168. doi:10.1016/j.cor.2014.10.016

Zografos, K. G., & Davis, C. F. (1989). Multi-objective programming approach for routing hazardous materials. *Journal of Transportation Engineering, 115*(6), 661–673. doi:10.1061/(ASCE)0733-947X(1989)115:6(661)

APPENDIX

Figure 1. Layout for Allsop and Charlesworth's network
(*Allsop and Charlesworth, 1977*)

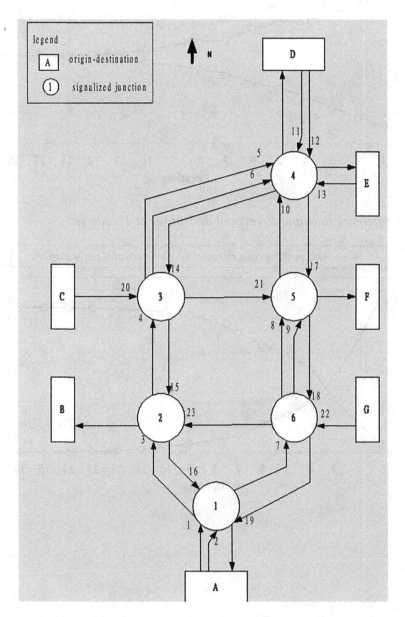

Figure 2. DDSBL solutions for 1ˢᵗ initial data set

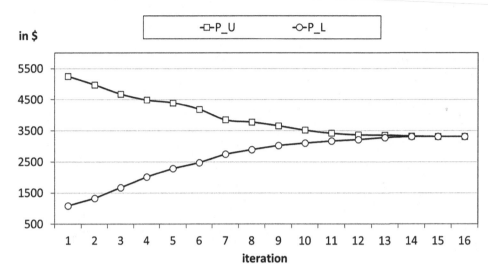

Figure 3. Percent difference ratio and directional derivatives at 1ˢᵗ data set

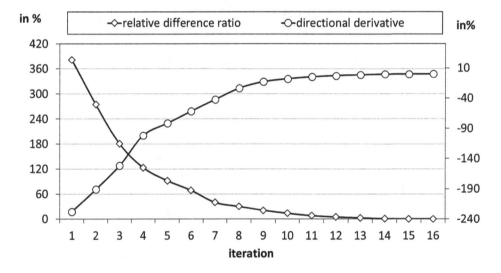

Figure 4. Trade-off between risk and cost at 1ˢᵗ data set

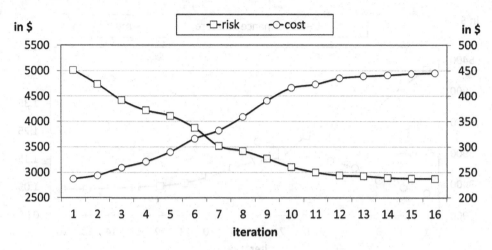

Figure 5. Trade-off between risk equity and cost at 1ˢᵗ data set

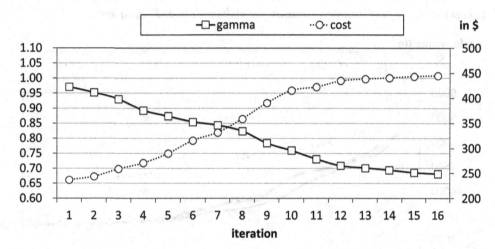

Figure 6. Trade-off between performance measure and flow factor at 1ˢᵗ data set

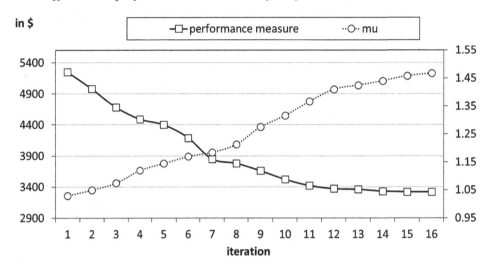

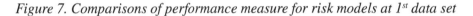

Figure 7. Comparisons of performance measure for risk models at 1ˢᵗ data set

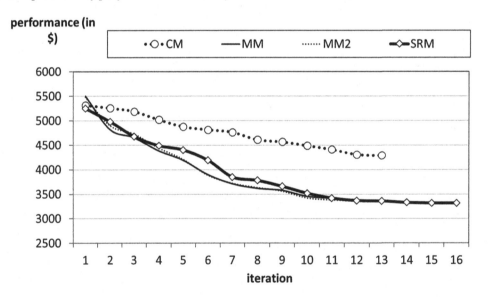

Figure 8. Comparisons of risk equity for risk models at 1ˢᵗ data set

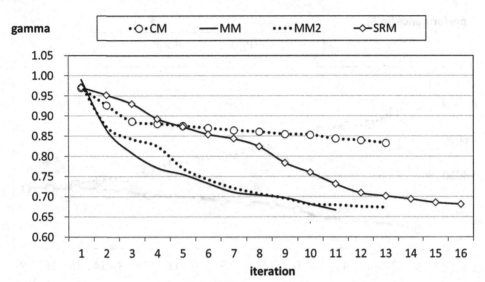

Figure 9. Trade-off between risk and flow factor for risk models at 1ˢᵗ data set

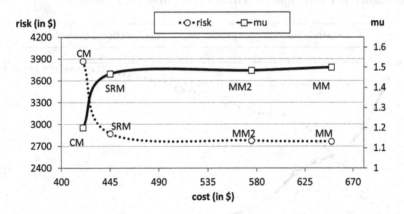

Figure 10. DDSBL solutions for 2nd initial data set

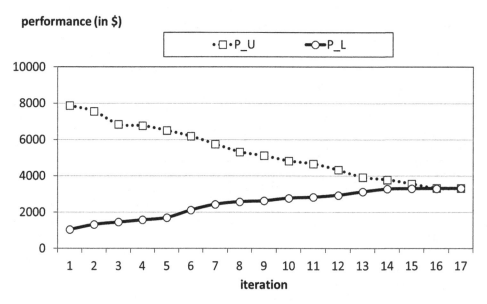

Figure 11. Percent difference ratio and directional derivatives at 2nd data set

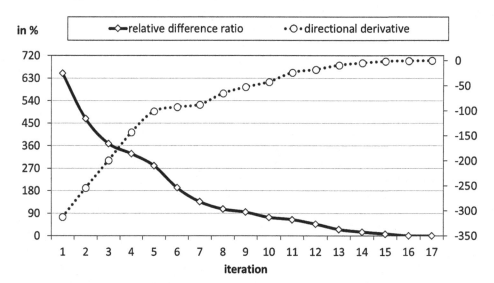

Figure 12. Trade-off between risk and cost at 2ⁿᵈ data set

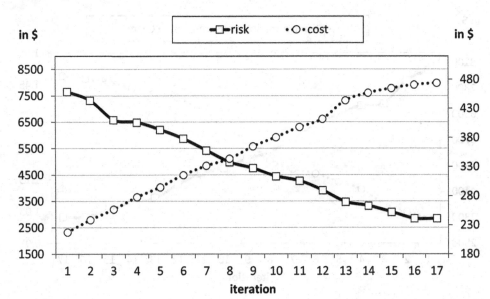

Figure 13. Trade-off between risk equity and cost at 2ⁿᵈ data set

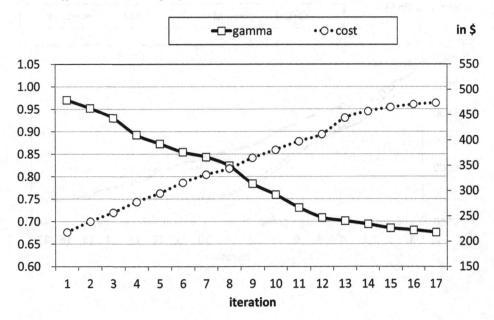

Figure 14. Trade-off between performance measure and flow factor at 2ⁿᵈ data set

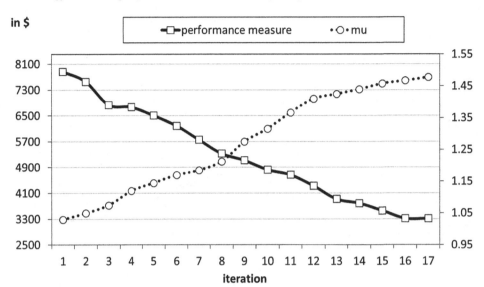

Figure 15. Comparisons of performance measure for risk models at 2ⁿᵈ data set

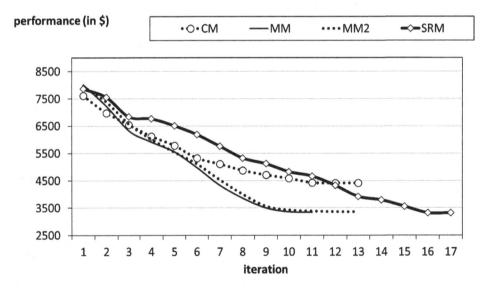

Figure 16. Comparisons of risk equity for risk models at 2nd data set

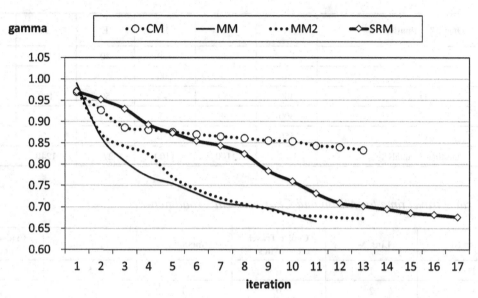

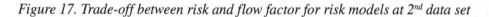

Figure 17. Trade-off between risk and flow factor for risk models at 2nd data set

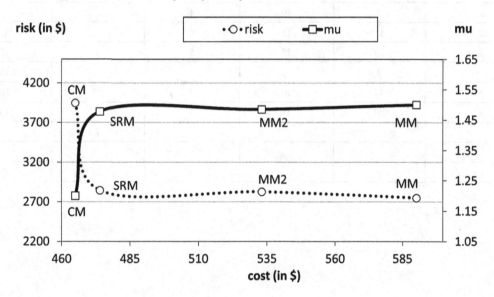

Table 1. Base travel demands for Allsop and Charlesworth's road network in veh/h

Origin/Destination	A	B	D	E	F	Origin Totals
A	-	250	700	30	200	1180
C	40	20	200	130	900	1290
D	400	250	-	50	100	800
E	300	130	30	-	20	480
G	550	450	170	60	20	1250
Destination totals	1290	1100	1100	270	1240	5000

Table 2. Cruise travel time for Allsop and Charlesworth's road network

Junction No.	Link No.	Cruise Travel Time (in s)	Junction No.	Link No.	Cruise Travel Time (in s)
1	1	0	4	5	20
1	2	0	4	6	20
1	16	10	4	10	10
1	19	10	4	11	0
2	3	10	4	12	0
2	15	15	4	13	0
2	23	15	5	8	15
3	4	15	5	9	15
3	14	20	5	17	10
3	20	0	5	21	15
			6	7	10
			6	18	15
			6	22	0

Table 3. Initial data sets for Allsop & Charlesworth' s road network

Signal Setting Variables	1ˢᵗ Initial Data	2ⁿᵈ Initial Data
$1/\varsigma$	70	75
φ_{11}/ς	30	32
φ_{21}/ς	30	33
φ_{31}/ς	70	75
φ_{12}/ς	30	32
φ_{22}/ς	30	33
φ_{13}/ς	30	32
φ_{23}/ς	30	33
φ_{14}/ς	18	20
φ_{24}/ς	18	20
φ_{34}/ς	19	20
φ_{44}/ς	41	45
φ_{54}/ς	42	45
φ_{15}/ς	18	20
φ_{25}/ς	18	20
φ_{35}/ς	19	20
φ_{45}/ς	41	45
φ_{16}/ς	30	32

continued on following page

Table 3. Continued

Signal Setting Variables	1st Initial Data	2nd Initial Data
φ_{26}/ς	30	33
PI (in \$)	5250	7870
γ	0.971	0.966
μ	1.030	1.035

where $1/\varsigma$ denotes the common cycle time and φ_{am}/ς denotes the green durations in seconds for signal group a at junction m.

Table 4. Optimal signal settings for the 1st initial data

Signal Setting Variables	CM-Based	MM-Based	MM2-Based	SRM-Based
$1/\varsigma$	90	115	118	105
φ_{11}/ς	40	54	49	48
φ_{21}/ς	40	51	59	47
φ_{31}/ς	90	115	118	105
φ_{12}/ς	42	55	56	50
φ_{22}/ς	38	50	52	45
φ_{13}/ς	39	53	55	48
φ_{23}/ς	41	52	53	47
φ_{14}/ς	22	37	35	32
φ_{24}/ς	26	34	35	29
φ_{34}/ς	27	29	33	29
φ_{44}/ς	53	76	75	66
φ_{54}/ς	54	71	73	66

continued on following page

Table 4. Continued

Signal Setting Variables	CM-Based	MM-Based	MM2-Based	SRM-Based
φ_{15}/ς	26	34	36	38
φ_{25}/ς	24	29	24	24
φ_{35}/ς	25	37	43	28
φ_{45}/ς	55	68	65	67
φ_{16}/ς	42	45	55	45
φ_{26}/ς	38	60	53	50
PI (in $)	4290	3416	3354	3318
μ	1.2	1.5	1.485	1.467
γ	0.833	0.667	0.673	0.682
CPU (in s)	1212	1044	967	201
γ_x^c (in %)	-	54.76	36.9	5.95
γ_x^e (in %)	-	-28.53	-28.19	-25.76
γ_x^s (in %)	-	-19.93	-19.21	-18.13

Table 5. Optimal signal settings for the 2nd initial data

Signal Setting Variables	CM-Based	MM-Based	MM2-Based	SRM-Based
$1/\varsigma$	100	106	120	120
φ_{11}/ς	50	34	57	52
φ_{21}/ς	40	62	53	58
φ_{31}/ς	100	106	120	120
φ_{12}/ς	45	66	56	51

continued on following page

Table 5. Continued

Signal Setting Variables	CM-Based	MM-Based	MM2-Based	SRM-Based
φ_{22}/ς	45	30	54	59
φ_{13}/ς	46	39	57	51
φ_{23}/ς	44	57	53	59
φ_{14}/ς	27	34	36	41
φ_{24}/ς	28	27	33	32
φ_{34}/ς	30	30	36	32
φ_{44}/ς	60	66	74	78
φ_{54}/ς	62	69	77	78
φ_{15}/ς	30	19	35	34
φ_{25}/ς	28	29	26	26
φ_{35}/ς	27	43	44	45
φ_{45}/ς	63	53	66	65
φ_{16}/ς	48	48	54	50
φ_{26}/ς	42	48	56	60
PI (in \$)	4415	3340	3358	3319
μ	1.19	1.496	1.485	1.477
γ	0.840	0.668	0.673	0.677
CPU (in s)	1094	995	922	197
γ_x^c (in %)	-	26.88	14.62	1.94
γ_x^e (in %)	-	-30.38	-28.48	-27.97
γ_x^s (in %)	-	-20.48	-19.88	-19.40

Table 6. DDSBL solutions for the 1ˢᵗ initial data set

$\mu^{(k)}$	$DP_1(\Psi^{(k)}; \Delta\Psi^{(k)})$	$P_u^{(k)}$	$P_l^{(k)}$	$\delta^{(k)}$	$100\% * \dfrac{\delta^{(k)}}{P_l^{(k)}}$	$\gamma^{(k)}$
1.030	-227.86	5250	1090	4160	381.65	0.971
1.050	-190.82	4980	1330	3650	274.44	0.952
1.075	-151.53	4680	1670	3010	180.24	0.930
1.120	-101.76	4490	2010	2480	123.38	0.893
1.145	-81.39	4400	2290	2110	92.14	0.873
1.170	-61.58	4190	2480	1710	68.95	0.855
1.185	-42.21	3850	2750	1100	40.00	0.844
1.213	-23.81	3780	2900	880	30.34	0.824
1.275	-13.00	3660	3030	630	20.79	0.784
1.316	-8.15	3520	3100	420	13.55	0.760
1.367	-4.91	3420	3170	250	7.89	0.732
1.410	-2.96	3370	3220	150	4.66	0.709
1.425	-1.65	3360	3280	80	2.44	0.702
1.440	-0.47	3330	3315	15	0.45	0.694
1.458	-0.19	3320	3316	4	0.10	0.686
1.467	-0.06	3318	3318	0	0.01	0.682

Table 7. DDSBL solutions for the 2nd initial data set

$\mu^{(k)}$	$DP_1(\Psi^{(k)};\Delta\Psi^{(k)})$	$P_u^{(k)}$	$P_l^{(k)}$	$\delta^{(k)}$	$100\% * \dfrac{\delta^{(k)}}{P_l^{(k)}}$	$\gamma^{(k)}$
1.035	-312.34	7870	1050	6820	649.52	0.966
1.042	-254.31	7560	1330	6230	468.42	0.960
1.081	-198.77	6840	1460	5380	368.49	0.925
1.110	-143.28	6770	1580	5190	328.48	0.901
1.144	-101.18	6510	1710	4800	280.70	0.874
1.176	-92.36	6190	2120	4070	191.98	0.850
1.189	-87.47	5760	2440	3320	136.07	0.841
1.222	-65.14	5330	2580	2750	106.59	0.818
1.285	-52.60	5120	2630	2490	94.68	0.778
1.314	-42.12	4830	2780	2050	73.74	0.761
1.355	-23.49	4670	2830	1840	65.02	0.738
1.399	-17.76	4330	2940	1390	47.28	0.715
1.416	-9.02	3920	3125	795	25.44	0.706
1.432	-4.57	3790	3279	511	15.60	0.698
1.451	-1.42	3560	3305	255	7.72	0.689
1.463	-0.49	3321	3315	6	0.17	0.684
1.477	-0.08	3319	3319	0	0.00	0.677

Chapter 13
Examining Visitors' Characteristics and Behaviors in Tourist Destinations Through Mobile Phone Users' Location Data

Masahide Yamamoto
Nagoya Gakuin University, Japan

ABSTRACT

This chapter uses Mobile Kukan Toukei™ (mobile spatial statistics) to collect the location data of mobile phone users in order to count the number of visitors at specific tourist destinations and examine their characteristics. Mobile Kukan Toukei is statistical population data created by an operational data of mobile phone networks. It is possible to estimate the population structure of a region by gender, age, and residence using this service of the company. The locations and characteristics of the individuals obtained herein are derived through a non-identification process, aggregation processing, and conceal-ment processing. Therefore, it is impossible to identify specific individuals. This chapter attempts to identify the number of visitors in different periods and their characteristics based on the location data of mobile phone users collected by the mobile phone company. In addition, it also attempts to demonstrate an alternative method to more accurately infer the number of visitors in specific areas.

INTRODUCTION

Since Prime Minister Koizumi's first term, the government of Japan had been attempting to boost the tourism industry, because authorities have come to recognize the importance of promoting tourism in order to stimulate sluggish regional economies in Japan. For example, the government launched the Visit Japan Campaign (VJC), which is the promotional effort of the government to activate inbound tourism with the objective of uniting the public and private sectors. The tourism industry, being labor intensive,

DOI: 10.4018/978-1-7998-0106-1.ch013

was expected to absorb some of the labor force from different regions of Japan. Therefore, various economic enterprises and local governments had been struggling to promote the industry.

Due to these efforts including the VJC, Japan's tourism industry has been enjoying a rapid increase in the number of incoming tourists from other countries. According to the Japan National Tourism Organization, the number has amounted to approximately 31.2 million people in 2018.

However, several famous tourist destinations such as Kyoto have come to suffer from so-called "over-tourism," whereas most places still have room to accept more tourists. Therefore, attracting visitors to not too popular places should create a win-win situation. Holding an event to attract visitors could be an alternative, especially for rural areas devoid of famous tourism resources.

Originally, Japan's tourism industry had been suffering from significant volatility in demand depending on the season and day of the week. Furthermore, there has been a significant loss of business opportunities because of congestion during the busy season. To cope with such volatility, tourism facilities, such as inns and hotels, have been trying to level the demand through daily and/or seasonal pricing adjustments. For example, room rates on the days before holidays are usually more expensive than they are on other days. Despite these efforts, the differences between on-season and off-season occupancy rates of rooms and facilities are still large. In other words, attracting customers in the off-season is an important challenge for tourism. Various events have been held to eliminate the seasonal gap.

Numerous events are currently held to attract visitors to Japan. Many events are newly launched. To date, it has been difficult to accurately grasp the extent to which these events attract visitors and the types of people who visit. However, by employing the recently provided Information and Communication Technology (ICT) services, it is possible to verify the number and characteristics of visitors to a particular event.

This chapter used "Mobile Kukan Toukei™" provided by NTT DOCOMO, Inc. and DOCOMO Insight Marketing, Inc to count the number of visitors at specific tourist destinations and examine their characteristics. Mobile Kukan Toukei is statistical population data created by a mobile phone network (see Figure 1). Although measuring the exact number of visitors to open tourist areas has been quite difficult so far, it has now become possible to estimate not only the number but also the population structure of a region by gender, age, and residence by using this service (see Figure 2). The locations and characteristics of the individuals obtained herein are derived through a non-identification process, aggregation processing, and concealment processing. Therefore, it is impossible to identify specific individuals.

Figure 1. Population statistics of Mobile Kukan Toukei
Retrieved July 2, 2019, from https://www.nttdocomo.co.jp/corporate/disclosure/mobile_spatial_ statistics/#p01

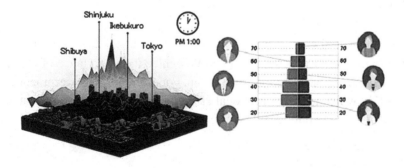

Figure 2. Population statistics of Mobile Kukan Toukei
Retrieved July 2, 2019, from https://www.nttdocomo.co.jp/corporate/disclosure/mobile_spatial_ statistics/#p01

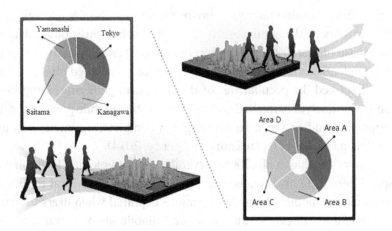

This chapter attempts to identify the number of visitors in different periods and their characteristics. In addition, it also attempts to demonstrate an alternative method to more accurately infer the number of visitors in specific areas.

RELATED RESEARCH

Nowadays, big data have become important in many research areas[1], such as data mining, machine learning, computational intelligence, information fusion, the semantic Web, and social networks (Bello-Orgaz et al., 2016, p. 46). To date, several attempts have been made to use large-scale data or mobile phone location data in tourism marketing studies.

Studies That Used Big Data in Tourism

Most studies dealing with big data in tourism were published after 2010. Fuchs et al. (2014, pp. 198-208) presented a knowledge infrastructure that has recently been implemented at the leading Swedish mountain tourism destination, Åre. Using a Business Intelligence approach, the Destination Management Information System Åre (DMIS-Åre) drives knowledge creation and application as a precondition of organizational learning at tourism destinations.

Xiang et al. (2015) tried to apply big data to tourism marketing. The study aimed to explore and demonstrate the utility of big data analytics to better understand important hospitality issues, namely, the relationship between hotel guest experience and satisfaction. Specifically, the investigators applied a text analytical approach to a large number of consumer reviews extracted from Expedia.com to deconstruct hotel guest experiences and examine the association with satisfaction ratings (pp. 120-129).

These studies are similar to this study in that they attempted to utilize big data in tourism. However, the research methods and objectives of these studies are different from that of the present study.

Studies That Used Mobile Phone Location Data in Tourism

Studies using mobile phone location data for tourism surveys can be traced back to 2008. Ahas et al. (2008, pp. 469-485) introduced the applicability of passive mobile positioning data for studying tourism. They used a database of roaming location (foreign phones) and call activities in network cells: the location, time, random identification, and country of origin of each called phone. Using examples from Estonia, their study described the peculiarities of the data, data gathering, sampling, handling of the spatial database, and some analytical methods to demonstrate that mobile positioning data have valuable applications for geographic studies. Japan Tourism Agency conducted a similar study using international roaming service in December 2014 (Japan Tourism Agency, 2014).

Since the creative work of Ahas et al. (2008), several studies employing location data have emerged. Liu et al. (2013, pp. 3299-3311) investigated the extent to which behavioral routines could reveal the activities being performed at mobile phone call locations captured when users initiate or receive voice calls or messages. Using data collected from the natural mobile phone communication patterns of 80 users over more than a year, they assessed the approach via a set of extensive experiments. Based on the ensemble of models, they achieved prediction accuracy of 69.7%. The experiment results demonstrated the potential to annotate mobile phone locations based on the integration of data mining techniques with the characteristics of underlying activity-travel behavior.

A variety of related studies have also been conducted. Gao and Liu (2013, pp. 252-260) attempted to examine the methods used to estimate traffic measures using information from mobile phones, accounting for the fact that each vehicle likely contains more than one phone because of the popularity of mobile phones. Steenbruggen et al. (2015, pp. 335-346) used mobile phone data to provide new spatio-temporal tools for improving urban planning and reducing inefficiencies in current urban systems. They investigated the applicability of such digital data to develop innovative applications to improve urban management.

The present study could be characterized as similar to Ahas et al. (2008). However, Ahas et al. (2008) is based on results obtained by analyzing data roaming activity. Mobile phone users in the study are obviously limited. Therefore, whether the knowledge gained applies to the average traveler is not clear. In the present study, I analyzed data provided by NTT DoCoMo, Inc., which is the largest mobile phone service provider in Japan. Therefore, their data should be more reliable in that the volume of data is quite large.

Another study needs to be mentioned here. The Project Report that Okinawa Prefecture (2013) used location data obtained from a domestic mobile phone network. However, that report is different from the present study in that this study examines the transitions of visitors over two years. Although the report was epoch-making, it did not contain a few experimental elements. Therefore, it will be deficient in the long term.

Yamamoto (2019) used the Mobile Kukan Toukei to identify the number of visitors of each period and their characteristics based on the location data of mobile phone users collected by the mobile phone company. The study sites of the survey are mainly Toyama city and Kanazawa city in Japan, which became nationally popular when the Hokuriku Shinkansen (high-speed railway) opened in 2015.

Yamamoto compared the effect of the opening of the Shinkansen in the two cities. A comparison of visitors at Kanazawa Station with those at Toyama Station found that Kanazawa Station attracted visitors from a wider area of Japan (see Table. 1). Mobile phone users around Kanazawa Station were from 235 municipalities, including Ishikawa Prefecture, whereas those at Toyama Station were from 43 municipalities, including Toyama Prefecture (12:00 a.m.–1:00 p.m. on holidays in October 2015). Although the Hokuriku Shinkansen stops at both stations, the results suggest that Kanazawa has been

Table 1. Residential distribution of the population at Kanazawa Station and Toyama Station (based on data collected between 12:00 a.m.–1:00 p.m. on holidays in October 2014 and 2015)

Kanazawa Station			Toyama Station		
Residence	**2015**	**2014**	**Residence**	**2015**	**2014**
Toyama, Toyama Pref.	131	147	Kanazawa, Ishikawa Pref.	67	60
Takaoka, Toyama Pref.	93	94	Fukui, Fukui Pref.	18	13
Fukui, Fukui Pref.	91	80	Setagaya Ward, Tokyo	16	n/a
Myoko, Niigata Pref.	47	n/a	Suginami Ward, Tokyo	15	n/a
Nanto, Toyama Pref.	34	31	Yamagata, Yamagata Pref.	14	n/a
Setagaya Ward, Tokyo	34	17	Takayama, Gifu Pref.	14	n/a
Imizu, Toyama Pref.	34	42	Nakamura Ward, Nagoya, Aichi Pref.	13	n/a
Oyabe, Toyama Pref.	33	39	Minami Ward, Niigata, Niigata Pref.	13	n/a
Sakai, Fukui Pref.	32	30	Gifu, Gifu Pref.	12	n/a
Omachi, Nagano Pref.	30	n/a	Hakusan, Ishikawa Pref.	12	20
Ota Ward, Tokyo	28	12	Ota ward, Tokyo	12	n/a
Tsubame, Niigata Pref.	28	n/a	Himeji, Hyogo Pref.	12	n/a
Bunkyo Ward, Tokyo	27	n/a	Nagano, Nagano Pref.	12	n/a
Nagano, Nagano Pref.	24	n/a	Nerima Ward, Tokyo	11	n/a
Hiratsuka, Kanagawa Pref.	24	n/a	Shinagawa Ward, Tokyo	11	n/a
Sanda, Hyogo Pref.	23	n/a	Hida, Gifu Pref.	11	10
Tonami, Toyama Pref.	23	26	Joetsu, Niigata Pref.	11	n/a
Suginami Ward, Tokyo	22	16	Kawaguchi, Saitama Pref.	10	n/a
Nerima ward, Tokyo	22	10	Adachi Ward, Tokyo	10	n/a
Tsu, Mie Pref.	22	n/a	Takatsuki, Osaka	10	n/a

Source: (Yamamoto, 2019)

Note: The figures above do not include visitors from Ishikawa Pref. for Kanazawa Station and Toyama Pref. for Toyama Station. Numbers less than ten are represented as "n/a."

more successful so far in attracting visitors. The number of visitors from Tokyo (gray column) increased in both the cities. Despite the fact that Toyama is nearer to Tokyo than Kanazawa, the latter successfully attracted more visitors from Tokyo.

Other Related Studies

This chapter also covers tourists' behavior concerning their keyword search. As Sheldon (1997) notes, tourism is an information intensive industry. The size of the tourism industry alone suggests that it generates large volumes of information to be processed and communicated. The Internet has fundamentally changed the manner in which tourism related information is distributed and people plan for travel. Thus, keyword advertising has become significantly important in tourism as well as in other industries. Studies on keyword advertising in tourism emerged after 2010, and few have attempted to analyze data about keyword ads in tourism.

Xiang and Pan (2011) pointed out that search engine marketing is gaining the status of a major online marketing strategy for many destinations. Search queries are perhaps the most important behavioral aspect of the use of search engines. Keywords in travelers' queries reflect their knowledge about the city and its competitors. Xiang and Pan attempted to identify the patterns in online travel queries across tourist destinations, and offered insights for the manner in which tourism destinations are searched online and implications for search engine marketing for destinations.

Pan and Li (2011) examined the linguistic structure of destination image. They attempted to demonstrate the importance of niche keywords in search engine marketing, in order to establish the importance of niche phrases for tourism destination image (TDI).

Xiang and Gretzel (2010) investigated the extent to which social media appear in search engine results in the context of travel-related searches. The study employed a research design that simulates a traveler's use of a search engine for travel planning by using a set of pre-defined keywords in combination with nine U.S. tourist destination names. The analysis of the search results showed that social media constitute a substantial part of the search results, indicating that search engines likely direct travelers to social media sites.

Pan et al. (2007) analyzed 701 Excite.com accommodation search queries and suggested that travelers most often search for their accommodations simultaneously with other aspects of their travel, such as destinations, attractions, transportation and dining; and that most commence their search by seeking specific hotels in conjunction with their destination city.

Ayanso and Karimi (2015) used a unique cross-sectional dataset of the top 500 internet retailers in North America and empirically investigated the moderating effects of keyword competition on the relationship between ad position and its determinants in the sponsored search market. The empirical analysis indicated that the position of ads for web-only retailers is dependent on bid values and ad relevancy factors, whereas multi-channel retailers are more reliant on bid values.

Although there are a large number of studies on online marketing today, there are still limited articles on the topic of tourism. Yamamoto (2018) conducted a survey for attracting tourists online and measured its effect[2]. He displayed ads[3] on keyword search results related to regional tourism and used these to attract participants. Then he measured the percentage of visitors who visited a download (PDF brochure) site through the keyword advertising. The keyword advertising was classified into two categories, and their relative cost-effectiveness was examined through a comparison. Ad group 1, which was displayed for tourism-related keywords such as "Noto tourism" and "Nanao tourism", cost 50,831 yen, there were 622 clicks. Ad group 2, which was displayed for keywords related to the region and history or to castles, cost 19,596 yen, and there were 339 clicks. Comparing the two ad groups, ad group 2 was superior to ad group 1 in the cost-effectiveness.

WHAT ATTRACTS TOURISTS TO A DESTINATION?

It is essential to examine factors such as the tourists' decision-making process, and what kind of tourist formation is critical to them, to correctly comprehend their behavior. And it is also necessary to identify what they would be interested in, what prompts them to visit destinations, and what affects their destination choices as well.

According to a 2003 poll by the Cabinet Office[4], the main reasons for domestic travel were as follows (multiple answers, the top four items):

· Beautiful nature and scenery (mountains, rivers, waterfalls, sea, natural parks, etc.) 65.0%
· Relaxing in the hot springs 60.1%
· Local foods at the travel destination 42.5%
· Historic sites, cultural heritage, and museums 34.8%

In the same survey, respondents were also asked about the primary activities at the domestic travel destination (multiple answers, the top four items):

· Beautiful nature and scenery (mountains, rivers, waterfalls, sea, natural parks, etc.) 61.1%
· Relaxing in the hot springs 54.5%
· Local foods at the travel destination 36.0%
· Historic sites, cultural heritage, and museums 31.9%

Based on these results, it appears as though when the travelers visit tourist sites, their travel is usually based on plural purposes and the actual activities are generally in line with them. I recognized the significance of this research in that it uncovered what kind of elements travelers consider with respect their chosen destinations. However, it was still unclear the level to which those elements affected travelers' visit intentions.

Yamamoto (2016) examined several factors that influence potential travelers' decision making processes with regard to sightseeing destinations, as based on three questionnaire surveys[5]. Based on the aggregate results of the questionnaire and subsequent correlation analysis, Yamamoto extracted the factors that might affect the visit intentions of those who were planning to travel. He selected the Noto region as a specific destination about which he asked the respondents whether or not they would like to visit. He asked about their degree of their interest and knowledge about the region and compared the relevance to the visit intention.

The first question of the questionnaire asked about their interest in tourism resources and local food in the Noto area. There were five degrees of interests with 5 equaling "very interested" to 1 equaling "not interested." Figure 3 shows the average for all answers to the question. Of the five items, it can be observed that interests in local food and hot springs were relatively high.

The third question[6] centered on whether the respondents wanted to visit the Noto area. A rating of "5" equaled "want to visit," while "1" equaled "do not want to visit." Respondents who lived in the area were asked to answer as if they lived outside the area. The means of Nagoya and Kanazawa were 3.50 and 3.73, respectively, suggesting that the students in Kanazawa were more familiar with the Noto area. Hence, slightly more students in Kanazawa compared to Nagoya indicated that they intended to visit the region.

In the fifth question[7], respondents were requested to list tourist sites with which they were familiar in the Noto area. As expected, students in Kanazawa knew the tourist sites in Noto well, while those in Nagoya were not very familiar with the sites. Any difference in terms of cities regarding the students' tendencies to visit familiar sightseeing spots could not be observed. The most frequently mentioned among them was Notojima Aquarium. The second was Wakura-onsen, followed by Chirihama Nagisa Driveway, and Shiroyone Rice Terrace (Figure 4).

Table 2 and 3 illustrates the correlation coefficient between the degree of the respondents' visit intention and their interest level indicated in the first question. The values of students in Nagoya can be

Figure 3. The average of the interest level
Source: (Yamamoto, 2016)

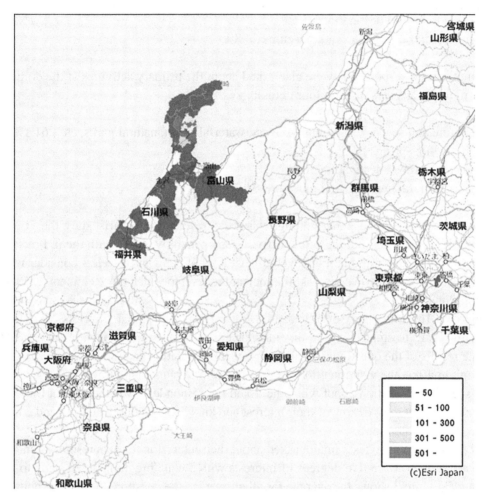

presented as follows: "tourism" (0.429), "hot springs" (0.365), "local food" (0.338), "nature" (0.310), and "history" (0.263), in the decreasing order of the sizes of the correlation coefficient (see Table 1)[8].

On the other hand, the highest among these in Kanazawa is "nature" (0.479), which is followed by "sightseeing" (0.433), "history" (0.342), "local food" (0.329), and "hot springs" (0.312).

Table 4 and 5 indicates the correlation coefficient between the degree of the respondents' visit intentions and their mean of the degree of interests among the five keywords. This table also illustrates the correlation coefficient between the visit intention and number of tourist sites with which the respondent is familiar in the Noto area. The values for the former were 0.447 (Nagoya) and 0.528 (Kanazawa), which exceeded those of the five keywords. Conversely, those for the latter were 0.238 (Nagoya) and 0.154 (Kanazawa), suggesting that the correlation was difficult to find.

Basically, the stronger the visit intention was, the more familiar the individual would be about the destination. However, traveler's curiosities might have been diluted if the individuals were familiar with the sites. In addition, some people may have lost their interests after several visits. In some cases, the

Figure 4. Familiar tourist sites in the Noto area
Source: (Yamamoto, 2016)

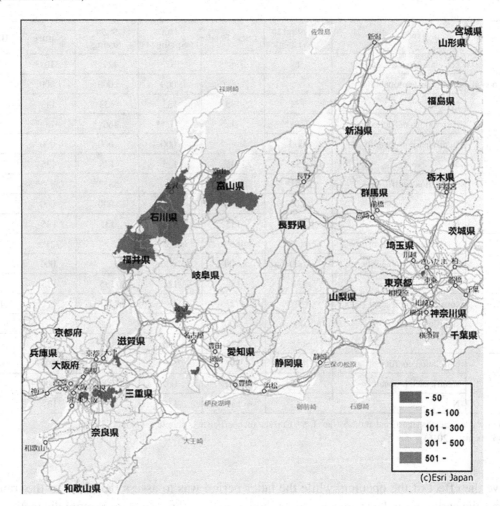

visit might have led to a revisit. However, some people never revisited sites. Therefore, it could be said that familiarity and recognition do not necessarily help tourist sites.

Overall, on comparing the results of Nagoya and Kanazawa, no major difference could be observed. In Nagoya, there were fewer students who had ever been to Noto and, hence, their recognition of tourist destinations in Noto was relatively low. In addition, they also showed less interest in "events."

This survey suggested that the higher the average interest level, the higher the intention to visit. In other words, it is important to present to potential tourists an accumulation of diverse tourism resources.

MOBILE KUKAN TOUKEI

This survey was conducted over two periods, the first from April 2014 to October 2015 and the second from December 27, 2015, to January 14, 2017. The sites studied in this survey are tourist destinations in Ishikawa Prefecture in Japan, including the Kanazawa city. The earlier period of the survey was

Table 2. The correlation coefficient between the degree of the respondents' visit intentions and their interest levels (Nagoya)

		Intention to Visit	Local Food	Hot Springs	Sight Seeing	Nature	History
intention to visit	correlation coefficient	1	.338**	.365**	.429**	.310**	.263**
	significance probability		.000	.000	.000	.000	.002
	N	133	133	133	133	133	133
local food	correlation coefficient	.338**	1	.507**	.466**	.378**	.289**
	significance probability	.000		.000	.000	.000	.001
	N	133	135	135	135	135	135
hot springs	correlation coefficient	.365**	.507**	1	.583**	.583**	.268**
	significance probability	.000	.000		.000	.000	.002
	N	133	135	135	135	135	135
sightseeing	correlation coefficient	.429**	.466**	.583**	1	.721**	.452**
	significance probability	.000	.000	.000		.000	.000
	N	133	135	135	135	135	135
nature	correlation coefficient	.310**	.378**	.583**	.721**	1	.469**
	significance probability	.000	.000	.000	.000		.000
	N	133	135	135	135	135	135
history	correlation coefficient	.263**	.289**	.268**	.452**	.469**	1
	significance probability	.002	.001	.002	.000	.000	
	N	133	135	135	135	135	135

*. Correlation coefficient is significant at the 5% level. **. Correlation coefficient is significant at the 1% level.
Source: (Yamamoto, 2016)

to observe the effect of the opening, while the latter period was to assess the effect of the transition. Sometimes the earlier period was selected to be shown because the results were more distinctive due to a shorter interval after the opening.

The survey areas are presented in Table 6 and Figure 5. There are two reasons the area around two hot springs was chosen. First, there are a number of hotels there, and therefore these places were likely to have a larger economic effect on the opening than other nearby areas. Second, the two hot springs are easily accessible from Kanazawa by train. Kenrokuen, which is one of the most famous gardens in Japan, about ten minutes by bus from the Kanazawa station, was added to the survey area to see the direct effect of the opening.

When selecting these areas, it was essential to identify their "regional mesh codes." A regional mesh code is a code for identifying the regional mesh. It stands for an encoded area that is divided into the same size squares (mesh) based on the latitude and longitude in order to use it for statistics. With regard to regional mesh, there are three types of meshes: primary, secondary, and tertiary. The length of one side of a primary mesh is about 80 km, and those of secondary and tertiary meshes are about 10 km and 1 km respectively.

In addition, split regional meshes also exist, which are a more detailed regional division. A half-regional mesh is a tertiary mesh that is divided into two equal pieces in the vertical and horizontal directions.

Table 3. The correlation coefficient between the degree of the respondents' visit intentions and their interest levels (Kanazawa)

		Intention to Visit	Local Food	Hot Springs	Sight Seeing	Nature	History
intention to visit	correlation coefficient	1	.329**	.312**	.433**	.479**	.342**
	significance probability		.000	.000	.000	.000	.000
	N	201	201	201	201	201	201
local food	correlation coefficient	.329**	1	.535**	.467**	.367**	.159*
	significance probability	.000		.000	.000	.000	.025
	N	201	201	201	201	201	201
hot springs	correlation coefficient	.312**	.535**	1	.517**	.421**	.177*
	significance probability	.000	.000		.000	.000	.012
	N	201	201	201	201	201	201
sightseeing	correlation coefficient	.433**	.467**	.517**	1	.589**	.347**
	significance probability	.000	.000	.000		.000	.000
	N	201	201	201	201	201	201
nature	correlation coefficient	.479**	.367**	.421**	.589**	1	.393**
	significance probability	.000	.000	.000	.000		.000
	N	201	201	201	201	201	201
history	correlation coefficient	.342**	.159*	.177*	.347**	.393**	1
	significance probability	.000	.025	.012	.000	.000	
	N	201	201	201	201	201	201

*. Correlation coefficient is significant at the 5% level. **. Correlation coefficient is significant at the 1% level.
Source: (Yamamoto, 2016)

Table 4. The correlation coefficient between the degree of the respondents' visit intentions and their average interest levels or knowledge (Nagoya)

		Intention to Visit	Interest Level (mean)	Number of Tourist Sites
intention to visit	correlation coefficient	1	.447**	.238**
	significance probability		.000	.006
	N	133	133	133
interest level (mean)	correlation coefficient	.447**	1	.321**
	significance probability	.000		.000
	N	133	135	135
number of tourist sites	correlation coefficient	.238**	.321**	1
	significance probability	.006	.000	
	N	133	135	135

*.Correlation coefficient is significant at the 5% level. **. Correlation coefficient is significant at the 1% level.
Source: (Yamamoto, 2016)

Table 5. The correlation coefficient between the degree of the respondents' visit intentions and their average interest levels or knowledge (Kanazawa)

		Intention to Visit	Interest Level (mean)	Number of Tourist Sites
intention to visit	correlation coefficient	1	.528**	.154*
	significance probability		.000	.029
	N	201	201	201
interest level (mean)	correlation coefficient	.528**	1	.258**
	significance probability	.000		.000
	N	201	202	202
number of tourist sites	correlation coefficient	.154*	.258**	1
	significance probability	.029	.000	
	N	201	202	202

*.Correlation coefficient is significant at the 5% level. **. Correlation coefficient is significant at the 1% level.
Source: (Yamamoto, 2016)

The length of one side is about 500 m. Furthermore, the length of one side of a quarter and 1/8 regional meshes is about 250 m and 125 m respectively.

For example, the mesh code of Wakura Hot Springs, which is one of the survey areas, is a third order code 5536-5703 (Figure 6). If the survey area cannot be covered in one mesh, it is possible to combine multiple meshes, like Kenrokuen in Table 1. Kenrokuen Park was added to the survey areas to compare with the hot springs and enable observation of their distinctions.

This chapter first analyzed the location data collected from NTT DOCOMO, Inc. to consider the effect of the opening of the Hokuriku Shinkansen on the survey areas. The periods during which the data were collected are 8.00-9.00, 12.00-13.00, and 14.00-15.00 hrs.

Transition in Number of Visitors in Each Time Period

Figure 7 shows that Kenrokuen Park attracted more visitors in the afternoons probably due to the large number of tourists who visit the park on single-day trips. On the other hand, Wakura, which is located on the Noto Peninsula, had more visitors (Figure 8) in the mornings (8:00 a.m.–9:00 am) than the other

Table 6. Survey areas and regional mesh codes

	Survey Areas	Regional Mesh Code	Type of Codes
Kanazawa	Kenrokuen	5436-6572+5436-6573-1,5436-6573-3	Tertiary, 1/2
Nanao	Wakura Hot Springs	5536-5703	Tertiary
Kaga	Yamanaka Hot Springs	5436-2299,5436-2390	Tertiary

Source: Provided by the author
Note: A regional mesh code is a code for identifying the regional mesh, which is divided into the same size of a square (mesh) based on latitude and longitude. The length of one side of a primary mesh is about 80 km, and those of secondary and tertiary meshes are about 10 km and 1 km respectively.

Figure 5. Survey areas

hot springs. Regarding Yamanaka hot springs, there was no significant difference in visits between different periods (Figure 9).

There are two possible explanations for these results. First, many visitors may have spent more than one night at Yamanaka hot springs. Second, the morning market held near Wakura hot springs may have increased the population there before noon.

Although both Wakura and Yamanaka hot springs are a little far from Kanazawa, their results were contrary. A TV drama might have increased the number of tourists in Wakura. "Mare," which was broadcast nationwide from March to September 2015, presented the story about a girl born in Noto Peninsula.

Figure 10 shows visitor transitions at the two hot springs and Kenrokuen. Notably, the transitions of the two hot springs show very similar fluctuations. The correlation coefficient between them is 0.586, whereas that between both hot springs and Kenrokuen is below 0.1 (see Table 7).

These values might suggest that the two hot springs are competitors. Visitors who like hot springs typically stay to enjoy them for more than one night, whereas many visitors might have enjoyed Kenrokuen without staying overnight.

Visitors' Characteristics: Gender, Age, and Residence

The Kenrokuen Park attracted a variety of visitors, including many female visitors. On the other hand, many elderly people (over 60 years old) visited the hot springs. I presume that the local people account for a large proportion of these visitors (see Figures 11, 12, and 13).

Figure 6. The regional mesh of Wakura Hot Springs

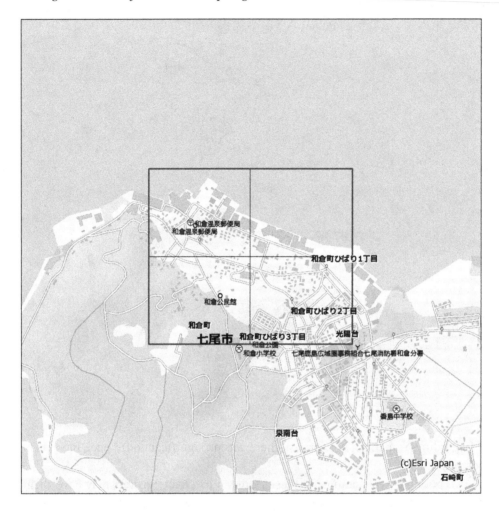

Figures 14, 15, and 16 illustrate the home residence areas of visitors to Kenrokuen, Wakura hot springs, and Yamanaka hot springs, respectively, on holidays in October 2015. These images show that Kenrokuen was successful in attracting many visitors from various areas in Japan. Wakura attracted more people from the Kanto region, whereas people in the Kansai region preferred Yamanaka (see Table 8).

These tendencies could be explained by accessibility. Yamanaka can be more easily accessed from the Kansai region, whereas Wakura is near to Noto Satoyama airport, which offers direct flights to Tokyo.

In general, visitors at the two hot springs were from smaller cities, perhaps due to tourist groups from those locations. Hot springs in the Hokuriku region are well known for their dependency on group tourism. Table 8 may suggest that dependency.

Figure 7. Visitor transitions at Kenrokuen
Source: Provided by the author

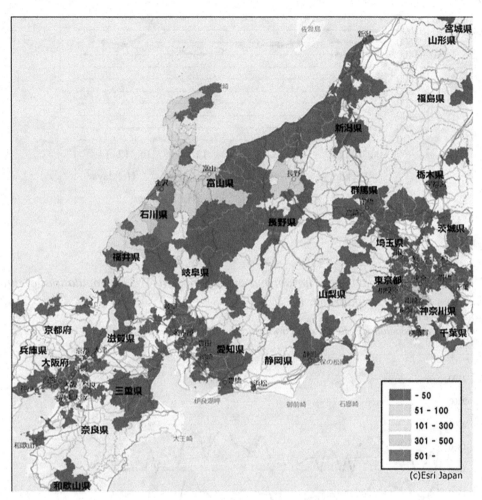

Figure 8. Visitor transitions at Wakura hot springs
Source: Provided by the author

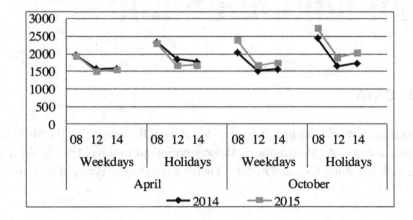

Figure 9. Visitor transitions at Yamanaka hot springs
Source: Provided by the author

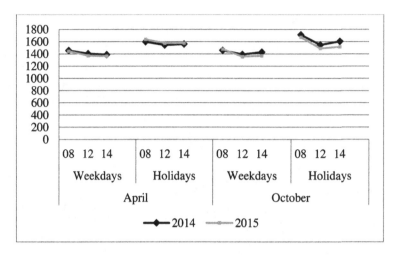

Figure 10. Visitor transitions at the two hot springs and Kenrokuen (Weekly populations of three tourist destinations from Dec. 27, 2015, to Jan. 14, 2017)
Source: Provided by the author
Note: Right axis indicates population at Kenrokuen Park; left axis indicates population at the two hot springs.

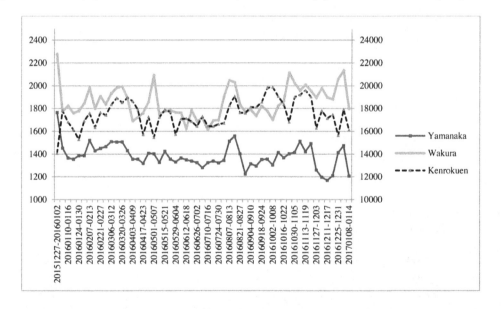

ANALYSIS OF DATA

From now on, this chapter would like to demonstrate an analysis by connecting the Mobile Kukan Toukei and keyword search volume. As shown above, those who intend to travel tend to show higher interest in various things such as nature, food and history. Their various interests might influence their keyword

Table 7. The correlation coefficient among the transitions of the population at tourist destinations

		Kenrokuen	Yamanaka	Wakura
Kenrokuen	correlation coefficient	-	.087	.011
	significance probability		.528	.937
	N	55	55	55
Yamanaka	correlation coefficient	.087	-	.586**
	significance probability	.528		.000
	N	55	55	55
Wakura	correlation coefficient	.011	.586**	-
	significance probability	.937	.000	
	N	55	55	55

**. Correlation coefficient is significant at the 1% level.

Source: Provided by the author

Figure 11. Visitors' gender distribution at Kenrokuen (2:00 p.m.–3:00 p.m., May 1–7, 2016)
Source: Provided by the author

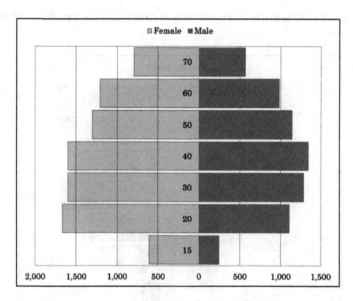

search before or during the travel, and ultimately emerge as some kind of trend in a specific keyword's search volume.

This survey obtained 42 keywords' search volume data through Google Trends[9], which Google Inc. provides, and attempted correlation analysis between the Mobile Kukan Toukei and the tourism related keyword (e.g., name of tourism site) search volume data (see Table 9). The latter was those from November 11th, 2015 to January 28th, 2017 in accordance with the former.

Table 10 shows that the transitions of the population at two hot springs indicated relatively higher correlation with the search volume of several keywords, whereas that of Kenrokuen Park had no correlations except for a phrase, *21st Century Museum of Contemporary Art*. As could be easily imagined,

Figure 12. Visitors' gender distribution at Wakura hot springs (2:00 p.m.–3:00 p.m., May 1–7, 2016)
Source: Provided by the author

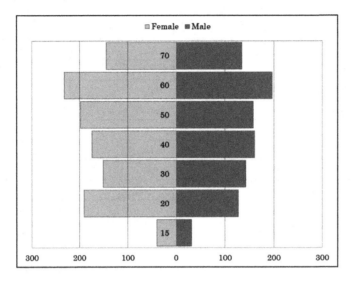

Figure 13. Visitors' gender distribution at Yamanaka hot springs (2:00 p.m.–3:00 p.m., May 1–7, 2016)
Source: Provided by the author

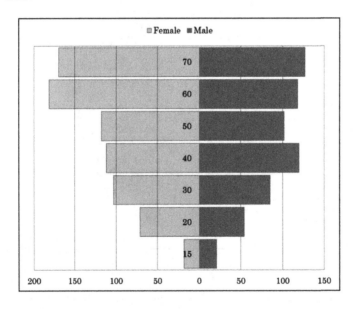

travelers do not necessarily search keywords of what they are currently enjoying but normally of what they are going to visit later.

Cross Correlation Analysis

Then, what kind of process should be done when faced with the case of the Kenrokuen? This chapter also attempted cross correlation analyses among them. With regard to the word *Kenrokuen*, its correlation

Table 8. Visitors' residential distribution at two hot springs (12:00 a.m.–1:00 p.m. on holidays in October 2015)

Wakura Hot Springs		Yamanaka Hot Springs	
Nanao City, Ishikawa Pref.	1706	Kaga City, Ishikawa Pref.	1222
Kanazawa City, Ishikawa Pref.	69	Kanazawa City, Ishikawa Pref.	31
Naka Noto Town, Ishikawa Pref.	42	Komatsu City, Ishikawa Pref.	23
Nagaoka City, Niigata Pref.	26	Toyama City, Toyama Pref.	22
Oyama City, Tochigi Pref.	25	Yokkaichi, Mie Pref.	22
Kaga City, Ishikawa Pref.	25	Fukui City, Fukui Pref.	15
Toyama City, Toyama Pref.	23	Suita City, Osaka Pref.	14
Kahoku City, Ishikawa Pref.	23	Uchinada Town, Ishikawa Pref.	14
Shiga Town, Ishikawa Pref.	22	Setagaya Ward, Tokyo	13
Ojiya City, Niigata Pref.	22	Nomi City, Ishikawa Pref.	13
Ritto City, Shiga Pref.	20	Hakusan City, Ishikawa Pref.	13
Ichikawa City, Chiba Pref.	20	Sakae Town, Chiba Pref.	12
Noto Town, Ishikawa Pref.	19	Higashi Nada Ward, Kobe City, Hyogo Pref.	11
Misato City, Saitama Pref.	18	Kita Ward, Kyoto City, Kyoto Pref.	11
Fukui City, Fukui Pref.	18	Moriyama Ward, Nagoya City, Aichi Pref.	10
Funabashi City, Chiba Pref.	18	Suminoe Ward, Osaka City, Osaka Pref.	10
Ichinomiya City, Aichi Pref.	18	Nonoichi City, Ishikawa Pref.	10
Aoba Ward, Yokohama City, Kanagawa Pref.	17	Otsu City, Shiga Pref.	10
Takaoka City, Toyama Pref.	17	Shinjuku Ward, Tokyo	10
Higashimurayama City, Tokyo	16	Adachi Ward, Tokyo	10

Source: Provided by the author

coefficient rises when it comes to one week later or before (Table 12). As for other keywords, *Kanazawa Tourism* showed higher correlation three to five weeks before, and *Kanazawa Station* from one week to three weeks before as well. In this way, people search each keyword at different times.

Similar findings which include negative correlations could be observed with Wakura and Yamanaka Hot Springs[10] (see Table 13 and 14). However, the tendency of the correlations to become more apparent in different periods is not so distinctive as the case with the Kenrokuen[11].

Regression Analysis

With the understanding above, a linear equation with regard to the population[12] at Kenrokuen Park could be derived (see Table 15, 16, and 17). In this manner, the linear equations of Wakura and Yamanaka hot springs can be obtained as well.

Figure 14. Visitors' residence at Kenrokuen (12:00 a.m. –1:00 p.m. on holidays in October 2015)

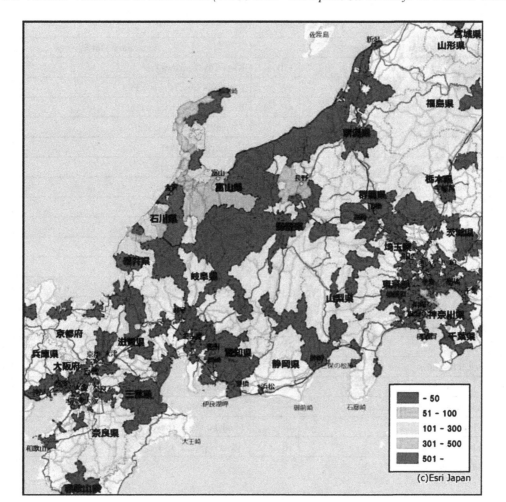

FUTURE RESEARCH DIRECTIONS

The linear equations illustrated above can be made more sophisticated by using an idea of average; for example, the linear equation for Kenrokuen used the keyword *Kenrokuen* search volume in one week before the transition of the population. Using the average volume of the three weeks (previous, present, and successive), the correlation coefficient (0.426) would be slightly but surely higher (Table 18).

Of course, these equations could be made more reliable by adopting several other factors such as the population of the same week (e.g., 14th of the year) in the previous year. Further search for better factors would be a future challenge of this study as well as attempting the same approach in different areas.

Figure 15. Visitors' residence at Wakura hot springs (12:00 a.m. –1:00 p.m. on holidays in October 2015)

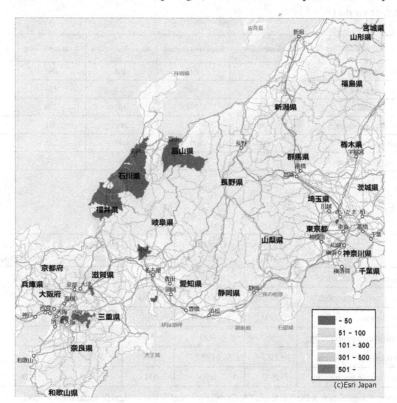

Table 9. The list of the keywords surveyed

Area	Keywords
Kanazawa	Kenrokuen, Kanazawa Tourism, Kanazawa Station, Kanazawa Castle, Higashichayagai, Korinbo, 21st Century Museum of Contemporary Art (21st CMCA), Omicho Market, Itaru (restaurant), Kazuemachi, Yuwaku Hot Springs, Toshiie Maeda
Wakura Hot Springs	Wakura Hot Springs, Wajima, Wajima Market, Notojima Island, Notojima Aquarium, Noto Tourism, Chirihama Beach, Suzu, Wakura Station, Noto Airport
Yamanama Hot Springs	Yamanama Hot Springs, Katayamazu Hot Springs, Yamashiro Hot Springs, Kaga Hot Springs, Kaga Station, Awazu Hot Springs, Komatsu Airport
Others	Hokuriku Tourism, Hokuriku Shinkansen, Gokayama, Shirakawago, Fukui Tourism, Fukui Station, Eiheiji Temple, Tojinbo, Awara Hot Springs, Toyama Tourism, Tateyama, Toyama Station, Unazuki Hot Springs

Source: Provided by the author

CONCLUSION

Tourism is likely to become increasingly important to local economies. However, tourism industry has been suffering significant volatility in demand depending on the season and day of the week. In addition, there was significant loss of business opportunities because of congestion during the busy season.

Table 10. The correlation coefficient between transitions of the population at tourist destinations and the keyword search volume (N=55)

		Kenrokuen	KanazawaTourism	KanazawaStation	KanazawaCastle	Higashi chayagai	Korinbo
Population of Kenrokuen	correlation coefficient	.265	-.023	.168	.085	.143	-.003
	significance probability	.051	.868	.221	.539	.297	.985
Population of Wakura	correlation coefficient	.438**	.161	.450**	.118	.442**	.434**
	significance probability	.001	.240	.001	.391	.001	.001
Population of Yamanaka	correlation coefficient	.444**	.369**	.449**	.253	.456**	.269*
	significance probability	.001	.006	.001	.062	.000	.047

Table 11.

		21st CMCA	Omicho Market	Itaru	Kazue machi	Yuwaku Hot Springs	ToshiieMaeda
Population of Kenrokuen	correlation coefficient	.403**	.039	.140	-.094	.131	-.179
	significance probability	.002	.780	.310	.497	.342	.191
Population of Wakura	correlation coefficient	.080	.635**	.200	-.029	.175	.011
	significance probability	.560	.000	.143	.836	.202	.936
Population of Yamanaka	correlation coefficient	.087	.619**	.269*	-.021	.250	.040
	significance probability	.530	.000	.047	.879	.065	.771

*. Correlation coefficient is significant at the 5% level. **. Correlation coefficient is significant at the 1% level.

Source: Provided by the author

To cope with such volatility, various events have been held to minimize the seasonal gap. Many events are newly launched. To date, it has been difficult to accurately grasp the extent to which these events attract visitors and the types of people who visit. However, by employing the recently provided Information and Communication Technology (ICT) services, it is possible to verify the number and characteristics of visitors to a particular event.

This study attempted to identify the number of visitors at two points in time at various places in Japan and their characteristics using the location data of mobile phone users collected by the mobile phone company. As explained above, Wakura hot springs received more visitors in the mornings, whereas there was no significant difference in visitor populations at Yamanaka hot springs at different times of day. Additionally, Wakura attracted more people from the Kanto region, whereas people in the Kansai region preferred Yamanaka.

This chapter demonstrated an analysis by connecting Mobile Kukan Toukei and keyword search volume. Tourists' various interests influence their keyword search before or during the travel, and ultimately emerge as some kind of trend in a specific keyword's search volume. This chapter also attempted cross correlation analyses among them. With the understanding here, a linear equation could be derived. These findings could lead to a model to forecast tourism demand in a destination.

Table 12. The cross correlation coefficient between the transition of the population at Kenrokuen and the keyword search volume (N=55)

		Kenrokuen	KanazawaTourism	KanazawaStation	Higashi chayagai	21st CMCA	Omicho Market
The same week	correlation coefficient	.265	-.023	.168	.143	**.403****	.039
	significance probability	.051	.868	.221	.297	.002	.780
1 week later	correlation coefficient	**.366****	-.129	.230	.185	.312*	.239
	significance probability	.006	.346	.091	.180	.020	.079
2 weeks later	correlation coefficient	.236	-.249	-.005	-.081	.197	.007
	significance probability	.082	.067	.974	.565	.150	.959
1 week before	correlation coefficient	**.354****	.208	**.460****	.314*	**.474****	.188
	significance probability	.008	.128	.000	.020	.000	.169
2 weeks before	correlation coefficient	.225	.249	**.552****	**.358****	**.506****	**.346****
	significance probability	.099	.067	.000	.007	.000	.010
3 weeks before	correlation coefficient	.183	**.432****	**.495****	.266*	**.465****	.254
	significance probability	.182	.001	.000	.050	.000	.062
4 weeks before	correlation coefficient	-.040	**.355****	.318*	.177	**.375****	-.008
	significance probability	.774	.008	.018	.196	.005	.953
5 weeks before	correlation coefficient	-.163	**.401****	.261	.134	.250	-.071
	significance probability	.234	.002	.054	.329	.066	.605
6 weeks before	correlation coefficient	-.081	.272*	.281*	.148	**.451****	.045
	significance probability	.556	.044	.038	.282	.001	.746

*. Correlation coefficient is significant at the 5% level. **. Correlation coefficient is significant at the 1% level.

Source: Provided by the author

Table 13. The cross correlation coefficient between the transition of the population at Wakura hot springs and the keyword search volume (N=55)

		NotojimaAquarium	Noto Tourism	Yamashiro	Kaga	Awazu	Hokuriku Tourism
The same week	correlation coefficient	.109	.000	**.421****	**-.478****	**.461****	-.247
	significance probability	.429	.999	.001	.000	.000	.069
1 week later	correlation coefficient	-.193	-.265	.027	**-.398****	.279*	-.227
	significance probability	.158	.051	.845	.003	.039	.096
2 weeks later	correlation coefficient	**-.436****	**-.458****	.242	-.263	.280*	**-.414****
	significance probability	.001	.000	.075	.052	.039	.002
1 week before	correlation coefficient	.030	-.178	**.382****	-.334*	.189	**-.351****
	significance probability	.825	.192	.004	.013	.167	.009
2 weeks before	correlation coefficient	-.192	-.319*	**.433****	-.316*	.212	**-.348****
	significance probability	.160	.018	.001	.019	.121	.009
3 weeks before	correlation coefficient	-.226	-.306*	**.364****	-.002	**.346****	-.258
	significance probability	.097	.023	.006	.990	.010	.057
4 weeks before	correlation coefficient	-.215	-.278*	.291*	.174	.315*	-.241
	significance probability	.114	.040	.031	.203	.019	.077
5 weeks before	correlation coefficient	.053	-.153	-.143	-.277*	-.159	.095
	significance probability	.702	.265	.299	.040	.246	.491
6 weeks before	correlation coefficient	.105	-.221	-.094	-.215	-.139	-.146
	significance probability	.447	.106	.496	.116	.312	.288

*. Correlation coefficient is significant at the 5% level. **. Correlation coefficient is significant at the 1% level.

ACKNOWLEDGMENT

This research was supported by JSPS KAKENHI Grant Number JP15K01970.

Table 14. The cross correlation coefficient between the transition of the population at Yamanaka hot springs and the keyword search volume (N=55)

		Kenrokuen	Yamanaka	Katayamazu	Yama shiro	Hokuriku Shinkansen	Goka yama
The same week	correlation coefficient	**.444****	**.395****	**.375****	.224	**.379****	**.375****
	significance probability	.001	.003	.005	.100	.004	.005
1 week later	correlation coefficient	.328*	**.386****	**.374****	-.068	.241	.256
	significance probability	.015	.004	.005	.621	.079	.059
2 weeks later	correlation coefficient	.216	.169	.095	.119	.251	-.017
	significance probability	.113	.217	.492	.387	.070	.903
1 week before	correlation coefficient	.113	**.402****	**.364****	**.374****	.305*	**.376****
	significance probability	.410	.002	.006	.005	.023	.005
2 weeks before	correlation coefficient	-.050	.138	.263	.328*	.302*	.201
	significance probability	.718	.316	.052	.014	.025	.142
3 weeks before	correlation coefficient	-.099	.081	.068	.131	.197	.172
	significance probability	.473	.559	.620	.342	.150	.209
4 weeks before	correlation coefficient	-.010	-.012	.170	.090	.191	.131
	significance probability	.940	.932	.216	.512	.163	.340
5 weeks before	correlation coefficient	.045	-.007	.002	.163	.235	.112
	significance probability	.742	.957	.988	.234	.084	.414
6 weeks before	correlation coefficient	.158	-.014	.126	.076	.320*	.234
	significance probability	.250	.916	.361	.582	.017	.086

*. Correlation coefficient is significant at the 5% level. **. Correlation coefficient is significant at the 1% level.

Source: Provided by the author

Table 15. The summary of the model

Model	R	R^2	Adjusted R^2	Standard Error of Estimated Value
1	.884[a]	.782	.664	720.10244

Source: Provided by the author

Table 16. The analysis of the variance

Model		Sum of Squares	Degree of Freedom	Average Square	F Value	Significance Probability
1	Regression	65161023.469	19	3429527.551	6.614	.000[b]
	Residual error	18149163.513	35	518547.529		
	Total	83310186.982	54			

Source: Provided by the author

Table 17. The factors of the model

Model		Non-Standardization Factor		Standardization Factor	t Value	Significance Probability
		B	Standard Error	β		
1	(constant)	9720.875	1740.550		5.585	.000
	Kenrokuen	8.908	9.094	.100	.980	.334
	Kanazawa Tourism	9.094	15.010	.096	.606	.549
	Kanazawa Station	27.271	25.828	.193	1.056	.298
	Higashichayagai	-2.773	11.500	-.032	-.241	.811
	21st CMCA	-2.350	12.498	-.029	-.188	.852
	Omicho	.731	12.365	.009	.059	.953
	Kazuemachi	-15.870	5.335	-.275	-2.974	.005
	Yuwaku	16.655	7.329	.238	2.273	.029
	ToshiieMaeda	14.418	8.880	.178	1.624	.113
	Wakura	-2.986	11.760	-.030	-.254	.801
	Wajima Market	11.086	9.627	.140	1.152	.257
	Notojima	-16.375	12.104	-.227	-1.353	.185
	Chirihama	-13.940	11.129	-.239	-1.253	.219
	Suzu	21.253	11.699	.259	1.817	.078
	Komatsu Airport	-8.343	13.956	-.078	-.598	.554
	Fukui Station	20.786	11.770	.187	1.766	.086
	Tojinbo	17.450	14.145	.192	1.234	.226
	Toyama Station	14.146	15.776	.118	.897	.376
	Unazuki	22.361	9.794	.289	2.283	.029

Source: Provided by the author

Table 18. The cross correlation coefficient between the transition of the population at Kenrokuen and the keyword search volume including average value (N=55)

		The Same Week	1 Week Before	1 Week Later	Average of 2 Weeks (Previous and Present)	Average of 2 Weeks (Successive and Present)	Average of the 3 Weeks
Population of Kenrokuen	correlation coefficient	.265	.354**	.366**	.356**	.361**	.426**
	significance probability	.051	.008	.006	.008	.007	.001

**. Correlation coefficient is significant at the 1% level.

Source: Provided by the author

REFERENCES

Ahas, R., Aasa, A., Roose, A., Mark, Ü., & Silm, S. (2008). Evaluating passive mobile positioning data for tourism surveys: An Estonian case study. *Tourism Management*, *29*(3), 469–485. doi:10.1016/j.tourman.2007.05.014

Ayanso, A., & Karimi, A. (2015). The moderating effects of keyword competition on the determinants of ad position in sponsored search advertising. *Decision Support Systems*, *70*, 42–59. doi:10.1016/j.dss.2014.11.009

Bello-Orgaz, G., Jung, J. J., & Camacho, D. (2016). Social big data: Recent achievements and new challenges. *Information Fusion*, *28*, 45–59. doi:10.1016/j.inffus.2015.08.005

Cabinet Office. (2003). *Jiyujikan To kankou Ni Kansuru Seron-Chousa* [The Public Opinion Survey on Tourism and Free Time]. Tokyo, Japan: Cabinet Office.

Fuchs, M., Höpken, W., & Lexhagen, M. (2014). Big data analytics for knowledge generation in tourism destinations – A case from Sweden. *Journal of Destination Marketing & Management*, *3*(4), 198–208. doi:10.1016/j.jdmm.2014.08.002

Gao, H., & Liu, F. (2013). Estimating freeway traffic measures from mobile phone location data. *European Journal of Operational Research*, *229*(1), 252–260. doi:10.1016/j.ejor.2013.02.044

Japan Tourism Agency. (2014). *Keitaidenwa kara erareru ichijouhou tou wo katuyousita hounichi gaikokujin doutaichousa houkokusho* [Foreign visitors' dynamics research report utilizing mobile phone location information]. Retrieved June 28, 2019, from http://www.mlit.go.jp/common/001080545.pdf

Kim, C., Park, S., Kwon, K., & Chang, W. (2012). How to select search keywords for online advertising depending on consumer involvement: An empirical investigation. *Expert Systems with Applications*, *39*(1), 594–610. doi:10.1016/j.eswa.2011.07.050

Liu, F., Janssens, D., Wets, G., & Cools, M. (2013). Annotating mobile phone location data with activity purposes using machine learning algorithms. *Expert Systems with Applications*, *40*(8), 3299–3311. doi:10.1016/j.eswa.2012.12.100

Okinawa Prefecture Culture, Sports, and Tourism Department. (2013). *Senryakuteki repeater souzou jigyou houkokusho* [Report on strategic creation of repeaters]. Retrieved June 28, 2019, from http://www.pref.okinawa.jp/site/bunka-sports/kankoseisaku/kikaku/report/houkokusixyo/documents/07dairokusiyou.pdf

Pan, B., & Li, X. R. (2011). The Long Tail of Destination Image and Online Marketing. *Annals of Tourism Research*, *38*(1), 132–152. doi:10.1016/j.annals.2010.06.004

Pan, B., Litvin, S. W., & O'Donnell, T. E. (2007). Understanding accommodation search query formulation: The first step in putting 'heads in beds'. *Journal of Vacation Marketing*, *13*(4), 371–381. doi:10.1177/1356766707081013

Qiao, D., Zhang, J., Wei, Q., & Chen, G. (2017). Finding competitive keywords from query logs to enhance search engine advertising. *Information & Management*, *54*(4), 531–543. doi:10.1016/j.im.2016.11.003

Sheldon, P. J. (1997). *Tourism Information Technology*. CABI Publishing.

Steenbruggen, J., Tranos, E., & Nijkamp, P. (2015). Data from mobile phone operators: A tool for smarter cities? *Telecommunications Policy, 39*(3-4), 335–346. doi:10.1016/j.telpol.2014.04.001

Xiang, Z., & Gretzel, U. (2010). Role of Social Media in Online Travel Information Search Original. *Tourism Management, 31*(2), 179–188. doi:10.1016/j.tourman.2009.02.016

Xiang, Z., & Pan, B. (2011). Travel Queries on Cities in the United States: Implications for Search Engine Marketing for Tourist Destinations. *Tourism Management, 32*(1), 88–97. doi:10.1016/j.tourman.2009.12.004

Xiang, Z., Schwartz, Z., Gerdes, J. H. Jr, & Uysal, M. (2015). What can big data and text analytics tell us about hotel guest experience and satisfaction? *International Journal of Hospitality Management, 44*, 120–129. doi:10.1016/j.ijhm.2014.10.013

Yahiro, K., & Oguchi, T. (2003). Kankouchi-Senkou Ni Oyobosu Kojinteki-Genfukei To Shinriga-kuteki- Kojinsa [Individual Preference for Sightseeing Destinations determined]. *The Tourism Studies Quarterly, 15*(1), 28–29.

Yamamoto, M. (2016). A comparative study on travelers' sightseeing intentions. *Journal of Global Tourism Research, 1*(2), 139–144.

Yamamoto, M. (2018). A comparative study on search keyword advertising to attract tourists. In *Proceedings of the Twelfth International Conference on Management Science and Engineering Management* (vol. 1, pp. 701-710). Cham, Springer.

Yamamoto, M. (2019). Furthering Big Data Utilization in Tourism. In F. P. G. Márquez & B. Lev (Eds.), *Data Science and Digital Business* (pp. 157–171). Cham: Springer. doi:10.1007/978-3-319-95651-0_9

ADDITIONAL READING

Chan, F., Lim, C., & McAleer, M. (2005). Modelling multivariate international tourism demand and volatility. *Tourism Management, 26*(3), 459–471. doi:10.1016/j.tourman.2004.02.013

Chu, F.-L. (2009). Forecasting tourism demand with ARMA-based methods. *Tourism Management, 30*(5), 740–751. doi:10.1016/j.tourman.2008.10.016

Frechtling, D. C. (2001). *Forecasting Tourism Demand: Methods and Strategies*. Butterworth-Heinemann.

Fuchs, M., Höpken, W., & Lexhagen, M. (2014). Big data analytics for knowledge generation in tourism destinations – A case from Sweden. *Journal of Destination Marketing & Management, 3*(4), 198–208. doi:10.1016/j.jdmm.2014.08.002

Pan, B., Litvin, S. W., & O'Donnell, T. E. (2007). Understanding accommodation search query formulation: The first step in putting 'heads in beds'. *Journal of Vacation Marketing, 13*(4), 371–381. doi:10.1177/1356766707081013

Song, H., Qiu, R., & Park, J. (2019). A review of research on tourism demand forecasting: Launching The Annals Of Tourism Research curated collection on tourism demand forecasting. *Annals of Tourism Research*, *75*, 338–362. doi:10.1016/j.annals.2018.12.001

World Tourism Organization. (2008). *Handbook on Tourism Forecasting Methodologies*. World Tourism Organization.

Xiang, Z., Schwartz, Z., Gerdes, J. H. Jr, & Uysal, M. (2015). What can big data and text analytics tell us about hotel guest experience and satisfaction? *International Journal of Hospitality Management*, *44*, 120–129. doi:10.1016/j.ijhm.2014.10.013

KEY TERMS AND DEFINITIONS

DOCOMO Insight Marketing, Inc.: The company that provides marketing research, communication, area marketing, and related consulting services.

Google Trends: A website provided by Google which indicates the search volume of specific keywords in Google Search over time and also analyzes the popularity of top search queries across various regions and languages.

Ishikawa Prefecture: A prefecture located in central Honshu, the main island of Japan.

Kenrokuen: One of the three most beautiful gardens in Japan. The name means a garden which possesses the six characteristics that an ideal garden should have.

Mobile Kukan Toukei: Statistical population data provided by NTT DOCOMO, Inc., DOCOMO Insight Marketing, Inc. and Mobile Kukan Toukei is a trademark of NTT DOCOMO, Inc.

Noto Peninsula: A peninsula that protrudes north into the Sea of Japan from the coast of the Ishikawa Prefecture.

NTT DOCOMO, Inc.: Japan's largest telecommunications company, which serves over 73 million customers in Japan via its wireless networks including a nationwide LTE network.

Visit Japan Campaign (VJC): The promotional effort of the Japanese government to activate inbound tourism into Japan, aimed to achieve a target of attracting 10 million foreign tourists to visit Japan by the year 2010.

Wakura Hot Springs: A hot spring resort on the edge of Nanao Bay at the base of the Noto Peninsula in the Ishikawa Prefecture, Japan.

Yamanaka Hot Springs: A hot spring resort in Kaga City, Ishikawa Prefecture, Japan.

ENDNOTES

[1]   Big data have also been attracting the attention of businesses so far. For example, convenience stores in Japan can now quickly predict the transition of their sales which include new products from the enormous amounts of information collected by cash register terminals and thereby optimize their purchases and inventories.

[2]   Yamamoto (2018) developed a website to provide information on tourism and gourmet food concerning the Noto region (http://noto-kankou.seesaa.net/). Then he measured the effectiveness of

attracting visitors through access analysis using Google Analytics. The study conducted the survey on keyword advertisements twice. The first survey was conducted from January 20 to April 30, 2015, whereas the second survey was conducted from July 15 to July 18, 2017. The advertising cost was 70,427 yen.

[3] The keyword ads concerned Komaruyama Castle Park (Nanao City, Ishikawa Prefecture), built by Toshiie Maeda in 1582. It included the park's name, the URL of its website (see Fig. 2), and a brief description of the park. When visitors clicked on the ad, the website was displayed.

[4] There was a related study on the factors that affect peoples' choices with regard to the travel destinations. Yashiro and Oguchi (2003) conducted a questionnaire survey on the tourist destination preferences. They surveyed 98 female college students in Tokyo, who ranged in age from 18 to 23. The question was "what kind of tourist destination would you prefer?" This was followed by a listing of options." Yashiro and Oguchi tabulated the number of respondents who answered "affirmative" or "very affirmative" for each choice. Consequently, the percentage of affirmatives was particularly high for places with natural resources such as "hot springs (86.7%)," "warm places (83.7%)," and "sea (77.3%)." Non-natural sites, "ruins (68.4%)," "theme parks (62.2%)," and "historic sites (57.1%)" also received relatively high affirmation rates. Although the subject was limited to female university students, these survey results suggested that the accumulation of tourism resources may be advantageous in order to attract tourists.

[5] The first survey spanned July 22-24, 2014; second was during July 15-17, 2015; and third was conducted on December 22, 2015. These surveys targeted university students in Nagoya and Kanazawa cities who attended tourism classes. In these classes, there were 459 (187 in Nagoya and 272 in Kanazawa) attendees on the date of survey administration; the total number of respondents was 337 (135 in Nagoya and 202 in Kanazawa). In terms of gender, there were 115 (45 in Nagoya and 70 in Kanazawa) male students, 220 (89 in Nagoya and 131 in Kanazawa) female students, and 2 (1 each in the two cities) unknowns. The questionnaire consisted of six items and did not require the respondents to disclose their identity. In order to obtain more data and perform a comparison, the survey was conducted in two universities. Nagoya city is more urbanized and at a greater distance from the Noto peninsula than Kanazawa city.

[6] The second question asked whether or not the respondents had been to (lived there or still living there) the Noto area. Approximately 67.2% (135) of the respondents in Kanazawa answered that they had visited the Noto area (27.9% said "no"), whereas 12.6% (17) in Nagoya answered that they had been there (85.9% said "no").

[7] The fourth question inquired about their prerequisites to visit the Noto area. The following multiple answers were provided: ① there is an event ② can eat delicious food ③ possible to see something unusual ④ easy to access ⑤ other. While many respondents chose answer ②, the second most popular choice could not be determined clearly; students in Nagoya chose ③, while those in Kanazawa preferred ①. This difference could be explained easily; numerous events are held in Nagoya city that the students can enjoy without going outside the city.

[8] Yamamoto also attempted to examine the correlation coefficient between the school year and the respondents' visit intentions. The result of -0.062 was hardly relevant.

[9] Through this service, people can obtain data of the keyword search volume described in percentages. If a keyword is frequently searched in a week, the percentage would be close to 100.

[10] Only keywords that have shown apparent correlation are included in Table 12 and 13.

11   Such tendency that the transition of the populations in Wakura and Yamanaka Hot Springs show relatively higher correlations with keyword search volume in the same week might be explained as follows: those who travel to these hot springs tend to visit nearby tourism spots later, and search also related keywords after their arrival in the hot springs.

12   Mobile Kukan Toukei estimates the population including the non-DOCOMO users with the penetration rate of DOCOMO's mobile phone.

APPENDIX

Table 19a. The cross correlation coefficient between the transition of the population at Kenrokuen and the keyword search volume (N=55)

		Kazuemachi	Yuwaku Hot Springs	Toshiie Maeda	Wakura Hot Springs	Wajima Market	Notojima
The same week	correlation coefficient	-.094	.131	-.179	-.079	.244	.012
	significance probability	.497	.342	.191	.567	.072	.930
1 week later	correlation coefficient	.002	-.045	-.248	-.192	.232	-.080
	significance probability	.987	.746	.067	.161	.088	.564
2 weeks later	correlation coefficient	**-.459****	-.014	-.257	**-.349****	.135	-.157
	significance probability	.000	.921	.059	.009	.327	.251
1 week before	correlation coefficient	.043	.102	-.088	.108	**.386****	.025
	significance probability	.755	.459	.524	.433	.004	.856
2 weeks before	correlation coefficient	.062	.304*	-.034	.229	.296*	.215
	significance probability	.655	.024	.806	.092	.028	.115
3 weeks before	correlation coefficient	.255	.327*	.136	**.406****	**.349****	.163
	significance probability	.060	.015	.321	.002	.009	.234
4 weeks before	correlation coefficient	.054	.102	.280*	.344*	.168	.162
	significance probability	.698	.457	.038	.010	.220	.237
5 weeks before	correlation coefficient	-.224	.264	.267*	.327*	.304*	.208
	significance probability	.101	.051	.048	.015	.024	.128
6 weeks before	correlation coefficient	.048	**.448****	**.376****	.291*	.122	**.372****
	significance probability	.730	.001	.005	.031	.374	.005

Table 19b. The cross correlation coefficient between the transition of the population at Kenrokuen and the keyword search volume (N=55)

		Chiri hama	Suzu	Komatsu Airport	Fukui Station	Tojinbo	Toyama Station	Unazuki
The same week	correlation coefficient	.111	.184	.097	.183	.103	.172	-.041
	significance probability	.420	.180	.483	.181	.454	.211	.764
1 week later	correlation coefficient	-.013	.123	.049	.165	.146	.254	-.040
	significance probability	.922	.373	.725	.229	.287	.061	.774
2 weeks later	correlation coefficient	-.078	-.074	.021	-.160	.003	.050	-.188
	significance probability	.573	.590	.880	.244	.984	.716	.170
1 week before	correlation coefficient	.303*	.264	.121	**.391****	.256	.255	.013
	significance probability	.024	.051	.379	.003	.059	.061	.925
2 weeks before	correlation coefficient	**.350****	.192	.250	.292*	**.371****	**.394****	.224
	significance probability	.009	.160	.066	.031	.005	.003	.100
3 weeks before	correlation coefficient	**.355****	.268*	**.424****	.232	**.449****	**.345****	**.487****
	significance probability	.008	.047	.001	.089	.001	.010	.000
4 weeks before	correlation coefficient	.272*	**.405****	.279*	.124	.339*	**.364****	.332*
	significance probability	.045	.002	.039	.368	.011	.006	.013
5 weeks before	correlation coefficient	.282*	**.475****	.322*	.215	.292*	.282*	.145
	significance probability	.037	.000	.017	.115	.030	.037	.290
6 weeks before	correlation coefficient	.339*	**.514****	.222	.340*	.234	**.408****	**.365****
	significance probability	.011	.000	.103	.011	.085	.002	.006

*. Correlation coefficient is significant at the 5% level. **. Correlation coefficient is significant at the 1% level.
Source: Provided by the author

Chapter 14
Machine Learning for Smart Tourism and Retail

Carlos Rodríguez-Pardo
Grupo de Inteligencia Artificial Aplicada. Universidad Carlos III de Madrid, Spain

Miguel A. Patricio
Universidad Carlos III de Madrid, Spain

Antonio Berlanga
Grupo de Inteligencia Artificial Aplicada. Universidad Carlos III de Madrid, Spain

José M. Molina
Grupo de Inteligencia Artificial Aplicada. Universidad Carlos III de Madrid, Spain

ABSTRACT

The unprecedented growth in the amount and variety of data we can store about the behaviour of customers has been parallel to the popularization and development of machine learning algorithms. This confluence of factors has created the opportunity of understanding customer behaviour and preferences in ways that were undreamt of in the past. In this chapter, the authors study the possibilities of different state-of-the-art machine learning algorithms for retail and smart tourism applications, which are domains that share common characteristics, such as contextual dependence and the kind of data that can be used to understand customers. They explore how supervised, unsupervised, and recommender systems can be used to profile, segment, and create value for customers.

INTRODUCTION

The growth in the amount and diversity of data that can be obtained from people's behaviour has seen an unprecedented growth in recent years. This growth is parallel to the popularization and development of machine learning algorithms that can detect patterns in vast amounts of data. Personal electronic devices, such as smartphones, tablets or wearables are becoming ubiquitous, and the amount and variety

DOI: 10.4018/978-1-7998-0106-1.ch014

of sensors that those devices possess are raising quickly. The combination of those factors creates the opportunity of finding patterns that explain consumers' behaviours, preferences or tastes.

In this chapter, we will explore the possibility of applying artificial intelligence algorithms into smart retail and tourism problems. We will explain what are the main challenges that we need to face when creating solutions for those two fields that can learn from the past preferences and behaviours of users, as well as what are the possibilities that machine learning methods can provide for companies, both in increasing customer value and improving decision-making.

First, we will explore the use of supervised learning methods for those tasks. The use of different learning algorithms (deep neural networks, random forest, decision trees, boosting, etc.) will be motivated and compared, so that we can have a better idea on what algorithms are more suited for each task that is involved in the process of creating smart tourism applications. We will study problems such as class imbalances, overfitting, missing values or dimensionality reduction, and different ways of tackling those problems correctly. Machine learning frameworks for different programming languages will also be compared.

The use of unsupervised learning methods is of interest for this problem. Most notably, automatically detecting groups of users that behave similarly can be of great value for retail and smart tourism companies, as, from those groups, they will be able to understand better their own customers. Clustering algorithms, including Self-organised maps (SOM), Expectation-maximization (E-M), K-means or density-based methods like DBSCAN, will be compared and reviewed, as in the supervised learning part of the chapter.

The ultimate goal of using machine learning for smart retail and tourism solutions is to offer customers products and services that maximize their value. A way to do so is through recommender systems, which learn from the characteristics of products that each user has liked in the past, as well as from preferences from similar users, in order to provide a recommendation that maximizes the chance of that users buying that particular product or service. Smartphones and wearables are equipped with several sensors that can provide information about what the user is doing (is it moving, driving, running, etc.) and what are its surroundings (weather, geolocalization, etc.). This is known as contextual information, and it can provide valuable information to recommender systems. Context-aware recommender systems are algorithms that learn from past preferences of users over product taking into account the context in which they interacted with the application (e.g., e-commerce) in the past. The way in which this contextual information should be integrated into recommender systems is, nevertheless, not obvious, and there is no clear consensus in the scientific literature on to which method is preferable. In this final part of our chapter, we will analyse and compare different context-aware recommender systems, as well as different ways of representing contextual information.

In sum, the main goal of this chapters is to explore the use of three different areas of machine learning in the setting of retail and smart tourism applications: Unsupervised and supervised learning, and recommender systems. Those three areas provide algorithms that are indubitably useful for retail and touristic companies and their customers, as they can provide insights that were undreamt of in the past. Different methods will be reviewed and compared with a critical point of view and with the final goal of helping whoever is interested in creating data-driven retail and smart tourism solutions.

MACHINE LEARNING FOR RETAIL AND SMART TOURISM APPLICATIONS

Supervised Learning for User Profiling

Supervised learning is the field in machine learning concerned with learning a function that transforms an input to an output given exemplar tuples input-output. A significant part of the popularization of machine learning in many domains is due to advancements and developments in supervised learning models and the creation of vast annotated datasets. Supervised learning is typically divided in two groups, depending on the nature of the output of the function that is being learned. As such, in *regression*, the output is a natural number, whereas in *classification*, the output is the probability of the input being a member of a specific class or group. Most supervised learning algorithms that can be used for classification can also be used for regression, and vice versa. In this chapter, we will focus on classification, but the techniques can also be transferred to regression tasks.

Classification algorithms create the opportunity of inferring or estimating information about customers by means of using raw data that does not provide us with valuable information about them as an input to models that can infer valuable information. User profiling is the process of categorizing users into predefined classes, given information about them. In the retail and smart tourism domains, those classes are typically related to categories that are useful for creating value for customers. For instance, given the age of one person and the street they reside in, a classification model could be able to classify them into different groups according to their purchasing power, which is a decisive factor when purchasing products. This toy example can be extended to more descriptive classes, such as "person who likes going to concerts", etc. Supervised learning is huge topic, and we will briefly mention the techniques we believe are most useful for user profiling in the domain of retail and smart tourism. We will assume that our input data is tabular (not images, text or audio, which require a completely different set of learning algorithms) and our output is the profile of the user.

The way in which classification algorithms are trained is common for most learning algorithms. We first need a raw dataset, which is comprised of a large set of examples {input, class}. The input data can be multivariate or univariate, and the variables can be numeric, classes, etc. This dataset is pre-processed so that learning algorithms can make the most out of it, by transforming the variables into what classification algorithms expect to receive. For example, numeric variables must be normalized so that their scale does not affect the final result; missing values must be replaced, outliers must be detected and replaced (Chauvenet criteria, Dixon's Q test, Grubb's test, Mahalanobis distance), classes must be balanced (via oversampling, undersampling or generating synthetic data)(Aksoy & Haralick, 2001; Chawla, 2005; Chawla, Bowyer, Hall, & Kegelmeyer, 2002; Dougherty, Kohavi, & Mehran, 1995; Grubbs, 1950; He & Ma, 2013; Kotsiantis & Kanellopoulos, 2006; Liu, Zhang, Zhang, & Liu, 2016; Minh Phoung, Lin, & Altman, 2005; Orlov, 2011; R. B. & W. J., 1951; Rohrer, 2015), etc. In domains in which there are too many variables compared with the number of examples, this number of variables is reduced by choosing the most important ones (wrapper methods, mutual information tests, etc.) or transforming the input space into one that represents the best trade-off of number of variables and their relative variance (principal component analysis, singular value decomposition or linear discriminant analysis are common ways of doing this) (MK, 2016; University, 2016).

This dataset is then divided into a training dataset, which is used to train the classification algorithm, and a test dataset, which is used to evaluate the algorithm. The training set usually has many more samples than the test set, so that the model can learn more patterns. Optionally, it is possible to create another dataset, typically called *validation dataset*, which is used to compare different models and to find a suitable set of training hyperparameters. To evaluate the algorithms fairly, this division is done many times and the algorithm is trained and tested on different random divisions of the dataset, in a process known as cross-validation.

Many machine learning algorithms can perfectly learn the patterns in the training set, but those patterns may not be present in the test dataset. This problem is known as overfitting, which happens when the model is over-parametrized: The model has too much flexibility and has fitted noise that is present in the training dataset but is not present on new samples. To avoid this phenomenon, the most common approaches are to simplify the model, reduce the number of variables, or gather more data.

Most learning algorithms work by minimizing a scoring function, that signals the algorithm on how different the predicted output is to the real output. This scoring function is known as the loss function, and there are many different loss functions available. In classification, the most typical loss function is the cross-entropy error, which is differentiable with respect to the model parameters, but there are other widely-used functions, such as the Kullback–Leibler divergence or the mutual information. Nevertheless, the way of evaluating classification algorithms rarely uses those functions directly. Instead, other metrics are used, which are either easier to understand or more related to the problem (or both). In classification, usually the confusion matrix is reported, which shows how much each class is wrongly classified as any of the other classes, and metrics such as Positive predictive value, True Positive Rate and F1-Score are also widely used. In many problems, being able to correctly classify in one particular class is more desirable than in some other classes. For example, in the medical domain, it may be very costly to incorrectly predict that one patient is healthy than it is to incorrectly predict that they are unhealthy. Both the loss function and the metric used for reporting the results should take into consider those factors. Once the error metric has been defined, it is now possible to train different learning algorithms and compare them. The best algorithm will be the one that showed the smallest error on the test dataset.

Supervised Learning: Algorithms

In this section, several classification algorithms will be mentioned, and their capabilities will be compared so as to provide an overview onto which of them is more suitable for each problem. We will not dive into implementation or mathematical details as it is not the goal of this chapter, please use the references for details on each of those algorithms.

Linear Models

A classifier is said to be linear if it makes its classification decision by computing a linear combination of the input variables, which should be represented using a vector of scalar numbers. Linear models are usually fast in test time, they converge to a solution easily, their results are highly interpretable and, when the dimensionality of the input data is high, their results are usually comparable to those of more complex methods. Nevertheless, most problems do not show a linear behaviour, so linear models are typically used as a baseline upon which to build more complex, non-linear, models. Four sets of algorithms that belong to this class can be highlighted.

A *Naïve Bayes* classifier is a probabilistic classifier that is based on the Bayes' rule (Barber, 2010). It owes its name to its main assumption: the input variables are conditionally independent given the class. That is, if we know the output class, the input variables are all independent of each other: if we know the value of one of them, we cannot infer anything about the value of the others. This assumption usually does not hold in most domains in the real world, but it simplifies the algorithm greatly, and it is its greatest disadvantage: the conditional independence assumption makes it less accurate than other linear models. However, they provide probabilistic results, which is important in domains in which we want to know how certain we are about our predictions, and they scale well, as there are not that many parameters to estimate.

A *perceptron* classifier is a linear classifier that estimates if its input belongs to a class or to another class. It is the basis of artificial neural networks, which stack multiple perceptrons together, as well as adding non-linearities. The perceptron is usually trained in an iterative fashion, using gradient descent as the optimization algorithm. It is a simple algorithm that is easy to train and converges to the exact solution if the problem is convex and linearly separable, but as in any other linear model, its accuracy is easily surpassed by other algorithms. Additionally, it is only useful in binary classification problems. If we want to classify the input into more than 2 classes, this method is not suitable. Finally, unlike other linear methods, it does not provide a probabilistic output.

The *logistic regression* model, also known as *logit*, works similarly to the perceptron: The output is a linear combination of the input variables. Nevertheless, it extends it by adding a probabilistic interpretation to the output and support for multiple output classes. They do this by, instead of estimating if the input belongs to one class, it estimates the probability that the input belongs to each class. Therefore, its results are more interpretable, typically as accurate as the perceptron and they are easy to train. Logistic regression is typically the baseline used to compare other algorithms with.

Support Vector Machines (Nefedov, 2016) are a set of classification algorithms that find the optimal linear separation between classes. They work by transforming the input space into a higher dimensional space, in which the input data can be separated maximally. That is, they not only find a separation between classes, they find the best separation. This characteristic makes them generalize better than logistic regression models to unseen data. Using a technique known as the *kernel trick*, they can be extended to non-linear problems, and they can also be used for regression or probabilistic classification. In many classification problems, support vector machines were the state-of-the-art models until deep learning surpassed them. Nevertheless, they are extremely powerful models and are relatively fast to test and train. Despite those advantages, they are hard to interpret, and finding the optimal set of hyperparameters and configuration can be problematic.

Decision Tree Learning

Decision trees are widely used decision mechanisms that represent decision-making in a tree or graph fashion, in which nodes are connected in a hierarchical fashion (Quinlan, 1983; Russell & Norving, 2014). To make a decision on whether the input belongs to a class, the input is fed to the first node in the tree, which checks the value of one of its attributes. Depending on the value of the attribute, a different path is taken. This process is done until a terminal node is reached, which will make the decision of the class that the input example belongs to. Decision tree learning is the process of learning the structure of this tree from data. Typically, the way this is done is by choosing the attribute that best separates the classes in the dataset according to a loss function, usually entropy. Then, the dataset is divided and each of the *child* nodes in the tree performs this operation again, until the classes can be perfectly separated. To avoid over-fitting, many times, the number of nodes is limited, in a process known as *pruning*. Several algorithms can be framed in the decision tree learning field, like ID3, CART, C5.0, SEE5.0. Decision trees are one of the most easily interpretable classification models, which is an advantage in domains such as medicine. They are fast to train and test, they can provide probabilistic results, and they can be combined easily with other methods. However, they tend to overfit and its results are usually surpassed by more complex methods.

Random forests (Ho, 1998) are one of the most powerful classification algorithms in terms of their accuracy. They work by combining the predictions of several (typically thousands) decision trees that were only trained on a random subset of variables in the dataset. They can detect interactions between variables, work well on big datasets and in high-dimensional domains and provide state-of-the-art results in many domains. However, they lack the interpretability of decision trees, they are harder to train than other methods and testing is slower than in many other algorithms (as many decision trees must be checked to make a decision). Additionally, they work better when the input variables are uncorrelated.

Artificial Neural Networks

Artificial neural networks are complex machine learning models that work by stacking several perceptrons (Clevert, Unterthiner, & Hochreiter, 2015; Cuadros & Domínguez, 2014; Glorot & Bengio, 2010; Hegenbart, 2015; Jaderberg et al., 2017; Nielsen, 2017), followed by a non-linearity operation, into several layers, known as *hidden layers*. Artificial neural networks also receive the name of *deep learning* when they have at least one hidden layer. They are trained using the *back-propagation* algorithm, which allows the model to have as many hidden layers as it is wanted. They are the state-of-the-art models in many machine learning problems, including computer vision, natural language processing, protein-to-protein interaction, etc. They provide the best results in many tasks because of the non-linearity operations and because they do not saturate when they are provided with more data: they can learn indefinitely if more data is provided and if the model has enough *neurons*. They are robust to contradictory data, they have high tolerance to noise and are easy to implement thanks to the availability of high-level APIs that provide support for them. Additionally, they can be trained on any differentiable loss function, which makes them suitable for many different tasks. However, they tend to overfit, training takes a long time, their results are not interpretable, are sensitive to *adversarial noise*, and are very data-hungry, which makes them unsuitable for domains in which little data is available.

Other Models

Bayesian Networks (Barber, 2010; Friston, Mattout, Trujillo-Barreto, Ashburner, & Penny, 2007; Penny, 2012) are probabilistic classifiers that model conditional dependencies of variables and the output classes using a graph structure. Unlike *Naïve Bayes*, they do not assume conditional independencies of variables, which makes them more accurate. Given a fixed graph, finding the model parameters is usually easy, but learning the graph structure is usually hard, and done using algorithms such as Expectation-Maximization, which do not necessarily converge to an optimal solution. They are highly interpretable, accurate and can handle missing values with easy. Moreover, they can be used to estimate those missing values. However, estimation in Bayesian Networks is not trivial, and techniques like D-separation or Markov blankets are needed for this process.

Boosting (Freund & Schapire, 1997; Friedman, 1999) algorithms are a set of machine learning algorithms that work by training *weak classifiers*, such as decision tree, and iteratively train algorithms on the data points in which the decision tree cannot correctly predict the class of the input. *Gradient boosting machines* are one of the most powerful boosting models, and it uses gradient descent for helping the boosting task. This set of algorithms is similar to random forests in their advantages and disadvantages: They are powerful, but they tend to overfit, are slow in inference time, and their results are not interpretable.

K-nearest neighbours is a classification (and regression) method that, given a new data point, predicts its class by finding the K closest points to that point, and finding their most common class. There is no learning phase, which can be beneficial in domains in which datasets change a lot over time, but they are very slow (you need to compare the input point to all the other points in the dataset) in inference time, they are not interpretable, finding the optimal K is usually hard, and its accuracy is usually worse to most other models.

Wrap-Up

Supervised learning provides retail and smart tourism companies with the capability of inferring information about their customers with an unprecedented level of detail and precision. In order to do so, machine learning and data science practitioners need to be careful in the way they obtain, process and use their data, so as to make the most value out of it. Several algorithms have been compared, most of which are the basis of many machine learning projects. Nevertheless, this is an active line of research, so it is likely that more models, training algorithms and datasets will be available in the future.

Unsupervised Learning for User Segmentation

Unsupervised learning is the field in machine learning which is concerned on the discovery of patterns from unlabelled data. Unlike in supervised learning, the goal is not to learn a function that maps from one known domain to another known domain, instead it is to find internal structures in the data that allows to represent the data more densely or more compactly. Among the typical algorithms that are belong in unsupervised learning, autoencoders, clustering algorithms and dimensionality reduction methods stand out as the most widely used.

User segmentation is a process which has the goal of building groups or segments of users that are similar to each other and different to the users which belong to the other groups or segments, according to some similarity criteria. A typical use of user segmentation is to create customer segments, which allows the definition of specific marketing campaigns for each segment, thus providing them with more value and a more personalised experience. Even if the best way to create value for each customer would be to personalize campaigns individually for each user, this can be costly and difficult to automate. Customer segmentation provides a middle ground between treating the whole customer population homogenously and assuming the cost of extremely individualised marketing campaigns. This process was traditionally hand-crafted, with experts manually defining both the customer segments and the marketing campaigns that those segments were going to receive. This is a risky endeavour, as it is possible that experts in retail companies do not fully understand their customers or they introduce their own biases into the segmentation process.

A family of unsupervised learning algorithms, known as clustering algorithms, can be used for the automatic discovery of such segments, by analysing the past behaviour of the customers. This has several advantages over hand-crafting the definition of the segments. Besides the fact that machine learning methods are unbiased (the biases they reflect are contained on the data or they were manually introduced by the machine learning practitioners, but not on the methods themselves), those algorithms typically find more complex patterns than what a typical customer segmentation would use. This allows the discovery of fine-grained groups of customers with very specific behaviours. Clustering algorithms provide the opportunity of automating this task, but the variety of available methods can make it hard to choose an optimal method for solving this task.

In this section of the chapter, we will briefly introduce the clustering algorithms that we find to be the most suitable for customer segmentation in the retail and smart tourism fields. The decision between which of those algorithms are most suitable for a task depends on the goal of the task, the amount and characteristics of the data that is available and other requirements, like visualization capabilities or interpretability. An important decision to make when using a clustering algorithm is the distance metric, which is equivalent to the loss function in supervised learning: It is used to measure how much one customer behaves like another customer. Amongst those metrics, we find the Euclidean distances (L norms) and non-euclidean distances (Hamming, Gaussian, cosine similarty, Jaccard, edit distance, etc.) (Commons, 2016). Please use the references for details on those distances. It is worth noting that most of the data pre-processing methods that were mentioned in the supervised learning part of this chapter should also be used before applying any clustering algorithm. We will assume that each customer will only be placed in one group of customers (clusters are separate of each other).

Clustering Algorithms

The *expectation-maximization* algorithm (E-M) is a optimization algorithm which is used to find maximum-a-posteriori parameter estimators in machine learning models which depend on unobservable latent variables. The algorithm alternates two phases: One *expectation* step, which computes the likelihood of the data given the estimated parameters, and a *maximization*, which re-estimates the parameters given the computed likelihood. If those two steps are computed interatively enough times, the algorithm typically converges to a local minimum, as there are typically many possible solutions to this task. In clustering, this algorithm is used to find the centers of clusters (groups of points) and the size of the cluster (typically measured in standard deviations). E-M is used for many tasks, including parameter estimation in Hidden Markov Models, but they can be used for clustering by using E-M to fit a Gaussian Mixture Model, which is a cluster analysis method that assumes that each cluster can be represented using a multivariate Gaussian (A.Bilmes, 1998; Choung B Do, 2008; Lab, 2015). The advantages of this method over other clustering algorithm include that the assignation of individuals to one cluster is probabilistic, so it provides an uncertainty measurement which is useful in many domains; and it generalizes to many different clustering requirements: It is possible to assume different characteristics for the clusters (e.g. gaussian or non-gaussian shape) and the algorithm will work. Nevertheless, E-M rarely converges to the global minimum, it is highly dependent on the parameter initialization and can be slow to train. Besides, it is necessary to indicate the number of clusters (or customer segments) that the algorithm needs to find.

K-means is a clustering algorithm which implicitly uses E-M as its optimization procedure. It groups the data into K clusters, based on some similarity criteria. Given an initialization of the cluster center, the algorithm assigns to each cluster those points that are closer to that cluster than to any other cluster. Then, the center of each cluster is re-computed so that it becomes the center of the data points that were assigned to it in the previous step. Those two steps are computed until a convergence criteria is met. K-means is a widely used algorithm due to its simplicity and because it typically converges faster than other clustering methods, but it has several disadvantages. Most notably, you need to specify the value of K (which in some sense introduces biases to the algorithm), the result highly depends on the initialization of the cluster centers, and it is not possible to provide a probabilistic assignment of customer over clusters. Nevertheless, several improvements have been proposed to alleviate some of those issues ((MathWorks), 2008; Arthur, 2007; Bin Mohamad & Usman, 2013; Towers, 2013). We believe that K-means is a good baseline upon which to build more sophisticated customer segmentations. Its results can be visualized using Voronoi diagrams (Riddhiman, 2016).

Self-organising maps (SOM) are a set of unsupervised learning algorithms loosely based on artificial neural networks(Burguillo, 2013; MathWorks, n.d.; Rey-López, Barragáns-Martínez, Peleteiro, Mikic-Fonte, & Burguillo, 2011). They were designed for finding a denser representation of the input data, in a similar way to what auto-encoders typically do. They can be used for finding customer segments, as they can be used seamlessly for clustering. Unlike in many other clustering methods, the resulting clusters have a neighbourhood property (there is a pre-defined notion of distance between clusters), and the clusters are organized automatically in a map of clusters, hence the name. Thus, despite the fact that it is necessary that we pre-define the number of clusters, those clusters can be further grouped together if we find the results to be too fine-grained. We believe that this family of algorithm provide an advantageous balance of cluster quality, interpretability and other desirable properties for customer segmentation. Their results can be visualized easily by means of the Unified Distance Matrix (Binwu Wang Danfeng Sun, 2014; Rodriguez-Pardo, Patricio, Berlanga, & Molina, 2017) However, they are typically slow to train, and they typically get stuck in a local minimum, as is usual in algorithms that are trained using gradient descent.

Density-based spatial clustering of applications with noise (DBSCAN) is a clustering algorithm which bases its similarity criteria in a density estimation. More precisely, it finds an indefinite number of clusters by grouping together points that are close to each other. This allows the discovery of clusters with complex shapes, which is a significant advantage over simpler clustering methods such as K-means, which can only find circular-shaped clusters. They can also be used for the discovery of outlier points. However, they can be slow and are very sensitive to hyperparameter specification (Martin Ester Jörg Sander, Xiaowei Xu, 1996).

Ordering points to identify the clustering structure (OPTICS) is another density-based algorithm that solves one of the main problems of DBSCAN, as it can find clusters with different densities. It uses hierarchical clustering for grouping points together. Despite this improvement, they suffer from most of the other disadvantages of DBSCAN, most notably the sensitivity to hyperparameter specification. Its results can be visualized using a reachability plot (Ankerst, Breunig, Kriegel, & Sander, 1999; Boe-Hansen, Berg, Amigo, & Babamoradi, 2015).

Hierarchical clustering is a clustering methods that groups points together into a hierarchy of clusters. This can be done in two ways: a divisive clustering, which starts with only one clusters and separates the clusters in a binary fashion, or agglomerative clustering (the most typical), which groups the two most similar points or clusters together until all points have been assigned to a cluster. The main advantages of this family of clustering algorithms is that there is no need for pre-defining the number of clusters, and their results are highly interpretable as they can be visualized using a *dendrogram*. However, they are very slow to train and do not scale well when the number of data points increase. (Dzobo, Alvehag, Gaunt, & Herman, 2014; Galili, 2015; Y.-S. Lee & Cho, 2011; Mathworks, n.d.; Schonlau, 2002; Vande-kerckhove, Tuerlinckx, & Lee, 2011). This method can be extended in many ways, including Ward's method (Minnesota, n.d.; Mojena, 2004; Mojena, Mojena, & Richard, 2006).

It can be burdensome to evaluate the quality of the clustering performed by the aforementioned algorithms. Unlike in supervised learning, where there are objective quality metrics that can be used to compare the results of the algorithms, in unsupervised learning those metrics do not exist to the same extent. However, there are some ways to empirically measure some desireable properties of the clusters, including the average and minimal distance between clusters, their densities, similarities, entropy, etc. (Hennig, 2013). Those results can also be analysed by domain experts (eg: What is the average age in this customer segment? What is the behaviour of this segment? Is it different to the other segments in a meaningful way?).

Wrap-Up

Unsupervised learning provides retail and smart tourism companies with the capability of automating segmenting their customers in meaningful ways. In this section we have summarised some of the state of the art algorithms that we find most suitable for this task, and briefly discussed ways of comparing the results of those algorithms.

Context-Aware Recommender Systems

Recommender Systems: Main Approaches and Their Capabilities

Recommender systems (RS) are filtering systems that are used to provide users with recommendations about items or products they have not seen, rated, or purchased yet. They gained popularity in the scientific literature in the 1990s (Schafer, Konstan, & Riedi, 1999), due to the growth of online stores, which led to an exponential increment in the amount of information that can be obtained about the preferences of users. Those circumstances created the necessary conditions for the boom in recommender systems. RS typically work by estimating how each user will rate (e.g., how much they will like) a specific item or product by analysing how they have rated similar products, using some similarity metric.

Accordingly, one of the most important decisions to make when designing a recommender system is how to represent how much a user liked an item(Bobadilla, Ortega, Hernando, & Gutiérrez, 2013; Ricci, Rokach, & Shapira, 2011). Traditionally, this is done by assigning a numeric value to those preferences. This is advantageous because numeric values are easy to work with by computers, users can easily and rapidly provide them, and they simple to store in structured databases, as opposed to more complex representations, such as user-written reviews, which require the use of complex natural language processing algorithms. Those numeric values that represent preferences of users can be obtained implicitly (eg., a user has watched a movie, listened to a song, bought a product), or explicitly (by asking the users to provide a numeric value to the product or item). Both methods have their advantages. Implicit methods are less invasive and require less user interaction, which is important for some user experiences, whereas explicit methods are more descriptive, and the users are provided with more control on the products they are recommender with. Regardless on the method, by using a numeric representation on those preferences, it is possible to predict the rating that users will give to products they do not know, by analysing how they rated similar products (the notion of similarity in recommender systems is one of their defining factors).

Recommender systems are typically classified into three groups in the scientific literature, depending on the information they use to model user preferences (Bobadilla et al., 2013; Isinkaye, Folajimi, & Ojokoh, 2015; Ricci et al., 2011). The way in which that information is beyond the introductory nature of this chapter, but many useful resources can be found in the references provided. Context-aware recommender systems are an extension of baseline recommender systems. Therefore, a brief overview of recommender systems is provided so that context-awareness can be easily understood in the context of providing users with recommendations.

Collaborative Filtering

Collaborative filtering recommender systems model user preferences over unseen products by assuming that, if one user has rated a set of items in a certain way, it is likely that they will rate unseen products similarly to how other users, who rated the first set of items in the same way, rated that product. This type of recommender system assumes that users that behaved similarly in the past will also behave similarly in the future (Ekstrand, Riedl, & Konstan, 2011; Isinkaye et al., 2015; Li, Lu, & Xuefeng, 2005; Schafer, Frankowski, Herlocker, & Sen, 2007; Schafer et al., 1999; C. Wang & Blei, 2011). Therefore, they do not use characteristics of the products themselves. Collaborative filtering has several advantages over other approaches. Most notably, they can provide more precise recommendations, over a greater variety of products, because it can find patterns that are more complex and meaningful than what other methods can handle, given enough data. They do not rely on descriptions of products, which could be used for finding characteristics that explain user preferences but can be hard to analyse robustly, and, most importantly, they do not assume that users are independent of each other. Most of those reasons explain why collaborative filtering is the basis of some of the most successful recommender systems. Nevertheless, they come with some problems. Most notably, they suffer from a problem known as cold start, which happens when not enough data has been gathered on the preferences of users, so recommendations that the system provides the users with are not accurate. Collaborative filtering works best when there are many users in the systems, which are actively rating products.

There are three common ways of implementing collaborative filtering in recommender systems. Traditionally, memory-based collaborative filtering (Baltrunas & Ricci, 2014; Kim, Lee, & Chung, 2014; J. Lee, Sun, & Lebanon, 2012; Su & Khoshgoftaar, 2009) has been the most used method. This method stores a matrix of (users, products, ratings), and then compute a similarity metric that finds, for a given user, the most similar users to them in the database (in the way they rated products in the past) and recommends products by weighting the preferences of users by that similarity metric, most typically the cosine similarity or statistical correlation. This approach has been substituted lately by model-based collaborative filtering (Breese, Heckerman, & Kadie, 1998; Chen, Liu, Huang, & Sun, 2010; Goldberg, Roeder, Gupta, & Perkins, 2001; Karatzoglou, Amatriain, Baltrunas, & Oliver, 2010; Koren & Yehuda, 2008; Lam, Vu, Le, & Duong, 2008; Rendle, n.d.; Roffo & Ing-Inf05, 2017; Schafer et al., 2007; Su & Khoshgoftaar, 2009; H. Wang, Wang, & Yeung, 2015; Yao et al., 2015), which uses complex machine learning algorithms for learning user preferences. Instead of using the raw aforementioned matrix, they learn a model from that matrix, with the goal of learning a denser representation of the preferences of users. This can be done in an unsupervised way (by using dimensionality reduction algorithms, such as singular value decomposition) or in a supervised way (most typically using Factorization Machines, Bayesian Networks, Artificial Neural Networks or decision trees). Finally, those approaches can be combined, in what is called hybrid collaborative filtering.

Content-Based Recommender Systems

Another group that is commonly studied in the literature is known as content-based recommender systems, which goes in the opposite direction to collaborative filtering. They assume that all the information that explains user preferences is contained on the descriptions of each product. Therefore, they define each product using a set of descriptors (e.g. price, name, categories, brand, color, latent spaces of neural networks, etc.), that can be used to extract the properties that are important for each user. They assume that if a user tends to like products with a particular property, they will like unseen products with that same property(Felfernig, Friedrich, Jannach, & Zanker, 2006; Lops, de Gemmis, & Semeraro, 2011; Martínez, Barranco, Pérez, & Espinilla, 2008). Content-based recommender systems are able to adapt dynamically to changes of the preferences of users and they are not as adversely affected by the cold start problem (Lam et al., 2008). Therefore, they are ideal for domains in which preferences change rapidly and there are not many users in the database that could be used to find patterns with. The success of those systems depends on the quality and quantity of the available descriptors, and how much the user interacts with the system. Despite their advantages, they show problems that can make them unsuitable for many domains. Most notably, they do not exploit inter-user similarity, the recommendations they provide their users with are typically very similar to what they have rated before (Isinkaye et al., 2015), each user must be modelled individually, which can be computationally costly, and, in general, the recommendations are not as accurate as what collaborative filtering is capable of.

Learning user preferences in content-based recommender systems can be modelled as a supervised learning problem, in which we are given a set of tuples (item descriptors, user rating), and we want to learn, from data, a function that maps the item descriptors to the user ratings, with the goal of generalizing to unseen products. As the domains in which content-based recommender systems are implemented are usually not populated with a great amount of data, learning in those systems is a typical few-shot supervised learning problem. Therefore, simpler learning algorithms, such as Naïve Bayes, Logistic Regression, Linear Discriminant Analysis or Support Vector Machines (Lops et al., 2011), are more popular in content-based recommender systems than more complex algorithms, such as neural networks or boosting methods. Moreover, simpler methods are faster to train and less memory-heavy, which is beneficial as one model is needed for each user in the system.

Hybrid Recommender Systems

The third group in our list is known as hybrid systems(Chen et al., 2010; Li et al., 2005; Su & Khoshgoftaar, 2009), which combine different sources of information to model user preferences. Usually, they combine collaboratively-sourced preferences with item descriptors, by weighting the predictions of collaborative filtering and content-based methods. They can also benefit from other data, such as user profiling (gender, age, nationality, etc.). A common way of implementing hybrid systems is having two independent models, a content-based system and a collaborative filtering system, and combine their predictions using a model on top on both. This model can be simple (averaging both predictions) or more complex (by training a learning model that learns to weight both predictions together).

Challenges and Future Trends

Despite the capabilities of the aforementioned models, which have shown success in different domains, there are challenges that neither approach have been able to fully address. Data sparsity and scalability concerns have been partially resolved by model-based recommender systems, which apply dimensionality reduction or machine learning methods to obtain a smaller representation of the preferences of the user without losing accuracy. The cold start problem in collaborative filtering systems has not been solved, which can create extremely inaccurate predictions. This is a problem for the user experience, and ultimately can be detrimental for obtaining new users or keeping current customers.

Hybrid recommender systems have the potential to solve the problems that content-based and collaborative filtering systems individually pose, but they come with a cost. One of the motivations behind using collaborative filtering is that defining the set of descriptors for each product is costly and can reduce the dynamism of the system because it can increase the time it takes to include a new product in the system. Nevertheless, for some domains, it is possible to automatically define this set of descriptors, by means of using natural language processing or by using a machine learning system to do this task (for example using an autoencoder to find a dense numeric representation of the product). In the future, we can expect that the use of new deep learning approaches can significantly increase the accuracy of the models, and better data storage systems and sources of information will enrich those systems.

Nonetheless, one of the challenges the recommender systems literature has not been able to fully solve is how to include dynamic, time-dependent, information that can influence the preferences of users. User preferences may change significantly in short periods of times, in different ways and time windows for each user. Failing to include those patterns in recommender systems will diminish their quality and will create less value for customer and revenue for companies. Context-aware recommender systems are a first approximation to tackling this problem.

Evaluating Recommender Systems

The way in which recommender systems are evaluated is typically related with the accuracy of the predictions they perform. Simply put, we compare the real ratings users give to products with the predicted ratings, using a similarity metric like the mean squared error, correlation or cross-entropy. This is advantageous in scientific terms, as learning can be done over those metrics via differentiation, and those metrics are widely used in many scientific domains. Nevertheless, there is some controversy on the use of those metrics, because they do not consider the value created for the user or the revenue created for the company that owns the recommender system (e.g. the system could be recommending products that the user likes but that do not provide a lot of revenue due to their price or financial or operating reasons).

Regardless of this controversy, there are empirical studies that provide insights onto which of the many available recommender systems is most beneficial for a particular domain (Baltrunas & Ricci, 2014; Hu, Koren, & Volinsky, n.d.; Isinkaye et al., 2015; J. Lee et al., 2012; Lombardi, Anand, & Gorgoglione, 2009; Pu, Chen, & Hu, 2012; Tamine-Lechani, Boughanem, & Daoud, 2010). From them, several interesting conclusions can be extracted. For instance, recommender systems that use matrix factorization or machine learning consistently obtain the best accuracies. Among them, singular value decomposition, probabilistic factorization machines and non-parametric principal component analysis stand out due to their balance of simplicity, lack of computational cost and accuracy. Other methods, such as memory-based collaborative filtering, provide less accurate predictions but their results are more easily interpretable.

As in many other problems in machine learning and data analysis, one of the deciding factors of the success of an automatic decision-making system is the amount of data that is available for learning patterns that can be used to make decisions. In the context of recommender systems, this is measured using the density of the ratings matrix (Panniello, Tuzhilin, Gorgoglione, Palmisano, & Pedone, 2009). For a fixed number of users and items in the database, this density increases when users provide more ratings, thus reducing the uncertainty of their preferences. The denser this matrix is, the more patterns can be learned, and the recommendations will be more accurate.

Context-Aware Recommender Systems

The widely-spread availability and popularity of portable electronic devices, such as smartphones or wearables, along with the development of algorithms capable of finding complex patterns on vast amounts of data has made it possible to estimate contextual information that can be used to feed recommender systems with additional data that they can use to improve their estimations.

Contextual information in recommender systems is information that can be used to understand the environment surrounding the user, which may influence the way they perceive the world, and therefore has an influence on their preferences (Dey, 2001). Contextual information is by nature dynamic and time-dependent. Therefore, the context in recommender systems is the set of items that can temporarily change the preferences of a user towards a set of items. Users may have different preferences depending on their location, the weather in that location, the time of the day, the activity there are doing, etc. Incorporating those variables in our predictive systems creates the opportunity of providing more value to the user, in unprecedented ways. Smartphones and wearables can be used to know the location of one user at any given time. This can be matched with external APIs to know the weather surrounding them, estimating the activity they are doing, knowing the amount of people in that same location, etc. Moreover, most smartphones provide activity recognition (the user is walking, running, in a bus, standing still, etc.) using data from the sensors they incorporate. It is likely, for instance, that users that are users that are running in the countryside have different preferences to users that are sitting on a restaurant in the city centre.

While in baseline recommender systems the basic database entry was <user, item, rating>, including contextual information adds another field to describe each rating, which becomes <user, **context**, item, rating>. This context is defined as a vector of smaller contextual variables. For example, weather, location, activity and time of the day. The more descriptive the representation of the context is, the bigger this vector will become, which can be problematic in terms of data sparsity. Simply put, if we are too granular when representing the context, we may not have enough observations for each possible <user, **context**, item, rating> tuples, which will make the recognition of patterns more difficult (Karatzoglou et al., 2010). Manually defining the granularity of the description of the contextual information can be cumbersome, which is why the typical approach is to store contextual information in the most granular way that is possible given the technology, and then reduce this granularity using a dimensionality reduction technique. For instance, the model will receive a contextual vector that represents 20 different contextual variables, and using principal component analysis or a wrapper method, the model will reduce those 20 variables to only 2 variables that represent the maximal amount of information. Nevertheless, the way in which contextual information is represented is an increasingly studied topic in the literature, so we may see changes to this approach in the future.

The goal of any context-aware recommender system is to find a function that maps the context, the user and the item to a numeric rating. The way in which context is included in the recommender system is not a fully solved problem and several approaches have been proposed in the literature. Three main approaches can be highlighted.

Pre-Filtering Context-Aware Recommender Systems

Pre-filtering context-aware recommender systems utilize a two-phased algorithm to predict ratings. As their name suggests, the first step when predicting new ratings is to filter the data that is relevant for the given context (G. Adomavicius & Tuzhilin, 2005; Gediminas Adomavicius, Sankaranarayanan, Sen, &

Tuzhilin, 2005; Gediminas Adomavicius & Tuzhilin, 2015). Then, that data is fed to a typical recommender system and the prediction is done without taking context into consideration anymore. In other terms, contextual information is used to take into account only the ratings that were done in a similar context. Then, those ratings are used by a typical collaborative filtering or content-based system for predicting the ratings over new items.

Pre-filtering systems have several advantages over other approaches. First, there is no need to pre-define the granularity of the contextual information. When predicting a new rating, it is possible to provide the model with different levels of granularity(Lombardi et al., 2009; Zheng, Burke, & Mobasher, 2012), so that it takes into account more samples or, so the context is more similar to the input context. This creates the possibility of being adaptive to the number of samples for a given context and creates flexibility for both users and the designers of the recommender system. Additionally, this approach completely separates the recommender system from its context-awareness part, which is beneficial in terms of modularity. As such, you can optimize the recommender system by itself, without considering the context, and vice-versa.

Nevertheless, those advantages can be outweighed by its limitations. When filtering ratings, it is possible to filter too many samples in the database, thus limiting the number and complexity of patterns found by the recommender system. It is hard to balance the descriptiveness of the context and having a sufficient number of samples for the recommender system to work with. Moreover, as each new query to the system is made with different data, model-based recommender systems are harder to train, as you either need a big number of models per user and context, or you need to train a new model in every query, which can take time and the output of the query could be obtained after the users' context has changed and therefore the query is no longer useful.

Post-Filtering Context-Aware Recommender Systems

Oppositely, post-filtering systems revert the two phases described in the pre-filtering section of this chapter. Here, in the first phase, all ratings are considered, ignoring the context in which those ratings were created, as in any other recommender system. This allows the system to use the maximal amount of data as possible and alleviates some of the problems that were mentioned in the pre-filtering section.

Then, we obtain an estimated rating for all the items the user has never seen before. For this set of items, a filtering is done to discard those that do not make sense due to the context of the user. There are two ways in which this can be done. First, one can eliminate the items that the user may like but in a completely different context, or the system can learn to modify those predicted ratings so as to consider the contextual information.

As in pre-filtering, one disadvantage is that is hard to balance the filtering of the contextual information and the quality of the predictions. In this case, it can be difficult not to discard too many or too little items for recommendations, or to overfit or underfit the filtered estimations. It is computationally more costly than pre-filtering, as all ratings are taken into account by the learning system, but its predictions can be more accurate. There is no consensus on the literature onto which of those two approaches is better (Panniello et al., 2009; White, Bailey, & Chen, 2009), and it has been proven that both can be better than the other, depending on the goals of the system, its domain, the amount of data available or how much interpretability we want to impose on the predictions of the system.

Model-Based Context-Aware Recommender Systems

Despite the simplicity of pre and post-filtering systems in the domain of context-aware recommender systems, those approaches have been recently substituted by model-based systems (Gediminas Adomavicius et al., 2005; Gediminas Adomavicius & Tuzhilin, 2015; Gavalas, Konstantopoulos, Mastakas, & Pantziou, 2014; Karatzoglou et al., 2010; Kim et al., 2014; J. Lee et al., 2012; Lombardi et al., 2009; Millard, De Roure, & Shadbolt, 2005; Tamine-Lechani et al., 2010; White et al., 2009; Yao et al., 2015; Zheng et al., 2012), which can learn more complex relationships between user preferences and contextual information. In model-based systems, there is no separation between the phase of rating predictions and the phase of including contextual information in the model. As such, the context is considered as just another variable for the model to learn with.

Due to the data sparsity that is typical in these systems, the most popular approaches have used matrix factorization algorithms, which can dramatically reduce the dimensions of the ratings tensor, making the whole system computationally and memory efficient than filtering algorithms whilst returning more accurate predictions and making use of all the available data. We can expect the popularization of model-based systems in this domain, despite their lack of interpretability.

FUTURE RESEARCH DIRECTIONS

There are other techniques in artificial intelligence that have a potential applicability into retail and smart tourism applications. Recently, generative models and new types of autoencoders (most notably variational autoencoders) have been proven to be effective for different generative tasks and latent space interpolation. Those models could be used in different tasks for retail and smart tourism. For example, for generating *synthetic* customers that are plausible, which could be useful for simulations, or for improving datasets by generating more data that can be used to train machine learning models.

Additionally, recent advancements in natural language processing and computer vision create the opportunity of understanding more about customers and tourists. For example, by analysing the images posted in social media, or by reading the reviews of products written by them, it should be possible to better understand their context and their preferences.

Besides, it is likely that more sensors will be incorporated into handheld devices, which opens the opportunity of having richer contextual information. The way in which the data obtained by those sensors can be transformed into valuable information to be used by context-aware recommender systems is unknown and an interesting research question.

CONCLUSION

In this chapter, we have provided an introductory overview on the capabilities of machine learning in the smart tourism and retail domains. More precisely, we have explained the usage of supervised, unsupervised and recommender systems with a focus on the algorithms that we believe to be most useful for those domains. We have ordered the sections in the chapter with the purpose of providing a logical and coherent view over the capabilities of those fields into the retail and smart tourism domains. In particular, we believe that supervised learning can be of a great use towards building smart systems that can learn from data. The result of supervised learning can be applied as input to unsupervised learning methods in a more seamless way than in the inverse of this process. Conversely, by applying supervised and unsupervised learning to understand users or customers, it is possible to feed recommender systems with data that can be used to understand customers' preferences over items more precisely. In sum, this chapter provides a brief overview on the basic machine learning models that are the most useful for the domains we wanted to focus on.

In the future, when better algorithms, more data, better hardware and software is available, it is likely that we see a more widespread use of those techniques. We believe that the interplay between the three kinds of learning mentioned in this chapter will create a significant opportunity for creating value for customers, revenue for companies and other interests that public and private institutions have.

REFERENCES

Adomavicius, G. (2015). Context-Aware Recommender Systems. In Recommender Systems Handbook. Academic Press. doi:10.1007/978-1-4899-7637-6_6

Adomavicius, G., Sankaranarayanan, R., Sen, S., & Tuzhilin, A. (2005). Incorporating contextual information in recommender systems using a multidimensional approach. *ACM Transactions on Information Systems*, 23(1), 103–145. doi:10.1145/1055709.1055714

Adomavicius, G., & Tuzhilin, A. (2005). Toward the next generation of recommender systems: A survey of the state-of-the-art and possible extensions. *IEEE Transactions on Knowledge and Data Engineering*, 17(6), 734–749. doi:10.1109/TKDE.2005.99

Aksoy, S., & Haralick, R. M. (2001). Feature Normalization and Likelihood-based Similarity Measures for Image Retrieval. *Pattern Recognition Letters*, 22(5), 563–582. doi:10.1016/S0167-8655(00)00112-4

Ankerst, M., Breunig, M. M., Kriegel, H.-P., & Sander, J. (1999). OPTICS: Ordering Points To Identify the Clustering Structure. *ACM SIGMOD'99 Int. Conf. on Management of Data*.

Arthur, D. (2007). *k-means++: The Advantages of Careful Seeding*. Academic Press.

Baltrunas, L., & Ricci, F. (2014). Experimental evaluation of context-dependent collaborative filtering using item splitting. *User Modeling and User-Adapted Interaction*, 24(1–2), 7–34. doi:10.100711257-012-9137-9

Barber, D. (2010). *Bayesian Reasoning and Machine Learning*. Academic Press.

Ben Schafer, J., Frankowski, D., Herlocker, J., & Sen, S. (2007). Collaborative Filtering Recommender Systems. In The Adaptive Web (pp. 291–324). Academic Press. doi:10.1007/978-3-540-72079-9_9

Ben Schafer, J., Konstan, J., & Riedi, J. (1999). Recommender systems in e-commerce. *Proceedings of the 1st ACM Conference on Electronic Commerce - EC '99*, 158–166. 10.1145/336992.337035

Bilmes, A. J. (1998). A Gentle Tutorial of the EM Algorithm and its Application to Parameter Estimation for Gaussian Mixture and Hidden Markov Models. International Computer Science Institute, U.C. Berkeley.

Bin Mohamad, I., & Usman, D. (2013). Standarization and Its Effects on K-Means Clustering Algortihm. *Research Journal of Applied Sciences, Engineering and Technology*, *16*(7), 3033–3299.

Binwu Wang Danfeng Sun, H. L. (2014). Social-Ecological Patterns of Soil Heavy Metals Based on a Self-Organizing Map (SOM): A Case Study in Beijing, China. *International Journal of Environmental Research and Public Health*, 3618–3638. PMID:24690947

Bobadilla, J., Ortega, F., Hernando, A., & Gutiérrez, A. (2013). Recommender systems survey. *Knowledge-Based Systems*, *46*, 109–132. doi:10.1016/j.knosys.2013.03.012

Boe-Hansen, G., van den Berg, F. W. J., Amigo, J. M., & Babamoradi, H. (2015). Quality assessment of boar semen by multivariate analysis of flow cytometric data. *Chemometrics and Intelligent Laboratory Systems*, 142.

Breese, J. S., Heckerman, D., & Kadie, C. (1998). Empirical Analysis of Predictive Algorithms for Collaborative Filtering. *UAI'98 Proceedings of the Fourteenth Conference on Uncertainty in Artificial Intelligence*, 43–52.

Burguillo, J. C. (2013). Playing with complexity: From cellular evolutionary algorithms with coalitions to self-organizing maps. *Computers & Mathematics with Applications (Oxford, England)*, 66.

Chawla, N. V. (2005). Data Mining for Imbalanced Datasets: An Overview. *Data Mining and Knowledge Discovery Handbook*, 853–867.

Chawla, N. V., Bowyer, K. W., Hall, L. O., & Kegelmeyer, W. P. (2002). SMOTE: Synthetic minority over-sampling technique. *Journal of Artificial Intelligence Research*, *16*(1), 321–357. doi:10.1613/jair.953

Chen, X., Liu, X., Huang, Z., & Sun, H. (2010). RegionKNN: A Scalable Hybrid Collaborative Filtering Algorithm for Personalized Web Service Recommendation. *2010 IEEE International Conference on Web Services*, 9–16. 10.1109/ICWS.2010.27

Choung, B., & Do, S. B. (2008). What is the expectation maximization algorithm? *Computational Biology*, *26*(8), 897–899. PMID:18688245

Clevert, D.-A., Unterthiner, T., & Hochreiter, S. (2015). Fast and Accurate Deep Network Learning by Exponential Linear Units (ELUs). *ICLR*, *2016*, 1–14. doi:10.3233/978-1-61499-672-9-1760

Commons, A. (2016). *Clustering algorithms and distance measures*. Retrieved from http://commons.apache.org/proper/commons-math/userguide/ml.html

Cuadros, A. J., & Domínguez, V. E. (2014). Customer segmentation model based on value generation for marketing strategies formulation. *Estudios Gerenciales*, *30*(130), 25–30. doi:10.1016/j.estger.2014.02.005

Dey, A. K. (2001). Understanding and using context. *Personal and Ubiquitous Computing*, *5*(1), 4–7. doi:10.1007007790170019

Dougherty, J., Kohavi, R., & Mehran, S. (1995). Supervised and Unsupervised Discretization of Continuous Features. *Machine Learning: Proceedings of the Twelfth International Conference*, 194–202.

Dzobo, O., Alvehag, K., Gaunt, C. T., & Herman, R. (2014). Multi-dimensional customer segmentation model for power system reliability-worth analysis. *International Journal of Electrical Power & Energy Systems*, *62*, 532–539. doi:10.1016/j.ijepes.2014.04.066

Ekstrand, M. D., Riedl, J. T., & Konstan, J. A. (2011). Collaborative Filtering Recommender Systems. *Human-Computer Interaction*, *4*(2), 81–173. doi:10.1561/1100000009

Ester, Sander, & Xu. (1996). A Density-Based Algorithm for Discovering Clusters in Large Spatial Databases with Noise. *KDD: Proceedings / International Conference on Knowledge Discovery & Data Mining. International Conference on Knowledge Discovery & Data Mining*, (96), 227–231.

Felfernig, A., Friedrich, G., Jannach, D., & Zanker, M. (2006). An Integrated Environment for the Development of Knowledge-Based Recommender Applications. *International Journal of Electronic Commerce*, *11*(2), 11–34. doi:10.2753/JEC1086-4415110201

Freund, Y., & Schapire, R. E. (1997). A Decision-Theoretic Generalization of On-Line Learning and an Application to Boosting. *Journal of Computer and System Sciences*, *55*(1), 119–139. doi:10.1006/jcss.1997.1504

Friedman, J. H. (1999). *Greedy Function Aproximation: A Gradient Boosting Machine*. Academic Press.

Friston, K., Mattout, J., Trujillo-Barreto, N., Ashburner, J., & Penny, W. (2007). Variational free energy and the Laplace approximation. *NeuroImage*, *34*(1), 220–234. doi:10.1016/j.neuroimage.2006.08.035 PMID:17055746

Galili, T. (2015). dendextend: An R package for visualizing, adjusting and comparing trees of hierarchical clustering. *Bioinformatics (Oxford, England)*, *22*(31), 3718–3720. doi:10.1093/bioinformatics/btv428 PMID:26209431

Gavalas, D., Konstantopoulos, C., Mastakas, K., & Pantziou, G. (2014). Mobile recommender systems in tourism. *Journal of Network and Computer Applications*, *39*, 319–333. doi:10.1016/j.jnca.2013.04.006

Glorot, X., & Bengio, Y. (2010). Understanding the difficulty of training deep feedforward neural networks. In Y. W. Teh & M. Titterington (Eds.), *Proceedings of the Thirteenth International Conference on Artificial Intelligence and Statistics* (pp. 249–256). Retrieved from http://proceedings.mlr.press/v9/glorot10a.html

Goldberg, K., Roeder, T., Gupta, D., & Perkins, C. (2001). Eigentaste: A Constant Time Collaborative Filtering Algorithm. *Information Retrieval*, *4*(2), 133–151. doi:10.1023/A:1011419012209

Grubbs, F. E. (1950). Sample Criteria For Testing Outlying Observations. *Annals of Mathematical Statistics*, *21*(1), 27–58. doi:10.1214/aoms/1177729885

He, H., & Ma, Y. (2013). *Imbalanced Learning: Foundations, Algorithms and Applications*. Hoboken, NJ: IEEE Press. doi:10.1002/9781118646106

Hegenbart, S. (2015). *Deep Learning with Convolutional Neural Networks*. Academic Press.

Hennig, C. (2013). *Measurement of quality in cluster analysis*. Londres: University College, London.

Ho, T. K. (1998). The Random Subspace Method For Constructing Decision Forests. *IEEE Transactions on Pattern Analysis and Machine Intelligence*, 832–844.

Hu, Y., Koren, Y., & Volinsky, C. (n.d.). *Collaborative Filtering for Implicit Feedback Datasets*. Retrieved from http://yifanhu.net/PUB/cf.pdf

Isinkaye, F. O., Folajimi, Y. O., & Ojokoh, B. A. (2015). Recommendation systems: Principles, methods and evaluation. *Egyptian Informatics Journal*, *16*(3), 261–273. doi:10.1016/j.eij.2015.06.005

Jaderberg, M., Dalibard, V., Osindero, S., Czarnecki, W. M., Donahue, J., & Razavi, A. (2017). Population Based Training of Neural Networks. Academic Press.

Karatzoglou, A., Amatriain, X., Baltrunas, L., & Oliver, N. (2010). Multiverse recommendation: n-dimensional tensor factorization for context-aware collaborative filtering. *Proceedings of the Fourth ACM Conference on Recommender Systems - RecSys '10*, 79. 10.1145/1864708.1864727

Kim, J., Lee, D., & Chung, K.-Y. (2014). Item recommendation based on context-aware model for personalized u-healthcare service. *Multimedia Tools and Applications*, *71*(2), 855–872. doi:10.100711042-011-0920-0

Koren, Y., & Yehuda. (2008). Factorization meets the neighborhood. *Proceeding of the 14th ACM SIGKDD International Conference on Knowledge Discovery and Data Mining - KDD 08*, 426. 10.1145/1401890.1401944

Kotsiantis, S., & Kanellopoulos, D. (2006). Discretization Techniques: A recent survey. *GESTS International Transactions on Computer Science and Engineering*, *32*, 47–58.

Lab, A. T. B. R. S. (2015). *Expectation Maximization On Old Faithful*. Retrieved from https://es.mathworks.com/matlabcentral/fileexchange/49869-expectation-maximization-on-old-faithful

Lam, X. N., Vu, T., Le, T. D., & Duong, A. D. (2008). Addressing cold-start problem in recommendation systems. *Proceedings of the 2nd International Conference on Ubiquitous Information Management and Communication - ICUIMC '08*, 208. 10.1145/1352793.1352837

Lee, J., Sun, M., & Lebanon, G. (2012). *A Comparative Study of Collaborative Filtering Algorithms*. Retrieved from https://arxiv.org/pdf/1205.3193.pdf

Lee, Y.-S., & Cho, S.-B. (2011). Activity Recognition Using Hierarchical Hidden Markov Models on a Smartphone with 3D Accelerometer. *Hybrid Artificial Intelligent Systems*, 460–467. doi:10.1007/978-3-642-21219-2_58

Li, Y., Lu, L., & Xuefeng, L. (2005). A hybrid collaborative filtering method for multiple-interests and multiple-content recommendation in E-Commerce. *Expert Systems with Applications*, *28*(1), 67–77. doi:10.1016/j.eswa.2004.08.013

Liu, Y., Zhang, Y.-M., Zhang, X.-Y., & Liu, C.-L. (2016). Adaptive spatial pooling for image classification. *Pattern Recognition*, *55*(C), 58–67. doi:10.1016/j.patcog.2016.01.030

Lombardi, S., Anand, S., & Gorgoglione, M. (2009). Context and Customer Behavior in Recommendation. *Work*. Retrieved from http://ids.csom.umn.edu/faculty/gedas/cars2009/LombardiEtAl-cars2009.pdf

Lops, P., de Gemmis, M., & Semeraro, G. (2011). Content-based Recommender Systems: State of the Art and Trends. In Recommender Systems Handbook (pp. 73–105). Academic Press. doi:10.1007/978-0-387-85820-3_3

Martínez, L., Barranco, M. J., Pérez, L. G., & Espinilla, M. (2008). A Knowledge Based Recommender System with Multigranular Linguistic Information. *International Journal of Computational Intelligence Systems*, *1*(3), 225–236. doi:10.1080/18756891.2008.9727620

MathWorks. (n.d.). *Cluster with Self-Organizing Map Neural Network*. Retrieved from https://es.mathworks.com/help/nnet/ug/cluster-with-self-organizing-map-neural-network.html

MathWorks. (2008). *Efficient K-Means Clustering using JIT*. Retrieved from https://es.mathworks.com/matlabcentral/fileexchange/19344-efficient-k-means-clustering-using-jit

Mathworks. (n.d.). *Dendrogram plot*. Retrieved from https://es.mathworks.com/help/stats/dendrogram.html

Millard, I., De Roure, D., & Shadbolt, N. (2005). *Contextually Aware Information Delivery in Pervasive Computing Environments*. doi:10.1007/11426646_18

Minh Phoung, T., Lin, Z., & Altman, R. B. (2005). Choosing SNPs using feature selection. *Bioinformatics (Oxford, England)*, *1*(1).

Minnesota, U. O. (n.d.). Ward's Method and Centroid methods. In Hierarchical Clustering (pp. 41–48). Academic Press.

MK, A. (2016). *Linear Discriminant Analysis (LDA)*. Retrieved from https://mlalgorithm.wordpress.com/tag/linear-discriminant-analysis/

Mojena, R. (2004). Ward's Clustering Algorithm. Encyclopedia of Statistical Sciences.

Mojena, R. (2006). Ward's Clustering Algorithm. Encyclopedia of Statistical Sciences. doi:10.1002/0471667196.ess2887.pub2

Nefedov, A. (2016). *Support Vector Machines: A Simple Tutorial*. Retrieved from http://svmtutorial.online/

Nielsen, M. (2017). *Deep learning*. Retrieved from http://neuralnetworksanddeeplearning.com/chap6.html

Orlov, A. I. (2011). Mahalanobis distance. *Encyclopedia Of Mathematics*. Retrieved from http://www.encyclopediaofmath.org/index.php?title=Mahalanobis_distance&oldid=17720

Panniello, U., Tuzhilin, A., Gorgoglione, M., Palmisano, C., & Pedone, A. (2009). Experimental comparison of pre- vs. post-filtering approaches in context-aware recommender systems. *Proceedings of the Third ACM Conference on Recommender Systems - RecSys '09*, 265. 10.1145/1639714.1639764

Penny, W. (2012). Bayesian model selection and averaging Bayes rule for models. *SPM for MEG/EEG*. Retrieved from http://www.fil.ion.ucl.ac.uk/spm/course/slides12-meeg/14_MEEG_BMS.pdf

Pu, P., Chen, L., & Hu, R. (2012). Evaluating recommender systems from the user's perspective: Survey of the state of the art. *User Modeling and User-Adapted Interaction*, *22*(4–5), 317–355. doi:10.100711257-011-9115-7

Quinlan, J. R. (1983). Learning Efficient Classification Procedures and Their Application to Chess End Games. In *Symbolic Computation: An Artificial Intelligence Approach* (pp. 463–482). Springer.

R. B., D., & W. J., D. (1951). Simplified Statistics for Small Numbers of Observations. *Analytical Chemistry*, 636–638.

Rendle, S. (n.d.). *Factorization Machines*. Retrieved from https://www.csie.ntu.edu.tw/~b97053/paper/Rendle2010FM.pdf

Rey-López, M., Barragáns-Martínez, A. B., Peleteiro, A., Mikic-Fonte, F. A., & Burguillo, J. C. (2011). moreTourism: Mobile recommendations for tourism. *Digest of Technical Papers - IEEE International Conference on Consumer Electronics*, 347–348. 10.1109/ICCE.2011.5722620

Ricci, F., Rokach, L., & Shapira, B. (2011). Introduction to Recommender Systems Handbook. In Recommender Systems Handbook (pp. 1–35). Academic Press. doi:10.1007/978-0-387-85820-3_1

Riddhiman. (2016). *Voronoi Diagrams in Plotly and R*. Retrieved from http://moderndata.plot.ly/voronoi-diagrams-in-plotly-and-r/

Rodriguez-Pardo, C., Patricio, M. A., Berlanga, A., & Molina, J. M. (2017). Market trends and customer segmentation for data of electronic retail store. Lecture Notes in Computer Science. doi:10.1007/978-3-319-59650-1_44

Roffo, G., & Ing-Inf05, S. S. D. (2017). *Ranking to Learn and Learning to Rank: On the Role of Ranking in Pattern Recognition Applications*. Retrieved from https://arxiv.org/pdf/1706.05933.pdf

Rohrer, B. (2015). Methods for handling missing values. *Cortana Intelligence Gallery*. Retrieved from https://gallery.cortanaintelligence.com/Experiment/Methods-for-handling-missing-values-1

Russell, S., & Norving, P. (2014). *Artificial Intelligence: A modern Approach*. Pearson.

Schonlau, M. (2002). The Clustergram: A graph for visualizing hierarchical and non-hierarchical cluster analysis. *The Stata Journal*, *3*, 316–327.

Su, X., & Khoshgoftaar, T. M. (2009). A Survey of Collaborative Filtering Techniques. *Advances in Artificial Intelligence*, *2009*, 1–19. doi:10.1155/2009/421425

Tamine-Lechani, L., Boughanem, M., & Daoud, M. (2010). Evaluation of contextual information retrieval effectiveness: Overview of issues and research. *Knowledge and Information Systems*, *24*(1), 1–34. doi:10.100710115-009-0231-1

Towers, S. (2013). *K-means clustering*. Retrieved from http://sherrytowers.com/2013/10/24/k-means-clustering/

University, P. S. (2016). *Principal Components Analysis (PCA)*. Retrieved from https://onlinecourses.science.psu.edu/stat857/node/35

Vandekerckhove, J., Tuerlinckx, F., & Lee, M. D. (2011). Hierarchical diffusion models for two-choice response times. *Psychological Methods*, *16*(1), 44–62. doi:10.1037/a0021765 PMID:21299302

Wang, C., & Blei, D. M. (2011). Collaborative topic modeling for recommending scientific articles. *Proceedings of the 17th ACM SIGKDD International Conference on Knowledge Discovery and Data Mining - KDD '11*, 448. 10.1145/2020408.2020480

Wang, H., Wang, N., & Yeung, D.-Y. (2015). Collaborative Deep Learning for Recommender Systems. *Proceedings of the 21th ACM SIGKDD International Conference on Knowledge Discovery and Data Mining - KDD '15*, 1235–1244. 10.1145/2783258.2783273

White, R. W., Bailey, P., & Chen, L. (2009). Predicting user interests from contextual information. *Proceedings of the 32nd International ACM SIGIR Conference on Research and Development in Information Retrieval - SIGIR '09*, 363. 10.1145/1571941.1572005

Yao, L., Sheng, Q. Z., Qin, Y., Wang, X., Shemshadi, A., & He, Q. (2015). Context-aware Point-of-Interest Recommendation Using Tensor Factorization with Social Regularization. *Proceedings of the 38th International ACM SIGIR Conference on Research and Development in Information Retrieval - SIGIR '15*, 1007–1010. 10.1145/2766462.2767794

Zheng, Y., Burke, R., & Mobasher, B. (2012). Differential context relaxation for context-aware travel recommendation. In *Lecture Notes in Business Information Processing* (Vol. 123, pp. 88–99). LNBIP. doi:10.1007/978-3-642-32273-0_8

KEY TERMS AND DEFINITIONS

Context-Aware System: Any system that can make use of contextual information to solve their tasks more efficiently or effectively.

Machine Learning: The field in computer science which is concerned on the development of algorithms that can make computers learn from data.

Recommender Systems: Informatics systems that aim to predict the ratings that users will give to an unseen product or item.

Retail: Economic sector that creates revenue by selling products or services to final customers.

Smart Tourism: The application of communication and computer science methods for the development of tools that are used in tourism.

Supervised Learning: The field in machine learning which is concerned on the development of algorithms that learn functions from labelled data.

Unsupervised Learning: The field in machine learning which is concerned on the development of algorithms that learn functions from unlabeled data.

Chapter 15
Predictive Analysis of Robotic Manipulators Through Inertial Sensors and Pattern Recognition

Jorge Alonso Moro
Universidad Europea de Madrid, Spain

Carlos Quiterio Gómez Muñoz
Universidad Europea de Madrid, Spain

Fausto Pedro García Márquez
ⓘ https://orcid.org/0000-0002-9245-440X
University of Castilla-La Mancha, Spain

ABSTRACT

Industrial robotics is constantly evolving, with installation forecast of about 2 million new robots in 2020. The predictive maintenance focused on industrial robots is beginning to be applied more, but its possibilities have not yet been fully exploited. The present study focuses on the applications offered by inertial sensors in the field of industrial robotics, specifically the possibility of measuring the "real" rotation angle of a robotic arm and comparing it with its own system of measure. The study will focus on the measurement of the backlash existing in the gearbox of the axis of a robot. Data received from the sensor will be analysed using the wavelet transform, and the mechanical state of the system could be determined. The introduction of this sensing system is safe, dynamic, and non-destructive, and it allows one to perform the measurement remotely, in the own installation of the robot and in working conditions. These features allow one to use the device in different predictive functions.

DOI: 10.4018/978-1-7998-0106-1.ch015

INTRODUCTION

Nowadays, the diagnosis of the structural state of the robotic manipulator arms is made in a slightly optimized way, which involves the supervision of an operator of the movement of each axis of the arm. Thus, it is not possible to have a clear measurement of the dysfunction of the robot arm by observing the evolution of the problems during the work of a robotic cell. It must be taken into account that there are mechanical breakdowns, due to backlash in their gearboxes, which involve production stops of around 12 hours. In the case that the spare part is not available in the necessary time, this stop would be extended until the arrival of the replacement. Moreover, the possibility of completely replacing an old robot with a new one involves a great investment and a time of intervention in the production line that would force to stop production during the same.

Currently, preventive and corrective rather than predictive maintenance is performed, replacing the mechanics parts when it reaches its useful life, as suggested by the manufacturer and making preventive ranges of change of greases and oils.

Several studies like Sarkar, Ellis, and Moore (1997), detects mechanical backlash through signal modelling of the torque produced by a motor in a series of gear wheels. This type of case is undesired since the mechanics of the robot itself are usually cycloidal gearboxes. It would be also necessary to take measurements with an external equipment at the ends of each axis of the robot. It is possible to find systems that try to reduce these problems during production, such as the TCP tool calibration. TCP tool is a device in a circular hollow shape, in which the robot tool moves every certain time to determine externally the real position in the space of the robot tool, and it allows to correct the trajectories of the same in dynamic (Cox and Freeman, 2005a). This type of device corrects the possible dispersions that may have during the process, but it will not indicate any information about the mechanical state of the manipulator.

There are patented systems which perform a neural network to determine what type of failure has the robot with the help of several sensors that run through the manipulator and the monitoring of these data (Sjöstrand, Blanc, and Tavallaey, 2010). The analysed parameters are: temperature of the gearboxes, friction of the axis and temperature of the motor, among others (Cox and Freeman, 2005b & Huang, 2017 & Stoica and Moses, 1997 & Vallely and Papaelias, n.d. & Shi et. Al, 2018).

Nowadays, it is possible to find integrated predictive maintenance systems that read different variables of the robot, such as the intensity, voltage and temperature of its motors (Amini, 2016 & Shi, Soua, and Papaelias, 2017 & Muñoz, Jiménez, and Márquez, 2017 & Jiménez et. Al, n.d. & Jiménez et. Al, n.d.). But the analysis of all this data is done externally to the robot, from embedded computers from other manufacturers.

It is necessary to be able to "predict" the behaviour of the mechanics of a robot in order to schedule interventions in them without affecting the other means of production. In addition, it helps the management of maintenance staff, allowing them to plan tasks and minimizing the unexpected of this type of breakdowns (Huang, Papaelias, and Lang, n.d. & Muñoz and Márquez, 2018 & Jiménez, Muñoz, and Márquez, 2018 & Sjöstrand, Blanc, and Tavallaey, 2010). Another advantage of predictive is to optimize the number of spare parts in the warehouse. This stock optimization will prevent the storage of expensive parts that may deteriorate over time.

EXPERIMENTAL SETUP AND CASE STUDY

In order to test the system in real conditions, the same data acquisition system has been installed in two real robots of similar characteristics. One robot was in perfect conditions (No damage or slack in any of its axes), while the other robot had backlash in one of its gearboxes. The type of robot is an ABB IRB 6400 of 1998, with a load capacity of 120 kilograms and a work area of 2.4 meters. The tool we have on its flange is a real production tool, weighing around 50 kilograms and symmetrically. On both robots it has been performed the same tests, which consist of cyclic movements have been programmed independent of axis 2 and later of axis 3 (Figure 1). The movement speed used in the tests has been 1000 millimetres per second.

The data acquisition system consists of a device controlled with Arduino to take angular values of the robotic arm in movement. Through an inertial sensor, it has been taken the inclination value of the robot during the programmed cycles. Figure 2 shows the implementation of the device on the robot at the end of the arm of axis 3.

The data acquisition system for the angular positions is shown in Figure 3. It consists of an Arduino prototyping plate, an MPU-6050 inertial sensor (three accelerometers and three gyroscopes) and a Bluetooth module for wireless serial transmission of data to a computer.

Two independent movements have been programmed in the robot software. The first is a repetitive movement of axis 3 of the robot, from -20 to 50 degrees. The second programmed movement is from axis 2 of the robot, from -20 to 50 degrees. In both programs, it is performed a stop between movements of 0.5 seconds of waiting in order to show better the backlash.

Figure 1. Movement of the robot IRB 6400 (ABB)

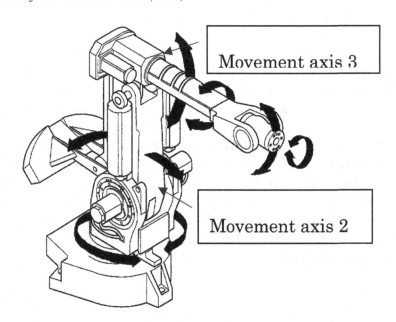

Figure 2. Picture showing position of the angular measuring device on the wrist of the manipulator

Data
Acquisition
System

Results

It is possible to observe in Figure 4 the mechanical backlash effect in the defective robot through the angular position of the device. The graph shows the higher oscillations in the robot's waiting points, indicating the backlash present in the gearbox of the rotor.

It has been analysed the results obtained on the defective robot. It shows how in the programmed movements the pattern of the described trajectory is repeated when the backlash manifests itself. It has been carried out the study on 5000 samples of the angular position taken every 10 milliseconds. Figure

Figure 3. Detail of the angular measuring device

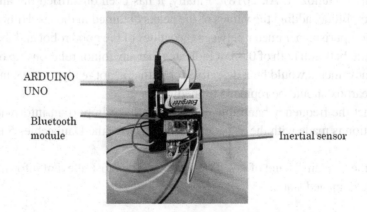

ARDUINO
UNO

Bluetooth
module

Inertial sensor

Figure 4. Comparison of the movement captured by the sensor in "healthy state" robot and in "defective" robot

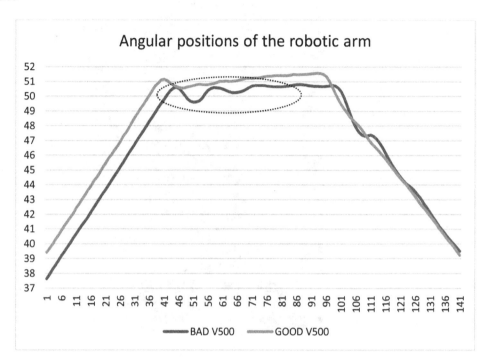

5 shows the signal in which a 15 Hz lowpass filter has been performed in order to remove undesired data like noise.

The following operations have been made to the obtained data. A low lowpass filter of 15 Hz has been performed to remove noise, since the frequencies of the oscillations have a range of 0.5 to 4 Hz ("Signal Processing", 2018). Later a Wavelet Transform has been applied using Daubechies 11 and reaching the level 7. From this last analysis the details at level 3 of Wavelet Transform has been choosen as a most representative information. Then, Hilbert transform has been applied for a better analysis of the "envelope" of the obtained graph and thus be able to compare it better with its equivalent graph of the values obtained from the robot without mechanical problems (Jiménez, Muñoz, and Márquez, 2019 & Jiménez, Gómez, and Márquez 2018 & Jiménez et. Al, 2019 & Papaelias et. Al, 2016 & Gómez Muñoz et. Al, 2017 & Gómez Muñoz et. Al, 2018) . Finally, it has been quantified the amount of frequency changes and their amplitude, adding the values of the peaks obtained in the last Hilbert graph (Figure 6).

This gives us a comparison parameter between the values of the good robot and the bad robot, obtaining a relationship ratio between both of 0.83. It indicates that any minor relationship between robots with the same types of movements would be a defective robot that is not ready to work in a daily production and the defective gearbox should be replaced immediately.

In order to extract the frequency band that contains the most important information for the case of study, a decomposition is made with the Wavelet Transform with the Daubechies 5 family with 5 levels (Figure 7).

Figure 8 shows the "Details" band of level 3. It contains the most relevant information to distinguish the healthy from the damaged state.

Figure 5. Samples taken from the angular position of the defective robot

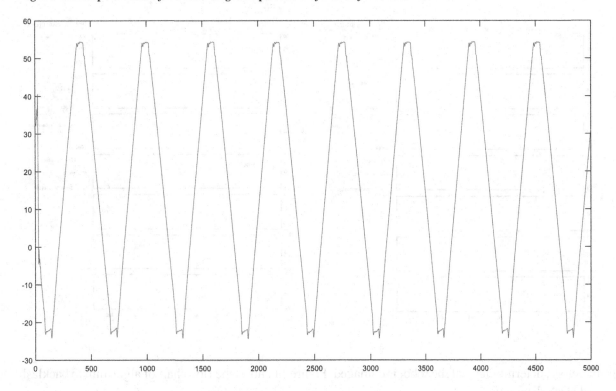

Figure 8Figure 9 shows the detail at level 3 in the Wavelet Transform for the complete wave, where the magnified oscillation of each cycle can be observed. It can be observed the clear pattern of the repetitions of the cycles for a spectrum of the specific frequency selected by the Wavelet analysis ("Wavelet Toolbox", 2002 & Misiti et. Al, 1996 & Gomez et. Al, 2017). This shows how many oscillations the robot has had during its trajectory and how large these have been. In other words, this give information about the severity of the backlash.

Finally, by applying Hilbert Transform the envelope is obtained and it is possible to compare the plot of the obtained graph with some reference samples. In this case, it will be the data obtained from a robot without mechanical problems. Figure 10 shows the differences between both robots.

The blue values correspond to the robot without damage and the red ones to the analyzed data of the robot with damage.

It can be seen that the values of the damaged robot have peaks of greater height and width. This is due to the greater oscillation that produces in each movement. By means of a peak detection algorithm and the sum of the maximum values, it can be detected when a "healthy" threshold is exceeded and

Figure 6. Flowchart of signal processing

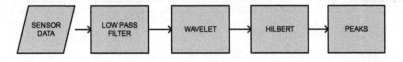

Figure 7. Wavelet decomposition of (a) healthy state of robot arm and (b) damaged state of robot arm

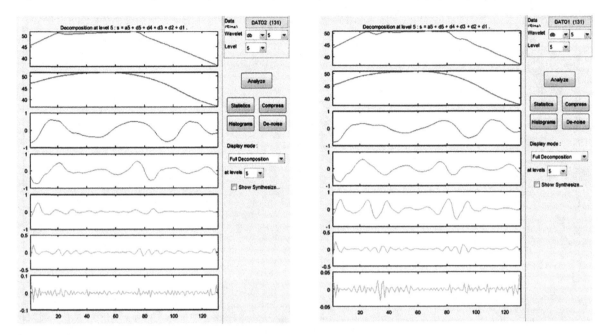

therefore, determining that the robot is damaged. Figure 11 shows the flowchart of algorithm to backlash and slack detection.

CONCLUSION

This work analyses the mechanical state of industrial robots through their "actual" angular positions monitored by inertial sensors. It is useful when the robotic system is not able to check correctly its positions due to a failure in their axis. A condition monitoring system based on an inertial sensor was built to collect the actual angular position of the robotic arm in a wireless and autonomous device.

It was studied the cyclic movement of two robots, one of them damaged and other robot with a "healthy state". A pattern recognition of the movements of both robots was performed to extract the feature characteristics of the damaged movement. The damaged robot presented an underdamped move-

Figure 8. Daubechies 5 wavelet decomposition. Healthy state of robot (a) and damaged state (b)

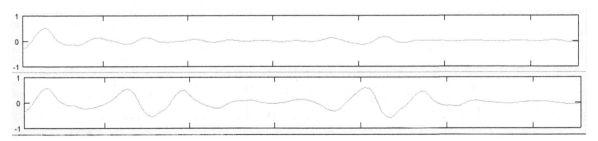

Figure 9. Detailed graph of level 3 of the applied wavelet transform

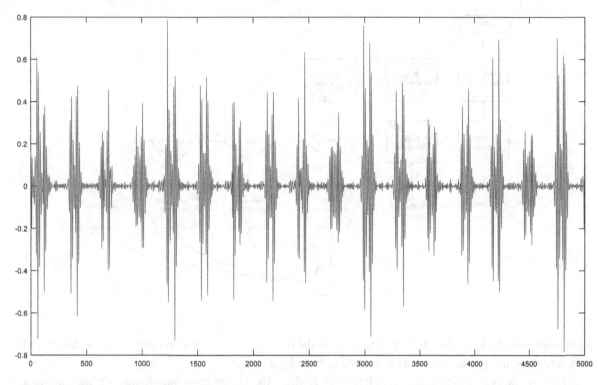

Figure 10. Hilbert transformation and comparison of healthy state data (blue) and damaged state (red)

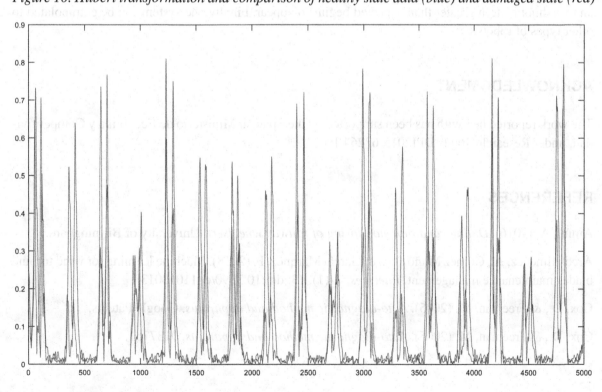

Figure 11. Flowchart of algorithm to backlash and slack detection

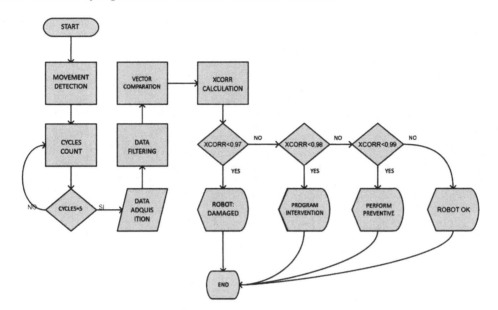

ment when arm brakes. Then it is compared with the obtained values in real time of the healthy robotic arm, and thus, the presence of backlash is determined.

The early detection of this incipient failure may allow the planning of maintenance works and could avoid unnecessary substitutions of parts. It minimizes the investment, since it allows to continue using it even if the working time of the manufacturer has been exceeded. The device generates an alarm when an overshoot pattern greater than expected begins to appear. Finally, the system can be extrapolated to other types of robots.

ACKNOWLEDGMENT

The work reported herewith has been supported by the Spanish Ministerio de Economía y Competitividad, under Research Grants DPI2015-67264-P.

REFERENCES

Amini, A. (2016). *Online condition monitoring of railway wheelsets*. University of Birmingham.

Arcos Jiménez, A., Gómez Muñoz, C., & García Márquez, F. (2018). Machine learning for wind turbine blades maintenance management. *Energies*, *11*(1), 13. doi:10.3390/en11010013

Cox, D., & Freeman, M. (2005). *Auto-diagnostic method and apparatus*. Google Patents.

Cox, D., & Freeman, M. (2005). *Auto-diagnostic method and apparatus*. 0137751.

Gomez, C. Q., Garcia, F. P., Arcos, A., Cheng, L., Kogia, M., & Papelias, M. (2017). Calculus of the defect severity with EMATs by analysing the attenuation curves of the guided waves. *Smart Structures and Systems*, *19*(2), 195–202. doi:10.12989ss.2017.19.2.195

Gómez Muñoz, C. Q., Arcos Jimenez, A., García Marquez, F. P., Kogia, M., Cheng, L., Mohimi, A., & Papaelias, M. (2018). Cracks and welds detection approach in solar receiver tubes employing electromagnetic acoustic transducers. *Structural Health Monitoring*, *17*(5), 1046–1055. doi:10.1177/1475921717734501

Gómez Muñoz, C. Q., García Marquez, F. P., Arcos Jimenez, A., Cheng, L., Kogia, M., & Mayorkinos, P. (2017). Calculus of the defect severity with EMATs by analyzing the attenuation curves of the guided waves. *Smart Structures and Systems*, *19*(2), 195–202. doi:10.12989ss.2017.19.2.195

Huang, Z. (2017). *Integrated railway remote condition monitoring*. University of Birmingham.

Huang, Z., Papaelias, M., & Lang, Z. (n.d.). Wayside detection of axle bearing faults in rolling stock through correlation processing of high-frequency acoustic emission signals. *Proceedings of First World Congress on Condition Monitoring-WCCM*.

Jiménez, A. A., Gómez, C. Q., & Márquez, F. P. G. (2018). Concentrated solar plants management: Big data and neural network. In *Renewable energies* (pp. 63–81). Springer. doi:10.1007/978-3-319-45364-4_5

Jiménez, A. A., Márquez, F. P. G., Moraleda, V. B., & Muñoz, C. Q. G. (2019). Linear and nonlinear features and machine learning for wind turbine blade ice detection and diagnosis. *Renewable Energy*, *132*, 1034–1048. doi:10.1016/j.renene.2018.08.050

Jiménez, A. A., Muñoz, C. Q. G., & Márquez, F. P. G. (2019). Dirt and mud detection and diagnosis on a wind turbine blade employing guided waves and supervised learning classifiers. *Reliability Engineering & System Safety*, *184*, 2–12. doi:10.1016/j.ress.2018.02.013

Jiménez, A. A., Muñoz, C. Q. G., & Márquez, F. P. G. (n.d.). Machine learning and neural network for maintenance management. *Proceedings of International Conference on Management Science and Engineering Management*, 1377-1388. 10.1007/978-3-319-59280-0_115

Jiménez, A. A., Muñoz, C. Q. G., Marquez, F. P. G., & Zhang, L. (n.d.). Artificial Intelligence for Concentrated Solar Plant Maintenance Management. *Proceedings of Proceedings of the Tenth International Conference on Management Science and Engineering Management*, 125-134. 10.1007/978-981-10-1837-4_11

Misiti, M., Misiti, Y., Oppenheim, G., & Poggi, J.-M. (1996). Wavelet toolbox. The MathWorks Inc.

Muñoz, C. Q. G., Jiménez, A. A., & Márquez, F. P. G. (2017). Wavelet transforms and pattern recognition on ultrasonic guides waves for frozen surface state diagnosis. *Renewable Energy*.

Muñoz, C. Q. G., & Márquez, F. P. G. (2018). Future maintenance management in renewable energies. In *Renewable Energies* (pp. 149–159). Springer. doi:10.1007/978-3-319-45364-4_10

Papaelias, M., Cheng, L., Kogia, M., Mohimi, A., Kappatos, V., Selcuk, C., ... Gan, T.-H. (2016). Inspection and structural health monitoring techniques for concentrated solar power plants. *Renewable Energy*, *85*, 1178–1191. doi:10.1016/j.renene.2015.07.090

Sarkar, N., Ellis, R. E., & Moore, T. N. (1997). Backlash detection in geared mechanisms: Modeling, simulation, and experimentation. *Mechanical Systems and Signal Processing, 11*(3), 391–408. doi:10.1006/mssp.1996.0082

Shi, S., Han, Z., Liu, Z., Vallely, P., Soua, S., Kaewunruen, S., & Papaelias, M. (2018). Quantitative monitoring of brittle fatigue crack growth in railway steel using acoustic emission. *Proceedings of the Institution of Mechanical Engineers. Part F, Journal of Rail and Rapid Transit, 232*(4), 1211–1224. doi:10.1177/0954409717711292

Shi, S., Soua, S., & Papaelias, M. (2017). Remote condition monitoring of rails and crossings using acoustic emission. *Proceedings of 2017 NSIRC Annual Conference*.

Signal processing Toolbox, User's Guide. (2018). Natick, MA: The MathWorks, Inc.

Sjöstrand, N., Blanc, D., & Tavallaey, S. (2010). *Method and a control system for monitoring the condition of an industrial robot*. 7,826,984 B2.

Sjöstrand, N., Blanc, D., & Tavallaey, S. S. (2010). *Method and a control system for monitoring the condition of an industrial robot*. Google Patents.

Stoica, P., & Moses, R. L. (1997). Introduction to spectral analysis. Prentice Hall.

Vallely, P., & Papaelias, M. (n.d.). Integrating Remote Condition Monitoring of Railway Infrastructure with High Speed Inspection. *Proceedings of First World Congress on Condition Monitoring-WCCM*.

Wavelet Toolbox. (2002). Natick, MA: The MathWorks, Inc.

Chapter 16
Call Masking:
A Worrisome Trend in Nigeria's Telecommunications Industry

Benjamin Enahoro Assay
https://orcid.org/0000-0002-2850-1718
Delta State Polytechnic, Ogwashi-Uku, Nigeria

ABSTRACT

The phenomenon of call masking and other related infractions have assumed frightening dimension in Nigeria. Apart from depriving the government and telecoms companies of huge revenue, the sharp practices also constitute a security threat to the nation. In a bid to curb the menace, the Nigerian Communications Commission, the industry regulator, had to suspend six interconnect exchange licenses in February 2018 and bar 750,000 lines belonging to 13 operators from the national network suspected to have been involved in the criminal act. However, in spite of the measures taken by NCC, the sharp practices have continued unabated. It is against this backdrop that this chapter proffers solutions and recommends ways to nip the infractions in the bud and save the telecoms industry from imminent collapse.

INTRODUCTION

There is no denying the fact that call masking and refilling, and other related infractions such as SIM Boxing have assumed worrisome dimension in the telecommunications industry in Nigeria. The industry which has posted impressive records in the last few years owing to good regulatory framework and a conducive operating business environment, has come under serious threats of telecoms fraudsters and criminals, who are determined to plunder the gains of the industry for personal interest.

Call masking/refilling is a practice in which callers hide their true numbers when making calls, especially international calls, in order to evade international call rates. A masked call happens when an international call coming into a country is concealed and presented as a local call in order to avoid payment of the correct international termination rate (ITR). For instance, if a number is masked as a lo-

DOI: 10.4018/978-1-7998-0106-1.ch016

cal call, the rogue network operator pays N3.90 Local Termination Rate (LTR) instead of the approved N24.40 ITR (Anuforo, 2018; Adepetun, 2019).

Anuforo (2018) has associated the phenomenon of call masking with the following:

1. It is powered by Voice APIs, a coding platform where a developer can set up phone number proxies to keep parties from knowing each other's phone numbers during a call.
2. It uses a short-lived phone number for each party, for example (5527, 00245). This allows the caller to communicate seamlessly during a specified time period, with no room for the recipient to speak.
3. It is one of the many platforms terrorists use to communicate in an anonymous manner.
4. It is used to disguise as a family, especially for fraudulent motives.
5. It is a method used to evade the international call rates.
6. Call masking amounts to revenue loss for licensed local telecom operators from international calls since they are being disguised as local calls.

SIM Boxing is a process of creating an artificial middle man with a device that alternates call rates. A SIM Box fraud is a practice whereby SIM boxes are installed with multiple prepaid SIM cards. This enables the fraudsters to bring calls through VoIP (through internet) and terminate international calls through local phone numbers in the respective country, just to make it appear as a local call, by initiating the call through local SIM installed in the SIM box.

Syed (2014), avers that the SIM box fraudsters mainly use the prepaid SIM, the ownership and address of which is hard to know whereas post-paid SIM are easily traceable because of address verification at the time of connection. The affected stakeholders are the mobile operators, the legal international carriers, and the government.

According to him, there are two major players involved in this activity: (1) the fraudsters inside the terminating country; and (2) the illegitimate international carriers from across the border. The fraudster could be a SIM box operator, a local loop operator or a national carrier license holder. The SIM box fraudster basically sets up everything-the SIM boxes, the connectivity, the manpower, and fresh suppliers of SIMs. The local loop operators, bringing in illegal traffic, may use their switches in place of a SIM box. This makes it look like a local call using their own numbering series to terminate the traffic onto mobile operators. The national carrier may bring in illegal traffic, change the 'A' number to fake local loop number for each call and terminate the same onto mobile operators on their national trunks instead of international trunks.

The perpetrators of these telecoms infractions have ulterior motives in tampering with international calls and disguising such calls as local calls because of the profit they hope to make from the price differential between international and local call termination rates (Okonji, 2018; Amanze-Nwachukwu, 2018).

This criminal activity according to the Nigerian Communications Commission (NCC), has been going on since September 2016 following the implementation of the N24.40 international termination rate (ITR). However, the effect of the abuse became public after the realization that the industry was losing so much money to the illicit activity of some telecoms operators. Apart from the colossal loss in revenue, these infractions are said to pose security risks to Nigeria. Telecoms industry expert cum Director-General, Delta State Innovation Hub (DSHUB), Chris Uwaje has expressed the fear that call masking could make it impossible to trace calls linked to terrorists groups such as Boko Haram that has been ravaging most parts of northern Nigeria.

In response to the persisting telecoms fraud, Executive vice chairman of NCC, Professor Umar Garba Danbatta said the commission, in collaboration with different stakeholders and security agencies held series of meetings which culminated in the barring of 750,000 numbers assigned to 13 operators from the national network and licensees in February 2018 for their involvement in call masking and refiling.

However, despite the drastic measures taken by NCC, the industry regulator, to stem the menace of call masking/refilling, and SIM boxing, the problem has continued unabated thus posing a major challenge to the industry that has witnessed many giant strides since the advent of the Global System for Mobile Communication (GSM) in 2001, and a major contributor to the nation's Gross Domestic Product.

This chapter thus examines the menace of call masking in Nigeria's telecommunications industry and how to tackle it. The objectives of the chapter are:

1. To point out the dangers call masking/refiling, and SIM boxing pose to the telecommunications industry in Nigeria.
2. To show why call masking and other infractions in Nigeria's telecommunications industry have continued unabated.
3. To highlight the role stakeholders can play in tackling the menace of call masking/refiling, and SIM boxing
4. To recommend ways to curb the menace of call masking and other related infractions in Nigeria's telecommunications industry.

BACKGROUND

Overview of Telecommunication

Telecommunication is the transmission of signs, signals, messages, words, writings, images and sounds of information of any nature by wire, radio, optical or other electromagnetic system (ITU 2012). Telecommunication occurs when the exchange of information between communication participants include the use of technology. It is transmitted through a transmission media, such as over physical media, for example, over electrical cable, or via electromagnetic radiation through space such as radio or light. Such transmission paths are often divided into communication channels which afford the advantages of multiplexing. Since the Latin term communication is considered the social process of information exchange, the term telecommunications is often used in its plural form because it involves many different technologies (Huurdeman, 2003).

Early means of communicating over a distance included visual signals, such as beacons, smoke signals, semaphore telegraphs, signal flags and optical heliographs. Other examples of pre-modern long-distance communication included audio messages such as coded drumbeats, long-blown horns, and loud whistles. 20th and 21st century technologies for long-distance communication usually involve electrical and electromagnetic technologies, such as telegraph, telephone, and teleprinter, networks, radio, microwave transmission, fibre optics, and communications satellites.

A revolution in wireless communication began in the first decade of the 20th century with the pioneering developments in radio communications by Guglielmo Marconi, who won the Nobel prize in Physics in 1909, and other notable pioneering inventors and developers in the field of electrical and electronic telecommunications. These included Charles wheatstone and Samuel Morse (inventors of the telegraph), Alexander Graham Bell (inventor of the telephone), Edwin Armstrong and Lee de Forest (inventors of radio), as well as Vladimir Zworykin, John Logie Baird and Philo Farnsworth (some of the inventors of television)

The word telecommunication is a compound of the Greek prefix tele meaning distant, far off, or afar, and the Latin communicare, meaning to share. Its modern use is adapted from the French because its written use was recorded in 1904 by the French engineer and novelist Edouard Estaunie (Dilhac, 2004; New Oxford American Dictionary, 2005). Communication was first used as an English word in the late 14th century. It comes from old French communication (14c., Modern French communication), from Latin communication em (nominative communication), noun of action from past participle stem of communicate "to share, divide out; communicate, impart, inform; join, unite, participate in," literally "to make common," from communis."

Telegraph and Telephone

On 25 July 1837 the first commercial electrical telegraph was demonstrated by English inventor Sir William Fothergill Cooke, and English Scientist Sir Charles Wheat stone (The Telegraph, 2017). Both inventors viewed their device as "an improvement to existing electromagnetic telegraph" not as a new device (Calvert, 2004).

Samuel Morse independently developed a version of the electrical telegraph that he unsuccessfully demonstrated on 2 September 1837. This code was an important advancement over wheatstone's signaling method. The first transatlantic telegraph cable was successfully completed on 27 July 1866, allowing transatlantic telecommunication for the first time (BernDibner, 1959).

The conventional telephone was invented independently by Alexander Bell and Elisha Gray in 1876 (Electronic Oberlin Group, 2006). Antonio Meucci invented the first device that allowed the electrical transmission of voice over a line in 1849. However, Meucci's device was of little practical value because it relied upon the electronic effect and thus required users to place the receiver in their mouth to hear what was being said. The first commercial telephone services were set-up in 1878 and 1879 on both sides of the Atlantic in the cities of New Haven and London (AT&T, 2006).

Modern Telecommunication

Modern Telecommunication is founded on a series of key concepts that experienced progressive development and transformation over a long period of time. Telecommunication technologies may primarily be divided into wired and wireless methods. Overall though, a basic telecommunication system consists of three main parts that are always present in some form or another:

1. A transmitter that takes information and converts it to a signal.
2. A transmission medium, also called the physical channel that carries the signal. An example of this is the "free space channel".
3. A receiver that takes the signal from the channel and converts it back into usable information for the recipient

For example, in radio broadcasting station the station's large power amplifier is the transmitter; and the broadcasting antenna is the interface between the power amplifier and the "free space channel". The free space channel is the transmission medium; and the receiver's antenna is the interface between the free space channel and the receiver. Next, the radio receiver is the destination of the radio signal, and this is where it is converted from electricity to sound for people to listen to.

Sometimes, telecommunication systems are "duplex" (two-way systems) with a single box of electronics working as both the transmitter and a receiver, or a transceiver. For example, a cellular telephone is a transceiver (Haykin, 2001). The transmission electronics and the receiver electronics within a transceiver are actually quite independent of each other. This can be readily explained by the fact that radio transmitters contain power amplifiers that operate with electrical powers measured in the microwatts or nanowatts. Hence, transceivers have to be carefully designed and built to isolate their high-power circuitry from each other, so as not to cause interference.

Telecommunication over fixed lines is called point-to-point communication because it is between one transmitter and one receiver. Telecommunication through radio broadcasts is called broadcast communication because it is between one powerful transmitter and numerous low-power but sensitive radio receivers (Haykin, 2001).

Telecommunications in which multiple transmitters and multiple receivers have designed to cooperate and to share the same physical channel are called multiplex system. The sharing of physical channels using multiplexing often gives very large reductions in costs. Multiplexed systems are laid out in telecommunication networks, and the multiplexed signals are switched at nodes through to the correct destination terminal receiver.

Telecommunication Networks

A telecommunication network is a collection of transmitter, receivers, and communications channels that send messages to one another. Some digital communication networks contain one or more routers that work together to transmit information to the correct user. An analog communications network consists of one or more switches that establish a connection between two or more users. For both types of network, repeaters may be necessary to amplify or recreate the signal when it is being transmitted over distances. This is to combat attenuation that can render the signal indistinguishable from the noise (ATIS Committee, 2001). Another advantage of digital system over analog is that their output is easier to store in memory, that is, two voltage states (high and low) are easier to store than a continuous range of states.

Communication Channels

The term "channel" has two different meanings. In one meaning, a channel is the physical medium that carries a signal between the transmitter and the receiver. Examples of this include the atmosphere for sound communications, glass optical fibres for some kinds of optical communications, coaxial cables for communications by way of the voltages and electric currents in them, and free space for communications using visible light, infrared waves, ultraviolet light, and radio waves coaxial cable types are classified by RG types or "radio guide," a terminology derived from world war II. The various RG designations are used to classify the specific signal transmission applications (Conwire, 2016). This last channel is called the "free space channel." The sending of radio waves from one place to another has nothing to do with presence or absence of an atmosphere between the two. Radio waves travel through a perfect vacuum just as easily as they travel through air, fog, clouds, or any kind of gas.

The other meaning of the term "Channel" in telecommunications is seen in the phrase communications channel, which is a sub division of a transmission medium so that it can be used to send multiple streams of information simultaneously. For example, one radio station can broadcast radio waves into space at frequencies in the neighbourhood of 94.5MHz (megahertz) while another radio station can simultaneously broadcast radio waves over a frequency bandwidth of about 180KHz (kilohertz), centred at frequencies such as the above, which are called the "carrier frequencies." Each station in this example is separated from its adjacent stations by 200KHz, and the difference between 200KHz and 180KHz is an engineering allowance for the imperfections in the communication system.

In the example above, the "free space channel" has been divided into communications channels according to frequencies, and each channel is assigned a separate frequency bandwidth in which to broadcast radio waves. This system of dividing the medium into channels according to frequency is called "frequency division multiplexing". Another term for the same concept is "wave length division multiplexing," which is more commonly used in optical communications when multiple transmitters share the same physical medium.

Another way of dividing a communications medium into channels is to allocate each sender a recurring segment of time (a "time slot," for example, 20 milliseconds out of each second), and to allow each sender to send messages only within its own time slot. This method of dividing the medium into communication channels is called "time division multiplexing" (TDM), and is used in optical fibre communication. Some radio communication systems use TDM within an allocated FDM channel. Hence, these systems use a hybrid of TDM and FDM.

Modern Telephone Network

In a telephone network, the caller is connected to the person they want to talk to by switches at various telephone exchanges. The switches form an electrical connection between the two users and the setting of these switches is determined electronically when the caller dials the number. Once the connection is made, the caller's voice is transformed to an electrical signal using a small microphone in the caller's handset. This electrical signal is then sent through the network to the user at the other end where it is transformed back into sound by a small speaker in that person's handset.

Hacker et al. (2015, p. 433) note that as of 2015, the landline telephones in most residential homes are analog that is, the speaker's voice directly determines the signal's voltage. Although short distance calls may be handled from end-to-end as analog signals, increasingly telephone service providers are transparently converting the signals to digital signals for transmission. The advantage of this is that digitized voice data can travel side-by-side with data from the internet and can be perfectly reproduced in long distance communication (as opposed to analog signals that are inevitably impacted by noise).

Mobile phones have a significant impact on telephone networks. Mobile phone subscriptions now outnumbered fixed-line subscription in many markets. Sales of mobile phones in 2005 for instance, totaled 816.6 million with that figure being almost equally shared amongst the markets of Asia/Pacific (204m), Western Europe (164m), CEMEA (Central Europe, the Middle East and Africa) (153.5m), North America (148m) and Latin America (102m). In terms of new subscriptions over the fives years from 1999, Africa has outpaced other markets with 58.2% growth (Mbarika & Mbarika, 2006). Increasingly these phones are being serviced by systems where the voice content is transmitted digitally such as GSM or W-CDMA with many markets choosing to deprecate analog systems such as AMPS (Australia Telecommunications Association, 2003).

In the past few years, Africa's telecoms ecosystem has witnessed dramatic changes that stakeholders have applauded. As the mobile telecoms market begins to mature, Africa service providers are beginning to offer new products. The focus has switched away from securing more subscribers, towards boosting their average revenue per user (ARPU) rate through encouraging greater data consumption and mobile banking. Yet although technology is paving the way for the sale of more products, regulators sometimes struggle to keep up, while some governments fear that competition is proving inadequate to drive down prices.

Although South Africa is at the forefront of the African 4G revolution, the government believes that data prices are far too high and are deterring poorer people from accessing the technology. In September 2016, South Africa's minister of telecommunications and postal services, Siyabonga Cwele, announced: "I strongly believe in the near future they will come down because innovation and the demand in Africa and South Africa in particular for social media is very high and increasing exponentially." He added: "All these dictate that those data costs should come down, but also as government we are putting measures to make sure that there is competition in this broadband market. The sector regulator will launch an investigation into the lack of competition amid fears that leading players in the market are preventing smaller companies from offering cheaper access" (African Business, 2016).

As ever, East Africa is proving an innovative test bed for the telecoms industry. The East African Community (EAC) has enabled the region to make the most progress on reducing cross-border roaming charges by implementing its "roam like home" policy. Although operators feared that revenues would be greatly reduced, much lower costs have encouraged people to make far more calls, thereby maintaining revenues. In addition, the Tanzanian government now requires mobile operating licenses, in trend that could become more common across the continent.

The availability of 4G Long Term Evolution (LTE) services in Africa has been limited but is starting to take off. The technology offers speeds similar to fixed line broadband and lower costs for operators. Uptake has been greatest in South Africa, parts of the rest of Southern Africa and Nigeria but is now starting to spread to cities in the rest of the continent. For instance, in late September 2016, Vodafone and Afrimax announced plans to launch 4GLTE data services for Vodafone Cameroon customers in Douala and Yaounde, and later elsewhere in the country (African Business, 2016).

Michel Matas, a telecoms partner at Bird & Bird, contrasted Vodafone's strategy in Africa with that of its rivals: "Orange, MTN, Bharti Airtel, Viettel or Maroc Telecom businesses in Africa [have] in general based their activities on firstly the creation of wholly or majority owned local subsidiaries after obtaining a licence or, secondly, a majority or total acquisition of assets in existing operators," he said that vodafone's strategy was "probably inspired by its older strategy put in place in Europe toward commercial partnerships with local operators. The new partnership with Afrimax enables Vodafone to carry out its business in Africa by limiting risky investments, in particular in Cameroom where the market is already addressed by Camtel, MNT, Orange and Viettel." Viettel is a relatively new entrant into the African telecoms market. The Vietnamese company operates in Burundi, Mozambique and Tanzania, as well as Cameroon.

New telecoms deals in Africa have accelerated the pace of development in the continent. In September 2016, the Libyan Post, Telecommunications and Information Company (LPTIC) won a licence to become the fourth mobile operator in Cote d' Ivoire, a rare success for a Libyan Company at a difficult time in its home market. LPTIC Chairman Faisal Gergab said: "The Ivorian market is one of the largest and fastest growing emerging markets." He added that he hoped that the expertise gained and revenues generated would help his company to improve its operations in Libya.

The government of Tanzania has agreed a rather unusual deal to buy back a 35% stake in Tanzania Telecommunications Corporation (TTCL) for just $7m from Bharti Airtel, bringing the company fully back under state control. TTCL held a monopoly on telecoms services in the country prior to the mobile boom but is now just a minor mobile operator. The government has sought for years to regain control of the company, which has been partly owned by Bharti Airtel since 2010. It seems likely that it will now seek to expand TTCL's operations, although it would be politically difficult for it to finance the company's expansion from state funds.

In October 2016, Blue Label Telecoms agreed to pay R5bn ($356m) for a 45% stake in fellow South African Company Cell C, which is struggling to reduce its debt and was forced to restructure its bond obligations last year. Blue Label, which sells prepaid airtime, has also agreed to sell a stake in itself to Net I UEPS Technologies for R2bn (African Business, 2016).

There have also been dramatic changes in telephone communication behind the scenes. Starting with the operation of TAT-8 in 1988, the 1990s saw the widespread adoption of systems based on optical fibres. The benefit of communicating with optic fibers is that they offer a drastic increase in data capacity. TAT-8 itself was able to carry 10 times as many telephone calls as the last copper cable laid at that time and today's optic fibre cables are able to carry 25 times as many telephone calls as TAT-8 (AT & T knowledge Ventures, 2006). This increase in data capacity is due to several factors: first optic fibres are physically much smaller than competing technologies. Second, they do not suffer from crosstalk which means several hundred of them can be easily bundled together in a single cable (CISCO Systems, 2006). Lastly, improvements in multiplexing have led to and exponential growth in the data capacity of a single fibre (CISCO Systems, 2006; Jander, 2006).

Assisting communication across many modern optic fibre networks is a protocol known as Asynchronous Transfer Mode (ATM). The ATM protocol allows for the side-by-side data transmission mentioned previously. It is suitable for public telephone networks because it establishes a pathway for data through the network and associates a traffick contract with that pathway. The traffick contract is essentially an agreement between the client and the network about how the network is to handle the data; if the network cannot meet the conditions of the traffick contract it does not accept the connection. This is important because telephone calls can negotiate a contract so as to guarantee themselves a constant bit rate, something that will ensure a caller's voice is not delayed in parts or cut off completely (Stallings, 2004). There are competitors to ATM, such as Multi-protocol Label Switching (MPLS), that perform a similar task and are expected to supplant ATM in the future (Dix, 2002).

Impact of Telecommunication on Society

Telecommunication has a significant social, cultural and economic impact on modern society. In 2008, estimates placed the telecommunication industry's revenue at $4.7 trillion or just under 3% of the gross world product (official exchange rate) (Internet Engineering Task Force, 2010). The following are some of the areas where the impact of telecommunication is felt.

Economic Impact

On the microeconomic level, companies have used telecommunication to help build global business empires. This is self-evident in the case of online retailer Amazon.com but, according to academic Edward Lenert, even the conventional retailer Walmart has benefited from better telecommunication infrastructure compared to its competitors (Lenert, 1998). In cities throughout the world, home owners use their telephones to order and arrange a variety of home services ranging from pizza deliveries to electricians. Even relatively poor communities have been noted to use telecommunication to their advantage. In Bangladesh's Narshingdi district, for example, isolated villages use cellular phones to speak directly to wholesalers and arrange a better price for their goods. In Cote d'Ivoire coffee growers share mobile phones to follow hourly variations in coffee prices and sell at the best price (Samaan, 2013).

On the Macroeconomic scale, some scholars have suggested a causal link between good telecommunication infrastructure and economic growth (Roller & Waverman, 2001). Few dispute the existence of a correlation although some argue it is wrong to view the relationship as causal (Riaz, 1997). Because of the economic benefits of good telecommunication infrastructure, there is increasing worry about the inequitable access to the telecommunication services amongst various countries of the world-this is known as the digital divide.

A 2003 survey by the International Telecommunication Union (ITU) revealed that roughly a third of countries have fewer than one mobile subscription for every 20 people and one-third of countries have fewer than one land-line telephone subscription for every 20 people. In terms of internet access, roughly half of all countries have fewer than one out of 20 people with internet access. From this information, as well as educational data, the ITU was able to compile an index that measures the overall ability of citizens to access and use information and communication technologies (ITU, 2008). Using this measure, Sweden, Denmark and Iceland received the highest ranking while the African countries Nigeria, Burkina Faso and Mali received the Lowest (ITU, 2003).

Social Impact

Telecommunication has played a significant role in social relationships. Nevertheless, devices like the telephone system were originally advertised with an emphasis on the practical dimensions of the device (such as the ability to conduct business or order home services) as opposed to the social dimensions. It was not until the late 1920s and 1930s that the social dimensions of the device became a prominent theme in telephone advertisements. New promotions started appealing to consumers' emotions, stressing the importance of social conversations and staying connected to family and friends (Fischer, 1988).

Since then the role that telecommunications has played in social relations has become increasingly important. In recent years, the popularity of social networking sites has increased dramatically. These sites allow users to communicate with each other as well as post photographs, events and profiles for others to see. The profiles can list a person's age, interests, sexual preference and relationship status. In this way, these sites can play important role in everything from organizing social engagements to courtship (CNN, 2008).

Prior to social networking sites, technologies like short message service (SMS) and the telephone also had a profound impact on social interactions. In 2000, market research group Ipsos MORI reported that 81% of 15 to 24 –year-old SMS users in the United Kingdom had used the service to coordinate social arrangements and 42% to flirt (IPSOS MORI, 2005).

Other Impacts

In cultural terms, telecommunication has increased the public's ability to access music and film. With television, people can watch films they have not seen before in their own home without having to travel

Table 1. News source preference of Americans in 2006

Local TV	59%
National TV	47%
Radio	44%
Local paper	38%
Internet	23%
National paper	12%

Survey permitted multiple answers.
Source: Pew Internet Project 2006

to the video store or cinema. With radio and the internet, people can listen to music they have heard before without having to travel to the music store.

Telecommunication has also transformed the way people receive their news. A 2006 survey of slightly more than 3,000 Americans by the non-profit Pew Internet and American life Project in the United States the majority specified television or radio over newspapers.

Telecommunication has an equally significant impact on advertising. TNS media intelligence reported that in 2007, 58% of advertising expenditure in the United States was spent on media that depend upon telecommunication (Advertising Age, 2008).

Menace of SIM BOXING in Africa

Africa owes much of its recent growth and development to telecommunications services. However, over the past few years, telecos in Africa have been hit by several telecos frauds. SIM box fraud is one of the major frauds affecting the dynamic telecos market in Africa. The impact is huge in terms of the loss in revenues to telecoms and taxes to the governments. It is estimated that Africa loses up to 150 million US dollars (https://standardtimespress.org/?p=5791) every year to interconnection frauds. Reports suggest

Table 2. Advertising expenditures in US in 2007

Medium	Percentage	Spending
Internet	7.6%	$ 11.31 billion
Radio	7.2%	$ 10.69 billion
Cable TV	12.1%	$ 18.02 billion
Syndicated TV	2.8%	$ 4.17 billion
Spot TV	11.3%	$ 16.82 billion
Network TV	17.1%	$ 25.42 billion
Newspaper	18.9%	$ 28.22 billion
Magazine	20.4%	$ 30.33 billion
Outdoor	2.7%	$ 4.02 billion
Total	**100%**	**$ 149 billion**

Source: Advertising Age 2008

that two years back SIM box fraud had brought in losses of 12 to 15 million minutes' worth of revenue to Kenyan government and operators, and about US $5.8 million to Ghana government.

While Nigeria had been battling the menace for the past two and half years, which had impacted negatively on security and costing the country about $3 billion losses, according to the Nigerian Communications Commission (NCC), Uganda has announced that it was losing about $ 60 million yearly to the challenge. Derrick Sebaale, independent ICT consultant said the amount in part led to revenue from voice services to remain flat or grow sluggishly in 2015, 2016 and 2017.

Upadhyay (2018) contends that SIM Box frauds target Africa because of the following:

1.   The mobile subscriber growth in Africa is largely driven by the lower call prices and availability of cheaper handsets. The competition arising from over-the-top (OTT) providers has put an additional pricing pressure on telecoms, forcing them to design new bundled offerings encompassing data, voice and SMS. Such bundles bring much lower per-minute revenue for the operators as compared to traditional services. Fraudsters operating the SIM boxes are taking advantage of this scenario to bypass the formal call termination system that fetch higher tariffs to telecoms. The calls routed through the IP networks are terminated using local SIM gateways, thus compromising the formal interconnection networks and bringing heavy losses to the telecoms who have invested in building the networks. Traditionally, African countries are known to have higher interconnection tariffs compared to other regions, which further explains why such frauds are prevailing in Africa.

2.   Technological advancements have also contributed to the rise in interconnection frauds. The growing sophistication around SIM Box technologies has made fraud detection difficult using traditional methodologies. SIM boxes are programmed to mimic the activities of a normal call user. The equipment can have SIM cards of different operators installed, so a single SIM can operate with several GSM gateways located in different parts of the world. The availability of SIM cards at cheaper prices and the lack of law enforcement over the sale of prepaid SIM cards have also favoured the growth of SIM box fraud, further.

3.   Globally, the difference in approaches adopted by different countries to deal with the fraud makes it difficult for operators to develop a unified strategy to fight these frauds. IP interconnection services are treated as legal in a few countries whereas they are banned in other countries due to the regulatory issues associated with such activities. For example, the Ghanian government has declared SIM boxes illegal and made several arrest in this regard. However, SIM boxes are now available in several open markets including popular e-commerce platforms for around $1000 per unit. To make the matter worse, OTT providers like Viber are now explicitly selling their call termination capabilities to lure roaming customers to such bypass activities. Another such OTT development noticed recently is Skype offering free calls to mobiles and landlines in the United States and Canada from India. These evolving trends convey the scale at which the SIM fraud is growing, calling for immediate action from telecos to safeguard their revenue streams.

Conclusively, the recent developments around SIM box fraud have further aggravated the challenges faced by African telecos. With no scope for regulatory remediation, the only way forward for them is to prevent these attacks using advanced technologies. Traditional approaches like Call Detail Record (CDR) analysis are becoming ineffective in dealing with modern SIM box strategies due to the latency and false positives associated with those methods. As the market evolves, operators are looking toward a unified approach that can help them address the crisis in a much proactive manner. The developments around machine learning and test call group (TCG) analysis have favoured the growth of an integrated solution that can help combat the fraud in a cost-effective manner. The approach builds the capabilities of the traditional models but integrates the advancements in artificial intelligence and self-learning rules.

Current Research Trend on Call Masking and SIM Boxing

Despite constituting serious threat to security and economy of some nations as well as the telecommunications industry, studies on call masking/refilling and SIM boxing are scanty. However, available studies show that the scourge is yet to abate in countries where the malaise is endemic, in spite of concerted efforts by individual countries to deal with it.

A survey conducted in 2015 by Communication Fraud Control Association (CFCA) on global bypass fraud show clearly an upward trend, although the overall global fraud is on a decline. Samuel (2019), notes that the trend will continue to grow if the root cause is not addressed. The revenue loss as CFCA puts it, amounts to USD 3.77billion. According to the survey, top 10 countries where the fraudulent calls originated, is listed in Table 3.

Further survey points out the percentage of top five frauds, in which interconnect Bypass fraud in network is around 5%, whereas in roaming status, interconnect bypass fraud amounts between 20-25%. Authorities in US say that hackers were involved in an international crime ring that scammed telecommunication companies out of an estimated USD 50 million in last few years (kala, 2019). FBI most wanted list of cyber criminals have been arrested by authorities in their native Pakistan. Serbian police have cracked down on illegal SIM Box scheme.

According to Serbia's interior ministry in cooperation with the special department of cyber crime of prosecutor's office and the ministry of interior Macedonia have identified miscreants using SIM boxes to bypass international communications via VolP and making low-cost calls in Serbia. More than 40,000 SIM cards were found in Macedonia of mobile operators from Serbia, Croatia, Slovenia, Albania, Bosnia and Herzegovina. There are incidents in Ghana where the fraudsters connived with partners abroad to route internet calls via VolP to make it appear as if the call is a local one. Even women have been arrested for alleged SIMbox fraud (Kala, 2019).

Table 3. Country wise fraudulent calls in percentage based on call origin

Countries	Fraudulent Calls Percentage
United States	5%
Pakistan	4%
Spain	4%
Cuba	3%
Italy	3%
Philippines	3%
Somalia	3%
United kingdom	2%
Dominican Republic	1%
Egypt	1%

Source: Kala 2019

Ghana's efforts to crack down on SIM boxing fraud have been given a boost by the efforts of Subah Infosolutions Ghana Limited, which now partners with the authorities in the fight against the crime. Subah Infosolutions has been contracted by the Ghana Revenue Authority (GRA) to assist in blocking revenue leakages in the system through monitoring, locating, identifying and apprehending illegal SIM box operators across the country. The company's assistance in surveillance is credited with helping the Joint Anti-Telecom Fraud Task Force chalk up a number of successes so far in 2015. The task force includes detectives from the CID headquarters, officials from the National Communications Authority (NCA) and officials from the various Telecoms Service Providers (Acquaye, 2015).

In India, a techie was recently arrested for operating telephone exchange for a Pakistan spy. According to the sources the Uttar Pradesh Anti-Terrorism squad busted an illegal telephone exchange and spying racket causing national security threat. This act has been committed by a software engineer from south Delhi and ten others from Lucknow and other parts of UP. The exchanges were not only making lakhs of rupees by routing international calls bypassing the legal gateways. These systems were used for Pakistan's Inter-Service Intelligence (ISI) to call Army officials to elicit information from them. The racket was busted after the defence ministry and Army alerted the military intelligence in Jammu and Kashmir. ISI has been spying over and innocent victims have been sharing information. Intelligence officials unearthed the racket and found network was using SIMbox to carry out their spying activities. The callers based in Pakistan, Bangladesh made calls using VoIP through SIMbox and connected to receivers in India. The receivers in India could only see Indian numbers on their phone screens. The law enforcement authorities have recovered 16 SIM Box units, 140 prepaid cards, 10 mobile phones and 28 data cards and five laptops (Kala, 2019).

Theoretical Framework

This chapter is hinged on the technological determinism theory. The theory posits that media technology shapes how we as individuals in a society think, feel, act and how society operates as we move from one technological age to another.

Most interpretations of technological determinism share two general ideas namely: that the development of technology itself follows a predictable, traceable path largely beyond cultural and political influence, and that technology in turn has effects on societies that are inherent, rather than socially conditioned or that the society organizes itself in such a way to support and further develop a technology once it has been introduced.

Croteau and Hoynes (2003, pp.305-307) define technological determinism as the approach that identifies technology advances, as the central causal element in processes of social change. They further assert that as a technology stabilizes, its design tends to dictate users' behaviours, consequently diminishing human agency. Postman (1992, pp.3-20) notes that the "uses made of technology are largely determined by the structure of the technology itself, that is, that its functions follow from its form".

The above statements are indeed true of the mobile technology, which fraudsters use to commit all forms of communication fraud.

MAIN FOCUS OF THE CHAPTER

Issue

Against the backdrop of the rising trend of call masking, call Refiling and SIM Boxing in Nigeria's telecommunications industry, the Nigerian Communications Commission gave a startling revelation that the telecoms industry lost as much as N1.06 trillion ($3 billion) revenue to these infractions within a space of two years.

The Executive Vice Chairman of NCC, Prof. Umar Garba Danbatta, at the 85th edition of the Telecoms Consumer Parliament organized by the Commission in Lagos disclosed that the revenue loss started in September 2016 when the NCC reviewed and implemented a new call termination rate for international in bound traffick from N3.90k per minute to N24.40k per minute. He said the operators involved in call masking and refiling took undue advantage of the hike in international termination call rate to tamper with international calls and terminate them as local calls in order to avoid paying the new rate, thereby defrauding the telecoms industry of trillions of naira within a space of two years.

According to him, what happened since 2016 was a clear indication that some unscrupulous elements in the telecoms industry wanted to continue to fraudulently profit from the earlier lopsidedness in the International Termination Rate (ITR), which was operational before the 2016 review.

Worried by the ugly development, Prof. Danbatta said NCC investigated the fraud and arrested some operators involved in call masking and call refiling. He hinted that in the process, NCC barred as much 750,000 lines assigned to 13 operators from the national network. The lines, which were barred in 2018 were suspected of being used for masking and NCC had to withdraw the use of such lines. The action of the commission was predicated on the series of complaints by telecoms consumers and other industry stakeholders on the rising wave of call masking and refiling, which the NCC helmsman said posed security and economic risks to the nation.

Controversy

Ever since these infractions became an issue in Nigeria's telecommunications industry, many including stakeholders, have expressed worry over the multi-billion naira sector. While some applaud NCC for the actions taken to arrest the drift, others who appeared to be more concerned about the disturbing trend want the commission to move beyond the barring of lines and withdrawal of licenses to taking pragmatic measures that will permanently rid the industry of all criminal tendencies.

While the industry regulator (NCC) basked in the euphoria of the punitive measures taken so far against the operators allegedly involved in the malfeasance, the critics are desirous of seeing a more radical change in the commission's approach towards the infractions that tend to rip the industry apart.

Problem

Unarguably, call masking, call refiling and SIM boxing have taken a toll on the nation's revenue and that of the telecommunications industry. It has also undermine the security of the nation especially with the threats of Boko Haram insurgents in the north. It is in realization of these breaches that NCC decisively moved against the perpetrators of these criminal acts.

Despite the regulatory actions of the commission, call masking, call refilling and SIM boxing have persisted as telecoms consumers continued to express outrage over call masking, even as security agencies constantly put pressure on NCC to find a lasting solution to the menace.

However, Prof. Danbatta has assured that as part of zero tolerance for communications fraud in the market, the NCC was determined to stamp out the practice in the industry at all cost.

Solutions and Recommendations

In view of the adverse effects of call masking, call refiling and SIM boxing on the telecommunications industry and the entire nation, the following solutions and recommendations are hereby proposed:

1. The Nigerian Communications Commission, in collaboration with the National Orientation Agency should increase its awareness campaign on eradication of call masking and other related infractions in the telecoms industry in Nigeria.
2. The NCC should impose severe sanctions on all those involved in the criminal act in order to save the telecoms industry from imminent collapse.
3. In order to reduce the rate of call masking in the country, the NCC should review the current exchange rate for international and local call termination.
4. NCC should create more public awareness on the implications of call masking and make the general public understand the issues around call masking and call refiling.
5. NCC should commit to prosecuting those involved in call masking and make such prosecution public.
6. Telecoms subscribers should duly and personally register all new SIM cards purchased and should avoid patronizing pre-registered SIM card dealers.
7. In order to completely address the issue, NCC should continue to monitor the networks and sanction more operators and individuals who are still involved in call masking, call refiling and SIM boxing.
8. Telecoms subscribers and the Nigerian populace should adhere to the advice of NCC to continue to report cases of call masking and refiling to a special free of charge code: 622 for proper tracking of such calls.
9. NCC should without delay come out with a technology solution that would help to detect SIM Boxes used by the fraudsters.

FUTURE RESEARCH DIRECTIONS

Call masking, Call refiling and SIM Boxing have assumed a worrisome dimension in Nigeria's telecommunications industry, hence stakeholders are unanimous in their call for a concerted effort in dealing with the malaise in order to secure the industry. Nigeria's telecom market had become vulnerable to interconnection frauds and the industry lacked a well coordinated, structured and effective approach to combat the malaise.

In line with the title of the book which has to do with " Advanced Multi – Industry Applications of Big Data Clustering and Machine Learning" it is urgent that government and stakeholders in the telecoms industry evolve digital solutions that would help curtail the growing trend of call masking, call refiling and SIM Boxing in Nigeria. To effectively checkmate the activities of the miscreants, the relevant stakeholders need to come together to deal decisively with call masking and other related infractions in the telecoms sector.

The stakeholder engagement model will apply here. Stakeholder engagement is the process by which an organization involves people who may be affected by the decisions it makes, or can influence the implantation of its decisions. They may support or oppose the decisions, be influential in the organization or within the community in which it operates, hold relevant official position or be affected in the long term (Wikipedia, n.d). It is a tool used by mature private and public sector organizations, especially when they want to develop understanding and agree to solutions on complex issues or issues of concern (Stakeholder Mapping, n.d)

The term stakeholder engagement has however emerged as a means of describing a broader, more inclusive public participation process. When executed effectively, stakeholder engagement can be used to improve communication, obtain wider support, gather useful data and ideas, enhance agency reputation, and provide for more sustainable decision making (PermNewsletter, 2012). A robust stakeholder engagement model is vital for organizations, governments and other entities to be able to understand and respond to legitimate stakeholder concerns such as call masking, call refiling and SIM Boxing. Interconnection fraud is a complex issue of public concern not only to Nigeria but other countries in Africa.

Fighting call masking and other related infractions is the responsibility of everyone. It is important to understand that no one person or institution can have the requisite capacity to deal with interconnection fraud. As a result, all segment of society including telecom operators, civil society, the media, subscribers, law enforcement agencies, government and the general public should be involved in efforts to deal with the menace at the earliest available opportunity. It is important to engage all stakeholders to ensure that they understand the issues and processes involved.

As the key stakeholders are engaged, it is imperative to monitor the implementation of the policies put in place to address interconnection fraud from time to time in order to realize the set objectives. This will form the direction of future research in this domain. Proper monitoring of the policies will ensure that the industry is protected against call masking, call refiling and SIM boxing

CONCLUSION

It is obvious that call masking, call refiling and SIM Boxing portend serious danger for Nigeria. The report that Nigeria lost over $3 billion or N1.06 trillion to call masking and other related infractions in the telecoms industry in a period of two years is disturbing. The situation Nigeria finds itself is deplorable. Apart from the economic sabotage, the activities of the criminals pose serious security risk to the nation.

Although the Executive Chairman of NCC, Prof. Umar Danbatta has assured that the Commission is on top of the matter, there are signs that the infractions may not go away so easily unless drastic measures are applied.

In spite of the efforts of the commission in tackling the menace through the suspension of the interconnect exchange licensees in February 2018 and the barring of 750,000 lines suspected of being used for the criminal acts, call masking, call refiling and SIM boxing have refused to abate.

Every Nigerian should condemn the activities of those that engage in call masking/refilling, and SIM boxing in the telecoms sector. It is good that NCC has sanctioned some licensed telecoms operators for the infractions. It should go a step further to sanction other telecom firms involved in SIM boxing. The overall aim of the NCC should be to eradicate the fraudulent practices in the sector forthwith. Since the NCC is aware of this economic sabotage, it must come up with punitive measures to stop the menace. The perpetrators of this crime must be apprehended and prosecuted for depriving the government of the huge revenue.

Besides, the NCC must equally address the problem of unsolicited text messages from telecoms operators, call dropping, over billing and poor quality of services. Nigerians can recall that the network operators were given up to June 30, 2016 to stop sending unsolicited short message service (SMS) or calls to subscribers or face sanctions. Despite the deadline and N5 million fine in the first instance, the problem is yet to abate.

In 2017, the NCC asked the network operators to create a data base for phone numbers of subscribers on the "Do-Not-Disturb" list in the bid to stop unsolicited message. Since part of the 8-point agenda of the Prof. Danbatta regime is to improve the quality of service, the NCC helmsman must ensure that all network operators improve the quality of their services to their customers. This is what Nigerians expect from the industry regulator.

REFERENCES

Acquaye, N. A. (2015). *SIM box task team steps up successes with help from the firm*. Retrieved from https://www.biztechafrica.com/article/sim-box-task- team –steps –successes- help-ict-firm/9592/

Adepetun, A. (2019, March 27). Governments charged as SIM Boxing menace rips Africa. *The Guardian*.

Advertising Age. (2008, June 23). *100 leading national advertisers*. Author.

African Business. (2016). *Telecoms: Business evolves as the market matures*. Author.

Amanze-Nwachukwu, C. (2018, October 29). Call masking: A worrisome trend. *THISDAY*.

Anuforo, C. (2018, August 1). All you need to know about call masking. *Daily Sun*.

AT & T Knowledge Ventures. (2006). *Milestones in AT & T history*. Retrieved from https://www.att.com/history/milestones.html

ATIS Committee. (2001). *ATIS Telecom Glossary*. Retrieved from http://www.atis.org/tg2k

AT&T. (2006). *History of AT & T*. Retrieved from https://www.att.com/history/milestones.html

Australia Telecommunications Association. (2003). *Ten years of GSM in Australia*. Retrieved from https://www.amta.org.au/default.asp?Page=142

Bern Dibner, B. Library Inc. (1959). *The Atlantic Cable*. Retrieved from https://www.sil.si.edu/digital/collections/hst/atlantic-cable/

Calvert, J. B. (2004). *The electromagnetic telegraph*. Retrieved from http://www.du/~calvert/tell/morse/morse.html

CISCO Systems. (2006). *Fundamentals of DWDM technology*. Retrieved from http://www.cisco.com/univercd/cc/td/doc/product/mels/cm1500/dwdm/dwdm_ovr.pdf

CNN. (2008). *How do you know your love is real? Check Facebook.* Retrieved from http://www.cnn.com/2008/LIVING/personal/04/04/facebook.love/index.html

Conwire. (2017). *Coax cable FAQ series: What is RG Cable?-Conwire.* Retrieved from http://www.conwire.com/coax-cable-rg-cable-blog

Croteau, D., & Hoynes, W. (2003). *Media society: Industries, Images & Audiences.* Thousand Oaks, CA: Pine Forge Press.

Dilhac, J. M. (2004). *From tele-communicare to telecommunications.* Retrieved from http://www.ieee.org/portal/cms_docs_iportals/about us/history_center/conferences/che2004/Dilhac.pdf

Dix, J. (2002). *MPLS is the future, but ATM hangs on.* Retrieved from https://www.networkworld.com/columnists/2002/0812edit.html

Electronic Oberlin Group. (2006). *Elisha Gray.* Retrieved from https://www.oberlin.edu/external/EOG/OYTT-images/ElishaGray.html

Fischer, C. S. (1988). Touch someone: The telephone industry discovers sociability. *Technology and Culture, 29*(1), 32–61. doi:10.2307/3105226

Hacker, M., Burgardt, D., Fletcher, L., Gordon, A., Peruzzi, W., Pretopnik, R., & Qaissaunee, M. (2015). *Engineering & Technology.* Boston: Cengage Learning.

Haykin, S. (2001). *Communication Systems* (4th ed.). Hoboken, NJ: John Wiley & Sons.

Huurdeman, A. A. (2003). *The world history of telecommunications.* Hoboken, NJ: John Wiley & Sons. doi:10.1002/0471722243

Internet Engineering Task Force. (2010). *Worldwide telecommunications industry revenues.* Retrieved from https://www.plunkettresearch.com/Telecommunications/telecommunicationsStatistics/tabid/96/Default.aspx

Ipsos Mori. (2005). *I just text to say I love you.* Retrieved from https://www.ipsos-mori.com/research publications/researcharchive/1575/1-Just-text-To-Say-I-Love-You.aspx

ITU. (2003). *World telecommunication development report.* Retrieved from https://www.itu.int/ITU-D/ict/publications/wtdr-03/index.html

ITU. (2008). *Digital access index (DAI).* Retrieved from https://www.itu.int/ITU-D/ict/dai/

ITU. (2012). *Article 1.3 ITU Radio regulations.* Retrieved from http://www.itu.int/dms_pub/itu-s/oth/02/20/502020000244501PDFE.PDF

Jander, M. (2006). *Report: DWDM no match for sonet.* Retrieved from http://www.lightreading.com/document.asp?doc_id=31358

Kala, N. (2019) A study on internet bypass fraud: national security threat. *Forensic Research & Criminology International Journal, 7*(1).

Lenert, E. (1998). A communication theory perspective on telecommunications policy. *Journal of Communication, 48*(4), 3–23. doi:10.1111/j.1460-2466.1998.tb02767.x

Mbarika, V., & Mbarika, I. (2006). *Africa calling*. Retrieved from http://www.spectrum.ieee.org/may06/3426

New Oxford American Dictionary. (2005). *Telecommunication, tele and communication*. Oxford, UK: Oxford University Press.

Okonji, E. (2018, October 11). *Curbing the menace of call masking, refilling*. THISDAY.

PermNewsletter. (2012, April). *Understanding the importance of stakeholder engagement*. Retrieved from http://www.cansr.msu.du/uploads/files

Pew Internet project. (2006). *Online News: For many home broadband users, the internet is a primary news source*. Retrieved from http://web.archive.org/web/2013/021122359/http://www.ccgrouppr.com/PIP_News.and.Broad.pdf

Postman, N. (1992). *Technology*. New York: Vintage Press.

Riaz, A. (1997). The role of telecommunications in economic growth: Proposal for an alternative framework of analysis. *Media Culture & Society*, *19*(4), 557–583. doi:10.1177/016344397019004004

Roller, L. H., & Waverman, L. (2001). Telecommunications infrastructure and economic development: A simultaneous approach. *The American Economic Review*, *91*(4), 909–923. doi:10.1257/aer.91.4.909

Samaan, M. (2003). *The effect of income inequality on mobile phone penetration*. Retrieved from http://web.archive.org/web/20070214102055/http://dissertations.bc.edu/cgi/viewcontent.cgi?article=1016&context=ashonors

Samuel, D. V. (2019). *Bypass fraud evolution detection through CDR analysis*. Retrieved from https://www.linkedin.com/pulse/bypass-fraud-evolution-detection-through-cdr-analysis-samuel-pmp

Stakeholdermapping. (n.d.). *Stakeholder engagement*. Retrieved from http://www.stakeholdermapping.com/smm-maturity-model/

Stallings, W. (2004). *Data and Computer Communications* (7th ed.). Pearson Prentice Hall.

Syed, A. N. (2014). *The grey market in prepaid: tactics to combat international bypass fraud via the SIM box*. Retrieved from https://www.bswan.org/sim_box_fraud.asp

The Telegraph. (2017). *Who made the first electric telegraph communications?* Retrieved from http://www.telegraph.co.uk/technology/connecting-britain/first-electric-telegraph/

Upadhyay, N. (2018). *Why SIM Box fraud is rampant in Africa?* Retrieved from http://www.subex.com/author/neeraj/

Wikipedia. (n.d.). *Stakeholder enegagement*. Retrieved from http://en.m.wikipedia.org/wiki/stakeholder-engagement

ADDITIONAL READING

Abdikarim, H; Ibrahim, R; Elmi, S; Sallehuddin, R. (2012) Detecting SIM box fraud using neural networking.

Akinola, K. (2018). NCC blasted over call masking sanctions errors. Retrieved from http://technology-times.ng

Becker, R. A., Volinsky, C., & Wilks, A. R. (2010). Fraud detection in telecommunications: History and lessons learned. *American Statistical Association and the American Society for Quality Technometrics.*, *52*(0), 1.

Wilson, J. (1998). *Telecom and network security: Toll fraud and teleabuse update*. Telecommunications Reports International Inc.

Yusoff, M. I. M., Mohammed, I., & Bakar, M. R. A. (2013). Fraud detection in telecommunication industry using Gaussian mixed model. International conference on Research and Innovation in Information Systems (ICR115) 27-28 November, Kuala Lumpur, Malaysia. IEEE Conference Publication. 10.1109/ICRIIS.2013.6716681

Zhao, Q., Chen, K., Tongxinli, Y. Y., & Wang, X. (2018). *Detecting telecommunication fraud by understanding the contents of a call* (Vol. 1, p. 8). Cybersecurity.

KEY TERMS AND DEFINITIONS

Fraudster: A person who commits fraud, especially in business dealings.

Interconnect Bypass Fraud: Is a new type of fraud that is based on interconnect telecom systems. Interconnect bypass fraud or SIM Box fraud is a growing challenge that network operators around the world are facing.

Interconnection Bandwidth: Is a metric that measure how ready a location or industry is to maximize its interconnection potential.

Interconnection Network: In telecommunications, interconnection is the physical linking of a carrier's network with equipment or facilities not belonging to that network. The term may refer to a connection between a carrier's facilities and the equipment belonging to its customer, or to a connection between two (or more) carriers.

International Mobile Subscriber Identity (IMSI): Is a unique number associated with all Global System for mobile communications (GSM) and Universal Mobile Telecommunications System (UMTS) network mobile phone users use for identifying a GSM subscriber. Each IMSI number has two parts.

IP Network: An IP network is a communication network that uses internet protocol (IP) to send and receive messages between one or more computers. As one of the most commonly used global networks, an IP network is implemented in internet networks, local area networks (LAN) and enterprise networks.

OTT: Over the top is a term used to refer to content that distribute streaming media as a standalone product directly to viewers over the internet, bypassing telecommunications, multi-channel television, and broadcast television platforms that traditionally act as a controller or distributor of such content.

SIM Box: Is a device used as part of VoIP gateway installation. It contains a number of SIM cards, which are linked to the gateway but housed and stored separately from it.

SIM Card: Is an integrated circuit that is intended to securely store the international mobile subscriber (IMSI) number and its subscribers on mobile telephony devices (such as mobile phones and computers).

Telecom Operator: Is a telephone company that provides telecommunications services such as telephony and data communications access.

Chapter 17
An Optimized Three–Dimensional Clustering for Microarray Data

Narmadha N.

https://orcid.org/0000-0003-4306-9641

Periyar University, India

R. Rathipriya

Periyar University, India

ABSTRACT

This chapter focuses on discrete firefly optimization algorithm (FA)-based microarray data, which is a meta-heuristic, bio-inspired, optimization algorithm based on the flashing behaviour of fireflies, or lighting bugs. Its primary advantage is the global communication among the fireflies, and as a result, it seems more effective for triclustering problem. This chapter aims to render a clear description of a new firefly algorithm (FA) for optimization of tricluster applications. This research work proposes discrete firefly optimization-based triclustering model first time to find the highly correlated tricluster from microarray data. This model is reliable and robust triclustering model because of efficient global communication among the swarming particles called fireflies.

1.1 INTRODUCTION

This chapter focuses on Discrete Firefly Optimization Algorithm (FA) based Microarray Data which is a meta-heuristic, bio-inspired, optimization algorithm based on the flashing behaviour of fireflies, or lighting bugs. Its primary advantage is the global communication among the fireflies, and as a result, it seems more effective for triclustering problem.

This chapter aims to render a clear description of a new Firefly Algorithm (FA) for optimization of tricluster applications. The chapter organization is given as follows. Section 2 discusses the Firefly Optimization Algorithm. Section 3 outlines the development of the proposed biclustering model. Hy-

DOI: 10.4018/978-1-7998-0106-1.ch017

brid Firefly Optimization Based Biclustering model is introduced and discussed in the Section 4. The experimental results analysis of the proposed models is elaborated in the Section 5. Section 6 concludes the chapter with the future research possibility.

1.2 Related Work

This subsection provides an overview of related works in the field of 3D microarray gene expression data analysis, in particular, the work related to the optimization technique that is Particle Swarm Optimization (PSO).

A pattern-driven local search operator is inbuilt with the binary Particle Swarm Optimization (PSO) algorithm is used to improve the search efficiency (Yangyang Li, 2014).BPSO encoding gene-to-class sensitivity (GCS) mainly used to perform gene selection. GCS is used to extract the samples with the help of extreme learning machine (ELM).ELM, K. nearest neighbour (KNN) and support vector machine (SVM) classifiers are used for prediction with high accuracy for microarray data, it gives the efficiency and effectiveness for gene selection method (FeiHan, 2015).

The Multi-Objective Particle Swarm Optimization is used for gene expression data to extract the bicluster. The main purpose of this technique is to cover all elements of the gene expression matrix amongst the overlapping bicluster (Mohsen lashkargir, 2009). Biclustering algorithm is used to identify the coherent bicluster with minimum MSR (Mean Square Residue) and with maximum row variance for gene expression data.

To solve this kind of problem various optimization approaches are used namely 1) Nelder Mead with Levy Flight and 2) Tabu search with Nelder Mead are proposed and compared. NM with Levy Flight shows better performance and it gives a better global optimal solution when compared to Tabu search with Nelder Mead (Kavitha M, 2016).

Biclustering algorithm is used to cluster the gene expression data, to improve the residue function for this algorithm. This improved function is more appropriate for the stochastic heuristic algorithm. The parallel genetic algorithm (GA) is used for biclustering optimization algorithm; it can prevent the local convergence in the optimal algorithm and make the probability for global convergence bigger (Wei Shen, 2012). EDA- GA hybrid is to analyze the gene expression data it not only gives converge quickly but it provides the global solution (Feng Liu, 2006). PSO with GA is used to solve the biclustering problem and it provides high accuracy (Baiyi Xie, 2007). Binary Particle Swarm Optimization (BPSO) is used to retrieve the global optimal bicluster from the web usage data. It provides the relationship between the web users and webpage (R.Rathipriya, 2011).

Firstly small disjoint tightly correlated submatrices are generated using the K-Means clustering algorithm. Secondly, the greedy search algorithm mainly used to enlarge the seeds. The output of the greedy search algorithm is used as an initial population of binary PSO, these steps are used to identify bicluster (Shyama Das, 2010). To solve the classification of gene expression data to implement the improved binary particle swarm optimization (IBPSO) for feature selection and K-nearest neighbour (K-NN) as an evaluator of IBPSO. These methods are helpful to reduce the total number of features as required (Li-Yeh Chuang, 2007).

The gene expression data clustering K-means, FCM and hierarchical techniques are used for clustering microarray data. But PSO based K-means gives better performance for clustering microarray data (Lopamudra Dey, 2014). Biclustering algorithm used shifting and scaling pattern on the merit function it is mainly used to grow the bicluster. But this measure has its own demerits for identifying scaling pattern and coherent evolution to grow bicluster (K.Thangavel, 2011).

Particle Swarm Optimization (PSO) is used for the best subset generation and for evaluating the subset to uses k-means as wrapper algorithm. The algorithm gives the good quality of cluster with an accuracy of 70-80% (Deepthi P S, 2015). The Firefly Algorithm is a meta-heuristic, nature-inspired, optimization algorithm which is based on the social flashing behavior of fireflies, or lighting bugs, in the sky. It was developed by Xin-She Yang at Cambridge University in 2009. In (K. Thangavel 2014), preliminary assessment of discrete version of FA (DFA) is presented and applied for mining coherent and large volume bicluster from web usage dataset. Moreover, authors have claimed that DFA outperforms the PSO for extraction of optimal bicluster.

The limitations identified from the study is given as:

- Most of the research works are concentrated on genetic algorithm and PSO to extract optimal cluster or bicluster or tricluster from microarray data. But, a very few research work uses firefly optimization algorithm.
- Mean Squared Residue based fitness functions is used to identify optimal set of genes but it fails to extract coherent pattern.

Therefore, this research work proposes Discrete Firefly Optimization based Triclustering model first time to find the highly correlated tricluster from microarray data. This model is reliable and robust triclustering model because of efficient global communication among the swarming particles called fireflies.

2. METHODS AND MATERIALS

2.1 Three Dimensional (3D) Dataset Matrix: Defnition

Three dimensional (3D) Dataset Matrix let A is represented by

- r is defined as number of genes (rows) X= $\{x_1, x_2 \ldots \ldots x_r\}$,
- c is defined as number of Samples (Columns) Y = $\{y_1, y_2 \ldots y_c\}$ and
- t is defined as number of (time point) Z= $\{z_1, z_2 \ldots z_t\}$.
- Element a_{ijk} is represented as gene (x_i), sample (y_i) and time point (z_k).

Other names for three dimensional data are 3D, Multidimensional data, cube data, and tridiac data.

2.2 Tricluster

Three dimensional (3D) dataset A with r (genes) is denoted as X, c (columns) is denoted as Y and t (time point) is denoted as Z; that is Tricluster B = (I,J,K) is the subset of original dataset, where I is the subset of X (I ⊆ X), J is subset of Y (J ⊆ Y) and K is subset of Z (K⊆Z).

2.3. GST Microarray Data / Triclustering

It is represented as

- G = {g1,g2,g3...gn} be a set of n genes
- S = {s1,s2,s3.....sm} be a set of m biological samples
- T = {t1,t2,t3......tl} be a set of l time points

A three dimensional microarray dataset is a real-valued n*m*l matrix D = G*S*T whose three dimensions correspond to genes, samples and time points is said to be GST Microarray data or Triclustering

2.4 Representation of Triclustering

See Figure 1.

2.5 Binary Encoding of Tricluster

3D gene expression dataset is represented by a binary string with three categories. A gene encodes a maximal tricluster. A time series / 3D gene expression dataset contains number of gene is represented by G, number of samples is represented by S and number of time point is represented by T.

In 3D dataset first g bits corresponding to the genes, the next s bits corresponding to the samples and the last t bits corresponding to the time points. Each string is denoted by g+s+t bits that are represented by either 0 or 1. If the value is 1 then it is said to be gene/sample/time point is presented in the tricluster. If the value is 0 then the gene/sample/time point are not presented in the tricluster.

Example

3D gene expression dataset is represented by a binary string {01101110010101001101} the total number bits in a string is 20. Table 1 shows the particular number of genes, samples and time points presented in the binary string.

The figure 2 shows the member of genes presented in the tricluster is g = { g_2, g_3, g_5, g_6, g_7 }, the member of samples presented in the tricluster is s = { s_1, s_3, s_5} and the member of time points presented in the tricluster is t = { t_2, t_3, t_5}. Thus the encoding representation shows the set of genes are presented for the same set of samples at the same set of time points. The encoded tricluster with subset of genes works at different set of sample at different time point.

2.6 Mean Correlation Value for Tricluster

Mean Correlation Value of a Tricluster (MCV) is defined as in equation 1, where

$$\bar{A} \frac{\sum_m \sum_n (A_{mn})}{m*n}, \bar{B} = \frac{\sum_m \sum_n (B_{mn})}{m*n} \tag{1}$$

Figure 1. Graphical representation of tricluster

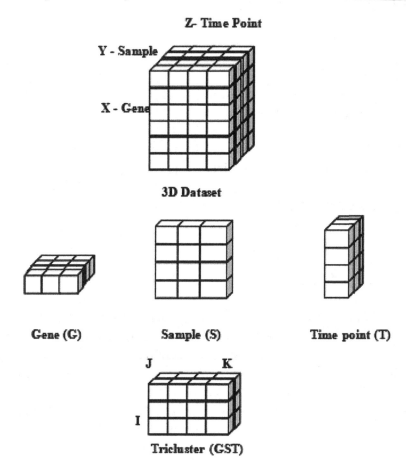

Table 1. Characteristic of a tricluster

3D Data	Genes	Samples	Time Points
	9	6	5

Figure 2. Binary encoding of a sample tricluster

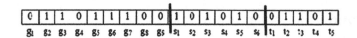

The range of MCV is [0, 1]. Value close to '1' signifies high correlated tricluster otherwise low or null correlated tricluster.

2.7 Fitness Function

The main objective of this work is to discover high volume triclusters with high MCV. The following fitness function F (I, J, K) is used to extract optimal tricluster is shown in equation 2 [10].

$$F\left(I,J,K\right) = \begin{cases} \left|I\right| * \left|J\right| * \left|K\right|, if\ MCV\left(Tricluster\right) \geq \delta \\ 0, Otherwise \end{cases} \tag{2}$$

Where |I|, |J|, |K| are number of rows, columns and the time points of Tricluster and δ is defined as follows
    Here, MCV threshold δ = Range from 0.95 to 0.98.

2.8 Firefly Optimization Algorithm: An Introduction

Fireflies' Behaviour

In 2009, Firefly algorithm, developed by Xin-She Yang, is inspired by the light attenuation over the distance and fireflies' mutual attraction, rather than by the phenomenon of the fireflies' light flashing. Algorithm considers what each firefly observes at the point of its position, when trying to move to a greater light-source, than his own. The firefly meta-heuristic relies on a set of artificial fireflies which communicate with each other to solve optimization problems. The behaviour of artificial fireflies is modeled according to the behaviour of fireflies in nature, which searches for a mating partner by emitting a flashing light.

The flashing light of fireflies is an awesome eye sight in the summer sky especially in the tropical and temperate regions. The bioluminescence process is responsible for flashing light in fireflies. However, two fundamental functions of such flashes are to attract mating partners (communication), and to attract potential prey. In addition, flashing may also serve as a protective warning mechanism. The rhythm of flashing, the rate of flashing and the amount of time form part of the signal system that brings both sexes together. It is noted that the light intensity at a particular distance r from the light source follow law of inverse square. That is, the light intensity 'I' decreases as the distance r increases in terms of $I \leq 1 \leq r2$. Moreover, the air absorbs light which becomes weaker and weaker as the distance increases. These two factors make most fireflies visible only to a limited distance, which is good enough for fireflies' foraging behaviour. The flashing light of fireflies can be formulated in such a way that it is associated with the objective function to be optimized, which makes it possible to formulate new optimization algorithms called Firefly Optimization Algorithm FOA.

In FOA, the following three rules are framed based on the flashing characteristics of fireflies:

1. Generally, all fireflies are unisex, i.e. one firefly is attracted to other fireflies irrespective of their sex.
2. Attractiveness is directly proportional to their brightness, thus for any two flashing fireflies, the less bright one will move towards the more brighter one. If no one is brighter than a particular firefly, it moves randomly.

3. The brightness of a firefly is determined by the objective function to be optimised. For a maximization problem, the brightness can simply be proportional to the value of the objective function.

Thus, pseudo code of FOA is shown in algorithm 1 (Table 2).

3. DISCRETE FIREFLY OPTIMIZATION BASED TRICLUSTERING (DFOT) ALGORITHM

Mapping concepts of the firefly algorithm to the triclustering problem will be discussed in this section elaborately. The real fireflies search for a mating partner by means of flashing lights whereas artificial fireflies search for the optimal tricluster in the solution space by means of objective function. Thus, map the attraction behaviour of fireflies to the optimal tricluster selection problem is as follows:

- a firefly becomes an artificial firefly
- the position of a firefly becomes a tricluster solution
- the brightness of a firefly becomes the quality of a tricluster solution evaluated with a correlation based fitness function
- the attractiveness between two fireflies becomes the hamming distance between two triclusters
- the movement of a firefly is mapped to a modification of the firefly's current position (i.e. tricluster)

3.1 Directed Movement of Discrete Firefly

In standard Firefly Optimization algorithm, firefly movement is based on light intensity and comparing it between each two fireflies. In Discrete Firefly algorithm, the movement is caused by the use of genetic crossover operator, and that is given as follows.

r = Hamming similarity (f_i, f_j)

Table 2.

Algorithm 1: Firefly Optimisation Algorithm(FOA)

Step 1 Initialize the initial population of fireflies F_i, i = 1, 2 ..., *mf*.
Step 2 Define light absorption coefficient λ (control parameter)
Step 3 while (*tmax* < MaxGeneration)
        for i = 1 to *mf-1*
            for j = i +1 to *mf*
                if fitness(F_i) > fitness(F_j)
                    Move F_i toward F_j;
                End if
a. Attractiveness varies with distance r via $e^{-\lambda r}$
        b. Evaluate fitness of new solutions
    End for *j*
    End for *i*
    Rank the fireflies
    End while
Step 4 Return the best fireflies

Table 3.

Algorithm 2: Discrete Firefly Optimization based Triclustering Algorithm

Input: N, number of fireflies,
 Output: optimal Tricluster
       Step 1 Initialize the binary encoded biclusters as initial fireflies
       $X = \{x_1, x_2, ..., x_n\}$.
       Step 2 Do
       for $i = 1: N$
       for $j = 1: i$
       if fitness $(x_i) <$ fitness (x_j) then
       $r =$ Compute_Distance (x_i, x_j)
       $xprob = r$ / number of bits in x_i
 $x_i =$ Crossover$(x_i, x_j, xprob)$
 end if
 end for
 end for
 until (Stopping_Condition())
 Step 3 Return optimal bicluster

$$x_i = \text{crossover}(f_i, f_j, r)$$

where function Hamming similarity(.) gives similarity between two fireflies f_i, f_j and r is used as crossover probability rate. But firefly f_i new position causes better cost, it will move to that new position. New firefly optimization algorithm can be summarized as the pseudocode is shown in algorithm 2. This strategy makes a social behaviour for all fireflies and they move towards global best.

3.2 Crossover Operator

The genetic crossover operator is used to produce new individuals by inheriting some parts of both parent's genetic material. In this research work, Multi-point Crossover operator is used to move firefly towards brighter fly as in nature.

For multi-point crossover *mpc*, crossover positions is given as $mpc = \{l_1, l_2, ..., l_{mp}\}$ where l is the length of the binary string. The bits between successive crossover points are exchanged between the two strings to produce two new offspring [136]. The disruptive nature of multi-point crossover appears to encourage the exploration of the search space, rather than favouring the convergence to highly fit fireflies (triclusters) early in the search, thus making the search more robust.

3.3 Proposed DFOB Model

In algorithm 2, each firefly is associated with a generated tricluster solution. These initial tricluster solutions will be improved in an iterative manner until (*Stopping_Condition*) is met or maximum number of iteration reached.

In the iterative process, if the fitness of the solution (firefly) is better than the fitness of the solution (another firefly) which means that the latter firefly will be attracted towards the first one and thus it will have its solution improved. The flowchart of proposed work is shown in figure 3.

Figure 3. Flowchart for discrete firefly optimization based triclustering model

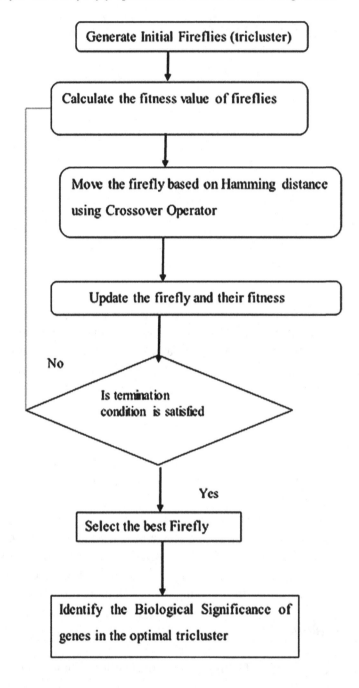

4. EXPERIMENTAL ANALYSIS

The performance of the proposed Discrete Firefly Optimization based Triclustering model is tested on 3D yeast cell cycle dataset is show in table 4. The yeast cell cycle analysis projects are public and available in http://genome-www.stanford.edu/cellcycle/.

Table 4. 3D microarray dataset description

Dataset	Genes	Sample	Time Point
CDC15 Experiment	8832	9	24

The main characteristic feature of the firefly algorithm is the fact that it simulates a parallel independent run strategy, wherein every iteration, a swarm of n fireflies is generated from n solutions. Each firefly works almost independently, and as a result the algorithm, will converge very quickly with the fireflies aggregating closely to the optimal solution.

Table 5 shows the characteristic of the optimal Tricluster extracted from yeast dataset using Discrete Firefly Optimization Triclustering (DFOT) model. This experiment is conducted using different MCV threshold ranges from 0.95 to 0.98 on 3D microarray dataset is tabulated. This tabulation contains the threshold value, number of genes, number of samples and number of time points, volume and the optimal correlated tricluster.

From the results, it has obvious that, the DFOT model extracts highly correlated triclusters called optimal tricluster. These triclusters contains highly relevant genes, samples over set of time points of a 3D microarray data with high volume.

Table 6 shows the Biological Significant for CDC15 dataset from yeast cell cycle. This tabulation contains values of Gene Ontology (GO) ID in the first column, GO term in the second column, Cluster Frequency in the third column, Background Frequency in the fourth column and P-Value in the fifth column.

Form the study, the proposed optimized three dimensional clustering approach using discrete firefly optimization has ability to extract highly expressive functional genes (in terms of tricluster) from Microarray data.

5. SUMMARY

In this chapter, a new application of the recently developed Discrete Firefly Optimization algorithm to the 3D microarray dataset has been proposed, presented and tested. The results of the implementation of

Table 5. Performance of DFOT for three dimensional microarray data

Optimal Tricluster	Threshold Value	No. of Genes	No. of Samples	No. of Time Points	Volume	Optimal Correlated Tricluster
Optimal Tricluster 1	0.95	419	7	16	46928	0.9504
Optimal Tricluster 2	0.96	387	5	14	27090	0.9601
Optimal Tricluster 3	0.97	260	7	15	27300	0.9700
Optimal Tricluster 4	0.98	119	5	15	17856	0.9800

Table 6. Biological significance of genes in the optimal triclusters

GO ID	GO_term	Cluster Frequency	Background Frequency	P-Value
5515	Protein Binding	348	633	0.00057
16740	Transferase Activity	445	839	0.00328
16301	Kinase Activity	119	194	0.0063
3677	DNA Binding	224	396	0.00203
17111	Nucleoside-Triphosphatase Activity	225	369	1.64E-07
16462	Pyrophosphatase Activity	236	390	1.64E-07
16817	Hydrolase Activity, Acting On Acid Anhydrides	236	390	1.64E-07
16818	Hydrolase Activity, Acting On Acid Anhydrides, In Phosphorus-Containing Anhydrides	236	390	1.64E-07
16787	Hydrolase Activity	475	897	0.00017
16887	Atpase Activity	158	266	0.00101
43168	Anion Binding	94	147	0.00219

this proposed model clearly showed the efficiency and effectiveness of the DFOB model for extracting the larger volume Tricluster with high correlation value.

REFERENCES

Deepthi, P. S. S. M. (2015). PSO Based Feature Selection for Clustering Gene Expression Data. IEEE.

Fei Han, C.-Q. W.-S.-H.-Q.-S. (2015). A Gene Selection Method for Microarray Data Based on Binary PSO Encoding Gene-to-class Sensitivity Information. *IEEE Transactions On Computational Biology And Bioinformatics.*

Kavitha, M. D. (2016). *A Hybrid Nelder-Mead Method For Biclustering Of Gene Expression Data.* International Journal Of Technology Enhancements And Emerging Engineering Research.

Li, Y. M. I. (2014). Biclustering of Gene Expression Data Using Particle Swarm Optimization Integrated with Pattern-Driven Local Search. *IEEE Congress on Evolutionary Computation (CEC).* 10.1109/CEC.2014.6900323

Li-Yeh Chuang, H.-W. C.-J.-H. (2007). *Improved binary PSO for feature selection using gene expression data.* Computational Biology and Chemistry Elsevier Ltd.

Liu, F. H. Z. (2006). Biclustering of Gene Expression Data Using EDA-GA Hybrid. *IEEE Congress on Evolutionary Computation Sheraton Vancouver Wall Centre Hotel.*

Lopamudra Dey, A. M. (2014). Microarray Gene Expression Data Clustering using PSO based K-means Algorithm. *International Journal of Computer Science and its Applications.*

Mohsen lashkargir, S. A. (2009). A Hybrid Multi-Objective Particle Swarm OptimizationMethod to Discover Biclusters in Microarray Data. *International Journal of Computer Science and Information Security*.

Rathipriya, R., Thangavel, K., & Bagyamani, J. (2011). Binary Particle Swarm Optimization based Biclustering of Web usage Data. *International Journal of Computers and Applications*, *25*(2), 43–49. doi:10.5120/3001-4036

Shyama Das, S. M. (2010). Greedy Search-Binary PSO Hybrid for Biclustering GeneExpression Data. *International Journal of Computers and Applications*.

Thangavel, K., & Bagyamani, J. (2011). Novel Hybrid PSO-SA Model for Biclustering of Expression Data. *International Conference on Communication Technology and System Design by Elsevier*.

Thangavel, K., & Rathipriya, R. (2014). Mining correlated bicluster from web usage data using discrete firefly algorithm based biclustering approach. *International Journal of Mathematical, Computational. Physical and Quantum Engineering*, *8*(4), 700–705.

Wei Shen, G. L. (2012). A Novel Biclustering Algorithm and Its Application inGene Expression Profiles. *Journal of Information and Computational Science*.

Xie, B. S. C. (2007). Biclustering of Gene Expression Data Using PSO-GA Hybrid. *1st International Conference on Bioinformatics and Biomedical Engineering IEEE Xplore*.

Yang, X.-S. (2009). Firefly algorithms for multimodal optimization, in: Stochastic Algorithms: Foundations and Applications, SAGA. *Lecture Notes in Computer Science*, *5792*, 169–178. doi:10.1007/978-3-642-04944-6_14

Chapter 18
Identifying Patterns in Fresh Produce Purchases:
The Application of Machine Learning Techniques

Timofei Bogomolov
University of South Australia, Australia

Malgorzata W. Korolkiewicz
University of South Australia, Australia

Svetlana Bogomolova
ⓘ https://orcid.org/0000-0003-4449-6514
Business School, Ehrenberg-Bass Institute, University of South Australia, Australia

ABSTRACT

In this chapter, machine learning techniques are applied to examine consumer food choices, specifically purchasing patterns in relation to fresh fruit and vegetables. This product category contributes some of the highest profit margins for supermarkets, making understanding consumer choices in that category important not just for health but also economic reasons. Several unsupervised and supervised machine learning techniques, including hierarchical clustering, latent class analysis, linear regression, artificial neural networks, and deep learning neural networks, are illustrated using Nielsen Consumer Panel Dataset, a large and high-quality source of information on consumer purchases in the United States. The main finding from the clustering analysis is that households who buy less fresh produce are those with children – an important insight with significant public health implications. The main outcome from predictive modelling of spending on fresh fruit and vegetables is that contrary to expectations, neural networks failed to outperform a linear regression model.

DOI: 10.4018/978-1-7998-0106-1.ch018

INTRODUCTION

Recent advances in technology have led to more data being available than ever before, from sources such as climate sensors, transaction records, scanners, cellphone GPS signals, social media posts, digital images, and videos, just to name a few. This phenomenon is referred to as Big Data, allowing researchers, governments, and organizations to know much more about their operations, thus leading to decisions that are increasingly based on data and analysis, rather than experience and intuition (McAfee & Brynjolfsson, 2012).

Big Data is typically defined in terms of its variety, velocity, and volume. Variety refers to expanding the concept of data to include unstructured sources such as text, audio, video, or click streams. Velocity is the speed at which data arrives and how frequently it changes. Volume is the size of the data, which for Big Data typically means large, given how easily terabytes to zettabytes of information are amassed in today's marketplace.

When it comes to consumer behavior and decisions, consumer data makes it possible to track individual purchases, to capture the exact time at which they occur, and to track purchase histories of individual customers. This data can be linked to demographics, advertising exposure, or credit history. Hence, researchers now have access to much more consumer data with greater coverage and scope, but also much less structure or much more complex structure than ever before. Traditional econometric modelling generally assumes that observations are independent, grouped (panel data), or linked by time. However, the Big Data we now have available may have more complex structure, and the goal of modern econometric modelling could be to uncover exactly what the key features of this dependence structure are (Einav & Levin, 2014). Developing methods that are well suited to that purpose is a challenge for researchers.

This chapter examines consumer food choices, in particular, purchasing patterns in relation to fresh fruit and vegetables. Consumption of fresh fruit and vegetables makes an important contribution to society in multiple ways. Increased consumption of fruit and vegetables can have a significant positive effect on population health (Mytton, Nnoahim, Eyles, Scarborough, & Mhurchu, 2014; World Health Organization 2015). Strong sales of fresh produce support primary production, contributing to rural and regional economies and farmers' livelihoods (Bianchi & Mortimer, 2015; Racine, Mumford, Laditka, & Lowe, 2013). Fruit and vegetable categories in supermarkets contribute some of the highest profit margins, compared to other product categories (e.g., packaged food), making these categories very important for supply-chain members. Therefore, better understanding and prediction of patterns of consumer purchases of fresh fruit and vegetables could have a substantial positive effect on a range of health, economic, commercial, and social outcomes.

Traditionally, consumer research into fresh fruit and vegetables has relied on consumer surveys, where consumers report their attitudes and intentions to buy fresh produce and barriers to doing so (Brown, Dury, & Holdsworth, 2009; Cox et al., 1996; Péneau, Hoehn, Roth, Escher, & Nuessli, 2006; Finzer, Ajay, & Ali, 2013; Erinosho, Moser, Oh, Nebeling, & Yaroch, 2012). The results were inherently biased by the indirect link between what consumers say in surveys and their actual behavior. When fresh produce purchases were examined, they were often based on self-reports, which typically are influenced by social desirability bias (Norwood & Lusk, 2011) and memory failures, resulting in over- or under-reporting of purchases (Ludwichowska, Romaniuk, & Nenycz-Thiel, 2017). Overcoming these limitations, this chapter draws on a more reliable Consumer Panel Dataset, which is one of the Nielsen datasets made available to marketing researchers around the world at the Kilts Center for Marketing, the University of Chicago Booth School of Business. Since participating households routinely scan all their purchases,

Nielsen Consumer Panel Dataset provides a complete and accurate account of their spending on fresh fruit and vegetables across all grocery outlets.

Leveraging off this unique and high-quality dataset, consumer purchasing decisions in relation to fresh fruit and vegetables are investigated using both unsupervised and supervised machine learning techniques, including clustering, artificial neural networks, and deep learning neural networks. By exploring the Nielsen Consumer Panel Dataset, the authors aim to illustrate the extent to which machine learning methods can lead to models that uncover previously unknown patterns of consumer behavior and that capture consumer purchasing decisions better. The specific objectives of this chapter are:

- To illustrate the application of unsupervised (clustering) and supervised (linear regression, artificial neural networks, and deep learning neural networks) machine learning techniques to household purchase data in fresh fruit and vegetables; and
- To highlight the advancement in knowledge and interpretation that could be obtained by the application of these machine learning techniques.

In economic terms, improved understanding of how consumers buy fresh produce could help growers and retailers to increase sales of fresh fruit and vegetables. This, in turn, would have a positive flow on effect on:

- Population health – fruit and vegetables are the healthiest of the foods, and research shows that people do not eat enough of them;
- Economic outcomes, especially for agrarian economies, including the United States and Australia;
- Social outcomes, by providing more jobs and income to food-growing communities and supply-chain members;
- The environment, by reducing consumption of meat products in favor of fruit and vegetables.

The structure of the chapter is as follows: the Nielsen Consumer Panel Dataset is introduced first, followed by an analysis of consumer purchasing decisions. The analysis begins with an exploration of consumer characteristics using clustering techniques. Groupings of households obtained from clustering are then compared in terms of their purchasing behavior, and observed differences are formally assessed using a non-parametric version of MANOVA. The second stage of the analysis incorporates household groupings resulting from clustering into supervised predictive modelling of consumer spending on fresh fruit and vegetables. The next section discusses main outcomes and contributions, followed by some suggestions for future research directions and a conclusion.

NIELSEN CONSUMER PANEL DATASET

In this chapter, patterns of customer purchases of fruit and vegetables are studied using the Nielsen Consumer Panel Dataset, which consists of a representative panel of households that continually provide information about their purchases using in-home scanners to record all their purchases intended for in-home use. Consumers provide information about their households and what products they buy, as well as when and where they make purchases. The dataset covers 13 years (2004 to 2016), with more than a billion purchases from up to 60,000 consumer households in any given year. It provides rich information about household purchasing patterns that allows researchers to study questions that cannot be addressed using other forms of data. For example, the dataset also includes purchases from retailers who traditionally do not cooperate with scanner data-collection companies. In addition, due to the national coverage (the entire United States divided into 52 major markets), there is wide variation in household location, seasonal patterns in availability of fresh produce, and demographics, adding to the richness of the captured consumer information. There are many examples of applications of this dataset in the economic and marketing literature, ranging from studies on tax effects, geography, price policies, in-store promotion and advertising to disaster relief sales, pharmaceutical products, liquor, etc. For a list of working papers that leverage Nielsen Consumer Panel Dataset, see additional reading. Yet, studies that use the Nielsen Consumer Panel Dataset and that focus on fresh fruit and vegetable purchases are relatively rare. A few exceptions are studies focused on organic purchases (e.g., Kim, Seok, & Mark, 2018; Kim, Seok, Mark, & Reed, 2018; Nelson, Fitzgerald, Tefft, & Anderson, 2017), and a study of retirement influence on fresh fruit and vegetable purchases (Hinnosaar, 2018).

The Nielsen Consumer Panel Dataset consists of the following files: Panelists, Trips, Purchases, Retailers, Products, Product Extra Attributes, and Brand Variations. Panelist files contain demographic, geographic, and product ownership information, which is updated annually. Demographic and product ownership variables are recorded for the entire household and the head of the household, as well as demographics for some other household members. Household describing variables (used in this analysis) include household size, income, presence and age of children in household, employment, education, marital status, occupation, type of residence, and race. There is also spatial information – ZIP code, state, county, region – as well as basic indicators of household assets – kitchen appliances, TV items, Internet connection.

Trips files provide summary information about each of the shopping trips made by panelists, such as the household ID, date, retail chain shopped, and the total amount spent for the trip. Since 2007, the number of shopping trips has varied between 10 and 11 million per year, and on average, there are about 180 shopping trips per household per year.

Purchases files provide information about the specific products a household bought on a shopping trip, including the product ID, the quantity, price paid, and any perceived deals. Specifically, there is a flag if a purchase was seen by the panelist as a deal, and the coupon value if the panelist used a coupon. For each year, there are more than 60 million transactions recorded.

Each Products file contains detailed product information for each unique product code, such as description, brand description, multipack and size. Products come from 10 Nielsen-defined food and non-food departments, approximately 4.2 million unique product codes in total for all years. The departments are dry grocery, frozen foods, dairy, deli, packaged meat, fresh produce, non-food grocery, alcohol, general merchandise, and health and beauty aids. Some products contain additional characteristics (e.g., flavor, variety, packaging, salt content, organic claim). These are recorded in Products Extra Attributes files for approximately one million products. Finally, the Retailers file contains an anonymized list of all retailers, each classified into one of 66 channel types (e.g., grocery, online shopping, discount store, hardware, drug store), from which products were purchased.

For the purposes of analyses presented in this chapter, only supermarket shopping is considered. That is, only shopping trips to retailers classified as "grocery" are analyzed, accounting for 66% of all shopping trips recorded. A single year (2013) was selected for the analysis, with data from other years (2014 and 2015) used for validation of outcomes. Given the authors' focus on fresh fruit and vegetables, products of interest belong to the "Fresh Produce" category.

ANALYSIS OF SUPERMARKET PURCHASING DECISIONS BY HOUSEHOLDS

The primary unit of analysis in this chapter is the household. In the field of shopper behavior, household level analysis is the most common, because many grocery purchases, especially from supermarkets, are made on behalf of the entire household. Purchases and trip information were therefore aggregated by household to produce the following variables to describe households' shopping behavior:

- Average number of shopping trips per month (num_trips).
- Average monthly number of items bought across all product categories (purchases).
- Average monthly spending on all product categories (spending).
- Average monthly number of purchases perceived as deals for all product categories (deals).
- Average monthly number of purchases labelled as organic for all product categories (organic).
- Average monthly number of items bought in the Fresh Produce category (fr_purchases).
- Average monthly spending on Fresh Produce (fr_spending).
- Average monthly number of Fresh Produce purchases labelled as organic (fr_organic).
- Average monthly number of perceived deals for Fresh Produce category (fr_deals).

Descriptive statistics for raw data from 2013 are reported in Table 1. On average, US households made 5.11 shopping trips to supermarket per month (median 4.25 trips). They bought 61.8 items (median 51.3) and spent on average $233.28 (median $189.14). That included 7.1 items (median 4.7) and $16.87 (median $11.63) on products from Fresh Produce category (fruit and/or vegetables). On average, households bought 0.8 (0.6) items labelled as organic, including 0.2 (0) items from Fresh Produce category. Also, households purchased on average 21.6 (10.5) items on a deal; only 1.6 (0.5) of them were from Fresh Produce category.

Figure 1 shows average monthly spending on items from Fresh Produce category for different states. Spending pattern correlates with overall wealth of households – coastal states tend to have higher household incomes, and as a result, they might be spending more on all products, including fruit and vegetables.

Next, unsupervised and supervised learning techniques are employed to understand household shopping behavior further. More specifically, clustering is used to explore household demographic information

Table 1. Descriptive statistics for variables representing shopping behavior of households

Key	Mean	Std. Dev.	Median	IQR	Min	Max
num_trips	5.11	3.49	4.25	3.88	1.00	38.33
purchases	61.78	46.74	51.25	55.67	1.00	701.08
spending	$233.28	$183.65	$189.14	$211.15	$0.89	$3935.32
organic	0.84	2.68	0.17	0.58	0.00	91.91
deals	21.62	29.09	10.50	29.75	0.00	501.42
fr_purchases	7.08	7.27	4.73	6.67	0.00	132.58
fr_spending	$16.87	$17.60	$11.63	$15.30	$0.00	$712.52
fr_organic	0.19	0.71	0.00	0.13	0.00	43.73
fr_deals	1.61	2.90	0.50	2.00	0.00	84.17

Figure 1. Average monthly expenditure on fresh produce in 2013

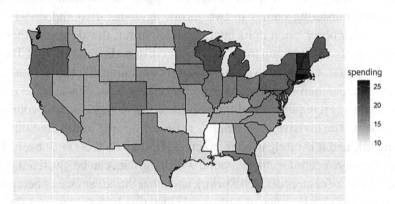

and to create groupings based on similar household characteristics. The resulting household clusters are then compared in terms of their shopping behavior using variables defined in this section. This is followed by predictive modelling of household spending on fresh fruit and vegetables using selected supervised learning techniques. In the case of both unsupervised and supervised learning, multiple methods of varying complexity are employed and compared in relation to outcomes of interest. The purpose of employing multiple methods is to illustrate the impact (if any) of different approaches to the same task on results from that task, and to explore the extent to which more advanced machine learning techniques can be expected to produce better outcomes or predictions with panel data and in the context of studying consumer behavior.

Exploratory Analysis of Nielsen Consumer Data Using Clustering Techniques

Unsupervised learning, more specifically, clustering techniques, are employed (a) to discover distinct clusters based on household characteristics, and (b) to determine how shopping patterns overall and in fresh fruit and vegetables differ between those clusters of households.

Clustering has been applied across many disciplines to place objects into groups or clusters suggested by available data so that objects in a given cluster are more similar (in some sense) than those placed in different clusters. The objective can be to find a hidden structure in the data or to reduce its dimensionality. Partitioning data into clusters may be an aim in itself or an input into further analysis.

Clustering is considered unsupervised learning, since there are no pre-defined classes into which to assign objects. In fact, the number of classes may need to be established as a part of the clustering process. Most commonly used clustering techniques are distance-based. As the name suggests, a distance metric of some kind (e.g., Euclidean distance) is used to separate observations into clusters with small within-cluster distances and large separation from other clusters. The algorithms involved are relatively simple to apply and interpret, but they suffer from a lack of well-defined rules on how to form clusters and how to assess the quality of clustering solutions. Despite numerous measures and criteria having been proposed in the literature, a decision what "similar enough" or "good enough" might mean in a particular application remains highly subjective. A comprehensive review of distance-based clustering methods and the underlying theory can be found in Hastie, Tibshirani, and Friedman (2009).

Distance-based clustering can be classified into two types: hierarchical clustering and partitional clustering. Hierarchical clustering comes in two forms, agglomerative and divisive. Agglomerative clustering starts with each observation in its own separate cluster; the algorithm then proceeds to find the most similar data points and to group them into larger clusters. In contrast, divisive clustering works in the other direction by first starting with a single cluster containing all observations and then dividing most dissimilar observations into separate, smaller clusters. Divisive clustering is more complex than agglomerative clustering, as it requires an additional clustering method as a sub-routine to divide existing clusters at each step. The divisive approach has not been studied in the literature as extensively as agglomerative methods, and it is rarely used in practice (Hastie et al., 2009; Jobson, 1992). Partitional clustering assumes there are central features around which the data can be clustered in non-overlapping partitions with the number of centers defined a priori, and it has the advantage of being relatively computationally inexpensive. One disadvantage of partitional clustering is that it requires the expected number of clusters to be known beforehand. In contrast, hierarchical clustering allows the researcher to decide the number of clusters in the data based on the analysis of a dendrogram, which is a tree-like graphical depiction of the structure produced by the algorithm. This makes hierarchical clustering a more flexible approach. Hierarchical clustering is also preferred when there is a perceived hierarchy in the data and for smaller datasets due to its computational complexity. In terms of distance-based clustering, this chapter focuses on hierarchical clustering, as it can be applied to categorical data.

However, clustering techniques are not limited to distance-based methods. There is also a range of model-based clustering techniques that rely on knowing the probability distribution of the data. Cases are assigned to clusters based on assessments of probability rather than a distance measure to find similarities between cases. Latent class analysis (LCA) is an example of a model-based clustering method, also referred to as a finite mixture model. As discussed in McCutcheon (1987) and elsewhere (e.g., Vermunt & Magidson, 2002), the method assumes that the population is composed of different unobserved groups, or latent classes, and the joint density of observed variables is a mixture of the class-specific density. The simplest form of a latent class model assumes that observed data come from a mixture of multivariate multinomial distributions. Cluster membership is decided based on probability calculated using the maximum likelihood method. As the method relies on distributional assumptions, it is possible to use formal tests or goodness-of-fit indices to decide the number of clusters. In that respect, the focus is on modelling the latent structure behind the data rather than looking for similarities, as is the case with distance-based cluster analysis. LCA is sometimes referred to as a "soft clustering" method, as it allows objects to belong to more than one class, and thus it offers more flexibility than a "hard clustering" method such as hierarchical clustering, where objects must be split into distinct clusters.

As argued in Anderlucci and Hennig (2014), cluster analysis is not a well-defined problem, in that differing meanings can be assigned to similar objects assigned to the same clusters. In distance-based clustering, the aim is to find well-separated clusters with low within-cluster distances whereas the model-based approach aims to uncover latent structure in the data. In both cases, "true" clustering of the data may be sought; however, there is not much literature to guide users as to which approach is most suitable for their particular application. In this chapter, both distance-based clustering (hierarchical) and model-based clustering (LCA) are applied to illustrate their use in the context of studying purchasing decisions by households. The authors' interest in LCA arises in part from its growing popularity facilitated by the availability of easily implemented LCA-based algorithms in statistical analysis software packages. Another reason for considering a model-based approach is the question of whether resulting partition represents true clustering of the data. It has been pointed out in the clustering literature (e.g.,

Figure 2. Cluster dendrogram for 2013 data

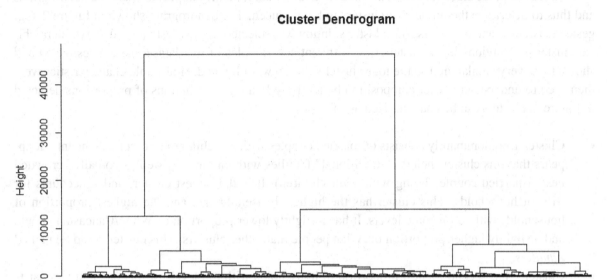

Ultsch & Lötsch, 2017) that by virtue of their design, commonly used algorithms including hierarchical clustering can impose structure on data even when there is actually none. Also, while a hierarchical cluster analysis always ensures that the most similar observations are in the same clusters, often there are situations where a cluster should be split and its members re-allocated to other clusters. However, no such step exists in the algorithm, and clusters created by hierarchical cluster analysis are commonly less homogeneous than clusters formed by other algorithms. This issue does not arise with LCA, and in addition, some researchers (Anderlucci & Henning, 2014; Vermunt & Magidson, 2002) have found the latent class approach relatively more successful at recovering the true cluster structure when such structure is known, albeit with artificial datasets. Other advantages of LCA clustering include being able to incorporate variables of different scale types, add covariates to the analysis, and overcome sparseness in the data (Vermunt & Magidson, 2002).

Both hierarchical clustering and LCA clustering are now applied to produce clusters of households based on their demographic characteristics. In both cases, the shopping behavior of the resulting clusters is compared. Similarities and differences between the two clustering solutions are also discussed.

Hierarchical Clustering

To investigate household purchasing behavior, clusters were first formed using agglomerative hierarchical clustering based on following household variables defined by Nielsen and stored in Panelist files: region_code, household_income, household_size, type_of_residence, household_composition, age_and_presence_of_children, race, and marital_status. As all these are categorical variables, they were converted into dichotomous dummy variables and then used to create a matrix of Manhattan distances. Ward's method of minimizing within-cluster variation was used to form clusters, as it produced the most interpretable clusters. The Manhattan distance metric is often chosen, as it is less sensitive to outliers (Jobson, 1992). It is also preferred for high-dimensional and categorical data, and a mathematical justification for using it with Ward's linkage is given in Strauss and von Maltitz (2017).

As a first step, the algorithm was executed for a few small random samples to study the dendrograms and thus to determine the number of clusters to be produced. The dendrogram shown in Figure 2 suggested between 3 and 6 clusters. A 4-cluster solution was selected as the most optimal. Next, hierarchical clustering solutions for 4 clusters over different sub-samples of the dataset were investigated and shown to be very similar, and so the four-cluster solution was obtained. Household characteristics were then used to understand cluster composition better. Based on the distributions of proportions depicted in Figure 3, clusters can be characterized as follows:

- Cluster 1 predominantly consists of married couples with 2-3 children or other dependents. It appears that this cluster includes "traditional" families with children as well as so-called crowded nests (married couples living with adult children). It is the largest cluster, and it accounts for 31% of households. This cluster has the highest household size and the highest proportion of households with top income levels. It has a slightly lower proportion of White/Caucasian people and a slightly higher proportion of Asian people than other clusters. This cluster could be named *Families*.

- Cluster 2 has second highest proportion of households with top levels of income, and it consists mostly of White/Caucasian married couples without children or other dependents. This cluster is the same size as Cluster 1, and it accounts for 30-31% of households. It is comprised of DINKs (double income, no kids) including empty nesters (50+ couples whose adult children have left home). This cluster could be named *DINKs*.

- Cluster 3 is composed of single-member households, that is, males or females living alone, never married or widowed, divorced, or separated; predominantly with no kids. It accounts for 25% of households, and it consists mainly of females living alone (approximately 73%). This cluster has the lowest level of income and a somewhat higher proportion of multi-family housing than other clusters. Race distribution in Cluster 3 is similar to that in Clusters 1 and 4. This cluster could be named *SINKs* (single income no kids).

- Cluster 4 is the smallest cluster, accounting for 12% of households. It is the third in terms of incomes and the second in terms of household size (2-4 members). Most households in this cluster are headed by females. All marital status categories are represented, with the highest proportion in the separated/divorced category. This cluster includes single parents with one or more children plus other remaining family and relationship groups (e.g., unmarried couples). This cluster could be named *Single Parents Plus*.

All clusters have very few differences in terms of region, residence type, or race distribution (except Cluster 2 as mentioned above). Hence, the major driving characteristics are household composition and marital status.

Figure 4 shows the average values of variables characterizing shopping behavior for each cluster relative to the average for all households in the dataset. As the distributions of the shopper behavior variables are highly right-skewed, log transformation was applied in all cases. Transformed values were then standardized to produce z scores (mean = 0, standard deviation = 1). A bar near zero indicates a cluster average close to the overall average, while a bar with a positive or negative value indicates a deviation from the overall average in terms of higher or lower spending or the number of items purchased.

When interpreting, it is important to look at the relative size of the bars within each cluster; a disparity between spending patterns overall and on fresh produce could indicate useful patterns. Also, positive

Figure 3. Household characteristics by cluster in the hierarchical solution

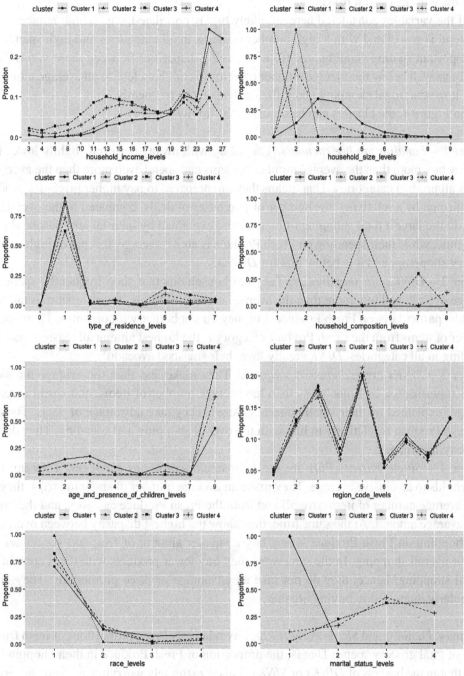

and negative deviations have different interpretations. For example, a high bar in the positive direction for total spending and a low positive bar in fresh produce spending means lower purchases of fruit and vegetables in relation to the total basket size. On the other hand, a high negative bar for the total spending and a low negative bar for the fresh produce spending means that the cluster has a higher proportion of fresh produce in the overall basket.

Many of the variables considered here are likely highly correlated, e.g., a high number of shopping trips in general is associated with a high number of items in all categories and high spending. Hence, the most important finding should come from observing disparities between these variables, e.g., if a household buys well below the average number of items overall but close to an average number of items with deals, it means frugal shopping and utilizing deals more frequently.

Based on Figure 4, the clusters can be described as follows:

- Cluster 1 – *Families* are *big spenders*. They shop with average or even slightly lower frequency, but they buy more than the average number of items and spend even more than the average amount across all product categories. That means they are prepared to pay higher prices for products. This is confirmed by a relatively low number of purchases of deals, compared to the overall shopping. They do the largest total shopping of all clusters, explained by their larger household size. At the same time, while their spending on Fresh Produce is above average, it is not as high as for the total grocery shopping, and it is below that for *DINKs*.

- Cluster 2 – *DINKs* are *shopaholics*. They are households that shop frequently, spend above the average overall, and buy more than the average number of items. They sometimes take advantage of deals, particularly on Fresh Produce, but they do not bother with organics. Their spending and number of items from the Fresh Produce category is the highest among all clusters and above their spending in all categories. *DINKs* really love their smashed avocado!

- Cluster 3 – *SINKs* are *economical shoppers*. They make less than the average number of trips to the supermarket, buy much less than the average number of items, and spend much less than average (explained by their small household size). They take advantage of deals. Their spending on Fresh Produce is relatively in line with the overall shopping and spending. They do not bother with buying organics.

- Cluster 4 – *Single Parents Plus* are the *least health-conscious shoppers*. They are the closest households to an elusive average. They make an average number of shopping trips, they buy close to an average number of items overall and from the Fresh Produce category, and they spend close to an average amount. At the same time, they show the highest disparity between overall shopping and shopping on Fresh Produce – they buy a smaller amount of fruit and vegetables compared to their overall shopping. In the same way, they buy fewer products with deals compared to their overall shopping; hence, they do not take an advantage of price promotions. They are also not particularly interested in buying organic.

In summary, *Families* and *Single Parents Plus* buy relatively lower proportions of fresh fruit and vegetables out of total grocery spend. That is, the proportion of Fresh Produce in their shopping baskets is lower than that in the baskets of *DINKs* or *SINKs*. This is extremely worrying, as both clusters represent household with children. From the public health perspective, these are the households that should be buying more fresh fruit and vegetables to support children's healthy development and to instill healthy dietary patterns in the next generation.

Managerially, it is also important to look at the absolute spending and the items bought, not just standardized figures, to ensure the differences between the clusters are substantial enough to develop actionable strategies for each cluster. Summary statistics in Table 2 are now discussed to gain further

Figure 4. Normalized shopping behavior (means) by cluster in the hierarchical solution

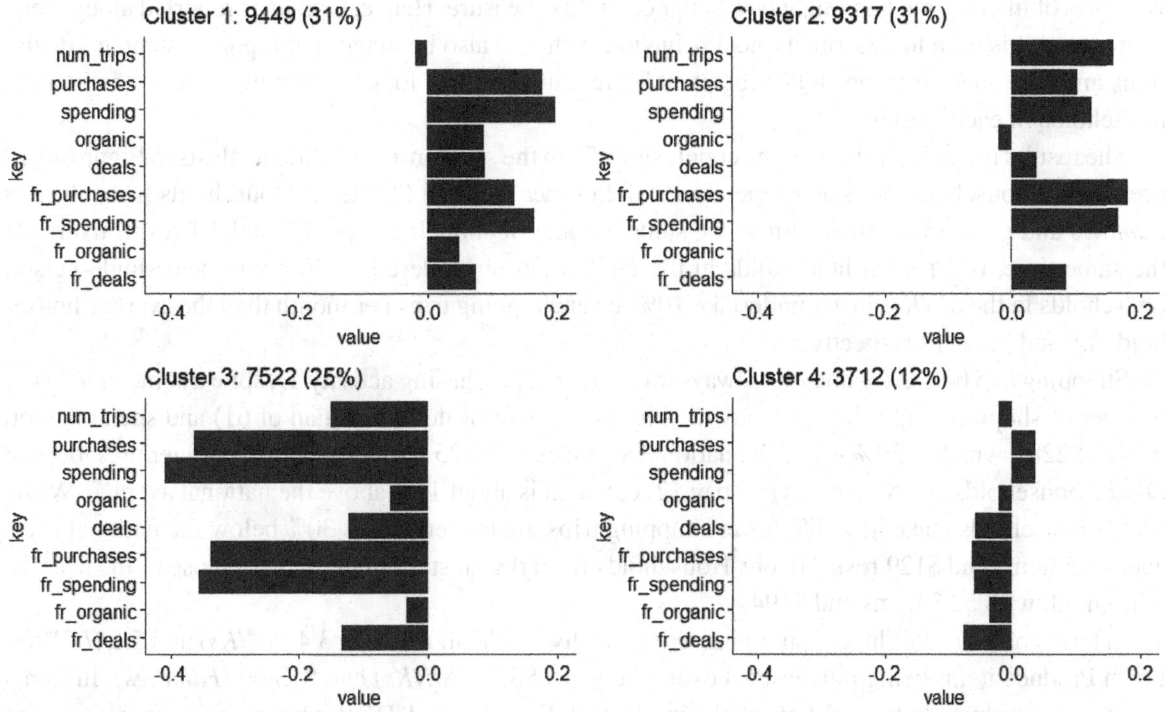

Table 2. Descriptive statistics for shopping behavior variables based on hierarchical clustering

	Mean (Std. Dev)	Median (IQR)	Mean (Std. Dev)	Median (IQR)	Mean (Std. Dev)	Median (IQR)	Mean (Std. Dev)	Median (IQR)
Cluster	**Families**		**DINKs**		**SINKs**		**Single Parents Plus**	
N	18,660 (31%)		18,726 (31%)		15,379 (25%)		7,586 (13%)	
num_trips	5.1 (3.6)	4.2 (3.9)	5.6 (3.6)	4.8 (4.2)	4.6 (3.1)	3.8 (3.4)	5 (3.5)	4.1 (3.7)
Purchases (item)	73.2 (55.1)	61 (67.7)	65.7 (44.3)	57.7 (56.7)	43 (30.6)	36.5 (36.8)	62 (45.8)	52.3 (54.4)
Spending ($)	277 (212)	228 (249)	252 (179)	216 (217)	157 (122)	129 (136)	233 (176)	194 (205)
Organic (item)	1.1 (3.3)	0.2 (0.8)	0.8 (2.6)	0.2 (0.6)	0.7 (2)	0.1 (0.5)	0.8 (2.2)	0.1 (0.6)
Deals (item)	26.2 (35.3)	12.3 (36.8)	22.4 (27.9)	11.8 (32.2)	15.5 (20.1)	8.1 (21.7)	20.7 (28.3)	9.9 (29.1)
fr_purchases (item)	8 (8.1)	5.4 (7.4)	8.1 (7.8)	5.6 (7.6)	5 (5.2)	3.4 (4.3)	6.5 (6.4)	4.4 (6)
fr_spending ($)	19.5 (20.4)	13.6 (17.5)	19 (18.3)	13.5 (17)	11.7 (12.2)	8.3 (10.4)	15.4 (15.1)	11 (13.8)
fr_organic (item)	0.2 (0.9)	0 (0.2)	0.2 (0.7)	0 (0.2)	0.2 (0.6)	0 (0.1)	0.2 (0.5)	0 (0.1)
fr_deals (item)	1.8 (3.2)	0.6 (2.3)	1.8 (3.2)	0.6 (2.3)	1.2 (2.1)	0.4 (1.6)	1.4 (2.5)	0.4 (1.8)

insights into the shopping behavior of households. Due to the right-skewness of the distributions for all variables of interest, median might be a better centrality measure. Hence, median is reported along mean values, and it is used to describe typical behavior. It should also be noted that reported standard deviations and interquartile range (IQR) values indicate that there is a lot of variability between individual households in each cluster.

The results in Table 2 reinforce the conclusions from the standardized values analysis in Figure 4. An average US household shops at a supermarket 4.25 times a month (Table 1). Households from clusters *Families* and *Others* undertake almost the same number of shopping trips, 4.2 and 4.1 respectively. At the same time, two-person households in the *DINKs* cluster undertake 13% more, and single-person households in the *SINKs* cluster undertake 10% fewer shopping trips per month than the average household, 4.8 and 3.8 trips respectively.

Shopping trip frequency does not always translate into purchasing activity. Despite a somewhat lower number of shopping trips, *Families* buy the highest number of items (median of 61) and spend the top dollar ($228), which is 20% above the national averages of 51.25 items and $189. Frequently shopping *DINKs* households buy 57.7 items and pay $216, which is about 13% above the national average. While *SINKs* households make just 10% fewer shopping trips, their spending is 30% below the national average, 36.5 items and $129 respectively. Households from the cluster *Other* are very close to the average household, with 52.3 items and $194.

In terms of Fresh Produce, a shopping trip typically results in between 3.4 (*SINKs*) and 5.6 (*DINKs*) Fresh Produce items being purchased, costing between $8.30 (*SINKs*) and $13.60 (*Families*). In terms of organic products, a typical household in clusters *Families* and *DINKs* buys one organic item for every five shopping trips. For clusters *SINKs* and *Single Parents Plus*, one organic product is typically purchased for every 10 shopping trips.

Looking at the ratio of Fresh Produce out of a total grocery basket items, it is clear that the two types of households with children (*Families* and *Single Parents Plus*) have lower proportions of fresh items (8.8% and 8.3% respectively) than the other two clusters (*DINKs* 9.8% and *SINKs* 9.4%). These results highlight a difference between clusters that is significant from the perspective of supply-chain managers and public health policy-makers. The overall picture also highlights that all households are buying relatively lower amounts of fresh produce, showing that less than 10% of their grocery baskets are fresh fruit and vegetables.

Real-life applications of clustering techniques suffer from non-replicability or instability of cluster solutions (see, for example, Ben-David, von Luxburg, & Pál, 2006; Leisch, 2015; Levine & Domany, 2001). To address this shortcoming in the present setting, the same clustering procedure was repeated independently for 30,000 panelists randomly sampled from the data for 2013, 2014 and 2015. Figure 5 shows the same nine shopping-related variables as in Figure 4, but for three different years. While there are some minor differences in cluster sizes and in the values of individual variables, the overall structure of clusters remains the same from year to year, which demonstrates the strong validity of the presented approach.

The differences in the shopping behavior of different groups of customers presented in Table 2 offer managerially significant insights. However, it is necessary to investigate whether there are statistically significant differences among the four clusters. The classical parametric MANOVA (multivariate analysis of variance) cannot be used for these data, as all nine shopping behavior variables are right skewed, and they do not follow a normal distribution. Hence, they do not meet the assumption of multivariate normality required for MANOVA. A nonparametric test for the comparison of multivariate data samples

Figure 5. Spending behavior means by cluster for 2013, 2014, and 2015

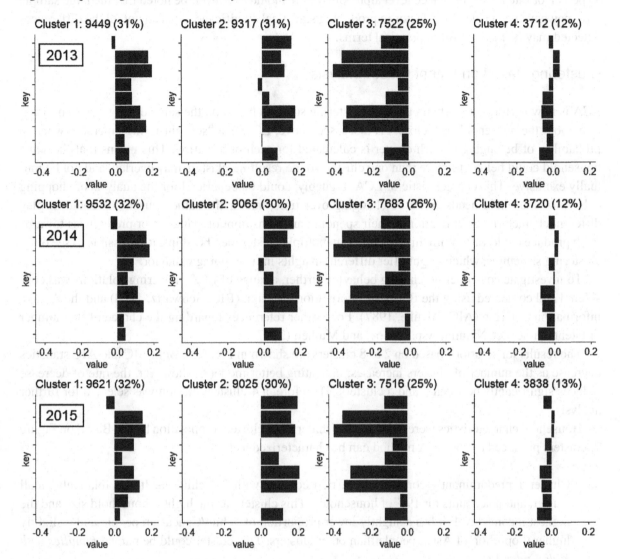

(Burchett, Ellis, Harrar, & Bathke, 2017) was employed to test statistical significance on the global level, as well as to identify statistically significant response variables and factor levels, while controlling the familywise error rate.

Global test results were highly significant (p-value $= 0$), indicating that there is a statistically significant difference among the clusters in relation to the nine spending pattern variables, namely the number of shopping trips plus the number of purchases made, the total amount spent, the number of purchases perceived as deals, and the number of organic products bought, both overall and in the fresh produce category. As the global hypothesis of no difference among clusters was rejected, a detailed follow up analysis was carried out to test for differences for all possible permutations of clusters and shopping behavior variables. A null hypothesis of equality for all appropriate subsets of factor levels (clusters) and response variables (shopping behavior variables) was rejected, while maintaining the maximum overall

Type I error rate at a significance level alpha of 0.05. It should, however, be noted that the large sample size may have been a deciding factor in producing statistical significance, and so not all the differences detected may be meaningful in practical terms.

Clustering Based on Latent Class Analysis

LCA is now performed to obtain another clustering solution based on the same demographic information about the households as before. As discussed above, LCA is a "soft clustering" method, where a probability of belonging to each cluster is calculated for each observation. This means that the same household could belong to more than one cluster, so the resulting clusters may overlap, and not be mutually exclusive. This characteristic of LCA, arguably, could be beneficial for the analysis of shopping behavior. Household needs could be changing over time, and/or the same households could display different characteristics in relation to their spending and consumption patterns, or preferences towards fresh produce could vary. With this flexibility in multiple cluster memberships, it is possible to see other clustering structures, which might offer different insights into shopping behavior.

To investigate consumer purchasing behavior further, a range of LCA clustering solutions was considered and compared using the Bayesian information criterion (BIC; Schwartz, 1978) and the Akaike information criterion (AIC; Akaike, 1987). For further references regarding the choice of the number of latent classes see Nylund, Asparouhov, and Muthén (2007).

The results for solutions based on 2 to 8 clusters are shown in Figure 6. Both BIC and AIC statistics decrease as the number of clusters increases, indicating better model fit; however, the rate of decrease reduces significantly between 4 and 5 clusters. Therefore, a 4-cluster solution was selected for further analysis.

Household characteristics were again used to understand cluster composition better. Based on Figure 7, clusters produced by the LCA method can be characterized as follows:

- Cluster 1 predominantly consists of married couples with 2-3 children. It is a relatively small cluster, and it accounts for 19% of households. This cluster has the highest household size and the highest income level. It has a slightly lower proportion of White/Caucasian people and a slightly higher proportion of Asian people than other clusters. This cluster could be named *Families with Kids Under 18*.
- Cluster 2 predominantly consists of White/Caucasian married couples without children under 18. It is the largest cluster, and it accounts for 44% of households. This cluster has the second highest proportion of top income levels. In most cases, these are 2-person households but there is also a

Figure 6. Scree plot based on model fit measures for different numbers of clusters in LCA

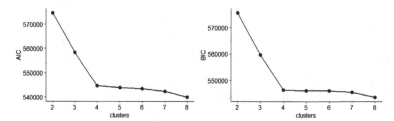

Figure 7. Household characteristics by cluster in the LCA solution

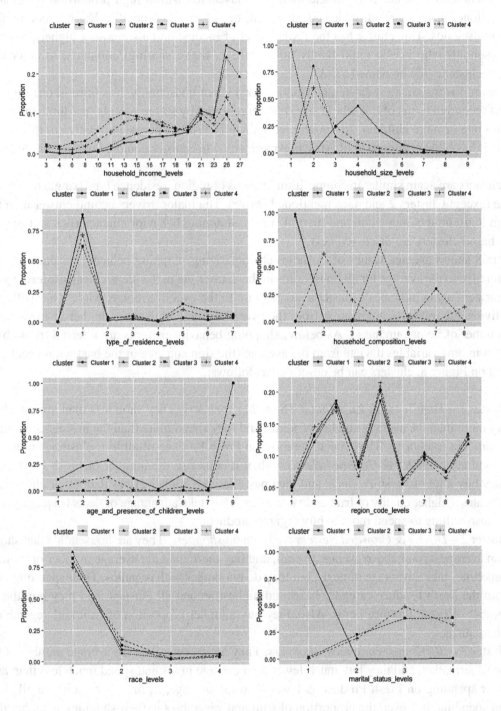

small proportion of households with one or two additional members. This suggests that this is a cluster of DINK households including the so-called empty nesters (parents whose grown up children have left home) plus crowded nesters (parents living with adult children). This cluster could therefore be named *DINKs & Crowded Nesters*.

- Households in Cluster 3 are single-member households with a high proportion of females living alone, never married, widowed, divorced, or separated, hence SINKs. It accounts for 26% of households. This cluster has the lowest level of income and a somewhat higher proportion of households who live in multi-family housing (e.g., house sharing) compared to other clusters. This cluster could be named *SINKs*.
- Cluster 4 is the smallest cluster, accounting for 11% of households. It is third in terms of income and second in terms of household size. It is represented by single parents (predominantly female) with one or more children. Although predominantly White/Caucasian, relative to the other clusters it has higher proportion of African Americans. This cluster could be named *Single Parents*.

All clusters are again similar in composition in terms of region, residence type (single family house), and race (except Clusters 2 and 4, as mentioned above). The major drivers behind cluster membership are again household composition and marital status. Shopping behavior characteristics of households in LCA-based clusters are discussed next.

Figure 8 shows average values of variables characterizing shopping behavior for each LCA-based cluster relative to the average for all households in the dataset. As in the hierarchical clustering solution, a bar near zero again indicates a cluster average close to the overall average, while a bar with positive or negative value indicates a deviation from the overall average in terms of higher or lower spending or the number of items purchased. As before, shopping behavior patterns are inferred from observing disparities in how variables deviate from the average (the sign and size of the bar) within each cluster.

Based on Figure 8, clusters can be described as follows:

- Cluster 1 – *Families with Kids Under 18* are *big spenders*. They shop less than average, but they buy more than the average number of items, and they spend more than the average amount across all product categories. They spend the most on Fresh Produce of all four clusters, but they come second after *DINKs & Crowded Nesters* when it comes to the number of Fresh Produce items. They buy a lot of Fresh Produce, and they pay relatively higher prices than other clusters, which indicates a higher quality of fruit and vegetables. They take advantage of deals frequently, but they are also willing to spend more to buy organic products.
- Cluster 2 – *DINKs & Crowded Nesters* are *frequent shoppers*. They are households that shop more than average, spend above average overall, and buy more than the average number of items. They sometimes take advantage of deals, but they do not bother with organics. Their spending on items from the Fresh Produce category is second highest among all clusters, and they buy the largest number of Fresh Produce items. Also, they buy a higher proportion of fruit and vegetables than other clusters.
- Cluster 3 – *SINKs* are *economical shoppers*. They make fewer than the average number of trips to the supermarket, and they buy much fewer than average items and spend much less than average. Their spending on Fresh Produce is lower than the average, in line with their overall shopping and spending; however, the proportion of fruit and vegetables in their shopping is higher than the average household. They do not bother with deals or buying organics.
- Cluster 4 – *Single Parents* are the *least health-conscious shoppers*. They are households that are very close to the average. They do an average number of shopping trips, they buy close to an average number of items overall and from the Fresh Produce category, and they spend close to an average amount. At the same time, they show the highest disparity between overall shopping and

shopping on Fresh Produce – they buy less fruit and vegetables compared to their overall shopping. They do not take advantage of price promotions overall, and even less so on Fresh Produce. They are also not interested in buying organic.

A comparison of the clusters shows the highest disparity between overall shopping and shopping for Fresh Produce category for *Families with Kids Under 18* and *Single Parents*. There is a much lower proportion of Fresh Produce items bought by these households compared to their counterparts from the *DINKs* and *SINKs* clusters and compared to the national average.

The summary statistics in Table 3 provide further insights into the shopping behavior of households in different clusters based on the LCA solution. Due to the lack of symmetry in the underlying distributions, median is again used to describe typical behavior in relation to the nine variables.

Compared to national averages of 4.25 shopping trips per month with 51.25 items, including 4.73 items from Fresh Produce category, and spending $189, including $11.63 on Fresh Produce items, *Families with Kids Under 18* shop at supermarkets on average 3.9 times per month, spend $242 for 64.9 items including $14 on 5.5 Fresh Produce items. That makes them the highest spending group – almost 30% above the national average.

Households from the *DINKs & Crowded Nesters* cluster shop in supermarkets more frequently – 4.7 times per month – and buy 57.1 items ($215) including 5.5 items ($13.40) from the Fresh Produce category. *SINKs* households are the lowest spenders – more than 30% below the national average – with 3.8 shopping trips per month, 36.5 items ($129) overall and 3.4 items ($8.30) from Fresh Produce category. *Single Parents* households are the closest to national averages, with 4.1 shopping trips per month, 51.8 items ($191), and 4.3 items ($10.80) from the Fresh Produce category.

Differences in shopping behavior of different groups of customers presented in Table 3 were assessed for statistical significance using the same non-parametric MANOVA approach as in the case of hierarchical clustering. The global hypothesis of no difference among the four clusters based on the nine shopping behavior variables was rejected (p-value $= 0$). The detailed follow-up analysis again showed statistically significant differences for all appropriate subsets of factor levels and response variables, while maintaining the maximum overall Type I error rate at a significance level alpha of 0.05.

As mentioned previously, LCA is a soft clustering method, in that a probability of belonging to each cluster is calculated for each observation. This means that clusters may overlap, because certain observations can have relatively high probabilities of belonging to multiple clusters. In the case considered here, most households have probability 1 or close to 1 of being in some cluster, so there is no doubt over their cluster membership. However, for about 3% of households, the LCA model produced probabilities that could place them in two clusters. For example, a household with probabilities (0.33, 0, 0.67, 0) could belong to Cluster 1 or 3.

There are two possible strategies to deal with this situation and to get cluster summary statistics. One is to treat households with questionable membership as outliers and to exclude them from the analysis. The other is to overinflate sample size by adding questionable households to all possible clusters. Both approaches were tried and the resulting clustering solutions compared to the one described above, where each household was assigned to a single cluster indicated by the highest of the probabilities. There was no discernible difference between the resulting clusters, and hence no significant differences for cluster interpretability.

Figure 8. Normalized shopping behavior (means) for LCA clusters

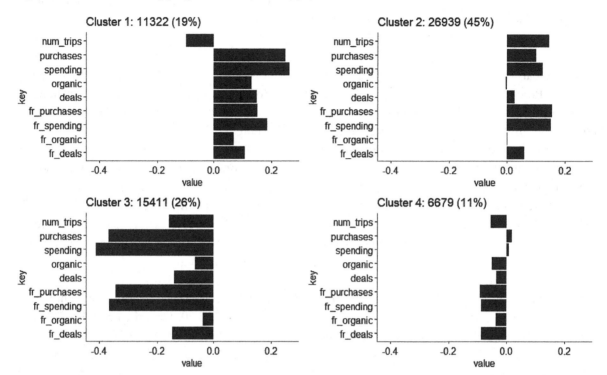

Table 3. Descriptive statistics for shopping behavior variables based on LCA clustering

	Mean (Std. Dev)	Median (IQR)	Mean (Std. Dev)	Median (IQR)	Mean (Std. Dev)	Median (IQR)	Mean (Std. Dev)	Median (IQR)
Cluster	Families with Kids Under 18		DINKs & Crowded Nesters		SINKs		Single Parents	
N	11,322 (19%)		26,939 (45%)		15,411 (26%)		6,679 (11%)	
num_trips	4.8 (3.4)	3.9 (3.6)	5.6 (3.7)	4.7 (4.2)	4.6 (3.1)	3.8 (3.4)	4.9 (3.5)	4.1 (3.7)
Purchases (item)	76.9 (56.3)	64.9 (70.8)	66.2 (46.8)	57.1 (58.2)	43 (30.7)	36.5 (36.8)	61.7 (45.8)	51.8 (54.1)
Spending ($)	289 (213)	242 (259)	254 (188)	215 (222)	157 (122)	129 (136)	230 (174)	191 (200)
Organic (item)	1.2 (3.7)	0.2 (0.8)	0.8 (2.6)	0.2 (0.6)	0.7 (2)	0.1 (0.5)	0.7 (2.2)	0.1 (0.5)
Deals (item)	28.2 (36.6)	14 (39.7)	22.6 (29.3)	11.2 (32)	15.5 (20.2)	8.1 (21.7)	20.8 (28.4)	10 (29)
fr_purchases (item)	8.1 (8)	5.5 (7.6)	8 (7.9)	5.5 (7.4)	5 (5.2)	3.4 (4.3)	6.3 (6.2)	4.3 (5.8)
fr_spending ($)	19.9 (19.9)	14 (17.9)	19 (19.1)	13.4 (17)	11.7 (12.2)	8.3 (10.4)	15 (14.6)	10.8 (13.3)
fr_organic (item)	0.3 (0.9)	0 (0.2)	0.2 (0.7)	0 (0.2)	0.2 (0.6)	0 (0.1)	0.2 (0.5)	0 (0.1)
fr_deals (item)	1.9 (3.3)	0.7 (2.4)	1.8 (3.2)	0.6 (2.3)	1.2 (2.1)	0.4 (1.6)	1.4 (2.5)	0.4 (1.8)

Table 4. Crosstabulation for cluster membership based on hierarchical and LCA clustering solutions

		LCA Clusters			
		Families with KIDS Under18	DINKs and Crowded Nesters	SINKs	Single Parents
Hierarchical Clusters	Families	11,199	7436	3	22
	DINKs	34	18,680	0	12
	SINKs	0	11	15,368	0
	Single Parents Plus	89	812	40	6,645

Comparing the Results of Hierarchical and LCA Clustering

The LCA solution thus described bears much similarity to the hierarchical clustering solution. The major difference in cluster membership between LCA and hierarchical clustering appears when it comes to households comprising married couples with children. As shown in Table 4, in the hierarchical clustering solution most two-parents-with-children households were placed in one separate cluster. In LCA clustering solution, they were split, and parents living with adult children were grouped together with married couples without children (DINKs) to form the largest cluster. The remaining married couples with children under 18 were assigned to a separate (smaller) cluster. Single parent and single person (SINKs) households appear to have been treated in the same way by the two methods, being placed into separate clusters of similar sizes.

Hence, the main source of disparity appears to be related to characteristics and consequently shopping behaviors of married couple households that include other adult relatives, most likely adult children. According to the LCA method, these households are more similar to DINK households than families with children.

In summary, managerially, it appears that both clustering methods – hierarchical and LCA, produce very similar four-cluster solutions, with largely similar shopping behaviors in respective clusters. Implications of these results are offered in the *Main Outcomes and Contributions* section.

Predictive Modelling of Household Spending on Fresh Fruit and Vegetables

This section describes an application of supervised machine learning techniques to the Nielsen Consumer Panel Dataset. Linear regression has been an important tool of data analysis since its introduction in the early 19th century. Traditionally it serves two purposes: (1) to make predictions for unobserved cases, e.g., out-of-sample or future observations; and (2) to identify the most important input variables (the strongest predictors in the model) through coefficient analysis. Linear regression remains one of the most popular types of data analysis today (Fox, Montgomery, & Lodish, 2004).

Artificial neural networks were introduced in the mid-1900s as an attempt to recreate human neural processing. A neural network is typically presented as three connected layers: an input nodes layer (independent variables or predictors), an output nodes layer (dependent variables or targets), and a hidden nodes layer between them. The number of nodes in the hidden layer can vary in a very wide range, and every node represents a multiple linear regression model with a possible addition of an activation function allowing it to control a process of results passing through. For more details, see Rojas (2013) or Hastie et al. (2009) and the references therein.

From the mathematical point of view, a neural network is a non-linear model resulting from a combination of many multiple linear regression models. Due to the very large number of coefficients in neural network models, their interpretations become much more problematic than linear regression models. However, their predictive ability seems to be superior to linear regression. Indeed, neural networks have been shown to be better predictive models than traditional predictive techniques for datasets where non-linear relationships might be expected or where relationships are simply unknown (Dasgupta, Dispensa, & Ghose, 1994; Sargent, 2001).

The most recent development in the area of machine learning is the introduction of so-called deep learning neural networks. These can be interpreted as neural networks with hierarchical architecture, created by adding multiple hidden layers of different sizes between input and output layers. Hence, a deep learning neural network becomes a non-linear model resulting from a combination of many neural networks. Deep learning techniques have demonstrated the ability to extract high-level, complex abstractions and data representations from large volumes of data in areas such as computer vision (Krizhevsky, Sutskever, & Hinton, 2012) and natural language processing (Mikolov, Sutskever, Chen, Corrado, & Dean, 2013), as well as customer behavior analysis (Shi, Xu, & Li, 2017).

In this chapter, all three types of supervised predictive models mentioned above (linear regression, neural network, and deep learning) are employed to predict household spending on products from the Fresh Produce category, that is, on fruit and vegetables, based on spending on other grocery product categories. For this purpose, transaction data was aggregated for individual trips in such a way that every observation is a vector of amounts spent in each of 119 product categories. The resulting dataset had 3.5 million observations (shopping trips) with the spending split across 119 product groups. Then, all observations were aggregated to calculate mean of monthly spending on each category for each household, and predictive models were run at the household level. The amount spent on fresh fruit and vegetables (variable Fresh Produce) was the target, and spending in all other product categories were predictors. Naturally, data were very sparse, as there were no purchases in many categories. All variables were log-transformed and normalized using min-max normalization, a typical process in machine learning that rescales all variables to take values between 0 and 1. This ensures that features measured on a larger scale do not exert undue influence on the overall results. One more variable had been added as a predictor – clustering membership to serve as a proxy for demographic information about each household.

Ordinary Least-Squares Regression

Ordinary least-squares regression was employed to predict the amount spent on Fresh Produce products by each household based on the information about the amount spent on products from other categories. More than 70% of the variables in the model were statistically significant due to the very large sample size. The model has an adjusted R-squared value of 0.57, which is considered a relatively good fit for consumer behavior data (Figure 9). There were no differences in prediction results from using different clustering solutions. Therefore, only results based on hierarchical clustering membership are reported below.

The model provides a few interesting insights into spending on Fresh Produce. The highest positive coefficient estimates, that is, product categories positively correlated with spending on Fresh Produce, were frozen unprepared meat, poultry, and seafood (0.2076), yogurt (0.1301), dried vegetables (0.1172), cheese (0.1135), salads and prepared food from the deli (0.0957), and canned vegetables (0.0875). Product categories with the highest negative coefficient estimates, that is, those negatively related to spending on Fresh Produce, were prepared food dry mixes (-0.0789), tobacco accessories (-0.0600), carbonated beverages (-0.0522), prepared frozen food (-0.0466), frozen pizza, snacks (-0.0437), and non-grocery types of products – shoe care, electronics, shaving. All these variables were highly statistically significant with *p*-values close to zero. These results seem logical: households that spend more on protein, dairy, and prepared vegetables – all healthful foods – also spend more on fresh fruit and vegetables. Conversely, households that spend more on unhealthy foods (carbonated beverages, frozen pizza) and tobacco spend less on fresh produce.

While the directional effects of these coefficient estimates are easy to interpret, one needs to be cautious in trying to assign practical significance to these estimates' values. The predictive model operates with normalized log-transformed values of monthly spending in each category, including the target, the Fresh Produce category. Hence, this is a log-log model, and the coefficient estimate interpretation should be given as an expected percentage change in the target variable when predictor value increases by some percentage. For example, an interpretation for a coefficient 0.2076 for frozen unprepared meat, poultry, and seafood, which is the largest coefficient, is as following: a 10% spending increase in this category will result in the spending on Fresh Produce equal to $\exp(0.2076 \log(1.1)) = 1.019983$, that is, almost a 2% increase in spending on Fresh Produce. Another large (negative) coefficient for carbonated beverages (-0.0522) means that a 10% increase in spending for this category is expected to decrease Fresh Produce spending by 0.5% – spending equal to $\exp(-0.0522 \log(1.1) = 0.9950$. These conversions across the largest coefficients suggest that most of these associations are small in value, and they might have limited managerial significance.

Coefficients for clustering membership were statistically significant but relatively low in value at 0.008 for Clusters 1 and 3 and 0.017 for Cluster 2. This means that with all other variables held constant, compared to a household in Cluster 4, a household in Clusters 1 or 3 would spend 0.8% more, whereas for a household from Cluster 2 the difference would be 1.7%.

Artificial Neural Network

As the next step, the same prediction task was attempted using another form of supervised machine learning – artificial neural networks. A neural network with 122 input nodes (spending in 118 product categories and 4 cluster membership categories), 1 output node (spending in the Fresh Produce category) and one hidden layer of 180 nodes was created and trained over 40 epochs with a 20% validation split. The model used mean squared error as a loss function, and an RMSProp optimizer and a ReLU activation function for each layer. The model had 22,321 trainable parameters. The prediction result on the test sample was marginally worse than after the linear regression with *R*-squared = 0.54 (Figure 10).

Figure 11 shows the history of the loss function for training and validation datasets over 40 epoch training process. The maximal improvements in the model – the lowest values of the loss function – were achieved after 10-15 epochs. After that, the neural network was overfitting the training dataset without any real improvements in the predictions on the validation dataset. Therefore, despite the expectation, the artificial neural network model did not produce better predictions than a much simpler multiple linear regression model.

Figure 9. Actual vs predicted plot based on the OLS regression model to predict spending on fresh produce

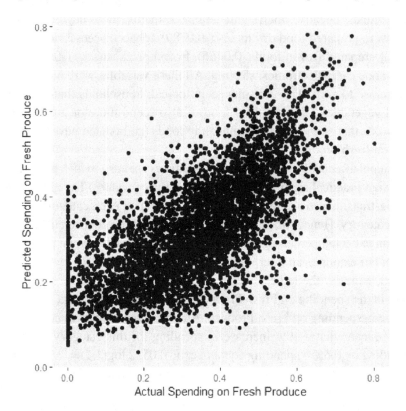

Deep Learning Neural Network

A deep learning modeling technique was also attempted for the same dataset. A new neural network had the same 122 input and 1 output nodes as before, plus 10 hidden layers of 180 nodes each. That resulted in 315,541 trainable parameters. The model was trained over 40 epochs with a 20% validation split. Figure 12 shows results of predicting spending on Fresh Produce for households from the test sample, while Figure 13 reports a history of the loss function over the 40 epochs of the neural networks training process. The lowest values of the loss function on the validation dataset were achieved after 4 epochs only. After that, the model was overfitting the training dataset and actually reducing the effectiveness of predictions on the out-of-sample data. That resulted in a quite poor quality of predictions with an R-squared of 0.46, which is below than R-squared for the one-layer neural network and the OLS regression model fitted previously.

MAIN OUTCOMES AND CONTRIBUTIONS

In this chapter, the authors aimed to illustrate the application of unsupervised and supervised machine learning techniques to consumer purchases panel data, with a particular focus on fresh fruit and vegetables.

First, the chapter has demonstrated a step-by-step application of two different clustering techniques: hierarchical (distance-based) and LCA (model-based). The key finding from the clustering analysis is

Figure 10. Actual vs predicted plot for the one-layer artificial neural network to predict spending on fresh produce

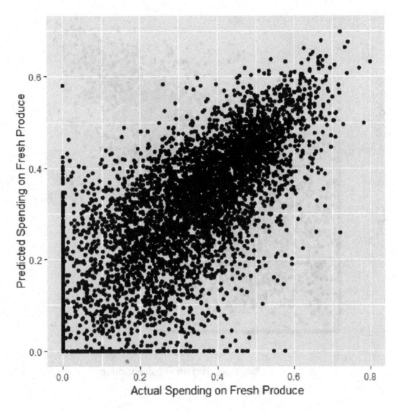

Figure 11. Loss function for training and validation datasets in the one-layer artificial neural network

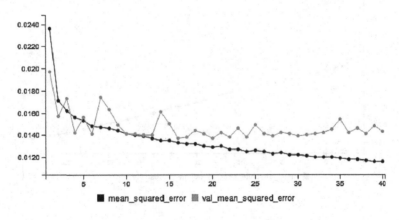

that the types of households that buy less fresh produce are those with children – an important insight that carries serious public health implications. Further, the authors showed that in the context of consumer purchases in fresh produce, it is possible to develop a clustering solution that is replicable over time (three years) and across two different clustering methods (distance- and model-based). Such replication over years and across clustering methods, and the resulting robust clustering solution, makes an

Figure 12. Actual vs predicted plot for the deep learning neural network

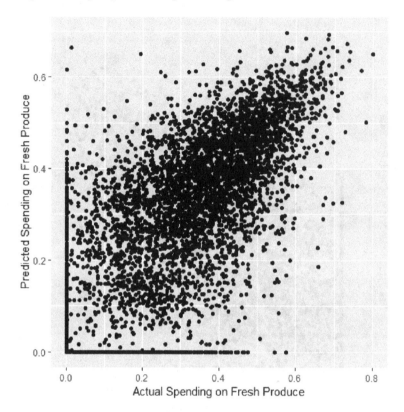

Figure 13. Loss function for training and validation datasets in deep learning neural network

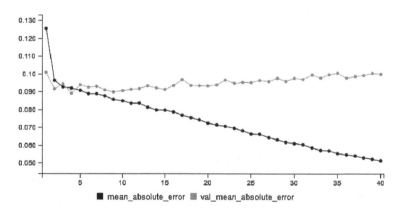

important contribution to the literature on clustering, where non-replicability of clusters is one of the major methodological challenges.

Second, the chapter has illustrated the application of three predictive modelling techniques – linear regression, artificial neural network, and deep learning, and it has compared the resulting models based on their predictive power. Despite common expectations, more advanced machine learning techniques (artificial neural network and deep learning neural network) were no more effective than a multiple regression model in predicting the amount spent on fresh fruit and vegetables based on household characteristics and spending in grocery categories other than fresh produce. This robust empirical evidence makes another valuable contribution to the field of machine learning, suggesting that in some circumstances (as presented here) more advanced techniques do not necessarily offer more insights or more predictive power. This finding is also useful for the field of marketing and econometrics to guide researchers' choices of analytical tools.

For the field of public health and agricultural economics, this chapter has offered a robust discovery of shopping patterns in fresh fruit and vegetables categories using scanner-based information, a major advancement on past studies dominated by survey-based information about consumer purchasing decisions. As such, this chapter has offered new insights into buying of fresh produce by US households, which is new knowledge that carries important implications for supply-chain and public health practitioners.

FUTURE RESEARCH DIRECTIONS

While promising, the analysis presented in this chapter offers only a glimpse into the wealth of insights that could be gained from Nielsen Consumer Panel Dataset regarding purchasing decisions made daily by US households. As discussed above, unsupervised learning in the form of clustering produced some results of practical significance; similarities and differences in spending on fresh produce were established for households grouped into clusters based on their demographic characteristics. Predicting the average amount spent on fresh produce using selected supervised learning techniques proved more challenging, and it could be subject of further study. The Nielsen dataset offers individual shopping trip information for all households, down to the exact contents of shopping baskets, which could be explored for patterns across time as well as cross-category purchase decisions.

Further replication of the observed patterns is needed. Specifically, the authors call for more studies that directly compare different clustering methods in a pursuit of developing procedures that provide more replicable clustering solutions. Similarly, while this chapter has demonstrated that in the context of consumer purchases of fresh fruit and vegetables, more advanced predictive models do not outperform the traditional models, more work is needed to compare these models on the same datasets to offer direct comparisons and to start building a body of evidence regarding their performance and predictive abilities in different contexts.

CONCLUSION

This chapter has illustrated the application of common machine learning techniques to a novel context of consumer purchases of fresh fruit and vegetables. The findings offer useful contributions to a number of academic disciplines: machine learning and statistics, marketing and econometrics, public health, and agricultural economics.

DISCLAIMER

1.   Researcher(s) own analyses calculated (or derived) based in part on data from The Nielsen Company (US), LLC and marketing databases provided through the Nielsen Datasets at the Kilts Center for Marketing Data Center at The University of Chicago Booth School of Business.
2.   The conclusions drawn from the Nielsen data are those of the researcher(s), and they do not reflect the views of Nielsen. Nielsen is not responsible for, had no role in, and was not involved in analyzing and preparing the results reported herein.

ACKNOWLEDGMENT

The authors acknowledge the support of the Ehrenberg-Bass Institute for Marketing Science, Business School, University of South Australia in gaining access to Nielsen Consumer Panel Dataset.

REFERENCES

Akaike, H. (1987). Factor analysis and AIC. *Psychometrika*, *52*(3), 317–332. doi:10.1007/BF02294359

Anderlucci, L., & Hennig, C. (2014). The clustering of categorical data: A comparison of a model-based and a distance-based approach. *Communications in Statistics. Theory and Methods*, *43*(4), 704–721. doi:10.1080/03610926.2013.806665

Ben-David, S., von Luxburg, U., & Pál, D. (2006). A sober look at clustering stability. In H. U. Simon, & G. Lugosi (Eds.), *Proceedings of the 19th Annual Conference on Learning Theory* (pp. 5-19). New York, NY: Springer. 10.1007/11776420_4

Bianchi, C., & Mortimer, G. (2015). Drivers of local food consumption: A comparative study. *British Food Journal*, *117*(9), 2282–2299. doi:10.1108/BFJ-03-2015-0111

Bodapati, A. V. (2008). Recommendation systems with purchase data. *JMR, Journal of Marketing Research*, *45*(1), 77–93. doi:10.1509/jmkr.45.1.77

Brown, E., Dury, S., & Holdsworth, M. (2009). Motivations of consumers that use local, organic fruit and vegetable box schemes in Central England and Southern France. *Appetite*, *53*(2), 183–188. doi:10.1016/j.appet.2009.06.006 PMID:19540288

Burchett, W., Ellis, A., Harrar, S., & Bathke, A. (2017). Nonparametric inference for multivariate data: The R package NPMV. *Journal of Statistical Software*, *76*(4), 1–18. doi:10.18637/jss.v076.i04 PMID:30220889

Cox, D. N., Reynolds, J., Mela, D. J., Anderson, A. S., McKellar, S., & Lean, M. E. J. (1996). Vegetables and fruit: Barriers and opportunities for greater consumption. *Nutrition & Food Science*, *96*(5), 44–47. doi:10.1108/00346659610129251

Dasgupta, C. G., Dispensa, G. S., & Ghose, S. (1994). Comparing the predictive performance of a neural network model with some traditional market response models. *International Journal of Forecasting, 10*(2), 235–244. doi:10.1016/0169-2070(94)90004-3

Einav, L., & Levin, J. (2014). The data revolution and economic analysis. *Innovation Policy and the Economy, 14*(1), 1–24. doi:10.1086/674019

Erinosho, T. O., Moser, R. P., Oh, A. Y., Nebeling, L. C., & Yaroch, A. L. (2012). Awareness of the Fruit and Veggies—More Matters campaign, knowledge of the fruit and vegetable recommendation, and fruit and vegetable intake of adults in the 2007 Food Attitudes and Behaviors (FAB) Survey. *Appetite, 59*(1), 155–160. doi:10.1016/j.appet.2012.04.010 PMID:22524998

Finzer, L. E., Ajay, V. S., Ali, M. K., Shivashankar, R., Goenka, S., Pillai, D. S., ... Prabhakaran, D. (2013). Fruit and vegetable purchasing patterns and preferences in South Delhi. *Ecology of Food and Nutrition, 52*(1), 1–20. doi:10.1080/03670244.2012.705757 PMID:23282188

Fox, E. J., Montgomery, A. L., & Lodish, L. M. (2004). Consumer shopping and spending across retail formats. *The Journal of Business, 77*(S2), S25–S60. doi:10.1086/381518

Hastie, T., Tibshirani, R., & Friedman, J. H. (2009). *The elements of statistical learning: Data mining, inference, and prediction* (2nd ed.). New York, NY: Springer. doi:10.1007/978-0-387-84858-7

Hinnosaar, M. (2018, July 30). *The impact of retirement on the healthiness of food purchases.* doi:10.2139srn.3235215

Jobson, J. D. (1992). Applied multivariate data analysis.: Vol. 2. *Categorical and multivariate methods.* New York, NY: Springer.

Kim, G., Seok, J. H., & Mark, T. (2018, February 13). *New market opportunities and consumer heterogeneity in the U.S. organic food market.* doi:10.2139srn.2916250

Kim, G., Seok, J. H., Mark, T., & Reed, M. R. (2018, January 1). *The price relationship between organic and non-organic vegetables in the U.S.: Evidence from Nielsen scanner data.* doi:10.2139srn.3176082

Krizhevsky, A., Sutskever, I., & Hinton, G. E. (2012). Imagenet classification with deep convolutional neural networks. In F. Pereira, C. J. C. Burges, L. Bottou, & K. Q. Weinberger (Eds.), Advances in neural information processing systems: Vol. 25. *NIPS 25* (pp. 1097–1105). Lake Tahoe, CA: Curran Associates.

Leisch, F. (2015). Resampling methods for exploring clustering stability. In C. Hennig, M. Meila, F. Murtagh, & R. Rocci (Eds.), *Handbook of cluster analysis* (pp. 637–652). Boca Raton, FL: Chapman and Hall/CRC.

Levine, E., & Domany, E. (2001). Resampling method for unsupervised estimation of cluster validity. *Neural Computation, 13*(11), 2573–2593. doi:10.1162/089976601753196030 PMID:11674852

Ludwichowska, G., Romaniuk, J., & Nenycz-Thiel, M. (2017). Systematic response errors in self-reported category buying frequencies. *European Journal of Marketing, 51*(7/8), 1440–1459. doi:10.1108/EJM-07-2016-0408

McAfee, A., & Brynjolfsson, E. (2012). Big data: The management revolution. *Harvard Business Review*, *90*(10), 60–68. PMID:23074865

McCutcheon, L. A. (1987). *Latent class analysis*. Newbury Park, CA: Sage. doi:10.4135/9781412984713

Mikolov, T., Sutskever, I., Chen, K., Corrado, G. S., & Dean, J. (2013). Distributed representations of words and phrases and their compositionality. In C. J. C. Burges, L. Bottou, M. Welling, Z. Ghahramani, & K. Q. Weinberger (Eds.), Advances in neural information processing systems: Vol. 26. *NIPS 2013* (pp. 3111–3119). Lake Tahoe, CA: Curran Associates.

Mytton, O. T., Nnoaham, K., Eyles, H., Scarborough, P., & Mhurchu, C. N. (2014). Systematic review and meta-analysis of the effect of increased vegetable and fruit consumption on body weight and energy intake. *BMC Public Health*, *14*(1), 1–11. doi:10.1186/1471-2458-14-886 PMID:25168465

Nelson, E., Fitzgerald, J. M., Tefft, N., & Anderson, J. (2017, September 1). *US household demand for organic fruit*. doi:10.2139srn.3081997

Norwood, F. B., & Lusk, J. L. (2011). Social desirability bias in real, hypothetical, and inferred valuation experiments. *American Journal of Agricultural Economics*, *93*, 528–534.

Nylund, K. L., Asparouhov, T., & Muthén, B. O. (2007). Deciding on the number of classes in latent class analysis and growth mixture modeling: A Monte Carlo simulation study. *Structural Equation Modeling: An Interdisciplinary Journal*, *14*(4), 535–569. doi:10.1080/10705510701575396

Péneau, S., Hoehn, E., Roth, H. R., Escher, F., & Nuessli, J. (2006). Importance and consumer perception of freshness of apples. *Food Quality and Preference*, *17*(1-2), 9–19. doi:10.1016/j.foodqual.2005.05.002

Racine, E. F., Mumford, E. A., Laditka, S. B., & Lowe, A. (2013). Understanding characteristics of families who buy local produce. *Journal of Nutrition Education and Behavior*, *45*(1), 30–38. doi:10.1016/j.jneb.2012.04.011 PMID:23073176

Rojas, R. (2013). *Neural networks: A systematic introduction*. Berlin, Germany: Springer Science & Business Media.

Sargent, D. J. (2001). Comparison of artificial neural networks with other statistical approaches: Results from medical data sets. *Cancer: Interdisciplinary International Journal of the American Cancer Society*, *91*(S8), 1636–1642. doi:10.1002/1097-0142(20010415)91:8+<1636::AID-CNCR1176>3.0.CO;2-D PMID:11309761

Schwartz, G. E. (1978). Estimating the dimension of a model. *Annals of Statistics*, *6*(2), 461–464. doi:10.1214/aos/1176344136

Shi, H., Xu, M., & Li, R. (2017). Deep learning for household load forecasting—A novel pooling deep RNN. *IEEE Transactions on Smart Grid*, *9*(5), 5271–5280. doi:10.1109/TSG.2017.2686012

Strauss, T., & von Maltitz, M. J. (2017). Generalising Ward's method for use with Manhattan distances. *PLoS One*, *12*(1), 1–21. doi:10.1371/journal.pone.0168288 PMID:28085891

Ultsch, A., & Lötsch, J. (2017). Machine-learned cluster identification in high-dimensional data. *Journal of Biomedical Informatics*, *66*, 95–104. doi:10.1016/j.jbi.2016.12.011 PMID:28040499

Vermunt, J. K., & Magidson, J. (2002). Latent class cluster analysis. In J. A. Hagenaars & A. L. McCutcheon (Eds.), *Applied latent class models* (pp. 89–106). Cambridge, UK: Cambridge University Press. doi:10.1017/CBO9780511499531.004

World Health Organization. (2015). *Increasing fruit and vegetable consumption to reduce the risk of noncommunicable diseases*. Geneva, Switzerland: Author.

ADDITIONAL READING

Agresti, A. (2012). *Categorical data analysis*. New York, NY: Wiley.

Athey, S. (2018). The impact of machine learning on economics. In A. Agrawal, J. Gans, & A. Goldfarb (Eds.), *The Economics of Artificial Intelligence: An Agenda* (pp. 507–547). Cambridge, MA: National Bureau of Economic Research; Retrieved from https://EconPapers.repec.org/RePEc:nbr:nberch:14009

Hennig, C. (2015). Clustering strategy and method selection. In C. Hennig, M. Meila, F. Murtagh, & R. Rocci (Eds.), *Handbook of cluster analysis* (pp. 703–737). Boca Raton, FL: Chapman and Hall/CRC. doi:10.1201/b19706

Johnson, R. A., & Wichern, D. W. (2008). *Applied multivariate statistical analysis*. Englewood Cliffs, NJ: Prentice Hall.

Jordan, M. I., & Mitchell, T. M. (2015). Machine learning: Trends, perspectives and prospects. *Science*, *349*(6245), 255–260. doi:10.1126cience.aaa8415 PMID:26185243

Najafabadi, M. N., Villanustre, F., Khoshgoftaar, T. M., Seliya, N., Wald, R., & Muharemagic, E. (2015). Deep learning applications and challenges in big data analytics. *Journal of Big Data*, *2*(1), 1–21. doi:10.118640537-014-0007-7

Von Luxburg, U., Wiliamson, R. C., & Guyon, I. (2012). Clustering: Science or art? In I. Guyon, G. Dror, V. Lemaire, G. Taylor, & D. Silver (Eds.), JMLR Workshop and Conference Proceedings 27 (pp. 65–79). Washington, DC: MIT Press. Retrieved from https://www.chicagobooth.edu/research/kilts/datasets/nielsen/working-papers

KEY TERMS AND DEFINITIONS

Artificial Neural Network (ANN): A predictive computer algorithm inspired by the biology of the human brain that can learn linear and non-linear functions from data. Artificial neural networks are particularly useful when the complexity of the data or the modelling task makes the design of a function that maps inputs to outputs by hand impractical.

Cluster Analysis: A type of an unsupervised learning that aims to partition a set of objects in such a way that objects in the same group (called a cluster) are more similar, whereas characteristics of objects assigned into different clusters are quite distinct.

Deep Learning: A type of machine learning based on artificial neural networks. It can be supervised, unsupervised, or semi-supervised, and it uses an artificial neural network with multiple layers between the input and output layers.

Hierarchical Clustering: The most common approach to clustering. The method proceeds sequentially, producing a nested assignment of objects into clusters. It is typically agglomerative, with cluster sizes increasing as the number of clusters decreases. At each step of the process, a clustering criterion based on a measure of proximity between groups must be computed to decide which groups of objects are to be joined together.

Latent Class Analysis (LCA): A statistical technique used in factor, cluster, and regression modelling, where constructs or latent classes are identified from multivariate categorical data and used for further analysis. The probability that a case belongs to a particular latent class is calculated using the maximum likelihood method. The resulting models can also be described as finite mixture models.

Machine Learning: A branch of artificial intelligence that focuses on data analysis methods that allow for automation of the process of analytical model building.

Partitional Clustering: A commonly used approach to clustering that begins with a preselected number of groups or clusters. An initial allocation of objects to clusters is followed by reassignment to new groups based on a measure of proximity between each object and each group. The process continues until all objects have been assigned to their closest groups. A commonly used partitioning method is the k-means algorithm.

Predictive Modelling: A process of using data mining or machine learning techniques to predict outcomes of interest. Once variables that are likely to influence the outcomes are identified and the relevant data is collected, a model is formulated and tested.

Supervised Learning: A machine learning task designed to learn a function that maps an input onto an output based on a set of training examples (training data). Each training example is a pair consisting of a vector of inputs and an output value. A supervised learning algorithm analyzes the training data and infers a mapping function. A simple example of supervised learning is a regression model.

Unsupervised Learning: A class of machine learning techniques designed to identify features and patterns in data. There is no mapping function to be learned or output values to be achieved. Cluster analysis is an example of unsupervised learning.

Chapter 19
Urban Spatial Data Computing:
Integration of GIS and GPS Towards Location–Based Recommendations

Uma V.
https://orcid.org/0000-0002-7257-7920
Pondicherry University, India

Jayanthi Ganapathy
https://orcid.org/0000-0001-9701-6241
Anna University, India

ABSTRACT

Urban spatial data is the source of information in analysing risks due to natural disaster, evacuation planning, risk mapping and assessments, etc. Global positioning system (GPS) is a satellite-based technology that is used to navigate on earth. Geographical information system (GIS) is a software system that facilitates software services to mankind in various application domains such as agriculture, ecology, forestry, geomorphology analysis in earthquake and landslides, laying of underground water pipe connection and demographic studies like population migration, urban settlements, etc. Thus, spatial and temporal relations of real-time activities can be analysed to predict the future activities like predicting places of interest. Time analysis of such activities helps in personalisation of activities or development of recommendation systems, which could suggest places of interest. Thus, GPS mapping with data analytics using GIS would pave way for commercial and business development in large scale.

INTRODUCTION

Urban spatial data, defines the spatial location and references of objects, people etc. They are generated from smart phones and other sources. They help in planning urban activities like disease management and control, traffic management etc. Internet of Things (IoT) is the recent advancement in information technology, electronic and telecommunication industry etc., which has led to the development of smart cities. Internetworking of devices and communication technologies has enabled wide range of applica-

DOI: 10.4018/978-1-7998-0106-1.ch019

tions in urban planning. Knowledge discovery on urban settlements is essential for decision making in demographic studies and urban growth (Allen, 1981 & Box et. al, 2012 & Campelo, 2013 & Claramunt and Theriault, 1995 & Rich et. al, 2009). In this view, the objective of this chapter is to present various computing methods for urban spatial data. These methods illustrate the importance of handing different data formats and utilisation of such acquired datasets in real time applications.

Data analytics and information management are intellectual property of every nation worldwide. Today, advancements in information technology have made it possible to acquire and process data efficiently. As technology advances, data storage and management becomes a fundamental issue as data is unstructured and differs in storage formats such as text, image, video. Data formats in terms of storage and computation demands high performance computing architectures (Li et. al, 2010 & Mohammady and Delavar, 2016). Today, the source of spatial data is plenty. They are multidimensional, unstructured and streaming in giga bits (Gbps). Such data differ in volume, velocity, veracity and variety and are termed as Spatial Big Data.

Machine Learning (ML) is scientific computation technology evolved from principles and concepts of Artificial Intelligence (AI). Today, ML is predominant in every domain application. Statistical method based computational models enable time series forecasting applications. Deep-learning is the recent advancement in ML using which data mining algorithms have evolved to equip parallel processing in information systems. These systems are enriched with data intensive computation using open source software frameworks. But, this chapter does not discuss about the application of machine learning for spatial data handling. This chapter actually focusses on Geographical Information System (GIS) and explains how it can be used in effective analysis of spatial data.

Raster and vector formats form the major category of spatial data. These datasets require pre-processing methods to make them useful in software systems for information retrieval and other decision support. Spatial computing algorithms are enriched with mathematical structures (Jayanthi and Uma, 2017a & Jayanthi and Uma, 2017b & Mondo et. al, 2010 & Randell, Cui, and Cohn, 1992 & Sudhira, Ramachandra, and Jagadish, 2004) . In this view, the objective of this chapter is to present various computing methods for urban spatial data. These methods illustrate the importance of handing different data formats and utilisation of such acquired datasets in real time applications.

GPS data processing using GIS helps in tracking and monitoring services. Point coordinates in the form of latitude and longitude of GPS data represents a spatial location on earth. This spatial information enables location based software service development such as travel information system, freight management, logistics and supply chain management in industries etc. An activity that has taken place in a spatial location at any given time represents temporal information.

Human activities are specific to location in general and their behaviour varies with respect to time. People visit a particular place for some need but at times they visit periodically. For instance, travelling to tourist spot location and shipping of goods is a temporal periodical activity. People navigate periodically to specific locations. This location when indexed by coordinate system represents points in latitudes and longitudes. Such location data are termed as spatial data. Temporal data of location is nothing but spatial data indexed in time series (Box et. al, 2012). Navigation system enables location tracking based on activities occurring at different time instants. Tracking such activities is possible using GPS navigation system. Geographical Information System (GIS) is a software system used for analysing GPS data. Spatial pattern analysis on GPS data is helpful in demographic studies in terms of analysis of human behaviour and activities so as to support decision making in business developments.

Spatial and temporal factors are prime elements in imparting location based services to mankind. Location data is generated when GPS is operated. Periodic storage and analysis of these location data are useful in decision making when appropriate computational techniques are applied (Allen, 1981 & Campelo, 2013 & Randell, Cui, and Cohn, 1992 & Sudhira, Ramachandra, and Jagadish, 2004 & Yong et. al, 2014 & Xiaoyi et. al, 2016 & Xin et. al, 2013). Spatio-temporal analysis is used to analyse the relation between different spatial locations using temporal information. Thus, space – time analysis of GPS data is essential in location tracking and location based services to mankind (Hornsby and Egenhofer, 2000 & Mondo et. al, 2010).

Spatio-Temporal Geographic Information system (GIS) has enormous information service applications to mankind in various domains such as agriculture, ecology, wildlife and forestry, earthquake and landslide assessment in geomorphology studies, demographic studies like population migration, urban settlements etc. Application specific software systems and services can be developed using spatio-temporal GIS that would provide location based software services like recommending nearby locations by personalising human activities.

The objective of the proposed chapter is to explain the importance of GPS data analytics using GIS and its applications in location based software services. The next 2 sections explain the terms related to GPS and GIS which would help in better understanding of the chapter.

GPS Navigation Systems

Location tracking and positioning is made easy today with the help of GPS Navigation systems. These systems help in locating a spatial location on map. These systems are helpful in tracking objects when appropriate data is present. Location data acquired by GPS navigation systems are useful in analyzing human activities such as mobility of people in different locations, environmental risk assessment and evacuation planning, migration and urban settlements, health care and disease spread etc. Hence it is essential to explore GPS data processing and management. The data acquired by GPS receivers are stored in GPX exchange format. This file format is used under public license, free of cost. GPS file contains fields like latitude and longitude for every point. GPS visualizer software packages are available to convert raw GPS data to text delimited comma separated value (.csv) files. Data in this format is used to describe waypoints, track objects and find routes. Apart from these applications, there are many applications of GPS data in various domains such as Recommendation systems, Fleet Management System, Location based services, Traveller Information system etc.

Basic Terms and Definitions

- **GPS** – Global Positioning System is a Navigation system comprising of following components.
  - *Space Segment* – Consists of constellation of satellites (24 satellites) used to measure spatial location using transmitted signals.
  - *Control Segment* - Consists of ground monitor stations, three antennas and master control station.
  - *User Segment* - Consists of GPS receiver that receives signal from minimum of four satellites to measure three dimensions namely direction, position (location) and time.
- **Geo-location** – The coordinate points that identify a specific object on earth is geo-location.

- **Data Dictionary** – The attributes produced by GPS receiver and the represented information collectively constitutes data dictionary.
- **Navigation System** – A system that uses an electronic equipment that determines position of a vehicle and its direction from a specified location. GPS is one such satellite navigation system.
- **Positioning System** - Mechanism used for determining location of an object in space.
- **Autonomous Positioning** – Represents a technique that uses GPS receiver to produce raw data with 10 meters minimum precision error.
- **Local Positioning system** – A navigation system that provides position of object within vicinity or within a given local area.
- **Location Tracking** – The process of identifying the path traced by remote object.
- In the next section the concepts related to GIS are explained to enable the naïve readers to have a basic understanding of the domain.
- **Geographic Information System (GIS)** is software system that integrates storage, analysis, mapping and visualization of both spatial and a-spatial data of a geographic area. This software system helps in visualizing geographic datasets in thematic layers. The underlying data store is Geo-database that helps data manipulation operations such as insert, delete, update and other aggregate operations on data. The underlying data store of GIS is Geo-database. It is organized collection of well-defined data (spatial) items in raster and vector format representing geographic entities.

Raster and Vector Data

Entity represents object in real world and such entities have attributes that describe characteristics of spatial data items such as feature type, color, shape, size etc. Spatial data holds point coordinates viz. latitude and longitude which identify location of a feature in a geographic space. Those properties of data that describe about features such as color, shape, size and type etc., other than location are all a-spatial data. Hence, spatial data is of two types (1) Raster data and (2) Vector data.

1. **Raster data** - The spatial data is stored as picture element (pixel) with row and columns in matrix form. Each pixel contains spatial information. Example: image in .tiff, .png
2. **Vector data** - The spatial data stored in the form of point, line and polygon constitute vector data. Example: shapefiles

Geographic Information Systems (GIS) is a software system that integrates software, thematic layers, Query processing engine, Visualization etc. Raster datasets are useful in identifying area of extent of a specific geography such as forestry, wet land, and agricultural growth. It is also significant in risk assessment, post assessment of disaster management. Digital elevation model is one such raster data that can identify likelihood of land-cover regions affected by flood and helps in decision on relief efforts thus, helps in evacuation planning, Gray scale images are captured using single band. Multi-spectral images contain different information which is captured on one or more bands. Raster image consumes large amount of space as each pixel carries digital information and occupies space in memory. Thus, raster data is useful in analysis continuous change in information over time.

Vector data provides precise location data. This data stores topology information that allows efficient operation on geometric features such as proximity and network analysis. However, vector data does not store continuous spatial change. To derive continuity in vector datasets specific interpolation and scientific computing is performed.

Spatial datasets are represented in geo-database using geometric data type such as point, line and polygon. Point is a geographic location represented in terms of Latitude and Longitude. Line is the path connecting any two spatial points. The distance between any two points is length of line connecting them. The line connecting each point in a given set of points thus forms a path. The start of the path is source vertex and end of the path is terminal vertex. Polygon is formed when a closed path passes through set of points. The closed path of finite length thus forms polygon. These geometric types are stored in vector format.

Vector formats define topological structures using which physical structures on earth are represented. Point, line, and polygon describe connectivity, adjacency and continuity. These structures are useful in buffering and proximity analysis. A buffer space is a polygon surrounding a geographic feature in selection which is used for proximity analysis. Two linear features A, B are said to be connected when there is a path to traverse from A to B and B to A. The details of various Vector and Raster Data Formats are given in Table 1 and 2 respectively.

Maps

The study of map making techniques is known as Cartography. The different types of maps are (1) Topography map (2) Base Map and (3) Thematic Map. Topography map is formed by mapping of earth surface that comprises of hilly terrains; land cover, natural and man-made structures etc. Base Map is the map that provides the fundamental information upon which other maps can be built. The density of data points representing geographic feature is analyzed using heatmap. Thematic map is a layer describing geographic features in a dataset represented using specific theme. Map clusters identify hotspot, outlier, spatial similarity based on geographic features that are statistically significant. Our chapter will discuss the importance and applications of clustering in detail. Clustering can be visualized as layers in GIS. Cartesian Co-ordinate is point coordinate on real axis. Control point is the point coordinate in real world that references the geographic features on map. Geo-referencing is mapping raster image by associating it with real co-ordinate system. Geocoding is the process of transforming physical identity of an object to location in point coordinates form. Map Projection is transformation of point coordinate on earth and projection on a plane. Map Algebra is mathematical set theory based algebraic operations used for analysis and manipulation of geographic data. Having understood the concepts associated with

Table 1. Vector data formats

Format	Description	Software
GeoJSON	Hierarchical arrangement of data series in the form of key-value pair	ArcGIS QGis ArcInfo
TopoJSON	Line segment stored as single arc which can be referenced multiple times by different polygons	
Esri –Shapefile	Generic format for exchanging vector data .shp, .shx, and .dbf files	
GeoPackage	Open format based on SQLite database format	
Keyhole Markup Language (KML)	A KML/KMZ file can also reference a series of rasters called overlays.	

Table 2. Raster data formats

Format	Description	Software
ArcInfo Grid	Software for viewing raster data files.	ArcCatalog ArcInfo Workstation
MrSID	The MrSID file extension is .sid. A companion file with a .sdw extension and the same prefix name as the .sid is used as a world file for georeferencing a MrSID image	
ECW	Proprietary format for ERMapper for imagery compression.	
JPEG	Non-proprietary image compression format. Compression ratios are similar to MrSID and ECW formats.	
TIFF	Grey scale TIFF images are compressed with MrSID to 10:1 or 15:1. Color images are usually compressed to 30:1 or 40:1.	

GPS and GIS, the next section will explain the importance of spatio-temporal analysis and the clustering methods used to achieve this.

Spatio-Temporal Analysis

Real world objects exhibit change over time. Evolving spatial features describe change over time scale. The phenomenal characteristics of such spatial features and their behaviors can be well studied using formal mathematical techniques known as spatial statistics. Spatial and temporal components of evolving geographic features help in various forms of raster and vector analysis like clustering, classification, buffer and proximity, spatial queries, spatial joins, etc. In this chapter, we discuss the clustering approaches and its applications in recommendations.

GPS DATA AND GIS BASED CLUSTERING METHODS

In this section, crime data[1] is analyzed to show the significance of clustering. First, we discuss the various clustering analysis techniques available and then we present discussions related to the case study.

Cluster Analysis

Point based Clustering analysis that helps in identifying behavior of activities using GPS data are

1. Cold spot analysis
2. Hot spot analysis.

Vector data can be used to identify the locations that are statistically significant. Z-score and p-values indicate the presence of statistically significant clusters in the data. A high z-score and p-value indicate the presence of hot spots and low negative scores indicate the presence of cold spots. Z-score nearer to zero indicate no spatial clustering. These analyses are performed on crime data the results are discussed below. The crime statistics data containing GPS locations of crime activities are used for analyzing behavior of burglary, robberies, theft etc. The crime dataset when analyzed using clustering approaches have provided interesting information which can be useful for the police department in making decisions. Burglary activity in residential areas is found to be minimal at some point of time while it is dense at different time instances in different spatial regions. Hence, behavior of such activities can be analyzed as shown in figure 1. Figure 1 shows which residential areas are sparsely affected by burglary. Whereas, figure 2 shows hot spot clusters describing a dense burglary activity. This location analysis can help in providing recommendations to concerned officials and they can make a decision on providing security in locations which are identified as hot spots.

SPATIAL QUERY OPERATIONS

Spatial queries are special type of query executed on geo databases. Spatial queries can be used to retrieve information from maps and in this section we explain how spatial queries help in retrieving information that can help in recommendations. Check in data of 2 cities New York and Tokyo is obtained from Four Square dataset[2]. The dataset has details about check-ins made in the two cities for a period of 10 months (from 12 April 2012 to 16 February 2013). The check-in details are time stamped and contains GPS coordinates. The details of semantic category of various places in the two cities are also provided. The semantic categories include Arts and Crafts store, Food and drink shop, Airport, Student center, Book shop etc. So, the dataset provides details about the check-ins in various places belonging to different semantic categories of the above mentioned 2 cities. If we consider New York city check-ins data, the base map obtained is shown in figure 3. Now over this base map a spatial query can be applied to get category-wise check-ins data. Figure 4 shows the result of the query. The spatial locations (GPS coordinate points) that represent check-in details of a particular day at various locations and that matches the

Figure 1. Cold spot burglary in residential areas

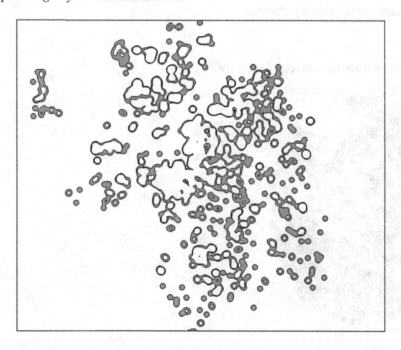

Figure 2. Hot spot of burglary activity in residential areas

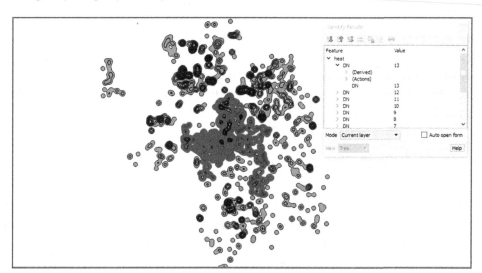

query conditions are identified. The pattern matching operation in the spatial query is *"LIKE"* where C is the attribute (category) on which the logical *AND* condition is performed. Those spatial locations that satisfy given category names are visualized as yellow color platelets.

Consider the spatial query using select by feature tool in GIS. The above retrieved information will help in knowing the check-ins made on a particular day at a particular place. When this spatio-temporal analysis is repeated considering various time stamps then it is possible to find out the point of interest of travelers. This would enable the tourist management system to provide recommendations like point of interest to travelers. Similarly, spatial query applied on check-in information for Tokyo dataset is shown in figure 5. It is found that the travelers are found to be more clustered than New York dataset. In this spatial query **D** represents category attribute.

Figure 3. Check-ins information in New York City

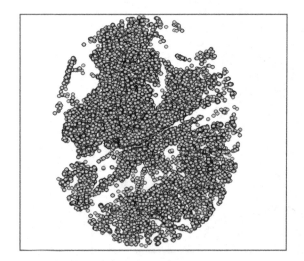

Figure 4. Spatial query on check-in information in New York City

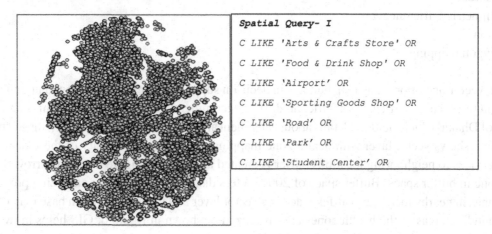

```
Spatial Query- I
C LIKE 'Arts & Crafts Store' OR
C LIKE 'Food & Drink Shop' OR
C LIKE 'Airport' OR
C LIKE 'Sporting Goods Shop' OR
C LIKE 'Road' OR
C LIKE 'Park' OR
C LIKE 'Student Center' OR
```

VECTOR OPERATIONS

Recommendations to human can be made based on vector operations which may be performed when GPS data and spatial datasets in other appropriate formats like .shp (shapfiles) etc. are available.

Buffer or Proximity Analysis

Buffer is a geographic space created on vector layer around a geographic feature of interest to analyze proximity of feature in a region of interest. The proximity analysis can be used further for various vector operations as given below.

1. Intersect

Figure 5. Spatial query on check-ins information in Tokyo City

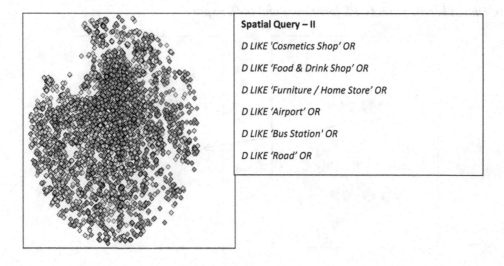

```
Spatial Query – II
D LIKE 'Cosmetics Shop' OR
D LIKE 'Food & Drink Shop' OR
D LIKE 'Furniture / Home Store' OR
D LIKE 'Airport' OR
D LIKE 'Bus Station' OR
D LIKE 'Road' OR
```

2. Difference
3. Symmetric Difference
4. Union
5. Polygon Clipping

These vector operations may help humans in decision support or in recommending planning services at the right time. The significance of buffer analysis in recommendation is illustrated in this section using datasets of Dhaka[3] which includes details about catchment area, slum areas (in shapefile (.shp)format) and

Figure 6 shows vector layer with health zone mapping. To analyze proximity of these health zones and its services to neighboring locations buffer is created as shown in Figure 6 and the arrow denotes a health zone in buffer space. Buffer space of 2000 meters distance is created for analyzing proximity of health zones in nearby locations. Buffer space is a vector layer and when overlaid on base map of Dhaka the surrounding areas of the health zones are visualized as shown in figure 6. GIS helps in overlaying of different layers to visualize aggregation on data.

1. Intersect

Intersect is a vector operation performed to extract portion of features common to both input layer and intersecting layer. The features in resulting intersect layer are assigned attributes of those features common to both the layers.

Thus, intersection operation does not modify the attributes instead outputs those features that are in common as shown in figure 7. The buffer space created around the health zones is overlaid with Dhaka catchment area. When intersect operation is performed those catchment areas within buffer space are given as results. This operation helps in analyzing distance proximity and can help in recommendation systems. Recommendations can be given to the user by considering their current locations and with the proximity analysis the health center nearer to their location can be given as recommendation.

Figure 6. Dhaka health zones (GPS locations) and buffer space

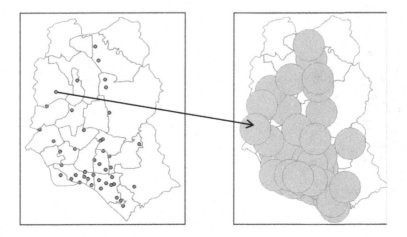

Figure 7. Intersection of buffer space and health zones within the Dhaka catchment area

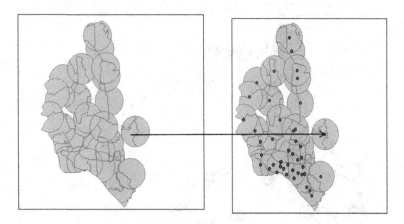

2. Difference

Difference operation creates a vector layer with those features that are not partially overlapping or fully overlapping or part of features present in input layer and difference layer. The difference layer resulted from buffer layer and residential areas of Dhaka are shown in figure 8. The residential areas outside the health zone buffer are the result of this difference operation. This vector layer thus, helps in visualizing and analyzing residential areas that are not served with health center facilities. These type of analysis will help in making decision about starting new health centers at places where they are not available. So such type of location based recommendation can help to cater the needs of people.

Symmetric Difference

Symmetrical difference operation removes those features overlapping with input layer and difference layer. It extracts features from input layer and difference layer in which overlapping features are not present. The result of symmetrical difference operation is shown in figure 9. The residential areas overlapping with buffer space are removed. This is visually shown in yellow color platelets in figure 9. Symmetrical difference operation helps in identifying those residential areas that are within close proximity of health zone facilities in Dhaka. This type of analysis will help in recommending health center that exists in close vicinity.

3. Union

Union operation creates a vector layer containing features that are overlapping and non-overlapping in both the input layers as shown in figure 10. Residential areas that are overlapping with buffer space and non – overlapping features as well are extracted in union vector layer.

4. Polygon Clipping

Clipping operation extracts features that fall within the space bounded by clipping layer. Figure 11 shows clipped residential regions that are within the buffer space.

Figure 8. Vector layer shown result of difference operation

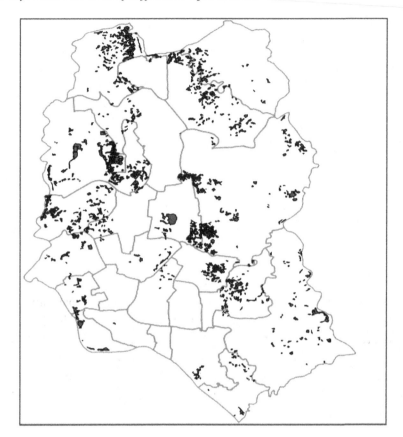

The mobility of people at various locations of Tokyo city using check – in dataset is made known using attribute based clustering on two attributes latitude and longitude present in check – in dataset. The check- in registered at various locations is shown in Table 3. The number of features present in each of classes as shown in figure 12 is retrieved using query shown below. The count of features present in each class is shown in Table 4. The feature records retrieved using cluster is shown in figure 13 which is attribute table containing class field.

Query 1 when executed on the geo database returns 7831 features on map.

Recommendations to human based on mobility of people is made possible using clusters on spatial location of spots check-in information. The method of mobility analysis is illustrated in this section using a large social network dataset. The different classes identified using K-Means clustering based on latitude and longitude spatial features is shown in figure 14. Gowalla is a social network where users share their location information during check-in at various locations (Yong et al. 2014; Xin et al. 2013). The features considered for this recommendation analyses are

1. Id – Unique number to identify record containing check-in information
2. created_at – Date of check-in
3. time – Time information of GPS location
4. latitude and longitude – Spatial location

Figure 9. Symmetrical difference vector layer

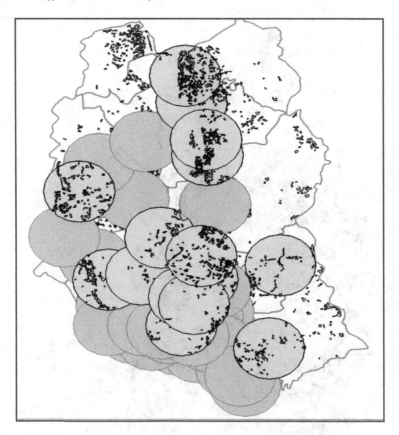

5. radius_meters – Check in made at various spots
6. spot categories – This dataset has following major categories
    a. Community
    b. Entertainment
    c. Food
    d. Outdoor
    e. Shopping
    f. Travel

The mobility of peoples in the year 2009 based on places of interest can be analyzed using the query. Those records whose radius is not within 1000 meter radius are retrieved as shown in figure 15.

The mobility of peoples in the year 2010 based on places of interest can be analyzed using the Query 3. The features returned by the query are shown in figure 16.

The mobility of peoples in the year 2009 analyzed based on check-in information using the Query 4 and returned features as shown in figure 17.

The places of interest at close proximity distance can be analyzed using Query 5 and result of the query is shown in figure 18.

Figure 10. Union operation

The query returned 49019 features out of 979635 as shown in figure 19 which is 5% of total check-in made in the month of February 2010. From the above mentioned analyses, it is evident that analysis of spatial and temporal data can help in recommending places of interest and in identifying the mobility patterns of people. Thus, it is clear that GPS and GIS when integrated can provide better recommendations.

CONCLUSION AND FUTURE RESEARCH DIRECTIONS

GPS data can contribute in understanding the mobility patterns of people. In this chapter, we have discussed the basic terminologies related to GIS and GPS. Clustering and analyzing GPS data can help in understanding the mobility patterns in the data. Recommendation systems play a major role in recom-

Figure 11. Polygon clipping operation

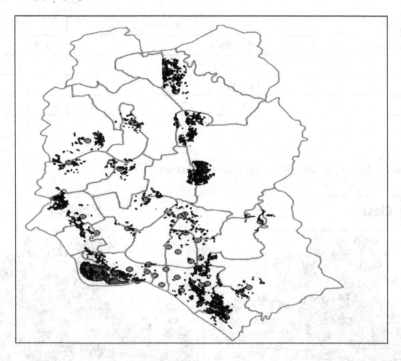

Query 1.

(CLASS = 3) AND (D LIKE 'Airport' OR D LIKE 'Bus Station' OR D LIKE 'Cosmetics Shop' OR D LIKE 'Food & Drink Shop' OR D LIKE 'Furniture / Home Store' OR D LIKE 'Road' OR D LIKE 'Subway')

Table 3. Locations identified in check – in dataset

Sl. No.	GPS Locations
1.	Food & Drink Shop
2.	Furniture / Home Store
3.	Cosmetics Shop
4.	Road
5.	Airport
6.	Subway
7.	Bus station

Table 4. Feature class

Sl. No.	Feature	Total
1.	CLASS 0	10489
2.	CLASS 1	27044
3.	CLASS 2	30132
4.	CLASS 3	7831

Figure 12. K means clustering on GPS locations (4 classes)

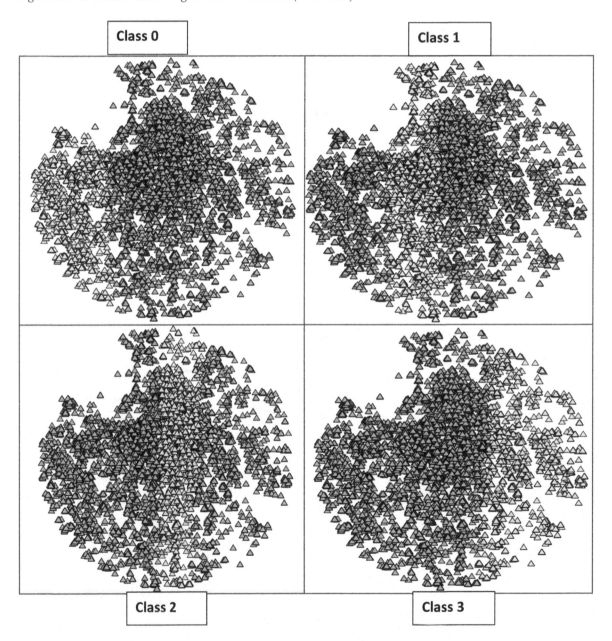

Figure 13. Attribute table showing K – means cluster filed class

	A	B	C	D	LAT	LONG	E	F	class
1	1541	4f0fd5a8e4b038...	4bf58dd8d48988...	Cosmetics Shop	35.70510108999...	139.6195899999...	540	Tue Apr 03 18:17...	2
2	868	4c178638c2dfc9...	4bf58dd8d48988...	Food & Drink Shop	35.72559198999...	139.7766325999...	540	Tue Apr 03 19:12...	2
3	1541	4b83b207f964a5...	4bf58dd8d48988...	Furniture / Home ...	35.70507417999...	139.6195022999...	540	Tue Apr 03 19:20...	2
4	589	4b5ed39cf964a5...	4bf58dd8d48988...	Airport	35.54896343000...	139.7846113999...	540	Tue Apr 03 19:59...	0
5	589	4e014c11c65b89...	4bf58dd8d48988...	Bus Station	35.57502802999...	139.7587865000...	540	Tue Apr 03 20:01...	0
6	1390	4e64a4e1a8095...	4bf58dd8d48988...	Bus Station	35.68389724000...	139.5684189000...	540	Tue Apr 03 20:40...	2
7	214	4c39423c1e06d1...	4bf58dd8d48988...	Road	35.67256545000...	139.4846641999...	540	Tue Apr 03 20:41...	1
8	1876	4b5da9e0f964a5...	4bf58dd8d48988...	Subway	35.74880450999...	139.7195988999...	540	Tue Apr 03 20:59...	3
9	499	4b8c5418f964a5...	4bf58dd8d48988...	Subway	35.68220662000...	139.7987669999...	540	Tue Apr 03 21:04...	2
10	1552	4d319572d7db6...	4bf58dd8d48988...	Bus Station	35.68288854000...	139.5673218000...	540	Tue Apr 03 21:32...	2
11	2085	4b5bac4af964a5...	4bf58dd8d48988...	Subway	35.55002895999...	139.6336770000...	540	Tue Apr 03 21:39...	0
12	1143	4b7481e1f964a5...	4bf58dd8d48988...	Subway	35.73027306000...	139.7113779000...	540	Tue Apr 03 21:52...	2
13	1029	4dc24f03b0fb49...	4bf58dd8d48988...	Food & Drink Shop	35.75502785999...	139.8769854999...	540	Tue Apr 03 21:53...	3
14	13	4c995e24b8e922...	4bf58dd8d48988...	Road	35.70163792999...	139.6883135999...	540	Tue Apr 03 21:53...	2
15	499	4b5ed34ef964a5...	4bf58dd8d48988...	Airport	35.55137976999...	139.7884082999...	540	Tue Apr 03 21:54...	0
16	13	4d998a1961a3a...	4bf58dd8d48988...	Road	35.70205956000...	139.6951683000...	540	Tue Apr 03 21:56...	2
17	1965	4b2692f9f964a5...	4bf58dd8d48988...	Subway	35.68859746999...	139.7106913000...	540	Tue Apr 03 21:56...	2
18	1324	4ddb7a4ffa7637...	4bf58dd8d48988...	Food & Drink Shop	35.57869226999...	139.5736492000...	540	Tue Apr 03 22:01...	0
19	1967	4b63a9e5f964a5...	4bf58dd8d48988...	Road	35.65857769000...	139.7107852000...	540	Tue Apr 03 22:02...	1
20	13	4ec6087993ad41...	4bf58dd8d48988...	Road	35.70929152000...	139.7033072000...	540	Tue Apr 03 22:04...	2

Figure 14. K-means clusters

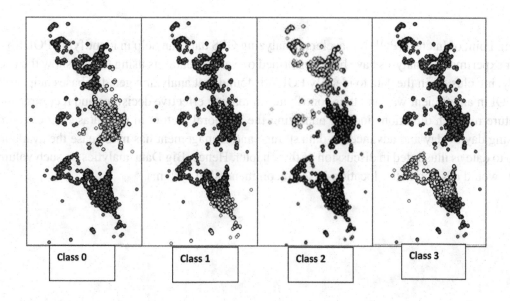

Class 0 Class 1 Class 2 Class 3

Figure 15. Places of interest beyond 1000 meters distance in the year 2009

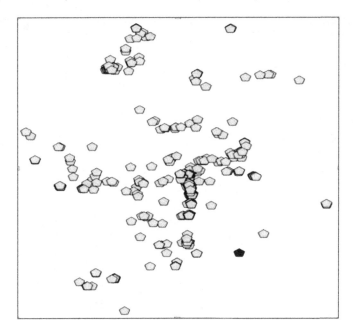

Query 2.

radius_meters NOT IN (1000)

mending Point of Interest (POI) to travelers. Analyzing GPS data can help in identifying POI. So, in this chapter experimental analyses have been performed on various datasets using GIS to show the necessity of analyzing clusters in the data to identify POI. It is found that analyzing geo databases helps in identifying POI in an efficient way and thus contributes in making effective decisions and recommendations. The future research directions include analyzing the temporal factors in the dataset. Location data is increasing day by day and advances in data storage and management has made ease the availability of data up to date as illustrated in discussion of this chapter. Hence, Big Data analytics on such voluminous datasets would develop better location-based recommendation systems.

Figure 16. Places of interest in the year 2010

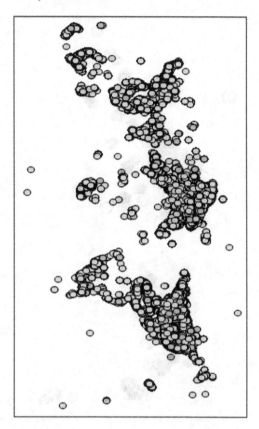

Query 3.

```
CASE
WHEN "radius_meters" NOT IN (100) THEN 'Hello'
END
```

Figure 17. Check-in made in the year 2009

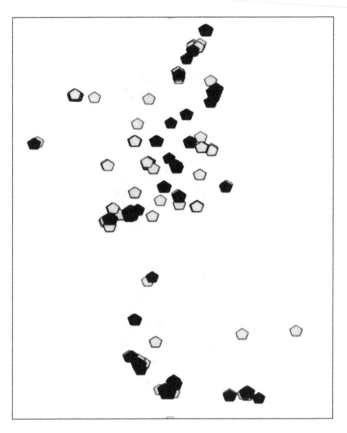

Query 4.

CASE
WHEN "created_at" IN ('27-03-2009') OR "created_at" IN ('28-03-2009') OR "created_at" IN ('29-03-2009') OR "created_at" IN ('31-03-2009') OR "created_at" IN ('30-03-2009') THEN 'NONE'
END

Figure 18. Places of interest in the year 2010

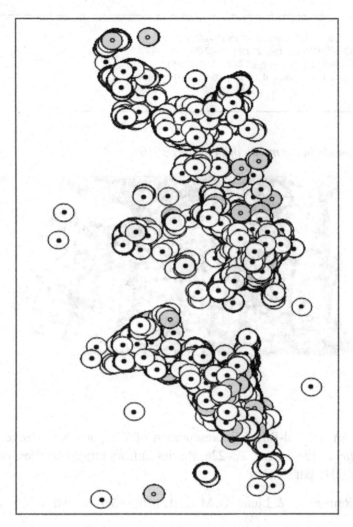

Query 5.

```
CASE
WHEN "radius_meters" IN (100)
or "radius_meters" IN (1000)
or "radius_meters" IN (2000)
or "radius_meters" IN (3000)
or "radius_meters" IN (4000)
OR "radius_meters" IN (10000)
THEN 'Success'
END
```

Query 6.

```
CASE
WHEN "created_at" IN ('6/2/2010') OR "created_at" IN ('7/2/2010')
OR "created_at" IN ('10/2/2010') OR "created_at" IN ('14-02-2010')
OR "created_at" IN ('17-02-2010') OR "created_at" IN ('19-02-2010')
OR "created_at" IN ('21-02-2010') OR "created_at" IN ('26-02-2010')
THEN 'Success'
END
```

Figure 19. Check- in made in the month of February 2010

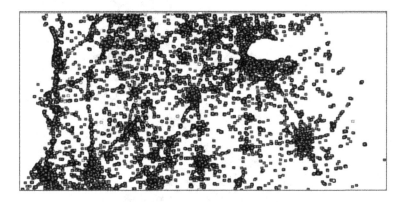

REFERENCES

Allen, J. F. (1981). An Interval-Based Representation of Temporal Knowledge. *International Joint Conferences on Artificial Intelligence*, 22–226. Retrieved from http://www.ijcai.org/Past Proceedings/ IJCAI-81-VOL 1/PDF/045.pdf

Box, P., Jankins, G., Reinsel, G., & Ljung, G. M. (2012). *Time Series Analysis Forecasting and Control*. Academic Press.

Campelo, C. E. C. (2013). Representing and Reasoning about Changing Spatial Extensions of Geographic Features. *LNCS*, *8116*, 33–52.

Claramunt, C. M., & Theriault, M. (1995). Managing time in GIS: An event -oriented approach. In *Proceeding of VLDB International Workshop on Temporal Databases*, (pp. 23-42). Springer Verlag. 10.1007/978-1-4471-3033-8_2

Hornsby, K., & Egenhofer, M. J. (2000). Identity - based change: A foundation for spatio-temporal knowledge representation. *International Journal of Geographical Information Science*, *14*(3), 207–224. doi:10.1080/136588100240813

Jayanthi, G., & Uma, V. (2017). *A qualitative inference method for prediction of geographic process using spatial and temporal relations. International Journal of Artificial Intelligence and Soft Computing.*

Jayanthi, G., & Uma, V. (2017). *Modeling Spatial Evolution: Review of Methods and its Significance. In Dynamic Knowledge Representation in Scientific Domains*. IGI Global.

Li, Q., Chen, X., Chen, J., & Tang, Q. (2010). An evacuation risk assessment model for emergency traffic with consideration of urban hazard installations. *Chinese Science Bulletin, 55*(10), 1000–1006. doi:10.100711434-009-0277-1

Liu, X., Liu, Y., Aberer, K., & Miao, C. (2013). Personalized Point-of-Interest Recommendation by Mining Users' Preference Transition. In *Proceedings of the 22nd ACM International Conference on Information and Knowledge Management (CIKM'13)*, (pp. 733-738). ACM. 10.1145/2505515.2505639

Liu, Y., Wei, W., Sun, A., & Miao, C. (2014). Exploiting Geographical Neighborhood Characteristics for Location Recommendation. In *Proceedings of the 23rd ACM International Conference on Information and Knowledge Management (CIKM'14)*, (pp. 739-748). ACM. 10.1145/2661829.2662002

Ma, X., Pei, T., Song, C., & Zhou, C. (2016). A new assessment model for evacuation vulnerability in urban areas. *International Journal of Geographical Information Science*, 29–39.

Mohammady, S., & Delavar, M. R. (2016). Urban sprawl assessment and modeling using landsat images and GIS. *Modeling Earth Systems and Environment, 2*(3), 155. doi:10.100740808-016-0209-4

Mondo, G. D., Stell, J. G., Claramunt, C., & Thibaud, R. (2010). A Graph Model for Spatio-temporal Evolution. *Journal of Universal Computer Science, 16*(11), 1452–1477.

Randell, D. A., Cui, Z., & Cohn, A. G. (1992). A Spatial Logic based on Regions and Connection. *Proceeding of KRR*, 165–176.

Rich, Knight, & Nair. (2009). *Artificial Intelligence*. Tata MacGraw Hill.

Sudhira, H. S., Ramachandra, T. V., & Jagadish, K. S. (2004). Urban sprawl: Metrics, dynamics and modelling using GIS. *International Journal of Applied Earth Observation and Geoinformation, 5*(1), 29–39. doi:10.1016/j.jag.2003.08.002

ENDNOTES

[1]   https://www.nij.gov/topics/technology/maps/pages/crimestat-downloads.aspx

[2]   https://www.kaggle.com/chetanism/foursquare-nyc-and-tokyo-checkin-dataset

[3]   https://www.healthpolicyproject.com/geoHealth/resources/Section_3_4.zip health zones (as GPS location data).

Compilation of References

(2014). Kumar, Yugal, & Sahoo, G. (2014). A Review on Gravitational Search Algorithm and its Applications to Data Clustering. *I.J. Intelligent Systems and Applications*, *6*, 79–93. doi:10.5815/ijisa.2014.06.09

Abbasi, A., Chen, H., & Salem, A. (2008). Sentiment Analysis in Multiple Languages: Feature Selection for Opinion Classification in Web Forums. *ACM Transactions on Information Systems*, *26*(3), 12. doi:10.1145/1361684.1361685

Abbasian, M. A., & Nezamabadi-pour, H. (2012). Multi objective gravitational search algorithm using non-dominated Fronts. *J. Electr. Eng.*, *41*(1), 67–80.

Abbasian, M. A., Nezamabadi-pour, H., & Amoozegar, M. (2015). A clustering based archive multi objective gravitational search algorithm. *J. Fund. Inf.*, *138*, 387–409.

Abdallah, A., Maarof, M. A., & Zainal, A. (2016). Fraud detection system: A survey. *Journal of Network and Computer Applications*, *68*, 90–113. doi:10.1016/j.jnca.2016.04.007

Abdou, H. A. (2009). Genetic programming for credit scoring: The case of Egyptian public sector banks. *Expert Systems with Applications*, *36*(9), 11402–11417. doi:10.1016/j.eswa.2009.01.076

Acquaye, N. A. (2015). *SIM box task team steps up successes with help from the firm.* Retrieved from https://www.biztechafrica.com/article/sim-box-task- team –steps –successes- help-ict-firm/9592/

Adepetun, A. (2019, March 27). Governments charged as SIM Boxing menace rips Africa. *The Guardian.*

Adomavicius, G. (2015). Context-Aware Recommender Systems. In Recommender Systems Handbook. Academic Press. doi:10.1007/978-1-4899-7637-6_6

Adomavicius, G., Sankaranarayanan, R., Sen, S., & Tuzhilin, A. (2005). Incorporating contextual information in recommender systems using a multidimensional approach. *ACM Transactions on Information Systems*, *23*(1), 103–145. doi:10.1145/1055709.1055714

Adomavicius, G., & Tuzhilin, A. (2005). Toward the next generation of recommender systems: A survey of the state-of-the-art and possible extensions. *IEEE Transactions on Knowledge and Data Engineering*, *17*(6), 734–749. doi:10.1109/TKDE.2005.99

Advertising Age. (2008, June 23). *100 leading national advertisers.* Author.

Affi, A., & Azen, S. (1979). *Statistical Analysis* (2nd ed.). London, UK: Academic press.

African Business. (2016). *Telecoms: Business evolves as the market matures.* Author.

Aggarwal & Reddy. (2013). *Data Clustering: Algorithms and Applications.* CRC Press.

Aggarwal, C.C., Hinneburg, A., & Keim, D.A. (2000). On the surprising behavior of distance metrics in high dimensional space. *IBM Research report*, RC 21739.

Aggarwal, C. C., & And Yu, P. S. (2000). Finding generalized projected clusters in high dimensional spaces. *SIGMOD Record, 29*(2), 70–92.

Aggarwal, C. C., Procopiuc, C., Wolf, J. L., Yu, P. S., & And Park, J. S. (1999a). Fast algorithms for projected clustering. *Proceedings of the ACM SIGMOD Conference*, 61-72.

Aggarwal, C. C., Wolf, J. L., & And Yu, P. S. (1999b). A new method for similarity indexing of market basket data. *Proceedings of the ACM SIGMOD Conference*, 407-418.

Agrawal, R., & Gupta, N. (2017). Educational Data Mining Review: Teaching Enhancement. In Privacy and Security Policies in Big Data (pp. 149-165). IGI Global.

Agrawal, R., & Gupta, N. (Eds.). (2018). *Extracting Knowledge from Opinion Mining*. IGI Global.

Agresti, A. (2007An Introduction To Categorical Data Analysis (2nd ed.). Wiley.

Ahas, R., Aasa, A., Roose, A., Mark, Ü., & Silm, S. (2008). Evaluating passive mobile positioning data for tourism surveys: An Estonian case study. *Tourism Management, 29*(3), 469–485. doi:10.1016/j.tourman.2007.05.014

Ahmadlou, M., & Adeli, H. (2010). Enhanced probabilistic neural network with local decision circles: A robust classifier. *Integrated Computer-Aided Engineering, 17*(3), 197–210. doi:10.3233/ICA-2010-0345

Ajami, A., & Armaghan, M. (2013). A multi-objective gravitational search algorithm based approach of power system stability enhancement with UPFC. *Journal of Central South University, 20*(6), 1536–1544. doi:10.100711771-013-1645-1

Akaike, H. (1987). Factor analysis and AIC. *Psychometrika, 52*(3), 317–332. doi:10.1007/BF02294359

Akdemir, C. (2016). *Detecting Fraud by Using Data Mining Techniques and an Application in Retail Sector* (Doctoral Dissertation). Marmara University Social Sciences Institute, Istanbul, Turkey.

Akoglu, L., Tong, H., & Koutra, D. (2015). Graph based anomaly detection and description: A survey. *Data Mining and Knowledge Discovery, 29*(3), 626–688. doi:10.100710618-014-0365-y

Aksoy, S., & Haralick, R. M. (2001). Feature Normalization and Likelihood-based Similarity Measures for Image Retrieval. *Pattern Recognition Letters, 22*(5), 563–582. doi:10.1016/S0167-8655(00)00112-4

Al Janabi, M. A.M. (2008, Summer). Integrating Liquidity Risk Factor into a Parametric Value at Risk Method. *Journal of Trading*, 76-87.

Al Janabi, M. A. M. (2010). Incorporating Asset Liquidity Effects in Risk-Capital Modeling. *Review of Middle East Economics and Finance, 6*(1), 3. doi:10.2202/1475-3693.1258

Al Janabi, M. A. M. (2013). Optimal and Coherent Economic-Capital Structures: Evidence from Long and Short-Sales Trading Positions under Illiquid Market Perspectives. *Annals of Operations Research, 205*(1), 109–139. doi:10.100710479-012-1096-3

Al Janabi, M. A. M. (2014). Optimal and investable portfolios: An empirical analysis with scenario optimization algorithms under crisis market prospects. *Economic Modelling, 40*, 369–381. doi:10.1016/j.econmod.2013.11.021

Al Janabi, M. A. M. (2019). Theoretical and Practical Foundations of Liquidity-Adjusted Value-at-Risk (LVaR): Optimization Algorithms for Portfolios Selection and Management. In N. Metawa, M. Elhoseny, A. E. Hassanien, & M. K. Hassan (Eds.), *Expert Systems: Smart Financial Applications in Big Data Environments*. London, UK: Taylor & Francis Group. doi:10.4324/9780429024061-1

Al Janabi, M. A. M., Arreola-Hernández, J. A., Berger, T., & Nguyen, D. K. (2017). Multivariate dependence and portfolio optimization algorithms under illiquid market scenarios. *European Journal of Operational Research*, *259*(3), 1121–1131. doi:10.1016/j.ejor.2016.11.019

Alexander, G., & Baptista, A. M. (2008). Active portfolio management with benchmarking: Adding a value-at-risk constraint. *Journal of Economic Dynamics & Control*, *32*(3), 779–820. doi:10.1016/j.jedc.2007.03.005

Alguliyev, R., Imamverdiyev, Y., & Sukhostat, L. (2018). Weighted Clustering for Anomaly Detection in Big Data Optim. *Information and Computation*, *6*, 178–188.

Allen, J. F. (1981). An Interval-Based Representation of Temporal Knowledge. *International Joint Conferences on Artificial Intelligence*, 22–226. Retrieved from http://www.ijcai.org/Past Proceedings/IJCAI-81-VOL 1/PDF/045.pdf

Allsop, R. E., & Charlesworth, J. A. (1977). Traffic in a signal-controlled road network: An example of different signal timings inducing different routeings. *Traffic Engineering & Control*, *18*, 262–264.

Alp, E. (1995). Risk-based transportation planning practice: Overall methodology and a case example. *INFOR*, *33*(1), 4–19. doi:10.1080/03155986.1995.11732263

Alvi, M. (2016). *A Manual For Selecting Sampling Techniques In Research*. MPRA Munich Personal RepPEC Archive.

Amanze-Nwachukwu, C. (2018, October 29). Call masking: A worrisome trend. *THISDAY*.

Amihud, Y., Mendelson, H., & Pedersen, L. H. (2005). Liquidity and Asset Prices. *Foundations and Trends in Finance*, *1*(4), 269–364. doi:10.1561/0500000003

Amini, A. (2016). *Online condition monitoring of railway wheelsets*. University of Birmingham.

Anderberg, M. R. (2014). *Cluster analysis for applications: probability and mathematical statistics: a series of monographs and textbooks* (Vol. 19). Academic Press.

Anderlucci, L., & Hennig, C. (2014). The clustering of categorical data: A comparison of a model-based and a distance-based approach. *Communications in Statistics. Theory and Methods*, *43*(4), 704–721. doi:10.1080/03610926.2013.806665

Angelidis, T., & Benos, A. (2006). Liquidity adjusted value-at-risk based on the components of the bid-ask spread. *Applied Financial Economics*, *16*(11), 835–851. doi:10.1080/09603100500426440

Ankerst, M., Breunig, M. M., Kriegel, H.-P., & Sander, J. (1999). OPTICS: Ordering Points To Identify the Clustering Structure. *ACM SIGMOD'99 Int. Conf. on Management of Data*.

Anuforo, C. (2018, August 1). All you need to know about call masking. *Daily Sun*.

Arcos Jiménez, A., Gómez Muñoz, C., & García Márquez, F. (2018). Machine learning for wind turbine blades maintenance management. *Energies*, *11*(1), 13. doi:10.3390/en11010013

Arreola-Hernández, J., Al Janabi, M. A. M., Hammoudeh, S., & Nguyen, D. K. (2015). Time lag dependence, cross-correlation and risk analysis of U.S. energy and non-energy stock portfolios. *Journal of Asset Management*, *16*(7), 467–483. doi:10.1057/jam.2015.33

Arreola-Hernandez, J., Hammoudeh, S., Khuong, N. D., Al Janabi, M. A. M., & Reboredo, J. C. (2016). Global financial crisis and dependence risk analysis of sector portfolios: A vine copula approach. *Applied Economics*, *49*(25), 2409–2427. doi:10.1080/00036846.2016.1240346

Arthur, D. (2007). *k-means++: The Advantages of Careful Seeding*. Academic Press.

Arunachalam, D., Kumar, N., & Kawalek, J. P. (2018). Understanding big data analytics capabilities in supply chain management: Unravelling the issues, challenges and implications for practice. *Transportation Research Part E, Logistics and Transportation Review*, *114*, 416–436. doi:10.1016/j.tre.2017.04.001

Assunção, M. D., Calheiros, R. N., Bianchi, S., Netto, M. A. S., & Buyya, R. (2015). Big Data computing and clouds: Trends and future directions. *Journal of Parallel and Distributed Computing*. doi:10.1016/j.jpdc.2014.08.003

Aster, R. C., Borchers, B., & Thurber, C. H. (2013). *Parameter estimation and inverse Problems*. New York, NY: Academic Press.

AT & T Knowledge Ventures. (2006). *Milestones in AT & T history*. Retrieved from https://www.att.com/history/milestones.html

AT&T. (2006). *History of AT & T*. Retrieved from https://www.att.com/history/milestones.html

ATIS Committee. (2001). *ATIS Telecom Glossary*. Retrieved from http://www.atis.org/tg2k

Australia Telecommunications Association. (2003). *Ten years of GSM in Australia*. Retrieved from https://www.amta.org.au/default.asp?Page=142

Ayanso, A., & Karimi, A. (2015). The moderating effects of keyword competition on the determinants of ad position in sponsored search advertising. *Decision Support Systems*, *70*, 42–59. doi:10.1016/j.dss.2014.11.009

Aydin, M. N., Kariniauskaite, D., & Perdahci, N. Z. (2018). Validity Issues of Digital Trace Data for Platform as a Service: A Network Science Perspective. Proceedings of Trends and Advances in Information Systems and Technologies. WorldCIST'18 2018. doi:10.1007/978-3-319-77703-0_65

Bachelier, L. (2011). *Louis Bachelier's theory of speculation: the origins of modern finance*. Princeton, NJ: Princeton University Press; doi:10.1515/9781400829309

Baltrunas, L., & Ricci, F. (2014). Experimental evaluation of context-dependent collaborative filtering using item splitting. *User Modeling and User-Adapted Interaction*, *24*(1–2), 7–34. doi:10.100711257-012-9137-9

Bangia, A., Diebold, F., Schuermann, T., & Stroughair, J. (1999). *Modeling Liquidity Risk with Implications for Traditional Market Risk Measurement and Management*. Working Paper, The Wharton School, University of Pennsylvania.

Baniassadi, Z., Nezamabadi-pour, H., & Farsangi, M. M. (2011). A multi-objective solution of gravitational search algorithm for benchmark functions and placement of SVC. *Intell. Syst. Electr. Eng.*, *1*(1), 59–78.

Barani, F., Mirhosseini, M., & Nezamabadi-pour, H. (2017). Application of binary quantum-inspired gravitational search algorithm in feature subset selection. *Applied Intelligence*, *47*(2), 304–318. doi:10.100710489-017-0894-3

Barber, D. (2010). *Bayesian Reasoning and Machine Learning*. Academic Press.

Bates, D. M., & Watts, D. G. (1988). *Nonlinear regression analysis and its applications*. Hoboken, NJ: Wiley Sons. doi:10.1002/9780470316757

Bchenne, S., Jacob, D., & Henze, G. P. (2011). Sampling Based On SOBOL, Sequences For Month Carlo Techniques Applied To Builing Simulations. *12th Conference Of international Building Performance Simulation Association*.

Bell, M. G. H. (2000). A game theory approach to measuring the performance reliability of transport networks. *Transportation Research Part B: Methodological*, *34*(6), 533–546. doi:10.1016/S0191-2615(99)00042-9

Bellman, R. E. (1961). *Adaptive control processes*. Princeton, NJ: Princeton University Press. doi:10.1515/9781400874668

Bello-Orgaz, G., Jung, J. J., & Camacho, D. (2016). Social big data: Recent achievements and new challenges. *Information Fusion*, *28*, 45–59. doi:10.1016/j.inffus.2015.08.005

Ben Schafer, J., Frankowski, D., Herlocker, J., & Sen, S. (2007). Collaborative Filtering Recommender Systems. In The Adaptive Web (pp. 291–324). Academic Press. doi:10.1007/978-3-540-72079-9_9

Ben Schafer, J., Konstan, J., & Riedi, J. (1999). Recommender systems in e-commerce. *Proceedings of the 1st ACM Conference on Electronic Commerce - EC '99*, 158–166. 10.1145/336992.337035

Ben-David, S., von Luxburg, U., & Pál, D. (2006). A sober look at clustering stability. In H. U. Simon, & G. Lugosi (Eds.), *Proceedings of the 19th Annual Conference on Learning Theory* (pp. 5-19). New York, NY: Springer. 10.1007/11776420_4

Ben-Tal, A., & Nemirovski, A. (1987). *Lectures on modern convex optimization: Analysis, algorithms and engineering applications. MOS-SIAM Series Optimization*. Philadelphia, PA: Philadelphia Society for Industrial and Applied Mathematics.

Berkhin, P. (2002). Survey of Clustering Data Mining Techniques. Accrue Software.

Berman, J. J. (2013). Introduction. In Principles of Big Data. Morgan Kaufmann.

Bern Dibner, B. Library Inc. (1959). *The Atlantic Cable*. Retrieved from https://www.sil.si.edu/digital/collections/hst/atlantic-cable/

Berry, M., Dumais, S., Landauer, T., & O'Brien, G. (1995). Using linear algebra for intelligent information retrieval. *SIAM Review*, *37*(4), 573–595.

Bezdek, J. C. (1981). *Pattern Recognition with Fuzzy Objective Function Algorithms*. Norwell: Kluwer Academic Publishers. doi:10.1007/978-1-4757-0450-1

Bhattacharya, A., & Roy, P. K. (2012). Solution of multi-objective optimal power flow using gravitational search algorithm. *IET Generation, Transmission & Distribution*, *6*(8), 751–763. doi:10.1049/iet-gtd.2011.0593

Bhogal, J., & Choksi, I. (2015). Handling Big Data Using NoSQL. *Proceedings - IEEE 29th International Conference on Advanced Information Networking and Applications Workshops, WAINA 2015*. 10.1109/WAINA.2015.19

Bianchi, C., & Mortimer, G. (2015). Drivers of local food consumption: A comparative study. *British Food Journal*, *117*(9), 2282–2299. doi:10.1108/BFJ-03-2015-0111

Bianco, L., Caramia, M., & Giordani, S. (2009). A bilevel flow model for hazmat transportation network design. *Transportation Research Part C, Emerging Technologies*, *17*(2), 175–196. doi:10.1016/j.trc.2008.10.001

Bijuraj, L. v. (2013). Clustering And Its Application. *Proceedings Of National Conference On New Horizones in.it-NCNHIT*.

Bilmes, A. J. (1998). A Gentle Tutorial of the EM Algorithm and its Application to Parameter Estimation for Gaussian Mixture and Hidden Markov Models. International Computer Science Institute, U.C. Berkeley.

Bin Mohamad, I., & Usman, D. (2013). Standarization and Its Effects on K-Means Clustering Algortihm. *Research Journal of Applied Sciences, Engineering and Technology*, *16*(7), 3033–3299.

Binwu Wang Danfeng Sun, H. L. (2014). Social-Ecological Patterns of Soil Heavy Metals Based on a Self-Organizing Map (SOM): A Case Study in Beijing, China. *International Journal of Environmental Research and Public Health*, 3618–3638. PMID:24690947

Birant, D., Kut, A., Ventura, M., Altınok, H., Altınok, B., Altınok, E., & Ihlamur, M. (2012). *A New Approach for Quality Function Deployment: An Application*. Paper presented at Akademik Bilisim 2010, Mugla, Turkey.

Bobadilla, J., Ortega, F., Hernando, A., & Gutiérrez, A. (2013). Recommender systems survey. *Knowledge-Based Systems*, *46*, 109–132. doi:10.1016/j.knosys.2013.03.012

Bodapati, A. V. (2008). Recommendation systems with purchase data. *JMR, Journal of Marketing Research*, *45*(1), 77–93. doi:10.1509/jmkr.45.1.77

Boe-Hansen, G., van den Berg, F. W. J., Amigo, J. M., & Babamoradi, H. (2015). Quality assessment of boar semen by multivariate analysis of flow cytometric data. *Chemometrics and Intelligent Laboratory Systems*, 142.

Bothtner, U., Milne, S. E., & Kenny, G. N. (2002). Bayesian probabilistic network modeling of remifentanil and propofol interaction on wakeup time after closed-loop controlled anesthesia. *Journal of Clinical Monitoring and Computing*, *17*, 31–36. PMID:12102247

Box, P., Jankins, G., Reinsel, G., & Ljung, G. M. (2012). *Time Series Analysis Forecasting and Control*. Academic Press.

Box, G., & Jenkins, G. (1976). *Time series analysis: forecast and control*. Hoboken, NJ: John Wiley & Sons.

Boyd, S., & Vandenberghe, L. (2004). *Convex optimization*. Cambridge, UK: Cambridge University. doi:10.1017/CBO9780511804441

Bramer, M. (2007). *Principles of data mining*. London: Springer.

Breese, J. S., Heckerman, D., & Kadie, C. (1998). Empirical Analysis of Predictive Algorithms for Collaborative Filtering. *UAI'98 Proceedings of the Fourteenth Conference on Uncertainty in Artificial Intelligence*, 43–52.

Breiman, L. (2001). Breiman. Random forests. *Machine Learning*, *45*(1), 5–32. doi:10.1023/A:1010933404324

Breiman, L. (2001). Statistical Modeling: The Two Cultures. *Statistical Science*, *16*(3), 199–231. doi:10.1214s/1009213726

Brown, E., Dury, S., & Holdsworth, M. (2009). Motivations of consumers that use local, organic fruit and vegetable box schemes in Central England and Southern France. *Appetite*, *53*(2), 183–188. doi:10.1016/j.appet.2009.06.006 PMID:19540288

Buja, A., Hastie, T., & Tibshirani, R. (1989). Linear smoothers and additive models (with discussion). *Annals of Statistics*, *17*(2), 453–555. doi:10.1214/aos/1176347115

Burchett, W., Ellis, A., Harrar, S., & Bathke, A. (2017). Nonparametric inference for multivariate data: The R package NPMV. *Journal of Statistical Software*, *76*(4), 1–18. doi:10.18637/jss.v076.i04 PMID:30220889

Burguillo, J. C. (2013). Playing with complexity: From cellular evolutionary algorithms with coalitions to self-organizing maps. *Computers & Mathematics with Applications (Oxford, England)*, 66.

Burnham, K. P., & Anderson, D. R. (2002). *Model selection and multimodel inference: A practical Information-theoretic approach*. New York, NY: Springer Verlag.

Button, M., & Brooks, G. (2016). From 'shallow' to 'deep' policing: 'crash-for-cash' insurance fraud investigation in England and Wales and the need for greater regulation. *Policing and Society*, *26*(2), 210–229. doi:10.1080/10439463.2014.942847

Cabinet Office. (2003). *Jiyujikan To kankou Ni Kansuru Seron-Chousa* [The Public Opinion Survey on Tourism and Free Time]. Tokyo, Japan: Cabinet Office.

Cai, X., Perez-Concha, O., & Coiera, E. (2016). Real-time prediction of mortality, readmission, and length of stay using electronic health record data. *Journal of the American Medical Informatics Association, 23*, 553–561. PMID:26374704

Calvert, J. B. (2004). *The electromagnetic telegraph.* Retrieved from http://www.du/~calvert/tell/morse/morse.html

Cambridge University Press. (2008). *Cambridge online dictionary.* Author.

Campbell, R., Huisman, R., & Koedijk, K. (2001). Optimal portfolio selection in a Value-at-Risk framework. *Journal of Banking & Finance, 25*(9), 1789–1804. doi:10.1016/S0378-4266(00)00160-6

Campelo, C. E. C. (2013). Representing and Reasoning about Changing Spatial Extensions of Geographic Features. *LNCS, 8116*, 33–52.

Carlsson, G., & Mémoli, F. (2010). Characterization, stability and convergence of hierarchical clustering methods. *Journal of Machine Learning Research, 11*, 1425–1470.

Carter, E. M., & Potts, H. w. (2014). *Predicting Length Of Stay From An Electronic Patient Record System: A Primary Total Knee Replacement Example.* Crter And Potts BMC Medical Informatics And Decision Making.

Celik, S. (2017). Applying Web Usage Mining for the Analysis of Web Log Files. *Istanbul Business Research, 46*(1), 62–75.

Chakraborty & Nagwani. (2011). Analysis and Study of Incremental DBSCAN Clustering Algorithm. *International Journal of Enterprise Computing and Business Systems, 1*(2).

Chawla, N. V. (2005). Data Mining for Imbalanced Datasets: An Overview. *Data Mining and Knowledge Discovery Handbook*, 853–867.

Chawla, N. V., Bowyer, K. W., Hall, L. O., & Kegelmeyer, W. P. (2002). SMOTE: Synthetic minority over-sampling technique. *Journal of Artificial Intelligence Research, 16*(1), 321–357. doi:10.1613/jair.953

Cheng, C., Fu, A., & And Zhang, Y. (1999). Entropy-based subspace clustering for mining numerical data. Proceedings of the 5th ACMSIGKDD, 84-93.

Cheng, S. F., Epelman, M. A., & Smith, R. L. (2006). CoSIGN: A parallel algorithm for coordinated traffic signal control. *IEEE Transactions on Intelligent Transportation Systems, 7*(4), 551–564. doi:10.1109/TITS.2006.884617

Chen, M. (2017). Soft clustering for very large data sets. *Comput Sci Netw Secur J., 17*(11), 102–108.

Chen, M., Mao, S., & Liu, Y. (2014). Bigdata:asurvey. *Mobile Networks and Applications, 19*(2), 1–39.

Chen, X., Liu, X., Huang, Z., & Sun, H. (2010). RegionKNN: A Scalable Hybrid Collaborative Filtering Algorithm for Personalized Web Service Recommendation. *2010 IEEE International Conference on Web Services*, 9–16. 10.1109/ICWS.2010.27

Chiou, S.-W. (2003). TRANSYT derivatives for area traffic control optimisation with network equilibrium flows. *Transportation Research Part B: Methodological, 37*(3), 263–290. doi:10.1016/S0191-2615(02)00013-9

Chiou, S.-W. (2016). A bi-objective bi-level signal control policy for transport of hazardous materials in urban road networks. *Transportation Research Part D, Transport and Environment, 42*, 16–44. doi:10.1016/j.trd.2015.09.003

Chira, C., Sedano, J., Camara, M., Prieto, C., Villar, J. R., & Cor-chado, E. (2014). A cluster merging method for time series microarray with product values. International Journal of Neural Systems, 24(6).

Chiralaksanakul, A., & Mahadevan, S. (2007). Decoupled approach to multidisciplinary design optimization under uncertainty. *Optimization and Engineering*, *8*(1), 21–42. doi:10.100711081-007-9014-2

Choung, B., & Do, S. B. (2008). What is the expectation maximization algorithm? *Computational Biology*, *26*(8), 897–899. PMID:18688245

Cil, I. (2012). Consumption universes based supermarket layout through association rule mining and multidimensional scaling. *Expert Systems with Applications*, *39*(10), 8611–8625. doi:10.1016/j.eswa.2012.01.192

Cil, I., & Turkan, Y. S. (2013). An ANP-based assessment model for lean enterprise transformation. *International Journal of Advanced Manufacturing Technology*, *64*(5-8), 1113–1130. doi:10.100700170-012-4047-x

CISCO Systems. (2006). *Fundamentals of DWDM technology*. Retrieved from http://www.cisco.com/univercd/cc/td/doc/product/mels/cm1500/dwdm/dwdm_ovr.pdf

Claramunt, C. M., & Theriault, M. (1995). Managing time in GIS: An event -oriented approach. In *Proceeding of VLDB International Workshop on Temporal Databases*, (pp. 23-42). Springer Verlag. 10.1007/978-1-4471-3033-8_2

Clarke, F., Ledyaev, Y., Stern, R., & Wolenski, P. (1980). *Nonsmooth Analysis and Control Theory*. New York: Springer-Verlag.

Cleveland, W. S. (1979). Robust locally weighted regression and smoothing Scatter plots. *Journal of the American Statistical Association*, *74*(368), 829–836. doi:10.1080/01621459.1979.10481038

Clevert, D.-A., Unterthiner, T., & Hochreiter, S. (2015). Fast and Accurate Deep Network Learning by Exponential Linear Units (ELUs). *ICLR*, *2016*, 1–14. doi:10.3233/978-1-61499-672-9-1760

CNN. (2008). *How do you know your love is real? Check Facebook*. Retrieved from http://www.cnn.com/2008/LIVING/personal/04/04/facebook.love/index.html

Cochrane, J. H. (2005). *Asset Pricing*. Princeton, NJ: Princeton University Press.

Cokluk, O. (2010). Logistic Regression: Concept and Application. *Educational Sciences: Theory and Practice*, *10*(3), 1397–1407.

Combes, C., Kadari, F., & Chaabane, S. (2014). Predicting Hospital Length of Stay Using Regression Models: Application To Emergency Department. *10eme Conference Francophone de Modelisation, optimization et Simulation-MOSIM'14*.

Commons, A. (2016). *Clustering algorithms and distance measures*. Retrieved from http://commons.apache.org/proper/commons-math/userguide/ml.html

Conwire. (2017). *Coax cable FAQ series: What is RG Cable?-Conwire*. Retrieved from http://www.conwire.com/coax-cable-rg-cable-blog

Cover, T. M., & Hart, P. E. (1967). Nearest neighbor pattern classification. *IEEE Transactions on Information Theory*, *13*(1), 21–27. doi:10.1109/TIT.1967.1053964

Cox, D., & Freeman, M. (2005). *Auto-diagnostic method and apparatus*. 0137751.

Cox, D. N., Reynolds, J., Mela, D. J., Anderson, A. S., McKellar, S., & Lean, M. E. J. (1996). Vegetables and fruit: Barriers and opportunities for greater consumption. *Nutrition & Food Science*, *96*(5), 44–47. doi:10.1108/00346659610129251

Cox, D., & Freeman, M. (2005). *Auto-diagnostic method and apparatus*. Google Patents.

Craven, P., & Wahba, G. (1979). Smoothing noisy data with spline functions: Estimating the correct degree of smoothing by the method of generalized cross-validation. *Numerische Mathematik*, *31*(4), 377–403. doi:10.1007/BF01404567

Croteau, D., & Hoynes, W. (2003). *Media society: Industries, Images & Audiences*. Thousand Oaks, CA: Pine Forge Press.

Cuadros, A. J., & Domínguez, V. E. (2014). Customer segmentation model based on value generation for marketing strategies formulation. *Estudios Gerenciales*, *30*(130), 25–30. doi:10.1016/j.estger.2014.02.005

Current, J., & Ratick, S. (1995). A model to assess risk, equity and efficiency in facility location and transportation of hazardous materials. *Location Science*, *3*(3), 187–201. doi:10.1016/0966-8349(95)00013-5

Dantzig, G. B. (2010). Linear programming under uncertainty. In *Stochastic programming* (pp. 1–11). New York, NY: Springer. doi:10.1007/978-1-4419-1642-6_1

Dasgupta, C. G., Dispensa, G. S., & Ghose, S. (1994). Comparing the predictive performance of a neural network model with some traditional market response models. *International Journal of Forecasting*, *10*(2), 235–244. doi:10.1016/0169-2070(94)90004-3

Das, N., Das, L., & Rautaray,, S.S., & Pandey, M. (2018). Big Data Analytics for Medical Applications I.J. *Modern Education and Computer Science*, *2*, 35-42.

De Boor, C. (1978). *Practical guide to splines*. New York, NY: Springer Verlag. doi:10.1007/978-1-4612-6333-3

Deepthi, P. S. S. M. (2015). PSO Based Feature Selection for Clustering Gene Expression Data. IEEE.

Dempe, S. (2003). Annotated bibliography on bilevel programming and mathematical programs with equilibrium constraints. *Optimization*, *52*(3), 333–359. doi:10.1080/0233193031000149894

Deshmukh & Ramteke. (2015). Comparing the techniques of cluster analysis for big data. *International Journal of Advanced Research in Computer Engineering & Technology*, *4*(12).

Devore, J. (2012). *Probability and Statistics for Engineering and the Sciences* (8th ed.). Belmont, CA: Cengage Publisher.

Dey, A. K. (2001). Understanding and using context. *Personal and Ubiquitous Computing*, *5*(1), 4–7. doi:10.1007007790170019

Dhamodharavadhani, S., Gowri, R., & Rathipriya, R. (2018). Unlock Different V's of Big Data for Analytics. *International Journal on Computer Science and Engineering*, *06*(04), 183–190.

Díez, F. J. (2014). *Introducción a los Modelos Gráficos Probabilistas*. UNED.

Dilhac, J. M. (2004). *From tele-communicare to telecommunications*. Retrieved from http://www.ieee.org/portal/cms_docs_iportals/about us/history_center/conferences/che2004/Dilhac.pdf

Dincerden, E. (2017). *Is Zekasi ve Stratejik Yonetim*. Istanbul: Beta Basım Dagitim Co.

Dix, J. (2002). *MPLS is the future, but ATM hangs on*. Retrieved from https://www.networkworld.com/columnists/2002/0812edit.html

Dontchev, A. L., & Rockafellar, R. T. (2002). Ample parameterization of variational inclusions. *SIAM Journal on Optimization*, *12*(1), 170–187. doi:10.1137/S1052623400371016

Dorigo, M., Maniezzo, V., & Colorni, A. (1991). *Positive Feedback as a Search Strategy*. Technical Report no. 91016. Politecnico di Milano.

Dougherty, J., Kohavi, R., & Mehran, S. (1995). Supervised and Unsupervised Discretization of Continuous Features. *Machine Learning: Proceedings of the Twelfth International Conference*, 194–202.

Dowd, K., Blake, D., & Cairns, A. (2004, Winter). Long-Term Value at Risk. *The Journal of Risk Finance*, 52-57.

Dowlatshahi, M. B., & Nezamabadi-pour, H. (2014). GGSA: A grouping gravitational search algorithm for data clustering. *Engineering Applications of Artificial Intelligence, 36*, 114–121. doi:10.1016/j.engappai.2014.07.016

Dowlatshahi, M. B., Nezamabadi-pour, H., & Mashinchi, M. (2014). A discrete gravitational search algorithm for solving combinatorial optimization problems. *Information Sciences, 258*, 94–107. doi:10.1016/j.ins.2013.09.034

Duda, P. E. H., & Stork, D. G. (2001). *Pattern Classification*. New York: Wiley.

Duggal, R., & Kharti, S. K. (2016). Impact Of Selected Pre-Processing Techniques On Prediction Of Risk Of Early Readmission For Diabetic Patient In India. *International Journal Of Diabetes In Developing Countries.*

Dunteman, G. H. (1989). *Principal components analysis (No. 69)*. Sage. doi:10.4135/9781412985475

Dzobo, O., Alvehag, K., Gaunt, C. T., & Herman, R. (2014). Multi-dimensional customer segmentation model for power system reliability-worth analysis. *International Journal of Electrical Power & Energy Systems, 62*, 532–539. doi:10.1016/j.ijepes.2014.04.066

Ebrahimi, M., Yazdavar, A., & Sheth, A. (2017). Challenges of Sentiment Analysis for dynamic events. *IEEE Intelligent Systems, 32*(5), 70–75. doi:10.1109/MIS.2017.3711649

Eilers, P. H. C., & Marx, B. D. (1996). Flexible smoothing with B-splines penalties. *Statistical Science, 11*(2), 89–121. doi:10.1214s/1038425655

Einav, L., & Levin, J. (2014). The data revolution and economic analysis. *Innovation Policy and the Economy, 14*(1), 1–24. doi:10.1086/674019

Ekstrand, M. D., Riedl, J. T., & Konstan, J. A. (2011). Collaborative Filtering Recommender Systems. *Human-Computer Interaction, 4*(2), 81–173. doi:10.1561/1100000009

Electronic Oberlin Group. (2006). *Elisha Gray*. Retrieved from https://www.oberlin.edu/external/EOG/OYTT-images/ElishaGray.html

Erinosho, T. O., Moser, R. P., Oh, A. Y., Nebeling, L. C., & Yaroch, A. L. (2012). Awareness of the Fruit and Veggies—More Matters campaign, knowledge of the fruit and vegetable recommendation, and fruit and vegetable intake of adults in the 2007 Food Attitudes and Behaviors (FAB) Survey. *Appetite, 59*(1), 155–160. doi:10.1016/j.appet.2012.04.010 PMID:22524998

Erkut, E., & Gzara, F. (2008). Solving the hazmat transport network design problem. *Computers & Operations Research, 35*(7), 2234–2247. doi:10.1016/j.cor.2006.10.022

Erkut, E., & Ingolfsson, A. (2000). Catastrophe avoidance models for hazardous materials route planning. *Transportation Science, 34*(2), 165–179. doi:10.1287/trsc.34.2.165.12303

Erkut, E., & Ingolfsson, A. (2005). Transport risk models for hazardous materials: Revisited. *Operations Research Letters, 33*(1), 81–89. doi:10.1016/j.orl.2004.02.006

Erkut, E., & Verter, V. (1998). Modeling of transport risk for hazardous materials. *Operations Research, 46*(5), 625–664. doi:10.1287/opre.46.5.625

Erol, O. K., & Eksin, I. (2006). A new optimization method: Big Bang–Big Crunch. *Advances in Engineering Software, 37*(2), 106–111. doi:10.1016/j.advengsoft.2005.04.005

Ertöz, Steinbach, & Kumar. (2003). Finding clusters of different sizes, shapes, and densities in noisy, high dimensional data. *SDM SIAM.*

Ester, M., Kriegel, H.-P., Sander, J., & Xu, X. (1996). A Density-Based Algorithm for Discovering Clusters in Large Spatial Databases with Noise. *Proceeding of 2nd international Conference on Knowledge Discovery and date Mining (KDD 96).*

Ester, Sander, & Xu. (1996). A Density-Based Algorithm for Discovering Clusters in Large Spatial Databases with Noise. *KDD: Proceedings / International Conference on Knowledge Discovery & Data Mining. International Conference on Knowledge Discovery & Data Mining*, (96), 227–231.

Ester, M., Kriegel, H. P., Sander, J., & Xu, X. (1996). A density-based algorithm for discovering clusters in large spatial databases with noise. In *Proceedings of the 2nd International Conference on Knowledge Discovery and Data Mining.* AAAI Press.

Everitt, B., Landau, S., Leese, M., & Stahl, D. (2011). *Cluster Analysis.* Wiley Series in Probability and Statistics. doi:10.1002/9780470977811

Fabozzi, F. J., Focardi, S., & Kolm, P. (2006, Spring). Incorporating Trading Strategies in the Black-Litterman Framework. *Journal of Trading*, 28-37.

Fahad. (2014). A Survey of Clustering Algorithms for Big Data: Taxonomy and Empirical Analysis. *IEEE Trans. Emerging Topics in Computing, 2*(3), 267-79.

Fama, E. F. (1965). The behavior of stock-market prices. *The Journal of Business, 38*(1), 34–105. doi:10.1086/294743

Fama, E. F. (1970). Efficient capital markets: A review of theory and empirical work. *The Journal of Finance, 25*(2), 383–417. doi:10.2307/2325486

Fan, J., & Gijbels, I. (1996). *Local polynomial modelling and its applications.* London, UK: Chapman & Hall.

Fan, Y., & Liu, C. (2010). Solving stochastic transportation network protection problems using the progressive hedging-based method. *Networks and Spatial Economics, 10*(2), 193–208. doi:10.100711067-008-9062-y

Fei Han, C.-Q. W.-S.-H.-Q.-S. (2015). A Gene Selection Method for Microarray Data Based on Binary PSO Encoding Gene-to-class Sensitivity Information. *IEEE Transactions On Computational Biology And Bioinformatics.*

Felfernig, A., Friedrich, G., Jannach, D., & Zanker, M. (2006). An Integrated Environment for the Development of Knowledge-Based Recommender Applications. *International Journal of Electronic Commerce, 11*(2), 11–34. doi:10.2753/JEC1086-4415110201

Fenz, S. (2012). An ontology-based approach for constructing Bayesian networks. *Data & Knowledge Engineering, 73*, 73–88. doi:10.1016/j.datak.2011.12.001

Finzer, L. E., Ajay, V. S., Ali, M. K., Shivashankar, R., Goenka, S., Pillai, D. S., ... Prabhakaran, D. (2013). Fruit and vegetable purchasing patterns and preferences in South Delhi. *Ecology of Food and Nutrition, 52*(1), 1–20. doi:10.1080/03670244.2012.705757 PMID:23282188

Fischer, C. S. (1988). Touch someone: The telephone industry discovers sociability. *Technology and Culture, 29*(1), 32–61. doi:10.2307/3105226

Fontanarava, J., Pasi, G., & Viviani, M. (2017). Feature Analysis for Fake Review Detection through Supervised Classification. *International Conference on Data Science and Advanced Analytics.* 10.1109/DSAA.2017.51

Fox, W. P., & Hammond, J. (2019). Advanced Regression Models: Least Squares, Nonlinear, Poisson and Binary Logistics Regression Using R. Data Science and Digital Business, 221-262.

Fox, W.P. (2011). Using the EXCEL Solver for Nonlinear Regression. *Computers in Education Journal, 2*(4), 77-86.

Fox, E. J., Montgomery, A. L., & Lodish, L. M. (2004). Consumer shopping and spending across retail formats. *The Journal of Business*, 77(S2), S25–S60. doi:10.1086/381518

Fox, J. (2001). *Multiple and generalized nonparametric regression, series: Quantitative applications in the social sciences*. London, UK: SAGE Publications.

Fox, W. P. (1993). The Use of Transformed Least Squares in Mathematical Modeling. *Computers in Education Journal*, *III*(1), 25–31.

Fox, W. P. (2011). Using Excel for nonlinear regression. *COED Journal*, 2(4), 77–86.

Fox, W. P. (2012). Importance of "good" starting points in nonlinear regression in mathematical modeling in Maple. *JCMST*, *31*(1), 1–16.

Fox, W. P. (2012). Issues and Importance of "Good" Starting Points for Nonlinear regression for Mathematical Modeling with Maple: Basic Model Fitting to Make Predictions with Oscillating Data. *Journal of Computers in Mathematics and Science Teaching*, *31*(1), 1–16.

Fox, W. P. (2012). *Mathematical Modeling with Maple*. Boston, MA: Cengage Publishers.

Fox, W. P. (2018). *Mathematical Modeling for Business Analytics*. Boca Raton, Fl.: CRC Press.

Fox, W. P., & Christopher, F. (1996). Understanding Covariance and Correlation. *PRIMUS (Terre Haute, Ind.)*, *VI*(3), 235–244. doi:10.1080/10511979608965826

Freund, Y., & Schapire, R. E. (1997). A Decision-Theoretic Generalization of On-Line Learning and an Application to Boosting. *Journal of Computer and System Sciences*, 55(1), 119–139. doi:10.1006/jcss.1997.1504

Friedman, J. H. (1999). *Greedy Function Aproximation: A Gradient Boosting Machine*. Academic Press.

Friedman, J., Hastie, T., & Tibshirani, R. (2001). *The elements of statistical learning* (Vol. 1). New York: Springer Series in Statistics.

Friedman, J. H. (1991). Multivariate adaptive regression splines. *Annals of Statistics*, *19*(1), 1–141. doi:10.1214/aos/1176347963

Friedman, J. H., & Stuetzle, W. (1981). Projection pursuit regression. *Journal of the American Statistical Association*, 76(376), 817–823. doi:10.1080/01621459.1981.10477729

Friston, K., Mattout, J., Trujillo-Barreto, N., Ashburner, J., & Penny, W. (2007). Variational free energy and the Laplace approximation. *NeuroImage*, *34*(1), 220–234. doi:10.1016/j.neuroimage.2006.08.035 PMID:17055746

Fuchs, M., Höpken, W., & Lexhagen, M. (2014). Big data analytics for knowledge generation in tourism destinations – A case from Sweden. *Journal of Destination Marketing & Management*, 3(4), 198–208. doi:10.1016/j.jdmm.2014.08.002

Fujii, Y., & Tanaka, K. (1971). Traffic capacity. *Journal of Navigation*, 24(4), 543–552. doi:10.1017/S0373463300022384

Galili, T. (2015). dendextend: An R package for visualizing, adjusting and comparing trees of hierarchical clustering. *Bioinformatics (Oxford, England)*, 22(31), 3718–3720. doi:10.1093/bioinformatics/btv428 PMID:26209431

Gandomi, A., & Haider, M. (2015). Beyond the hype: Big data concepts, methods, and analytics. *International Journal of Information Management*, 35(2), 137–144. doi:10.1016/j.ijinfomgt.2014.10.007

Ganesan, T. (2013). Swarm intelligence and gravitational search algorithm for multi-objective optimization of synthesis gas production. *Appl. Energy*, *103*, 368–374.

Gang, J., Tu, Y., Lev, B., Xu, J., Shen, W., & Yao, L. (2015). A multi-objective bi-level location planning problem for stone industrial parks. *Computers & Operations Research*, *56*, 8–21. doi:10.1016/j.cor.2014.10.005

Gao, H., & Liu, F. (2013). Estimating freeway traffic measures from mobile phone location data. *European Journal of Operational Research*, *229*(1), 252–260. doi:10.1016/j.ejor.2013.02.044

Gavalas, D., Konstantopoulos, C., Mastakas, K., & Pantziou, G. (2014). Mobile recommender systems in tourism. *Journal of Network and Computer Applications*, *39*, 319–333. doi:10.1016/j.jnca.2013.04.006

Ghalambaz. (2011). A hybrid neural network and gravitational search algorithm method to solve well known wessinger's equation. *International journal of MAIMM Engineering*, 5.

Giordano, F., Fox, W., & Horton, S. (2013). *A First Course in Mathematical Modeling* (5th ed.). Boston, MA: Cengage Publishers.

Glorot, X., & Bengio, Y. (2010). Understanding the difficulty of training deep feedforward neural networks. In Y. W. Teh & M. Titterington (Eds.), *Proceedings of the Thirteenth International Conference on Artificial Intelligence and Statistics* (pp. 249–256). Retrieved from http://proceedings.mlr.press/v9/glorot10a.html

Glugnn, N., Owens, L., Bennett, K., Healy, M. L., & Silke, B. (2014). Glucose As A Risk Predictior In Acute Medical Emergency Admissions. Elsevier. *Diabetes Research and Clinical Practice*.

Go, A., Bhayani, R., & Huang, L. (2009). Twitter sentiment classification using distant supervision. CS224N Project Report, 1(12).

Goel, A. (2014). Study of Different Partitioning Clustering Technique. International Journal for Scientific Research & Development, 2(8).

Goil, S., Nagesh, H., & And Choudhary, A. (1999). *MAFIA: Efficient and scalable subspace clustering for very large data sets*. Technical Report CPDC-TR-9906-010, Northwestern University.

Goldberg, K., Roeder, T., Gupta, D., & Perkins, C. (2001). Eigentaste: A Constant Time Collaborative Filtering Algorithm. *Information Retrieval*, *4*(2), 133–151. doi:10.1023/A:1011419012209

Golub, G. H., Heath, M., & Wahba, G. (1979). Generalized Cross-Validation as a method for choosing a good Ridge Parameter. *Technometrics*, *21*(2), 215–223. doi:10.1080/00401706.1979.10489751

Gómez Muñoz, C. Q., Arcos Jimenez, A., García Marquez, F. P., Kogia, M., Cheng, L., Mohimi, A., & Papaelias, M. (2018). Cracks and welds detection approach in solar receiver tubes employing electromagnetic acoustic transducers. *Structural Health Monitoring*, *17*(5), 1046–1055. doi:10.1177/1475921717734501

Gomez, C. Q., Garcia, F. P., Arcos, A., Cheng, L., Kogia, M., & Papelias, M. (2017). Calculus of the defect severity with EMATs by analysing the attenuation curves of the guided waves. *Smart Structures and Systems*, *19*(2), 195–202. doi:10.12989ss.2017.19.2.195

Gopalan, R., Batta, R., & Karwan, M. (1990). The equity constrained shortest path problem. *Computers & Operations Research*, *17*(3), 297–307. doi:10.1016/0305-0548(90)90006-S

Grubbs, F. E. (1950). Sample Criteria For Testing Outlying Observations. *Annals of Mathematical Statistics*, *21*(1), 27–58. doi:10.1214/aoms/1177729885

Guha, S., Rastogi, R., & Shim, K. (1998). Cure: An efficient clustering algorithm for large databases. *Proceedings of the 1998 ACM SIGMOD International Conference on Management of Data*, 73–84.

Guha, S., Rastogi, R., & Shim, K. (1998). CURE: an efficient clustering algorithm for large databases. *Proceedings of the 1998 ACM SIGMOD international conference on Management of data*, 73-84. 10.1145/276304.276312

Gupta, N., & Agrawal, R. (2017). Challenges and Security Issues of Distributed Databases. In *NoSQL* (pp. 265–284). Chapman and Hall/CRC.

Gupta, N., & Agrawal, R. (2018). NoSQL security. *Advances in Computers, 109*, 101–132. doi:10.1016/bs.adcom.2018.01.003

Hacker, M., Burgardt, D., Fletcher, L., Gordon, A., Peruzzi, W., Pretopnik, R., & Qaissaunee, M. (2015). *Engineering & Technology*. Boston: Cengage Learning.

Haghbayan, P., Nezamabadi-pour, H., & Kamyab, S. (2017). A niche GSA method with nearest neighbor scheme for multimodal optimization. *Swarm and Evolutionary Computation, 35*, 78–92. doi:10.1016/j.swevo.2017.03.002

Halliday, D., Resnick, R., & Walker, J. (2000). *Fundamentals of Physics* (6th ed.). Delhi: Wiley.

Han. (2014). Feature subset selection by gravitational search algorithm optimization. *Inf. Sci., 81*, 28-146.

Han, J., & Kamber, M. (2001). *Data Mining: Concepts and Techniques*. Morgan Kaufmann Publishers.

Han, X., Chang, X. M., Quan, L., Xiong, X. Y., Li, J. X., Zhang, Z. X., & Liu, Y. (2014). Feature subset selection by gravitational search algorithm optimization. *Inf. Sci., 281*, 128–146. doi:10.1016/j.ins.2014.05.030

Han, X., Quan, L., Xiong, X. Y., Almeter, M., Xiang, J., & Lan, Y. (2017). A novel data clustering algorithm based on modified gravitational search algorithm. *Engineering Applications of Artificial Intelligence, 61*, 1–7. doi:10.1016/j.engappai.2016.11.003

Hartshorn, S. (2016). *Machine Learning With Random Forests And Decision Trees: A Visual Guide For Beginners*. Kindle Edition.

Hashem, I. A. T., Yaqoob, I., Anuar, N. B., Mokhtar, S., Gani, A., & Ullah Khan, S. (2015). The rise of "big data" on cloud computing: Review and open research issues. *Information Systems, 47*, 98–115. doi:10.1016/j.is.2014.07.006

Hassanzadeh, H. R., & Rouhani, M. (2010). A multi-objective gravitational search algorithm. *Computational Intelligence, Communication Systems and Networks (CICSyN), Second International Conference*.

Hastie, T. J., & Tibshirani, R. J. (1990). *Generalized additive models*. New York, NY: Chapman and Hall.

Hastie, T., & Tibshirani, R. (1986). Generalized Additive Models. *Statistical Science, 1*(3), 297–318. doi:10.1214s/1177013604

Hastie, T., & Tibshirani, R. (1987). Generalized additive models: Some applications. *Journal of the American Statistical Association, 82*(398), 371–386. doi:10.1080/01621459.1987.10478440

Hastie, T., Tibshirani, R., & Friedman, J. H. (2001). *The element of statistical learning*. New York, NY: Springer Verlag. doi:10.1007/978-0-387-21606-5

Hastie, T., Tibshirani, R., & Friedman, J. H. (2009). *The elements of statistical learning: Data mining, inference, and prediction* (2nd ed.). New York, NY: Springer. doi:10.1007/978-0-387-84858-7

Hastie, T., Tibshirani, R., & Wainwright, M. (2015). *Statistical learning with sparsity: the lasso and generalizations*. CRC Press. doi:10.1201/b18401

Hatamlou, Abdullah, & Othman. (2011). Gravitational Search Algorithm with Heuristic Search for Clustering Problems. *Proceeding of 3rd IEEE on Data Mining and Optimization (DMO)*, 190 – 193.

Hatamlou, A., Abdullah, S., & Nezamabadi-pour, H. (2012). A combined approach for clustering based on K-means and gravitational search algorithms. *Swarm and Evolutionary Computation, 6,* 47–55. doi:10.1016/j.swevo.2012.02.003

Haykin, S. (2001). *Communication Systems* (4th ed.). Hoboken, NJ: John Wiley & Sons.

Hearst, M. A. (1999). Untangling Text Data Mining. In *Proceedings of the 37th Annual Meeting of the Association for Computational Linguistics on Computational Linguistics.* Association for Computational Linguistics. 10.3115/1034678.1034679

Heckerman, D. (1996). *A Tutorial on Learning With Bayesian Networks.* Technical Report MSR-TR-95-06, Microsoft Corporation.

Hegenbart, S. (2015). *Deep Learning with Convolutional Neural Networks.* Academic Press.

He, H., & Ma, Y. (2013). *Imbalanced Learning: Foundations, Algorithms and Applications.* Hoboken, NJ: IEEE Press. doi:10.1002/9781118646106

He, L., Huang, G. H., & Lu, H. W. (2011). Greenhouse gas emissions control in integrated municipal solid waste management through mixed integer bilevel decision making. *Journal of Hazardous Materials, 193,* 112–119. doi:10.1016/j.jhazmat.2011.07.036 PMID:21816539

Hennig, C. (2013). *Measurement of quality in cluster analysis.* Londres: University College, London.

He, R. (2017). A Kernel-Power-Density Based Algorithm for Channel Multipath Components Clustering. *IEEE Transactions on Wireless Communications, 16*(11), 7138–7151.

Hidri, M. S., Zoghlami, M. A., & Ayed, R. B. (2017). Speeding up the large-scale consensus fuzzy clustering for handling Big Data. *Fuzzy Sets and Systems.*

Hinneburg, A., & Keim, D. (1999). Optimal grid-clustering: Towards breaking the curse of dimensionality in high-dimensional clustering. *Proceedings of the 25th Conference on VLDB,* 506-517.

Hinnosaar, M. (2018, July 30). *The impact of retirement on the healthiness of food purchases.* doi:10.2139srn.3235215

Hisata, Y., & Yamai, Y. (2000). *Research toward the practical application of liquidity risk evaluation methods.* Discussion Paper, Institute for Monetary and Economic Studies, Bank of Japan.

Holland, J. H. (1975). *Adaptation in Natural and Artificial Systems.* Ann Arbor, MI: University of Michigan Press.

Hornsby, K., & Egenhofer, M. J. (2000). Identity - based change: A foundation for spatio-temporal knowledge representation. *International Journal of Geographical Information Science, 14*(3), 207–224. doi:10.1080/136588100240813

Hosmer, D., Lemeshow, S., & May, S. (2008). Regression Modeling of Time-to-Event Data. Willey Series in Probability and Statistics, second edition. doi:10.1002/9780470258019

Hosmer, D., & Lemeshow, S. (2013). *Applied Logistic Regression* (3rd ed.). Willey Series in Probability and Statistics. doi:10.1002/9781118548387

Ho, T. K. (1998). The Random Subspace Method For Constructing Decision Forests. *IEEE Transactions on Pattern Analysis and Machine Intelligence,* 832–844.

Hovy, E. H. (2015). *What are Sentiment, Affect, and Emotion? Applying the Methodology of Michael Zock to Sentiment Analysis.* Springer International Publishing Switzerland. doi:10.1007/978-3-319-08043-7_2

Ho, W.-M., Lin, J.-R., Wang, H.-H., Liou, C.-W., Chang, K. C., Lee, J.-D., ... Lee, T.-H. (2016). Prediction OF In-Hospital Stroke Mortality In Critical Care Unit. *SpringerPlus, 5*(1), 1051. doi:10.118640064-016-2687-2 PMID:27462499

Ho, Y., & Pepyne, D. (2002). Simple explanation of the no-free-lunch theorem and its implications. *Journal of Optimization Theory and Applications*, *155*(3), 549–570. doi:10.1023/A:1021251113462

Hsieh, N.-C. (2005). Hybrid mining approach in the design of credit scoring models. *Expert Systems with Applications*, *28*(4), 655–665. doi:10.1016/j.eswa.2004.12.022

Hu, S. (2007). *Akaike Information Criterrion*. Academic Press.

Hu, Y., Koren, Y., & Volinsky, C. (n.d.). *Collaborative Filtering for Implicit Feedback Datasets*. Retrieved from http://yifanhu.net/PUB/cf.pdf

Huang, Z. (2017). *Integrated railway remote condition monitoring*. University of Birmingham.

Huang, Z., Papaelias, M., & Lang, Z. (n.d.). Wayside detection of axle bearing faults in rolling stock through correlation processing of high-frequency acoustic emission signals. *Proceedings of First World Congress on Condition Monitoring-WCCM*.

Huddleston, S., & Brown, G. . (2018). INFORMS Analytics Body of Knowledge. John Wiley & Sons and Naval Postgraduate School updated notes.

Huurdeman, A. A. (2003). *The world history of telecommunications*. Hoboken, NJ: John Wiley & Sons. doi:10.1002/0471722243

Hyndman, R., & Athanasopoulos, A. (2018). *Forecasting: principles and practices* (2nd ed.). OTexts. Retrieved from https://otexts.com/fpp2/ets.html

Ibrahim, A. A., Mohamed, A., & Shareef, H. (2012). A novel quantum-inspired binary gravitational search algorithm in obtaining optimal power quality monitor placement. *Journal of Applied Sciences (Faisalabad)*, *12*(9), 822–830. doi:10.3923/jas.2012.822.830

Ibrahim, A. A., Mohamed, A., & Shareef, H. (2014). Optimal power quality monitor placement in power systems using an adaptive quantum-inspired binary gravitational search algorithm. *International Journal of Electrical Power & Energy Systems*, *57*, 404–413. doi:10.1016/j.ijepes.2013.12.019

Ican, O. (2013). *Determining the Functional Structure of Financial Time Series by Means of Genetic Learning*. Anadolu University, Graduate School of Social Sciences.

Imandoust, S. B., & Bolandraftar, M. (2013). Application of k-nearest neighbor (kNN) approach for predicting economic events: Theoretical background. *International Journal of Engineering Research and Applications*, *3*(5), 605–610.

Internet Engineering Task Force. (2010). *Worldwide telecommunications industry revenues*. Retrieved from https://www.plunkettresearch.com/Telecommunications/telecommunicationsStatistics/tabid/96/Default.aspx

Ipsos Mori. (2005). *I just text to say I love you*. Retrieved from https://www.ipsos-mori.com/research publications/researcharchive/1575/1-Just-text-To-Say-I-Love-You.aspx

Isinkaye, F. O., Folajimi, Y. O., & Ojokoh, B. A. (2015). Recommendation systems: Principles, methods and evaluation. *Egyptian Informatics Journal*, *16*(3), 261–273. doi:10.1016/j.eij.2015.06.005

ITU. (2003). *World telecommunication development report*. Retrieved from https://www.itu.int/ITU-D/ict/publications/wtdr-03/index.html

ITU. (2008). *Digital access index (DAI)*. Retrieved from https://www.itu.int/ITU-D/ict/dai/

ITU. (2012). *Article 1.3 ITU Radio regulations*. Retrieved from http://www.itu.int/dms_pub/itu-s/oth/02/20/502020000244501PDFE.PDF

Jabbar, M. A., Deekshatulua, B. L., & Chandra, P. (2013). Classification of Heart Disease Using K-Nearest Neighbor and Genetic Algorithm. In *Proceedings of International Conference on Computational Intelligence: Modeling Techniques and Applications* (CIMTA) 2013 (*vol. 10*, pp. 85 – 94). Kalyani, India: Elsevier Ltd. 10.1016/j.protcy.2013.12.340

Jackson, J. E. (2005). *A user's guide to principal components* (Vol. 587). John Wiley & Sons.

Jacob, S.S., & Vijayakumar, R. (2018). Modern Techniques used for Big Data Clustering: A Review. *International Journal of Engineering Science Invention, 7*(6), 1-5.

Jaderberg, M., Dalibard, V., Osindero, S., Czarnecki, W. M., Donahue, J., & Razavi, A. (2017). Population Based Training of Neural Networks. Academic Press.

Jagota, A. (2013). *Machine Learning Basics Kindle Edition* [Kindle Fire version]. Retrieved from Amazon.com.

Jain & Dubes. (1990). *Algorithms for Clustering Data*. Prentice hall advanced references series, Michigan state University.

Jain, A. (2010). Data clustering: 50 years beyond K-means. *Pattern Recognition Letters, 31*(8), 651–666. doi:10.1016/j.patrec.2009.09.011

Jain, A. K., & Dubes, R. C. (1988). *Algorithms for Clustering Data*. Upper Saddle River, NJ: Prentice-Hall.

James, G., Witten, D., Hastie, T., & Tibshirani, R. (2013). *An introduction to statistical learning* (Vol. 112). New York: Springer.

Jamshidi, Y., & Kaburlasos, V. G. (2014). gsaINknn: A GSA optimized, lattice computing knn classifier. *Engineering Applications of Artificial Intelligence, 35*, 277–285. doi:10.1016/j.engappai.2014.06.018

Jander, M. (2006). *Report: DWDM no match for sonet*. Retrieved from http://www.lightreading.com/document.asp?doc_id=31358

Japan Tourism Agency. (2014). *Keitaidenwa kara erareru ichijouhou tou wo katuyousita hounichi gaikokujin doutaichousa houkokusho* [Foreign visitors' dynamics research report utilizing mobile phone location information]. Retrieved June 28, 2019, from http://www.mlit.go.jp/common/001080545.pdf

Jarrow, R., & Subramanian, A. (1997). Mopping up Liquidity. *Risk (Concord, NH), 10*(12), 170–173.

Jayanthi, G., & Uma, V. (2017). *A qualitative inference method for prediction of geographic process using spatial and temporal relations. International Journal of Artificial Intelligence and Soft Computing*.

Jayanthi, G., & Uma, V. (2017). *Modeling Spatial Evolution: Review of Methods and its Significance. In Dynamic Knowledge Representation in Scientific Domains*. IGI Global.

Jiang, H., Li, J., Yi, S., Wang, X., & Hu, X. (2011). Expert Systems with Applications A new hybrid method based on partitioning-based DBSCAN and ant clustering. *Expert Systems with Applications, 38*(8), 9373–9381. doi:10.1016/j.eswa.2011.01.135

Jiang, J., Ji, Z., & Shen, Y. (2014). A novel hybrid particle swarm optimization and gravitational search algorithm for solving economic emission load dispatch problems with various practical constraints. *International Journal of Electrical Power & Energy Systems, 55*, 628–644. doi:10.1016/j.ijepes.2013.10.006

Ji, B., Yuan, X., Li, X., Huang, Y., & Li, W. (2014). Application of quantum-inspired binary gravitational search algorithm for thermal unit commitment with wind power integration. *Energy Conversion and Management, 87*, 589–598. doi:10.1016/j.enconman.2014.07.060

Jiménez, A. A., Gómez, C. Q., & Márquez, F. P. G. (2018). Concentrated solar plants management: Big data and neural network. In *Renewable energies* (pp. 63–81). Springer. doi:10.1007/978-3-319-45364-4_5

Jiménez, A. A., Márquez, F. P. G., Moraleda, V. B., & Muñoz, C. Q. G. (2019). Linear and nonlinear features and machine learning for wind turbine blade ice detection and diagnosis. *Renewable Energy, 132*, 1034–1048. doi:10.1016/j. renene.2018.08.050

Jiménez, A. A., Muñoz, C. Q. G., & Márquez, F. P. G. (2019). Dirt and mud detection and diagnosis on a wind turbine blade employing guided waves and supervised learning classifiers. *Reliability Engineering & System Safety, 184*, 2–12. doi:10.1016/j.ress.2018.02.013

Jiménez, A. A., Muñoz, C. Q. G., & Márquez, F. P. G. (n.d.). Machine learning and neural network for maintenance management. *Proceedings of International Conference on Management Science and Engineering Management,* 1377-1388. 10.1007/978-3-319-59280-0_115

Jiménez, A. A., Muñoz, C. Q. G., Marquez, F. P. G., & Zhang, L. (n.d.). Artificial Intelligence for Concentrated Solar Plant Maintenance Management. *Proceedings of Proceedings of the Tenth International Conference on Management Science and Engineering Management,* 125-134. 10.1007/978-981-10-1837-4_11

Jin, H., & Batta, R. (1997). Objectives derived from viewing hazmat shipments as a sequence of independent Bernoulli trials. *Transportation Science, 31*(3), 252–261. doi:10.1287/trsc.31.3.252

Jinquan. (2011). Hitune: dataflow-based performance analysis for big data cloud. Proc. of the 2011 USENIX ATC, 87-100.

Jobson, J. D. (1992). Applied multivariate data analysis.: Vol. 2. *Categorical and multivariate methods*. New York, NY: Springer.

Jobson, J. D., & Korkie, B. M. (1981). Putting Markowitz Theory to Work. *Journal of Portfolio Management, 7*, 70–74.

Johnson, I. (2012). *An Introductory Handbook on Probability, Statistics, and Excel*. Retrieved from http://records.viu. ca/~johnstoi/maybe/maybe4.htm

Johnson, R. A., & Wichern, D. W. (2002). Applied multivariate statistical analysis: Vol. 5. *No. 8*. Upper Saddle River, NJ: Prentice Hall.

Jolliffe, I. (2011). Principal component analysis. In *International encyclopedia of statistical science* (pp. 1094–1096). Berlin: Springer. doi:10.1007/978-3-642-04898-2_455

Jorion, P. (1991). Bayesian and CAPM Estimators of the Means: Implications for Portfolio Selection. *Journal of Banking & Finance, 15*(3), 717–727. doi:10.1016/0378-4266(91)90094-3

Jorion, P. (2007). *Value At Risk: The New benchmark for Managing financial Risk* (3rd ed.). McGraw-Hill.

Joshi, A., Bhattacharya, P., & Mark, J. (2017). Automatic Sarcasm Detection: A Survey. ACM Computing Surveys, 50(5).

Jung, Kang, & Heo. (2014). Clustering Performance Comparission Using K-means And Expectation MaximiZation Algorithm. *Bio Technology And Biotechnological Equipment, 28.*

Jun, S., Lee, S. J., & Ryu, J.-B. (2015). A Divide Regression Analysis For Big Data. *International Journal Of Software Enginnering And Its Applications.*

Kaewprag, P., Newton, C., & Vermillion, B. (2017). Predictive models for pressure ulcers from intensive care unit electronic health records using Bayesian networks. *BMC Medical Informatics and Decision Making, 17*(Suppl 2), 65. PMID:28699545

Kaggle Inc. (2019). *Loan data set.* [Data file]. Retrieved from https://www.kaggle.com/prateikmahendra/loan-data

Kala, N. (2019) A study on internet bypass fraud: national security threat. *Forensic Research & Criminology International Journal, 7*(1).

Kalisch, M., Fellinghauer, B. A., & Grill, E. (2010). Understanding human functioning using graphical models. *BMC Medical Research Methodology, 10*, 14. PMID:20149230

Kang, Y., Batta, R., & Kwon, C. (2014). Generalized route planning model for hazardous material transportation with VaR and equity considerations. *Computers & Operations Research, 43*, 237–247. doi:10.1016/j.cor.2013.09.015

Kanungo, T., Mount, D. M., Netanyahu, N. S., Piatko, C. D., Silverman, R., & Wu, A. Y. (2012). A local search approximation algorithm for k-means clustering. *18th Annual ACM Symposium on Computational Geometry*, 10-18.

Kara, B. Y., & Verter, V. (2004). Designing a road network for hazardous materials transportation. *Transportation Science, 38*(2), 188–196. doi:10.1287/trsc.1030.0065

Karaboga, D. (2005). *An Idea based on Honey Bee Swarm for Numerical Optimization.* Technical Report TR06. Computer Engineering Department, Engineering Faculty, Erciyes University.

Karaboga, D., & Ozturk, C. (2011). A novel clustering approach: Artificial bee colony (ABC) algorithm. *Applied Soft Computing, 11*(1), 652–657. doi:10.1016/j.asoc.2009.12.025

Karatzoglou, A., Amatriain, X., Baltrunas, L., & Oliver, N. (2010). Multiverse recommendation: n-dimensional tensor factorization for context-aware collaborative filtering. *Proceedings of the Fourth ACM Conference on Recommender Systems - RecSys '10*, 79. 10.1145/1864708.1864727

Karmarkar, N. (1984). A new polynomial-time algorithm for linear programming. *Combinatorica, 4*(4), 373–395. doi:10.1007/BF02579150

Kartal, B. (2015). *Financial Portfolio Optimization with Artifical Bee Colony Algorithm.* Istanbul University, Social Sciences Institute.

Kavitha, M. D. (2016). *A Hybrid Nelder-Mead Method For Biclustering Of Gene Expression Data.* International Journal Of Technology Enhancements And Emerging Engineering Research.

Keeney, R. (1980). Equity and public risk. *Operations Research, 28*(3-part-i), 527–534. doi:10.1287/opre.28.3.527

Kennedy, J., & Eberhart, R. C. (1995). In Particle swarm optimization. *Proceedings of IEEE International Conference on Neural Networks.* 10.1109/ICNN.1995.488968

Keogh, E., Chakrabarti, K., & Mehrotra, S. (2001). Locally adaptive dimensionality reduction for indexing large time series databases. *Proceedings of the ACMSIGMOD Conference.*

Ketchen, D. J. Jr, & Shook, C. L. (1996). The application of cluster analysis in strategic management research: An analysis and critique. *Strategic Management Journal, 17*(6), 441–458. doi:10.1002/(SICI)1097-0266(199606)17:6<441::AID-SMJ819>3.0.CO;2-G

Khajooei, F., & Rashedi, E. (2016). *A New Version of Gravitational Search Algorithm with Negative Mass.* Academic Press.

Kılıçaslan, H., & Giter, M. S. (2016). Kredi Derecelendirme ve Ortaya Çıkan Sorunlar [Credit Rating and Emerging Issues]. *Maliye Araştırmaları Dergisi, 2*(1), 61–81.

Kim, G., Seok, J. H., & Mark, T. (2018, February 13). *New market opportunities and consumer heterogeneity in the U.S. organic food market*. doi:10.2139srn.2916250

Kim, G., Seok, J. H., Mark, T., & Reed, M. R. (2018, January 1). *The price relationship between organic and non-organic vegetables in the U.S.: Evidence from Nielsen scanner data*. doi:10.2139srn.3176082

Kim, C., Park, S., Kwon, K., & Chang, W. (2012). How to select search keywords for online advertising depending on consumer involvement: An empirical investigation. *Expert Systems with Applications, 39*(1), 594–610. doi:10.1016/j.eswa.2011.07.050

Kim, J., Lee, D., & Chung, K.-Y. (2014). Item recommendation based on context-aware model for personalized u-healthcare service. *Multimedia Tools and Applications, 71*(2), 855–872. doi:10.100711042-011-0920-0

Kiwiel, K. C. (1990). Proximity control in bundle methods for convex nondifferentiable minimization. *Mathematical Programming, 46*(1-3), 105–122. doi:10.1007/BF01585731

Knagenhjelm, P., & Brauer, P. (1990). Classification of vowels in continuous speech using MLP and a hybrid network. *Speech Communication, 9*(1), 31–34. doi:10.1016/0167-6393(90)90042-8

Koren, Y., & Yehuda. (2008). Factorization meets the neighborhood. *Proceeding of the 14th ACM SIGKDD International Conference on Knowledge Discovery and Data Mining - KDD 08, 426.* 10.1145/1401890.1401944

Kotsiantis, S., & Kanellopoulos, D. (2006). Discretization Techniques: A recent survey. *GESTS International Transactions on Computer Science and Engineering, 32,* 47–58.

Krieg. (2001). A Tutorial on Bayesian Belief Networks. Surveillance Systems Division Electronics and Surveillance Research Laboratory.

Krizhevsky, A., Sutskever, I., & Hinton, G. E. (2012). Imagenet classification with deep convolutional neural networks. In F. Pereira, C. J. C. Burges, L. Bottou, & K. Q. Weinberger (Eds.), Advances in neural information processing systems: Vol. 25. *NIPS 25* (pp. 1097–1105). Lake Tahoe, CA: Curran Associates.

Kumar, V., Chhabra, J. K., & Kumar, D. (2014). Automatic cluster evolution using gravitational search algorithm and its application on image segmentation. *Engineering Applications of Artificial Intelligence, 29,* 93–103. doi:10.1016/j.engappai.2013.11.008

Kurzynski, M. W. (1983). The optimal strategy of a tree classifier. *Pattern Recognition, 16*(1), 81–87. doi:10.1016/0031-3203(83)90011-0

Lab, A. T. B. R. S. (2015). *Expectation Maximization On Old Faithful*. Retrieved from https://es.mathworks.com/matlabcentral/fileexchange/49869-expectation-maximization-on-old-faithful

Lacave, C., & Diez, F. J. (2003). *Knowledge Acquisition in PROSTANET-A Bayesian Network for Diagnosing Prostate Cancer*. Berlin: Springer-Verlag. doi:10.1007/978-3-540-45226-3_182

Lakshmi, T. M., Sahana, R. J., & Venkatesan, V. R. (2018). Review on Density Based Clustering Algorithms for Big Data Integrated Intelligent Research (IIR). *International Journal of Data Mining Techniques and Applications, 7*(1), 13–20. doi:10.20894/IJDMTA.102.007.001.003

Lam, X. N., Vu, T., Le, T. D., & Duong, A. D. (2008). Addressing cold-start problem in recommendation systems. *Proceedings of the 2nd International Conference on Ubiquitous Information Management and Communication - ICUIMC '08*, 208. 10.1145/1352793.1352837

Landajo, M., Andres, J. D., & Lorca, P. (2007). Robust neural modeling for the cross-sectional analysis of accounting information. *European Journal of Operational Research*, *177*(2), 1232–1252. doi:10.1016/j.ejor.2005.10.064

Langlois, R. N., & Cosgel, M. M. (1993). Frank Knight on risk, uncertainty, and the firm: A new interpretation. *Economic Inquiry*, *31*(3), 456–465. doi:10.1111/j.1465-7295.1993.tb01305.x

Le Saout, E. (2002). *Incorporating liquidity risk in VaR models*. Working Paper, Paris 1 University.

Lee, J., Sun, M., & Lebanon, G. (2012). *A Comparative Study of Collaborative Filtering Algorithms*. Retrieved from https://arxiv.org/pdf/1205.3193.pdf

Lee, Y.-S., & Cho, S.-B. (2011). Activity Recognition Using Hierarchical Hidden Markov Models on a Smartphone with 3D Accelerometer. *Hybrid Artificial Intelligent Systems*, 460–467. doi:10.1007/978-3-642-21219-2_58

Lee, K., Eoff, B. D., & Caverlee, J. (2011). *Seven Months with the Devils: A Long-Term Study of Content Polluters on Twitter*. ICWSM.

Lee, S. (2005). Application of logistic regression model and its validation for landslide susceptibility mapping using GIS and remote sensing data. *International Journal of Remote Sensing*, *26*(7), 1477–1491. doi:10.1080/01431160412331331012

Lee, T. C. M. (2003). Smoothing parameter selection for smoothing splines: A simulation study. *Computational Statistics & Data Analysis*, *42*(1-2), 139–148. doi:10.1016/S0167-9473(02)00159-7

Lee, T.-S., & Chen, I.-F. (2005). A two-stage hybrid credit scoring model using artificial neural networks and multivariate adaptive regression splines. *Expert Systems with Applications*, *28*(4), 743–752. doi:10.1016/j.eswa.2004.12.031

Leisch, F. (2015). Resampling methods for exploring clustering stability. In C. Hennig, M. Meila, F. Murtagh, & R. Rocci (Eds.), *Handbook of cluster analysis* (pp. 637–652). Boca Raton, FL: Chapman and Hall/CRC.

Lenert, E. (1998). A communication theory perspective on telecommunications policy. *Journal of Communication*, *48*(4), 3–23. doi:10.1111/j.1460-2466.1998.tb02767.x

Leung, H., & Wu, J. (2000). Bayesian and Dempster-Shafer target identification for radar surveillance. *IEEE Transactions on Aerospace and Electronic Systems*, *36*(2), 432–447. doi:10.1109/7.845221

Levi, M., & Burrows, J. (2008). Measuring the impact of fraud in the UK: A conceptual and empirical journey. *British Journal of Criminology*, *48*(3), 293–318. doi:10.1093/bjc/azn001

Levine, E., & Domany, E. (2001). Resampling method for unsupervised estimation of cluster validity. *Neural Computation*, *13*(11), 2573–2593. doi:10.1162/089976601753196030 PMID:11674852

Liaw, A., & Wiener, M. (2002). Classification and regression by randomForest. *R News*, *2*(3), 18–22.

Li, C., & Zhou, J. (2014). Semi-supervised weighted kernel clustering based on gravitational search for fault diagnosis. *ISA Transactions*, *53*(5), 1534–1543. doi:10.1016/j.isatra.2014.05.019 PMID:24981891

Lin, H., Wang, C., Liu, P., & Holtkamp, D. J. (2013). Construction of disease risk scoring systems using logistic group lasso: Application to porcine reproductive and respiratory syndrome survey data. *Journal of Applied Statistics*, *40*(4), 736–746. doi:10.1080/02664763.2012.752449

Li, Q., Chen, X., Chen, J., & Tang, Q. (2010). An evacuation risk assessment model for emergency traffic with consideration of urban hazard installations. *Chinese Science Bulletin, 55*(10), 1000–1006. doi:10.100711434-009-0277-1

Liu, F. H. Z. (2006). Biclustering of Gene Expression Data Using EDA-GA Hybrid. *IEEE Congress on Evolutionary Computation Sheraton Vancouver Wall Centre Hotel.*

Liu, F., Janssens, D., Wets, G., & Cools, M. (2013). Annotating mobile phone location data with activity purposes using machine learning algorithms. *Expert Systems with Applications, 40*(8), 3299–3311. doi:10.1016/j.eswa.2012.12.100

Liu, X., Liu, Y., Aberer, K., & Miao, C. (2013). Personalized Point-of-Interest Recommendation by Mining Users' Preference Transition. In *Proceedings of the 22nd ACM International Conference on Information and Knowledge Management (CIKM'13)*, (pp. 733-738). ACM. 10.1145/2505515.2505639

Liu, Y., Wei, W., Sun, A., & Miao, C. (2014). Exploiting Geographical Neighborhood Characteristics for Location Recommendation. In *Proceedings of the 23rd ACM International Conference on Information and Knowledge Management (CIKM'14)*, (pp. 739-748). ACM. 10.1145/2661829.2662002

Liu, Y., Zhang, Y.-M., Zhang, X.-Y., & Liu, C.-L. (2016). Adaptive spatial pooling for image classification. *Pattern Recognition, 55*(C), 58–67. doi:10.1016/j.patcog.2016.01.030

Li, Y. M. I. (2014). Biclustering of Gene Expression Data Using Particle Swarm Optimization Integrated with Pattern-Driven Local Search. *IEEE Congress on Evolutionary Computation (CEC)*. 10.1109/CEC.2014.6900323

Li, Y., Lu, L., & Xuefeng, L. (2005). A hybrid collaborative filtering method for multiple-interests and multiple-content recommendation in E-Commerce. *Expert Systems with Applications, 28*(1), 67–77. doi:10.1016/j.eswa.2004.08.013

Li-Yeh Chuang, H.-W. C.-J.-H. (2007). *Improved binary PSO for feature selection using gene expression data.* Computational Biology and Chemistry Elsevier Ltd.

Ljubesic, N., & Fiser, D. (2016). *A global analysis of emoji usage.* ACL.

Lkhagva, B., Suzuki, Y., & Kawagoe, K. (2006, April). New time series data representation ESAX for financial applications. In *22nd International Conference on Data Engineering Workshops (ICDEW'06)* (pp. x115-x115). IEEE. 10.1109/ICDEW.2006.99

Løkketangen, A., & Woodruff, D. L. (1996). Progressive hedging and tabu search applied to mixed integer (0, 1) multistage stochastic programming. *Journal of Heuristics, 2*(2), 111–128. doi:10.1007/BF00247208

Lombardi, S., Anand, S., & Gorgoglione, M. (2009). Context and Customer Behavior in Recommendation. *Work.* Retrieved from http://ids.csom.umn.edu/faculty/gedas/cars2009/LombardiEtAl-cars2009.pdf

Lopamudra Dey, A. M. (2014). Microarray Gene Expression Data Clustering using PSO based K-means Algorithm. *International Journal of Computer Science and its Applications.*

Lops, P., de Gemmis, M., & Semeraro, G. (2011). Content-based Recommender Systems: State of the Art and Trends. In Recommender Systems Handbook (pp. 73–105). Academic Press. doi:10.1007/978-0-387-85820-3_3

Ludwichowska, G., Romaniuk, J., & Nenycz-Thiel, M. (2017). Systematic response errors in self-reported category buying frequencies. *European Journal of Marketing, 51*(7/8), 1440–1459. doi:10.1108/EJM-07-2016-0408

Ludwig & Simone, A. (2015). MapReduce-based fuzzy c-means clustering algorithm: Implementation and scalability. *International Journal of Machine Learning and Cybernetics, 6*, 923–934.

Luo, C., Wu, D., & Wu, D. (2017). A deep learning approach for credit scoring using credit default swaps. *Engineering Applications of Artificial Intelligence, 65*, 465–470. doi:10.1016/j.engappai.2016.12.002

Luo, G. (2016). *Automatically Expalining Machine Learning Prediction Results: A Demonstration On Type 2 Diabetes Risk Prediction.* Luo Health Inf Sci Syst.

Luo, Z. Q., Pang, J. S., & Ralph, D. (1996). *Mathematical Programs with Equilibrium Constraints.* Cambridge, UK: Cambridge University Press. doi:10.1017/CBO9780511983658

MacQueen, J. (1967). Some methods for classification and analysis of multivariate observations. In *Proceedings of Fifth Berkeley Symposium on Mathematics Statistics and Probability.* University of California Press.

Madhavan, A., Richardson, M., & Roomans, M. (1997). Why do security prices change? A transaction-level analysis of NYSE stocks. *Review of Financial Studies, 10*(4), 1035–1064. doi:10.1093/rfs/10.4.1035

Madoroba, S. B. W., & Kruger, J. W. (2014). Liquidity effects on value-at-risk limits: Construction of a new VaR model. *Journal of Risk Model Validation, 8*(4), 19–46. doi:10.21314/JRMV.2014.127

Maes, S., Tuyls, K., Vanschoenwinkel, B., & Manderick, B. (2002). *Credit card fraud detection using Bayesian and neural networks.* Paper presented at 1st International Naiso Congress on Neuro Fuzzy Technologies, Havana, Cuba.

Mahajan, V., Jain, A. K., & Bergier, M. (1977). Parameter estimation in marketing models in the presence of multicollinearity: An application of ridge regression. *JMR, Journal of Marketing Research, 14*(4), 586–591. doi:10.1177/002224377701400419

Malhotra, K. G., Mohan, C. K., & Huang, H. (2017). *Anomaly detection principles and algorithms. Terrorism, Security, and Computation.* Springer.

Mandelbrot, B. B. (1963). The variation of certain speculative prices. *The Journal of Business, 24*, 392–417.

Maninderjit, K., & Garg, S. K. (2014). Survey on Clustering Techniques in Data Mining for Software Engineering. *International Journal of Advanced and Innovative Research, 3*, 238–243.

Marianov, V., & ReVelle, C. (1998). Linear non-approximated models for optimal routing in hazardous environments. *The Journal of the Operational Research Society, 49*(2), 157–164. doi:10.1057/palgrave.jors.2600506

Markowitz, H. (1959). *Portfolio Selection: Efficient Diversification of Investments.* New York: John Wiley.

Marquardt, D. W., & Snee, R. D. (1975). Ridge regression in practice. *The American Statistician, 29*(1), 3–20.

Martínez, L., Barranco, M. J., Pérez, L. G., & Espinilla, M. (2008). A Knowledge Based Recommender System with Multigranular Linguistic Information. *International Journal of Computational Intelligence Systems, 1*(3), 225–236. doi:10.1080/18756891.2008.9727620

MathWorks. (2008). *Efficient K-Means Clustering using JIT.* Retrieved from https://es.mathworks.com/matlabcentral/fileexchange/19344-efficient-k-means-clustering-using-jit

MathWorks. (n.d.). *Cluster with Self-Organizing Map Neural Network.* Retrieved from https://es.mathworks.com/help/nnet/ug/cluster-with-self-organizing-map-neural-network.html

Mathworks. (n.d.). *Dendrogram plot.* Retrieved from https://es.mathworks.com/help/stats/dendrogram.html

Ma, X., Pei, T., Song, C., & Zhou, C. (2016). A new assessment model for evacuation vulnerability in urban areas. *International Journal of Geographical Information Science*, 29–39.

Mbarika, V., & Mbarika, I. (2006). *Africa calling.* Retrieved from http://www.spectrum.ieee.org/may06/3426

McAfee, A., & Brynjolfsson, E. (2012). Big data: The management revolution. *Harvard Business Review, 90*(10), 60–68. PMID:23074865

McCutcheon, L. A. (1987). *Latent class analysis*. Newbury Park, CA: Sage. doi:10.4135/9781412984713

Meucci, A. (2009). Managing Diversification. *Risk (Concord, NH)*, *22*(5), 74–79.

Michaud, R. O. (1989). The Markowitz Optimization Enigma: Is 'Optimized' Optimal? *Financial Analysts Journal*, *45*(1), 31–42. doi:10.2469/faj.v45.n1.31

Mikolov, T., Sutskever, I., Chen, K., Corrado, G. S., & Dean, J. (2013). Distributed representations of words and phrases and their compositionality. In C. J. C. Burges, L. Bottou, M. Welling, Z. Ghahramani, & K. Q. Weinberger (Eds.), Advances in neural information processing systems: Vol. 26. *NIPS 2013* (pp. 3111–3119). Lake Tahoe, CA: Curran Associates.

Millard, I., De Roure, D., & Shadbolt, N. (2005). *Contextually Aware Information Delivery in Pervasive Computing Environments*. doi:10.1007/11426646_18

Minghao, H. (2011). A novel hybrid K-harmonic means and gravitational search algorithm approach for clustering. *Expert Systems with Applications*, *38*(8), 9319–9324. doi:10.1016/j.eswa.2011.01.018

Minh Phoung, T., Lin, Z., & Altman, R. B. (2005). Choosing SNPs using feature selection. *Bioinformatics (Oxford, England)*, *1*(1).

MINITAB ©. (2019). Retrieved from https://support.minitab.com/en-us/minitab/18/help-and-how-to/graphs/how-to/time-series-plot/before-you-start/example/

Minnesota, U. O. (n.d.). Ward's Method and Centroid methods. In Hierarchical Clustering (pp. 41–48). Academic Press.

Mirjalili, S., & Gandomi, A. (2017). Chaotic gravitational constants for the gravitational search algorithm. *Applied Soft Computing*, *53*, 407–419. doi:10.1016/j.asoc.2017.01.008

Mirjalili, S., & Hashim, M. (2012). Training feed forward neural networks using hybrid particle swarm optimization and gravitational search algorithm. *Applied Mathematics and Computation*, *218*(22), 1125–11137. doi:10.1016/j.amc.2012.04.069

Misiti, M., Misiti, Y., Oppenheim, G., & Poggi, J.-M. (1996). Wavelet toolbox. The MathWorks Inc.

Mizumoto, K., Yanagimoto, H., & Yoshioka, M. (2012). IEEE/ACIS 11th *International Conference on Computer and Information Science. IEEE*.

MK, A. (2016). *Linear Discriminant Analysis (LDA)*. Retrieved from https://mlalgorithm.wordpress.com/tag/linear-discriminant-analysis/

Mohammady, S., & Delavar, M. R. (2016). Urban sprawl assessment and modeling using landsat images and GIS. *Modeling Earth Systems and Environment*, *2*(3), 155. doi:10.100740808-016-0209-4

Mohsen lashkargir, S. A. (2009). A Hybrid Multi-Objective Particle Swarm OptimizationMethod to Discover Biclusters in Microarray Data. *International Journal of Computer Science and Information Security*.

Mojena, R. (2004). Ward's Clustering Algorithm. Encyclopedia of Statistical Sciences.

Mojena, R. (2006). Ward's Clustering Algorithm. Encyclopedia of Statistical Sciences. doi:10.1002/0471667196.ess2887.pub2

Mondo, G. D., Stell, J. G., Claramunt, C., & Thibaud, R. (2010). A Graph Model for Spatio-temporal Evolution. *Journal of Universal Computer Science*, *16*(11), 1452–1477.

Montgomery, D. C., Peck, E. A., & Vining, G. G. (2012). *Introduction to linear regression analysis* (Vol. 821). John Wiley & Sons.

Morgan Guaranty Trust Company. (1994). *RiskMetrics-Technical Document*. New York: Morgan Guaranty Trust Company, Global Research.

Mucherino, A., Papajorgji, P. J., & Pardalos, P. M. (2009). K-nearest neighbor classification. In *Data mining in agriculture. Springer Optimization and Its Applications, 34*. New York, NY: Springer. doi:10.1007/978-0-387-88615-2_4

Mukhajee, S., & Shaw, R. (2016). *Big Data, Concept, Applications, Challenges And Future Scope* (Vol. 5). International Journal Of Advanced Research In Computer And Communication Engineering.

Muñoz, C. Q. G., Jiménez, A. A., & Márquez, F. P. G. (2017). Wavelet transforms and pattern recognition on ultrasonic guides waves for frozen surface state diagnosis. *Renewable Energy*.

Muñoz, C. Q. G., & Márquez, F. P. G. (2018). Future maintenance management in renewable energies. In *Renewable Energies* (pp. 149–159). Springer. doi:10.1007/978-3-319-45364-4_10

Mytton, O. T., Nnoaham, K., Eyles, H., Scarborough, P., & Mhurchu, C. N. (2014). Systematic review and meta-analysis of the effect of increased vegetable and fruit consumption on body weight and energy intake. *BMC Public Health, 14*(1), 1–11. doi:10.1186/1471-2458-14-886 PMID:25168465

Nakamoto, S. (2008). *Bitcoin: A Peer-to-Peer Electronic Cash System*. Satoshi Nakamoto Institute.

Narmanlioglu, O., & Zeydan, E. (2018). Mobility-Aware Cell Clustering Mechanism for Self-Organizing Networks. *Access IEEE, 6*, 65405–65417. doi:10.1109/ACCESS.2018.2876601

Nefedov, A. (2016). *Support Vector Machines: A Simple Tutorial*. Retrieved from http://svmtutorial.online/

Nelder, J. A., & Wedderburn, R. W. M. (1972). Generalized linear models. *Journal of Royal Statistical Society. A, 135*(3), 370–384. doi:10.2307/2344614

Nelson, E., Fitzgerald, J. M., Tefft, N., & Anderson, J. (2017, September 1). *US household demand for organic fruit*. doi:10.2139srn.3081997

Nemirovski, A., & Todd, M. J. (2008). Interior-point methods for optimization. *Acta Numerica, 17*, 191–234. doi:10.1017/S0962492906370018

Nerurkar, P., Shirke, A., Chandane, M., & Bhirud, S. (2017). Empirical Analysis of Data Clustering Algorithms. *6th International Conference on Smart Computing and Communications*.

Neter, J., Kutner, M., Nachtsheim, C., & Wasserman, W. (1996). Applied Linear Statistical Models (4th ed.). Irwin Press.

Neves, P.C., & Bernardino, J. (2015). Big Data in Cloud Computing: features and issues. *Open Journal of Big Data, 1*(2).

New Oxford American Dictionary. (2005). *Telecommunication, tele and communication*. Oxford, UK: Oxford University Press.

Newman, M. (2010). *Networks: an introduction*. Oxford, UK: Oxford University Press. doi:10.1093/acprof:oso/9780199206650.001.0001

Niculescu-Mizil, A., & Caruana, R. (2005). *Predicting good probabilities with supervised learning*. ICML. doi:10.1145/1102351.1102430

Nielsen, M. (2017). *Deep learning*. Retrieved from http://neuralnetworksanddeeplearning.com/chap6.html

Nistal-Nuño. (2018). *Tutorial of the probabilistic methods Bayesian networks and influence diagrams applied to medicine*. Wiley.

NM, D. S., T, E., P, S., & S, L. (2015). Predictive Methodology For Diabetic Data Analysis In Big Data. *Procedia Computer Science*.

Nobahari, H., Nikusokhan, M., & Siarry, P. (2012). A multi-objective gravitational search algorithm based on non-dominated sorting. *International Journal of Swarm Intelligence Research, 3*(3), 32–49.

Norwood, F. B., & Lusk, J. L. (2011). Social desirability bias in real, hypothetical, and inferred valuation experiments. *American Journal of Agricultural Economics, 93*, 528–534.

Nuarmi, E. A., Neyadi, H. A., Mohamed, N., & A1-jaroodi, J. (2015). Application Of Bigdata To Smartcities. *Springer Open Journal*.

Nylund, K. L., Asparouhov, T., & Muthén, B. O. (2007). Deciding on the number of classes in latent class analysis and growth mixture modeling: A Monte Carlo simulation study. *Structural Equation Modeling: An Interdisciplinary Journal, 14*(4), 535–569. doi:10.1080/10705510701575396

O'Driscoll, A., Daugelaite, J., & Sleator, R. D. (2013). "Big data", Hadoop and cloud computing in genomics. *Journal of Biomedical Informatics, 46*(5), 774–781. doi:10.1016/j.jbi.2013.07.001 PMID:23872175

Okinawa Prefecture Culture, Sports, and Tourism Department. (2013). *Senryakuteki repeater souzou jigyou houkokusho* [Report on strategic creation of repeaters]. Retrieved June 28, 2019, from http://www.pref.okinawa.jp/site/bunka-sports/kankoseisaku/kikaku/report/houkokusixyo/documents/07dairokusiyou.pdf

Okonji, E. (2018, October 11). *Curbing the menace of call masking, refilling. THISDAY*.

Opsomer, J., & Ruppert, D. (1997). Fitting a bivariate additive model by local polynomial regression. *Annals of Statistics, 25*(1), 186–211. doi:10.1214/aos/1034276626

Orlov, A. I. (2011). Mahalanobis distance. *Encyclopedia Of Mathematics*. Retrieved from http://www.encyclopediaof-math.org/index.php?title=Mahalanobis_distance&oldid=17720

Oussous, A., Benjelloun, F., Ait Lahcen, A., & Belfkih S. (2018). Big Data technologies: A survey. *Journal of King Saud University – Computer and Information Sciences, 30*, 431–448.

Oussous, A., Benjelloun, F., Lahcen, A. A., & Belfkih, S. (2015). *Comparison and Classification of NoSQL Databases for Big Data*. Big Data Analytics.

Owais, S. S., & Hussein, N. S. (2016). *Extract Five Categories CPIVW From The 9v's Characteristics of Big data*. Academic Press.

Pan, B., Litvin, S. W., & O'Donnell, T. E. (2007). Understanding accommodation search query formulation: The first step in putting 'heads in beds'. *Journal of Vacation Marketing, 13*(4), 371–381. doi:10.1177/1356766707081013

Pan, B., & Li, X. R. (2011). The Long Tail of Destination Image and Online Marketing. *Annals of Tourism Research, 38*(1), 132–152. doi:10.1016/j.annals.2010.06.004

Pang, B., & Lee, L. (2008). Opinion mining and sentiment analysis. *Foundation and Trends in Information Retrieval, 2*(1-2), 1–135.

Panniello, U., Tuzhilin, A., Gorgoglione, M., Palmisano, C., & Pedone, A. (2009). Experimental comparison of pre- vs. post-filtering approaches in context-aware recommender systems. *Proceedings of the Third ACM Conference on Recommender Systems - RecSys '09*, 265. 10.1145/1639714.1639764

Papaelias, M., Cheng, L., Kogia, M., Mohimi, A., Kappatos, V., Selcuk, C., ... Gan, T. H. (2016). Inspection and structural health monitoring techniques for concentrated solar power plants. *Renewable Energy*, *85*, 1178–1191. doi:10.1016/j. renene.2015.07.090

Papa, J. (2011). Feature selection through gravitational search algorithm. *Acoustics Speech and Signal Processing (ICASSP), IEEE International Conference.*

Park & Hyeoun. (2013). An Introduction To Logistic Regression From Basic Concepts To Interpretation with Particular Attension To Nursing Domin. *J Korean Acad Nurs, 43.*

Pathak, S., & Agrawal, R. (2019). Design of Knowledge Based Analytical Model for Organizational Excellence. *International Journal of Knowledge-Based Organizations*, *9*(1), 12–25. doi:10.4018/IJKBO.2019010102

Paul, W., & Baschnagel, J. (2013). *Stochastic processes.* Heidelberg, Germany: Springer. doi:10.1007/978-3-319-00327-6

Pavithra, P., Nandhini, R., & Suganya. (2018). A Research on Different Clustering Algorithms and Techniques. *International Journal of Trend in Scientific Research and Development*, *2*(5).

Pearl, J. (1988). *Probabilistic Reasoning in Intelligent Systems: Networks of Plausible Inference.* San Francisco, CA: Morgan Kaufmann.

Peffer, M. E., & Ramezani, N. (2019). Assessing epistemological beliefs of experts and novices via practices in authentic science inquiry. *International Journal of STEM Education*, *6*(1), 3. doi:10.118640594-018-0157-9

Pei, L., & HaiBin, D. (2012). Path planning of unmanned aerial vehicle based on improved gravitational search algorithm. *Science China*, *55*, 2712–2719.

Péneau, S., Hoehn, E., Roth, H. R., Escher, F., & Nuessli, J. (2006). Importance and consumer perception of freshness of apples. *Food Quality and Preference*, *17*(1-2), 9–19. doi:10.1016/j.foodqual.2005.05.002

Penny, W. (2012). Bayesian model selection and averaging Bayes rule for models. *SPM for MEG/EEG.* Retrieved from http://www.fil.ion.ucl.ac.uk/spm/course/slides12-meeg/14_MEEG_BMS.pdf

PermNewsletter. (2012, April). *Understanding the importance of stakeholder engagement.* Retrieved from http://www.cansr.msu.du/uploads/files

Pew Internet project. (2006). *Online News: For many home broadband users, the internet is a primary news source.* Retrieved from http://web.archive.org/web/2013/021122359/http://www.ccgrouppr.com/PIP_News.and.Broad.pdf

Postman, N. (1992). *Technology.* New York: Vintage Press.

Price, B. (1977). Ridge regression: Application to nonexperimental data. *Psychological Bulletin*, *84*(4), 759–766. doi:10.1037/0033-2909.84.4.759

Punj, G., & Stewart, D. W. (1983). Cluster analysis in marketing research: Review and suggestions for application. *JMR, Journal of Marketing Research*, *20*(2), 134–148. doi:10.1177/002224378302000204

Pu, P., Chen, L., & Hu, R. (2012). Evaluating recommender systems from the user's perspective: Survey of the state of the art. *User Modeling and User-Adapted Interaction*, *22*(4–5), 317–355. doi:10.100711257-011-9115-7

Qiao, D., Zhang, J., Wei, Q., & Chen, G. (2017). Finding competitive keywords from query logs to enhance search engine advertising. *Information & Management*, *54*(4), 531–543. doi:10.1016/j.im.2016.11.003

Quinlan, J. R. (1983). Learning Efficient Classification Procedures and Their Application to Chess End Games. In *Symbolic Computation: An Artificial Intelligence Approach* (pp. 463–482). Springer.

Quirk, R., Greenbaum, S. G. L., & Svartvik, J. (1985). A comprehensive grammar of the English language. Longman.

R. B., D., & W. J., D. (1951). Simplified Statistics for Small Numbers of Observations. *Analytical Chemistry*, 636–638.

Racine, E. F., Mumford, E. A., Laditka, S. B., & Lowe, A. (2013). Understanding characteristics of families who buy local produce. *Journal of Nutrition Education and Behavior*, *45*(1), 30–38. doi:10.1016/j.jneb.2012.04.011 PMID:23073176

Raghuvanshi, N., & Patil, J. M. (2016). A Brief Review on Sentiment Analysis. *International Conference on Electrical, Electronics, and Optimization Techniques (ICEEOT). IEEE Conferences*.

Rajagopal, Anamika, Vinod, & Niranjan. (2018). *gsa–fapso-based generators active power rescheduling for transmission congestion management*. Academic Press.

Ramezani, N. (2015). Approaches for missing data in ordinal multinomial models. In *JSM Proceedings, Biometrics section, New Methods for Studies with Missing Data Session*. Alexandria, VA: American Statistical Association Journal.

Ramezani, N. (2016). Analyzing non-normal binomial and categorical response variables under varying data conditions. In *Proceedings of the SAS Global Forum Conference*. Cary, NC: SAS Institute Inc.

Ramezani, N., & Ramezani, A. (2016). *Analyzing non-normal data with categorical response variables. In proceedings of the Southeast SAS Users Group Conference*. Cary, NC: SAS Institute Inc.

Ramos, C. C. O., de Souza, A. N., Falcao, A. X., & Papa, J. P. (2012). New insights on nontechnical losses characterization through evolutionary-based feature selection. *IEEE Transactions on Power Delivery*, *27*(1), 40–146. doi:10.1109/TPWRD.2011.2170182

Randell, D. A., Cui, Z., & Cohn, A. G. (1992). A Spatial Logic based on Regions and Connection. *Proceeding of KRR*, 165–176.

Rao, N., Cox, C., Nowak, R., & Rogers, T. T. (2013). Sparse overlapping sets lasso for multitask learning and its application to fmri analysis. In Advances in neural information processing systems (pp. 2202-2210). Academic Press.

Rashedi, E., Nezamabadi-pour, H., & Saryazdi, S. (2009). GSA: A Gravitational Search Algorithm. *Information Sciences*, *179*(13), 2232–2248. doi:10.1016/j.ins.2009.03.004

Rashedi, E., Nezamabadi-Pour, H., & Saryazdi, S. (2010). BGSA: Binary gravitational search *algorithm. Natural Computing*, *9*(3), 727–745. doi:10.100711047-009-9175-3

Rathipriya, R., Thangavel, K., & Bagyamani, J. (2011). Binary Particle Swarm Optimization based Biclustering of Web usage Data. *International Journal of Computers and Applications*, *25*(2), 43–49. doi:10.5120/3001-4036

Raychaudhuri, S., Stuart, J. M., & Altman, R. B. (1999). Principal components analysis to summarize microarray experiments: application to sporulation time series. In Biocomputing 2000 (pp. 455-466). Academic Press. doi:10.1142/9789814447331_0043

Refaeilzadeh, P., Tang, L., & Liu, H. (2009). Cross-Validation. In L. Liu & M. T. Özsu (Eds.), *Encyclopedia of Database Systems*. Boston, MA: Springer.

Reinsch, C. H. (1967). Smoothing by spline functions. *Numerische Mathematik*, *10*(3), 177–183. doi:10.1007/BF02162161

Rendle, S. (n.d.). *Factorization Machines*. Retrieved from https://www.csie.ntu.edu.tw/~b97053/paper/Rendle2010FM.pdf

Rey-López, M., Barragáns-Martínez, A. B., Peleteiro, A., Mikic-Fonte, F. A., & Burguillo, J. C. (2011). moreTourism: Mobile recommendations for tourism. *Digest of Technical Papers - IEEE International Conference on Consumer Electronics*, 347–348. 10.1109/ICCE.2011.5722620

Rezaei, M., & Nezamabadi-pour, H. (2014). *A prototype optimization method for nearest neighbor classification by gravitational search algorithm. Intelligent Systems*. ICIS.

Rezaei, M., & Nezamabadi-pour, H. (2015). Using gravitational search algorithm in prototype generation for nearest neighbor classification. *Neurocomputing*, *157*, 256–263. doi:10.1016/j.neucom.2015.01.008

Riaz, A. (1997). The role of telecommunications in economic growth: Proposal for an alternative framework of analysis. *Media Culture & Society*, *19*(4), 557–583. doi:10.1177/016344397019004004

Ricci, F., Rokach, L., & Shapira, B. (2011). Introduction to Recommender Systems Handbook. In Recommender Systems Handbook (pp. 1–35). Academic Press. doi:10.1007/978-0-387-85820-3_1

Rich, Knight, & Nair. (2009). *Artificial Intelligence*. Tata MacGraw Hill.

Riddhiman. (2016). *Voronoi Diagrams in Plotly and R*. Retrieved from http://moderndata.plot.ly/voronoi-diagrams-in-plotly-and-r/

Roch, A., & Soner, H. M. (2013). Resilient price impact of trading and the cost of illiquidity. *International Journal of Theoretical and Applied Finance*, *16*(6), 1–27. doi:10.1142/S0219024913500374

Rockafellar, R. T., & Wets, R. J. B. (1991). Scenarios and policy aggregation in optimization under uncertainty. *Mathematics of Operations Research*, *16*(1), 119–147. doi:10.1287/moor.16.1.119

Rodriguez M.Z., Comin, C.H., Casanova, D., Bruno, O.M., Amancio D.R., & Costa, L.F. (2019). Clustering algorithms: A comparative Approach. *PLoS One*.

Rodriguez-Pardo, C., Patricio, M. A., Berlanga, A., & Molina, J. M. (2017). Market trends and customer segmentation for data of electronic retail store. Lecture Notes in Computer Science. doi:10.1007/978-3-319-59650-1_44

Roffo, G., & Ing-Inf05, S. S. D. (2017). *Ranking to Learn and Learning to Rank: On the Role of Ranking in Pattern Recognition Applications*. Retrieved from https://arxiv.org/pdf/1706.05933.pdf

Rohrer, B. (2015). Methods for handling missing values. *Cortana Intelligence Gallery*. Retrieved from https://gallery.cortanaintelligence.com/Experiment/Methods-for-handling-missing-values-1

Rojas, R. (2013). *Neural networks: A systematic introduction*. Berlin, Germany: Springer Science & Business Media.

Rokach, L., & Maimon, O. (2005). Clustering Methods. In O. Maimon & L. Rokach (Eds.), *Data Mining and Knowledge Discovery Handbook*. Boston, MA: Springer.

Roller, L. H., & Waverman, L. (2001). Telecommunications infrastructure and economic development: A simultaneous approach. *The American Economic Review*, *91*(4), 909–923. doi:10.1257/aer.91.4.909

Roll, R. (1992). A mean/variance analysis of tracking error. *Journal of Portfolio Management*, *18*(4), 13–22. doi:10.3905/jpm.1992.701922

Romesburg, C. (2004). *Cluster analysis for researchers*. Lulu.com.

Rubio-Largo, A., & Vega-Rodriguez, M. A. (2013). *A multi-objective approach based on the law of gravity and mass interactions for optimizing networks*. Lect. Notes Comput. Sci., 7832, 13–24).

Ruozi, R., & Ferrari, P. (2013). *Liquidity Risk Management in Banks: Economic and Regulatory Issues*. Springer Briefs in Finance. doi:10.1007/978-3-642-29581-2

Russell, S., & Norving, P. (2014). *Artificial Intelligence: A modern Approach*. Pearson.

Sajana, T., Sheela Rani, C. M., & Narayana, K. V. (2016). A Survey on Clustering Techniques for Big Data Mining. *Indian Journal of Science and Technology, 9*(3).

Samaan, M. (2003). *The effect of income inequality on mobile phone penetration.* Retrieved from http://web.archive.org/web/20070214102055/http://dissertations.bc.edu/cgi/viewcontent.cgi?article=1016&context=ashonors

Samuel, D. V. (2019). *Bypass fraud evolution detection through CDR analysis.* Retrieved from https://www.linkedin.com/pulse/bypass-fraud-evolution-detection-through-cdr-analysis-samuel-pmp

Sarafrazi, S., & Nezamabadi-pour, H. (2013). Facing the classification of binary problems with a GSA-SVM hybrid system. *Mathematical and Computer Modelling, 57*(1-2), 270–278. doi:10.1016/j.mcm.2011.06.048

Saraoglu, A. C. (2017). *Stock Price Reactions to Dividend Changes: a Comparative Test of Signalling Theory and Market Efficiency in The Emerging Emea Stock Markets* (Doctoral Dissertation). Kadir Has University, Istanbul, Turkey.

Sargent, D. J. (2001). Comparison of artificial neural networks with other statistical approaches: Results from medical data sets. *Cancer: Interdisciplinary International Journal of the American Cancer Society, 91*(S8), 1636–1642. doi:10.1002/1097-0142(20010415)91:8+<1636::AID-CNCR1176>3.0.CO;2-D PMID:11309761

Sarkar, N., Ellis, R. E., & Moore, T. N. (1997). Backlash detection in geared mechanisms: Modeling, simulation, and experimentation. *Mechanical Systems and Signal Processing, 11*(3), 391–408. doi:10.1006/mssp.1996.0082

Sasi Kiran, J., Sravanthi, M., Preethi, K., & Anusha, M. (2015). Recent Issues and Challenges on Big Data in Cloud Computing. IJCST, 6(2).

Sathya, R., & Abraham, A. (2013). Comparison of supervised and unsupervised learning algorithms for pattern classification. *Int J Adv Res Artificial Intell, 2*(2), 34–38. doi:10.14569/IJARAI.2013.020206

Schölkopf, B., Smola, A., & Müller, K. R. (1999). *Kernel principal component analysis: Advances in kernel methods-support vector learning.* Cambridge, MA: MIT Press.

Schonlau, M. (2002). The Clustergram: A graph for visualizing hierarchical and non-hierarchical cluster analysis. *The Stata Journal, 3*, 316–327.

Schwartz, G. E. (1978). Estimating the dimension of a model. *Annals of Statistics, 6*(2), 461–464. doi:10.1214/aos/1176344136

Seber, G. A. F., & Wild, C. J. (1989). *Nonlinear regression.* New York, NY: Wiley and Sons. doi:10.1002/0471725315

Segal, M. R. (2004). *Machine learning benchmarks and random forest regression.* Academic Press.

Seifi, F., Kangavari, M. R., Ahmadi, H., Lotfi, E., Imaniyan, S., & Lagzian, S. (2008). Optimizing twins decision tree classification using genetic algorithms. *7th IEEE International Conference on Cybernetic Intelligent Systems*, 1–6. 10.1109/UKRICIS.2008.4798957

Shafiq, M. O., & Torunski, E. (2016). A Parallel K-Medoids Algorithm for Clustering based on MapReduce. *Proceedings of 2016 15th IEEE International Conference on Machine Learning and Applications*, 502-507.

Shamsudin, H. C. (2012). A fast discrete gravitational search algorithm. *Computational Intelligence, Modeling and Simulation (CIMSiM), Fourth International Conference.*

Shanhe, Wenjin, & Yanmei. (2018). An improved hybrid particle swarm optimization with dependent random coefficients for global optimization. *33rd Youth Academic Annual Conference of Chinese Association of Automation (YAC)*, 666-672.

Shanmugapriya, B. (2017). Clustering Algorithms for High Dimensional Data – A Review. *International Journal of Computer Science and Information Security, 15*(5).

Sheen, J. N. (2005). Fuzzy financial profitability analyses of demand side management alternatives from participant perspective. *Information Sciences, 169*(3-4), 329–364. doi:10.1016/j.ins.2004.05.007

Sheldon, P. J. (1997). *Tourism Information Technology.* CABI Publishing.

Shelokar, P. S., Jayaraman, V. K., & Kulkarni, B. D. (2004). An ant colony approach for clustering. *Analytica Chimica Acta, 509*(2), 187–195. doi:10.1016/j.aca.2003.12.032

Shi, S., Soua, S., & Papaelias, M. (2017). Remote condition monitoring of rails and crossings using acoustic emission. *Proceedings of 2017 NSIRC Annual Conference.*

Shi, B., Chen, N., & Wang, J. (2016). A credit rating model of microfinance based on fuzzy cluster analysis and fuzzy pattern recognition: Empirical evidence from Chinese 2,157 small private businesses. *Journal of Intelligent & Fuzzy Systems, 31*(6), 3095–3102. doi:10.3233/JIFS-169195

Shi, H., Xu, M., & Li, R. (2017). Deep learning for household load forecasting—A novel pooling deep RNN. *IEEE Transactions on Smart Grid, 9*(5), 5271–5280. doi:10.1109/TSG.2017.2686012

Shi, S., Han, Z., Liu, Z., Vallely, P., Soua, S., Kaewunruen, S., & Papaelias, M. (2018). Quantitative monitoring of brittle fatigue crack growth in railway steel using acoustic emission. *Proceedings of the Institution of Mechanical Engineers. Part F, Journal of Rail and Rapid Transit, 232*(4), 1211–1224. doi:10.1177/0954409717711292

Shor, N. (1998). *Nondifferentiable Optimization and Polynomial Problems.* Boston: Kluwer Academic Publishers. doi:10.1007/978-1-4757-6015-6

Shyama Das, S. M. (2010). Greedy Search-Binary PSO Hybrid for Biclustering GeneExpression Data. *International Journal of Computers and Applications.*

Signal processing Toolbox, User's Guide. (2018). Natick, MA: The MathWorks, Inc.

Silahtaroglu, G. (2016). *Veri madenciliği.* Istanbul: Papatya Press.

Silverman, B. W. (1985). Some aspects of the spline smoothing approach to non-parametric regression curve fitting. *Journal of the Royal Statistical Society. Series B. Methodological, 47*(1), 1–21. doi:10.1111/j.2517-6161.1985.tb01327.x

Singh, A. S., Masuku, & Micah, B. (2014). Sampling Techniques And Determination Of Sample Size in applied Statistical Research: An Overview. *International Journal Of Economics, Commerce And Management.*

Singh, S. P., & Jaiswal, U. C. (2018). Machine Learning for Big Data: A New Perspective. *International Journal of Applied Engineering Research, 13*(5), 2753-2762.

Sisodia, D., Singh, L., & Sisodia, S. (2012). Clustering Techniques: A Brief Survey of Different Clustering Algorithms. *International Journal of Latest Trends in Engineering and Technology, 1*(3).

Sjöstrand, N., Blanc, D., & Tavallaey, S. (2010). *Method and a control system for monitoring the condition of an industrial robot.* 7,826,984 B2.

Sjöstrand, N., Blanc, D., & Tavallaey, S. S. (2010). *Method and a control system for monitoring the condition of an industrial robot.* Google Patents.

Smith, C. (2017). *Decision trees and random forests: a visual introduction for beginners.* Blue Windmill Media.

Sohrab Mahmud, Md., Mostafizer Rahman, Md., & Nasim Akhtar, Md. (2012). Improvement of K-means Clustering algorithm with better initial centroids based on weighted average. *7th International Conference on Electrical and Computer Engineering*, 647-650.

Solak, S. (2007). *Efficient solution procedures for multistage stochastic formulations of two problem classes.* Georgia Institute of Technology.

Soleimanpour-moghadam, M., & Nezamabadi-pour, H. (2012). An improved quantum behaved gravitational search algorithm. *Electrical Engineering (ICEE), 20th Iranian Conference.* 10.1109/IranianCEE.2012.6292446

Soleimanpour-moghadam, M., Nezamabadi-pour, H., & Farsangi, M. M. (2011). A quantum behaved gravitational search algorithm. *Proceeding of Int. Conf. Computational Intelligence and Software Engineering.*

Soleimanpour-moghadam, M., Nezamabadi-pour, H., & Farsangi, M. M. (2014). A quantum inspired gravitational search algorithm for numerical function optimization. *Inf. Sciences, 267,* 83–100. doi:10.1016/j.ins.2013.09.006

Sönmez, F., & Bülbül, S. (2015). An intelligent software model design for estimating deposit banks profitability with soft computing techniques. *Neural Network World, 25*(3), 319–345. doi:10.14311/NNW.2015.25.017

Srivastava, A., Kundu, A., Sural, S., & Majumdar, A. (2008). Credit card fraud detection using hidden Markov model. *IEEE Transactions on Dependable and Secure Computing, 5*(1), 37–48. doi:10.1109/TDSC.2007.70228

Stakeholdermapping. (n.d.). *Stakeholder engagement.* Retrieved from http://www.stakeholdermapping.com/smm-maturity-model/

Stallings, W. (2004). *Data and Computer Communications* (7th ed.). Pearson Prentice Hall.

Steenbruggen, J., Tranos, E., & Nijkamp, P. (2015). Data from mobile phone operators: A tool for smarter cities? *Telecommunications Policy, 39*(3-4), 335–346. doi:10.1016/j.telpol.2014.04.001

Stoica, P., & Moses, R. L. (1997). Introduction to spectral analysis. Prentice Hall.

Stone, C. (1977). Consistent nonparametric regression. *Annals of Statistics, 5*(4), 595–645. doi:10.1214/aos/1176343886

Storn, R., & Price, K. (1995). *Differential Evolution – A simple and Efficient Heuristic for Global Optimization over Continuous Spaces.* International Computer Science Institute.

Strack, B., DeShazo, J. P., Gennings, C., Olmo, J. L., Ventura, S. J., & Cios, K. (2014). *Impact OF HbAlc Measurement on Hospital Readmission Rates: Analysis of 70,000 Clinical Database Patient Records.* Hindawi Publishing Corporation BioMed research International.

Strauss, T., & von Maltitz, M. J. (2017). Generalising Ward's method for use with Manhattan distances. *PLoS One, 12*(1), 1–21. doi:10.1371/journal.pone.0168288 PMID:28085891

Strehl, A., Ghosh, J., & Mooney, R. (2000). Impact of similarity measures on web-page clustering. *Proc. AAAI Workshop on AI for Web Search,* 58–64.

Sturn, A., Quackenbush, J., & Trajanoski, Z. (2002). Genesis: Cluster analysis of microarray data. *Bioinformatics (Oxford, England), 18*(1), 207–208. doi:10.1093/bioinformatics/18.1.207 PMID:11836235

Subramaniyaswamy, V., Vijayakumar, V., Logesh, R., & Indragandhi, V. (2015). Unstructured data analysis on big data using map reduce. *Procedia Computer Science, 50,* 456–465. doi:10.1016/j.procs.2015.04.015

Sudhira, H. S., Ramachandra, T. V., & Jagadish, K. S. (2004). Urban sprawl: Metrics, dynamics and modelling using GIS. *International Journal of Applied Earth Observation and Geoinformation, 5*(1), 29–39. doi:10.1016/j.jag.2003.08.002

Suganya, R., Pavithra, M., & Nandhini, P. (2018). *Algorithms and Challenges in Big Data Clustering. International Journal of Engineering and Techniques*, *4*(4), 40–47.

Suman & Mittal. (2014). Comparison and Analysis of Various Clustering Methods in Data mining On Education data set using the weak tool. *International Journal of Emerging Trends & Technology in Computer Science, 3*(2).

Sun & Zhang. (2013). A hybrid genetic algorithm and gravitational using multilevel thresholding. *Pattern Recognition and Image Analysis*, 707–714.

Sushmita, S., Khulbe, G., Hasan, A., & Newman, S. (2015). *Predicting 30-Day Risk And Cost Of "All Cause" Hospital Readmissions*. The Workshop Of The Thirtieth AAA 1 Conference On Artificial Intelligence Expanding The Boundaries Of Health Informatics Using A1: Technical Report ws-16-08.

Su, X., & Khoshgoftaar, T. M. (2009). A Survey of Collaborative Filtering Techniques. *Advances in Artificial Intelligence*, *2009*, 1–19. doi:10.1155/2009/421425

Syed, A. N. (2014). *The grey market in prepaid: tactics to combat international bypass fraud via the SIM box*. Retrieved from https://www.bswan.org/sim_box_fraud.asp

Takahashi, D., & Alexander, S. (2002). Illiquid Alternative Asset Fund Modeling. *Journal of Portfolio Management*, *28*(2), 90–100. doi:10.3905/jpm.2002.319836

Tamine-Lechani, L., Boughanem, M., & Daoud, M. (2010). Evaluation of contextual information retrieval effectiveness: Overview of issues and research. *Knowledge and Information Systems*, *24*(1), 1–34. doi:10.100710115-009-0231-1

Taylan, P., Weber, G. W., & Ozkurt, F. Y. (2010). A new approach to multivariate adaptive regression splines by using Tikhonov regularization and continuous optimization. *Top (Madrid)*, *18*(2), 377–395. doi:10.100711750-010-0155-7

Taylan, P., Weber, G.-W., & Beck, A. (2007). New approaches to regression by generalized additive models and continuous optimization for modern applications in finance, science and technology. *Optimization*, *56*(5-6), 675–698. doi:10.1080/02331930701618740

Teddie & Yu. (2007). Mixed Methods Sampling A Typology with examples. *Journal Of Mixed Methods Research, 1*.

Teräsvirta, T. (2009). An Introduction to Univariate GARCH Models. In T. Mikosch, J. P. Kreiß, R. Davis, & T. Andersen (Eds.), *Handbook of Financial Time Series*. Heidelberg, Germany: Springer. doi:10.1007/978-3-540-71297-8_1

Thangavel, K., & Bagyamani, J. (2011). Novel Hybrid PSO-SA Model for Biclustering of Expression Data. *International Conference on Communication Technology and System Design by Elsevier*.

Thangavel, K., & Rathipriya, R. (2014). Mining correlated bicluster from web usage data using discrete firefly algorithm based biclustering approach. *International Journal of Mathematical, Computational. Physical and Quantum Engineering*, *8*(4), 700–705.

The Telegraph. (2017). *Who made the first electric telegraph communications?* Retrieved from http://www.telegraph.co.uk/technology/connecting-britain/first-electric-telegraph/

Thornton, D., van Capelleveen, G., Poel, M., van Hillegersberg, J., & Mueller, R. (2014, April). *Outlier-based health insurance fraud detection for us medicaid data*. Paper presented at 16th International Conference on Enterprise Information Systems, ICEIS 2014, Lisbon, Portugal.

Towers, S. (2013). *K-means clustering*. Retrieved from http://sherrytowers.com/2013/10/24/k-means-clustering/

Uitter, J. S. (1984). Faster Methods for Random Sampling (Vol. 27). Academic Press.

Ukkusuri, S. V., Ramadurai, G., & Patil, G. (2010). A robust transportation signal control problem accounting for traffic dynamics. *Computers & Operations Research*, *37*(5), 869–879. doi:10.1016/j.cor.2009.03.017

Ultsch, A., & Lötsch, J. (2017). Machine-learned cluster identification in high-dimensional data. *Journal of Biomedical Informatics*, *66*, 95–104. doi:10.1016/j.jbi.2016.12.011 PMID:28040499

Ulusavas, O. (2010). *Short Term Predictable Patterns Following Price Shocks Conditional On Characteristics of Information Signals, Foreign Investment and Investor Confidence: Evidence from Istanbul Stock Exchange* (Doctoral Dissertation). Yeditepe University, Istanbul, Turkey.

University, P. S. (2016). *Principal Components Analysis (PCA)*. Retrieved from https://onlinecourses.science.psu.edu/stat857/node/35

Upadhyay, N. (2018). *Why SIM Box fraud is rampant in Africa?* Retrieved from http://www.subex.com/author/neeraj/

Ursem, R. K. (1999). Multinational evolutionary algorithms. *Proceedings of Congress of Evolutionary Computation*, 1633–1640.

Uzar, C. (2013). *The Usage of Data Mining Technology in Financial Information System; an Application on Borsa Istanbul* (Doctoral Dissertation). Dokuz Eylül University Social Sciences Institute, Izmir, Turkey.

Vallely, P., & Papaelias, M. (n.d.). Integrating Remote Condition Monitoring of Railway Infrastructure with High Speed Inspection. *Proceedings of First World Congress on Condition Monitoring-WCCM*.

Van Vlasselaer, V., Eliassi-Rad, T., Akoglu, L., Snoeck, M., & Baesens, B. (2016). Gotcha! Network- based fraud detection for social security fraud. *Management Science*, *63*(9), 3090–3110. doi:10.1287/mnsc.2016.2489

Vandekerckhove, J., Tuerlinckx, F., & Lee, M. D. (2011). Hierarchical diffusion models for two-choice response times. *Psychological Methods*, *16*(1), 44–62. doi:10.1037/a0021765 PMID:21299302

Velmurugan, T., & Santhanam, T. (2011). A survey of partition based clustering algorithms in data mining: An experimental approach. *Inf Technol J*, *10*(3), 478–484. doi:10.3923/itj.2011.478.484

Vermunt, J. K., & Magidson, J. (2002). Latent class cluster analysis. In J. A. Hagenaars & A. L. McCutcheon (Eds.), *Applied latent class models* (pp. 89–106). Cambridge, UK: Cambridge University Press. doi:10.1017/CBO9780511499531.004

Veter, V., & Kara, B. Y. (2008). A path-based approach for hazardous transport network design. *Management Science*, *54*(1), 29–40. doi:10.1287/mnsc.1070.0763

Vijayalakshmi, K., & Priya, M. (2019). A K- Nearest Neighbors' based on Clustering for High Performances and High Volumes of the Data. *International Journal of Scientific Research & Engineering Trends, 5*(3).

Vincent, R. A., Mitchell, A. I., & Robertson, D. I. (1980). *User Guide to TRANSYT, TRRL report, LR888*. Crowthorne: Transport and Road Research Laboratory.

Vural, A. G., Cambazoglu, B. B., & Karagoz, P. (2014). Sentiment-Focused Web Crawling. *ACM Transactions on the Web*, *8*(4), 22. doi:10.1145/2644821

Wahba, G., & Wold, S. (1975). A completely automatic French curve: Fitting spline functions by cross-validation. *Communications in Statistics*, *4*(1), 1–17. doi:10.1080/03610927508827223

Walmart Recruiting - Store Sales Forecasting. (n.d.). Retrieved from https://www.kaggle.com/c/walmart-recruiting-store-sales-forecasting/data

Wang, H. W., Zheng, L. J., & Liu, Z. Y. (2012). Sentiment feature selection from Chinese online reviews. *China Journal of Information Systems, 11.*

Wang, W. (2012). Harnessing twitter big data for automatic emotion identification. *Privacy, Security, Risk and Trust (PASSAT), International Conference on Social Computing (SocialCom) IEEE.*

Wang, C., & Blei, D. M. (2011). Collaborative topic modeling for recommending scientific articles. *Proceedings of the 17th ACM SIGKDD International Conference on Knowledge Discovery and Data Mining - KDD '11*, 448. 10.1145/2020408.2020480

Wang, D., Zhang, Z., Bai, R., & Mao, Y. (2018). A hybrid system with filter approach and multiple population genetic algorithm for feature selection in credit scoring. *Journal of Computational and Applied Mathematics, 329*, 307–321. doi:10.1016/j.cam.2017.04.036

Wang, H., Wang, N., & Yeung, D.-Y. (2015). Collaborative Deep Learning for Recommender Systems. *Proceedings of the 21th ACM SIGKDD International Conference on Knowledge Discovery and Data Mining - KDD '15*, 1235–1244. 10.1145/2783258.2783273

Wang, Q., Ai, B., He, R., Guan, K., Li, Y., Zhong, Z., & Shi, G. (2017). A Framework of Automatic Clustering and Tracking for Time-Variant Multipath Components. *IEEE Communications Letters, 21*(4), 953–956. doi:10.1109/LCOMM.2016.2637364

Wang, Y., & Vassileva, J. (2003). Bayesian Network-Based Trust Model. *Proceedings of the IEEE/WIC International Conference on Web Intelligence (WI'03).* 10.1109/WI.2003.1241218

Watson, J. P., & Woodruff, D. L. (2011). Progressive hedging innovations for a class of stochastic mixed-integer resource allocation problems. *Computational Management Science, 8*(4), 355–370. doi:10.100710287-010-0125-4

Wavelet Toolbox. (2002). Natick, MA: The MathWorks, Inc.

Wei Shen, G. L. (2012). A Novel Biclustering Algorithm and Its Application inGene Expression Profiles. *Journal of Information and Computational Science.*

White, R. W., Bailey, P., & Chen, L. (2009). Predicting user interests from contextual information. *Proceedings of the 32nd International ACM SIGIR Conference on Research and Development in Information Retrieval - SIGIR '09*, 363. 10.1145/1571941.1572005

Wickham, H., & Grolemund, G. (2016). *R for data science: import, tidy, transform, visualize, and model data.* O'Reilly Media, Inc.

Wiegleb, G. (1980). Some applications of principal components analysis in vegetation: ecological research of aquatic communities. In *Classification and Ordination* (pp. 67–73). Dordrecht: Springer. doi:10.1007/978-94-009-9197-2_9

Wikipedia. (n.d.). *Stakeholder enegagement.* Retrieved from http://en.m.wikipedia.org/wiki/stakeholder-engagement

Witten, I. H., Paynter, G. W., Frank, E., Gutwin, C., & Nevill-Manning, C. G. (2005). KEA: Practical Automated Keyphrase Extraction. In Design and Usability of Digital Libraries: Case Studies in the Asia Pacific (pp. 129-152). IGI Global.

Wold, S., Esbensen, K., & Geladi, P. (1987). Principal component Analysis. *Chemometrics and Intelligent Laboratory Systems, 2*(1-3), 37–52. doi:10.1016/0169-7439(87)80084-9

World Health Organization. (2015). *Increasing fruit and vegetable consumption to reduce the risk of noncommunicable diseases.* Geneva, Switzerland: Author.

Wu, J. Y. (2011). MIMO CMAC neural network classifier for solving classification problems. *Applied Soft Computing*, *11*(2), 2326–2333. doi:10.1016/j.asoc.2010.08.013

Xiang, J., Han, X. H., Duan, F., Qiang, Y., Xiong, X. Y., Lan, Y., & Chai, H. (2015). A novel hybrid system for feature selection based on an improved gravitational search algorithm and k-NN method. *Applied Soft Computing*, *31*, 293–307. doi:10.1016/j.asoc.2015.01.043

Xiangtao, Yin, & Ma. (2011). Hybrid differential evolution and gravitation search algorithm for unconstrained optimization. *International Journal of Physical Sciences*, *6*, 5961–5981.

Xiang, Z., & Gretzel, U. (2010). Role of Social Media in Online Travel Information Search Original. *Tourism Management*, *31*(2), 179–188. doi:10.1016/j.tourman.2009.02.016

Xiang, Z., & Pan, B. (2011). Travel Queries on Cities in the United States: Implications for Search Engine Marketing for Tourist Destinations. *Tourism Management*, *32*(1), 88–97. doi:10.1016/j.tourman.2009.12.004

Xiang, Z., Schwartz, Z., Gerdes, J. H. Jr, & Uysal, M. (2015). What can big data and text analytics tell us about hotel guest experience and satisfaction? *International Journal of Hospitality Management*, *44*, 120–129. doi:10.1016/j.ijhm.2014.10.013

Xie, B. S. C. (2007). Biclustering of Gene Expression Data Using PSO-GA Hybrid. *1st International Conference on Bioinformatics and Biomedical Engineering IEEE Xplore*.

Yadav, A., & Kim, J. H. (2014). A niching co-swarm gravitational search algorithm for multi-modal optimization. *Proceedings of Fourth International Conference on Soft Computing for Problem Solving*. 10.1007/978-81-322-1771-8_55

Yahiro, K., & Oguchi, T. (2003). Kankouchi-Senkou Ni Oyobosu Kojinteki-Genfukei To Shinrigakuteki- Kojinsa [Individual Preference for Sightseeing Destinations determined]. *The Tourism Studies Quarterly*, *15*(1), 28–29.

Yamamoto, M. (2016). A comparative study on travelers' sightseeing intentions. *Journal of Global Tourism Research*, *1*(2), 139–144.

Yamamoto, M. (2018). A comparative study on search keyword advertising to attract tourists. In *Proceedings of the Twelfth International Conference on Management Science and Engineering Management* (vol. 1, pp. 701-710). Cham, Springer.

Yamamoto, M. (2019). Furthering Big Data Utilization in Tourism. In F. P. G. Márquez & B. Lev (Eds.), *Data Science and Digital Business* (pp. 157–171). Cham: Springer. doi:10.1007/978-3-319-95651-0_9

Yang, C., Huang, Q., Li, Z., Liu, K., & Hu, F. (2017). Big Data and cloud computing: Innovation opportunities and challenges. *International Journal of Digital Earth*, *10*(1), 13–53. doi:10.1080/17538947.2016.1239771

Yang, X.-S. (2009). Firefly algorithms for multimodal optimization, in: Stochastic Algorithms: Foundations and Applications, SAGA. *Lecture Notes in Computer Science*, *5792*, 169–178. doi:10.1007/978-3-642-04944-6_14

Yao, L., Sheng, Q. Z., Qin, Y., Wang, X., Shemshadi, A., & He, Q. (2015). Context-aware Point-of-Interest Recommendation Using Tensor Factorization with Social Regularization. *Proceedings of the 38th International ACM SIGIR Conference on Research and Development in Information Retrieval - SIGIR '15*, 1007–1010. 10.1145/2766462.2767794

Yazdani, S., & Nezamabadi-pour, H. (2011). A new gravitational solution for multimodal optimization. *18th Iranian Conference on Electrical Engineering*.

Yazdani, S., Nezamabadi-pour, H., & Kamyab, S. (2014). A gravitational search algorithm for multimodal optimization. *Swarm and Evolutionary Computation*, *14*, 1–14. doi:10.1016/j.swevo.2013.08.001

Yildiz, E. G. (2017). *Analysis of Online Customer Complaints by Data Mining* (Doctoral Dissertation). Trakya University Social Sciences Institute, Edirne, Turkey.

Yilmaz, S. E. (2017). *Evaluation of the Ability of the Social Network Analysis Method about Establishment of the Relations and Contradictions in Prescribing Characteristics, with the Real World Data* (Doctoral Dissertation). Istanbul University, Institute of Health Science, Istanbul, Turkey.

Yiu, K. F. C. (2004). Optimal portfolios under a value-at-risk constraint. *Journal of Economic Dynamics & Control, 28*(7), 1317–1334. doi:10.1016/S0165-1889(03)00116-7

Younghoon, K., Kyuseok, S., Min-Soeng, K., & Sup, L. J. (2014). DBCURE-MR: An efficient density-based clustering algorithm for large data using MapReduce. *Information Systems, 42*, 15–35. doi:10.1016/j.is.2013.11.002

Yu, Ying, & Wang. (2011). Immune gravitation inspired optimization algorithm. *International Conference on Intelligent Computing, Springer.*

Zandevakili, H., Rashedi, E., & Mahani, A. (2017). Gravitational search algorithm with both attractive and repulsive forces. *Soft Computing.* doi:10.100700500-017-2785-2

Zan, H., Hsinchun, C., Chia-Jung, H., Wun-Hwa, C., & Soushan, W. (2004). Credit rating analysis with support vector machines and neural networks: A market comparative study. *Decision Support Systems, 37*(4), 543–558. doi:10.1016/S0167-9236(03)00086-1

Zanoon, N., Al-Haj, A., & Khwaldeh, S. M. (2017). Cloud Computing and Big Data is there a Relation between the Two: A Study. *International Journal of Applied Engineering Research, 12*, 6970-6982.

Zhang, H., Shoa, L., & Xi, C. (2014). Predicting The Treatement Effect in Diabetes Patient Using Classification Models. *International Journal Of Digital Content Technology And Its Applications, 8.*

Zhang, Y., & Zhou, W. (2015). Multifractal analysis and relevance vector machine-based automatic seizure detection in in-tracranial. *International Journal of Neural Systems, 25*(6). doi:. doi:10.1142/S0129065715500203

Zhang, B., Hsu, M., & Dayal, U. (2000). K-harmonic means. *International Workshop on Temporal, Spatial, and Spatio-temporal Data Mining.*

Zhang, L., Yin, Y., & Chen, S. (2013). Robust signal timing optimization with environmental concerns. *Transportation Research Part C, Emerging Technologies, 29*, 55–71. doi:10.1016/j.trc.2013.01.003

Zhang, T., Ramakrishnan, R., & Livny, M. (1996). BIRCH: an efficient data clustering method for very large databases. *Proceedings of the 1996 ACM SIGMOD international conference on Management of data*, 103-114. 10.1145/233269.233324

Zhang, X., & Huang, G. (2013). Optimization of environmental management startegies through a dynamic stochastic possibilistic multiobjective program. *Journal of Hazardous Materials, 246-247*, 257–266. doi:10.1016/j.jhazmat.2012.12.036 PMID:23313898

Zhang, Y., & Bu, H. (2017). Can extracted features from stock forum amount for the stock return? *International Conference on Service Systems and Service Management.*

Zhao, J., & Verter, V. (2015). A bi-objective model for the used oil location-routing problem. *Computers & Operations Research, 62*, 157–168. doi:10.1016/j.cor.2014.10.016

Zheng, Y., Burke, R., & Mobasher, B. (2012). Differential context relaxation for context-aware travel recommendation. In *Lecture Notes in Business Information Processing* (Vol. 123, pp. 88–99). LNBIP. doi:10.1007/978-3-642-32273-0_8

Zografos, K. G., & Davis, C. F. (1989). Multi-objective programming approach for routing hazardous materials. *Journal of Transportation Engineering*, *115*(6), 661–673. doi:10.1061/(ASCE)0733-947X(1989)115:6(661)

About the Contributors

Fausto Pedro Marquez works at UCLM as Full Professor (Accredited as Full Professor from 2013), Spain, Honorary Senior Research Fellow at Birmingham University, UK, Lecturer at the Postgraduate European Institute, and he has been Senior Manager in Accenture (2013-2014). He obtained his European PhD with a maximum distinction. He has been distingueed with the prices: Advancement Prize for Management Science and Engineering Management Nominated Prize (2018), First International Business Ideas Competition 2017 Award (2017); Runner (2015), Advancement (2013) and Silver (2012) by the International Society of Management Science and Engineering Management (ICMSEM); Best Paper Award in the international journal of Renewable Energy (Impact Factor 3.5) (2015). He has published more than 150 papers (65% ISI, 30% JCR and 92% internationals), some recognized as: "Renewable Energy" (as "Best Paper 2014"); "ICMSEM" (as "excellent"), "Int. J. of Automation and Computing" and "IMechE Part F: J. of Rail and Rapid Transit" (most downloaded), etc. He is author and editor of 25 books (Elsevier, Springer, Pearson, Mc-GrawHill, Intech, IGI, Marcombo, AlfaOmega,…), and 5 patents. He is Editor of 5 Int. Journals, Committee Member more than 40 Int. Conferences. He has been Principal Investigator in 4 European Projects, 5 National Projects, and more than 150 projects for Universities, Companies, etc. His main interest are: Maintenance Management, Renewable Energy, Transport, Advanced Analytics, Data Science. He is Director of www.ingeniumgroup.eu.

* * *

Rashmi Agrawal is working as Professor in Department of Computer Applications in MRIIRS, Faridabad, India. Dr. Agrawal has a rich teaching experience of more than 17 years. She is UGC-NET(CS) qualified. She has completed PhD, M.Phil, MTech, MSc and MBA(IT). Her area of expertise includes Artificial Intelligence, Machine Learning, Data Mining . She has published more than 40 research papers in various national and International conferences and peer reviewed Journals and authored many books and chapters in edited books. She has been editor in many edited books with international publishers. She has organized various Faculty Development Programmes and participated in workshops and Faculty development Programmes. She is a life time member of Computer Society of India. She has been a member of the editorial board in various journals and Technical Programme Committee in various conferences of repute.

Mazin A. M. Al Janabi is Full Professor of Finance at Tecnologico de Monterrey, EGADE Business School, Santa Fe Campus, Mexico City, Mexico. Professor Al Janabi holds a Ph.D. degree from the University of London, UK, and has over 30 years of real-world experience in diverse academic institutions and financial markets, and in many different roles. Professor Al Janabi has strong interest for research, publications and developments within emerging economies. Professor Al Janabi has published in top-tiered journals such as: International Review of Financial Analysis, European Journal of Operational Research, Annals of Operations Research, Applied Economics, Economic Modelling, Review of Financial Economics, Journal of Asset Management, Service Industries Journal, Studies in Economics and Finance, International Journal of Financial Engineering, Journal of Emerging Market Finance, Emerging Markets Finance and Trade, Review of Middle East Economics and Finance, Journal of Economic Research, Journal of Risk Finance, Journal of Banking Regulation, Journal of Financial Regulation and Compliance, Journal of Derivatives & Hedge Funds, Annals of Nuclear Energy, among others.

Benjamin Assay teaches mass Communication at Delta State Polytechnic, Ogwashi-Uku, Nigeria. He holds BA and MA degrees in Mass Communication from Delta State University, Abraka and University of Nigeria, Nsukka respectively. Assay is on the verge of being awarded a doctorate degree in mass communication by the Benue State Universality, Makurdi, Nigeria. He has published articles in scholarly journals and contributed chapters in several books locally and internationally. His research interests cover areas such as information and communication technology and national development; international communication and comparative media studies; media, democracy and good governance; population and health communication; and public relations and advertising. He is a member of several professional bodies, including African Council for Communication Education (ACCE) Nigeria Chapter, Advertising Practitioners Council of Nigeria (APCON), Association of Communication Scholars and Professional of Nigeria (ACSPN), Nigeria Institute of Public Relations (NIPR), National Association for Research Development (NARD), among others.

Timofei Bogomolov is a Lecturer in Data Science at the University of South Australia. He specialises in big data analysis and data mining methods. He applies his expertise to different contexts from marketing and consumer behaviour to financial markets and optimisation of hospital systems. He has published in applied mathematics and business journals.

Svetlana Bogomolova is an Associate Professor at the Ehrenberg-Bass Institute for Marketing Science, at the University of South Australia Business School. Svetlana's area of expertise covers consumer behavior and decision-making in relation to healthy and less healthy behaviours. Svetlana's discoveries feed into the practice of industry partners (e.g., national and international commercial and non-for-profit organisations), as well as inform government policies about protecting consumer interests. Svetlana's academic contributions have been recognized with a national fellowship, and multiple awards for research excellence and community engagement and numerous publications in leading marketing and health promotion journals.

Bhanu Chander is a Research Scholar at Pondicherry University, India. Graduated from Acharya Nagarjuna University and Post Graduated from the Central University of Rajasthan. WSN, Machine learning, Deep learning, Cryptography are his interesting research areas.

Pallavi Chavan is working as a professor in department of Information TEchnology at RAIT nerul, navi mumbai. she is having 14 years of teaching experience. Her area of interest is image processing, deep learning and soft computing.

Suh-Wen Chiou received her Ph.D. degree in Transport Studies in 1998 from UCL, University of London, UK. She also served as a Research Associate at KCL. In 2008 she took a chair as a fully Professor. She has published over 50 papers in international SCI journals such as Transportation Science, Transportation Research Part B, Computers and Operations Research, IEEE Trans. on Automatic Control, Decision Support Systems, Knowledge-based Systems, Applied Mathematical Modeling, Information Sciences and Automatica. Her research interests include nonlinear system control, data-driven robust control, area traffic signal control, stochastic modelling, network optimization, and operations research. Prof. Chiou is currently members of editorial advisory board of The Open Transportation Journal, The Open Operational Research Journal and The Open Management Journal.

William Fox is an Emeritus Professor in the Department of Defense Analysis at the Naval Postgraduate School. Currently, he is currently on the faculty in the Department of Mathematics at the College of William and Mary. He received his BS degree from the United States Military Academy at West Point, New York, his MS in operations research from the Naval Postgraduate School, and his Ph.D. in Industrial Engineering from Clemson University. He has taught at the United States Military Academy for twelve years until retiring for active military service, at Francis Marion University where he was the chair of mathematics for eight years, and twelve years at the Naval Postgraduate School. He has many publications and scholarly activities including twenty books, twenty-two chapters of books & technical reports, over one hundred and fifty journal articles, and over one hundred and fifty conference presentations and mathematical modeling workshops. He has directed several international mathematical modeling contests through the Consortium of Mathematics and its Applications (COMAP): the HiMCM and the MCM. His interests include applied mathematics, optimization (linear and nonlinear), mathematical modeling, statistical models, model for decision making in business, industry, medical and government, and computer simulations. He is a member of INFORMS, the Military Application Society of INFORMS, Mathematical Association of America, and Society for Industrial and Applied mathematics where he has held numerous positions.

Jayanthi Ganapathy is presently pursuing Ph.D in Machine Learning from Anna University, Chennai, India under faculty of Information and Communication Engineering. She has completed M. Tech Computer Science and Engineering in the year 2016 from Pondicherry Central University, Puducherry, India. She was awarded Pondicherry University Gold Medal in the year 2017. She has an interdisciplinary postgraduate degree in Remote Sensing completed in the year 2007 from Anna University, India. She is the university rank holder both in graduate and under graduate engineering studies. She has 9 years of teaching experience in engineering education (Computer Science and Engineering and Civil Engineering). She has authored two chapters in book published by IGI Global in 2017 and 2019. She has authored a paper published in International Journal of Artificial Intelligence and Soft Computing, Inderscience, indexed in ACM digital library. She has contributed in research areas that includes Artificial Intelligence, Knowledge Engineering, Statistical & Machine Learning, Machine learning applications in highway traffic management, etc.

Jayashree K. by qualification is an Engineer, having done her Doctorate in the area of Web services Fault Management from Anna University, Chennai and Masters in Embedded System Technologies from Anna University and Bachelors in Computer Science and Engineering from Madras University. She is presently Associate Professor in the Department of Computer Science and Engineering at Rajalakshmi

Engineering College, affiliated to Anna University Chennai. Her research interest includes Web services, Cloud Computing, Data Mining and distributed computing. She is an active member of ACM and CSI.

Malgorzata Korolkiewicz is a Senior Lecturer and Program Director for Data Science at the University of South Australia. Her research interests include include mathematical finance, risk management, environmental modelling, as well as data analytics and challenges posed by big data.

Anh Ninh is an Assistant Professor in the Computational Operations Research (COR) unit in the Department of Mathematics at the College of William & Mary. He holds a PhD in Operations Research from Rutgers Center for Operations Research (RUTCOR), Rutgers University. He is a member of the Supply Chain Analytics Labs at Rutgers Business School. His research experiences are in modeling and optimization, and he has conducted studies in the application areas of pharmaceutical and clinical trial supply chains. The focus of his research is on developing methodologies to optimize stochastic systems. Besides modeling and optimization, his research interest also includes machine learning applications and resource allocation.

Shanthi Bala P. currently working as an Assistant Professor in the Department of Computer Science, School of Engineering and Technology, Pondicherry University, India. Her research interests are in Artificial Intelligence, Machine Learning, Deep Learning, Distributed Computing Systems, Knowledge Engineering, Cyber Security, Networks, and Ontology.

Miguel A. Patricio received his BSc in Computer Science in 1991, his MSc in Computer Science in 1995 and his PhD in Artificial Intelligence in 2002 all from the Universidad Politecnica de Madrid. He has held an administrative position at the Computer Science Department of the Universidad Politecnica de Madrid since 1993. He is currently Associate Professor at the Escuela Politecnica Superior of the Universidad Carlos III de Madrid and research fellow of the Applied Artificial Intelligence Group (GIAA). He has leaded several Artificial Intelligence research projects sponsored by public and private institutions and has supervised four PhD. students, some of them related to information fusion and distributed sensor networks. He is the co-author of over 100 books, book chapters, journal papers, technical reports, etc. published by organizations such as Elsevier, IEEE, ACM, AAAI, Springer Verlag, Kluwer, etc., most of these present practical and theoretical achievements of computer vision and distributed systems. He has carried out a number of consulting activities in the areas of automatic visual inspection systems, video-surveillance systems, texture recognition, data minig and industrial applications.

Chithambaramani R. completed his Bachelor of Engineering in Computer Science and Engineering and Master of Engineering in Software Engineering from Rajalakshmi Engineering College affiliated to Anna University. Currently doing is PhD in Anna University Chennai.

Niloofar Ramezani is an Assistant Professor of Statistics at the Department of Statistics in George Mason University, and Section Councilor in the Applied Public Health Statistics Section at the American Public Health Association. She holds a PhD and a master's degree in applied statistics and research methods as well as a bachelor's degree in statistics. She is a statistician and research methodologist actively involved in applied and collaborative research. Her areas of expertise span both applied and theoretical statistics including optimal sample size estimation, missing data methods, longitudinal and multilevel modeling, big data, data analytics, time series, and survey research methodology. Her focus is on developing new methods and simplifying existing techniques in correlated and clustered data analysis in addition to categorical data analysis, data visualization, high-dimensional data modeling, and missing data strategies. Her work focuses on developing innovative research tools to answer questions across different fields, especially biomedical and social science.

Sajad Rather is currenty pursuing his PhD in the department of Compuet Science, School of Engineering and Technology, Pondicherry University, India. His research interests are in Machine Learning, Optimization of Nature Inspired Algorithms and Deep Learning.

Aditya Salunkhe is a 21-year-old college student who is working towards becoming an Information Technology engineer by the end of this current semester. He will be graduating from Ramrao Adik Institute of Technology which a very well ranked college in New-Mumbai. His areas of interest are Machine Learning & Image Processing. He has shown a consistent rise in his CGPA over all the 4 years of engineering. He is working on a project in the field of "Sentiment Analysis of Handwritten Documents" using the concepts of Image Processing & Graphology. He has also contributed to several other projects on web design, java framework, data management etc. He also has done an internship & developed a data management project for the HR services. Cloud Computing, Machine Learning and Artificial Intelligence are in particular his fields of interest.

Ferdi Sonmez has taken graduate degree from Marmara University and undergraduate degree from Bogazici University, Istanbul-Turkiye. He is currently chair of Computer Engineering Department at Arel University. Dr. Sönmez's research area includes: Artificial Neural Networks, Machine Learning, Big data, Deep learning, Database Management Systems, Scalable Data Analysis and Query Processing, Data Storage and Physical Design, Data Cleaning, Data Transformation and Crowdsourcing, Secure Data Processing, RDBMS and IMDB security. Dr. Sönmez has two years industrial experience, as a project manager for Turkey section of an international ICT consulting company. Dr. Sönmez worked on three international (COST EU) and a couple of national research projects. Dr. Sönmez has supervised several graduate students at master and co-supervised at PhD level.

Pakize Taylan joined the Art and Science Faculty, Mathematics Department, of Dicle University in Diyarbakir, Turkey, in February 1990. She received an Msc. degree in 1993 and Ph.D. degree in 1999 from Dicle University in the field of mathematical statistics, and she earned her assistant professor degree in 2000. She tought courses in Turkish language, Probability and Statistics and Mathematical Statistics. She worked at Middle East Technical University, Ankara and Bowling Green State University, Ohio, USA, at a Post-Doctoral position. Her research interests are lineer regression, nonlinear regression, spline regression, optimization. She has published journal articles and has presented her studies at national and international conferences. She still works at the Department of Mathematics, Art and Science Faculty, of Dicle University.

Masahide Yamamoto is a professor of the Faculty of Foreign Studies, Nagoya Gakuin University. He earned a Ph.D. in economics from Matsuyama University. Before joining the faculty of Nagoya Gakuin University, he taught at Kanazawa Seiryo University and St. Catherine University. His research interests include tourism economy studies. His major publications include Data Science and Digital Business (English: co-authored, Springer, 2019).

Index

A

additive model 181-183
ARIMA 24, 100, 115, 119-120, 125-126, 128, 131-132
artificial intelligence 17, 46-47, 75, 88, 99, 102, 148, 312, 326, 356, 410, 412
Artificial Neural Network (ANN) 66, 87, 91, 401, 403-404, 410

B

Bayesian Networks 50, 316, 321
big data 1-7, 10-12, 17-23, 29, 34-38, 43-47, 49, 75, 135, 148, 152-157, 160, 166, 170, 217, 226, 281, 359, 381, 412, 428

C

challenges of big data 1-2
classification 2-3, 16, 27-28, 50, 52-53, 55-56, 58, 61, 74-76, 84-85, 87-89, 91-92, 99, 135-136, 138, 141, 143-144, 148, 152-154, 156-157, 180, 205, 208-209, 212, 313-317, 367, 416
cluster analysis 86, 136, 141, 146-147, 165, 318, 386-387, 410, 416
clustering 1-7, 11, 50-53, 55-62, 64-66, 74-76, 84-87, 89-90, 92, 99, 143, 146-148, 158, 160-162, 166, 169, 215, 312, 317-319, 359, 366-367, 375, 380, 382, 384-388, 392, 394, 396-397, 399-405, 410, 415-416, 422, 424, 426
clustering techniques 1-3, 5, 7, 55, 382, 385-386, 392, 402
condition monitoring 340
Conic Quadratic Programming 180
Context-Aware System 333
correlated tricluster 366, 368, 370, 375
correlation analysis 285, 295-296
Credit Risk Analytics Use Case 26

D

data-driven approach 234
data science 7, 75, 317
deep learning 148, 315-316, 323, 380, 382, 400, 402, 404, 410
deep learning neural network 400, 402, 404
Discrete Firefly algorithm 372
DOCOMO Insight Marketing, Inc. 307

E

economic-capital 214-215, 217, 220-226
emerging markets 215-217, 226, 351
estimation 14, 16, 28-29, 66, 88, 91, 137, 163, 177-181, 184-185, 191, 198, 215, 217-218, 222, 316, 318-319
exploitation 82-84, 86, 89, 99
exploration 82, 84, 86-87, 89, 99, 143, 146, 373, 382
exponential smoothing 100, 115, 117, 119, 125, 128

F

financial econometric models 11
firefly algorithm 366, 368, 371-372, 375
forecasting 11, 29, 100-102, 104, 115, 127, 131, 156, 169-170, 412
fraudster 26, 346, 365
Fraud Use Case 22

G

GCC financial markets 217
Google Trends 295, 307
GPS data 17, 412-413, 416, 419, 424, 428
Gravitational Search Algorithm (GSA) 74-76, 85, 92, 99

H

hazmat transportation network design 234

Heuristic Algorithms 74, 83, 99
hierarchical clustering 3, 5, 60-61, 319, 380, 386-388, 396-397, 399-400, 410
high dimensional data 5, 64, 135, 141, 148, 181, 183
hybridization 74, 82-83, 86, 99

I

Interconnect bypass fraud 356, 365
Interconnection Bandwidth 365
Interconnection Network 365
International Mobile Subscriber Identity (IMSI) 365
IP network 365
Ishikawa Prefecture 282, 287, 307

K

Kenrokuen 288, 290-298, 307
kernel function 87, 179, 197-198
keyword search volume 294, 300
K-Means clustering 76, 147, 160-162, 166, 367, 422

L

Latent Class Analysis (LCA) 380, 386, 394, 410
Liquidity-Adjusted Value at Risk 214-216
liquidity risk 215-221
location based services 413
location data 35, 38, 279, 281-282, 290, 300, 412-414, 428
logistic models 136, 139-140, 148

M

machine learning 3, 5, 11-12, 15-16, 19-20, 22-23, 27-28, 50-52, 55, 84, 86-87, 92, 102-104, 118, 130, 135-138, 144-145, 148, 153-154, 160-161, 210, 217, 226, 281, 311-314, 316-318, 321-323, 326-327, 333, 356, 359, 380, 382, 385, 399-402, 404-405, 410, 412
MARS 177, 180-181, 189-191, 196, 201
mathematical modeling 75, 99, 101
microarray data 86, 148, 366-369, 375
Mobile Kukan Toukei 279-282, 287, 294-295, 300, 307
mobile phone 279-282, 300, 350, 365
moving average 24, 100, 115, 119, 125, 166
multiple linear regression 137, 142, 144-145, 399-401

N

nature-inspired algorithms 99

neural networks 15-17, 24, 82, 102, 141, 312, 315-316, 319, 321-322, 380, 382, 399-402, 410
Nielsen Consumer Panel Dataset 380, 382-383, 399, 405-406
nonlinear regression 113, 123, 177-178
nonparametric regression 177-178, 180, 189
Noto Peninsula 290-291, 307
NTT DOCOMO, Inc. 280, 282, 290, 307

O

optimization 10-11, 14-15, 17, 29, 74-75, 77-89, 91-92, 99, 112, 115, 117-118, 137, 177, 180, 187-188, 191-192, 196, 200-201, 214-215, 217, 221-222, 224-227, 231-232, 234-235, 237, 243, 245, 247-249, 252, 254-255, 315, 318, 335, 366-368, 371-375, 377
optimization models 10-11, 14, 29
OTT 365

P

Particle Swarm Optimization (PSO) 75, 83, 99, 367-368
Partitional Clustering 386, 410
portfolio management 29, 214, 216, 222-224, 226
prediction 12, 17, 28, 104, 115, 136, 144, 152-153, 166, 169-170, 180, 209, 282, 325, 367, 381, 400-401
predictive maintenance 334-335
predictive modelling 380, 382, 385, 399, 404, 410

R

random forest 136, 141-144, 148, 312
Raster Data 414-415
recommendation systems 411, 413, 420, 424, 428
recommender systems 311-312, 320-327, 333
regression 3, 27-28, 87-88, 100, 102, 104-109, 112-115, 119, 121, 123-126, 135-146, 152-154, 156-160, 163, 166-170, 177-178, 180-183, 189-190, 197-198, 297, 313, 315, 317, 322, 380, 399-402, 404-405, 410
regression analysis 3, 87-88, 105, 152-153, 156, 166, 297
retail 311-313, 317-318, 320, 326, 333, 383
risk equity 234-235, 244-246, 248-250, 256-259, 265, 267, 269, 271
robotic arm 334, 336, 340, 342

S

signal processing 338-339

SIM box 346, 354-357, 365

SIM Card 365

slack detection 340, 342

smart tourism 311-313, 317-318, 320, 326, 333

Social Media Analytics and Sentiment Analytics 22

software systems 412-413

spatio-temporal GIS 413

Statistical Modeling 135

stochastic optimization 231, 235, 243

supervised learning 15, 56, 87-88, 91, 102-104, 137, 312-314, 317-319, 322, 326-327, 333, 384-385, 405, 410

Swam Intelligence (SI) 74, 84, 99

T

Telecom Operator 365

three dimensional clustering 375

tourism 279-287, 292, 295, 297, 299-300, 307, 311-313, 317-318, 320, 326, 333

tricluster 366, 368-373, 375-377

U

unsupervised learning 2, 16, 50-52, 55, 91, 103, 146, 148, 312, 317, 319-320, 327, 333, 385, 405, 410

V

Vector data 414, 416

Visit Japan Campaign (VJC) 279, 307

Vs of Big Data 156

W

Wakura hot springs 290-293, 296, 299-300, 307

Wavelet Transform 334, 338-339, 341

Y

Yamanaka hot springs 291-292, 294, 296-297, 300, 307

Ensure Quality Research is Introduced to the Academic Community

Become an IGI Global Reviewer for Authored Book Projects

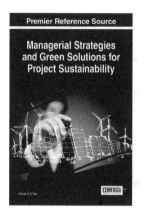

The overall success of an authored book project is dependent on quality and timely reviews.

In this competitive age of scholarly publishing, constructive and timely feedback significantly expedites the turnaround time of manuscripts from submission to acceptance, allowing the publication and discovery of forward-thinking research at a much more expeditious rate. Several IGI Global authored book projects are currently seeking highly-qualified experts in the field to fill vacancies on their respective editorial review boards:

Applications and Inquiries may be sent to:
development@igi-global.com

Applicants must have a doctorate (or an equivalent degree) as well as publishing and reviewing experience. Reviewers are asked to complete the open-ended evaluation questions with as much detail as possible in a timely, collegial, and constructive manner. All reviewers' tenures run for one-year terms on the editorial review boards and are expected to complete at least three reviews per term. Upon successful completion of this term, reviewers can be considered for an additional term.

If you have a colleague that may be interested in this opportunity,
we encourage you to share this information with them.

Printed in the United States
By Bookmasters